CHARLEMAGNE

CHARLEMAGNE

JOHANNES FRIED

Translated by Peter Lewis

HARVARD UNIVERSITY PRESS
Cambridge, Massachusetts
London, England
2016

This book was originally published as
Karl der Grosse © Verlag C. H. Beck oHG, München 2013

Library of Congress Cataloging-in-Publication Data
Names: Fried, Johannes, author. | Lewis, Peter, 1958– translator.
Title: Charlemagne / Johannes Fried ; translated by Peter Lewis.
Other titles: Karl der Grosse. English
Description: Cambridge, Massachusetts : Harvard University Press, 2016. |
"This book was originally published as Karl der Grosse (c)
Verlag C.H. Beck oHG, München 2013"—Title page verso. |
Includes bibliographical references and index.
Identifiers: LCCN 2016013071 | ISBN 9780674737396 (alk. paper)
Subjects: LCSH: Charlemagne, Emperor, 742–814. | Holy Roman Empire—
Kings and rulers—Biography. | France—History—To 987. |
Holy Roman Empire—History—To 1517.
Classification: LCC DC73 .F7513 2016 | DDC 944/.0142092 [B]—dc23
LC record available at https://lccn.loc.gov/2016013071

FIGURE I, TITLE PAGE Ninth-century coin showing Charlemagne as emperor. The obverse side reads KAROLUS IMP(erator) AUG(ustus); the "F" is thought to indicate the place where it was minted, Frankfurt am Main. It dates from sometime after 800 (Charlemagne's year of coronation as emperor), possibly 810. The reverse of this coin can be seen in Figure 52.

CONTENTS

PREFACE

THE FOLLOWING BOOK IS NOT A NOVEL, but it is a work of fiction all the same—a fiction based on this author's visualization of Charlemagne. And even though the resulting image does, quite properly, adduce all the available evidence from the period in question, it is nonetheless subjectively formed and colored. It is impossible nowadays to fathom the depths of a life lived more than twelve hundred years ago, so the only thing remaining for a writer to fall back on is his own imagination. Not every topic that could have been touched on is touched on. Experts on Charlemagne will no doubt spot these omissions just as surely as critics will point to them as failings. Perhaps those same critics will also censure this author for the way he has chosen to approach his subject, although all they would be able to offer would be a different, no less subjective and fragmentary image. An objective portrayal of the great Carolingian ruler is simply not possible.

The world twelve hundred years before our current era is an alien landscape barely recognizable to us anymore. Charlemagne lived from 748 (a putative birth date) to 814 (a definite death date). At that time, Constantinople was not yet called Istanbul. There was no soaring cathedral at Cologne, the cathedral at Bamberg would not be built for another two hundred years, and the one at Speyer was an unimposing affair compared with the magnificent edifice that looms over the Rhine there today. In Paris, there was no Louvre, while Notre-Dame on the Île de la Cité was still an episcopal church of modest proportions. In Venice, engineers had not yet driven oak pilings into the mud of the lagoon to provide firm foundations for St. Mark's Basilica or the magnificent palazzi of the Venetian nobility, and no gondoliers plied their trade on the Grand Canal, serenading their passengers. The Vatican, meanwhile, was nothing more than a hill outside the walls of the Eternal City; it was home to a church built in late antiquity housing the tomb of the apostolic prince St. Peter, but not yet a lavish papal palace.

Nor did the Holy Roman Empire exist. Whenever there is mention of an "empire" in the following pages, this refers strictly to a territorial entity, not the grand political institution of later centuries. The term is also occasionally used to denote the personal rule of Charlemagne.

Europe's populace was spread thin on the ground. Extensive tracts of land did not witness a human presence for weeks or even years on end. Cities that had survived from classical antiquity existed in name only; in many cases, they were full of nothing but ruins. They were not melting pots of immigrants from far-off lands, still less the proud, independent municipalities they became half a millennium later. The great migrations of people that had typified the ancient world, and that have continued to characterize human history right up to the present day, had ground to a temporary halt as a result of the great plague of the sixth century. The continent was covered with dense, almost impenetrable forests. Oar and sail power still dominated the oceans, and birds ruled the skies. The mountain summits of the Alps were shrouded in solitude and silence. Nights were illuminated by nothing but the light of the moon and stars; candles, which still cost a fortune, burned in churches and palaces but not yet in the lowly abodes of ordinary folk. People's lives followed the course of the sun; things proceeded at a sedate pace. Handicraft was in demand, and apart from mills, manual labor was not yet facilitated by any machines—hard work without a doubt, but on a human scale. The world was a placid place, time was not precious, and no one except fugitives from the law was hounded.

We are thus confronted with an alien world, and with people whose social and technical knowledge is utterly strange to us, who spoke a now wholly unfamiliar language, and whose entire mode of speech and thought and logic is far removed from our own. We do not share their emotions, we no longer have their skills at our fingertips, their aspirations and plans appear backward to us, and to us modern citizens of the world who are still grappling with the onset of globalization and its consequences, their values and ethics are virtually meaningless. For instance, no one in the age of Charlemagne wrote or drew caricatures; instead, both the common people and the ruling elites were in the habit of demonizing all opponents, heretics, or anyone who thought differently. Nor was irony common intellectual currency in this period. One notable feature of the time was the king's claim to exclusive sovereignty over interpretation of the past. This "authoritative memory" was evident throughout society and yielded to different perceptions and interpretations only in the rarest of cases.

As a result, we can open up and present this world only in the vaguest and most hypothetical way. The reader will search in vain for any wide-ranging reflections on methodology in the following pages. Yet it should be borne in mind that every beginning has its own preamble and starting point, and that every effect generates further effects of its own. Many historians ignore this fact and take the view that anyone seeking to understand the start of the beginning or the resulting effects must be thinking in teleological terms. But there are whole worlds between cause, effect, and telos. All the same, we have to take into account processes, systematically interacting processes, in which an uncontrollable abundance either of intertwining co-incidences in the environment and society or of unintentional simultaneity in human activity produces just as lasting and perhaps even more effective results than any systematic definition of objectives. In retrospect, this result might take on the appearance of something deliberate and planned.

I have sometimes, mostly in very different contexts, repeated certain facts where I felt that these would help the reader get his or her bearings. Occasionally, I have also—in some instances even without drawing attention to the fact—quoted some earlier works of mine; conversely, no citations from other sources have been left unattributed except by error. The large number of endnotes, which are designed to help substantiate the statements I make, offer a somewhat imperfect substitute; these focus primarily on texts that are readily at hand. Brief pointers to chapters, more extensive passages, or the dates of works of history given in the form of abbreviations inserted in the text are intended to make the endnote apparatus less cumbersome without interrupting the flow of the text; these always refer to the most recent historical record I consulted. Dates are styled as CE (Common Era) or, in the case of the Byzantine chronicler Theophanes, as the year since the creation of the world, the annus mundi, or AM. Allusions to "the biographer" always refer to Einhard and his *Life of Charlemagne* (*Vita Karoli*). "Ms." denotes the holding library's reference number for the manuscript cited. Academic works of secondary literature, indispensable though they are, are nevertheless generally mentioned in the text only when they are essential to the argument or when I am swimming against the tide of interpretation and need, however briefly, to explain the reasons I do so. I do not pretend to offer a comprehensive bibliography of works on Charlemagne and his age; for that, the interested reader is referred to two invaluable resources: Rudolf Schieffer's *Die Zeit des karolingischen Großreiches* and (albeit focusing on German history) Jörg W. Busch's *Die Herrschaften der Karolinger.* The bibliography at the end of this volume includes only the works I have cited repeatedly; other references are given in the relevant note.

Bearing in mind that I intended my book to appeal to a readership beyond academic circles, where historical records from the Carolingian period are concerned, I have mainly endeavored to quote from bilingual editions (Frankish/German); the same goes for the works in Old High German I have cited. For the dating of the "capitularies," those expressions of royal or imperial authority, I have basically followed Hubert Mordek's *Bibliotheca capitularium,* although it remains a moot point to what extent the individual numbers in this still most authoritative of editions actually correspond to individual documents among the capitularies included in the Monumenta Germaniae Historica (MGH); recent studies have questioned this. Alcuin's letters, a hugely important resource from Carolingian times, follow the dating in Donald A. Bullough's monograph on Alcuin.

This author is particularly indebted to two preceding works of scholarship on the same topic: British historian Donald A. Bullough's book on Charlemagne (*The Age of Charlemagne,* 2nd edition, 1973), which first appeared almost fifty years ago, and the latest work on Charlemagne, by Wilfried Hartmann (*Karl der Grosse,* 2010). The breadth of vision offered by Bullough and the precise historical analysis presented by Hartmann make reading these two fine works equally rewarding.

The list of those to whom my thanks are due is extensive. In particular, I would like to express my gratitude to two of my colleagues in the history faculty at Frankfurt: Jörg W. Busch, who took on the task of reading through the manuscript of this book and saved me from making a number of errors, and the Byzantine specialist Wolfram Brandes, to whom I am indebted for certain key points on the situation in Byzantium during Charlemagne's reign. I also recall with pleasure and gratitude the conversations about Charlemagne that I had with Bernhard Jussen, Max Kerner, Heribert Müller, and Matthias M. Tischler; this book has benefited greatly from their valuable suggestions. My heartfelt thanks are also owed to my tireless assistants in Frankfurt, Sinja Lohf and Janus Gudian, who constantly advised, assisted, and took the weight off my shoulders in all sorts of ways and whose patience and helpfulness knew no bounds. The editor in chief at C. H. Beck, Detlef Felken, showed his customary aplomb and skill in taking this book under his wing and steering it through the editorial process, including acquiring some wonderful illustrations; without his input and that of his colleagues Bettina Corßen-Meier and Janna Rösch, this volume would never have emerged in the very pleasing form it has. Last but not least, I would like to thank my wife, who once again had to suffer me reading draft chapters aloud to her and running half-formulated ideas past her; fortunately, she endured this all with a tolerant smile.

I am especially delighted that the German edition was published in the 250th anniversary year of the C. H. Beck publishing house. My thanks are due to Wolfgang Beck for encouraging me to write it, for taking a lively interest in its progress, and for his patience in watching it come to fruition. I dedicate this *Charlemagne* to him and to his publishing house, which has played such a significant role in the study of history through the ages.

Charlemagne's Empire

Frankish empire in 768
Gains by Charlemagne
Border marchlands
Frankish sphere of influence
Carolingian palaces
Transport and trade routes

The Mediterranean World

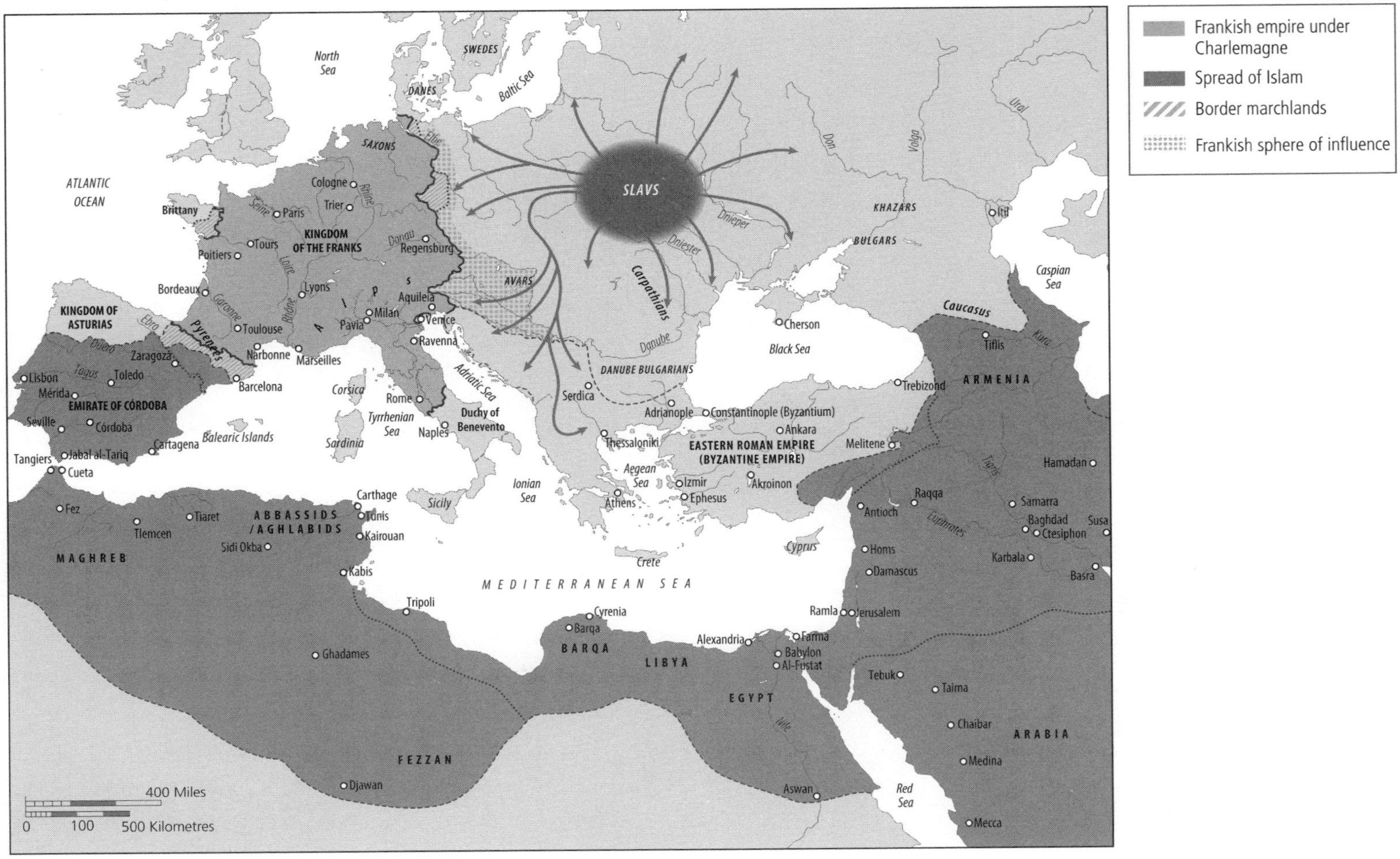

PROLOGUE

RAIN, POURING RAIN. A man was standing in the deluge, at the foot of the Mountain of Purgatory. The rain beat down incessantly on him but seemed incapable of washing away the sins that stained him. All the while, a hideous beast was gnawing at his manhood, which promptly grew back only to be eaten once more, over and over again. A venerable monk by the name of Wetti, who had formerly been a schoolmaster and was now himself at death's door, was profoundly shocked to see this penitent beneath the mountain. Wetti rallied and became lucid for a few hours, although he hardly dared to reveal the name of the departed sinner he had seen. But everyone recognized the unfortunate wretch who was being forced to do penance in Purgatory as the great ruler Charlemagne. The vision the dying man had seen was directed at those still alive, in the here and now. It compelled those in power to make sweeping changes. Years after Charlemagne's death, it served as a warning to the living about the perils of the afterlife, exhorting them to repent and reminding them of their duty to remember the departed in their prayers. For the emperor had died in sin.

This was the first recollection of Charlemagne to gain widespread currency after his death. It was created in 824, ten years after he passed away,[1] at the behest of his son and successor, Louis I. Louis had barely ascended the throne in Aachen (Aix-la-Chapelle) when he set about purging the royal court of the sinfulness with which his father had stained it by banishing those he deemed unworthy to be there and who were, moreover, his political opponents. The purpose of the vision of the monk Wetti, from Reichenau Abbey, was to persuade the living to lend succor to the suffering dead emperor through their intercession; the commemoration of the dead was to be given a firmer foundation than ever before. This was the clear agenda of salvation set forth by the new emperor and his spiritual adviser, Abbot Benedict of Aniane and Inden (Kornelimünster). Just as the litany did in life, so intercession was designed to solicit God's grace in death and at the same time remind those praying of the impending Day of Judgment. Would God keep the sinner Charlemagne in mind and take pity on him?

"Have mercy on me, O God" (Psalm 51). A blessed death: that was what people strove for. To be able to die strengthened by the sacraments of the Church, by confession, penitential psalms, extreme unction, and Communion, to be accompanied by priests and be armed by their prayers against the dangers of the afterlife, where the hosts of Heaven and Hell assailed a person's soul (as portrayed in the contemporary Old High German epic poem *Muspilli*),[2] where the inquisitions of the Day of Judgment and its martyrs lurked, where no one and nothing could help a person any longer, no compurgator and no false witness, and where only one's own actions, be they sinful or agreeable to God, were weighed in the balance, and where one's only source of hope was a belief in redemption through Christ and his saints. At this time, twelve hundred years ago, a person's ultimate aim was to meet a blessed end. As Psalm 31 put it: "Into thine hand I commit my spirit; thou hast redeemed me, O Lord God of truth."

And what of Charlemagne? How could he be so freely accused of sinning? At this time, in a peculiar form of authority that the living exercised over the dead, a person's life was interpreted from his or her death. Unlike the plague several centuries later, death was not some kind of great leveler. Rather, death revealed to posthumous interpreters whether a particular life had been lived piously or had fallen prey to Satan, whether a person would remain in God's thoughts or be scratched from the book of life and cast into the burning pit of Hell. Death was a measure of a person's past life and rewarded or penalized it accordingly. And the expectation of death awakened a foreknowledge that every action and every life would have to be accounted for. Faith shaped people's reality.

Yet the pious Louis I was not without enemies. Powerful leadership elites among the Franks remembered quite another Charlemagne and opposed the reign of his son, pressuring him, forcing him to do public penance, repeatedly change his advisers, and alter his plans and objectives, and plunging him into bloody conflicts. The Charlemagne they recalled was a warrior, a victor, and a wise emperor. Yet nothing, it seemed—no admonition, warning, prayer, or recollection—was able to halt the ongoing struggle for the throne and the kingdom. Before long, the Franks were embroiled in a murderous round of internecine battles, and their empire fragmented.

As all this was just starting to loom on the horizon, a slim pamphlet appeared—a memoir in the tradition of Ciceronian oratory[3]—titled *Vita Karoli Magni* (*Life of Charlemagne*), the work of the Frankish scholar Einhard. When still a young man, he had come to the Carolingian court, where he was given the courtier's name Bezaleel; over time, he was appointed Charlemagne's paladin and was on intimately friendly terms with him and his children, but by this stage he had withdrawn from courtly life. His *Life*, which before long had been copied several times and widely disseminated, held a mirror up to the disputatious offspring of the former emperor. The work depicted a quite different man from the penitent dreamer of Wetti's vision, showing instead the successful king, the hero, the great emperor, and the paragon for all other rulers. Not long after completing the work (ca. 836), Einhard died at the age of seventy-two, secure in the comfort of Holy Communion. Yet the emperor for whose attention the book was primarily intended, Louis the Pious, was not given a prominent mention in it at all, merely being noted as Charlemagne's successor and legal executor. Implicitly, this amounted to harsh criticism.

Einhard's life of Charlemagne also presented an image of its subject that continued to resonate. It was written when no one was left alive who could remember Charlemagne's boyhood any longer; his cousin Adalhard, who had grown up with him at the Frankish court, had died in 826.[4] Over time, and with the decline of the Frankish Empire, this image also became romanticized. But Einhard's "great king" had not reached the pinnacle, the summit of his fame; at this stage, he was still not regarded as Charles the Great. Nor was this the case even by the time the Swiss monastic chronicler Notker of St. Gall put pen to paper around 885.[5] Notker lauded the victorious, just, generous, farsighted, and God-fearing monarch. His account of Charlemagne's deeds—truncated at the beginning and end and little known—has handed down to us a collection of anecdotes about the great ruler and other Carolingians. Not unlike Einhard's biography, these evoked feelings of nostalgia and over time became so gilded and fantastically embellished as to attain almost mythical status. But even here, Charles was still not "the Great."

When, on the occasion of a visit to a monastery, Notker's tales were recounted to Charlemagne's great-grandson Charles III, he is said to have delighted in them and to have requested that they be written down. Henceforth, they served continually to remind him of one and the same thing: the hero Charlemagne, the *invictissimus imperator* (most unconquered emperor), the ideal ruler figure, of decisive action, power, and assertiveness—all qualities that the raving mad and profoundly ill Charles III thoroughly lacked. Each one of these episodes from Charlemagne's life proclaimed the same message to the man who commissioned them, namely, through commemorating his illustrious ancestor, to become aware of his own destiny: "Charles, become a Charlemagne!" Nevertheless, that which had eluded the influential courtier Einhard in the center of power was also denied to Notker in his remote Alemannic monastery. However much Charlemagne's deeds might thrill those who read or heard them, they could not prevent the downfall of the empire that he had created. Yet heroes are eternally wont to arise from such decline as comforters, givers of hope, and proclaimers of a brighter future despite all current misery, embodying, as it were, a bright, human place of remembrance far removed from all hardship.

It took a long while for Charlemagne to attain the final stage of historical heroizing, a peak that only Alexander, Constantine the Great, and Theodosius had scaled before him. The first hints of the personal greatness reflected in his regnal sobriquet appeared around 900 in the writings of the anonymous Saxon poet known as Poeta Saxo. But it was only around the turn of the first millennium that he began to be regularly vaunted—in both the western and eastern halves of the former Carolingian Empire—as Carolus Magnus, "Charles the Great."[6]

The recollection of a hero thus endured, a figure under whose rule the empire had grown in external power, while domestically it was able to live in peace and witness great events and experience a period of unprecedented splendor. And so a Charles who embodied a sense of nostalgia that was critical of the present entered the cultural canon of the West, offering the image of a past that augured a brighter future. He left none of his real deeds behind, whether good or bad. Rather, he went down in history equally as an evildoer and sinner, as a scourge of the feudal aristocracy, and as a hero and saint. However outstanding Charlemagne's reign was and however devoted to sensual pleasures his personal life may have been, after his death a process of mythmaking set in that was all-embracing. Collective memory, which modulated and distorted everything, filtered out revolts and campaigns of extermination, such as the one he conducted against his cousin Tassilo of Bavaria—at least in the first instance, since the narrative literature of a later era sought to paint an entirely different picture, reviving the motif of sin and the theme of rebellion and even heaping ridicule on the figure of Charlemagne.[7]

Charlemagne's significance was felt even beyond the frontiers of his empire. The Slavs, who originally had no conception of kingdoms and monarchy, adapted his given name as the title of their kings; just as the German *Kaiser* was derived from Caesar, and "Augustus" became a component of the imperial and royal title, right up to the demise of the Holy Roman Empire of the German Nation, so "Charles" became the basis of *korol*, *król*, or *král*, generic terms for "king." It may also be the case, though, that the initial impetus for this came from Charles III, Charlemagne's great-grandson, who was named after him.

What kind of man was this Charlemagne, then, that he should suffer such a mixed fate at the hands of posterity? That he should in turn be praised, castigated, and mocked or enter into legend, become the archetype of a king, and eventually become indisputably the most renowned ruling figure in the Middle Ages? That his name should still, to date, remain one of the most common names of kings throughout Europe: Charles (English), Karl (German), Charles (French), Carlos (Spanish), and so on? What do we know about him or his life or personality? The answer to this is disappointing. A biography of Charlemagne in the modern sense of the term would be an impossible undertaking. All we have to go on are a few isolated deeds of his, a handful of instructions that he may have issued, various results of his reign, a few impersonal traces of his life, and the basic fact that he ruled as king and emperor from 768 to 814. In sum, there is virtually nothing private and absolutely nothing personal about him extant, and aside from the few contemporary historians and chroniclers mentioned, there are no particular eyewitness accounts of his reign, while from his lifetime all the source material we possess is just a few odd works of historiography such as brief annals, a series of legislative or administrative decrees (the so-called capitularies), and some other documents, but, with one exception, no letters. These are all stylized texts firmly in the tradition of ancient historical record keeping. Not one of these dicta can be traced back with absolute certainty to Charlemagne, even though scholarly research does at least believe that his personal stamp is evident in this or that specific case.[8] No words of his four or five wives have come down to us, or of the many concubines, known or unknown, whom he may have loved, or even of his sons and daughters. These figures are all shrouded in silent mystery.

Only a faint hope exists that we may still be able to tease out some utterance or other, or even just some regal hint, from this eternally silent subject of ours. Even he, the great king and emperor, wished to have some memory of his deeds preserved for the future in his foundation, the Royal Church of St. Mary in Aachen, alongside commemorations of the dead. At least we have good grounds for assuming that the so-called *Annales regni Francorum* (Royal Frankish Annals) was compiled officially and with the approval of the court, a fact first established by the historian Leopold von Ranke in 1854. Every sentence of these imperial annals placed the ruler in the center of things and had, we may reasonably conjecture—in its first version shortly after 788—been written down under Charlemagne's supervision.[9]

Our justification for this premise may be illustrated by the example of the subsequent, quite incorrect, and well-documented fabrication of guilt against Duke Tassilo of Bavaria, which is given a surprising amount of coverage in precisely these annals (and only in them and their later counterparts), being spread over several years' entries.[10] This could hardly have happened without an express instruction from the king, a cousin of the Bavarian duke. We may surmise that Charlemagne would have had this work, along with others that he deemed important, read out to him for his approval.[11] Accordingly, it was he and not some historiographer who set the priorities that were apportioned by these almanacs.

Further instances may be cited that point to the king's personal involvement in these annals.[12] Charlemagne quite publicly promoted the writing of history. Just a few years earlier, between 783 and 787, a Benedictine monk and historian, Paul the Deacon, wrote a work titled *Gesta episcoporum Mettensium* (Deeds of the bishops of Metz). This history, which referred to the king by name, was clearly favorable to the Carolingian dynasty, praising Charlemagne and justifying his ascent to the throne. Metz had once been the see of St. Arnulf, one of the founding fathers of the Carolingian line, and in the same year in which Paul began his work (783), the funeral of Charlemagne's second wife, Hildegard, was held in the cathedral there. Paul, the son of a noble Lombard family, wrote his *Gesta* at the request of Charlemagne's royal chaplain Angilram, who by this time was also bishop of Metz. This work marked the true beginning of historiography within the Carolingian court.[13] In Paul's account, Charlemagne emerges as the great conqueror of Italy, as victor over the Lombards, who as a descendant of the founder of Rome, the Trojan Aeneas, had now managed to subdue Rome, the city of his ancestors. What was more worthy of admiration: his martial prowess, the splendor of his great wisdom, or his broad knowledge of all the liberal arts?

Charlemagne would no doubt also have had this history read out loud to him. He must have approved it and been so delighted by the picture it painted that he commissioned the Lombard writer to compose epitaphs for his sisters, who had died young. These poems took up the theme of the Carolingians' descent from Troy first broached in the *Gesta episcoporum* and also sang the praises of their patron, the conqueror of Italy. Here, then, historiography and poetry were placed in the service of praising and legitimizing the present. Admittedly, the saintly ancestor, whose cult had just begun to flourish from the early eighth century on, was only initially revered by Charlemagne; this attitude soon gave way to a curious distancing that now preferred to emphasize the dynasty's "Pepinid" forebears instead.[14]

The *Royal Frankish Annals,* the first version of which appeared shortly after 788, and which was briefly supplemented a few years later to update it to the year 792, performed this task with positively exemplary clarity. Its main feature was reflected in the Tassilo episode, which justifies us in interpreting this annalistic text as an account of the king's deeds.[15] Yet even if this is the case, we still possess no self-portrayal by the great man. Therefore, we cannot claim that things definitely happened in the way the annals described them; indeed, we must seriously doubt this. But we can state with certainty that Charles was concerned to ensure that his childhood, the early years of his reign, and his rule in general were analyzed, assessed, and viewed in the manner that the annalist had adopted. Wars predominated in this account, the Carolingians' protection of the Roman Church was emphasized, and now and then the text was interlaced with a personal anecdote, which surely must have been contributed by Charlemagne himself.[16]

In all probability, a decade later, around 805, he encouraged the nuns of the convent at Chelles, under the supervision of his sister Gisela, whom he had visited there the year before, to compile another work of history, the so-called *Earlier Annals of Metz* (*Annales Mettensis priores*). These offered an exhaustive account, albeit on the basis of largely unknown sources, of the rise of the Carolingian dynasty, first to the position of mayors of the palace and then to kings and emperors. Although they drew on the *Royal Frankish Annals,* they presented a somewhat different picture of Charlemagne and his deeds.[17] The narrative had a broader sweep, was more comprehensive, and moved purposefully toward its endpoint, the attainment of the title of emperor. And it was evident that this narrative was quite deliberately skewing its view of past events. Thus, for instance, it is claimed of Pepin (II) of Herstal, Charlemagne's great-grandfather, who died in 714: "Strengthened by the warnings of his holy ancestors, Pepin trod the paths of justice and finally seized the reins of royal power." The text goes on to reveal that Pepin proceeded to subjugate the Alemanni, the Bavarians, and the Saxons to the Frankish imperium.[18] The clear implication was that Charlemagne's imperial role was predestined from the earliest times.

How, then, are we to do Charlemagne justice, this ruler on whom contemporaries heaped panegyrics of praise and whom they secretly berated? Does any single one of the biographical sketches or patterns of memory ring true? Or all of them, viewed in the round? Or none at all? Interpretations from his age, namely, the late eighth and early ninth centuries, require a knowledge of the yardsticks by which all actions then were measured. These were applied across the board, from the mightiest ruler of the Middle Ages to each of his subjects. Yet these are now wholly alien to us skeptical denizens of the early twenty-first century and therefore allow us only tentative guesses at what life was really like in past eras. They require instead that we practice an archaeology of historical memory, which lays bare the strata of superimposed civilizations, one by one, until it has penetrated to the one under investigation and exposed it, while still being incapable of giving us a truly vivid overview of the polychromatic richness of life in that period.

So how might we approach an alien, dead, long-faded period, in which the threads of knowledge, faith, and action, of social values and personal emotions, were drawn together quite differently from nowadays? And how are we to approach Charlemagne, a king, a ruler, and a human being about whom no one knows the slightest thing anymore, who has become a mythical figure, a symbol, a cipher? Or his friends and confederates and his opponents, especially viewed from this contemporary age of instant experience and gratification, where only the here and now and self-fulfillment count for anything? How can we grasp the desires and disappointments of the deceased long after they have dissipated? Or their transgressions—now so foreign to us—or their beliefs and objectives?

No act of remembering can bring back yesterday; rather, every remembered past is a half-conscious, half-unconscious memory constructed from a present state with all its attendant joys, worries, enmities, and fears, with its totality of experiences, with its knowledge and its evaluations of information that has flowed to it from the past, and with its wishes, goals, and hopes.[19] Nor can remembering hope to reproduce anything that was once experienced without distorting it in the recollection. This goes for both the modern writer of history and for his or her ancient counterpart, and for each and every report from the distant past, for Einhard and his readers and interpreters, as it does for every annalist. Everything is the present, in which the past is reflected. This is particularly true of the legacies of cultures in which the written word had such limited currency as it did in the era of Charlemagne. We read Einhard's *Vita Karoli* with the advantage of the knowledge of the twelve hundred years that have elapsed since it was written. What is past can never be heard or seen again in its original form a second time.

History flows incessantly onward because it is rooted in human memory; it must constantly be rethought and recounted afresh since it is constantly called on to inform and educate younger generations of people. It does not convey some eternally unchanging message that "this is the way things were"; indeed, the most it can hope to do is to preserve a dried-out skeleton of inconsequential facts, which the "visionary" historian alone can then make sense of. History possesses a past that can be recalled only in a fragmentary way and is scarcely manageable, and a future as opaque as the future of humanity in general. Its bedrock, human memory, never rests but is subject instead to endlessly enduring powers of modulation because it, memory, is already embedded in the events themselves and constantly addresses new groups of listeners and readers. Likewise, the so-called *Royal Frankish Annals* rapidly found itself revised once it came within the purview of the royal court. Only ecclesiastical remembrance in prayer, namely, the memorial element enshrined in liturgical practice, was able to offer a more tenacious resistance to this tendency to distort, although even this could not entirely escape it. After all, essentially what was being remembered here were just the names of those for whom prayers were being offered, nothing more.

Therefore, only approximations to those distant eras of history are possible. Supported by historians such as Paul the Deacon, Einhard, Notker, and the anonymous annalists, together with the nuns of Chelles and others, these approximations follow various visions, warnings, and particular instructions that accounted for the powers of distortion already mentioned and let themselves be led by them. Some traces of the many changes that took place in, or were stimulated by, the age of Charlemagne still remain, although it is also true that those that have not been swept away entirely by the turbulence of ensuing ages have in many cases left only an unclear and faint impression on the written record. Yet historians can uncover even these scant remains and with some patience trace them back to their origin—acting as archaeologists of knowledge who, armed with their sheaves of questions, gradually work back from the present to the past. But it must be remembered that for all this, they still belong decidedly to the here and now.

With all these provisos, then, what might we identify about the childhood and boyhood of the future hero figure Charlemagne? What image did his contemporaries paint of the world surrounding the Frankish Empire, and what impression did it make on the young Frankish king as he set off on his campaigns of conquest? What expectations did he have to fulfill? How were the Franks and their leaders persuaded to reach a consensus on the constant round of wars waged by the king, and how was this maintained? Ultimately, Charlemagne emerges as a Christian ruler and his royal court as the focal point of a lasting process of renewal. Then the way becomes clear for the rebirth of the Western emperorship and the emergence of the struggles, during the final years of the reign of the "Imperator Augustus," to fashion from scant and often widely dispersed residues an empire founded on the noblest values and on peace and justice.

The tools used by historians in delving into the depths of the past consist of knowledge rather than the spade and trowel of the archaeologist. Thus, what they hope to uncover reflects their own present; they find this mirrored in the values and yardsticks they discover, in the beliefs and superstitions, in the learning and skills, in the environments and modes of existence, and in the ways the past perceived and recalled things. All that modern historians who engage with this period are doing is creating their own images of Charlemagne in precisely the same way as the painter Albrecht Dürer did in the late Middle Ages in his idealized portrait of Karolus Magnus Imperator (Figure 60), a work that undoubtedly obeys this or that artistic canon to the letter but is far removed from the historical reality of Charlemagne. This subject is treated at length in the Epilogue.

This sense of an unattainable past, which still resides in the most recent rules of art, dictates our whole mode of thought, action, and research. Every glance back into the past is like looking into a mirror, where what we see turns out to be a refraction of the skill and knowledge of our own times, along with its passions and doubts. We are the ones, not Charlemagne, who pose questions about modes of perception and structures of rulership; we are the ones who revere the art of double-entry bookkeeping and costs and profits, not the great king and emperor who scored great successes and overcame failures. In the end, history always comes down to us. Strictly speaking, then, no one Charlemagne resembles another.

So, an approximation to Charlemagne. He died, as the Church commanded, forewarned by omens and composed and calm. There was no question of doing penance. Lamentations for the deceased emperor were held only briefly in monasteries, dirges such as the still-extant *Planctus Karoli* were sung (this may have originated at Bobbio Abbey, the institution founded by St. Columbanus, which enjoyed a revival during Charlemagne's rule), and tears were shed; however, there were no excessive displays of grief, since these would not have been fitting.[20] "O Christ, you who command the heavenly Host, grant Charlemagne peace in Your Kingdom!" "Seated on Your Holy Throne, O Christ, receive your devoted servant Charlemagne with Your Apostles!" With incantations such as these, the living publicly commemorated the great man who had died, and who was now, hopefully and in pious trust, seeking an audience with the King of Heaven. These were decidedly not the kind of lavish funeral orations that became customary during the Baroque.

Having been taught by the eminent Anglo-Saxon scholar Alcuin of York, whom he managed to attract to his court at Aix as his personal tutor, Charlemagne was well aware that the Day of Judgment was nigh.[21] He was as devout a Christian as it was possible to be at this time. But he was also a man who enjoyed to the full the sensual pleasures of life. He had actively sought out and enjoyed the delights of physical love, time and time again. Charlemagne's life was certainly lived on a grand scale and was pious by the standards of his age, but it was not saintly. To be sure, the king and emperor had erected the magnificent Church of St. Mary and Our Savior in Aachen and had decorated and furnished it lavishly with gold and silver; he also regularly attended Mass every morning and evening and, as long as his health permitted, observed the nighttime canonical hours. Yet lust was regarded as one of the seven deadly sins and required penitence. Why didn't Charlemagne simply refrain from it? Did he somehow hope to evade its consequences in the hereafter? Furthermore, Charlemagne was no stranger to anger, revenge, and violence. Could all these faults be outweighed by good deeds? And did he do such deeds of his own volition, or was he spurred on by the need to receive God's grace? Many contemporaries had their doubts on this score. The theologians of the period presently began to indulge themselves in formulating doctrines of sin and predestination. Handbooks of penance, often imported into the Frankish Empire from Ireland, contained ready-made catalogs of sins and tariffs for purging oneself of them; only gradually did the practice of lifetime confession become established. Yet in Charlemagne's case, help for the suffering sinner might also be guaranteed by the thousandfold intercession of monks throughout the length and breadth of the kingdom.

What factors would be weighed in St. Michael's scales? Charlemagne had had messengers of the faith dispatched and had promoted the expansion of the cathedral church, as well as founding and endowing new bishoprics where these were required. In deep concern for the good order of the Church and the observance of ecclesiastical norms, he set in train a series of reforms that afforded protection, as far as possible, for the clergy and church property. Eternal praise of God resounded from the monasteries and would henceforth not fall silent in Charlemagne's realm. Moreover, it would ring forth in correct language that was worthy of God and pleasing to Him. The revival of education that Charlemagne set in motion was designed to fulfill this sacred purpose. In a way no ruler before him had done, the king had paid homage to the pope, the successor of St. Peter, on whose rock the Church was founded. He was the first king and emperor to seriously enact the legal principle according to which the pope was beyond the reach of all human justice—a decision that would have major ramifications in the future. Charlemagne also endeavored to make the protection of the poor that religion demanded a reality. He took up the cause of Christians overseas, sending them alms to rebuild their churches.

All the good works could now be weighed in the angel's scales of justice, at least in the eyes of Charlemagne's friends. Those he had conquered and ostracized may well have taken a different view. They might have remembered him rather as a despot, an oppressor, and a tyrant. Yet posterity chose to ignore their voices, at least at first. If one were to believe contemporary accounts, they appear to have been condemned to silence for all time. Only centuries later did their view begin to make any headway, articulated in this or that chanson de geste or other legends, such as the story of the Four Sons of Aymon, and fed by oral storytelling traditions and later revised accounts. Legends such as this testify to a groundswell of hostility and rebellion against the emperor and of rejection and criticism of his reign, especially in the southwest of the old Carolingian Empire, namely, in Aquitaine, which indeed was finally bound more firmly to the French crown only after the crusades against the Albigensians in the thirteenth century. Charlemagne appeared in these chansons as an antihero, a positive caricature of a ruler, sometimes even distorted to the point of ridicule.[22]

And what about Charlemagne himself? The king and emperor never brought himself to set down any autobiographical utterances. Even so, there is not a total absence of indications of his personality; they are just of a different kind. They can be found, for instance, in the *res gestae* of the *Royal Frankish Annals*. They are hidden in the theological polemic against the Greek "veneration of images" that he commissioned after the Second Council of Nicaea in 787. The finished work was read out to him, a layperson, for his scrutiny, and he duly commented on a number of individual sentences, by no means always just with brief, clipped instructions.[23] The sentences that provoked him to such exclamations give us some insight into Charlemagne's innermost self: a devout, earnest, and artless character.[24] Take, for example, the following dictum, falsely attributed to St. Ambrose: "In the same way in which God exists, lives, and reflects, so too does the soul exist, live, and reflect according to its scope." ("Good!" is Charlemagne's commentary.) According to its scope! So how did Charlemagne measure his own soul? And on another quotation from the same Pseudo-Ambrose— "The more an individual embodies virtues within himself, the closer he is to God and to being made in his Creator's own image"—Charlemagne remarks "Very good!" The king guided by virtue, close to God, and a facsimile of his Maker—this amounts to nothing less than a claim to absolute legitimacy by the ruler that transcends all panegyrics. Finally, there is this homily by the apostle St. Paul: "Therefore glorify God and carry Him in your body!" "*Catholice!*" comments Charlemagne. Here, the king is presenting himself as beholden to the Church, as a spirit-imbued agent of God, as the successor of Christ. In sentences such as these, then, Charlemagne wanted to identify aspects of his own psyche and to act in accordance with them: in a Catholic way, close to God and as befitted his soul.

So it was that, alongside Charlemagne's renown and his exquisite cathedral church, with its throne and imperial tomb, an undercurrent of skepticism and hostility also endured. Yet he remained a symbol of faith and hope, and the locus of his torments after death—the Mountain of Purgatory, not Hell—only served to foster them. And it is indeed the case that later generations considered the emperor absolved of all sins. As early as the apocalyptic year 1000, Emperor Otto III, a Saxon on his father's side, planned to canonize Charlemagne, the "Apostle" of the Saxons (a position that he, as victor, had occupied in the realm of the Ottonians since the late ninth century). Otto failed in this, however, and Charlemagne's canonization became a reality only 150 years later, in 1165, as the result of a calculated political move by the ruling emperor from Swabia, Frederick Barbarossa, and under the supervision of the excommunicated Archbishop Rainald of Cologne.[25] The pope who endorsed it, Paschal III, is also now regarded as an antipope; as a result, the late emperor's name was never included in the *Martyrologium Romanum,* the official register of all the Catholic saints. But in Aachen and Frankfurt, as well as in Reims, Zurich, and many other places, he has been revered as a saint ever since, with his feast day being celebrated on 28 January, the anniversary of his death in the year 814.

I

BOYHOOD

HORSE DUNG AND CESSPITS, chicken coops and pig rearing, oxen and a leisurely pace of life—Charlemagne grew up in a rural environment. From an early age, he knew his way around saddles and bridles, and his daily routine was filled with the smell of the stables, the shouts of farmhands, and the groaning of heavily laden carts. In such surroundings, a boy could let off steam, test his strength, and quickly mature to manhood. The Merovingians, the Carolingian dynasty's predecessors on the Frankish throne, had mostly resided in towns.[1] But, doubtless for reasons of easier accommodation and supply, Charlemagne's family tended to prefer spacious residences in the country known as *Pfalzen* (palaces)—though not exclusively, as Charlemagne's many sojourns in Worms or Regensburg attest. The *Pfalzen* were large estates, or villas, comprising a central manor house, possibly of half-timbered construction, with various outbuildings, workshops, workhouses for women (so-called *genicia*), smithies and farriers' workshops, stables, mills, and houses for clergymen, courtiers, and servants, and were suitable places for hosting the king and his entourage for several days or weeks. Every palace also had its own chapel, in which the royal family could attend daily mass and pray.

In addition, country living entailed constant change. Charlemagne's father, his children and their mother (pregnant or not), the servants and the retinue of armed men—this large group was constantly on the move, mainly in the "royal country" between the Loire, the Seine, the Meuse (Maas), and the Rhine, journeying from palace to palace and from one tented encampment to the next. This was a restless, itinerant life, but an unhurried one too (time was not precious), and the children were either carried in a palanquin or rode on horseback. This, then, was how Charlemagne was raised.

Certainly, although his usual milieu was country estates, Charlemagne was also familiar with several cities—Paris, Trier, Cologne, Vienne, Arles, Mains, Worms, Regensburg, and many others. He had visited most of them in the company of his father. These dated from Roman times but, as remains everywhere from this era attested, had shrunk considerably in the meantime or lay in ruins, and although they offered sufficient space for a bishop and the requisite churches, they were hardly large enough any longer for extended royal sojourns. Moreover, with the possible exception of Italy, they did not form their own jurisdiction; at this stage, there was still no specifically municipal law, still less any properly constituted arrangement between towns and their surrounding territory; nor was there any such thing as an organized citizenry or bourgeoisie. As a result, the societal basis for such abstract concepts as "equality" was entirely lacking. According to the understanding of that time, all people were not considered equal even where divine judgment was concerned. The aristocratic society that Charlemagne grew up in was characterized by inequality, and for all that this society proclaimed that its guiding and preserving principle was "justice," in actual fact it was governed by rivalry and conflict.

The only surviving reminiscence of Charlemagne's childhood is found in a later legend. It told the story of how the young Charlemagne, just seven years old at the time and extremely boisterous, started playing around among the graves that had been opened up for an ecclesiastical ritual of transferring the bones of saints in St. Germain (near Paris)—a ritual that was attended by miracles—and in the process lost a tooth for the first time. The myth may be an appealing tale well told, but it is fabricated for all that. The fact that children play and that even future emperors are capable of rampaging around wildly is scarcely surprising. Yet the story is simply not true. Charlemagne supposedly told it about himself. But no grown person remembers exactly when and how he or she lost the first of his or her twenty milk teeth; also, the chronological information does not tally. There is no absolute certainty about what year Charlemagne was born. His biographer Einhard, who knew the king and emperor for decades and served at his court, remembered incorrectly when he spoke of his death at the age of seventy-two. It is highly probable that Charlemagne was born in 748, reputedly on 2 April.[2] But this year doesn't chime in with the story of the missing tooth.

This episode, which historians have so eagerly grasped at for want of anything else to report about Charlemagne's childhood, was in fact fabricated far away from the emperor's court sometime in the ninth century—in a document commonly called the *Translatio* of St. Germanus—in order to secure possession and legal title over those same saints' graves in St. Germain. By then, Charlemagne had legendary status, and the tale of his having been present, even as just a small boy, would stand the claimants in good stead: a common pattern of fabrication, but one that tells us nothing about the childhood of its hero. The boyhood years of all early medieval rulers, insofar as they had not already ascended the throne when they were still children, are unknown to us. The reasons for this lie in the fundamental lack of interest shown by all historians in the reality of children's development and in education. They have traditionally preferred writing about dying and leaving the world rather than a person's entry into it. Actions are celebrated, not conditions. Stereotypical patterns of childhood were therefore promulgated, as opposed to people's real fates.

Einhard, too, thought it unnecessary to recall Charlemagne's childhood and youth, since by then no one was alive who had firsthand knowledge of that period. His place of birth is unknown; however, given the journey his parents were undertaking at the time, it may well have been situated in the Ver Palatinate somewhere between Paris and Compiègne; this region was the heartland of the dominion of Charlemagne's father, Pepin the Short.[3] Pepin would have made known his great joy at the birth of a son—something he had long wished for—far and wide. Yet nobody preserved any recollections of the future king's early years for posterity. All we really know are the identities of his closest relatives: his father, Pepin, and mother, Bertrada; his younger brother Carloman, who died aged twenty; another brother, also named Pepin, who only survived to the age of two; and his sister Gisela, whose poorly attested marriage plans with Adelchis, the son of the Lombard king, and with Leon, son of the Byzantine emperor, came to nothing, and who as the abbess of Chelles and Soissons died just under four years before her brother. Two other sisters, Rothaid and Adelheid, who died when they were still very young, are known only through their epitaphs at the Abbey of St. Arnulf in Metz.[4]

In any event, the young Charlemagne may have encountered even his closest relatives only when they were summoned by his father to attend special ceremonial occasions. But his mother, who was presumably responsible for his education as a young child, would still have exerted some influence over her son during his first years as king and over the Franks as a whole, before Charlemagne began to disengage himself from her. Bertrada was a daughter of one of the most powerful families in Austrasia, which owned estates around Laon and especially in the Eifel Mountains; it was through their marrying into this family that the Carolingians came into possession of the important Benedictine abbey at Prüm in Lorraine, together with its extensive landholdings.[5] Pepin's father, Charles Martel, had already taken an aunt of Bertrada as his first wife. No doubt Pepin's subsequent connection through marriage with this family helped smooth and promote his rise to the throne.

With such a deafening silence on the subject in the material that has been passed down to us, we can only guess at what impressions Charlemagne's childhood may have left on him. No chronicler recorded the name of his wet nurse—he was most probably breast-fed up to the age of three—or the names of his religious tutors and teachers. Yet these individuals definitely existed and must have made a major contribution to the future monarch's greatness. They will have joked with the boy Charlemagne, chided him when necessary, taught him—in all likelihood from the age of six onward—how to read and pray, and probably instructed this son of the man who had just become king in Latin also.[6] Did the teacher's cane ever swish down on this pupil's back? These first, highly formative years of the royal child's life can at best be presented as a kind of collective biography, which agglomerates a variety of information from here and there and forms it into a composite picture of a life that is typical of the era but is by no means an individual portrait.[7] The great man does not emerge from such an exercise with a distinct youth of his own. Key moments of his biography are unfortunately closed off from us forever.

Despite the existence of various (in the main, later) mirrors for princes, the principles, objectives, and ideals of the worldly education of a particular prince were not specially written down on parchment, even though they must have had just as formative an influence on a young person's maturing psyche as such ideals still have today. How did Charlemagne learn to master his emotions and to get through puberty, the stage of life when a person reached the age of consent and legal capacity, and how did he acquire the social graces? He was undoubtedly told the story that claimed that the Franks originated in Troy, and he seems to have taken this to be the truth; in any event, Paulus Diaconus (Paul the Deacon), the Lombard historian at the court of Charlemagne, declared "the Trojan Anchises," the father of Aeneas, to be the titular patron saint of Charlemagne's great-great-grandfather

Anschise, the son of St. Arnulf of Metz.[8] Charlemagne truly believed, then, that his ancestors were cousins of the legendary founder of Rome. Did such an ancestry condition the ranking, status, and self-regard of the family? The simple fact remains that we do not know how the lordly boy was raised. Consequently, the decisive formative influences remain hidden from the historian and can only be the subject of all kinds of speculation. In terms of his character, Charlemagne's later greatness remains a mystery.

We therefore have to search for isolated traces of recollection, for what Charlemagne himself might have remembered and wished to retain, souvenirs for himself and for wider courtly society. Only a narrow trace, barely detectable, emerges that might lead us to the experiences of his childhood and youth and their effect on the future ruler. Under the supposition previously established,[9] namely, that the entries on his first decades in power that appear in the *Royal Frankish Annals*—whose writers were very close to the court—all came about under the direct influence of Charlemagne the ruler, these might give us an insight into those events that had a particularly strong influence on the boy and the burgeoning king's son. What do these documents reveal?

These semiofficial records delve back into the past only very briefly. The annals began with the death of Charlemagne's paternal grandfather, Charles Martel, in 741 and the succession of his sons Carloman and Pepin (the latter of whom was Charlemagne's father). Everything that, even then, could have been included from well-known older reports was either suppressed or presented in a thoroughly distorted way. Until 767–768, when Charlemagne himself came to the throne, the annual entries are something of a feeble trickle. Other annals from the same period, such as the *Continuation* of the so-called *Chronicle of Fredegar*[10] or the *Earlier Annals of Metz*[11]—which were also connected with the royal court and used the *Royal Frankish Annals* as their basis—are much fuller and more informative. But everything changed the year Charlemagne ascended the throne. From this point on, the *Royal Frankish Annals* also becomes much more informative. Did the work before this date, with its terse reports, merely form a kind of guideline through the history of the realm before the accession of the great ruler? Or a collection of key words for souvenirs? Or a personal aide-mémoire? Or was it intended to set the basic tone for how future historiography should depict the past?[12] In short, was this Charlemagne's own snapshot of the most important experiences of his youth?

The *Annals* provide instances that would appear to corroborate this supposition. The entry for the year 759 is particularly striking in this respect.

Apart from mentioning the celebration of Christmas, all it contained was this surprising piece of news: "In this year, a son was born to King Pepin, whom the said king gave his own name, so that he should be called Pepin, like his father. He survived for two years and died in the third." This is the only entry within the *Annals* that cites a birth within the Carolingian dynasty; not even Charlemagne's birth or those of his children are mentioned. The birth of this Pepin and his death—the only place where this is spoken of—stand out all the more starkly as a result. This is an obituary of a quite extraordinary kind. No other passage here is devoted to the demise of a minor. We may surmise that the death of his little brother affected Charlemagne deeply.

This entry does not reflect the grief of some unknown annalist, but rather the king's commemoration of the dead.[13] The thirteen- or fourteen-year-old Charlemagne had just returned from the first or second military campaign he undertook in the company of his father.[14] Did he feel the death of little Pepin keenly at this point? Or was this the time, around 761, when his father introduced the concubine Himiltrud to Charlemagne, who then gave him his first son? This child was given the same name as Charlemagne's father and his dead infant brother.[15] So, does the death notice in the *Annals* also contain a hidden announcement of a birth? Charlemagne had not forgotten his little brother. In general, he was greatly moved by the untimely death of his siblings, as attested by the two epitaphs in Metz for his sisters, who also passed away when they were young.[16]

Whatever the case, the entry for the year concerning the unfortunate Pepin reflects Charlemagne's personal engagement with the *Royal Frankish Annals* and at the same time provides a retrospective insight into the formative influences at work in the story of his youth. Viewed in this way, the other entries may also, by analogy, be swiftly assessed for their relevance to Charlemagne. What do they point to?

The entry for the year 747 contains the first mention of the appeal for help issued by Grifo, Pepin's brother, to the Franks' enemies the Saxons, while the only details given for the following year, apart from a mention of developments in Bavaria, concern Grifo's flight through Saxony and Bavaria to take refuge with Duke Waiofar of Aquitaine—a clear hint at the legitimacy of the fratricidal war and the campaigns waged against Waiofar, Saxony, and Bavaria. But it also hints at the legitimacy of Pepin the Short's ascent to the throne. The entries for 749 and 750 duly report this great success. Nothing was recorded, by contrast, for the two years thereafter. The 753 entry, then, following on from 747, recounts Pepin's second war against the Saxons, the death of Grifo, and above all the arrival of Pope Stephen II in France, for whom, as we shall presently see, the six-year-old Charlemagne had to fulfil an important task;[17] the following year, Pepin and his two sons were anointed by the pope.

The entry in the *Annals* for 755 is dominated by Pepin's first Italian campaign and the restitution of the landholding of the Roman Church, the prelude, in other words, to Charlemagne's own campaign against the Lombards; another announcement in this year, of great importance for the succession, is that of the death of Pepin's brother Carloman. In 756, we see the second Italian campaign crowned with similar success and even greater donations to the heirs of St. Peter, which Charlemagne himself was allowed to affirm.[18] Great emphasis was placed on his alliance with the apostolic princes and their representatives, while in contrast, great play is made of the nefariousness, the untrustworthiness, and the unreliability of the Lombards and their king—an experience that Charlemagne was not to forget.

Alongside another note on the Bavarian duke Tassilo, the entry for 757 commemorates the arrival at court of an "imperial" (water) organ from Greece, whose tones clearly resounded long in Charlemagne's ears. An auspicious sign! The following year recalls yet another campaign by Pepin against the Saxons, who had by now been sentenced to pay annual compensation to the Franks of three hundred horses, but who proved to be tough adversaries. The years 760 through 764 are entirely filled with mention of Pepin's struggle against Waiofar of Aquitaine, in the course of which Charlemagne's first participation in a military campaign—specially inserted into the standard formulation used—is emphasized. It was this same conflict that saw Charlemagne launch his first military operation in his own right after coming to the throne, and that he brought to a successful conclusion. The year 765 notes, alongside a court assembly in Attigny, Christmas celebrations in the palatinate of Aix—the first time it is given this title; 766 sees another attack on Aquitaine, as do the two subsequent years. The first of these entries recalls the capture of Toulouse and Albi and, along with these towns, the whole of southwestern Aquitaine, while the second records the fall of Waiofar, the death of Pepin, and the succession of his sons Charlemagne and Carloman. The "glorious Lord and King Charlemagne" then celebrated his first Christmas in Aix (Aachen).

The wars in Aquitaine and against the Lombards and the Saxons, the elimination of the "collateral branch" of the Carolingian family and the rise of Charlemagne's line to autocracy and kingship, the "infidelity" of Tassilo of Bavaria, and the veneration of St. Peter and Rome—these were the events and impression that Charlemagne, after coming to the throne, recalled from his childhood and wished to have written down for posterity, alongside the death of young Pepin, his own first experience of war, and his love for Aix. This nexus of events was to dominate Charlemagne's deeds as king for years to come: the swift, successful war in Aquitaine; the long years of bitter struggle against the Saxons; his seizure of the Lombard kingdom; his first, surprising visit to Rome; the close connection with the Apostolic See; his propensity for memorializing events; and his momentous first encounter with the city of Aix. It seemed as though the son was fulfilling his father's legacy. Was it Charlemagne's wish that the Franks regard his own history in the same light? He could still rely on Pepin's ruling elite for support. One can sense, even see, how the son followed his father hither and thither in rapt admiration, be it in thought or in action, how his father's deeds seemed to him pointers for his own future kingship and to demand completion, and how compelling this act of remembrance was for him.

Miraculous tales were later told about Aix. One claimed that when hot springs had suddenly erupted there quite unexpectedly, Pepin had dressed himself in just a shirt and sandals and, protected by the sign of the Cross, thrust with his sword against a demon in the form of a shadow, plunging his blade in so deeply that filth, blood, and foul-smelling fat gushed out before a stream of pure, clean, healing water began to issue forth.[19] Behind this legend lay a reminiscence of the ancient Roman spa in the town. Did the images of pagan gods there, the devotional inscriptions, and temple remains betray the presence of impure spirits? The Celtic deity Grannus, for example, for whom Aachen, *Aquisgrani* (literally, "at the waters of Grannus"), was named?[20] Were these ancient remains completely destroyed? As always, one thing emerges clearly from this anecdote: namely, that Charlemagne had inherited his love for Aix (Aachen) from his father.

Thus it was the experience of war, an agonal social environment that did not spare even his own family, that dominated Charlemagne's childhood. The socialization of the future ruler was shaped by it. Indeed, waging war was the most urgent task of an early medieval ruler; at best, the *Annals* mention the internal organization of the empire over the coming years only in passing. It was essential for a king to prove himself as a military commander, to master his horse, to ride competently, to wield a sword, a hunting lance, and a boar spear effectively, and to successfully overcome and slay a wild boar. All this was seen as training for the body, fighting, and war and as a mark of leadership. We know that more than one of Charlemagne's great-grandsons were involved in hunting accidents with a fatal outcome.

Hunting was meant to be proof of kingly resolve and outstanding courage. A telling anecdote was recounted in this regard also: it told how Pepin cut through a lion's neck and severed a bull's head from its body, both together with one single mighty blow. A bullfight, then, served as a legitimation of his rulership: "They [his followers] fell to the ground, as though a thunderbolt had struck them, and cried: 'Who but a madman would deny your right to rule over all mankind?'" The monk Notker of St. Gall recounted this story in his *Life of Charlemagne,* written in 883–884 (2.15).

Charlemagne, too, was a great hunter. "Father Charlemagne rushes past . . . faster than birds fly, and plunges his spear into the beast's heart, thrusting the cold steel deep into the body of the monster . . . and causing the boar to fall to the ground." This celebration of the king's hunting prowess was written by a court poet around 800.[21] As a father, Charlemagne brought up his sons "in accordance with the custom of the Franks . . . to learn horsemanship, and to practice war and the chase" and his daughters "to familiarize themselves with cloth-making, and to handle distaff and spindle," as his biographer Einhard reports (chap. 19). The latter of these statements was perhaps said more for effect than as an accurate account of their schooling, for the king's daughters were also taught Latin and learned how to lead others, manage estates, ride, and travel from court to court—in short, how to participate in the business of ruling.

A youth spent in this way was no mere child's play. A king, as was said at the time of the duke of Bavaria, was expected to "lead an army and be capable of issuing orders with a loud voice." A ritualized way of speaking may well have been what was meant here, like the language of military commands in modern armies. The king was supposed to be gifted at oratory; delivering speeches was a key requirement of rulership, not least to his vassals and his army. The art of kingly oration, *adnuntiatio,* is later well attested for Charlemagne's grandsons. Charlemagne would doubtless have also learned this facility at an early age. He "was an eloquent, rousing speaker," his biographer tells us (chap. 25), blessed with a "clear, strong voice" (*clara voce*), but one that "scarcely befitted his stature" (chap. 22). Admittedly, public speaking demanded not only a voice that carried; it also required knowledge and education, as Charlemagne himself later emphasized.[22]

The *Annals* said nothing about royal virtues, such as a love of justice and protection of the poor, widows, and orphans. Only his protection and organization of the Church were occasionally mentioned, a clear indication that this function was seen as an aspect of royal authority rather than a matter of private piety. Individual testimonies that have come down to us from a later period and from different sources tell us more; although these likewise reveal nothing about Charlemagne's boyhood and youth, they do take the experiences of these years for granted and so enable us once again to make some cautious inferences.

Education as a Scholar and Instruction in the Christian Faith

Above all, education was in dire need of improvement, having atrophied in the seventh and eighth centuries. Yet the Christian faith—the Church and the act of worship—was thirsting for it. A new scholarly elite, devoted to the faith but also rigorously educated, needed to be trained afresh. In all likelihood, Charlemagne recognized or at least intuited this pressing requirement from early on and as a boy himself enjoyed the benefit of a full religious and scholarly education.

Later, as king, he would candidly proclaim his faith: "Since divine clemency ceaselessly protects us in both war and peace, . . . so we desire, because we are concerned for its welfare, to constantly improve the state of our Church, and to zealously renew [*reparare*] the discipline of learning [*litterarum officina*], which through the neglect of our forefathers is now almost forgotten, and—insofar as we are able—admonish others through our example to engage in intensive study of the liberal arts."[23] To mend what was defective, to renew, and to urge people to study: this sums up the key task that Charlemagne would set himself as king.

Charlemagne's educational program was not, however, an end in itself. It was in the service of worship and, by extension, the consolidation and legitimizing of his own authority. As a boy, he learned the necessity of devotion to God and his saints, and even to the pope; the royal unction of his father, himself, and his brother and the benediction of his mother and of the Franks and of the whole future royal dynasty clearly pointed him toward this. Being blessed by the successor, heir, and representative of the apostolic princes made an indelible impression on the future emperor in his early years, imparting to him a promise of the strengthening and legitimizing power of St. Peter. He was to remain true to this power for the whole of his life.

After unction by the pope, everything was better—or so it seemed: the Franks willingly followed the father who had eliminated his brother and nephews and appointed himself king, and the double victory over the Lombards, the capture of Septimania and Narbonne from the Saracens, and the increasingly successful war against Waiofar in Aquitaine all served to indicate that divine good fortune would henceforth rest on Pepin and Charlemagne.

The boy must have been receptive to the teachings of his spiritual educators. His humility before the mysteries of faith, which he still displayed as a ruler, his respect for the sanctity of the Church and its priests, his subjugation to the power of the saints and of God himself, of which he gave evidence from the very first day of his rule—in short, his piety and his unswerving religious observance (*cultus divinus*)—were all likely to have been awakened in his childhood and reinforced in his youth.

A certain degree of scholarly education was expected of a king's son. In this, Charlemagne outstripped all his forebears and predecessors. He is said to have spoken Latin like a native tongue, according to his biographer Einhard, who was writing long after the emperor's death (chap. 25), although this may have been a piece of posthumous panegyric exaggeration on Einhard's part. And as a king, he is reputed to have practiced dialectics, a fact that his tutor Alcuin not only corroborated but also defended against criticism that it was a useless undertaking (epistle 174); this further stresses his Latin skills, since such a thing would have been quite impossible in Old Frankish.

Charlemagne also displayed a practical interest in the natural sciences. The foundations of this may have been laid by his instruction in the seven liberal arts when he was still a boy. The king supposedly even understood a little Greek, at least according to Einhard (chap. 25). Charlemagne's later well-attested interest in the calculation of time, the *computus,* and astronomy may also have been stimulated at the same time. As king, he set great store by his children's education in the liberal arts, "which he took charge of in person," as Einhard again reported (chap. 19). The experiences of his youth would doubtless have inculcated this attitude in him. Henceforth, even though there is no direct evidence of this, Carolingian princes would have had a thorough grounding in Latin; this would customarily have begun around the age of seven. Reading and reciting, disciplines that were taught separately from writing, were also expected of a king's son.

To what extent Charlemagne actually met these high educational aims is a moot point, but as a mature ruler, he was surrounded by too much Latin to imagine that it would not have been intelligible to him. Riddles and jokes, songs and waspish instances of irony from the precincts of his court were all conveyed in Latin. We must ask ourselves who would have dared to laugh and puzzle if the king had not been able to join in these activities. In fact, Charlemagne is said to have gone to school with his cousin Adalhard, the later abbot of Corbie, who for his part (and, we must assume, Charlemagne too) showed a particular interest not only in learning Latin but also in mathematics, astronomy, and computistics (the science of calendrical calculation) and also proved adept in dialectics.[24] Even after he became king, Charlemagne would still recall this period of his life. Admittedly, writing—which at that time was regarded as more of a craft than a scholarly aptitude—was something that the emperor never mastered, despite a few attempts to do so late in life; his hand, which would have been used to clutching a sword, was likely too heavy and clumsy to manipulate the delicate goose-feather quill.

We may speculate whether the boy Charlemagne was really predisposed to a spiritual upbringing. If this was indeed the case, then surely not exclusively. Einhard (chap. 29) recalls that he was also very fond of contemporary songs in the vernacular, along with heroic epic poems, "heathen and ancient lays" (*barbara et antiquissima carmina*) that told of the deeds and wars of early kings. Charlemagne had them collected and written down. It would be wonderful to know what treasures this songbook contained, but in a fit of piety befitting his common sobriquet, Charlemagne's son Louis I had the only copy destroyed. We can only speculate. Alboin and Rosamund, Attila the Hun and Dietrich von Bern, Günther von Worms and Siegfried, and the Nibelungs may well have been the hero figures of Charlemagne's youth. After he became king of Italy in 774, he had a bronze statue of Dietrich von Bern brought from Rome to Aix—for what reason, we do not know;[25] this also disappeared in the reign of Louis the Pious. Charlemagne undoubtedly took great pleasure in the deeds of ancient heroes and in the tales of the worldly goings-on at this or that court. All the same, we can never know for certain what Charlemagne read during his formative years. As a young boy, he was presumably told all about how the Franks and his ancestors originally hailed from the ancient city of Troy. Yet there is no evidence of an epic lay about Troy having existed in Old Frankish. Has this been lost? Whatever the case, "King David," as his courtiers later took to calling Charlemagne, loved songs accompanied by the panpipes and stringed instruments plucked with a plectrum. And these would surely not all have been religious chants.

Granted, much of what Charlemagne read would have been of a religious nature. As his later life as a ruler showed, this reading matter had a lasting influence on him as he was growing up. The Psalms would not have been familiar only to monks during this period. Precious manuscripts were produced, such as the Dagulf Psalter, which Charlemagne had made as a gift for Pope Hadrian I. The king and emperor is said to have especially admired St. Augustine of Hippo's *On Christian Doctrine* and *The City of God;* once more, Einhard (chap. 24) makes specific mention of the latter work.

Charlemagne may well have been given a copy of *On Christian Doctrine* as a young boy, by way of introduction to his education in the tenets of the Christian faith. This work offered instruction in reading biblical passages and taught how the eternal and spiritual might become ensnared in and corrupted by physical and temporal concerns (1.4.10). As a father, he encouraged his son Louis to read Augustine's treatise.

As a king, however, he came up against the linguistic unreliability of the handwritten dissemination of the Word of God and the Scriptures, and the erroneous rendition of the Psalms. What he found was a state of utter confusion in the transmission of sources. Two Bible translations from late antiquity, the Vetus Latina and the Vulgate, existed side by side. For the most part, individual books of the Bible, or groups of books, circulated in individual manuscript copies, and only very few complete Bibles (pandects) were in existence. Moreover, Bible texts in Italy, Gaul, and Spain or among the Irish by no means corresponded with one another. In many cases, the copyist had made them illegible, or they were grammatically incorrect. Accordingly, in 789, Charlemagne ordered his scribes to undertake a full revision and correction of the text. The first fruits of their labor may be the Bible of Abbot Maurdramnus of Corbie (now only partially preserved), which was produced some time before 781 and may originally have comprised twelve or thirteen separate volumes.[26] But the most influential Bible of this period (still extant in a number of manuscripts) was edited by the Anglo-Saxon scholar Alcuin of York; in some ways, this was to form the basis of the modern Latin Vulgate Bible.

Biblical scholar Bonifatius Fischer, writing in 1965, summed up the importance of the Frankish king's intervention:

> Charlemagne's role does not simply reside in the fact that he
> commissioned Alcuin to produce a Bible revision, which he
> then introduced throughout his realm. More important, he laid
> vital foundations, stimulated religious interest and lively cultural
> exchange, and lent impetus to scholarly activity in general. He
> stressed the vital importance of a corrected Bible text.[27]

The most valuable Bible revision in scholarly terms, which did not even shy away from textual criticism, was edited by the Visigoth Theodulf, whom Charlemagne had elevated to the position of bishop of Orléans; this version employed a very small script that would later become known as Carolingian minuscule, which crammed the whole of the Scriptures, both the Old and New Testaments, into a single manageable codex. The psalter existed in three versions, which were occasionally combined synoptically in a single manuscript: the Hebrew (*iuxta Hebraeos*), Roman, and Gallic versions, the last of which Charlemagne preferred, without, however, declaring it obligatory within his realm.[28] This urge to hear the Word of God proclaimed error-free may well even have been awakened before Charlemagne's reign.

There could be no doubt that the future ruler would follow the Church's commandments, later lead his people to the Christian faith, attend Mass in person, be versed in the disciplines of fasting and prayer, provide welfare for the poor, widows, and orphans, defend the Church, and so on. A God-fearing life would surely bring divine blessings on his reign: time and again, this was suggested to the king and no doubt must also have been impressed on him as a child. A growing body of religious specialist literature, in the form of monitory letters and mirrors of princes and kings, helped spread knowledge of such values among those who could read.[29] Charlemagne's tutors must have been well aware of such doctrines.

Later, as a young monarch, Charlemagne was the recipient of biblical letters of admonition and exhortation. An Irish or possibly Anglo-Saxon cleric by the name of Cathuulf sent him such a missive around 775, just after Charlemagne had returned from his first Italian campaign:[30] "My Lord King, I urge you always to be mindful of Him who—I fervently believe—created you from nothing and raised you from insignificance to the most exalted state . . . and to the glory of kingship over Europe." Cathuulf went on, "Always be aware, my King, that you are God's representative, and that you have been entrusted with safeguarding and directing all the limbs of His Church and must account for them at the Day of Judgement—as well as for yourself." Cathuulf also explained that Charlemagne had God to thank for the beneficence that had set him on high. Now, though, the cleric continued, he should be mindful of his obligations: to always consult the *lex Dei* (law of God) (including the Holy Scripture), never to sell a Christian to a heathen (a remarkable reference to slavery), and to undertake to clothe the "Bride of Christ," that is, the Church. Cathuulf exhorted the king to always carry the "eight columns" of kingship with him, in order that he might "support the citadel of God" (*castra Dei . . . sustentare*): truth, patience, generosity, persuasiveness, punishment of evildoers, exaltation of the good, low taxes, and fairness in the dispensation of justice. Furthermore, a king ought periodically to renew the laws throughout his entire kingdom and root out injustice, as well as ordering High Mass to be sung on the appointed feast days for St. Michael, the conqueror of Satan (Revelation 12:7–9) and the weigher of souls at the Last Judgment, and for St. Peter, prince of the apostles.

Did Charlemagne read these admonitions? Did he take such pieces of moral instruction to heart? Did he even comprehend them? We cannot be sure, but—an example of the continuing fruits of education even today—we can conjecture. In any event, the twofold group of eight things in which Charlemagne was blessed and the eight columns of kingship may well have left a deep impression on the religiously receptive Charlemagne when, many years later, he started planning his own citadel of God, the palatinate church in Aix (Aachen Cathedral). Even when he was growing up, he would also have received similar admonishments, and he would likewise have been taught to appreciate the importance of observing ecclesiastical law as a boy, long before Cathuulf wrote to him. As king, he endeavored to strengthen the law and to enforce it throughout his kingdom; however, various rules within his realm contradicted one another, and Charlemagne was unable to resolve them. Nor did such legalism prevent him from flying in the face of certain Church norms. For example, his marriages were not remotely in accordance with the ecclesiastical law in force at the time; in fact, they were in flagrant violation of it.

Charlemagne's religiosity was in keeping with that of his age. He believed what his religious advisers—popes, bishops, abbots, and other clerics—advised and taught him. He shared the religious horizons of his contemporary world. Yet this allows us, albeit with due caution, to extrapolate from this and draw some conclusions about Charlemagne himself and the childhood influences that shaped him. Throughout his life, he set great store by the observance of religious rites and commandments. He acquired religious relics and venerated them. At the same time, he also took care that the widespread trade in bogus relics did not get out of hand. Relics proved their authenticity by their ability to work miracles.[31] Visions of the afterlife described what the soul could look forward to after death, and what a person should prepare for during his or her lifetime. The kind of faith that was expected of the common people was very straightforward. Very little in the way of liturgy was required to adopt this simple form of religiosity. Charlemagne's scholars exerted all the dialectical acuity that the age could muster in justifying and defending these simplified forms of liturgy. The people needed to be satisfied with these formulas.

Practiced in them since childhood, the king performed all the rituals that were then expected of a Christian ruler. He attended church each morning and evening (matins and vespers), took Mass every day, and occasionally even attended the nighttime canonical hours. As Einhard reported (chap. 26), he was also punctilious about seeing that services were conducted in a dignified manner, especially where the readings and the singing of psalms were concerned. During his whole life, he also devoted much time and effort to the good work of ministering to the poor; they were even remembered in his last will and testament (chap. 33). He is even said to have supported the Eastern Christians with donations of money (chap. 27). The aspects that Einhard emphasized were in line with a ritualized form of piety, although Charlemagne did not content himself with just that. The emperor took part in fasts and public demonstrations of humility, which were announced throughout the realm.[32] It was only on the subject of penitence, let alone acts of public penitence like those staged by his son Louis the Pious, that his biographer was silent. There is no mention of this observance, not even with signs of Charlemagne's impending death. Could it be that Charlemagne was a follower of the practice of undemonstrative penitence by tariff, which had been introduced from Ireland, and which prescribed the set amount of expiation required for each particular sin? Or was it the case that no one dared accuse the emperor of sins that required expiation in the first place?

After Charlemagne was crowned king, he demanded that all his subjects should confess these few simple articles of faith: *Hloset ir, chindo liupostun, rihti dera calaupa.*

> Dearest children, obey the commandment of faith. . . . Indeed, faith resides in few words, despite holding very profound mysteries. The Holy Ghost truly did dictate these words to the teachers of Christianity, the sacred messengers, with this degree of brevity in order that everyone might understand and be able to remember the things that all Christians should believe in and confess for all eternity. How can a person who can neither learn or want to retain in his memory these few words of belief, in which his redemption resides and through which he will be saved, nor recite the words of the Lord's Prayer, which Jesus himself taught his disciples, call himself a Christian? . . . Now every person who professes to be a Christian should hurry to confess his faith, to learn the Lord's Prayer with all haste, and also to teach these lessons to those who are baptized, so that he shall not be compelled to account for himself on the Day of Judgment. For this is both God's commandment and . . . the injunction of our Lord and Master [the Emperor].

Daz ist . . . unsares herrin capot (This is . . . the injunction of our Lord and Master). Through orders such as this, Charlemagne instructed and admonished his people.[33] Royal command and the threat of judgment combined to form the everyday practice of religion among the people. The Day of Judgment hung over everyone equally. Organized religion was an instrument of power, but the ruler himself had also been subject to this power from his earliest days. All Christians were expected to be able to recite the litanies by heart, to "acquire" faith, and to fear the Last Judgment. This form of faith knew no inwardness. Fear of God and of the torments of Hell drove people to a hope of salvation through humble observance of religious ritual. In fact, the Harrowing of Hell—Christ's descent into the underworld—was incorporated into the profession of faith in Gaul, from where it was also adopted by Rome. As a child, Charlemagne would have been encouraged to recite this creed and would have internalized such demands. They did not preclude a person from later penetrating more deeply into religious truths, but without constraining the king on these grounds from acts of violence. Punishment was an intrinsic element of faith. God and the saints scourged the insubordinate with illness, torments, fear of death, and untimely demise. Likewise, the king was required to punish the godless.

The creed and the Our Father (the Lord's Prayer) were translated into the "German" vernacular. "Gilaubiu in got fater almahtîgon, scepphion himiles enti erda. Endi heilenton Christ . . . Nidhar steig ci helliu, in thritten dage arstuat fona tóotem, úf steif ci himilom . . . thanan quemendi ci ardeileinne quecchêm endi dóodêm," (I believe in God the Father Almighty, Maker of heaven and earth. And in Jesus Christ . . . He descended into Hell; the third day He rose again from the dead; He ascended into Heaven . . . From thence He shall come to judge both the quick and the dead) in the words of the Frankish Weissenburg catechism, while an Alemannic (South German) Lord's Prayer from St. Gallen began: "Fater unseer, thu pist in himile, uuihi namun dinan, qhueme rihhi din." Charlemagne could have recited both in Latin. Baptismal vows and formulas of renunciation, confession, and penitence were on hand for the illiterate populace: "Forsahhistu unholdun? Ih forsahu, Forsahhistu unholdun uuerc indi uuilon? Ih fursahhu" (Do you forsake the Devil? I forsake him. Do you renounce the Devil in all your deeds and thoughts? I renounce him). All baptized Saxons were required to profess their faith in this way, in order to then confess: "Ich uuirdu gote almahtigen bigihtig enti allen gotes heilagon allero minero suntono . . . meinero eido, ubilero fluocho, liogannes, stelannes, huores, manslahti" (I hereby confess all my sins to Almighty God and His saints . . . all the false oaths, evil

---

30

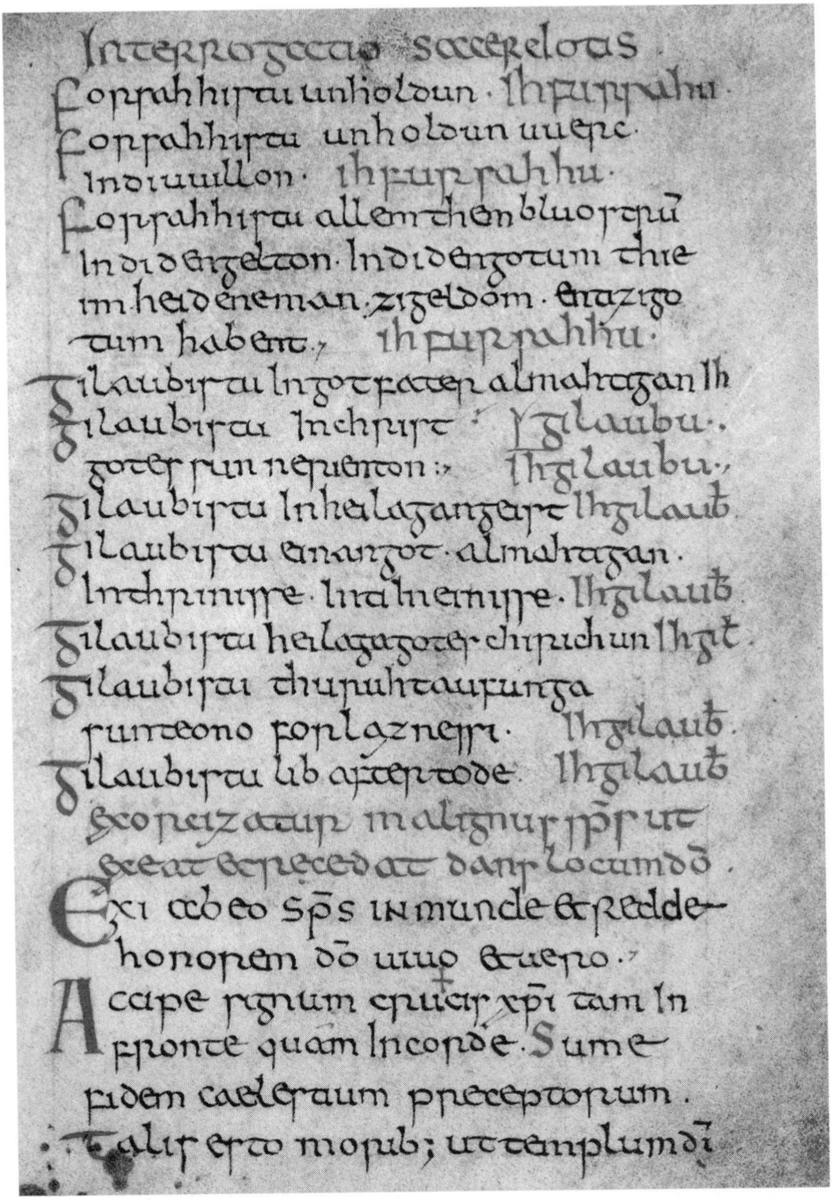

FIGURE 2 Text of a ninth-century Frankish baptismal vow. Cathedral chapter library, Merseburg (Cod.136, f. 16r).

curses, lies, theft, fornication, and manslaughter I have committed). Saxons who had been captured in battle were undoubtedly subjected to this kind of interrogation and on the orders of the king were also forcibly baptized. Thus we can observe a form of formalized Christianity at work here too. Charlemagne would have classified this as conversion.

The faith of the people beyond such formulaic expressions eludes the historian's understanding. Magic customs and heathen traditions endured in part for several centuries, creating in the process a number of syncretic forms of living and religion. Charlemagne grew up surrounded by these. The common people continued to believe in magic long after his death. The famous Merseburg Incantations are a prime example. "Eiris sazun idisi, sazun hera duoder. / Suma hapt heptidun, suma heri lezidun, / suma clubodun umbi cuoniouuidi: / insprinc haptbandun, inuar uigândun" (Once sat women, they sat here, then there. / Some fastened bonds, some impeded an army, / Some unraveled fetters: / Escape the bonds, flee the enemy!).[34] The magical allusions are no longer intelligible today; to what extent they were at the time is also open to question. But people believed that muttering them could do no harm.

In many cases, ancient magical elements were given just a thin veneer of Christianity, such as a blessing from Trier that was meant to guard against a horse going lame: "Quam Krist endi Sancte Stephan zi ther burg zi Saloniun: thar uuárth Sancte Stephanes hros entphangan. Soso Krist gibuozta themo Sancte Stephanes hrosse thaz entphangan, so gibuozi ihc it mid Kristes fullêsti thessemo hrosse. Pater noster. Uuala Krist, thu geuuertho gibuozian thuruch thina gnatha thessemo hrosse thaz antphangana atha thaz spurihalza, sose thû themo Sancte Stephanes hrosse gibuoztos zi thero burg Saloniun. Amen" (Christ and St. Stephen arrived in the town of Salonium; there, St. Stephen's horse was struck down by an illness. Just as Christ cured St. Stephen's horse, so may I cure this horse with Christ's help. O Christ, through your grace show compassion and cure this horse, which has become lame, just as you once cured St. Stephen's horse in Salonium).[35] This was sympathetic magic, which sought to invoke mysterious names and exemplary (alleged) miracles in order to cure a similar injury, just as St. Stephen's lame horse was once cured through the Word of Christ. Charlemagne would have been familiar with these kinds of practices; he now strove to wipe them out.[36]

Religiosity at this time, no doubt including that of the king, had nothing to do with theological speculations but rather comprised ritual practice, simple and tied to formulas, though not exclusively so. Charlemagne called for knowledge and understanding, for justifications. To this end, the ruler consulted his scholars. He also expected his children to familiarize themselves with the writings of the Church Fathers. His biographer records that Charlemagne himself was in the habit of having their works read aloud, say, when he was at mealtimes. Did Charlemagne first introduce this practice to his court, or had he perhaps adopted it from his father's table? We do not know which chapters of St. Augustine's *City of God* he especially admired, still less how he interpreted them. Perhaps it was precisely the last books, which dealt with the impending Last Judgment. In any event, we know that anticipation of the Day of Judgment and the Apocalypse held the faithful in its thrall, and Charlemagne was no exception. He, too, expected the Last Judgment at any time and would have been made aware of its approach. His tutor, Alcuin, was later to admonish him by invoking its threatening omens. Prognostication of a Christian nature would have been a well-known phenomenon to the king and emperor. In his old age, questions about the age of the world and the calendar bothered him more and more. Admittedly, the emperor also noted the inconsistency of all time calculations.[37] Nevertheless, his anxiety about the Day of Judgment was ever present.

The Last Judgment was the subject of vivid and terrifying portrayals. These were achieved through the use of urgent, rousing words, which were menacing, violent, evoking fear, and calling for good deeds. "And when men look for Him to come from heaven as the judge of the quick and the dead," St. Augustine's *De doctrina christiana* (1.15.14.31) stated, "it strikes great terror into the careless, so that they betake themselves to diligent preparation and learn by holy living to long for His approach, instead of quaking at it on account of their evil deeds."[38] No calendar could divest such words of their power. Visions of the Apocalypse handed down from late antiquity—available in copies from the Carolingian era such as the Trier Apocalypse[39]—did not as yet capture its full horrors in images, although they did picture Satan, first bound in chains and then released in the form of a serpent, along with the thousand years of Church history. At this stage, it was the spoken word that had a truly powerful impact, spreading fear of the Day of Judgment through sermons and moral exhortations (paraeneses).

Nor was the king spared this fear of the punishments that awaited in the hereafter, of the terrors of Hell, and of the Day of Judgment. Charlemagne learned to live at the End of Days, before the rise of a new and final era of world history. Even when his calendrical calculations later led him to determine that the world was younger than he had first imagined—so apparently prolonging the advent of that End of Days—uncertainty still prevailed. The

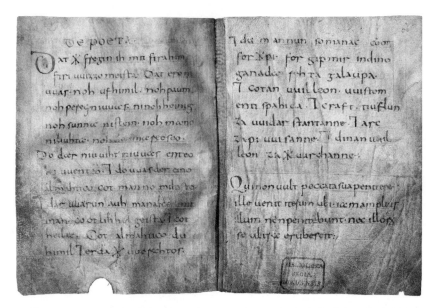

FIGURE 3 Manuscript of the "Wessobrunn Prayer." This work, also called the "Wessobrunn Creation Poem," dates from around 800 and comes from the Benedictine abbey of that name in Bavaria. Munich, Bavarian State Library.

world had been created, and it would pass away again, and moreover in the foreseeable future, in historical time. This was in accordance with God's will. Saints had taught and predicted that this would occur. Yet exactly when that time would come remained a secret. Even so, the king and emperor could read the signs of the impending end every bit as well as the scholars of his retinue; in general, he closely observed the signs in the heavens and on Earth so as to be able to prepare himself for the coming disaster. His biographer Einhard hinted at this (chap. 32). Charlemagne personally saw earthquakes, drought, and famine as unmistakable signs of God's wrath. The services that Charlemagne performed for God and the Church can be regarded as the fruits of his upbringing. When he became emperor, he still made them into the moral maxims guiding his every action.[40]

Perhaps even as a schoolboy he had been told about the "twelve evils of the world" (*duodecim abusiva saeculi*), an idea that was sometimes attributed to St. Patrick, sometimes to the Church Fathers Augustine of Hippo or Isidore of Seville, and which roundly castigated "men without virtue" and "unjust rulership." Whoever originated the concept, it certainly became widespread in the time of Charlemagne. According to this doctrine, not only was the "just king" required to offer leadership to his subjects and correct them, but also his rule was expected to spread joy among people, and, it was claimed, it would bring plenteous bounty to the world and engender "hope for future happiness." By contrast, at the Last Judgment, the king who "dispenses no justice" would get "a primacy of torment" (*in poenis primatum*). "For all the sinners whom he currently rules over will in the time of torments to come weigh down heavily on him as a reminder of all the harm he has inflicted on them."[41] Charlemagne had learned about the "twelve evils" during his father's reign, as guidance on how to strengthen a king's rule; and the same thing would hold good in his reign as well: he would be a warlike king, but also a God-fearing one who constantly had peace and justice in mind.

The Forces That Shaped Carolingian Kingship

Wherever he looked, all he could see was the tumult of battle; Charlemagne could not escape the surroundings into which he was born. And this environment, which resounded to the clash of weapons, was a lethal and worldly one that shaped his whole psyche. But the proximity of death and divine justice could neither dispel nor alloy the pleasures of the world; quite the contrary, in fact—it fostered them rather than curtailing them, while at the same time repeatedly and loudly calling for penance. As men, princes, including Charlemagne, experienced decidedly earthly urges, and feelings of ruthlessness, anger, and revenge and felt the temptations of both power and of lust. Charlemagne was far removed from being an ascetic. His whole being was shot through with a refreshing sensuality. We have no idea how he performed acts of penitence, but we do know that Charlemagne combined his worldly lifestyle with a concern for ecclesiastical liturgy and the Church, for the spread of the faith and educating his subjects in religious matters. His youth had taught him a great deal.

The world in which Charlemagne was educated was driven by greed, power struggles, violence, and perjury. He grew up in an agonal society, characterized by jealousy and envy and played out within an atmosphere of aristocratic rivalry and treachery, with deaths only too frequent an occurrence. These tendencies dominated the recent past of his own family, as well as the childhood and youth of the future emperor himself. Popular recollections of this period were shot through with references to insurrection and conflict: "The Franks rose up against one another," "Terrible persecution among the Frankish people," "The Franks attacked Charles Martel," "Charlemagne pushed forward against [the Frisian duke] Ratbod, but lost many men and hastily retreated," "A massive mutual slaughter"—but chronicle also recorded great victories: "Charles Martel came back with plentiful spoils of war," and "Charlemagne returned victorious."[42]

The nobility that was engaged in these struggles had already established itself in the pre-Carolingian period, admittedly not yet as a class with any legal status, but certainly as a social elite that was elevated by virtue of its prestige, kinship, property, influence, autogenous power, and status. Charlemagne's family belonged to these "mighty ones" or "great ones," as contemporary writers were wont to call them. This aristocracy was split by conflicting interests. Anyone who wanted to prevail and advance had to cover up his personal interests and unite these aristocratic forces around himself. Conflict between individual families and among the Franks in general filled the entire eighth century with the din of battle; nor were these antagonisms forgotten. The rise of the Carolingians and their early period of ruling were characterized by a constant keynote of betrayal, war, and death. It was precisely to this phenomenon—albeit often only in allusions—that the terse, information-poor historiography of the early Carolingian period referred. More specific or detailed data remained hidden as yet. Would the future king Charlemagne be able to alter this situation and exert lasting control over the Frankish nobility?

Although he would largely have had to rely on the oral tradition, including various myths and legends, as a boy Charlemagne would surely have heard about the history of his family and its rise to prominence. Charlemagne himself told Paulus Diaconus (Paul the Deacon) the anecdote about his saintly ancestor Arnulf of Metz, whose lost episcopal ring was miraculously found again in the belly of a fish caught from the river.[43] History books of the period either did not include this tale or recounted it in insufficient detail. Little has survived in written form to the present day except for the continuations of the chronicles of so-called Fredegar—which traced the illegitimate Carolingians, Childebrand and Nibelung, the uncle and cousin, respectively, of Pepin the Short, up to the era of Charlemagne—and the so-called *Liber historiae Francorum* (Book of the history of the Franks).[44] Only during Charlemagne's reign would things change and a broader approach to the writing of history set in, albeit one that skipped over and omitted the unpalatable past. In particular, the *Royal Frankish Annals* was highly selective, filtering what it reported in line with the king's wishes.

Thus, violence, persecution, and death accompanied the rise of the Carolingians. For instance, Charlemagne's grandfather, the "mayor of the palace," Charles, who was later given the sobriquet "Martel" (the hammer, i.e., of the Moors), and who in ecclesiastical circles in the ninth century was damned for his depredations of Church property, was able to rise to power only after a military campaign against his half brothers.[45] His sons were cut from the same cloth. Bloody family vendettas and wars dominated the expansion of Carolingian power, just as later, in the ninth and tenth centuries, they were to hallmark the dynasty's decline. Between 714 and 768, there were just five years when war was not being waged. Autarchy and its expansion across the south of Gaul and the whole of Provence beckoned as the major prize for those "great ones" who chose to engage in the struggle.

The empire over which this Charlemagne had de facto extended his sway[46] still observed several Roman traditions—more so in the south, with its high level of literacy and continued use of Roman common law, less so in the north. At first, this revealed a certain cultural decline but at the same time triggered a form of development aid exported from the culture-rich south to the heartland of the Frankish Empire between the Loire, the Meuse, and the Rhine. Although the ancient cities had also shrunk in the south, they had not entirely relinquished their urban mode of life. The ports remained open to long-distance trade to Constantinople and the East; meanwhile, the Muslim rulers of the most southerly regions of Gaul, with Narbonne at their center, turned their gaze toward Spain and Africa. Last but not least, the large Jewish communities at various locations must have maintained a network of far-flung contacts. A number of episcopal sees were prominent—Tours, Poitiers, Vienne, Arles, and Marseilles—despite the fact that even they were only a pale shadow of their former selves. The Franks, who had subjugated the territory north of the Loire, remained firmly rooted in peasant culture. The Carolingian mayors of the palace and kings acted not least as landlords and farmers, carrying out animal husbandry, forestry, and agriculture.

The rise of the Carolingians could not have come about without an effective army. Originally, the Frankish king could call on all free Franks in the event of war; the resulting force was a lightly armed infantry unit. But by this time, techniques of warfare had moved on, with effective armies now based on a swift, well-armed cavalry force. Warhorses had become prized possessions. The last kings of the Merovingian dynasty, who had been more symbolic idols than rulers, lacked the necessary resources to put together such a mounted unit and were forced to leave its formation up to the kingdom's aristocracy. The independent wealth of the churches, the nobility, and especially the Carolingian mayor of the palace (*maior domus*), who had formerly been nothing more than the foremost "servant" of the Merovingian king, had long since outstripped the royal stipend that was still distributed to them. Yet even the not-inconsiderable independent means of the Carolingians were not enough to enable them to raise and equip large-scale armies. Other sources therefore had to be tapped for this.

Stabling warhorses, the ownership of weapons and coats of mail, and military training grounds required major landownership and freed warriors from the necessity of earning an independent living. A helmet cost 6 pence (*denarii*), a coat of mail twice that, a sword and sheath 7 pence, cuisses (leg armor) 6, a spear and shield 2, a stallion 7 (but a mare just 3)—all told, then, a total outlay of 40 pence, or the cost of no fewer than 18 to 20 cows.[47] In the agrarian society of the eighth century, livestock represented an appreciable fortune. Over an entire year, to feed the number of cattle that it took to raise the revenue for a sizable army required at least twelve, or likely more, farmsteads with their tied farm laborers (some of whom were free men and some serfs) plus small manorial farms, managed by tied men without any landholdings of their own (so-called manse servants).

Under these circumstances, a warrior horde could in no way be financed simply from the war booty it hoped to seize. Rather, the constant state of conflict of necessity brought with it great social upheaval, which saw all forms of organization geared to war alone and gave rise to a warrior aristocracy, which was organized around the figure of the provider of land and army commander. It was Charles Martel's signal achievement that he was able to plan this reorganization program and implement it with brutal force. Henceforth, land concessions on a grand scale bound warriors to their feudal lord, but first and foremost to the Carolingians.

In order to equip this fighting force, Charles Martel requisitioned the extensive property held by the Church. This had grown continually since ancient times and, taken as a whole, exceeded any other institution's holdings. Charles, though, summarily confiscated large parts of it—perhaps, in his capacity as mayor of the palace, in the name of the king, but in truth for personal advantage—so as to be able to equip and pay his own followers. In return for this vast program of "secularization"—one might also call it enforced borrowing—the Church was granted a tithe (a tenth part of the economic yield of these lands; sometimes, additionally, a ninth part was also paid); before this, the payment of tithes had been very uncommon. The consequences of this could as yet not be foreseen. These tithes were a burden on the faithful, especially small farmsteads, while at the same time scarcely compensating for the losses the clergy had suffered. The real beneficiaries were the nobility, whose landed estates grew in size. But in actual fact, what

Charles managed to achieve with measures like this was to extend his control over those of his own class, too, and to group and concentrate them. His success in this regard hallowed his reign and legitimized his methods of rulership, at least for the time being. Charles's grandson, who bore his name, would in time have recourse to the same methods and likewise assign military roles to bishops and abbeys, with their still-extensive landownership.

Military successes to legitimize Charles Martel's reign were not long in coming. In 732, a victory at Tours/Poitiers over a Muslim force that had ventured far to the north—in itself of little consequence—was declared to be a major triumph and established Charles's fame; news of the victory even reached Rome. Overall, the military successes of this Charles appear to have earned him (from when we do not know) the sobriquet *Tudites* or *Martellus,* "the hammer"; admittedly, the earliest written evidence of this name occurs only at the end of the ninth century.[48] The pope invested new hope in this victorious warrior and asked for his help in combating his enemies in his own country, the Lombards, who ultimately set their sights on conquering the whole of Italy, including Rome. However, the Carolingian ruler turned down the apostolic father's request. Charlemagne never knew the grandfather whose name he carried; he knew only about his exploits.

The older Charles's power base was not so firmly established that he could risk waging a campaign in Italy; moreover, he was actually in league with the Lombards. He could hardly have gained the necessary consent of his confederates to go to war. In addition, southern Gaul, or Septimania—the area around Narbonne—was still not in Frankish hands and thus remained a potential source of danger. Only in 759 did this area finally succumb, when Martel's son Pepin the Short first overran the region and then, after a three-year siege, captured the city itself. The pope's request for help to the older Charles was nonetheless kept safe and well preserved. His namesake grandson knew of it and had it placed at the head of his collection of copies of papal correspondence, the so-called Codex Carolinus, as a document demonstrating an especially close bond between the papacy and the Frankish kings.

Just as his renowned grandson did later, Charles Martel shared his camp with several women, with whom he fathered children. When the question of the succession arose, this made for bloody internecine conflict between various claimants, which continued to resonate far into the childhood of the young Charlemagne and which, like the situation that blighted the reigns of the early kings of the Merovingian house, culminated in devastating and deadly struggles. Charles Martel's sons Pepin, Carloman, and Grifo vied with one another for power and for the position of mayor of the palace. At first, the Franks followed the two elder sons only very reluctantly and by no means unanimously. The aristocracy saw itself forced to take sides, which for them involved no less a risk to the security of their property, influence, and lives than the Carolingians themselves. To maintain their power, Pepin and Carloman jointly raised a Merovingian, the last in the line, to the throne: Childeric III, a puppet ruler who was king in name only. Ultimately, only Charlemagne's father, Pepin, succeeded in gaining any lasting power. He and his blood brother Carloman conspired to exclude their younger half brother Grifo from power; he eventually fled to Aquitaine and was killed when he tried to raise an army in Burgundy against Pepin and to escape to Italy. The future emperor Charlemagne was five years old when this happened.

Carloman also saw himself ousted from power and was forced to flee, first to the monastery of St. Andreas on Monte Soratte north of Rome and then, after too many Franks arrived in the region, farther south to Monte Cassino "to live the monastic life" (*monachyrio ordine perseveraturus*).[49] Nor was his eldest son, Drogo, able to maintain his position for long. Drogo was entrusted beforehand to the protection of his uncle Pepin, who at that stage was still childless, but when Pepin's first son was born in 748, followed soon after by a second, Drogo and his brothers were eliminated from the succession in perpetuity and joined monastic orders. Charlemagne's birth was accompanied by civil commotion, "by insurrection among the people" according to a contemporary chronicler, Willibald of Eichstätt.[50] In vain, Drogo's father, Carloman, left his monastery and his position in the retinue of Pope Stephen II in 753 and hurried back to the Frankish Kingdom to try and intervene with his brother on behalf of his son. He died the following year, even before he could make it back to the monastery. But Drogo and his five brothers found themselves condemned to spend the rest of their lives tonsured and to languish in permanent nameless obscurity in a succession of monasteries; there is no record of where and when they died. No one remembered them in their prayers. Being a Carolingian was clearly a dangerous business. The future emperor experienced this from his earliest childhood—and resolved to take after his father.

This all proved to be a heavy burden for the future. The memory of the acts of violence that his father and grandfather committed against their own relatives, which had accompanied the Carolingians' seditious ascent to the royal throne, weighed heavily on first Pepin the Short's and in turn Charlemagne's reign after he had ascended the throne. It was imperative that this memory be expunged from the popular consciousness. Accordingly, an extremely brief and sugar-coated depiction is given in the *Royal Frankish Annals* that is remarkable for its radical suppression of any hint of conflict and is full of omissions of fact and patent errors, with scarcely a mention of Pepin's ascent to the throne in 751. Incorrect dates, most of them too early, are given for events, making this account quite misleading and obfuscating even today. Instead, it simply proclaims, "Henceforth, reports of his, Pepin's, power and fear of his bold daring spread like wildfire throughout all the lands."[51]

Any recollection of the terrors that had been endured was to be extinguished for good. A papal ruling, the acquiescence of at least part of the nobility, and even an election "according to the [hitherto-unattested] usage of the Franks" and an anointing with holy oil by bishops or St. Boniface now lent legitimacy to the revolution.[52] How all this turned out in reality can no longer be determined. Only Grifo was given a mention in the *Royal Frankish Annals,* where he was denigrated as a supposedly illegitimate scion and a troublemaker, while all the tensions that existed between his half brothers Carloman and Pepin were concealed. Toward the end of his life, however, Charlemagne may well have had cause to recall the suppressed memories of his childhood and the forcible exclusion from the succession of his uncle and cousin and may well have speculated on a better way of doing things when he found himself having to organize a peaceful resolution of the question of who should succeed him. Yet in this, too, the agonal ethics of his era and society were to prove stronger than any sense of good will.

Only a subsidiary branch of Charles Martel's progeny escaped (for the time being) total exclusion or extinction. The mayor of the palace had a son named Bernhard from a liaison with an unknown lady. His sons Adalhard (who went to school with Charlemagne) and Wala, who were also the children of different mothers—a Frankish woman in the former's case, a Saxon woman in the latter's—together with their sisters Gundrada and Theodrada, attained a position of some influence at court under their cousin Charlemagne. But at no time were they ever regarded as entitled to inherit, a fact that probably saved their lives. Glittering careers lay ahead of them until distrust and envy at the court of Louis the Pious threatened to topple them and drove the Frankish Empire to its inexorable downfall.

The Young Charlemagne's First Encounter with a Pope

Even as a young child, from the age of six, Charlemagne was habituated to the duties of kingship. His assignment was to receive the beneficent donor of his own royal status, Pope Stephen II. On this occasion, the boy was dispatched on a journey of almost one hundred miles in order to greet the

Roman pontiff with "exultation, joy, and great extravagance" and to escort him to the royal palace at Ponthion,[53] where he was to meet the delighted king on the feast of Epiphany in the year 754. Before the boy's astonished eyes, there unfolded the pomp of the papacy, the whole ritualized procedure, which—although the young man would naturally not have realized it at the time—was modeled on the ceremonial of the Byzantine Empire: the solemn procession, the waving flags, the crosses, and the sheer opulence and magnificence of the ecclesiastical regalia. Pepin must also have been in awe of the pomp that the Romans displayed in his presence. Without more ado, he instructed Bishop Chrodegang of Metz to send priests to Rome with instructions to study the *cantus Romanus,* the liturgical style of singing employed in the Roman Church, and to introduce it to the Frankish Empire.

The son looked on as his father rode out three miles from his palace to bid the pope welcome. On meeting him, Pepin dismounted, stooped low, and prostrated himself before offering the customary courtesy of acting as the pope's *strator,* that is, leading his horse by the reins for a stretch: the king, the victor, the most powerful man in the Frankish Empire performing the duties of a stable boy. The boy also saw how a procession formed and heard the pope and his retinue start to intone the Gloria, followed by endless Laudes—a laudatory chant developed in the Frankish realm, like a litany but for the glorification of the ruler.[54] Finally, still singing hymns, the procession reached the palace. This is how a Roman historian, the author of the "Life of Stephen" in the *Liber pontificalis* (Book of the popes), portrayed the scene, taking great care to exclude everything that might have appeared to detract from the dignity and the self-esteem of the emperor-like successor to the apostolic prince.[55] But a similar impression may also have been left on the memory of the young Charlemagne: a spectacle that seemed both alien and amazing, the miracle of Rome.

For sure, there were certain moments that seemed to compromise such dignity and self-esteem, although the astonished boy would not have noticed them. In fact, they were recorded for posterity only by the *Royal Frankish Annals.* The pope came as a petitioner to the Franks, whose ruling elite, with the queen at their head, were by no means unanimous in being prepared to accede to his wishes. Extreme measures were required to win over the doubters. And in his desperation, Stephen would have been prepared to take them.

Indeed, at Charlemagne's court, many would later claim to remember the scene vividly. According to these accounts, on the day after the grand reception, the young Charlemagne looked on as the pope and his entire entou-

FIGURE 4 An eleventh-century fresco from the Basilica di San Clemente al Laterano in Rome showing Saints Cyril and Methodius bringing the relics of St. Clement to Rome.

rage came like supplicants, in sackcloth and ashes, to throw themselves at his father's feet and, "calling on Almighty God and the services of Saint Peter and Saint Paul to have mercy on them," to implore Pepin to free them and the Roman people from the clutches of the Lombards. Then, supposedly, the king summoned Charlemagne and his brother to help him and the assembled Frankish dignitaries raise Stephen and his retinue from the floor as a sign of their future protection and liberation. Finally, Charlemagne witnessed his father yielding to the pope's pleas.[56]

No more extreme measure than the self-abasement of this emperor-like man could possibly be imagined. Looking back, did Charlemagne at some stage realize that this visit of the Roman pontiff marked a momentous decision that served to detach Rome for all time from the empire of the (Eastern) Roman emperor, the successor of Constantine the Great, yet did not achieve independence for Rome but instead pushed it into dependence on the empire of the Carolingians?

This was the first time a Frankish king had come face-to-face with a successor to the apostolic princes. New rituals were called for. There was certainly no desire on the part of the Franks to measure themselves against the

Lombards, against whom their military help was now being sought. Rather, Roman ritual was taken as the model, insofar as it was known to the Franks. In Rome, for example, it was customary for people to ride out for six miles to welcome the emperor, though not for his representative the exarch; there too, Roman dignitaries performed the service of *strator* for the newly crowned pope. Later, in 800, Pope Leo III would receive the future emperor Charlemagne fully twelve miles outside the city.[57] But now, in 754, the Frankish king rode for three miles to meet the vicar of the Apostolic See and performed the *strator* service for him like a Roman worthy—if we are to believe the account given in the *Liber pontificalis*.

What a piece of theater, what a spectacle it must have been! Whatever the individual rituals that were performed, they must have been impressive instances that in their diversity and strangeness left a lasting impression on the young Charlemagne. This was a key moment in the boy's life, notwithstanding the fact that no written account reveals what he felt when he went to meet the party from Rome at that time, at this highly impressionable age, and when he stood there marveling at the magnificence of their entrance and the brilliance they radiated, and their humility and the reaction of his father and the other Franks. Even the *Royal Frankish Annals* has nothing to say on the subject. It merely records the arrival of the pope and his plea for assistance, and also the fact that the monk Carloman was sent by his abbot to oppose the pope's request; there is no mention whatsoever, though, of the ceremony or of Charlemagne's involvement. And, later on, the *Annals* also has nothing to say about the reception ceremony. Was the intention perhaps to leave this event open for future remodeling?

Only once, it seems, was this conspiracy of silence broken, namely, when Theodulf—surely with the agreement of his king—in his treatise attacking the Greek cult of images reminded the monarch of Stephen II's visit to Gaul and of the significance that Roman plainchant held henceforth for the king. Back then, Theodulf claimed, his father, Pepin, in concert with the pope, had ensured that the Roman method of psalmody, the *ordo psallendi*, was adopted among the Franks, so that Gaul and Rome might be united, just as they were united in faith, "in the honorable tradition of one mode of singing [*unius modulaminis*] and should not differ in having distinct ways of celebrating the liturgy [*officiorum varia celebratio*]." The first time Charlemagne had gone to Rome himself, Theodulf maintained, he had ordered, with the support of Pope Hadrian I, that plainchant should be adopted throughout the whole of Gaul, in Germania (the territory on the far bank of the Rhine), in Italy, and indeed even among the Saxons and other northern peoples. Listening to Theodulf, the king is said to have nodded in recollection of his childhood and his first trip to Rome almost twenty years before: "Yes," he answered, "it was all as you say [*totum bene*]."[58]

All the same, at this initial encounter with the pope, in 753–754, the boy Charlemagne gained a first inkling of the greatness of Rome, an impression that would remain with him throughout his life, and at the same time a sense of the sublimity of the successor and vicar of St. Peter, the guardian of Heaven. Devout humility before the sacred office of the pope was to accompany him for his whole lifetime. Later on, he explicitly acknowledged the teaching authority of the Roman Church and its bishops: "Everything is correct" (*bene omnia*).[59] He regarded the pope as the cradle and guarantor of orthodoxy and as the supplicant who implored God to bring salvation to the faithful, and who furthermore had the capacity to consolidate and strengthen his kingship; yet he also saw the pontiff's vulnerability and weakness. Even in this state of helplessness, the heir to St. Peter and his representative on Earth must be a powerful figure, sacrosanct and a source of salvation; the growing boy could not have construed things otherwise.

The apostolic father had hastened to Gaul in person to make a more urgent plea than that of his predecessor for help against the Lombards. It was a timely move on his part. The Carolingian usurper Pepin needed help to quell unrest among his own people. Consequently, he concluded an "alliance of friendship" (*amicitia*) with the pope, in which he swore to be a friend to his friends and an enemy to his enemies.[60] This "friendship" between the pope and the Frankish king would last until the eleventh century—in combination with a written agreement—and would be repeatedly renewed. The boy Charlemagne would have observed ritual acts but have been as unaware of their political import as he was of the "spiritual alliance" that Pepin formed with Stephen II at that time, in which he accepted the pontiff as his godfather; however, the ceremony that sealed this bond—presumably a baptism or confirmation—is not mentioned in the records. In time, Charlemagne would also renew this alliance with Hadrian I and Leo III, although from the Frankish side not even the briefest of notes was written to acknowledge this, whereas all popes up to Leo III never tired of pointing to this *compaternitas* (compaternity).[61] Admittedly, Pepin's or Charlemagne's missives to Rome have either not been preserved at all or at best only in a very brief and random selection, so these missing letters may have contained much in the way of clarification.

Pepin required more than just verbal support from the pope. The king endowed an *altarmensa*, most likely denoting a portable altar at which Mass could be celebrated before confession in St. Peter's Church. Stephen's brother and successor Paul I solemnly consecrated it.[62] This gift was a symbolic and ritual way of ensuring the presence of the Carolingian monarch in the rites of the Apostolic Church and formed a constant reminder of the benefactor at the tomb of St. Peter. The apostolic prince would, it was hoped, thereby feel obliged to offer the king his assistance in perpetuity. Finally, it was probably on Pepin's instructions that around that same time, 757, the mortal remains of St. Petronilla, who was traditionally regarded as the daughter of St. Peter, were transferred from a catacomb on the Via Ardeatina in Rome to their own chapel that had been specially built onto the southern transept of St. Peter's Basilica.[63] This chapel too was aimed at evoking "eternal remembrance" (*memoria aeterna*) of the Frankish king and at establishing his liturgical presence in St. Peter's.[64] Yet the young Charlemagne would have been aware of none of this, nor did it find any echo in the *Royal Frankish Annals*. Nonetheless, the devotion that King Pepin the Short showed toward the apostolic prince and his successor cannot fail to have left a lasting impression on his son.

The pope was escorted to the Royal Abbey of St. Denis, his winter quarters. There, the annals record, he anointed Pepin and his sons as kings and declared them *patricii Romanorum* (patricians of the Romans).[65] The meaning of this title was unclear because, strictly speaking, it was connected with a Byzantine courtly rank, which only the Byzantine emperor could bestow. The exarch, the Eastern emperor's representative in Italy, had once borne this honorific title, but the Frankish king could hardly take his place. Rather, this new patriciate served to keep the Carolingians' commitment to protecting the Roman Republic fresh in their minds. Pepin never took on this novel title, and even Charlemagne assumed it only after the first occasion on which he prayed at the tombs of the apostles. The anointing, meanwhile, was meant to absolve the new king of all blame for the exclusion from the succession and the death of his relatives and for his breaches of contract and the law in general, to legitimize his usurping of power, and to reinforce Pepin's authority among the Franks.

Pepin and Pope Stephen met again at Easter, this time at the palace in Quierzy, in order to announce Pepin's impending campaign in Italy, a decision he had just managed to implement beforehand at a second imperial assembly. Once again, as in Ponthion, the king assured the pope that he would secure the return of the Exarchate of Ravenna and of other land easements "belonging to the Roman Republic of St. Peter" (*beati Petri rei publicae Romanorum*),[66] which the Lombard king Aistulf had recently seized, and would hand control of these over to the prince of the apostles and his vicar rather than to the emperor in far-off Constantinople, who had formerly ruled over them ever since the days of Justinian.

The Carolingian king, who had only just ascended the throne and whose rule was still far from undisputed, was risking a lot with this pledge. By no means did all the Frankish nobility support him, nor did they relish a war against the Lombards. It was essential that Pepin's military adventure succeed, since nothing other than victory would silence his opponents. Accordingly, the many acts of devotion he showed to the prince of the apostles not only fulfilled the wishes of the bishop of Rome but also were undoubtedly designed to appease Frankish opponents of the enterprise. Now, they were expected to ride over the Alps to fight for the apostle and for the freedom of his Church, rather than for a foreign ruler.

Despite their youth, Pepin's sons were also included in the obligation: the six-year-old Charlemagne affirmed the promise of restitution, and even the name of Carloman, then just three years old, was added to the treaty.[67] This Donation of Pepin, whose territorial extent can no longer be fully grasped, would in time form the foundation of the Papal States, the final remnants of which still exist today. As king, Charlemagne would also have recalled the meetings at Ponthion and Quierzy, especially as successive popes regularly urged him to fulfill his promise. But as a boy, he could hardly have comprehended the agreement between his father and the honored guest from Rome. Nor, indeed, did Charlemagne as king ever implement the Donation, despite renewing it several times. As a result, the *Royal Frankish Annals* also forbears to make any mention of Pepin's and Charlemagne's pledges; the only sources that refer to them are Roman ones.

So, however nefariously it had been attained, Pepin's status as king was hallowed in 754 by papal unction. The *Annals* has nothing to say about the ceremony; however, an anonymous memorandum of 767, whose authenticity has long been disputed, reveals more about the occasion and above all about its purpose. According to this source, Pepin and his two sons were anointed and blessed (*unctus et benedictus, consecrati*) by Pope Stephen II in St. Denis on one and the same day.[68] Pepin's wife, Bertrada, also received the pope's blessing, as did the Frankish dignitaries present; moreover, they were enjoined never to elect a king henceforth "from the loins of another," but solely from those whom divine grace had now resolved to sanctify via the hand of the bishop of Rome.[69] This declaration excluded for all time the Merovingians and Pepin's nephew Drogo and his brothers from the royal succession. Charlemagne, the six-year-old boy, experienced here for the first

time the overwhelming allure of a papal consecration and the hugely stead-
ying effect that it radiated. He never forgot this and was later to have his sons
whom he regarded as legitimate anointed in the same way, this time in Rome.

Pepin marched on Italy. Aistulf was forced to sue for peace, which he
promptly broke the following year. The Frankish king and his army hurried
once more to Italy to support the pope in his struggle against the Lombards.
On this occasion, some of the Frankish nobility, with Queen Bertrada at
their head, tried to dissuade him; to counter this, one of the papal letters
preserved in the *Codex Carolinus* adopts the voice of the apostolic prince of
St. Peter himself to exhort Pepin to take action: "I, Peter, the Apostle of God,
who took you into my care as children, . . . who selected you Franks as my
chosen people above all others, . . . I urge and admonish you, . . . protect my
people, . . . defend Rome . . . and the Romans from the heinous Lombards! . . . Come, come, in the name of the living and one true God, I adjure
you, come and lend your assistance before the life-giving spring from which
you drink and which gives you new life, dries up, before the last glimmer
of the bright flame that lights your way gutters and dies, and before your
sacred mother, God's holy Church, is violated."[70] This letter achieved its
desired effect; it tells us much about the mentality of the Frankish king,
nobility, and general populace. Supernatural forces were intervening in the
fate of peoples, but above all the prince of the apostles was on the side of
the new dynasty. The boy Charlemagne could almost witness his intervention with his own eyes. Charlemagne clearly took great care to have this
letter preserved.

Byzantium observed these developments in the West with great concern.
In a move that circumvented the pope, Emperor Constantine V attempted
to involve himself in Italian affairs by dispatching a high-ranking envoy to
open direct negotiations with the Frankish king, who at that time was laying
siege to the city of Pavia.[71] At least in retrospect, Charlemagne must also have
learned of this. The envoy, a man by the name of Georgios, promised the king
"lavish imperial gifts" if he would agree to "restore Ravenna and the other
cities and castles of the exarchate to the Byzantine emperor's authority."
Pepin, though, stood firm and refused to recant his earlier promise. He
swore an oath in which he affirmed that he had thrown himself into the
conflict only out of love for St. Peter, and that the cities in question could
never be "wrested from the control of St. Peter and the authority of the
Roman Church and the Apostolic See." The king dismissed the Byzantine
envoy, who proceeded to journey via Rome (who knows for what reason;
he could achieve nothing there) back to Constantinople.

Yet the *Liber pontificalis*, the only source in which this event is recounted, says nothing about another matter; unusually numerous finds of Byzantine coins and the lead seals of imperial estate administrators in Sicily from the mid-eighth century onward, after Pepin's new Donation, have led astute observers to conclude that the prosperous and productive papal holdings there had shortly before been definitively confiscated by the Byzantine emperor, and that the loss of these affected papal assistance to the poor and other welfare programs (a matter later touched on in Charlemagne's correspondence with Hadrian I). In light of this, then, Pepin's allocations of lands captured from the Lombards in northern and central Italy were meant to compensate for these losses. At that time, in 757, it is possible that the Carolingian ruler even colluded with the Byzantine emperor by engaging in a mutual exchange arrangement; however, this must remain a matter of pure speculation for the time being.[72] After all, Sicily was a key naval base for the Byzantine Empire.

Eventually, Aistulf was defeated and forced both to hand over the territories he had seized to the Roman "Republic of St. Peter" and to pay a large sum in tribute to the pope. All this was allegedly affirmed in a document placed in the papal archives. Abbot Fulrad of St. Denis, a long-standing confidant of the pope, was sent to arrange the transfer of the cities and deposit all the city keys he had collected at the Confessio of the apostolic prince. These facts are recorded in the *Liber pontificalis*, in which every city in question is noted by name. This was tantamount to a carving up of territories according to victor's justice, and the constituting of a *res publica* where none had formerly existed. Yet Pepin spared the Lombard kingdom, allowing it to remain as an independent realm, though one that was now liable to pay tribute. The *Royal Frankish Annals* likewise says nothing on this matter.

The young Charlemagne, the future king, learned at an early age that the principal task of any ruler was to wage war. His childhood was filled with the sound of clashing arms and entirely subsumed within the conflicts that his father was engaged in: wars against the Saxons, the Aquitainians, the Bavarians, and the Lombards followed by peace covenants, broken oaths, and new rounds of fighting, year after year. Whatever happened between bouts of war was not worthy of an entry in the *Royal Frankish Annals*. The young man also learned that the aristocracy, who were required to fight alongside the king in these wars, had to be cajoled afresh into joining every new campaign. Yet alongside war, a second major factor came into play: Rome and faith in the might of St. Peter, the guardian of the gates of Heaven, a power that the boy saw enacted before him. Charlemagne appreciated the necessity of satisfying both requirements. War and renewal thus became the prime movers of the second Carolingian king and the first medieval emperor.

The young boy surely did not accompany his father to Italy, but he must have subsequently heard how his father burned down villages, laid waste to entire regions, brought home treasure troves, and ensured that his commanders also returned with ample war booty and were furnished with enough to pay their retinues. This was an early object lesson and mental practice in the business of Carolingian rulership. In any event, Charlemagne would later follow exactly in his father's footsteps, waging war, seizing booty, and rewarding his confederates.

In line with Salic law, Pepin's sons were deemed to have come of age when they turned twelve. Charlemagne was a countersignatory with his father of a document for the first time in 760; there are also some later instances of this. Now he was taken along on campaigns by his father, too. The next year he accompanied Pepin on a military foray to Aquitaine that, according to the *Royal Frankish Annals,* was Charlemagne's first campaign. Soon after, when the younger boy Carloman had also reached the age of majority (763), both sons were given their own domains to govern, comprising various earldoms. Charlemagne's territory seems to have been around Le Mans.[73] Further campaigns with his father followed. As a rule, Pepin wanted to have his growing, mature sons accompany him into battle on a regular basis, which could just as easily have been an educational as a precautionary measure on his part.

It is likely that this period also saw the young men's first encounters with women. The world demanded its tribute, which did not always accord with the commandments of religion and the Church, which called for chastity and sexual abstinence. Charlemagne was assigned his first wife at the age of fifteen or sixteen, although no formal marriage involving legal dowry and *wittum* (legal provision for the wife in the event that she was widowed) was concluded in this case; this took place in 763 at the latest, when his father bestowed his first earldom on him.[74] All the same, the pope at the time, Stephen II, declared the marriage valid. Charlemagne enjoyed the company of women; he would pay for this indulgence in the afterlife. His first spouse, Himiltrud, bore him a son who was given the name of his grandfather, Pepin. The young Charlemagne had fulfilled the first duty of a crown prince by siring a successor of his own. He had thus proved himself to be a fit and proper ruler. But what did he know of the world that he set out to conquer? What could he know? And what benefit did he derive from it?

2

THE FRANKISH EMPIRE AND
THE WIDER WORLD

"**T**HE VENERABLE LIGHTHOUSE OF EUROPE" (*Europae veneranda pharus*)[1] was how one poet once lauded the emperor Charlemagne. This gave the impression that his power had a continent-wide scope. But what did this bard know about Europe? Or about the world? And what did the ruler being praised here know, for that matter? Or his court, which echoed to the sounds of war? Or the court of his father, where he had been raised? The knowledge that Charlemagne may have amassed there must have prepared him for his future rule in an environment where various crowned heads were busy hatching their own plans. So, how reliable was this courtly learning? As always, we are confronted with the same answer: the rise of the Frankish Kingdom from a marginal to a Mediterranean power demonstrates just how adept and successful Charlemagne was at applying the knowledge he acquired.

Did education at the Frankish court sustain itself on pure book learning of the kind offered, say, by Isidore of Seville's *Etymologies*, a text that we know was used at the court of Pepin the Short? Or was it based instead on real experience? Charlemagne, his father, Pepin, and his grandfather before him had greatly expanded the frontiers of their empire. Endless wars had led his father and Charlemagne himself across the Alps and into Italy as far south as Benevento, north of Naples, as well as westward over the Pyrenees to the banks of the river Ebro, eastward down the Danube to Pannonia, and north as far as the rivers Eider and Elbe. Put together end-on-end, the journeys they had undertaken were equivalent to riding around the entire world. What geographical knowledge, then, and what conceptions of space guided these expeditions? And did the experiences gained through these military campaigns corroborate the conception of the continents of Europe, Asia, and Africa (or rather "Libya," as the third continent still continued to be known in accordance with ancient tradition) that had been gleaned from reading about them, and did they confirm written accounts of their size, their peoples, their religions, their structures of governance, and their networks of contacts? Or did the wars bring about a new understanding of Europe?

The Franks and their kings directed their gaze primarily toward the Near East and those parts of southern Europe closest to their empire, but seldom toward the west, the area inhabited by the Irish and the Anglo-Saxons, and never—at least not before Charlemagne's reign—to the north. So it was that, however far its rulers advanced, the empire of the Carolingians remained strictly delimited and on the periphery and did not shift, even for a few brief years, into the center of the world. Contemporary realms, in the shape of the Byzantine Empire and the Islamic caliphate, reigned supreme by deploying the global knowledge of the ancient Greeks, by keeping an eye on their powerful neighbors, and by fostering extensive connections that stretched as far as India and the Far East. They exchanged envoys and knowledge with these far-off lands. For example, so-called arabic numerals were modeled on a system of numerals used in India. In their pursuit of slaves and gold, Arabic merchants penetrated deep into Africa.

The Franks remained oblivious to such cosmopolitanism. From a geographical point of view, only China represented a marginal culture comparable to their empire. But the Chinese ruler, the "Son of Heaven," ruled over a realm that was simply too large and too powerful for the small, up-and-coming Frankish Empire, which was in any event subject to dynastic vicissitudes, to possibly be considered on a par with it. The great intermediary between the Far East and the Far West proved to be the Muslim Arab empire that had been established by the Umayyads and taken over by the Abbasids around 750. Only Siberia remained beyond the ken of all the various heirs of classical antiquity, while Scandinavia was at least known to the Irish and now, during the reign of Charlemagne, came within the Franks' purview also as a result of raids conducted by Nordic pirates.

Yet there was no talk of such matters at the courts of either Pepin or Charlemagne. No surviving text with any close association to these monarchs had foreign peoples and their lands as its subject. It was as if nothing whatsoever was known about neighboring regions and their peoples. Nobody learned to speak their languages. The dragon-prowed longships of those Viking raiders are invariably described as having appeared "suddenly" on the horizon, and all the more dangerously for that, as if from some unspecified far-distant realm. Silk came from Constantinople or from "Persia," not from the regions beyond the Silk Route. Foreign trade brought back only the occasional Oriental spice, so the Frankish palate seldom tasted such delicacies. And if anyone happened to buy a small bag or jar containing some, how was he supposed to know where the cinnamon had been grown, or where the secretion of the musk ox had come from? These kinds of luxury goods were brought by Jewish long-distance traders from Italy, southern Gaul, or al-Andalus (Muslim Spain). But no extant document mentions the ultimate source of these goods. China would have meant nothing to Frankish contemporaries. "Europe" was also just a pale specter.

It was a similar story where conceptions of physical space were concerned. Nowadays we measure distances in miles or kilometers, areas in square miles or square kilometers, and velocities in miles or kilometers per hour. We have maps drawn to various different scales, still use street maps for the whole of Europe, Asia, and America, possess globes, and click on Google Earth. We are used to seeing the earth from above, from airplanes and in pictures taken from space stations. But people in the Carolingian age lived closer to the ground. They were familiar with the soil, with sowing and harvesting, and with field edges for horse fodder while they were under way. Frankish descriptions of the marches or settlement enterprises of the Carolingian period reveal contemporaries' keen sense for all aspects of the natural world.

However, the Franks were not given to attempting a comprehensive abstraction to try to gain a spatial awareness of the whole empire or of individual sections of it, or even an understanding of how these fitted into a complete picture of the world. No map of their realm aided orientation. No one made any calculations concerning infrastructure or urban spatial design. Even so, Charlemagne the strategist did inquire how he might travel from Mainz to the rivers Main and Danube with greater ease, had a bridge built over the Rhine, and made plans to dig a navigable canal linking the Main and the Danube. But both these civil engineering undertakings failed and were not revived by his successors. Unpaved roads ran from settlement to settlement, and even the long-distance routes were traveled on foot or on horseback; at best, only light carts pulled by oxen (rarely horses) could be used on them.

Space within the Frankish Empire was organized according to the ecclesiastical provinces, each of which was headed by an archbishop, the dioceses, each with a bishop in charge, the parishes and ecclesiastical court regions, the counties, and the plethora of local districts. Corresponding to the tortuous travel routes, these did not adjoin one another but rather formed an endless succession of disparate units. No contemporary commentator ever described Charlemagne's empire through reference to any of these provinces, let alone the position of this empire among foreign realms. It is highly likely that even Charlemagne did not have an overview of all of them. Even in the ninth century, no ruler knew all these more or less strictly delimited regions. No one from the Alemannic region (southwest Germany) or Bavaria, no count or bishop would have been able to list all the districts of eastern Franconia or Saxony, and in all likelihood none could even have named every part of his home territory. Even the king was required to tap into the knowledge of those who knew a particular region when required. Ignorance threatened all forms of authority. When plans were drawn up in 842 to divide up the empire, a special commission had to be installed just to record the respective border regions.[2]

When the Bavarians or Saxons were incorporated into the Carolingian Empire, and when the rule of the Avars in Pannonia was ended, no chronicler picked up his pen to record in writing the areas that had been acquired. No Frankish king ever commissioned a description of the realm. The wealth of a country remained hidden. Nobody paid heed to or assessed the future presence in the country of those foreign peoples the Franks knew about, or of their population numbers; no one estimated the social and political consequences of absorbing them into the empire. All that happened was that the bishops of dioceses bordering on Pannonia—Passau, Salzburg, and Aquileia—squabbled about who should be given the responsibility to send missionaries there. When Norman pirates threatened the coasts of the empire, Charlemagne was keen to have ships built, but there was no attempt to acquire intelligence about the enemy, nor was any effective fleet ultimately launched to counter them. The tendency was to react rather than to take any preemptive action. At best, isolated scraps of information devoid of any context were brought to the Frankish king's attention. Where recording for posterity was concerned, at no time was that Europe of which Charlemagne was vaunted as the beacon ever truly reflected, nor did it take any real shape beyond the mere listing of province names.

And what of the people involved? Aside from the later biography by Einhard (the *Vita Karoli*), there is no contemporaneous description of Charlemagne, and apart from a depiction on the classical model of his head on coinage and perhaps also the famous equestrian statuette in the Louvre (although some authorities claim that it portrays Charles the Bald), no contemporary image of him as a ruler exists either. The templates of perception in which the social environment was recorded were geared toward the family, status, and rank; personal achievements played no part. Accordingly, the Franks' deficient awareness of space went hand in hand with a distinct lack of curiosity about those who inhabited it. People lived in a very widely scattered pattern, often with fewer than a dozen inhabitants to each square kilometer. At best, the overwhelmingly unfree population was regarded as a ruler's property, as individuals who were liable to pay tribute and render service to their feudal lord. The only distinction that Charlemagne drew was between free men and serfs; but only the upper echelons of society—known as *primores, optimates, maiores, potentes,* or various other terms—were of any significance. Not a single servant or handmaiden at the royal court ever received a mention in the records, despite the fact that even at Aix-la-Chapelle, unfree serving personnel outnumbered the lords present.

A number of city-like settlements or *civitates,* legacies of Roman antiquity, existed within the Frankish realm: Marseilles, Arles, Narbonne, Orléans, Paris, Cologne, Mainz, Augsburg, Regensburg, and others. But who was there to record the exchange that was already going on at that time between city and countryside, a subject of intensive study by modern geographers and historians? No one chronicled such matters as how the infrastructure coped with the demands placed on it, or the constraints of a fragmented system of administration, or the yields of various salt and metal-ore mines. Who was documenting the differences between Marseilles and Augsburg or between Arles and Regensburg? Or between the north and the south or the east and the west of the Carolingian Empire? Several of Pepin's or Charlemagne's lords served as envoys to Rome, Constantinople, or Jerusalem, but none of them left behind an account of their travels or a description of foreign peoples or countries. Whatever information they imparted to their rulers remains largely a mystery to us.

Admittedly, the period shortly after Charlemagne's death saw monastic and ecclesiastical estates beginning to keep records and audits in the form of registers and polyptychs. These also recorded the people who lived on each of the "farmsteads" surveyed, albeit without naming them—men, women, and children alike. However, the registers made no attempt to add them all up to form a general census of population, even one that merely embraced the estate under scrutiny or the region in question. The tenant farmers there were attached to the manorial lord or to his agent, the land steward or *judex,* to the neighborhood, and to the parish and the judicial community. The king was a distant entity, virtually unreachable even for free men, while the local count, the king's representative, was rather to be feared than approached for help. Detailed records were kept at best only on a small scale. No one at that time would have been capable of grasping the fact that Charlemagne reigned over an empire that may, according to the findings of modern historians, have encompassed as many as twenty million people.

As a rule, the free man who was a tied laborer was required to pay tribute, while the serf farmer had to do compulsory labor, for three days per week or several weeks annually, tilling the fields. No one, however, expressed all this in terms of a gross national product. Who could have done such a thing? After all, nobody would have known how to estimate the value of such information.

Certainly, the nobility was familiar with thinking in terms of the whole population, the *populus Francorum* (Frankish people); but as a rule, what they understood by this totality was just the aristocracy and perhaps a few freedmen, but not the common people. In addition to the Franks, there were also the other peoples of the Frankish Empire, the *gentes* (distinct ethnic groups) of the Goths, the Burgundians, the Alemanni, the Bavarians, the Saxons, the Lombards, and the Romans. They differed greatly in their sense of self-identity, their awareness of their origins, their laws and dress, their patterns of settlement, and their ways of life, even though the marriages that took place between these peoples at the level of the nobility, the "imperial aristocracy,"[3] began to efface these differences. But these people's sense of identity and their different legal codes (e.g., the *Leges Alamannorum* and the *Lex Baiuvariorum*) survived until far into the High and late Middle Ages, as the chronicles known as the *Sachsenspiegel* (ca. 1220) and the *Schwabenspiegel* (ca. 1275) make clear.

As for the inhabitants of foreign countries, they were accorded no attention whatever, and no interest was shown in their mode of rule or social order, their way of life, the kind of food they ate, or their different national forms of dress. Things foreign remained alien. No Frank bothered to inquire what impelled the Nordic peoples to undertake their audacious voyages. It is recorded in the *Royal Frankish Annals* for 782 that Charlemagne ordered 4,500 rebellious Saxons to be executed—one of the few figures regarding population to have come down to us. This figure is undoubtedly exaggerated, but what seems clear is that Charlemagne was concerned to have it documented, possibly as a deterrent. But who would have been in a position to conduct a census at this period? Later, in 798, we read that a third of all men under arms had been deported—a figure we might very cautiously estimate at 1,600 people all told.[4] But the fact is that there is no way of checking such figures. The methods used to count populations in a census at this time are not known, still less how any assessments of enemy troop strengths were conducted on this basis. The density of the population and the continual growth that was surely taking place, which modern historians would maintain could be deduced from the halving and quartering of farmsteads that went on throughout the ninth century,[5] remained unnoticed at the time, and the consequences of this development also went unheeded.

Life expectancy, even average life expectancy, did not loom large in people's thoughts at this time. Abstractions from real life, from human experiences that related directly to the individual, were unfamiliar; at most, there was just a mention of the *populus,* which, generally speaking, did not mean ordinary people but rather those prominent and powerful members of the community who were present at the event in question. The only voices that were heard belonged to those rare few who could read and write and who belonged to the ruling elite. Village communities, insofar as these existed at the time, and the people who lived on estates and who at best had a mouthpiece only in the court of their landlord or his reeve will remain forever unheard by historians.

Many people died in infancy, some in maturity, and others in old age. Charlemagne, for example, was a little over sixty-five when he died, while his brother Carloman was just twenty, his sister Gisela, abbess of Chelles and Notre-Dame-de-Soissons fifty-three, and his brother Pepin barely two years old. Of Charlemagne's eighteen children, the abbess Theodrada reached the age of sixty-three, the emperor Louis the Pious sixty-two, and Abbot Hugh of Saint-Quentin fifty-four. Three others died in infancy, while the rest, as far as we know for sure, reached somewhere between the ages of twenty and forty.[6] Many of the poor found themselves forced by sheer poverty to kill their infant offspring, above all, girls. Many other babies were exposed and left to die—archetypes for the fairy tale of Hansel and Gretel. It was just a fact of life then that sometimes people found it impossible to feed their children. People lived in their respective worlds, rich or poor, sated or hungry, and not a few of them in desperate need. In any event, there were not many of them, at most a couple of million living in a space inhabited nowadays by twenty times that number.

Supraregional and intercultural communication, which is seldom seen, was the preserve of the numerically small elites. A few hundred people come to prominence in this regard. For instance, in the *Royal Frankish Annals* compiled in the age of Charlemagne (768–814), only 150 names are cited: confidants of the king, friends, and foes. Letters and other documents that have been preserved might increase the number of names somewhat but could not dispel the overall impression; the king's retinue of advisers and assistants and the number of his close confidants would still be astonishingly small. And in the same way in which personages are seldom named, so their connections with foreign rulers are extremely rare.

Aside from rare pilgrimages, only isolated "diplomatic" occasions presented opportunities for encounters with foreigners. Technical difficulties restricted contacts. When Charlemagne sent a diplomatic mission to Baghdad in 797, it took three years—and several deaths along the way—before news finally reached him from the city. Arabic envoys at the court of Charlemagne were more marveled at than comprehended; Jews were therefore allowed to work as interpreters. As well as being beset by the attendant dangers of the unknown, traveling was dependent on the viability of overland and sea routes and affected by sickness, weather, and the time of year. It was advisable to take it easy and not attempt to hurry.

Only very few people possessed the necessary language skills for such an enterprise. Translators were few and far between but essential; sometimes communication had to be achieved by means of several interpretive interim stages. The business of making oneself understood—even with the Greeks— confined itself to the most vital and immediate concerns. Misunderstandings were the order of the day. In this way, intercultural exchange between the Frankish Empire and Byzantium or the Arab world was more a rough- and-ready affair than efficient. It consequently found itself relegated to a very few limited contact zones, such as Spain, southern Italy, Rome, or Venice, with a correspondingly delayed growth of such places in the northern regions of Europe.

As a result, cultural in-house developments and emphasis on differences drowned out intercultural contacts. Although these were not out of the question, their frequency and intensity were highly variable, and, taken as a whole, they were too scarce to be the source of really solid information. Conflicts brought war booty first and foremost and much less in the way of contact with alien cultures. Pilgrimages to Rome and the Holy Land, meantime, merely furnished strange travelers' tales. We may cautiously conclude that under Charlemagne's father, Pepin, the Frankish Empire and its peoples were still too caught up in themselves to be in a position to take an interest in the wider world beyond. Only during Charlemagne's reign did this situation begin to change for a few decades.

All the same, the scholars who gathered at the court of Charlemagne—Irishmen, Anglo-Saxons, Goths, and Lombards—represented diverse cultures of learning, from which the Frankish Empire drew benefit. This was at least one way in which geographical knowledge could be expanded. Alcuin of York, for example, acquainted Charlemagne's court with Anglo-Saxon realms of experience. Likewise, a man such as the Visigoth Theodulf of Orléans likely knew a smattering of Arabic; in any event, it was through him and others like him that people's intellectual horizons began to open up to Muslim Spain. Lombards like Paul the Deacon, in their turn, became conduits for Byzantine Greek culture to reach northern Europe. Only the world of the Slavs and the Scandinavians remained shrouded in obscurity; no one from these civilizations ever appeared at Pepin's or Charlemagne's court.

Learning from books was dependent on the intelligibility of a manuscript and spread only slowly. For instance, as far as we know, around 850/860 Tacitus's *Germania*, which had something to say about the peoples who inhabited the lands east of the Rhine as far as Finland, existed only in one or two manuscripts held in Fulda and Hersfeld.[7] It is widely assumed that Charlemagne possessed a remarkable library, although it has been possible to piece together only fragments of it.[8] Authors from classical antiquity—at least those who wrote in Latin rather than Greek—imparted an educational canon that was in the main no longer underpinned by firsthand experience. Moreover, by this stage Tacitus's "Germanic peoples," namely, the peoples east of the Rhine, did not exist anymore. Also, we cannot be certain that texts from ancient times or late antiquity were ever consulted in preparation for diplomatic, political, or military action.

The text with the widest distribution was in all probability Isidore of Seville's *Etymologies*. Its individual volumes contained information about the earth, which was known to be round, about Paradise, and about the various parts of the world, as well as general knowledge on cities, agriculture, and the dimensions of fields. Book 14 began by stating: "The inhabitable Earth is located in the central region of the world" (14.1.1) and "The world is surrounded on all sides by ocean" (14.2.1). There followed descriptions of the continents of Asia (where earthly Paradise was supposedly located), Europe, and "Libya" (i.e., Africa). An area described as *Arabia beata* (Blessed Arabia) had, as yet, no knowledge of Islam (14.3.15). Islands and mountains were mentioned, but no people. The picture of the world presented here was hopelessly antiquated.

Although the next book, 15, cited numerous cities and their mythical founders, along with places of human habitation, public buildings, fortifications, and so on, again no people or their daily activities are mentioned. Certainly, the *Etymologies* boasted a rich store of knowledge, including names and classifications handed down from one generation to the next, but no one could have used it, say, to follow the actual route from Aix to Rome or Constantinople, or to Jerusalem or Baghdad. It was virtually impossible to get one's bearings in the world, or even in Europe, with the aid of the encyclopedia from Spain.

There was nothing to be found in this work on the different cultures of the ancient world, all without exception premodern societies but with widely varying forms of social organization and degrees of closeness. Nor were any comparisons drawn between the "barbarian" civilizations of northern and eastern Europe—the comparatively unsophisticated arable and livestock farmers of the lands east of the Rhine and north of the Danube—and the advanced civilizations of the Mediterranean. Meanwhile, the Avars in the Carpathian basin were nomads, but at this stage no one had yet described their way of life. The collective consciousness of identity among the elites, which was based on rank, status, and kinship in order to participate in the important decisions of their respective groups, was not a topic of discussion in any contemporary work of scholarship. All in all, people knew little about one another.

Admittedly, this view of things can also readily be reversed; the world, likewise, knew little about the Franks, their kings, and their efforts to fashion a new golden age. It was only in Byzantium that intelligence was gathered at an early stage about them. Also, Muslim rulers may well have sent Christians as envoys to Christian lands. For example, Harun al-Rashid exchanged diplomatic missions with Charlemagne, although only faint indications of this exchange appear in the works of Arab historiographers, and even these have only lately come to light.[9]

Yet not even things that were closer at hand were described in detail in the Frankish Empire. Was it really the case that the king and his elites had such little interest in the countries and peoples surrounding them? Even Einhard, who listed all the wars that his ruler engaged in against foreign peoples, had nothing to say about these adversaries. Did this ignorance, then, lie behind the heavy defeat suffered by the rear guard of Charlemagne's army under the leadership of Roland at the battle of Roncevaux Pass in the

Basque country in 778? What did the Carolingian court really know about the Basques, the Avars, the Vikings—whom they regarded as pirates—or the Slavs, the Veleti, and the Obotrites, against whom a ban on the export of swords was imposed? How did it perceive them all? To what extent did it respect them? The most cursory reading of contemporary mirrors of princes and educational tracts reveals that tolerance was not on their agenda. Insofar as foreigners were not merchants, envoys, or guests, their foreignness was scarcely paid any heed; if anything, it was regarded as a threat. Communicating with them was an onerous business and failed all too frequently. There was a distinct lack of appropriate patterns of perception and interpretation enabling people to comprehend and value others in their otherness.

Charlemagne tolerated foreigners at his court; indeed, he liked having them there so much that, as Einhard noted, the presence of so many of them in the palace and in the kingdom at large began to be seen by many as positively irritating. When he wrote this, the biographer must have had in mind the many learned Irishmen, Anglo-Saxons, Visigoths, and Lombards in the empire and the fact that they had "snatched" so many ecclesiastical positions from Frankish or Alemannic candidates: "Yet Charlemagne in his magnanimity did not let such criticism annoy him, since all the drawbacks were offset by the praise he received for his generosity and his enhanced reputation" (chap. 21). Although Einhard's remarks betray no animosity, they do still reveal a somewhat deprecatory attitude toward "foreign infiltration" of courtly society and of the royal retinue. Under Louis the Pious, this defensive attitude began to manifest itself in practical antiforeign measures, which weakened the dynamic of cultural development.

Reports from foreign countries in the environs of the Frankish Empire, which, as far as we can ascertain, were circulated in the empire, offered little information on these lands. Contemporary travel reports are few and far between, derive from a variety of different periods, and at best contain only fragmentary accounts. As long as fifty years after the event, Willibald, who later became the first bishop of Eichstätt, recounted the story of his pilgrimage to Jerusalem to a nun named Huneberc, who committed it to paper (the *Hodoeporicon*). He had embarked on his journey in 720. The nun described his progress from place to place, noted the difficulties he encountered when he entered the territory controlled by the "Saracens," and gave a brief account of his return route, which took him around Calabria to Catania and Reggio and supposedly even included a visit to the volcano at Stromboli. There, he had been intending to cast a curious glance into the very abyss of

Hell, but clouds of volcanic ash thwarted his plans. His pilgrimage finally ended in the monastery at Monte Cassino.[10]

Yet despite the fact that this Anglo-Saxon cleric traveled through and spent time in lands controlled by the Saracens, under the sign of the crescent moon, he paid not the slightest attention to their religion and made no report of it. Every church he passed was recorded, but he skipped over his encounters with Muslims and Jews completely. At least Willibald remembered the title of the *Myrmumni* (often mistaken for a proper name), in other words, the "emir of Mummenin," the "leader of the faithful." The cleric also gave a detailed description of the Holy Sepulchre.[11] But all the oral travel accounts given in this period have been lost forever. What kind of information Charlemagne's envoys later came back with from Constantinople, Jerusalem, or Baghdad is a complete mystery. Unusual gifts from these far-off lands still stimulated the greatest interest; hidden behind such gifts was a knowledge of the alien culture in question.

Certainly, some aspects of geographical knowledge did accrue to the Carolingian age from antiquity. Walahfrid Strabo, for example, who laid the foundations of his wide-ranging knowledge only after Charlemagne's death and who may have studied under Hrabanus Maurus in Fulda, referred to the *Histories* of Orosius (1.2.60) in pinpointing the position of Alemannia or Swabia in his geographical view of the world. He also knew and cited Solinus's *Polyhistor* (21.2) in this context. He had an absolutely clear conception of the location of the Alps, Lake Constance, the Rhine, Aare, Danube, Drava, and Sava Rivers, the provinces of Noricum, Rhaetia, and Pannonia, and the city of Bregenz—in other words, the close environs of his monastery at Reichenau. By contrast, he was able to place Ireland, Britain, and Spain only very approximately. Yet this monk with his book learning did manage to correct the incorrect views of "many," suggesting that he was well aware of the lack of geographical knowledge among his contemporaries.[12] It seems reasonable to expect that Charlemagne's court was acquainted with the work of Orosius at the very least.

However, his contemporaries wrote hardly any ethnographic or geographical treatises of their own. Probably around the middle of the eighth century, a remarkable cosmological treatise was produced, the *Cosmographia*, a difficult text to interpret and very possibly written with satirical intent by a fictitious author named Aethicus. The anonymous actual author must "have been a person with an uncommon gift for fantasy."[13] This work had allegedly been translated from the Greek and edited by the Church Father St. Jerome; it was a kaleidoscopic compendium of book learning, with information that may have come originally from Byzantium, and it combined myths (e.g., Romulus warring against Francus), imaginative passages, and fiction: "a sophisticatedly structured description of the world, whose subject matter alone afforded a great deal of latitude for invention." Even regions that were comparatively close at hand were larded with fictitious places and events. This construct clearly had very little foundation in personal experience. It was wholly unsuitable as a tool for orientation in the real world, much less as an instrument of spiritual power. Rather, it reveals how geographical space and conceptions of the world at this time were assembled from a mixture of handed-down knowledge, fantasy, and imagination.

The oldest fragments of manuscripts of this work date from before 800. They may—although this is still disputed—point to Salzburg as the place where it was produced; Bobbio in Emilia-Romagna is also cited as a possible place of origin. The author began in proper scholarly fashion with the Creation, describing the earth, the sea, and the firmament, and then went on to recount the fictitious Aethicus's travels around the globe before finally turning to peoples who are not mentioned in the Bible; at this point the text once again intertwines mythical and real elements. In any event, the *Cosmographia* provided a view of the world stretching from the Spanish West through the land of the Amazons, Byzantium, and the Caucasus and on as far as central Asia, and from the Scandinavian North to the North African desert zone in the south. In this picture, no portion of the earth, however small, remained unfilled and empty. Yet even this inventive author, who evidently knew full well about the spherical form of the earth, did not allow his fantasy to stray beyond the confines of the areas of the West, East, and South that he chose to describe. Beyond this, it seemed, there was nothing, absolutely nothing, that was worthy of mention.

Another work that shows close affinity both to countries visited and to contemporary modes of perception, and that was almost certainly available to read in the Frankish Empire even during Pepin's reign, was Adamnan's report on the pilgrimage undertaken by Arculf (most probably a Franconian) to Jerusalem. This account provided no political information. Bishop Arculf went on his pilgrimage around 670/680, that is, some fifty years after the Arabs had conquered the city.[14] The author, Adamnan (who died in 704), ultimately became the abbot of Iona, St. Columba, the Elder's foundation on a tiny island off the coast of Scotland. One of the Irish or Anglo-Saxon monks there could have brought a manuscript over with him to the Frankish Empire, presuming, that is, that the text did not originate there in the first place. In any event, the oldest manuscripts likely date from before the mid-ninth century or shortly thereafter and are removed from the original by just a few intermediate stages.[15] In addition, the Venerable Bede also edited this same itinerary; this version might well have been known at Charlemagne's court too, given his Anglo-Saxon tutor Alcuin's great reverence for Bede.[16]

Arculf provided a brief description of his route through Byzantine- and Arab-controlled regions before giving an extensive account, in the manner of a travel guide, of all the holy sites in Jerusalem. In describing the sites in the Holy Land, the author relied repeatedly on Eusebius's *Onomasticon* in the translation by St. Jerome,[17] whose style he attempted to imitate; he also drew on other ancient sources. As a result, the work blends reportage and literary allusion. When it came to be known in the Frankish Empire, it did at least provide its readers with some recent knowledge of the Near East. Then again, it was nothing more than scholarly knowledge that was of only limited use for getting one's bearings in the real world.

Anyhow, for the most part it was only buildings, especially Christian churches and the mausoleums of venerable saints, that were described in this work; even in Constantinople, only the "great circular Church," namely, the Hagia Sofia, but not a single palace was deemed worthy of mention, although the author did describe the city's defensive walls (as he did in Jerusalem, where he gave an account of the Tower of David citadel and the Jaffa Gate). Very occasionally, for instance, in the heavily fortified city of Damascus, reference is made to a "Saracen church," that is, a mosque (2.28). On the Temple Mount in Jerusalem, Arculf saw the building that preceded the al-Aqsa mosque that stands there today, and even this—"it is rumored"—could accommodate three thousand worshippers (1.1.14); however, he did not venture inside. The coexistence in this city of Jews, Christians, and Muslims was touched on only fleetingly.

Some of the observations in this work are particularly noteworthy. The pilgrim turned up his nose at the amount of dung left behind on the streets by camels, horses, donkeys, and oxen and marveled at all the livestock and teeming crowds of people that streamed into the city for the annual fair on 12 September (1.1.17). Arculf found the sepulchre of the Virgin Mary, the Mother of God, in the Josaphat Valley empty (2.12.2–3); "How, when, and by whom her sacred body was removed and where it now awaits resurrection, no one knows." Unlike for the Anglo-Saxon Willibald,[18] the Ascension of the Mother of God had by this stage not been proclaimed. In his travel journal, Arculf expressed distances, in familiar Frankish fashion, in terms of days' travel. Thus, from Mount Tabor to Damascus, the residence of the "king of the Saracens," was seven days (2.29), while the journey from Jerusalem to Jaffa and by thence by ship across the Mediterranean to Alexandria was forty days (2.30). Nothing was said about the journey from Europe to the Holy Land, but we know that his voyage back from Alexandria to the "metropolis of the Roman Empire" took him via Crete (3.1); he also revealed that the distance from Constantinople along the shores of the Black Sea to the Danube estuary was forty miles (3.1).

The ceremony of the veneration of the Cross that he witnessed in Constantinople was an affront to this deeply pious man. The kind of elaborate staging that was laid on there was unknown in the West and appeared scandalous to Western eyes. On three successive days of the year, the fragments of the True Cross were presented at the altar: the first on the day celebrating the Last Supper, that is, Maundy Thursday, when first the emperor and then all the court officials in strict hierarchical sequence came up to kiss the relics. The next occasion was on Good Friday, when the "queen" and her ladies-in-waiting kissed the Cross fragments, and then finally on Easter Saturday, when the bishops and the entire assembled clergy kissed the "victorious Cross" before putting it away in its reliquary once more for another year (3.3.5–10). Arculf also heard tales of a picture of St. George and one of the Virgin Mary, and in particular of how oil kept miraculously dripping constantly from the picture of the latter (*imaginis tabula;* 3.4–5). In this work, then, a colorful cluster of information had been brought together, although it lacked any internal systematic organization and was scattered throughout the whole volume. The kind of information that circulated around Pepin's court and that the young Charlemagne may have taken notice of would have been no different.

The geographical knowledge that was current at the late court of Charlemagne was attested by the Irish scholar Dicuil, who lived and wrote at the Carolingian court under Louis the Pious. For his *Liber de mensura orbis terrae,* he referred back to classical authors, whose works were, at least in part, available to consult at Charlemagne's court, such as the *Mensuratio orbis.* This work had been commissioned in 435 by Emperor Theodosius II, and a copy was kept in Charlemagne's court library. Dicuil also cited Pliny the Elder, Solinus, Orosius, Isidore of Seville, and others;[19] he even managed to build some contemporary travelers' reports into his slim volume. Europe, Asia, and Africa ("Libya") were all treated province by province according to their size, followed by the rivers, the most significant islands, the Tyrrhenian Sea, and the highest mountains.

In the process, Dicuil did not shy away from correcting his sources or sometimes calling into question their reliability. "They are in error," he noted self-confidently (7.13). His book was the first to look as far north as Iceland, while to the east his descriptions went beyond Arabia and Persia and extended as far as the Ganges and the Indus rivers in India; in the south, though, apart from the Nile valley, his reportage did not go beyond the coastal provinces. The author spent an especially long time on the Nile and Egypt, the land of Moses, describing the flooding, the river delta, the great Mosaic "storehouses" (i.e., the pyramids), and several other features. In the process, he learned something that did not derive from a classical source, namely, that a pilgrim had managed to voyage on board a ship (by means of a canal) from the Nile to the Red Sea. When he was writing on India, he mentioned rhinoceroses and elephants, and he referred to hyenas in Africa. However, he had his doubts concerning the fabled African people spoken about by the geographer Solinus. This was not a topic he felt he could expand on.

Dicuil proudly displayed his firsthand knowledge of the north of the British Isles in describing the many larger and smaller islands that made up the coastline there: "I lived on some of them, I visited some, while others I merely saw or even just read about" (7.6). These were islands that no ancient classical author knew about, and that had originally been uninhabited, but that ultimately the Normans began using for grazing cattle and sheep (7.15). Dicuil may also have visited Ultima Thule, that is, Iceland, which lay on the Tropic of Cancer; certainly he was the first to describe the phenomenon of the midnight sun, which appeared, "so to speak, as though it were shining from behind a low hill," but which nevertheless brought no darkness, so that "people could go about their business as they wished"; it was even light enough for Dicuil to be able to pluck a louse off his shirt (7.8–13). For all its incompleteness, this work's critical stance toward the ancient authorities, combined with its accounts of personal experiences and plausible descriptions of foreign lands, bore witness to Charlemagne's interest in acquiring knowledge, along with a desire to turn toward the outside world and for realistic descriptions of that world that he might use to determine his actions. Above all, though, it testified to the ever-increasing body of knowledge that the king now had at his disposal to inform and guide his trading activities.[20]

Despite the fact that so few travelers set out from the Carolingian Empire, experience and reading still complemented each other. Knowledge gained through experience expanded correspondingly slowly. Texts handed down from the ancient world offered little help for orientation in the present, while the impressions conveyed by pilgrims scarcely went beyond the biblical pattern. And not even when external dangers loomed, such as hostile

Norman incursions, was any attempt made to understand or investigate the social differentness of the enemy, notwithstanding the fact that intelligence about the empire's neighbors must have been more precise and detailed in the frontier regions.[21] The world that lay beyond the borders was all too often simply viewed with suspicion, a feeling that the scant pieces of hard-and-fast information available would scarcely have been able to dispel. References to foreigners are correspondingly sparse in contemporary accounts, insofar as these are still extant.

Foreign peoples, languages, and lifestyles are almost completely excluded from the reports that have been preserved. No Frankish writer, it seems, ever sharpened his quill to describe Constantinople or the alien, incomprehensible modes of living that existed in the Byzantine Empire, although several of them spent time there, living on the Bosphorus and the Golden Horn. Misunderstandings further hampered communication. Complaints were regularly raised about miserable lodgings and dismissive treatment.

Even when the Lombards were subjugated by the Frankish king, no Frank saw fit to make a note of the qualities of his own and this conquered people by way of comparison, or of the Lombards' power structures, such as the economic potential of their financial administration, their social system, or their ways of life—let alone the characteristics of any of the other peoples in the region. Paul the Deacon may well have regaled the Carolingian court with stories from the history of his people and family, but no one deemed them worthy of being written down. Yet at this stage he had not produced his history of the Lombard people. Intercultural learning processes were similarly slow to arrive.

Such a comparison would above all have had systematic questioning as its premise, involving such concepts as "class" and "type," "the familiar" and "the foreign," their "peculiarity" (*proprium*) and their "difference," or their respective "chance traits" (*accidentia*). Yet it was at this very time that the Franks, prompted by the impetus given by the court of Charlemagne, began to practice modes of thought, perception, and examination that entertained such grand abstract concepts. Even so, it would take until the late Middle Ages before this method became widely familiar and proved its worth in practice. The intellectual horizons of scholars broadened only gradually. Nonetheless, it was at Charlemagne's court that a start was made. Knowledge about foreign matters started to intensify, while people's conceptions of foreignness became clearer, and information on the subject grew more pertinent. Charlemagne also knew how to exploit what little data he had at his disposal.

Certainly, the more remote a foreign country and people, the scantier the information became. The routes into the Near East were known through pilgrims—who were often suspected of being spies—and repeated diplomatic missions, and possibly also through occasional trade contacts. There are, however, no records of Frankish merchants venturing to Spain, Africa, or Constantinople. Only the Italian maritime cities, primarily ports belonging to the Eastern Roman Empire, such as Venice and Naples, now set about forging far-reaching mercantile networks. But the merchants did not commit their experiences to paper, with the result that we have no knowledge of them. Charlemagne, though, was able to solicit their advice from time to time.

In Rome, which until the mid-eighth century and a few years beyond was part of the Eastern Roman Empire, certain contacts were maintained with Constantinople, as well as with Jerusalem and its monasteries. Pope Zachary, who is reputed to have dispensed such beneficial advice to the Carolingians on the matter of regality, was the last Greek on the throne of St. Peter. He came from Santa Severina in Calabria. Yet nowhere in the official book of the popes, the *Liber pontificalis,* do we find any treatment of conditions in the Byzantine Empire or ways of life in Constantinople, Sicily, or the south of the Italian Peninsula. Charlemagne attempted to restrict commerce with the West Slavs to just a few trading posts (this does at least prove that such trade existed). However, we learn virtually nothing about the Slavs from contemporary accounts from the Carolingian period.

Byzantine trade, which was still extensive at this time, was able to reach China via the Silk Route, although with the West it ground to a halt over time. The last traces of it come to light in 776 in a missive by Pope Hadrian I to Charlemagne, in which he mentioned the appearance of Greek slave traders on the coast of Latium, who had allegedly acquired a number of serfs (*mancipia*) from the Lombards with a view to selling them to "the unspeakable race of the Saracens." Hadrian reported that he had ordered their ships to be set on fire after they entered the port of Civitavecchia and that the Greeks be detained. The intention of this was not to suppress the slave trade as such, but to stop Christians from selling their coreligionists to non-Christians. Starvation had allegedly driven the poor wretches to offer themselves for sale; some of them were said to have voluntarily surrendered themselves to the Greek slave merchants out of sheer desperation.[22]

Here, then, protection for the poor and a turning away from Byzantium went hand in hand. Admittedly, these Greeks who were trading with the Saracens would in all likelihood have come from Sicily or southern Italy rather than from Constantinople. There is no firm evidence that ports in Gallia—Marseilles or Narbonne, for instance—which had been retaken by the Muslims in 759, were being used at this time. During the reign of Charlemagne, alongside Naples and Amalfi, Venice increasingly began to take over the trade link that joined Constantinople with the West; the rise of the lagoon republic commenced in this period. The Franks, too, would doubtless have been familiar with the slave trade, although there is no direct evidence to this effect.[23]

The only merchants who ventured halfway around the globe were Jews; they acted as middlemen between the continents, from China to the Frankish Empire and Spain. The last vestiges of ancient Rome's global trading were evident in their activities. The Radhanites, as these traders were known, had a clear geographical grasp of the world and supposedly, according to the Arab chronicler Ibn Khordadhbeh, writing in the late ninth century, traversed the globe from west to east and vice versa; they were polyglot, reputedly speaking Arabic, Persian, "Roman" (i.e., Greek or Latin), Frankish, Spanish, and Slavonic. They were said to have traded slaves of both sexes, boys, brocade, castor oil, animal pelts, and swords from the West.

Ibn Khordadhbeh gave a detailed account of the routes they took. The route to the East began by ship from the Frankish Empire or Spain to Tangier and then by caravan along the North African coast to Suez, where the merchants boarded ships bound for India or China. From there, the Radhanites imported musk, spices, aloes, cinnamon, and other products of the Orient; it appears that silk was not mentioned in the Arab's account. On their return journey, the Jewish merchants either reached Antioch and Constantinople from Egypt or traveled overland to Baghdad, from where they went on to the Persian Gulf; they were also said to have visited the palace of the king of the Franks. Some of them ventured to the land of the Slavs and the Khazars and from there, Ibn Khordadhbeh maintained, had also got as far as China via the northern Silk Route.

The origin of the name of these traders (Radhanites, ar-Rhadaniya, Radhanim) is a mystery, and we do not know where these long-range merchants were based. Interpretations vary wildly, linking the name to Ragha in Persia, to Radhan, a suburb of Baghdad, or even to the Rhône River; those who take the last view claim that the Radhanites' homeland was around the Rhône and the Meuse (Maas).[24] Yet regardless of their different religion, the chronicler describes the routes taken by these merchants as regularly beginning farther to the West, in the Frankish Empire and Spain, and also says that they returned there. Perhaps this conceals a hint at their origins. Did they constitute a kind of "international" trading company? We may even know one of them by name—a man called Isaak, the Jewish merchant whom Charlemagne dispatched to Baghdad in 797 and who came back to the Frankish Empire three years later (by the route via North Africa described in Ibn Khordadhbeh's writings) leading the elephant Abul-Abbas, a present to Charlemagne from the Abbasid caliph Harun al-Rashid. In sending Isaak, Charlemagne, it appears, availed himself of knowledge that was lacking at his court. According to all accounts in the texts that have come down to us, the meticulous geographical knowledge of these Radhanites was unknown to the Franks and the Latin Christians, in marked contrast to the lands under Muslim rule. Even so, this body of learning revealed nothing about the internal affairs of the many polities that lay along the route from China to Spain.

Far-off Byzantium and the Even More Remote Dar al-Islam

After the Carolingians came to rule over the immediate environs of the Frankish Empire, this region had, so to speak, to be newly explored and somehow to be reinvented by the king and his elites. This took place in critical engagement with a changing reality. Yet, apart from perhaps the Anglo-Saxon kingdoms, this process did not yield any comprehensive knowledge of the foreign realms, nor did it engender any particular urge to investigate them, let alone describe them. As far as we can tell from the surviving accounts, their achievements and difficulties, both internal and external, received scant attention at the court of Pepin and his illustrious son. Accordingly, the foreign was scarcely understood in its otherness.

Both kings concluded treaties with foreign powers. These agreements were regarded as instances of "friendship" (*amicitia*), but for the Franks, they were also mutual commitments by both parties, with formal legal status and confirmed by oath.[25] Friendship was not simply friendship, however; it meant different things in different places. It was applicable only to a limited extent to contracts between foreign realms and peoples with diverse traditions, laws, and religions. Even under the Franks, it did not foster longevity. Foreign powers' contractual behavior was not restrained by it. Even the ways in which treaties were ratified differed considerably. For example, the convention of swearing an oath on religious relics or the Holy Scriptures was common only among Christian societies.

A few years after his coronation, Pepin exchanged ambassadors with the emperor in Constantinople (the Byzantines had actually taken the initiative).

The catalyst for this had been the Frankish ruler's two military campaigns against Italy, in 755 and 756, and the Carolingian king's actions there for the benefit of the *res publica Romanorum*. Constantinople—the Eastern Roman or Byzantine Empire—was at that time suffering great internal disruption due to the onset of the iconoclastic controversy, while externally it was under attack by both the Arabs and the Bulgars. The Byzantines were unable effectively to counter either the attack by the Lombards or Pepin's military campaign because their forces were all tied up in the East. As was often the case, the only course left open to them was diplomacy.

Frankish kings were, of course, aware of the existence of the Eastern Roman Empire but knew very little about it. The rule of the *basileus* (Byzantine emperor) was a continuation of the old Roman emperorship in the East. The metropolis of Constantinople had formed the center of the empire since the days of Constantine the Great and Justinian. The Byzantines' designation of themselves as "Romans" (*Rhomaioi*) and their realm as "Romania" reflected the traditional claim of the *basileus* to be the one legitimate ruler, the sole emperor of the Romans, despite the fact that his actual title only proclaimed him as king. The West, however, rejected this conceit and was in the habit of using the somewhat disparaging term "Greeks" to describe these Eastern "Romans."

Although it was true that the Eastern Roman Empire had successfully withstood many centuries of conflict to emerge intact from the Persian Wars, since that time it had found itself embroiled in extremely damaging rearguard actions fighting off the advance of the Arab caliphate. Before long, another threat materialized in the form of attacks by the (Proto-)Bulgars, who from the late seventh century had been menacing the northern borders of the empire.[26] In some years—say, 759–760[27]—this war on two fronts raged with full ferocity. Like the Khazars on the northern shore of the Black Sea, this mounted tribe remained even during Charlemagne's reign an unknown ethnic factor; it was only when his grandsons came to power that the Franks encountered these people face-to-face.

While Byzantium was beset by a number of different external threats, the Latin West was reaping the benefit of the very real protection that the Byzantine Empire afforded it. Indeed, this made the West's rise possible. Yet at no stage did the Franks appear to be conscious of the debt they owed to the oft-maligned "Greeks." Furthermore, as time went by, the long coastlines of Italy lost the protection of the dromons, the heavy galleys of the Byzantine fleet. The defense of Constantinople saw the deployment of Greek fire, a chemical weapon that burned even on the sea and whose terrifying efficacy was due to the use of a magnesium compound. Emperor Constantine V's reorganization of the Byzantine provinces into so-called themes (or *themata*), especially in Asia Minor and later in southern Italy, enabled land-based defenses to become more efficient too. Sicily was placed under the command of a military governor (*strategos*) and served as an operational base for the Byzantine fleet.

Internally, the Byzantine Orthodox Church did not foment any dogmatic rifts with Western Christianity, especially since Rome, the papacy, was strongly influenced by Eastern Orthodoxy during the Carolingian period; nevertheless, many different liturgical practices existed between the two churches. Thus, the Eastern Church fasted on Saturdays as well as Sundays and used leavened bread for Holy Communion, whereas the Western Church used unleavened bread as the Host. Both visibly and as a palpable undercurrent, over time such differences began to provoke irritation, skepticism, and rejection—or even undisguised hostility—notably among the Franks. One particular bone of contention that came to dominate discussion concerned the Orthodox Church's attitude to icons. In the Eastern Church, whose offshoots extended even as far as Rome, images of Christ, the Virgin Mary, and the saints were much venerated. Yet precisely at this time, a more or less vehement rejection of sacred images—iconoclasm—made its presence felt in Constantinople.[28] This movement was bound up with internal power struggles and was unable to assert itself in the long run. Before long, the cult of images returned, a phenomenon that had never been suppressed in the border provinces of the empire anyway. Charlemagne would subsequently call on the brilliance of his foremost scholars to root out any supposed outgrowths of this revitalized cult within his own realm.

Veneration of images had a long tradition especially in the city of Rome.[29] A series of venerable icons that still exist to this day testifies to this fact: the icon of the Virgin Mary at the Pantheon, dating from the sixth or early seventh century, the empress-like *Madonna della Clemenza* in Trastevere from the early eighth century, the seventh-century icons that were removed from Santa Maria Antiqua and rehoused in the church of Santa Francesca Romana (likewise located on the Forum Romanum), the *Maria Advocata* (also called the Madonna of San Sisto) in Santa Maria del Rosario, the Virgin Mary icon *Salus Populi Romani* or its original model in Santa Maria Maggiore, or the *Acheiropoieton*—literally "made without hands" (i.e., supposedly divinely created), and the icon of Christ in the pope's private chapel, the Sancta Sanctorum in the Lateran Palace.

The Church and the populace alike venerated these images, and many legends grew up around them. Lamps or candles were placed in front of them, and they were carried in procession through the streets. As donations from private or ecclesiastical benefactors, they were incorporated into public religious ritual. As a result, we read in the life of Pope Stephen II, the pontiff who anointed Pepin and his sons, that he led the penitential procession to pray for the lifting of the Lombards' siege of Rome "with that most sacred image of the Lord, our Savior Jesus Christ, which is generally known as the *Acheiropoieton*," carrying the panel, along with other clerics, on his shoulders from the Lateran to the church of Santa Maria ad Praesepe (Santa Maria Maggiore); there they put ashes in their hair as a sign of penitence and beseeched the Lord for help in their plight.[30] The icon served as nothing less than a guarantee of divine assistance. Every year on Maundy Thursday, this panel of the Savior was anointed with consecrated oil on the places showing the stigmata of Christ. Charlemagne probably attended this ceremony at least once. Admittedly, nothing can be made out on the panel today, as a result of the centuries-long veneration accorded to this painting; only copies of the image from the High Middle Ages give us some inkling of what it once looked like.[31]

After Justinian, the Latin civilization in Constantinople was completely subsumed within Greek culture. No Latin texts were disseminated any longer—no Cicero, Horace, Tacitus, St. Augustine, or St. Jerome. Instead, people began studying Plato and Aristotle, along with Origen and the other Greek Church Fathers. Medical texts like Galen's extensive body of work and that of Hippocrates were also in wide circulation. Even ancient texts like Homer's *Iliad* and *Odyssey* were saved for posterity in Byzantium, along with works by the historians Herodotus and Thucydides. Nor was technological learning lacking. The Byzantines still maintained an expensive fleet of warships. Yet ever since the reign of Justinian, social life, politics, the economy, and culture had increasingly come to focus on Constantinople. Gold, silk, and wealth in general began to be amassed around the Bosphorus; all trade routes ran to the imperial capital. The flip side of such magnificence, however, was the fact that the provinces were neglected in virtually every respect, be it political, economic, or cultural. Nor did it help that the long-distance trade connections fostered by the Byzantine Greeks led overland to central Asia and Persia. The catastrophic consequences of this insularity became apparent when the Arabs embarked on their campaigns of conquest.

The Byzantine emperor Constantine V had his scholars keep a close eye on developments in the West. It is astonishing to realize the accuracy of the information he was supplied with. The chronicler Theophanes, who wrote somewhat later, at the beginning of the ninth century, around 810–813, cites a note that he wrongly dates to the year AM 6216 (corresponding to 723–724 CE) but that nevertheless gives a precise sketch of events in the West: the attack of the Lombard king Aistulf and Pope Stephen II's "flight" to the Franks and their mayor of the palace Pepin, who, the report maintains, held real power in the realm, while the Frankish king sat idly at home, eating and drinking and showing himself to his subjects only on 1 May, when he exchanged gifts before hurrying back to the palace once more. The Frankish kings, Theophanes's source claimed, were known at the "long-haired ones" because they let their hair grow right down their backs "like hogs." And it was this Pepin (here Theophanes confuses Pepin the Short with his father, Charles Martel, wrongly stating that it was the former who beat the Moors at the battle of Poitiers on the Loire) on whom Pope Stephen conferred royal power while at the same time compelling the former king to take holy orders and enter a monastery. Pepin, the report continues, had two sons: Charlemagne and Carloman. No similar memorandum about the Eastern Roman Empire, embracing all the political background of the events of the period, is to be found in any annalistic text from the Frankish Empire.

It was therefore with full knowledge of what was going on in the West that Constantine turned to the Carolingians. Pepin turned down the emperor's request to place Ravenna and the cities of the exarchate, which Aistulf had conquered and which the Frankish ruler had restored to the Roman See, under imperial rule once more. In his state of powerlessness, the *basileus* was forced to accept this decision. So as not to lose all influence in Italy, he nevertheless concluded a friendship treaty with the barbarians. Pepin may well have regarded this as a tacit recognition of his rule, but in actual fact the Byzantine Rhomaioi were merely acting in accordance with a long-standing Roman tradition that considered "friends" lower-ranking, dependent office-holders.[32] In any event, it is possible that the Frankish king agreed to an exchange whereby the exarchate was ceded to the Byzantines in return for the papal patrimonies on Sicily confiscated by Byzantium.[33]

The self-confident and forceful intervention south of the Alps by the Carolingian ruler, his unsettling meeting with the Western patriarch, and the transfer of the exarchate to the papacy, which saw Pentapolis, Tuscia (Etruria), Spoleto, and other Italian provinces donated to the pope rather than being restored to the Eastern Roman Empire—all this must have been deeply unnerving for the *basileus*. Later, possibly around 766–767, when the full ramifications of the Donation of Pepin began to take effect, Constantine V proposed a marriage alliance to the Frankish king, a union whose aim was doubtless to get this donation revoked. To this end, the Byzantine emperor sought the hand of Pepin's daughter Gisela for his own son Leon.[34] Once again, Pepin refused. This decision was most probably reached at the Synod of Gentilly, which met at the beginning of 767, and at which both Byzantine and papal envoys were present. Points at issue at this synod included the Holy Trinity and the images of saints; it is also possible that the Franks were already at this time promulgating their creed, according to which the Holy Ghost did not proceed only from the Father but also from the Son (the *filioque* controversy).[35] Admittedly, though, no further details are known about this meeting. It is probable, however, that the Greek side sought to defend the iconoclastic Council of Hieria of 754, which must have provoked vehement opposition from Rome, with its thriving cult of icons. The Franks gradually began to involve themselves in the power struggle taking place around the Mediterranean.

Here, then, was a clash between two profoundly divergent Christian worlds that understood each other less and less and viewed each other with skepticism and mistrust. The Franks were irritated by matters that appeared alien to them. Thus, Byzantine diplomacy, which upheld the ancient Greco-Roman tradition, struck them as suspect and tantamount to artful mendacity. Time and again, they accused the Greeks of arrogance and of engaging in the wickedest intrigues. The theological differences concerning the creed and the question of iconoclasm that would presently take center stage only added to the growing list of prejudices.

Pepin's response to Constantine was not simply conditioned by the question of icons.[36] Rather, it was a declaration of devotion to St. Peter; any revisions in favor of the Eastern Roman Empire were excluded, and the dynastic marriage request was turned down. Thus, the friendship with Byzantium dissolved as swiftly as it had been formed. Even at this early stage, before he was named his father's successor, Pepin's son Charlemagne may well have noted the dogmatic unreliability of the Greeks and the necessity—but also the opportunity—of organizing effective resistance to them in alliance with Rome. After a few years, he was even able, unhindered by any diplomatic considerations, to incorporate Istria, which had hitherto been a Byzantine possession, into his realm (778). Only in 781 did East-West relations improve for a short while; on this occasion the initiative came from Constantinople once more, and once again it ended in failure.

Charlemagne's envoys got to know Constantinople and the imperial palace there well. They would surely have been constantly amazed, although no contemporary commentator described their impressions, and despite the fact that they must also, to counter this positive view, have despised the courtly pomp in evidence there. Not a single Frankish report on Constantinople at the time of Charlemagne has been preserved. But with its unfamiliar rituals and liturgies, what went on there would have repelled the Western envoys rather than stimulating them to imitation. Yet the legendary wealth of the Rhomaioi, the Roman tradition that was still alive and well there, the opulent style of living of the Byzantines, and the level of cultural learning that gave them a painfully palpable superiority over the Franks were guaranteed to provoke envy. A few isolated reflections by Carolingian envoys to the city appear only later in the oral tradition, and with their content doubtless distorted.[37] Yet for all that, some sort of cultural exchange did take place precisely in this response of criticism and rejection.

It is no coincidence that, in the final years of Pepin's reign, we learn that the Frankish king exchanged diplomatic representation with the caliph in Baghdad.[38] This was the first time such a thing had happened in the history of the Franks, and it underlines the newly enhanced status that their monarchy had attained through the Carolingian dynasty. For its part, the Baghdad caliphate could boast a unique history of success, embracing an unstoppable rise and an alarming expansion of power. Through Islam, the Prophet Muhammad had achieved what Christianity—which was not unknown in Arabia—had been unable to do, namely, to unify the previously disunited Arab tribes. They had originally been Bedouins with all manner of religious cults, who also had urban centers such as the trading cities of Mecca and Medina; especially there, Judaism and Christianity were by no means unknown. Their social structure resembled that of a diffuse clan society. Groups that had hitherto been disunited were unified, not just in religious terms but also where their form of rule was concerned, by the Qur'an and the life of the Prophet Muhammad, supplemented by the oral tradition. Even so, regional unrest and violence remained the order of the day; from the outset, Islam was a warlike religion.

The Latin West barely registered this development; no one even investigated the rise of this new adversary in retrospect. Meanwhile, the Eastern Roman Empire had grown extremely wary, for obvious reasons. A number of extraordinary tales began to circulate, painting the rise of these sons of the desert in apocalyptic colors. One such story claimed that Jews had taken Muhammad to be the Messiah and had adopted his faith. When he started to eat camel meat, they realized their mistake but remained loyal to him all the same. The Byzantine chronicler Theophanes recounted this tale in describing the year of the Prophet's death (AM 6122) and followed it with further details from the life and teachings of Muhammad, although these were distorted for polemical purposes. Theophanes concluded that he died as "the ruler of the Saracens and a false prophet." But the Latin Christians far from the borders of the Arab caliphate did not possess even this kind of knowledge.

Muhammad's death in 632 and the first conflicts arising from the succession to the Prophet, however, did nothing to halt the rapid conquests and the massive extension and construction of the Dar al-Islam (House of Islam). Completely in accordance with Arab social organization, Muhammad's tribe, the Quraysh, assumed the leadership role. The "successor of the prophet of Allah" (Arabic: *Khalifat rasuli 'llah,* or "caliph" for short) filled the position of both religious and political leader.

The expansion of the caliphate took place with breathtaking, scarcely believable speed over just a few decades: Jerusalem was taken in 638, while Egypt, the breadbasket of Constantinople, fell two years later, followed by Carthage in 647–649. In 711, Arabs landed in Spain for the first time, reaching the Pyrenees in just two years and crossing them to subdue the land north of the mountains, with the city of Narbonne at its center. Raiding parties were soon probing deep into Aquitaine; it was once such force that was confronted and defeated by Charles Martel in 732, a minor success that Carolingian propaganda hailed as a major victory. After Charlemagne's death, Arab attacks on Sicily were not long in coming.

Despite the fact that they were originally land dwellers, even before the seventh century had drawn to a close, the Arabs managed to build a powerful naval fleet with astonishing speed; this force proceeded to instill fear in the Greeks, who until then had ruled the Mediterranean, and even began to threaten Constantinople. The burgeoning Arab empire stretched from the Indus to the Pyrenees and from the Caucasus down to Aden at the mouth of the Red Sea, so covering a larger territory than the Roman Empire at its greatest extent. Arabian long-distance trade reached as far as India and China, Zanzibar, and the coast of East Africa; for a short period in the decades around 700, merchant shipping in the Latin world of the West was restricted or even interrupted. The most enduring effect of the Arab conquests was evident in the absence of any papyrus from Egypt, which until then had been widely used as writing material. Henceforth, the West was obliged to use expensive parchment.[39]

Conquered peoples beyond the confines of the Arabian Peninsula were not forced to convert to Islam. As fellow "peoples of the Book" (*dhimmi*), Jews and Christians were expressly spared conversion, although this by no means excluded harassment and persecution at a local level. The constant burden they were forced to bear was payment of high poll taxes (*jizya*) to the Muslim authorities. Christians in particular were permitted to serve in the civil administration of the caliphate. It was they who were responsible for countless translations from the Greek during the first decades of Arab rule. This greatly facilitated and hastened the reception of ancient Greek learning. The Arabs held medicine, technology, astronomy, and mathematics in especially high esteem. Philosophy, on the other hand, was regarded with suspicion on religious grounds.

It was not opposition by any foreign power but rather internal conflict that finally brought a halt to Arab expansion, when the dispute about the rightful successor to the Prophet escalated. The third caliph, Uthman, and his successor, Ali, were both assassinated, events that led to the split between the Sunni and Shia branches of Islam. Ultimately a clan of the Quraysh, the Umayyads, emerged victorious from the power struggle but was unable to heal the rift. For around a century thereafter, up to the reign of the first Carolingian monarch, Pepin the Short, all the caliphs came from this clan. These developments were all closely watched in Constantinople.

Around the time of Pepin, the first cracks began to appear in the powerful empire created by the Umayyads. Not least, as time went on, the native traditions of conquered peoples—for example, the Berbers in North Africa—proved ever more effective as a dividing force. The Arab West, as well as Africa and the provinces around the ancient settlement of Carthage, increasingly went their own way. The distant ripples from this upheaval reached as far as the Latin West. Admittedly, at first the Franks had no inkling of these fundamental developments, despite the fact that they, too, now had Muslims as their neighbors; by the time the Carolingians took power, the whole of the southwestern Mediterranean coast from Spain to Narbonne was under Muslim control.

The Umayyads established the capital of their caliphate at Damascus, a city with a predominantly Christian population. It was precisely these Christians who facilitated the adaptation of their new Arab rulers and their realm to the learning of late antiquity. Concerned, though not without a hint of schadenfreude, the Byzantine chronicler Theophanes, for example, wrote of the year AM 6251 (759/760 CE) that the Arabs had banned Christians from working as public scribes. He went on to report that they had been forced to rescind the ban, however, "because they [the Arabs] found themselves incapable of recording legal judgments." Of course, this kind of malicious gibe could not mask the fact that a high intellectual standard existed in the domain of the caliphs nor conceal that Christians in particular had played a key part in the caliphate's success story. The few historians from the Latin West who chose to write about this period omitted to mention any of these facts.

In the mid-eighth century, the Umayyads were replaced by the Abbasids, descendants of Muhammad's uncle Abbas. This would prove to be a glittering new start for the Arab caliphate. Al-Mansur, a staunch advocate of rationalistic Islam (the Mu'tazila school of Islamic theology), abandoned Damascus and moved his residence in 762 to Baghdad, on the Tigris River, stating, "This is the place where I intend to build." Astrologers and horoscopes had recommended it to him. "Commodities can be carried here on the Euphrates and Tigris Rivers, and via a network of canals. Only a place like this will be able to feed both the army and the populace at large." These words—displaying the kind of reasoning that would take a considerable time to take root among the Franks—were imputed to the caliph a century and a half later by the historian at-Tabari.[40] In general, this caliph set great store by learning, which he was wont to contrast with the ignorance of earlier rulers. He alone possessed a God-given, accurate power of judgment; it was up to him to direct and educate his people.[41]

A single Umayyad prince, 'Abd-ar-Rahman, had by chance escaped the fate suffered by the rest of his family, having traveled overland through North Africa and having reached Spain, where he founded an independent emirate (756)—a truly rare outcome indeed for an émigré. Over the following years, this refugee and first Umayyad ruler of al-Andalus, who later became known by the honorific title ad-Dakhil (the newcomer), secured the borders to the north against the Christians and the Franks. Yet he never lost sight of the light of the Orient, the palm trees, and his home of Damascus. The sight of a single palm tree in Spain was enough to remind him of what he had relinquished:

> O horseman making your way to my homeland,
> Be dispatched to my friends with salutations.
> As you can see, my body languishes in this country;
> But my heart and my loves lie back home.
> Separation was our destiny, we had to part;
> But parting has robbed me of sleep.

God ordered this separation;
Perhaps He will also grant us a reunion one day.

Allah did not will this, however; all that remained were this and other verses by the Umayyad exile.[42] But the country he ruled, al-Andalus, became a land of thriving Arab culture. Water, wood, and energy were there in abundance, plus the existing knowledge pool of the "Romans," the Visigoths, the Christians, and the Jews. This merged with the cultural capital that the Arabs brought to the country. Christians and Jews listened to the stories told by Arabs and followed ever more willingly the example set by the Muslims, whose poetry displayed a beauty and perfection unmatched by the verse being produced by the Latins at that time. Shortly before his death, 'Abd-ar-Rahman I embarked on the new, architecturally daring construction of the magnificent Great Mosque of Córdoba, while lush gardens surrounded his residence on the banks of the Guadalquivir. His successors, though, assumed the title of caliph only from the tenth century onward.

The usurper and Abbasid caliph al-Mansur now looked around for allies to fight this last Umayyad ruler; this quest made him turn his gaze northward, to the realm where, at almost exactly the same time, a successful coup had just been staged to topple the ruling Merovingian dynasty.[43] In addition, the Franks had already checked the military successes of the Umayyads and were preparing to launch a counteroffensive. We may presume that al-Mansur was responsible for dispatching the delegation to Pepin that arrived at the Frankish court around 764 or 765;[44] the king gave them an immediate response. Unfortunately, the official messages that were exchanged between the two sides have not survived. Another reciprocal legation sent three years later by the caliph, which like the previous one was in all probability headed by Christians, came bearing lavish gifts.[45] Evidently, the Carolingian king had given a favorable answer to the first delegation. We may speculate whether the Carolingian court registered its own cultural deficits and backwardness on the occasions of these official visits, and whether this experience remained like a thorn in the side of its intellectual culture, perhaps acting as a spur to catch up. Did the young Charlemagne perhaps entertain such feelings? We cannot prove it, but it seems plausible. Charlemagne was not blind to foreigners' intellectual achievements.

At this stage, it was too soon for the Franks to launch an attack against Umayyad rule in Spain, however. Such an enterprise could take place only under Charlemagne. Even so, the delegations sent by the Byzantines and the Arabs emphasize that the regimes of the eastern Mediterranean not only took note of changes in the West but also reacted to them and attempted to exploit them to their own advantage. This kind of diplomatic skill was lacking on the Frankish side. Despite this, at least these developments helped drag the Frankish Empire from its former marginal position back into the thick of momentous events that were shaping the Mediterranean world.

Whatever merchants, pilgrims, or migrants across borders may have learned firsthand about the Muslims initially counted for little against the hostile prejudices that were then circulating in the West. Nobody sought enlightenment, but intercultural exchange still managed to take place in this atmosphere, albeit not in any purposeful way; instead, it was a surreptitious, gradual process. Likewise, for a long time there was a paucity of correct information in the West about Islam and the Dar al-Islam, as indeed there was about all alien religions. Therefore, there were no analytical templates for analyzing foreign cults and cultures. These developed only over time. Biblical references countenanced no other gods and rejected any approach that sought to understand and engage with different religions. The religion of other people was the very factor that served to differentiate and demarcate cultures and generate animosity.

Along with control of the empire, Pepin's son Charlemagne also inherited his father's high reputation in both the West and the East. But by the time, from the early 780s onward, he resumed relations with Constantinople—and toward the end of the century with Baghdad—circumstances had changed completely. The Frankish king had elevated himself to the position of king of the Lombards and had extended the frontiers of his empire far beyond Rome to southern Italy, to the borders with Calabria and Apulia, and in the east to Pannonia. Charlemagne had also led a military expedition to the banks of the Ebro in Spain and had made great efforts to raise his own intellectual culture to be on a par with that of the Greeks and the "Saracens"; ultimately, he was striving for the imperial crown.

The Nearest Neighbors

The Frankish Empire was characterized by its lively cultural exchanges, especially with the Irish and the Anglo-Saxons. Yet communication with other neighboring peoples was restricted by virtue of their heathen nature; at best, trade contact close to the border helped break down cultural barriers. Although it came from two very distinct traditions, literacy was relatively widespread among the Irish and the Anglo-Saxons. Some Irish scholars even had a knowledge of Greek, although it is not clear what tradition this was based on. Ireland's social and ruling order was totally dissimilar to that on the Continent. Its church did not follow Roman practices; it became subject to the authority of the papacy only after being conquered by England in the twelfth century. St. Patrick—or whoever brought Christianity to the Irish in late antiquity—ushered in a development that followed a quite different course than on the Continent or among the Anglo-Saxons. This was conditioned by Ireland's long-standing isolation and hallmarked by a culture of high monasticism, which also held sway over theological scholarship and canon law in the country.

Despite the high oral culture of the *filid,* the country's poets and guardians of tradition, the Irish do not appear to have developed their own historiography during the early Middle Ages (although a sophisticated tradition of book illumination certainly evolved there). Nor was their church hierarchically structured, although there were bishops, that is, priests with the capacity to consecrate. Frequently, a majority of them lived in monasteries and were subservient to their abbot. The curious tradition of the *peregrinatio sancta* was widespread, aimless ventures into the wider world to proclaim the faith wherever pilgrims happened to gather. Charlemagne would benefit from this practice.

Things were quite different among the Anglo-Saxons. The end of Roman occupation of Britain and the immigration of Angles and Saxons saw the return of paganism to the island. In his history of the Anglo-Saxons (written around 730), Bede recounts that Wotan was regarded as the progenitor of most of their ruling tribes. Only at the end of the sixth century did missionaries appear among them once more, sent by Pope Gregory the Great. Those who were converted remained continuously bound to the Roman Church until the reign of Henry VIII in the sixteenth century. The church in England was organized by St. Augustine of Canterbury; it soon embraced two archdioceses, York and Canterbury, as well as several bishoprics. Unlike on the Continent, bishops' churches were linked to monasteries. These were responsible for nurturing and spreading literate Latin culture, although Greek, it must be admitted, was never taught there. The earliest textual evidence of the *Rule of St. Benedict* comes from here, incorporated around 670 into a set of regulations for nuns. The great cathedral schools, such as that in York, contained valuable libraries stocked with priceless manuscripts; many copies of these were sent to the Frankish Empire over time.

The connection to Rome forged by the missionaries led numerous Anglo-Saxon pilgrims to travel to the tombs of the apostles. Some, like the West Saxon king Ina in the early eighth century or Offa of Mercia at the end of that same century, sent voluntary donations to Rome for the upkeep of the churches there—contributions that later became known as "Peter's pence." And from the early eighth century, the Anglo-Saxons were ready and willing to undertake missionary work themselves. The Frankish Empire was to profit from this. Saints Willibrord, Winfried/Boniface, Willibald of Eichstätt, and his brother Wunibald all came to the empire on missions, founding monasteries and refounding churches. Willibald's sister Walburga followed in her brother's footsteps, and the religious order she founded in Eichstätt is still thriving today.

Charlemagne's church reform, however, called for more than simply missionaries, no matter how effective their involvement had once been. He craved the learning of the Irish and the Anglo-Saxons. He deliberately set his sights on the scholar Alcuin, whose services he was ultimately able to secure. Alcuin came to the Frankish Empire initially for a few years but thereafter settled there, teaching in both Aix-la-Chapelle and Tours. Henceforth, the mission could proceed with the authorities of his adopted homeland behind it. The Carolingians also entertained active relations with Offa, the most significant and successful king of Mercia. When he was still king, Charlemagne even chose a daughter of the Anglo-Saxon monarch as a wife for his second son, Charles. Offa, however, demanded in return one of Charlemagne's daughters for his own son. When Charlemagne refused, the projected alliance through marriage collapsed. Charlemagne took umbrage at this and responded by imposing a three-year blockade on English merchant ships, a fact that highlights not least the significance of trade at this time with England. The city of Dorestad (now in the Netherlands) was a leading trade center in the Frankish Empire. From the reign of Pepin, Offa had copied Frankish models in devising his penny coinage.

Occasionally, the Mercian kings even minted gold coins. Were these intended for trade, or did they rather serve as prestigious gifts to foreign dignitaries, such as the pope? A golden dinar from this realm, now on display at the British Museum, has an odd appearance. Its obverse is decorated with an (upside-down) Arabic embossed text, into which the name of the ruler responsible for minting it is incorporated: OFFA REX. On the reverse, however—rather clumsily executed but clearly identifiable nevertheless—can be seen the first statement of the *shahada* (the Islamic creed): *La ilaha illa 'llah* (There is no God but God).[46] What did anyone in Mercia, or for that matter in the Frankish Empire, know about the provenance of Arab money? Contemporaries would almost certainly not have been able to read the inscription. Nevertheless, the concept of currency must inevitably have led

FIGURE 5 This eighth-century coin, struck and issued by Offa, ruler of the Anglo-Saxon kingdom of Mercia in England, is a copy of an Abbasid gold dinar. It bears the king's name on the obverse and the first line of the *shahada,* the Muslim declaration of faith, on the reverse. British Museum.

people to turn their gaze toward the Arab East and the Mediterranean. Did Charlemagne also feel this pull? Except for a very few instances, though, we know that he did not use gold for the purpose of minting coins.

In the event, Alcuin brokered peace between Charlemagne and Offa and secured a trade treaty. In 796, Charlemagne had made this learned man abbot of St. Martin in Tours, a move that ensured that he remained in the Frankish Empire. The troubled situation in his homeland did the rest; in a letter to King Offa, he railed against his own people and claimed that he would not know what to do in England if he were to come back. Norman raiders were plundering and desecrating churches, altars were being tainted by perjury, monasteries were defiled with adultery, and the earth was besmirched with the blood of abbots, he told the Mercian king. "Woe unto the sinful people, this people of evil injustice, these sons of felony. They have abandoned God and in committing their crimes have heaped blasphemies on their Holy Savior," lamented Alcuin in prophetic tones (quoting Isaiah 1:4), and he admonished the king to be a good shepherd to his people.[47] For all that, though, it was through the close contacts that Alcuin continued to maintain with his homeland that the Frankish court came to know how things stood there.

Now peace reigned once more between Charlemagne and the king of Mercia; a formal treaty set out the detailed arrangements. For instance, the Frankish king guaranteed that pilgrims to Rome would not be molested in his territory; trade would continue to enjoy the customary protection, although this did not preclude the levying of duty payments, nor were pilgrims who also engaged in trade exempted from paying customs duty.[48] Anglo-Saxon refugees and emigrants from Mercia had taken refuge at Charlemagne's court and in his empire at large.[49] Charlemagne pledged to Archbishop Athilhard of Canterbury that he would stand surety for them and their safe return.

The wars waged by the Franks against the neighboring Saxons also brought with them a new proximity to the Slavs and the tribes who would become the Danes. But in Charlemagne's time, relations with these two peoples basically did not go beyond securing the borders and launching occasional raids across the river Elbe. These latter actions may have been undertaken in order to capture slaves.

The original homeland of the Slavs is a matter of dispute, although it may, according to linguistic evidence, have been located in the northeastern Carpathians. Historians lack full insight into how Slavic culture spread thereafter. Authors of classical antiquity had scarcely any knowledge of them. From the sixth century onward, historians began to distinguish among the Wends, the Antae, and the Slavs; some commentators shifted their homeland to the environs of the Sea of Azov. A Saxon author of the tenth century, Widukind of Corvey, spread a story of witches inhabiting this region. Like the Germanic language, Slavonic was divided into a number of subgroups. Therefore, it was hardly a unifying factor; numerous small groupings established themselves under various names on the banks of the Elbe and the Oder and farther east toward the river Don. The separation into Western, Southern, and Eastern Slavs is an invention of modern scholarship. The so-called Bavarian Geographer, an anonymous author working in the second half of the ninth century, listed around sixty different ethnic groups east of the Frankish Empire, from the Bulgars in the south to those inhabiting the lands bordering the Baltic in the north.[50] Accordingly, the era of Charlemagne had to deal with a series of minor peoples, who in the West at best were bound together by similar religious cults. More accurate information really becomes known only from the tenth century onward and at this stage already indicates a progressive differentiation between groups.

In the eighth and early ninth centuries, there were still no signs of the Slavs attempting to establish their own realm. A certain Samo, who was said to have originally been a French merchant, and who emigrated to live among the Wends in 623–624, seems—at least according to the so-called *Fredegar Chronicle* (4.48)—to have organized the Slavs in that region into a successful defensive unit against the Avars and to have established a regime there that over the space of just under three decades prevailed against all comers, even the Franks (4.68), and collapsed only after Samo's death. We know nothing more about this early Slavic state, however. Even up to Charlemagne's reign, only snatches of information about the Slavs continued to trickle down to the Franks, including written documents.

The Avars, who in the sixth century had advanced into the Carpathian basin as far as Pannonia, remained for all the surrounding peoples, including the Byzantines, nothing but dangerous adversaries until they were finally conquered in 796 and a decade later converted to Christianity. The Franks did not forge any alliance with Byzantium against them. Their envoys appeared at Charlemagne's court only infrequently, as the revised *Royal Frankish Annals* for the year 782 noted, registering it as a sign of weakness in claiming that they had come "to sue for peace"; Charlemagne, the *Annals* continued, "listened to what they had to say and dismissed them." No writers of Charlemagne's time said anything about the Avars' nomadic way of life, their social structure, or their culture.

Even nowadays, the origins of the Avars remain obscure.[51] It even seems questionable whether we can speak here of a single ethnicity, or whether the tribes bordering on Bavaria, whom Byzantine authors sometimes call Scythians and sometimes Huns, and whom Western historians generally refer to by the latter term, constituted a more or less firm confederation of peoples. The linguistic evidence that has survived is far too scanty to provide a definitive answer to the ethnic question. Their place of origin seems almost certain to have been the Asiatic steppe, somewhere in western Turkestan; they appear in Chinese records. Fleeing from attacks by "Turkic" peoples, they were found from 463 onward in areas north of the Black Sea, while from around 568 they pushed westward into the Carpathian basin, which the Lombards were vacating at the time in their migration to Italy. In the period 791–796, the campaigns against the Avars conducted by Charlemagne and his son Pepin, king of the Lombards, put an end to their rule in the Carpathian region.

No contemporary author recounted what took place in Moravia immediately after the collapse of the kingdom of the Avars. Only in the course of the later ninth century, around 820–830, in this location where, at various times, Byzantine, Roman, and Frankish-Bavarian influences all met, did new attempts emerge to form an empire that may have extended as far as Pannonia. Once again, long-distance trade may have provided the impetus. Trade routes ran from the streets of Regensburg down the Danube to Constantinople and in another direction via Prague and Kraków to Kiev, and from there down to Constantinople and Samarkand, bringing Regensburg merchants considerable prosperity, particularly from the commerce in slaves and wax. In turn, they were able to use their wealth to fund the creation of military retinues.

The customs code of around 902–906 for Raffelstetten, a toll station on the Danube in the eastern marches of Bavaria, provides evidence of long-distance trade that can hardly have begun only around 900; rather, it is far more likely to have already existed, at least in embryonic form, in the era of Charlemagne. The capitulary of Didenhofen from the year 805 makes it clear that trade was going on in the vicinity of the frontier with the Slavs and Avars. In these legislative acts, the emperor decreed that Frankish merchants were not permitted to venture farther than Bardovic, a site called Schezla (no longer identifiable), Magdeburg, Erfurt, Hallstadt (a remote location near Bamberg in Franconia), Forchheim, Pfreimt (near the town of Nabburg in the Upper Palatinate), Regensburg, and Lorch (on the river Enns in Upper Austria). Furthermore, they were not allowed to sell weapons or coats of mail.[52] The ban on trading in weapons hints at the existence of a Slavic upper class who wanted to emulate the Franks. In return, though, these Slavic noblemen could well have traded in unbaptized slaves from among their own people.

No Frankish trader ever strayed among the Danes; this people remained a mystery. Indeed, as a general rule, only very sparse information from the Scandinavian world reached the Frankish royal court either before or during Charlemagne's reign. Likewise, empires began to form and peoples to coalesce only during the era of the Frankish emperors, initially among the Danes and the Svea—the people for whom the future state of Sweden was named[53]—around Lake Mäleren. Despite carving occasional runic inscriptions, these peoples were all illiterate, nurturing instead the practice of oral transmission of history in a highly sophisticated bardic tradition that only partially (and even then with the content much altered) found its way into later written histories.[54] Scandinavia's many islands and heavily indented coastline predisposed its peoples to seafaring from a very early period, but the seagoing capability of their longships, the range of their voyages, and the audacity of their explorations remained hidden to their neighbors, including the Franks, for a very long time.

On 8 June 793, Vikings (from the Old Norse term *víkingr*, meaning "corsair" or "pirate") sacked the monastery of Lindisfarne on Holy Island off the coast of Northumbria, northern England, a major pilgrimage site, and soon afterward (in 795) the monastery on the island of Iona in the Inner

Hebrides, which had been founded by St. Columba. Iona was raided on two subsequent occasions (802 and 805); the Vikings proceeded to sack a succession of targets in Great Britain and Ireland. Their organization in small raiding parties comprising just a few ships, which gave them an unrivaled degree of mobility, made these pirates extremely dangerous. Before long, however, they were operating in larger groups. Even the earliest raids yielded a rich haul in the form of gold and slaves and prompted a seemingly endless series of assaults and plunderings of settlements along all the coastlines of Europe. Their activities were driven by commerce and the expectation of booty. Charlemagne quickly learned of these dreadful events through Alcuin, the Anglo-Saxon scholar at his court. Consequently, he was not surprised, although he was still unprepared, when a fleet of "Danes" in two hundred longships landed on the shores of his realm in 810 and pillaged areas in Frisia.[55]

The reasons that lay behind the voyages of the Vikings were a mystery to the Franks; they regarded these "men from the North" as nothing other than robbers, pirates, and heathens whose religion was alien to them; their only impulsion, according to the Franks, was their lust for gold. The various pagan cults were more or less unknown, while the texts of the *Edda* came to light far too late to afford any true insight into the faith world of the Scandinavians around 800. Snorri Sturluson's *Prose Edda* was written around 1220–1230, while the *Poetic Eddas* appeared around fifty years later.[56] The social order of these "pirates," meanwhile, was completely hidden from the Franks; it remained incomprehensible to them, and as a result, its effects were far more dangerous.

What drove these people out into the world, then? And what did Charlemagne know of this exodus? From the early ninth century, these new arrivals from the north strove to seize land, to settle it, and to establish their dominion over it. Later tradition spoke of overpopulation in the Viking homelands as a motivating factor. But it is more likely that the driving forces behind these lucrative voyages were as follows: the first concentrations of power in Scandinavia, a monarchy that was intent on subjugating free lords of manors, power struggles between individual members of the royal clan, and simply a quest for new areas to settle. Success in such enterprises boosted a person's social prestige and individual power. Certainly, the routes the Vikings took from Scandinavia down the rivers of eastern Europe to Constantinople were not known to the Franks in the era of Charlemagne; they did not even learn of them through hearsay accounts. Nor were those in the West familiar with the Vikings' long-distance connections, which extended as far as Samarkand and have been proved through coin finds.

Charlemagne's World

Charlemagne grew up in a world that in many places found itself in a state of intense upheaval. The advanced civilizations of the Mediterranean no longer formed a coherent religious unit during his time, although they had by no means drifted completely apart in economic terms. The plethora of cultures that had begun to develop from the seventh century onward promoted and hastened this change; intercultural exchange was not long in coming. This started even in Charlemagne's time, albeit tentatively at first. The neighboring peoples surrounding the Frankish Empire—Saracens, Anglo-Saxons, Danes, Slavs, Avars, and Greeks—constituted Charlemagne's world, through which knowledge flowed to him, within which he had to assert himself and survive with his realm, in which he intervened with his actions, and indeed which he was to fundamentally change.

The even more remote regions of the "Old World" were too far off for the Franks to register them on their horizon. They knew the name of this or that far-flung realm from works of antiquity but were unable to corroborate this abstract information through firsthand geographical knowledge. With just a few exceptions, all references to Persia, India, or Samarkand—cultural regions whose effects radiated out directly, if unnoticed, to the Western world—were absent from the works of authors of the Carolingian period, let alone any mention of Siberia, Mongolia, China, or Japan. Not even the ancient Greek or Latin geographers were familiar with these regions.

Although the great upheavals taking place in China had only an indirect effect on the West, they nevertheless led to mass migrations of people that—as with recent movements of the Huns and the Avars—finally ended only in the West. However, scholars in the West had no inkling of the ultimate causes of such migrations. Conversely, the Chinese paid no attention to the extreme West, of which they had just as little an idea as the West did of them; even the momentous events in Arabia and the Near East were of no consequence to the Middle Kingdom. The intensity of reciprocal knowledge was low, haphazard, fragmentary, and at best conveyed by merchants.

The same was true of sub-Saharan Africa. Arabian traders had by this time already ventured as far as the island of Zanzibar, had set foot on the African mainland in their search for slaves, gold, and ivory, and before long had even penetrated into its interior, but the Franks knew nothing at all about this. It is fair to say that developments there still largely elude even the modern historian. Even Egypt, aside from biblical references to the country, was unknown to the Franks; and the events in the Maghreb re-mained hidden, too, notwithstanding the direct impact these were to have on the Frankish Empire. There on the North African coast, however, a do-minion that was disengaged from the central authority of the Abbasid cali-phate in Baghdad began to arise in the form of the Berber kingdom. Only the events in Spain were not an entirely closed book to the Franks. In par-ticular, Visigoths who emigrated to Gaul were responsible for telling the Frankish king about what was happening south of the Pyrenees. It was from there, as well as from Italy, that cultural and technical innovations from the Arab world began to filter through to the Christian North.

According to traditional accounts, Charlemagne was not noticeably per-turbed or affected by these developments. His attention was focused on matters that were closer to hand. He led military campaigns to all the frontiers of his empire, threatening, conquering, securing borders, and ex-changing diplomatic legations. Over the years, various important foreign cities—Constantinople, Jerusalem, Baghdad, Kairouan, and Córdoba (barely), but most definitely Toledo—came within the purview of the Franks. But at first, admittedly, the business of waging war was all-consuming, and so it was to confronting his nearest neighbors that Charlemagne first turned his attention.

3

♛

THE WARRIOR KING

CHARLEMAGNE WAS TALL, a giant in stature, a fine figure of a man; he towered over most of his contemporaries by a head. This is revealed by the remains of his bones in Aix, which were preserved and revered as relics. From his earliest years, he had practiced how to bear arms and wield them in combat. His social standing demanded as much, and his followers expected it of him. Every fall, Charlemagne went off on a hunting expedition, indulging himself in the pleasurable sport for a few weeks. He continued this custom even as an old man. Hunting was not simply a pastime but also a necessity, a lordly gesture, and a ritual of kingship. This activity could prove a person's power, courage, and boldness and was also—since it was organized in the form of a drive hunt—not unlike a military maneuver. It served to fire up the king's whole retinue and presented ample opportunities for participants to display their manly virtues. A monarch who excelled at hunting could inspire terror in others and instill in his subjects respectful fear for their lord and king. It is well attested that Charlemagne's grandchildren and great-grandchildren rode to hunt as children and young men, rampaging about with sharp-edged weapons and endangering their own lives. The young Charlemagne would surely have been no different. At the age of thirteen at the latest, he accompanied his father on campaign. His growing powers were conditioned from an early age to confront increasingly difficult tasks. Later, as king, Einhard claimed in his biography, Charlemagne personally fought in the line of battle on two occasions.

Charlemagne was around twenty years old when he ascended to the throne in 768, and his brother Carloman was seventeen. Shortly before his death, their father, Pepin, had divided his realm between his two sons. The elder boy thus gained control over Austrasia, the greater part of Neustria, and half of Aquitaine, while his younger sibling received Burgundy and parts of Francia that bordered on it to the north, extending as far as Paris and St. Denis, along with Provence, Gothia (the stretch of Mediterranean coast from Narbonne to Nîmes), Alsace, Alemannia, and the remainder of Aquitaine. This dividing up of the empire saw Charlemagne hold sway over large parts of the Frankish heartland, eastern Francia, the frontier regions bordering on Saxony, and the peripheries of Aquitaine. As a consequence, his domain surrounded the area under his brother's control to the north and west. Charlemagne rarely sojourned in his own southern realm. Was it the case that he had no trustworthy confederates there? Or were there no palaces suitable for hosting a king's visit? Whatever the case, it so happened that the very first military campaign he embarked on in his own right, in 768 against Hunold, son of Waiofar, the last independent duke of Aquitaine, took him precisely through Carloman's territory. Or was it simply the fact that Charlemagne saw it as his first task to consolidate his rule in the Frankish heartlands? The two brothers and their retinues regarded one another with deep mistrust right from the outset. Even on later occasions, though, Charlemagne ventured into the territory south of the Loire only very infrequently. He appeared to regard it as almost an inconsequential adjunct to his realm.

No testamentary partition at this time was implemented without conflict arising. The empire of the Franks, which had been evolving for over half a century by this stage, could not simply forget that it had once been a unified entity. The holdings of the churches and monasteries or of the leading noblemen, on whose loyalty each of the two kings was now forced to depend, along with their families and commercial interests, transcended the boundaries drawn by the partition. Charlemagne quickly learned to exploit this situation, entirely to his brother's detriment.

In Alemannia and Provence, Carloman's realm bordered on Italy, a situation that raised tensions with the kingdom of the Lombards. At first, certainly, both rulers sent their bishops to a synod in Rome in 769 at the invitation of Pope Stephen III.[1] The situation on the Tiber had changed dramatically since Pepin's intervention in Italy and the death of Pope Paul II in 767. Just a few years previously, that pontiff had exulted in the fact that Desiderius, Aistulf's successor on the Lombard throne, had come to the Apostolic See peacefully disposed and in great humility, had made restitution, and had, with the pope as intermediary, sought to conclude a peace treaty with Pepin, "in order that the people of God on both sides might live in greater safety and in the tranquility of peace."[2] Now, though, events happened thick and fast.

Despite defeats by the Franks and reciprocal assurances in treaties, Lombard pressure on Rome did not abate. The division of the Frankish Empire after Pepin's death could not help but embolden Desiderius to launch a fresh wave of attacks on his rivals. Unrest broke out in Rome. After Paul I's death, a violent struggle saw Constantine II installed as the new pope; his opponents, under the leadership of the *primicerius* (head of a Church college) Christophorus, managed to escape, gain Lombard support, and reconquer Rome. They, in turn, after the Lombard candidate had been murdered, now placed a confidant of the former popes, Stephen III, on the throne of the apostolic prince. But he found that he needed external help to survive, which he sought and found from the Franks. In this way, the tables were turned once again.

By invoking the perils of the Last Judgment, Stephen urgently implored the two Frankish kings to champion the rights of the throne of St. Peter against the Lombards.[3] The synod of April 769 damned Constantine as a usurper and also condemned the Greeks' practice of iconoclasm. In acquiescing to this, the Franks implicitly adopted the Roman variant of the veneration of images.[4] Ultimately, a lesson was learned from the crisis that had been faced and overcome, and new rules were put in place for the election of popes: henceforth, only those who had followed the proper rules by passing through all levels of ordination up to that of deacon or cardinal could be elected pope; no laypeople or lower-ranking clerics were eligible.[5]

Before long, rumors began to reach the Tiber that one of the Frankish kings intended to marry a Lombard princess and to betroth one of his sisters, Gisela, to the Lombard heir apparent. Which of the kings was to be the groom was as yet unknown. This plan for a double dynastic marriage must have deeply troubled the pope. Stephen duly sent an urgent missive to both kings. He did not mince words in roundly condemning this "devilish" plan. How could such a magnificent dynasty of rulers, from the noble, sublime Frankish people, even begin to entertain the insane notion of allying themselves with the perfidious Lombards, this stinking brood not even worthy to be counted among the peoples of the earth, who had descended from a race of lepers? How could they possibly besmirch themselves by marrying into this repulsive, damned race of people, especially after their father had already chosen the most beautiful brides for them from among their own people?[6] They had pledged, Stephen reminded them, to be the friends of St. Peter and his representative, the pope, and to treat his enemies as their enemies. At the risk of their souls' salvation, they were not to be permitted to choose spouses from a foreign people. If they defied him, they would be threatened with anathema, namely, excommunication.

The young Charlemagne—he was the intended bridegroom—was not cowed by the pope's threats. Urged by his mother, Bertrada of Laon, and one or another of his great noblemen, he went ahead and forged an alliance with Desiderius, cemented by marriage. Bertrada had intervened once before, when Pepin was still on the throne, to avert a war against the Lombards; she now hastened to Rome to try to mollify the pope. On the return journey, however, she escorted the chosen Lombard bride back to her son. Stephen immediately, in response to a delegation sent by Carloman, formed an alliance with Charlemagne's younger brother, the "most Christian of all kings," offering to be godfather to his son Pepin and to anoint him, Carloman, at his investiture.[7]

Under Bertrada's influence, Charlemagne really did appear to execute an about-face. When he entered into his marriage in 770,[8] it formed part of a wider net of dynastic marriages, with two sisters of his bride, Liutperga and Adalperga, being wed to Charlemagne's cousin Tassilo of Bavaria and to Duke Arichis II of Benevento. In addition, although the connection lay a long way back in time, the Lombard royal house belonged to the same lineage, the Agilolfings, as the Bavarian duke himself. At around the same time, the intention was also, in return, to marry Bertrada's daughter Gisela to Desiderius's son Adelchis, although this never came to pass. Stephen's successor, Pope Hadrian I, baptized Tassilo and Liutperga's eldest son Theodo in 772[9]—a sign that marriages such as these opened up horizons that meant more than just dynastic connections. Charlemagne may have construed that baptism as a warning.

A new round of fighting broke out in Rome, in which the opponents of Christophorus gained the upper hand. Stephen III, meanwhile, threw in his lot with those who, under the leadership of one Paulus Afiarta, sought an alliance with the Lombards. Carloman suddenly saw himself isolated, and rumors began to circulate in Rome that he was planning a campaign against both the Lombards and Rome. But in the spring of 771, Stephen recanted

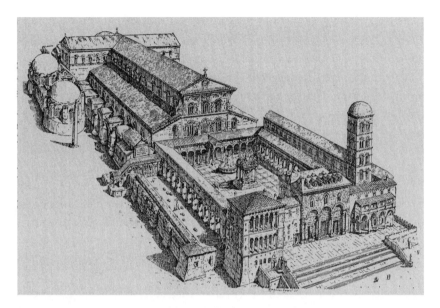

FIGURE 6 The former Church of St. Peter in Rome as it is thought to have looked during Charlemagne's reign. The rear cupola near the church's southern transept housed the chapel of the early Christian martyr St. Petronilla, devotion to whom was cultivated by Pepin and his son Charlemagne. This sixteenth-century artist's impression of the original basilica is taken from Pietro Crostarosa, *Le basiliche cristiane* (Rome, 1892).

and in a letter to Bertrada and Charlemagne praised King Desiderius and his people, that same people he had lambasted as the dregs of humanity not long before, and hailed him as the man who saved Rome from the murderous plans being hatched jointly by Christophorus and Carloman's ambassador. It is even possible that the pope invited the Lombard king to Rome at this time. In any event, under Desiderius's protection he was able to take refuge in St. Peter's Basilica and hold out until Christophorus was blinded and his supporters were eliminated. He appears to have allied himself with the Lombard king in good faith and to have received from him all the privileges of the Petrine See.[10] It was impossible for those in the far-off Frankish Empire to know what was really going on in Italy and Rome. After Stephen's death, the *Liber pontificalis* accused Desiderius of all kinds of nefarious activities, although this was totally at variance with this pope's letter mentioned earlier; *the Liber pontificalis* pinned the blame for the entire disaster on him.[11] But how did Charlemagne view these events, this internal game of intrigue and subterfuge in the city of the Apostolic See that could be ended only by violent external intervention?

The young king doubtless registered all this as an experience he would later be able to exploit. For now, though, he turned his energies in another direction. Was he perhaps receiving secret intelligence from inside Rome? Whatever the case, he dispatched his chancellor, Hitherius, to the Tiber around this time—"truly your and our honest and faithful servant," as Stephen lauded him—and tasked him with ensuring the restitution of papal patrimonies in the Duchy of Benevento.[12] As early as the beginning of 771, before Desiderius set out for Rome, Charlemagne separated from his wife, Desiderius's daughter, an act tantamount to a declaration of war. His mother was upset at this; until the end, she had wanted to save the marriage she had set in motion. But Charlemagne refused to comply with her wishes. In the short time Charlemagne and his bride were married,[13] the Lombard woman, whose name was not recorded for posterity (no doubt quite deliberately), had borne her husband no children; moreover, he did not like her and did not need her. In spite of his mother's urgings and in defiance of ecclesiastical law, he sent her back to her father. This must have happened several months before the death of his brother[14] (in early December 771) and ensured that there would be war sooner or later. Perhaps the divorce was also a calculated act of emancipation by the twenty-two-year-old king from his domineering mother, who had tried in vain to mediate between her warring sons.

The pope said nothing, raising no objection to the ensuing third marriage of the Frankish king, to Hildegard in the spring of 771,[15] a totally illegitimate union given that the Lombard wife was still alive at the time. Hildegard was a young girl barely thirteen years old, from the highest echelons of the Alemannic nobility; before her premature death at the age of twenty-six, she would bear her husband no fewer than nine children. Just as he would set off annually on military campaigns, so she would give birth to a child year in, year out.[16]

Yet Alemannia, whose ruling elite Charlemagne doubtless aimed to win over with this marriage alliance, was part of his brother's realm. Conflict with Carloman now appeared inevitable, and not just with him. The most important routes and mountain passes to Italy ran through Alemannia, and Charlemagne's third marriage was clearly bound up with his expansionist ambitions there. Charlemagne's cousin Adalhard criticized the young king for his illegitimate marriage, withdrew from courtly life, and became a monk—an act of protest, it was later claimed.[17] How far that is true is a matter of speculation; in later life, certainly, Adalhard became one of the emperor's most trusted advisers. But in 771, Charlemagne began arming himself to do battle with the Lombards. Later accounts from the Carolingian court also claimed to recall that preparations for war against Carloman were also being made at this time.

There is no denying that Charlemagne's marriage to Hildegard tore a gaping hole in the fine network of existing marriage alliances and created a wholly new one that required the utmost skill to manipulate, but that at the same time promised larger catches. It reveals the young king, in his first truly independent act as a ruler, as a bold schemer fully prepared to take risks. On her mother's side, his wife was a member of the ancient line of Alemannic dukes, which was widely and plausibly taken to be a side branch of the Agilolfing dynasty, the very family that produced the dukes of Bavaria and also—through a more distant set of relatives—occupied the royal throne of Pavia. Odilo, father of Tassilo of Bavaria, and Hildegard's mother, Imma, may well have been siblings. As a result, Charlemagne's new marriage meant conflict both with the Lombards and with his own brother. But did it also, as a long-term aim, raise the prospect of a struggle for control of Bavaria? For the time being, the Frankish king was content to conclude a treaty of "friendship" with his Bavarian cousin.[18]

Very few accounts were written of Carloman's three-year reign. A total of twelve documents that mention him—particularly relating to the monastery of St. Denis—have survived, three more than for his brother during the same period. His marriage with Gerberga, whose origins are unknown, was blessed with two sons, the elder of whom was given his grandfather's name, while Charlemagne likewise had a son called Pepin from one of his relationships, broken off due to his marriage to the Lombard princess. The tensions between the two brothers were more or less kept secret by the historians commissioned by Charlemagne. According to Einhard and the revised *Royal Frankish Annals,* Carloman allegedly refused to lend his brother any assistance when Charlemagne advanced through Aquitaine as far as Gascony in order to bring the war his father had begun to a successful conclusion and to subjugate the region definitively under his control. This was, as Einhard pointed out, Charlemagne's first war. Before long, the open hostility between the two brothers was palpable,[19] especially after Carloman began first to lend support to the Lombard king Desiderius's military actions against Rome and then to combat them.[20] Had the brothers entered into a contest over control of Italy? If Charlemagne thought that this was the case, then he was compelled to act: he needed to secure the support of the pope against his brother. As usual, death intervened to forestall the threatened civil war. Carloman died on 4 December 771—a sudden death, but of natural causes.

Because Carloman's sons, Charlemagne's nephews, were still only minors when their father died, Charlemagne saw his chance to seize the whole of his father's inheritance. Key magnates from Carloman's realm—Archbishop Wilchar of Sens, Abbot Fulrad of St. Denis, and Counts Warin and Adalhard—paid homage to him in December before anointing him their king at Corbény.[21] Had they been expecting Carloman to die? And was it Charlemagne who thwarted his nephews' succession? Or did the initiative come instead from these magnates, who did not want to be ruled by a child king? Whatever the case, Charlemagne's realm now bordered on Italy as well. No sooner had Carloman died than his widow was filled with fore-boding. She fled with her children to Pavia—placing herself under the pro-tection of the Lombard king, who cannot have been well disposed toward his former son-in-law, who had violated the terms of their agreement—before moving on to Verona. What was Gerberga hoping for? Was she plan-ning to escape to Bavaria, which at that stage was still ruled by Duke Tassilo III and not yet under the sway of the Frankish king? Or did she perhaps in-tend to get even farther away, to Constantinople, where a number of en-forced exiles from the Lombard kingdom had already taken refuge, and where Desiderius's son Adelchis would later flee?

For the time being, though, she entrusted her safety to the protection of the Lombards. Desiderius appeared ready to help the sons of Carloman, or at least Gerberga's eldest son, Pepin, to take the Frankish crown. To this end, he asked Pope Hadrian I to come to his court and anoint the boy.[22] His in-tention was clear: on the one hand, he could exploit this new rift among the Franks, and on the other, he could entice the pope to side with him. But his efforts were all to no avail. The very fact that Carloman's sons fled so precipi-tately after their father's death may well have cost them their inheritance—and Desiderius his crown.

The Call of Italy

In any event, Charlemagne got warning of what was afoot. Switching sides, he presented himself as the pope's natural ally and as Desiderius's opponent; feigning concern, he sent messages to Rome inquiring whether the pope had actually received the restitutions to the Apostolic See and the Roman people he had previously been promised, and put pressure on him when the answer came back in the negative.[23] The Carolingian king was clearly trying to force a definitive decision from the pope; a new appeal to him for help on the part of Pope Hadrian I only strengthened his position. It was around this time that Charlemagne first encountered Alcuin; the Anglo-Saxon scholar duly accompanied the legation the king sent to Rome. For their part, Hadrian's envoys were forced to travel by sea because the Lombards had blocked the Romans' overland routes.[24]

Desiderius ignored Charlemagne's warnings. However, the Carolingian king used the delay to launch an attack on Saxony. For centuries, these neighbors of the Franks had been the source of innumerable threats and conflicts, which the Franks had sought to combat, with varying degrees of success. Charlemagne conducted his first campaign against the Saxons in 772. He might well have been hoping for a swift success, and indeed, events seemed to bear out his optimism. His forces advanced rapidly to the castle of Eresburg (nowadays known as Niedermarsberg, on the Diemel River) and destroyed the major Saxon shrine called the Irminsul, which was situated either at this site or just to the north of it.[25] The *Royal Frankish Annals* for 772 triumphantly claimed that huge amounts of treasure, consisting of "gold and silver," had fallen into Charlemagne's hands, plunder that may have been pagan sacrificial offerings; this booty also seemed to fire the enthusiasm of the king's retinue for waging war.[26] Charlemagne distinguished himself as a successful military commander on his Saxon campaign, a leader it paid to follow. He pushed farther forward to the banks of the Weser, "laying waste the countryside with sword and fire," and after taking a number of prominent hostages withdrew once more with his forces.

After this triumph, the king immediately prepared to embark on a campaign against the Lombards. In late 773, he duly set off via Geneva to Italy with two columns of troops. He put himself at the head of one of these, leading it over Mt. Cenis in Savoy, while the other column, under the command of his uncle Bernhard, crossed the Alps through the Great St. Bernard Pass. The *Annals* claimed that a final attempt to reach a peaceful settlement was "maliciously" (*malignam mentem*) thwarted by Desiderius's obduracy. This rebuff, whether fabricated or true, served to justify the ensuing assault.[27] Charlemagne set up his campaign headquarters at the monastery of Novalese near Susa. A story still making the rounds there in the eleventh century recounted how, when Charlemagne had exhausted all the monks' supplies at his quarters, a "singer" (*ioculator*) appeared and intoned, "What reward will a person receive who can lead Charlemagne into the kingdom of Italy on paths where no spear will be cast at him, and no shield smashed?" In the interim a collaborator had picked up his fiddle—an Italian prepared to lead the Frankish force on secret paths that would allow them to attack his own king's army from the rear.[28] Had the monks perhaps persuaded him to make his approach? All we know for sure is that Frankish sources certainly report that a special unit of seasoned troops (*legionem ex probatissimis pugnatoribus*) did use a series of hidden mountain tracks to circumvent the Lombards' defensive lines at the Susa defile. Bernhard may also have arrived at this engagement with his force. In any event, suddenly finding himself threatened from the rear, Desiderius had no choice but to retreat, without giving battle, back to his capital, the heavily fortified city of Pavia. He was accompanied by Autcar, the man who had helped Carloman's widow, Gerberga, take flight to the city.[29] Desiderius duly found himself surrounded in Pavia. He was able to withstand the siege for nine months before finally surrendering.

After Charlemagne, probably still in 773, had pushed forward to Verona, where Carloman's widow had taken refuge, the former queen and her children were detained and handed over to her brother-in-law. Nothing is heard of either her or her sons thereafter. History is written by the victors, and the triumphant Charlemagne was concerned to hush up anything that might in later recollection have harmed his own rule. The only source to report anything of the incident, the contemporary semiofficial history of the popes, the *Liber pontificalis,* merely mentioned that Charlemagne's nephews had surrendered to their uncle,[30] whereupon they disappeared without trace. No writer recorded what became of them thereafter or definitively reported their demise; henceforth, no one would ever learn how these boys—who were, after all, proper scions of the Carolingian line with a legitimate claim to rulership—met their end, know where they were buried, or be able to commemorate them. Might they have been forced to take holy orders? Or did an act of murder smooth Charlemagne's ascent to power?

Charlemagne, though—whom the *Liber pontificalis* praised as "the great king, protected by God" and "the most Christian king of the Franks"[31]—interrupted the siege of Pavia, which was still dragging on, and hurried "to the threshold of the Apostles" (i.e., Rome) to celebrate Easter there.[32] At Pavia, he had ordered his wife, Hildegard, who was pregnant, to be brought to him. Now he simply left her at the tented encampment, where she would subsequently give birth. Apart from his wish to pray at the tombs of the apostles, our sources do not cite any particular reason for Charlemagne's visit to Rome. Could the king, as his father before him had once done, have been seeking the pope's approval for the cataclysmic changes he was planning to visit on Italy? Or was he seeking absolution from the heir and successor to St. Peter for his sins, for having murdered his nephews? Or the pope's blessing on his third marriage? Or did he simply want to verify in reality the image of the city of Rome he had cherished in his heart and mind's eye since childhood?

According to the "Vita Hadriani" in the *Liber pontificalis,* Hadrian was astonished and shocked when the Frankish king appeared outside the city walls, admittedly not at the head of an army, but still with a strong retinue. No Lombard king had ever been permitted to enter Rome. In his brief moment of consensus with the Apostolic See, Desiderius had been allowed to venture only as far as the church of St. Peter outside the Walls. However, Charlemagne came as a "friend," as a "patrician of the Romans" (the title bestowed on Pepin the Short and his sons by Stephen II). The gates could not remain closed to him. Indeed, it was solely thanks to Charlemagne's armed invasion of the Lombard kingdom that the key cities of Spoleto and Rieti, as well as Fermo, Ancona, Osimo, and Città di Castello, had voluntarily submitted themselves once more to the pope's control. The long-sought-after independent authority of the papacy now seemed to be coming to fruition. But was it now being put in jeopardy by the Frankish king? The pope's dilemma was how he should receive the king and *patricius Romanorum.*

In the event, under pressure to quickly improvise a ceremonial welcome, the pope took recourse to the protocol governing the summoning of the exarch, the representative of the Eastern Roman emperor in Ravenna. With banners flying, the papal militia and the Roman judiciary hurried to receive the approaching Charlemagne at Novae thirty miles outside the city, while at the one-mile marker outside the city walls, a welcoming party consisting of bands of city militia and groups of schoolchildren and their teachers awaited his arrival. They greeted the foreign ruler by waving palm and olive branches and singing songs of praise and acclamation, "as befitted the reception of an exarch or a patricius." As a mark of respect for the crosses carried by the papal envoys, Charlemagne dismounted, and he and his magnates continued on foot to the Basilica of St. Peter, where the pope and the entire Roman clergy and people were waiting for him. As he ascended the flight of stairs leading up to the church, Charlemagne kissed every single step. In the atrium, the pope and the king embraced each other; the monarch held the pontiff's hand as they entered the Apostolic Church together. The assembled clergy intoned the psalm "Blessed is he who comes in the name of the Lord!" and, as Hadrian and Charlemagne proceeded to confession over the tomb of St. Peter, called on God's power "to grant them victory through the succor of the Apostolic Prince."[33]

Then, at least according to the *Liber pontificalis,* the king formally requested the pope's permission to enter the city. Hadrian had to consent. They

FIGURE 7 The Pola Casket (ca. 400), an ivory reliquary originally from Pola in Istria, now held at the Archeological Museum in Venice, includes a depiction of the original shrine built to contain the relics of St. Peter in Rome; details include the throne (*hetoimasia*) and above it, the baldachin or canopy (*ciborium*).

swore to preserve each other's safety and presumably also took this opportunity to renew the *pactum,* the treaty Charlemagne's father, Pepin, had earlier concluded with Stephen II. Thereupon, the Frankish king and *patricius Romanorum* was granted access to the city. On Holy Saturday 774, he stood on the top of the Caelian Hill, one of the seven hills of Rome, within the bounds of the Eternal City, some 274 years after the Ostrogothic king Theodoric the Great, the last barbarian ruler, and 112 years after Constans II, the last emperor of Rome, had stood on the same spot. Yet despite all the demonstrative affirmations of friendship, this was a humiliation of the city and its bishop, which had not allowed a foreign ruler to set foot within its walls for centuries. The sea change in the balance of power was plain for every Roman to see, irrespective of who turned out to line the streets and welcome the new interloper.

Charlemagne's route on horseback around the capital led him from the Basilica of St. Peter across the bridge over the Tiber near the emperor Hadrian's mausoleum (the site of Castel Sant'Angelo today), right past the Circus Flaminius (Piazza Navona), left beneath the Capitoline Hill, straight through the heart of the city across the forum and past the church of Santa Maria Antiqua on his right and the arches of Titus, Severus, and Constantine and the Colosseum on his left, and past San Clemente and the forbidding Basilica of Quattro Coronati. The last leg of his route saw him ride up the steep, vineyard-strewn rise leading to the Caelian Hill, where he would have greeted the bronze equestrian statue supposedly depicting the emperor Constantine that presided over this vantage point, and glanced around the broad square, the Campus Lateranensis, observing what he would have taken to be the remains of that emperor's palace that had survived the intervening centuries. He and his small entourage dismounted and entered the magnificent porphyry-clad octagon of Constantine's baptismal pool, where he attended the baptisms and the subsequent confirmation by the pope the Cross Chapel of the Baptistery (see Figure 8). Finally, he and Pope Hadrian together visited the Basilica Constantiniana, which since time immemorial had been dedicated to St. Savior and St. John the Baptist, namely the episcopal church of the Roman pontiff, founded by Constantine.[34] There, in the heart of Rome, which no king of the Lombards had ever set foot in and where his own father had never been, the Frankish king knelt down to pray. Then he returned to St. Peter's, where he had elected to make his temporary residence, at Santa Petronilla outside the Aurelian Walls.

The king spent the Easter festival in the company of the pope. The Resurrection of Our Lord was a feast the whole city celebrated according to an ancient rite. Processions bearing flags and crosses made their way through the streets to the stational churches of the day. The pope, the clergy, the highest officers of the pontiff (*iudices*), the militias, all in their ceremonial finery, plus the whole of the citizenry and those who had been baptized on Easter Saturday, and now the king of the Franks and patrician of the Romans too were all involved in the celebrations, visiting the large patriarchate churches. This city, which even though ruined in parts was still extensive, received the Frankish king, its protector. Charlemagne saw the magnificence of its places of worship, each more awe inspiring, splendid, and spectacular than the one before, and prayed in the churches of Constantine the Great and celebrated with the pope.

Memories of his childhood may have welled up in Charlemagne on this occasion, when he, still a boy, had been sent out to greet Pope Stephen II and escort him to his father, and when he had gazed in wonder at the pomp of the Roman papacy.[35] It was only now, though, that the full magnificence of papal ceremony and rituals and the reflected glory of the greatness of

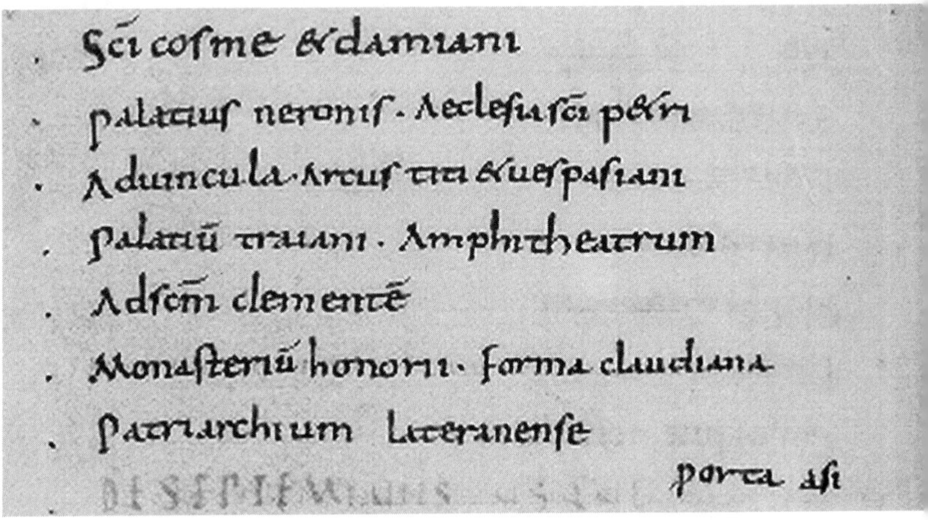
Sci cosme & damiani
palatium neronis. Aeclesia sci petri
Adruncula. Arcus titi & uespasiani
palatiu traiani. Amphitheatrum
Ad scm clemente
Monasteriu honorii. forma claudiana
Patriarchium Lateranense
porta asi

FIGURE 8 Detail from a double page of a description of Rome that was written around 800 by an unknown scribe from the monastery at Einsiedeln in Switzerland, tracing the route from Old St. Peter's to the Basilica of St. John Lateran. Einsiedeln Abbey Library.

ancient Rome was revealed to "the most Christian king of the Franks," and the recollections of his childhood coalesced, forming a vision perhaps not yet of a revival of Rome but certainly of a close connection between martial prowess and religion and a confluence of secular power, faith, and learning in the Frankish Empire so that it might be able to keep pace with Rome. What, though, could he see from up on the Caelian Hill? And how did he interpret and use it for his own reign?

With a practiced eye, the twenty-six-year-old king entered the place made famous by the story of Emperor Constantine being cured of leprosy through life-giving baptism: "Constantine, who was not a worshipper of demons, but of the true God Himself," as St. Augustine of Hippo describes him in *The City of God*. Pope (later Saint) Sylvester was said to have conducted the baptism at the precise spot where Charlemagne was now standing; tradition maintained that this act was followed by generous gifts by the emperor to the Roman Church. Knowledge of this kind on Charlemagne's part must have conditioned how he viewed the site and placed particular interpretations on what he perceived, as well as shaping his future attitudes.[36] Charlemagne was very familiar with this story. But unlike more recent scholars, he would no doubt not have categorized the *Passio sancti Silvestri,* as the

Adsčm theodorum
palatinuſ
Teſtamencum · Arcuſ conſtancini
mčſa fudinte
Cipuc affricae
Quactuor coronati
Sčioh̄anniſ inlateraniſ
nana

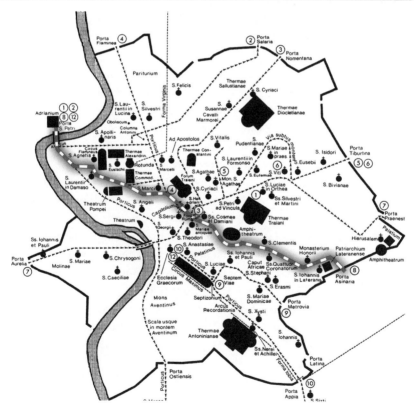

FIGURE 9 Charlemagne's route through Rome from St. Peter's to the Caelian Hill (after Bauer, *Bild der Stadt Rom im Frümittelalter*).

oldest manuscript of the acts of St. Sylvester, dating from the mid-eighth century, was called, as an unreliable legend.

There was another family association with Sylvester: it was to the monastery named for the saint on Monte Soratte north of the city that Pepin the Short's elder brother Carloman had withdrawn in 747, thus allowing Pepin to ascend the throne. The saint himself had once taken refuge in this monastery from persecution by the emperor, who was hostile to Christians; in this context, the *Royal Frankish Annals* for the year 746 specifically identifies this emperor as Constantine. Moreover, as reported later by Charlemagne's cousin Adalhard von Corbie and his biographer Radbert,[37] a number of Charlemagne's (unnamed) companions and advisers also knew and revered this traditional tale, without seeing through it as some "fabulous historical novel of the saints."[38] But it was, and still is, the only source of information available about the history of the site Charlemagne and his retinue visited at Easter in 774.

At that time, when Charlemagne reached this place so steeped in tradition, he may have learned to regard the Constantine portrayed in the *Passio sancti Silvestri* as a role model, the archetype of a Christian emperor who ruled Rome. Just a few years later (in 778), Pope Hadrian was able—and not just in expectation of currying favor with the emperor, but primarily to gain his approbation for the allusion—to recall the "great emperor Constantine, that most pious ruler of sacred remembrance" (*sanctae recordationis piisim[us] Constantin[us] Magn[us] imperator*) and his generous gifts and to dub him, the Carolingian monarch, "the new Emperor Constantine, the most Christian ruler in the sight of God" (*novus christianissimus Dei Constantinus imperator*).[39] In Charlemagne's Frankish Empire, too, Constantine was evoked time and again as the archetype of the Christian ruler.[40] Yet Constantine's later lapse from orthodoxy—banning hymns of praise and, where the Latin West was concerned at least, the Honors of the Altar (canonization)—was not concealed and darkened the image somewhat. But we may ask ourselves what the legend of Constantine really meant to the Frankish king.

The legend was passed down in the *Actus beati Silvestri*, which was written in the fifth or sixth century and refers repeatedly, consistently, and exclusively to the Caelian Hill site as an official imperial site, a palace complex of the emperor. Here, in his Palatium Lateranense, Constantine followed the inspiration of Roman piety. It was here that he saw in a dream the images of the apostolic princes, who told him to go to Bishop Sylvester to have his leprosy cured, and where he immersed himself in the healing baptismal font. He established the Basilica of Our Savior (now the Archbasilica

FIGURE 10 In the age of Charlemagne, this bronze equestrian statue of Marcus Aurelius, now at the Capitoline Museum in Rome, was wrongly thought to portray Constantine the Great and was referred to as *Caballus Constantini,* "the horse of Constantine."

FIGURE II The Basilica of Santi Quattro Coronati in Rome, from a painting by Ettore Roesler Franz in 1884. This picture shows how undeveloped Rome was even in the nineteenth century; the city must have looked very similar in the time of Charlemagne.

of St. John Lateran), although he did not donate it to the pope,[41] and passed laws that exalted the Roman Church. No explicit testimony, not even the "Life of St. Sylvester" in the *Liber pontificalis*, refers to this imperial palace complex being transferred to ecclesiastical ownership, even though de facto the Basilica Constantiniana, as it was regularly referred to at that time—in other words, the Church of Our Savior—had become the episcopal church of the pope.

Accordingly, over the following centuries, everything assigned to the emperor—who now resided in Constantinople—remained beyond the Church's grasp. Not even the Sessorium Palace, the former residence of Constantine's mother, Empress Helena, whose atrium she had converted into the church of Santa Croce in Gerusalemme, devolved to papal control, and over time it crumbled to ruins.[42] The solemn orations on Easter Sunday for the emperor, the king of the Franks, and others could still be heard during the early years of Charlemagne's reign.[43] It was only now that the long process of disengagement by papal Rome from the Byzantine Empire reached its decisive phase.[44] But up to this point, including when Charlemagne entered the city, the rights of the emperor were observed.

This was particularly true for those buildings that, according to the legend of St. Sylvester, were to be regarded as the imperial Lateran Palace. At the time when the *Passio* was written, they existed alongside the papal "House," the "Bishops' House" or "Patriarch's House" (*episcopium* or *patriarchium*), and were therefore not identical with that building and were clearly situated some distance from it. As a result, the latter edifice remained unchanged right up to Charlemagne's time, for the same length of time, indeed, as imperial power was represented in the city in the person of the exarch. What kind of picture, then, did this area on the Caelian Hill present when the Frankish king and his retinue entered the city and visited Constantine's Basilica of Our Savior and its baptistery? What exactly did he and his companions see? With their foreknowledge of the *Passio*, how would they have interpreted what they saw?

The area in question on the Caelian Hill, which stood on the fringes of the city at that time, surrounded by vineyards and right up against the Aurelian Walls, was named for its former owners, the consular family of the Laterani, whom Nero had dispossessed in the first century CE and whom Emperor Septimius Severus had later restored to part of their former estate, before the area for some unknown reason fell into the emperor's hands once more. It was therefore known as "the home of the Laterani," a name it retained until the start of the High Middle Ages. Consequently, in the age of Charlemagne, "Lateran" was not the name of the papal *patriarchium*, not the residence of the pope, but simply a place name denoting the inner-city site on the Caelian Hill. The episcopal church of the pope was the Constantinian or Lateran Basilica, namely, the basilica Constantine had founded or that was situated at "the home of the Laterani." Admittedly, during Charlemagne's reign, as far as we can tell, no one recalled the ancient origin of this name any longer.

Yet for a visitor like Charlemagne, who stood surveying the area with the legend of St. Sylvester in his mind, this complex of buildings might well have simply represented the center of imperial power. To the east, on the far side of the road that led to the nearby Porta Asinaria, lay the papal *patriarchium*. Pope Zachary had had it restored in the eighth century. To the southeast, the massive Church of Our Savior marked the bounds of the area and thereby created a large square, the Campus Lateranensis. The square was dominated by the so-called *Caballus Constantini*, the bronze equestrian statue of Marcus Aurelius, which in the early Middle Ages was wrongly identified as a likeness of the church's founder, Constantine (and hence escaped destruction), and which was moved to the Capitoline Hill only in the

FIGURE 12 Seventeenth-century engraving of the Lateran Basilica in medieval times. The numbers mark various locations, for instance, the entrance to the basilica (1), to the right of which stands the domed octagonal Lateran Baptistery (San Giovanni in Fonte). Number 6 denotes the *Caballus Constantini,* while the remaining buildings in the center of the engraving formed part of the papal palace. From Giovanni Giustino Ciampini, *De sacris aedificiis a Constantino Magno constructis* (Rome, 1693).

sixteenth century. To the west lay the baptistery, nowadays San Giovanni in Fonte, and behind both churches stood the city wall. Still farther to the west, at some distance from the *patriarchium,* stood the buildings that came to be identified as "Constantine's" palace. The northern edge of the square was marked by the Claudian Aqueduct, which since ancient times had supplied the buildings on the Caelian Hill with water. To the northwest, close at hand and standing in front of the (supposed) imperial palace, lay the Lateran Baths (Plate VIII).

This configuration of buildings, as it appeared to Charlemagne at "the home of the Laterani," must have made a lasting impression on the young ruler, still basking in the glow of his first military triumphs. Its basic layout could be analyzed as follows: church, square, palace, and equestrian statue. And so this place became a visible symbol of Christian sovereignty and grandeur; moreover, as we shall see, after several years this ground plan would be revived in Aix. Henceforth, the king knew what objectives he needed to achieve. His kingdom, his empire, would emulate the image of Rome.

FIGURE 13 Interior of the Constantinian Baptistery in the Lateran Basilica, today called San Giovanni in Fonte.

Over the ensuing days, Charlemagne participated in all the church rites conducted by the pope. We may even picture him riding alongside in procession with the apostolic father as he took Mass in the stational churches. There he listened to the papal liturgy and to the *schola cantorum* (choir school) and its magnificent songs of praise. He spent Easter night at his baptismal mass and in the Church of Our Savior, after which he returned to his quarters near St. Peter's in order to spend the following morning in a solemn procession of Roman dignitaries to attend a papal Easter celebration in Santa Maria ad Praesepe (now Santa Maria Maggiore). After the mass, the whole procession, including the pope and the Frankish king, moved to the *patriarchium,* where they took a ritual communal meal together. On Easter Monday, Pope Hadrian celebrated Mass in St. Peter's, where lauds were sung to the king, while on Tuesday he officiated at St. Paul outside the Walls—the two burial churches of the apostolic princes. On Wednesday, the two met once more in St. Peter's, where Hadrian requested from the king confirmation of the so-called Donation of Pepin and that he fulfill the pledge to honor his father's allocation of certain territories to the pope (remarkably, this act is very poorly attested),[45] a promise Charlemagne and his brother Carloman had already affirmed as boys at Quierzy. The confirmation was read out and renewed by the king, although it is unclear whether the Donation related to seigneurial, ecclesiastical, or fiscal rights.

The *Liber pontificalis* recorded the details, even the mysterious frontier to the north of the territories in question—puzzling because its origin and purpose were obscure—and delineated the bounds of the future Papal States and its environs, an area that was to become the subject of untold disputes over the coming centuries: "A Lunis cum insula Corsica, deinde in Suriano, deinde in Monte Bardone, id est in Verceto, deinde in Parma, deinde in Regio; et exinde in Mantua atque Monte Silicis, simulque et universum exarchatum Ravennantium, sicut antiquitus erat, atque provincias Venetiarum et Istria; necnon et cunctum ducatum Spolitinum seu Beneventanum" (from Luna with the island of Corsica, from there to Sarzana, from there to Monte Bardone, that is, Verceto, from there to Parma, from there to Reggio, and from there to Mantua and Monselice [near Padua], together with the whole exarchate of Ravenna, as it was originally, and the provinces of Venetia and Istria, and the entire duchies of Spoleto and Benevento). The first part of this statement evidently described the route of a road, although whether this constituted a frontier is unclear, while the second part enumerates provinces. The whole document is odd, however, insofar as none of the territory outlined ever originally belonged to the Roman Church.

The Liber pontificalis goes on to report that Charlemagne signed the document with his own hand, followed by all the bishops, abbots, dukes, and counts. One copy was laid on the Altar of the Apostolic Prince under the Gospels, while a second was deposited in the Confessio, the prayer room above the tomb of the Apostle. All the Franks present, including the king, the *Liber* claims, committed themselves to St. Peter and his representative

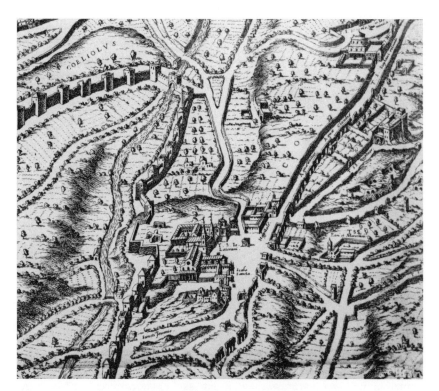

FIGURE 14 This map of Rome from 1577 by Étienne Dupérac highlights how the papal Lateran complex (foreground) formed an "island" within the city's walls. To the left of the Palace of the Popes is the Basilica of St. John Lateran, built by Emperor Constantine, while further to the left stands the Aurelian Wall. Immediately to the right of the papal palace is the Campus Lateranensis, and above the basilica the cloister and the canons' buildings; to the right of them, the octagonal tower of the Baptistery is visible. At the head of the two adjacent roads leading up to the Campus stands the famous Hospital of St. John; around and beneath this site were found the ruins of what was thought to have been Constantine's palace. Northeast of the Campus, the ruins of the ancient Aqua Claudia aqueduct are still visible, and to the right of it, near the top right edge of the map, is the Church of the Santi Quattro Coronati. Apart from the extensions to the papal palace and the hospital, the overall layout of this part of Rome would have corresponded to how the area looked in Charlemagne's time.

on Earth, Pope Hadrian, to adhere to the promise of the donation. Finally, a third copy of this renewed pledge was destined for the papal archives.

None of them have survived.[46] Nor was the promise kept in the sense of seigneurial rights, at least not by Charlemagne or to the extent envisaged in the document. Anyhow, Frankish sources glossed over the whole event; even the so-called *Royal Frankish Annals,* which had a semiofficial status, had nothing to say about what took place in the Eternal City.[47] It made do with just a laconically brief note that was still significant despite having a very pro forma feel to it: the king, the *Annals* recorded, had celebrated "Easter in Rome" before returning from there to the siege of Pavia. "In Rome"—phrased as prosaically as if he had spent the time in one of his palaces in Francia.

It is a moot point whether such brevity indicated a claim to sovereignty made only after the event, or whether it conveyed Charlemagne's intentions in 774. But it is evident that by around 790, when the *Royal Frankish Annals* was composed, Charlemagne was concerned to have all references to the Donation of Pepin—which was now the Donation of Charlemagne too—along with its causes and the circumstances surrounding it, wiped from the records. Einhard too made no mention of the Donation; even he would not have had the relevant document to hand when writing his biography. Nevertheless, knowledge of the act of renewal was kept alive, documented in the *Liber pontificalis,* and as late as the sixteenth century an image was painted by Taddeo Zuccaro on a wall of the Sala Regia, the official reception room in the Vatican palace, showing Charlemagne signing a document that by that time had not existed for several centuries.[48]

The pope's concerns, though, were evident in the measures he took after the king left the city. He did not pray for, or endow institutions solely in the name of, the Carolingian monarch.[49] Henceforth, he no longer dated his documents according to the Roman-Byzantine imperial regnal years but instead "under the sovereignty of Jesus Christ," in other words, according to the years of his own pontificate. He wanted to make clear who now ruled Rome. Hadrian also had coins minted that no longer had the head of the emperor on the obverse but instead his own name, *Hadrianus papa,* or even a head-and-shoulders portrait of himself encircled by the legend *Dominus noster Adrianus papa.* To be sure, Hadrian did not produce any gold coins, any imperial solidi. But even so, the silver coins were enough to proclaim his program of independence from the emperor—and from the Frankish king, for that matter. Indeed, for the first time, the pope took up arms and, in order to forestall an attack by Duke Arichis of Benevento—as he was at pains to let Charlemagne know—seized the city of Terracina;[50] from the

FIGURE 15 A coin of Pope Hadrian I (reigned 772–795). Fitzwilliam Museum, Cambridge, England.

High Middle Ages onward, papal military campaigns became increasingly frequent. Yet the *Liber pontificalis* was silent henceforth about the worldly interests of the Roman Church. The fact that the gates of the Eternal City were opened to the Carolingian ruler and the overt air of sovereignty the Frankish king displayed in staging his procession to the heart of Constantine's Rome were not reported by the writer of the *Liber*. Instead, he chose to focus solely on the spiritual activities of the pope.

Charlemagne likewise had little to say about the developments in Rome. After the Eastertide celebrations and an absence of around four or five weeks, he returned to resume the siege of Pavia. Anyone who controlled the city, which finally surrendered after a siege lasting nine months, would also gain mastery over the Lombard kingdom. In contrast to his father, after the defeat of Desiderius, Charlemagne proclaimed himself king of the Lombards. Presumably he had planned it thus after rejecting the king's daughter, his wife. And unlike his father, from now on he stressed that Rome was subject to his rule. Henceforth he styled himself "king of the Franks and Lombards and patricius of the Romans." Whatever the term *patricius* may have meant before, it was now a title of rulership. Just as Charlemagne ruled as king over the Franks and Lombards, so he reigned as *patricius* over the Romans.

A sad fate awaited those besieged in Pavia. The victorious Charlemagne took Desiderius and his wife, Ansa, captive and transported them back to the Frankish Empire, where he consigned them to a monastery and nunnery whose names are not recorded, as he did also with the former Lombard king's unnamed daughter, the wife he had spurned.[51] The expressions of those thus humiliated could convey nothing but hatred when their eyes met those of their captor. The north and center of Italy were now incorporated into Frankish rule; even so, the towns of Cividale in Friuli and Treviso had yet to be taken (this duly happened in 775 and 776, respectively), uprisings continued to break out, and the pope strove symbolically to maintain his own sovereignty.

The Organization of the Frankish Army

The wars against Saxony and the Lombards were the prelude to an endless succession of campaigns and conflicts. The Saxons themselves only added to the number, having exploited the absence of a king to rise up against the Franks (at least, this is how Frankish chroniclers interpreted the situation). And so Charlemagne spent over thirty years rushing from one war to another, year in, year out. A king had to prove himself in war in order to survive, and he had to provide his troops with regular booty if he wanted to stay in power. Einhard praised Charlemagne's actions. Looking back, he counted a total of eight wars, which meant that the Frankish king had fought on eight fronts against eight separate adversaries on whom he visited destruction: the Aquitanians, the Saxons, the Lombards, the Saracens, the Bavarians, the Bretons, the Beneventani, and the Slavs. But the king's biographer contented himself with allusions and did not go into detail. He wanted to celebrate peace in the crisis-threatened age in which he wrote. There was no denying, however, that Charlemagne was a warlike king, although he always had peace as his objective. He took a rest from fighting for only two years of his reign. Once Charlemagne had secured the imperial crown for himself, he turned his attention primarily to internal order within his massively expanded empire and stepped back from military campaigns.

The organization for waging war took its cue from Frankish traditions and the achievements of Charlemagne's grandfather Charles Martel. Methods of waging war at this time—strategy, tactics, equipment, and ways of fighting—can be reconstructed only very approximately.[52] It is possible that some knowledge about ancient techniques of warfare was still applied. It is even more difficult to determine the social composition of the fighting men. Many modern scholars now dispute the former assumption that all free men were liable for military service.[53] Instead, attention is now focused on the magnates and their retinues, who formed the backbone of the Frankish armies. So whom could the king call to arms? It appears that he had at his disposal a small standing army, with the potential to deploy small contingents of troops to various places.

Other than that, though, was he reliant on the consent of his magnates to assemble a truly effective fighting force in the event of war? How was such an agreement reached—through the outright gifting of land or bestowing fiefdoms? Or through giving his noblemen a regional or local stake in power by enlisting them as counts or stewards of the royal estates? Or through the prospect of war booty? Through gold and silver? Or through a combination of all of these? We know for certain that Charlemagne endowed his royal vassals in southern Gallia, for example, with generous estates. But they came at a price: anyone who owned twelve "manses" (a unit of cultivation or demesne, also called a *Hufe* [farmstead] in the Frankish Empire) was required to serve as a horseman with a coat of mail,[54] while those with fewer landholdings were merely warriors.

In recompense for the lands they had been given, most warriors were required to provide their own arms; if they were "homeless" (*non casati*), however, their master supplied weapons and horses. Men who joined up were responsible for bringing three months' provisions with them. If they were in the field any longer than this, the occupied land had to feed the troops. No campaign of any great length could be waged without foraging. Hardly any fodder for the horses was carried by the ox-drawn baggage train, only tents, at most, and even then only those for the commanders. The distances covered in a day's march were very small, hampered as the contingent was by the speed of the oxen; no force could advance at much more than fifteen—or at the very outside, twenty—kilometers a day. The Frankish war machine, like life in general at this time, rolled along at a sedate pace, on poor roads with the speed of oxcarts and, as subsequent events would show, helpless against the swift longboats of the Vikings. An army column of around a thousand mounted warriors, always riding two abreast, with a vanguard and a rear guard and the baggage train of oxcarts in between, would roll through the countryside over a length of some five or more kilometers; admittedly, we do not actually know how large armies at this time were. Yet they spelled danger at all times, come what may—for both friend and foe alike.

In comparison with later periods, armaments were light.[55] Most soldiers carried a spear, a long or a short sword and a shield, and a bow and arrows; wealthier fighters who owned twelve or more farmsteads, presuming they and their entourage were obliged to do war service, were equipped with a coat of mail. Bishops, abbots, abbesses, and counts were all expected to maintain a stock of arms with which to equip their people. Most warriors went into battle on foot. Warhorses—which needed to be around fourteen hands tall at the withers (sixteen hands in more recent times)[56]—could be afforded only by wealthier Franks; then again, they were essential, given the heavy mail such warriors wore. By this time, the formerly widespread "francisca," the traditional throwing ax of the Franks, was no longer in use. Spears were the preferred weapon for close-quarters combat. Sometimes, two spears would be taken into battle, one for throwing and the other for stabbing. Anyone who wielded a sword had to have undergone special training. Originally, a helmet was the preserve of the nobility, possibly even being reserved solely for commanders, but by 800 it may well have become more widespread.

In addition to the king, those entitled to raise a body of fighting men were the greater and lesser vassals, as well as bishops and abbots. The only Frankish conscription orders that have survived date from the reign of Louis the Pious, for example, a letter from an envoy responsible for mustering troops in his region, Archbishop Heti of Trier, to Bishop Frothard of Toul, dating from the year 817. In it, Heti tells his bishop that a strict command (*terribile imperium*) has been issued by the emperor "to all abbots, abbesses, counts, royal vassals, and the populace at large" in his archdiocese "who are obliged by the king's authority to undertake war service," ordering them to be in such a state of readiness that if the order to march should come in the morning, they would be ready to assemble at the rallying point by that same evening, and conversely, if the order were issued in the evening, by the following morning.[57] Twelve years later, a similar order ran: "All inhabitants of the entire empire who are bound to do military service should make themselves ready with horses, weapons, military garb, carts, and provisions, so that when they receive an order to this effect, they should be able to move without delay."[58] Moreover, the messengers who carried the mobilization orders were expected to be fed by the lords and ladies liable for war duty; to identify themselves, they carried with them a so-called *tractoria,* a royal warrant confirming their credentials.[59]

Things were no different under Charlemagne. A draft order sent by the emperor to Abbot Fulrad of St. Denis in 806 provides us with useful information.[60] In it, the emperor asks the abbot to supply the usual weapons and other war materiel—axes, knives, entrenching tools, iron spades, and the like—together with provisions and clothing. Charlemagne's directive runs: "From the moment the army sets off, there must be sufficient provisions to hand for three months in the field, while enough weapons and clothes for six months are also to be carried."

When they were shaping up for battle, the opposing forces may well have advanced to within calling distance of one another. To try to lure the enemy out from their cover, insults were hurled, or audacious riders were sent out to provoke a reaction. When battle was joined, the troops rushed forward "at a quick run." Charlemagne's grandson Nithard notes these details (*History*, 3.6). One well-established technique at this time was to feign a retreat; this same author described the training for such a maneuver: "One section of the troops, with their shields covering their backs, made as if they were retreating to their own lines in the face of their pursuers before turning back to pursue those whom they were fleeing from, until finally both kings, surrounded by their young bodyguard, burst forth with a loud roar and waving their spears, menacing first one and then another who tried to make good their escape." The individual units were led by individual magnates; records cite Margrave Roland, Seneschal Eggihard, and Count Palatine Anshelm as commanders of the rear guard during the retreat from Spain. In battle, fighting tactics concentrated on a series of duels, either knight against knight or foot soldier against foot soldier.

"They prepared their armor and buckled their swords over their chain mail, before riding out to battle. . . . Then they let sail their ashen spears, sharp showers, sticking in their shields. They came closer on foot, splitting each other's bright boards, striking fiercely until their weapons shattered their shields." This description of a fierce duel between two noble knights comes from the Old High German *Hildebrandslied* (Song of Hildebrand), written during Charlemagne's reign.[61] Furthermore, some manuscript illuminations from this time—for example, the Utrecht Psalter, the Stuttgart Psalter, and the Golden Psalter in St. Gallen (Plate VII)—depict battle scenes, although it is impossible to determine with any certainty to what extent these represented contemporary practice in warfare or simply followed templates from late antiquity.

Battles were also sung about in the *Waltharius*, a Latin poem from the tenth century:

> With a glance he surveyed the battlefield and organized his line of
> battle across the broad expanse of flat lands and fields. The two
> armies had already advanced within spear-throwing distance of
> one another and come to a halt. Then a great warlike cry rose
> into the air from both sides; at the same time signal horns rang
> out with their dreadful sound, and a rain of spears was flung
> from each battle line; spears of ash and cherry wood flew

together through the air followed, like lightning bolts, by the shimmer of hurled pikes. . . . When the whole supply of throwing weapons from both sides was exhausted, every man's hand clutched at his sword. Pulling the gleaming blades from their scabbards, they raised their shields once more, and now the armies clashed together, and resumed the fight all over again. As the horses crashed headlong into one another, so great was the force that some of their breastbones shattered. . . . In the midst of this clash, Waltharius battled forward in the mêlée, mowing down all who stood in his way with his sword.[62]

This no doubt echoes the way in which Charlemagne and his magnates would have ridden into battle. We know for certain that he flung himself into the mêlée of close combat on at least two occasions.

Thirty Years of War in Saxony

Their swift triumph against the Lombards emboldened the Franks to attempt to score a decisive victory against the Saxons too. The Saxons exploited their king's absence to exact revenge for the destruction of the Irminsul. Churches close to the Frankish border, like the monastery in Fritzlar or the diocesan town of Büraburg (near Marburg), founded by St. Boniface, were razed to the ground.[63] Charlemagne regarded these attacks as a breach of treaty, although admittedly he was in no position to appreciate the complex interplay of all the various factors involved—the relationship between the Saxon social and political system, ritual observances, treaties of unification, and resistance. Over the years up to 785, he concluded no fewer than fifteen treaties with Saxony and complained about an equal number of breaches.[64] Over time, the king became steadily angrier. Although he had won some Saxons over to baptism and peaceful coexistence, other groups clung to their traditional pagan cults and remained implacably opposed to him. No treaty, it appeared, could embrace all Saxons, whose settlements were spread across an area bounded by the rivers Rhine, Elbe, and Schlei.

The social order and the popular culture of the Saxons were completely unlike those of the Franks, making it difficult for the latter to properly grasp their adversaries.[65] The Saxons had no integrated leadership; in fact, they were less a single people and more a group of small ethnicities. St. Boniface, indeed, mentions eight groups by name in his letter (Epistle 43): the Thuringi, the Hessi, the Borthari, the Nistresi, the Uuedrecii, the Lognai, the

Suduodi, and the Grafelti,[66] although by the beginning of the ninth century only the first two and the last two were still to be found. Alongside these were the Harudi, the Bardi, and several others. The region the Franks thought of as "Saxony" was said to be divided into three areas, the *Heer-schaften,* or military districts, of Eastphalia, Westphalia, and Angria, which in turn did not represent coherent ethnic or political units; in addition, there were also the following areas: Wigmodien, around Bremen and possibly stretching as far as the banks of the Elbe, the Bardengau region on the lower Elbe, the regions north of the Elbe (Transalbingia), and a series of other small regions, districts, and areas of settlement. Charlemagne had to vanquish every one of these peoples, or at least win over their noblemen to his side. In the process, much importance was also placed on missionary work, notably the founding of dioceses and parish churches.[67] The Franks' ignorance of this foreign people was to come back to haunt them, however.

In 775, the Eastphalians were led by the tribal leader Hessi, and the Angrians by Brun;[68] a little later, the Westphalians joined the fray under the leadership of "Duke" Widukind. Some of the Saxon regions were ruled by "satraps," a kind of petty ruler. The Saxon people, it was claimed, had organized themselves into three social classes: the nobility, free men, and *Laten* (serfs).[69] They were reputed to gather annually at Marklo, a place on the Weser that has so far never been identified, for a "general assembly," at which laws were revised, legal judgments were passed, and joint decisions were taken about war, peace, and religious affairs. Present at these meetings were all the satraps, plus twelve elected representatives from each of the social classes.[70] This sounds too neat and ordered, however, for it not to have been a later invention.

The Saxons had no king. Instead, when war was imminent, they chose by lot one of their satraps to be their military commander (*dux*), according to the Venerable Bede, writing in the early eighth century.[71] The only report on the yearly general assembly appears in the later *Life of St. Lebuin,* an Anglo-Saxon missionary during the era of Charlemagne, which was written in the second half of the ninth century. Lebuin was said to have preached in Marklo: "God, the king of Heaven and Earth, and His Son Jesus Christ, announces to you that, if you devote your lives to Him and agree to do what He commands through His servants, He will give you greater gifts than you have ever received before." Lebuin then supposedly added a threat: "In the neighboring country, a king has taken up arms to invade your land, sack it and lay waste to it, and to visit all manner of enmity on you, send you into exile, dispossess you, and slaughter you."[72]

It is impossible to say how much the Saxons understood of the Anglo-Saxon missionary's sermon. Perhaps he used gestures to underline the gravity of the situation. But Lebuin's thumbnail sketch of Charlemagne's war against the Saxons and its objectives could scarcely have been put more succinctly: baptism or exile and death. Charlemagne used all three methods. In the midterm, though, the conflict brought him considerable cultural gain, namely, the connection of the extensive barbarian lands between the Rhine, Elbe, and Schlei to the advanced civilizations of the Mediterranean region—a coup even the Roman emperor Augustus and his successors had never managed to pull off. Soon, this proved to be a stroke of good fortune for the vanquished peoples of this region also. A century after their defeat, they were venerating Charlemagne as their great prophet, their apostle.

The Saxons had never developed their own tradition of historiography; not even a set of particularly enlightening runic inscriptions has been found preserved. Nor have any Old Saxon pagan songs or other such traditions come down to us from the Carolingian period. Later traditions, like those enumerated, say, by the chronicler Widukind of Corvey in the tenth century, may well already have been corrupted by scholarly accretions and no longer represent the original forms. Literacy was as alien a concept to the Saxons as monotheism.

As a result, we know about the original social and political system of the Saxons only through one late piece of evidence provided by the *Life of St. Lebuin,* which by the time it was written was already overlaid with various more recent developments. The brief chapter on Marklo, for instance, which older scholarship took to be reliable, must be open to doubt. Admittedly, Charlemagne soon recognized the danger and potential for resistance posed by such popular assemblies and summarily forbade them. The only permissible gatherings were assemblies convened by the king and the court hearings organized by lords appointed by the ruler. Even at these latter assemblies, priests were present to monitor the lords.[73]

Charlemagne was determined to dispel the danger the Saxons posed once and for all. He made himself a solemn pledge to this effect. The war that had now begun dragged on for almost thirty-three years, Einhard reported (chap. 7). Only in 805 did the original objective appear to have been finally reached: the absorption of all Saxons into the Frankish Empire and their baptism. Many Saxons fiercely resisted this liberation through subjugation—a policy that became ever more visible and palpable in the new castles and churches the king erected and the tributes he exacted from the region. For a long time, Saxons remained impervious to the message of Jesus Christ, of the Last Judgment, and of Heaven and Hell. The common people clung to their old rites and magical practices, to their "cult of demons," as Christians disparagingly referred to it. Suppression of this cult became one of the methods by which the Frankish king waged war against the Saxons, while missionary activity, the building of baptisteries and episcopal churches, the setting up of courts-martial, and the introduction of a tithe system all served as further techniques of oppression. They must have struck the Saxons as being nothing but the continuation of war and stripping of their freedoms by other means. But over time, it appeared that their incorporation into the Frankish kingdom did succeed in forging the Saxons into a single people.

Yet missionary activity at the End of Days was an essential requirement in the history of salvation. Pope Gregory the Great had stressed time and again how vital this task was. The Anglo-Saxons, who were converted through his efforts, were well aware of its importance[74] and proceeded to spread St. Gregory's teaching across the Continent.[75] Charlemagne cannot have been oblivious to this. The Gregorian doctrine required that heathen demonic cults be smashed. Yet the Frankish king had already embarked on just such a mission in his first campaign against Saxony in 772, when he had had the Irminsul torn down; this initial success led to an escalation of violence on both sides. The Saxons attacked, sacked, and destroyed churches, and in response the Franks pushed forward—sometimes from Frankfurt and sometimes along the main route from the Rhine to the Weser—ever deeper and more destructively into Saxon territory and attempted to place those they conquered under the yoke of an alien religion.

"With a mighty army and the name of Christ on his lips, Charlemagne sallied forth to Saxony," recalled a later chronicle, generalizing rather than referring to a specific campaign. "In his retinue were many bishops, priests, and countless other devout people well versed in the Christian faith, who had joined the campaign so that they might use sacred teachings to bind the Saxon people, who since time immemorial had been ensnared by demons, to a belief in the gentle and sweet yoke of Christ."[76] But this was, it seemed, all in vain. The longer the subsequent battles continued, the more savage the fighting became, perhaps for this very reason; as early as 774, Charlemagne is said to have coined the slogan that thereafter became the rallying call for almost the entire duration of the conflict: Baptism or Death. This phrase, then, was not just some reflection in retrospect from the reign of Louis the Pious.[77] Nevertheless, mass enforced baptisms did not help promote the Franks' missionary work in Saxony.

Very little is known about the persecuted religious cults and deities of the Saxons; the *Royal Frankish Annals* says absolutely nothing on the subject. Charlemagne's biographer Einhard (chap. 7) was of the opinion that the Saxons were "devoted to a demonic cult," whatever that may have meant; he made no attempt to glean more detailed information. Meanwhile, the Fulda schoolmaster Rudolf,[78] writing in 860, by which time the Saxons had long since converted to Christianity, reported that the Irminsul, that "universal pillar," had been a massive, upright tree trunk and had been given its name "because it supported, as it were, the whole world" (*quasi sustinens omnia*). But this explanation did not reveal a great deal, and Rudolf had no further insights to impart. On the matter of the Saxons' religion, he quoted the Roman historian Tacitus's *Germania*—the sole instance of this text being cited in the Middle Ages. However, these quotations give no hint of any first-hand knowledge of actual ritual practices.

An Old Saxon incantation found in a manuscript from Fulda or possibly Hersfeld and dating from around 800 does, though, reveal some knowledge of Thunaer, Woden, and Saxnote (the pagan gods Thor, Wotan, and Saxnot), whom new Christian converts were expected to renounce.[79] It seems that images of specific deities were alien to the Saxons, although they probably had cultic idols. Unlike the Christians worshipping in their churches, pagans conducted sacrifices on cliff tops or in sacred groves of trees; they would dust idols with flour or form them from cloths and carry them through the fields, all practices pointing to a fertility cult. Magic and sorcery were widespread.[80] Archaeologists have discovered burial mounds from this period; a special rite relating to the dead and their graves may well have been observed there. After the introduction of Christianity, anyone who cremated his or her dead would be punished by death; likewise, anyone who made sacrifices to the Devil or who "in the pagan manner" offered up the Communion wafer to demonic spirits. And anyone who swore oaths on natural springs, trees, or groves would be required to atone, according to rank, by means of a smaller or larger fine.[81] These penalties were imposed by Charlemagne during the course of the war. It is impossible to gauge how quickly these kinds of proscriptions became firmly established, but it must have taken some time.

The mission to the Frisians was instigated by St. Boniface, who suffered a martyr's death. Likewise, the first missionaries to be active among the Saxons were "tribal kin" Anglo-Saxon preachers like Ewald the Black and Ewald the Fair, one of whom was dark haired and the other blond, whom Abbot Willibrord sent from the monastery at Echternach to Westphalia, where they too were murdered. Nothing more is known about them. But Charlemagne capitalized on these early efforts and brought his might to bear on the matter of Christianizing the Saxons; not least, according to the Christian way of thinking, this legitimized the war he was waging. In retrospect, he claimed that he preached to them "with an iron tongue" (*ferrea lingua*),[82] as well as with warfare, executions, and death sentences. Einhard maintained that the Saxons had repeatedly promised to embrace Christianity but in their disloyalty had broken all these pledges.

The clash between these two religions was a matter of life and death. Missionary activity was a truly perilous enterprise, threatened time and again by "rebellions."[83] The missionaries showed great courage, and many of them were martyred; the heathens, though, thought that they were insane. A few of their names have been preserved for posterity. From around 780, the Anglo-Saxon Willehad, in his capacity as missionary bishop of Wigmodia, was responsible for the area around the present-day city of Bremen and possibly an area even farther east toward the Elbe. He built churches, preached the Gospel to the native peoples there (who must have found it somewhat unintelligible), and showed them the way to Eternal Life. At least, these are the details given in his *Life*, which was written only around 845 and, rather than presenting real details of Willehad's mission, offers instead more an archetypal trajectory. Liudger, a Frisian who had attended both St. Gregory's school in Utrecht and Alcuin's in York, first did missionary work among his own people, east of the lower river Ems, before moving deep into Westphalia, to the town of Münster, where he ultimately founded the diocese in 805, with Charlemagne's support.

Similarly, Liudger's missionary work was described only many decades later, shortly before the middle of the ninth century, by his relative and successor-but-one as bishop of Münster, Altfrid; by this time, many of the facts of his life were already shrouded in legend.[84] Yet he himself had been responsible for writing a *Life of St. Gregory of Utrecht*, his erstwhile teacher, around 790/791, in which he revealed something about his own missionary work.[85] This work was not like the king's approach but instead prescribed the "correct norm for life" (*rectissima norma vivendi*). Liudger praised the example set by the apostle Paul, for whom he named the cathedral church he founded in Münster (Sankt-Paulus-Dom). This missionary activity was underpinned by church building, preaching, and worship and was conducted by a host of indigenous pupils who were suited to missionary work and had been specially tutored in it.

Liudger set great store by conversion through good example and through conviction and understanding, rather than through coercion: "teaching and proceeding along the path set by God."[86] His founding of a monastery on his family's estate at Werden on the Ruhr, which would soon flourish, served at the same time as a rearward mission station. He had prepared for this step with a long sojourn at Monte Cassino, during which he got to know all the customs of a Benedictine monastery.[87] Yet even Liudger's preaching was accompanied by the destruction of pagan idols.[88] This alien cult and its symbols had to be eradicated and could not be permitted to exist alongside the religious signs of Christianity. Then, as now, this was what every existential struggle between religions demanded.

Charlemagne penetrated deep into the Saxon interior.[89] In 775, he advanced as far as Oker, where he took hostages from all three Saxon military districts. The following year, he convened a meeting at the source of the river Lippe, at which he required from all those present a twofold commitment: first, to submit to baptism, and second, to recognize Frankish rule. A year later, at the Karlsburg, almost certainly the later city of Paderborn, the first mass baptism took place. Yet the Saxons did not capitulate so quickly. Conflicts kept erupting afresh throughout the region, and the fighting intensified after Widukind took over the leadership on the Saxon side.[90] Widukind came from a high-born Westphalian family that would play an outstanding role in the following century.

Widukind skillfully organized the resistance. At the Süntel Mountains, he dared—in breach of a peace treaty, it was claimed—to engage in combat a Frankish force sent out to take punitive action against the Slavs and proceeded to wipe it out. Charlemagne, who might well have thought that he had subjugated the Saxons by this stage, was furious. In retaliation, he now personally led an advance to the confluence of the rivers Aller and Weser and exacted revenge for the "breach of treaty." At a place called Verden in October 782, he is said to have ordered the execution of some 4,500 Saxons who had been handed over to the Frankish king by "loyal" Saxons.[91] The *Royal Frankish Annals* recorded this for posterity. Although this figure may be exaggerated, the basic truth of the event is not in doubt. The earth and the waters of the river ran red with blood. At the princely assembly held at Lippspringe later that same year, the first counties in Saxony were established and immediately placed under the control of Saxon lords. Hostage taking and deportations were designed to break any last vestiges of resistance. Charlemagne himself, meanwhile, became more heavily involved in the campaign, donning his chain mail, taking up his sword, and launching himself into battle. Einhard (chap. 8) reports that, in the course of 783, Charlemagne was twice impelled by his fury to personally engage in the fighting.

Widukind at least managed to escape the bloody massacre at Verden unscathed. But the following year, even he was finally forced to capitulate in the face of overwhelming Frankish superiority after many years of brave and imaginative resistance and to surrender alongside his stepson, Abbi. Widukind was baptized in Attigny at Christmas 785. Charlemagne is said to have acted as his godfather and to have bestowed generous gifts on him. The brave warrior was allowed to withdraw to his country estates and was spared the fate of being consigned to a monastery, as usually happened to the enemies of the Frankish king. The memory of this resistance fighter remained alive among the Saxons for a long time; he was still being commemorated in the tenth century. The pope ordered liturgical services of thanksgiving to mark Charlemagne's victory.[92]

During this period of intense fighting, sometime between 780 and 782, the Diocese of Mainz was upgraded to an archdiocese, thus gaining ecclesiastical sovereignty over large tracts of the Saxon lands. However, even the Archdiocese of Cologne found itself extending out toward Saxony, with the accretion to its existing territory of the new dioceses of Münster, Osnabrück, Minden, and Bremen. The new archbishop of Mainz, Lull, a former assistant of Boniface and another Anglo-Saxon, is thought to have devoted his energies to expanding the bureaucracy of the church. It is tempting to speculate that he was the author of the thirty-three chapters of the *Capitulatio de partibus Saxoniae*, a legal ordinance enacted around this time by Charlemagne, which prescribed a series of draconian punishments, including the death penalty, for anyone who engaged in hostilities against Christian institutions or the person of the king.[93]

Churches were henceforth to enjoy greater sanctity (*honorem*) than pagan cultic sites had ever had (chap. 1) and were to be considered a special zone of peace in which a person might safely take refuge (chap. 2). Contravening this law was punishable by burning at the stake (chap. 3). Anyone who partook of meat during Lent was to be put to death unless a priest declared a state of emergency in which everyone was permitted to eat meat (chap. 4). Execution likewise awaited anyone who killed a bishop, priest, or deacon (chap. 6). The death penalty was also imposed on anyone who was deceived by the Devil into believing, like the pagans, that certain of their fellow citizens were witches who would eat human flesh, and who therefore took it on himself to burn these supposed witches and eat them instead (chap. 6). Similarly, anyone who followed the pagan practice of cremating a corpse would also face execution (chap. 7). The same punishment was meted out to those who plotted against a Christian or who engaged in a conspiracy against the king or the Christian populace (chap. 10). Everyone was expected to go to church on Sundays (chap. 18); clearly, church attendance was employed as a means of social control. Other clauses in the *Capitulatio* required that the inhabitants of any particular region were liable to cede two farmsteads for the use of every newly founded parish church, subjected new Christian converts to tithe laws, forbade illegitimate marriages, demanded that children should be baptized within a year of their birth, ordered that churchyards be used exclusively for Christian burials, and so forth.

We do not know to what extent these legal statutes accorded with the real lives of the Saxon people, or whether they were actually enforced, and if so, for how long; they have come down to us only in a single manuscript. Nevertheless, they do reveal a great deal about the bitterness with which the war was waged on both sides, and about the pagan community's hostility to the cult of Christianity. These proscriptions were intended to crush the Saxon people's autonomy, destroy their cults, and make the populace itself subject to the authority of the king and its system of free administration of justice subject to the jurisdiction of overlords appointed by the ruler (chaps. 28–31 and 34). Decades later, when once again the end of hostilities seemed within sight, these proscriptions were toned down, and the Saxons were placed legally more or less on a par with the Franks.[94] The *Lex Saxonum* put in place at that time therefore took greater account of the ancient legal customs of this people.

The final pocket of Saxon resistance was in northern Albingia, the place where Widukind had once taken refuge. There, in 791, a new uprising broke out against Frankish rule while Charlemagne was engaged in a campaign against the Avars. Once more, it would take several years for the Frankish king to regain control of the situation. The brutality of these clashes also comes across in the reports given in the revised *Royal Frankish Annals*:

> Although the Saxons had handed over hostages the previous
> summer [in 794] and had, as they were commanded, given solemn
> pledges of their loyalty, the king had not forgotten their earlier
> treachery and so . . . convened a general assembly, and invaded
> Saxony with his army, advancing right across the region and
> visiting almost total destruction on it. When he arrived in the
> Bardengoi region, he set up camp at a place called Bardowick
> and awaited there the arrival of the Slavs, whom he had

ordered to appear before him. It was there that the following news came to him: just as he was about to cross the river Elbe, Wizzin, king of the Slavic Obotrites, had been ambushed by the Saxons and killed. This crime enraged the king, spurring him on to conquer the Saxons with even greater haste, and provoking in him an even greater hatred of this accursed people. This heinous act prompted him to lay waste most of their lands and to return to Francia with a large group of hostages.[95]

A number of different tactics were employed in this conflict. Particularly, the Saxon nobility were more amenable than the common people to being annexed to the Franks. After all, they stood only to gain from being locked into Mediterranean culture and the Frankish system of rule. In addition, the king appointed loyal Saxons as counts, a powerful stimulus to joining the Franks. Indeed, the resistance was led first and foremost by the free men and the serfs; they rose up on two further occasions, in 841 and 843, during the Stellinga Rebellion. A program of annual campaigns, castle building, and repeated overwintering by the king and his army on Saxon territory took a heavy toll on the populace and the land. Hostages were required to be handed over on a regular basis, and deportations and mass executions were also the order of the day. The imposition of the administrative system of counties—alien to the Saxons—and missionary work completed the work begun through the force of arms. County regions and the foundation of churches and dioceses divided the land up into a newfangled network of parishes. We do not know whether the old districts (*Gaue*) were taken into consideration in this reorganization. For example, in his capacity as a priest, Liudger was put in charge of five such districts. The laconic reports found in the *Annals*—the only sources available to the modern historian—generally have nothing to say about how the founding of dioceses was carried out and organized in practice.

The story of Liudger and the bishopric of Münster is uniquely remarkable for the relatively large amount of information that has survived about it. No comparable testimonies are available for the other Saxon dioceses; instead, we must content ourselves with simply listing them. The foundations up to Charlemagne's death were Bremen (787), Paderborn (799), Minden and Verden on the Aller (ca. 800), Halberstadt and Osnabrück (804), and Münster (805), although precisely how they were administered thereafter remains a mystery. Monasteries appeared in Saxony only after Charlemagne's death. Corvey, or New Corbie, as it was called at the time, was the first of these to be set up, an institution founded by Charlemagne's cousins Adalhard and Wala, which at first was a satellite of its mother monastery of Corbie. Before this, missionary work in Saxony was supported by Frankish monasteries such as Echternach, Hersfeld, Fulda, or Liudger's foundation of Werden on the Ruhr. By 800, Saxony was even host to its first nunnery, at Herford.

In Paderborn, the founding of the diocese was preceded twenty years earlier by the building of a royal palace, the Karlsburg (*Urbs Caroli*) on the river Lippe, which may have been given that antique-style name only in 776. Its founding was accompanied by a mass baptism. In any event, the palace was so magnificently appointed that Charlemagne convened a princely assembly there in 777 and even more than two decades later, in 799, held a reception in the palace for Pope Leo III; it was on this latter occasion that the pontiff, in conjunction with the king, is reputed to have founded the diocese.[96] The palace complex included a Church of St. Savior as well as a Grand Hall, which at that time was decorated with lavish tapestries, and in which banquets were held.[97] Having the bishop of Rome come to visit Saxony, which had only just been won for Christendom, was clearly a very effective programmatic act. It gave Charlemagne an opportunity to present himself to the vicar of St. Peter, the head of the Church, as a vanquisher of heathens and a promoter of Christianity, and as the defender of the faith and future emperor.

The Lack of Information on Spain and Benevento

Not all the subsequent wars that Charlemagne fought, even when they ended in victory for him, were closely followed by intensive missionary activity. Unquestionably, the campaigns against Muslims were aimed at the expansion of Christianity. The upheavals taking place in the Islamic world at this time cast their shadow as far as the Frankish Empire. Although Arab forces had invaded Spain in 711 and within just a few years had advanced as far as the Pyrenees, presently crossing them as well, they had not conquered the whole of the Iberian Peninsula. Pockets of Christianity survived in the north and the northwest, such as the Basque region around Pamplona and above all the stronghold of the "last Visigoths" in Cantabria, Asturias, and Galicia. These "Visigoths" formed the nucleus of the new Christian kingdom of Asturias, and they are traditionally regarded as having formulated, from the late ninth century onward, the ideology of the Reconquista—the Christian reconquest of the Iberian Peninsula (al-Andalus) from the Moors. The energetic King Alfonso II, who ruled Asturias for forty-nine years from 791 and proved himself a highly effective military commander against the Muslims, may be regarded as the most successful architect of the young, up-and-coming kingdom, whose capital he relocated to Oviedo. Alfonso looked for support from the Franks in his struggle. According to Einhard (chap. 16), this "king of Galicia and Asturias" proclaimed himself in letters and through messages carried by envoys to be Charlemagne's vassal (*proprium*). To what extent this was an accurate description of their relationship is a moot point.

Christians living under Moorish rule, the so-called Mozarabs, mainly inhabited the cities. They were to benefit greatly from the high Arab culture that developed in al-Andalus. For the wider Christian community, though, they were a source of concern rather than hope, since they showed signs of heretical tendencies. Archbishop Elipand of Toledo, for example, expounded a theology ("Adoptionism") that he ascribed to St. Paul, but that in fact had distinct Islamic undertones to it and saw Christ as merely the adopted son of God in view of his human corporeality. Allah, likewise, had no son.

This new theological fallacy infiltrated the Pyrenean diocese of Urgell, which belonged to the Frankish Empire. Yet this spread of heresies met Christianity's eschatological expectations for the near future, as realized by the Arab invasion of Spain. The commentary on the Apocalypse written by Abbot Beatus of Liébana (in the kingdom of Asturias) in 779—and impressively illustrated, possibly according to the author's own scheme—gave voice to these imminent expectations.[98] Beatus personally was an opponent of Adoptionism but still extensively quoted (albeit without recognizing it as such) the work of the late fourth-century Donatistic heretic Ticonius, whose own commentary on the Apocalypse, now lost, can largely be reconstructed from these quotations. Eschatological expectations were therefore intimately bound up with the struggle against Moorish rule in Spain. For Charlemagne, the events taking place in the Pyrenean region were not just a military matter.

The Emirate of Córdoba did not represent itself in the slightest as a pacified country, a fact that not only was indicated by the annual reports of the Mozarab chronicle of 754[99] but also was well known in Charlemagne's empire. The Arabs were in a constant state of feuding with one another. It took a new arrival, in the form of the last Umayyad emir, ʿAbd ar-Rahman (756–788), to finally unify al-Andalus. Even so, the internal tensions still continued among his sons and successors. So it was that a prominent Muslim, Sulaiman al-Arabi of Barcelona, who had arrived at Charlemagne's court in 777, asked the Frankish king for help against the Umayyad emir.[100]

Charlemagne identified a marvelous prospect of winning victories against the "despicable" Saracens,[101] as his father and grandfather had done before him, and to expand his empire. Other rebels against Muslim rule appeared to be stirring: the rulers of the cities of Zaragoza and Huesca longed for independence from the emir of Córdoba. The governors of Barcelona and Girona also began to threaten insurrection and strove to bring about the breakup of the emirate—though in their case possibly only as a gesture of loyalty to the Abbasids. When it seemed that they were about to be suppressed, Sulaiman al-Arabi, allegedly in alliance with al-Husain al-Ansari of Zaragoza, sought Charlemagne's help against ʿAbd ar-Rahman. Accordingly, he appeared in Paderborn and—as the editor of the *Royal Frankish Annals* claimed in a legitimizing but at the same time obfuscating piece of backdating—"surrendered himself and the cities that the King of the Saracens had assigned to him."[102] Indeed, what was actually a war of aggression was proclaimed to be a defensive war, designed first and foremost to protect the Christians in Spain. This effectively gave Charlemagne "legitimate" grounds for advancing across the Pyrenees or at least indicates that he required such justification in the eyes of the Franks.[103]

The king embarked on this Spanish adventure without acquiring sufficient intelligence and, resolving that he would go to war in the coming year, called all free landowners to the ranks and marched south. He took his queen, Hildegard, with him on campaign but left her behind at Chasseneuil, a palace in northern Aquitaine, before proceeding to Spain, because she was pregnant. Ultimately, she had to thank God that she saw her husband again because he had gravely underestimated the danger of this campaign.

Despite the fact that they had encountered Muslims some decades before, during the Arab advance as far as the Loire at Poitiers, Charlemagne and his Franks possessed no reliable information about Islam, had no experience whatsoever of the diplomatic conventions of the Arab conquerors of Spain, and knew absolutely nothing about the actual situation in al-Andalus. Charles Martel's triumph over the "Saracens" lived on in Frankish folk memory, but this victory had not been followed up with any intelligence gathering about the foreigners, not even under Charlemagne. They had no inkling of the Moors' social or power structure or their methods of waging war. Instead, any knowledge on the part of the Franks about their adversaries was precluded by a stereotypical image of them as bogeymen. The Venerable Bede, Alcuin's great authority, had been the prime mover in giving the early Middle Ages this notion of the "Saracens" as beyond the pale. As a result, they came to be regarded as worshippers of the Devil and false gods, devotees of Lucifer.[104] The conception of their alien language, their daunting religion, their mysterious modes of rule, and the unfathomable culture of the Arabs meant that the Franks had no real notion of the likelihood of success in the war they had embarked on.

Charlemagne reaped the consequences of this ignorance almost immediately. Against expectation, al-Ansari did not open the gates of his city to the invaders. All the Frankish king could do was take a few hostages captive and sound the retreat. Al-Arabi was presumably also to be taken back to Francia as a prisoner. In the valley of Roncesvalles, the Frankish rear guard was ambushed by a force of Christian Basques. The reasons for this attack are unclear. It was probably the case that the perpetrators were taking revenge for the sacking of Pamplona, an act that Charlemagne felt driven to commit in order to "return home as a victor."[105] Einhard (chap. 9) reported that the heavy weaponry of the Franks was of no avail in the narrow defile. Arab sources claim that al-Arabi was freed from Frankish captivity during this clash.[106] Were Muslim forces therefore also involved in this battle? It is not out of the question. The famous "Chanson de Roland" about this engagement, written in the eleventh or twelfth centuries, certainly portrays it as an exclusively Frankish-Moorish clash.

The *Royal Frankish Annals* is silent about this embarrassing defeat for the much-vaunted king. The incident gets only a brief mention in the revision of this work, which was undertaken in the 820s; Charlemagne's biographer Einhard, too, openly commemorated this disaster, at somewhat greater length, even mentioning the commanders of the rear guard by name: the seneschal Eggihard, Count Palatine Anshelm, and Hruodland/Roland, count of the Breton Marchlands. Einhard wrote that all of them were killed, along with many others. Up to the time he was writing, Einhard claimed, this heinous act had not been avenged. Was he trying to warn against precipitate action? Or was he hoping that the Franks would retaliate? In any event, in the year 827, there was cause for both action and circumspection.[107]

Charlemagne returned unscathed from the Spanish debacle in 778. At Chasseneuil, north of Poitiers, he was able to embrace his wife once more and meet his new son for the first time, who had been christened Chlodwig/Ludwig/Clovis, the name of the most illustrious members of the now-defunct Merovingian ruling dynasty. His twin brother Chlothar/Lothar had died immediately after being born. By choosing these names, the Carolingians were consciously claiming kinship with the Merovingians.[108] Why, at this particular juncture straight after his defeat, and only now, was Charlemagne seeking to associate himself with the earlier dynasty and the triumphant

King Clovis and the two Merovingian rulers named Chlothar, who had also been victorious? Outside Poitiers, Clovis had received the promise of victory over the heretical Visigoths, which guaranteed the expansion of his Frankish realm.[109] Was Charlemagne attempting to link himself with this tradition and, despite his defeat, ensure that he was celebrated as a victor, to the extent that the setback was entirely eclipsed? As so often, the lack of any information in the surviving records precludes any deeper insight into this matter. Even so, it does tell us a great deal about the manipulative impulses of early medieval historiography.

The failure of the Spanish campaign in 778 revealed a fundamental absence of knowledge about this foreign country and a lack of information about conditions beyond the borders of the empire, as well as about foreign law, foreign ethics, foreign religion, foreign methods of fighting, and the ways in which such matters might play a key role in determining another people's loyalty and observance of treaties. Charlemagne had, it seemed, counted on the practice of subinfeudation, which he was very familiar with, existing among the Muslims, which it did not. Later, when people who knew Spain well, such as Theodulf, came to the Frankish court, things might have turned out very differently. However, over the course of the 780s, the tally of successes against the Moors increased, albeit in small steps and not without setbacks, but still steadily. For example, sometime before 790, the Diocese of Urgell was established. By this stage also—according to a later Arab historian, Ahmad al-Maqqari—'Abd ar-Rahman, pressed by Charlemagne's victories, supposedly instigated peace negotiations and attempted to forge a relationship through marriage with the Frankish king. Charlemagne is said to have been amenable to a peace deal but not to the prospect of marriage.[110]

Meanwhile, the dramatic events in Spain inspired contemporary poets. After all, the heroic battle of Roncesvalles and the death of the main protagonists were not unlike the theme of "woeful fate" in the *Hildebrandslied* and were wholly consonant with the taste of the age. The battle in the Pyrenees formed the starting point for the famous "Chanson de Roland," whose original version has not been preserved, but which incorporated countless other motifs with earlier story lines, for instance, from the time of Archbishop Hincmar of Reims. Its earliest traces can be found in various references from Catalonia dating from the eleventh century; the first complete version in French that has survived comes from around 1100, while the first German text of the story—leaving aside countless other versions, right up to Ariosto's epic poem *Orlando furioso* of 1516—was written at the court of Duke Henry the Lion at the behest of his wife, Matilda, daughter of King

Henry II of England and a member of the Angevin (Plantagenet) dynasty, whom he married in 1168.[111]

The "Chanson de Roland" is useless as a testimony of real events, but as a classic example of the imaginative and vivifying power of cultural memory, it is invaluable. Eggihard and Anshelm disappeared from the legend, and only Roland remained, being made into a nephew of the emperor, who was now shown, as a crusader figure, becoming involved himself in the battle in order to avenge his slaughtered companions. The legend could be regarded as a gross misrepresentation of a thirty-year period of history that actually culminated in the Christian conquest of Barcelona. But in the context of Charlemagne's canonization in 1165, this epic lay about a heathen-slayer and his paladins had a powerful influence on real historical events.

It did not take long for the Frankish Empire to get over Charlemagne's defeat; reform measures affecting the Church and the monarchy,[112] alongside strenuous ongoing efforts to integrate the Saxons into Charlemagne's realm, would soon eclipse this event. But Italy and Rome also demanded his presence at this time. Since his first visit there, Charlemagne had never lost sight of the Eternal City. He returned to Italy on three subsequent occasions, in 776, 780/781, and 787, before a decisive change came about. For the pope, conditions had improved markedly in the interim, not least as a result of the repeated intervention of the Carolingians and the eradication of the Lombard kingdom.

Nevertheless, in 775 Pope Hadrian I became gravely concerned about conspiracies being hatched against him and Charlemagne by Dukes Hilbrand of Spoleto, Arichis of Benevento, and Rodcausus of Friuli. These adversaries were reputed to have made a pact with the Byzantine Greeks to bring back Desiderius's exiled son Adelchis from Constantinople and install him on the throne.[113] It appeared, then, that Charlemagne's rule in Italy was not nearly as secure as the (uniformly later) Frankish sources maintained. Consequently, the king hurried across the Alps and crushed the insurrection in Friuli but then returned north without proceeding on to Rome, since he had in the meantime received news of a new wave of unrest in Saxony that required his presence there. Rome could wait, and Pope Hadrian would have to take control of his own fate.

Indeed, during this period the papacy did begin to exercise its own authority, taking no account any longer of the Eastern emperor in Constantinople. This new confidence manifested itself in attacks on the ships of Greek slave traders lying at anchor in the port of Civitavecchia[114] and was reflected in the fact that the pope began to mint his own coinage, in silver rather than gold, which was regarded as the exclusive preserve of emperors. In 778, Hadrian took the bold step of launching an assault on the south. In the first verifiable military campaign by a pope, papal troops overran the town of Terracina in the Duchy of Naples.[115] Yet rather than bringing any relief, this only served to heighten the danger for Rome, since Naples responded by forming an alliance with the Byzantines and Benevento against Rome.

Moreover, in central and northern Italy, no one actually acted in accordance with the Donation of Pepin and handed over to the papacy what had been promised, not even the Frankish royal messengers who resided there. This was the subject of frequent and bitter recriminations by Hadrian. He admonished Charlemagne, who was engaged on his Spanish adventure at the time, with the example of the devout Constantine the Great, who had provided St. Sylvester with rich patrimonies in Italy: in Tuscia, Spoleto, Benevento, Corsica, and Sabina.[116] Decades later, somewhere around 830–834, this letter of Pope Hadrian served as the catalyst for a Frankish counterfeiter to come up with the notorious "Constantinian Donation," which admittedly related to the ecclesiastical order rather than to seigneurial rights.[117]

It was not until four years after his last Italian campaign that Charlemagne set off to the south once more, in order, so it was claimed, that he might pray in Rome.[118] He celebrated Christmas of 780 in Pavia and spent Easter in the City of the Apostles. On Holy Saturday, he had his four-year-old son, Carloman, baptized with the name Pepin by Hadrian, and two days later Carloman and his brother Louis were anointed and crowned as kings— the former as king of the Lombards and the latter as king of Aquitaine. The change of name for his elder son may seem puzzling until we realize that names at this time carried great symbolic value. In any case, in Italy, all the name Carloman put people in mind of was a monk first and foremost, then a king, who had died in opposition to the Apostolic See. Yet while Carloman's name was discredited in Italy and Rome, Pepin recalled the victor over the Lombards, a loyal ally of St. Peter, and the protector of the Roman Church. Their newly acquired status as kings may well have been the catalyst for changing the name of the elder of the two boys.

It was around the time of Pepin's baptism that a masterpiece of Frankish book illumination was created—the renowned Godescalc Gospels, which was jointly commissioned by Charlemagne and Queen Hildegard just before their departure for Italy and was lavishly decorated with gold and silver; the volume takes its name from its principal illuminator. Aside from its splendor, the Godescalc Gospels is also an early example of the adoption

FIGURE 16 This ninth-century manuscript showing a baptism is thought to come from Wessobrunn Abbey. Munich, Bavarian State Library.

and development of foreign influences that may have come from a variety of sources—antiquity or late antiquity, Italy, Anglo-Saxon models, or Byzantium—and drew their inspiration from other book decoration or frescoes (Plates II and III).[119] "In this year [781]. King Charlemagne was in St. Peter's [in Rome], where his son Pepin was baptized," runs a marginal note to the Easter table at the end of the manuscript. This was the auspicious prelude to a school of book illumination that modern art historians ascribe directly to Charlemagne's court scriptorium. On the return journey to Francia, the archbishop of Milan baptized Charlemagne's newborn daughter Gisela.[120] Once again, Charlemagne's heavily pregnant wife had to endure the arduous journey across the Alps—either on horseback or carried in a litter.

The subsidiary or joint kingship arrangement Charlemagne set in motion with the coronation of his sons was designed to safeguard power. The coronation of a king was an unfamiliar event for the Franks, but the Lombard kings wore crowns, and even the prince of Benevento, Arichis II, employed this symbol of authority to emphasize his status. The young Pepin could not take a back seat in this matter; likewise, his young brother Louis also took part in the new ceremony. The presence of a king, even if he was only a child, symbolically promoted the unification and consolidation of the country and would also serve as a visual reminder of Carolingian authority in the lands they had conquered. Italy now once again had a center and presently a royal household in Verona, with its own court chapel—most probably established by Angilbert, the lay abbot of Centula and one of the king's closest confidants—and a royal assizes too.[121] In Italy, many Franks now took control of newly created earldoms, where there had been none previously. Experienced magnates were brought in to lead Pepin's regency: acting alongside, or possibly after, Angilbert in this role, there was Adalhard of Corbie, an uncle of Pepin on his father's side and his closest male relative, as well as others, such as Abbot Waldo of Reichenau. Appointed bishop of Pavia by Charlemagne in 791, Waldo was the figure whom, after his death in 814 and on account of his meteoric rise to prominence, Walahfrid Strabo depicts as undertaking a long spell of penance on the slopes of Purgatory Mountain (in his *Visio Wettini*). Waldo undertakes his act of atonement for his "inconsiderate deeds" on behalf of his dying fellow Benedictine monk Wetti, who had been a teacher at Reichenau when Waldo was abbot there (786–806).[122] These machinations meant that Charlemagne was now a king who ruled over other kings, like an emperor.

In Rome, meanwhile, feathers were ruffled by such special favors being shown to the Carolingian monarch. Contrary to what the pope might have hoped for, Charlemagne did not march south to take on the Byzantines but instead concluded a pact with the Eastern Roman Empire, where the emperor Leon IV had just died and the regency had been assumed by his widow, Empress Irene, for their ten-year-old son, Constantine VI. With a mixture of military force and diplomacy, Irene attempted to consolidate her position against a succession of changing but always dangerous opposition forces. Charlemagne committed himself to this alliance.[123]

The *Liber pontificalis*, which even as recently as 774 had given an extremely detailed and exuberant account of the confirmation of the Donation of Pepin, was henceforth silent on this matter. Despite the fact that Pope Hadrian had urged the Frankish king to fulfill the promise made at Ponthion and reconfirmed in Quierzy and Rome, all Charlemagne was prepared to do now, in 781, was to assign to the pope various patrimonies in Sabina, along with some estates in the Duchy of Spoleto and Tuscany. In return, Hadrian seems to have relinquished all claims to the transfer of at least Spoleto and Tuscia to his control, a concession for which he was required to provide documentary evidence.[124] Henceforth, he did not, as before, keep reminding the king of that promise. Although this remarkable papal letter has been lost over time, the collective cultural memory continued to recall the Donation of Pepin for centuries to come and kept invoking and breathing new life into it, in spite of the lack of documentary proof.

No account of Hadrian's papacy from 774 onward was committed to paper. All that is recorded in the *Liber pontificalis* is the internal achievements of the Roman Church or the city of Rome, for example, a mention of a church being renovated, the dedication of candles or altar decorations at this or that monastery, and the like. There could be no more eloquent testimony to the profound shift that Charlemagne's appearance in Rome brought about. No statement, however brief, about Rome's close relationship with the Frankish king; no indications of the loosening ties between the bishop of Rome and the *basileus* in Constantinople, which Hadrian was just then in the process of effecting; indeed, absolutely nothing about the prevailing political environment was now forthcoming. Charlemagne's visit to the city had struck Rome dumb; only under Hadrian's successor, Leo II, did it briefly regain its voice. Hadrian, who had wanted to dispel the danger posed by the Lombards and to avoid falling beneath the sway of Constantinople, now found himself having to bend his knee to the Frankish king.

Five years later, in 786, the time seemed ripe for the Frankish king to embark on a new expedition to Italy. Charlemagne, who had just finished suppressing an uprising led by the Thuringian nobleman Count Hardrat[125] and had returned from a successful campaign against the Bretons, was already spending Christmas in Florence and without more ado proceeded immediately onward to Rome. The *Royal Frankish Annals* did not reveal the reason for his journey. Instead, in stereotypical fashion it noted his purpose as being "to pray on the threshold of the apostles" and "to put his Italian affairs in order and to negotiate with the envoys of the *basileus*." Only the revision of the *Annals* from the reign of Louis the Pious made things clearer; there, it is said that Charlemagne believed that he might be able to overthrow Benevento and in so doing annex the last independent Lombard principality to his realm.[126]

Around 786–787, the princely court at Benevento was basking in the glow of a brilliant intellectual and artistic culture.[127] Eastern and Western influences met here and were expressed in the lavish household maintained by the prince, the magnificent Byzantine-influenced ceremonial it practiced, and the coinage it issued (which also owed much to Constantinople). The duchy profited not just from its close relations to the Byzantine Empire but also from its connections to the increasingly important monasteries at Monte Cassino and San Vicenzo al Volturno. As a result, its princes were in a position to defy Charlemagne.[128] As had earlier been the case in Pavia, Benevento also had a court scriptorium. Via the account given of it in the works of Paul the Deacon, Charlemagne might have used it as a model for his own court. Painting and book illumination were flourishing at the time, a fact still evidenced today by the remains of frescoes and monuments from this period. A minuscule script peculiar to the area, which used unconventional letters—the so-called Beneventan script—was developed there and remained in use for hundreds of years.[129] The vibrant culture of Benevento supplied models and stimuli to the Frankish Empire in general and Charlemagne's court in particular.[130] Paul the Deacon may be regarded as one of its principal exponents.

The court chapel of Duke Arichis II—constructed "for the redemption of our soul and the good of our people and country" and soon enlarged with the addition of a convent—was, like the court chapel of Justinian in Constantinople, consecrated in the name of St. Sophia, the "true wisdom of God," and so even in its dedication paid homage to its Greek model. Moreover, its ground plan, with two concentric passageways around a main central building, quite deliberately recalled the architectural concept behind the Hagia Sophia. Classical pillars and capitals supported the hexagon-shaped cupola. Charlemagne may have learned about this building and its attached convent through the work of Paul the Deacon; accordingly, any other layout for his own church foundation in Aix, which he set in motion immediately after his return from Italy, was out of the question. How else could he hope to keep up with the *basileus's* and the prince's manifestations of their prestige? And just as St. Sophia in Benevento was assigned a convent, so the Frankish king—possibly not Charlemagne but Louis the Pious—added an Augustinian monastery to the palatine church in Aix, dedicated to Our Savior and the Mother of God.

Arichis II, who reigned as the duke of Benevento from 758 on and who since the demise of the Lombard kingdom in Pavia had taken to styling himself "prince" (*princeps*), thereby emphasizing that he saw his realm as a continuation of Lombard sovereignty, soon managed, partly through alliances and partly through breaching agreements, to assert his independence from the Byzantine Greeks, the Lombard kingdom, and the Carolingian ruler. His son and heir Grimoald continued to consolidate the principality of Benevento on these bases and to lay the foundations of this polity for centuries to come.

In Rome, Charlemagne and the pope now hatched a plan to wage war against Benevento. Hadrian hoped to regain certain papal patrimonies. However, Arichis preempted the conflict by sending gifts to Rome and, as a way of fending off a Frankish assault on his principality, offered his son Grimoald as a hostage. According to the *Royal Frankish Annals,* the pope mistrusted this peace overture by the duke and in concert with the Frankish magnates urged Charlemagne to launch his invasion. Even so, for the time being, his army advanced only as far as Capua.

As Charlemagne's force approached his realm, Arichis took evasive action by withdrawing to Salerno. He "did not dare to meet Charlemagne face-to-face" but sent his two sons, Grimoald and Romuald, to negotiate with the king. "So that the country might avoid devastation and that its dioceses and monasteries might not be laid waste," an agreement was concluded to the effect that the duke would offer up twelve hostages, adding as a thirteenth his younger son, Grimoald, and that Arichis himself and his heir apparent, Romuald, and the people of Benevento should swear to abide by the treaty. Charlemagne had to content himself with this outcome, although he had achieved little by it. It was only with great difficulty that he managed to emerge from the process with his prestige undiminished.

At least, on his advance toward Benevento, he had visited Monte Cassino,[131] where he commissioned a copy of the *Rule of Benedict,* the original of which had supposedly been written by the saint himself, and had been given a collection of model sermons by his old acquaintance Paul the

Deacon. In Monte Cassino, it was said that in the mid-eighth century Pope Zachary had donated the *Benedictine Rule,* along with various other artifacts belonging to the saint, to the recently founded monastery.[132] So it was that, in a monastery that was generally poorly endowed with relics of St. Benedict, the *Rule* was seen as an important relic of the founder of the Western monastic tradition. Thus, in a special way, a transcript of this codex had also to be regarded as authentic. In gratitude, as he passed through Rome on his return journey, Charlemagne granted the monastery the privilege of immunity with the right to freely elect its own abbot.[133] Yet however precious the text of the *Benedictine Rule* and the collection of homilies may have been, the political outcome of this expensive enterprise was meager. Charlemagne withdrew north without having incorporated the Lombard south into his empire or even having gained some form of suzerainty over it. He did, though, enter Rome once more, where he was able to celebrate Easter with Pope Hadrian for the third time. Paul the Deacon, however, who had returned once more to his monastery by this time, was involved in writing the so-called *Epistola generalis,* one of the texts commonly regarded as being among the early works that epitomize Charlemagne's revival of learning.[134]

But new trouble was brewing in the south of Italy.[135] In violation of the agreement reached with Charlemagne, Arichis of Benevento made contact with the Byzantine Greeks and declared himself willing, in return for being granted control of the Duchy of Naples (still in Byzantine hands at the time) and the status of *patricius,* to mandate his own principality to Byzantium. The retreating Franks posed no danger to him, nor did the distant Eastern emperor on the Bosphorus. However, Arichis died on 26 August 787, before Byzantium's agreement to this arrangement reached him; his son Romuald had predeceased him. Paul the Deacon sent Arichis's widow, Adelperga, a former pupil of his, a laudatory and moving poem in condolence for her loss,[136] which spoke of a "great prince," a "most illustrious hero," and lamented, "Most excellent Arichis, what a credit to your age, what sorrow at your passing!"

Hadrian was deeply concerned by these developments. The rumored event that had caused repeated alarm in the past, namely, that Desiderius's son Adelchis might return to Italy with the Greeks to lay claim to his father's legacy, had now become a reality. In these circumstances, Adelperga negotiated with Charlemagne about the release of her son and present heir apparent to the throne of Benevento, Grimoald. During his brief spell in captivity, he had succeeded in winning the trust of the Frankish king.

Charlemagne duly released him, in defiance of the pope's warnings. At first, Grimoald kept faith with the Franks, perhaps because the Byzantine Greeks refused to cede Naples to him and took up arms against them. In alliance with Duke Hildebrand of Spoleto and a small Frankish force, he emerged victorious. Adelchis was forced to return to Constantinople, where he lived the rest of his days "in retirement."[137] He never again attempted an incursion into Italy. Grimoald, though, was now able to assert Benevento's independence between the great powers and even to further consolidate it, even though (or perhaps precisely because) he once more effected a rapprochement with the Greeks a few years later, around 791. This resulted in a succession of attacks against Benevento over the following years by King Pepin of the Lombards.

Increasing Rivalry with Byzantium

In the meantime, Charlemagne's relations with the Eastern Roman Empire had grown decisively worse. The Frankish advance toward southern Italy threatened the Byzantine sphere of influence. Like Sicily, Calabria and Apulia were "Rhomaic" territories; these latter two regions bordered on Benevento, whose affiliation with the Lombard kingdom was more nominal than real; furthermore, this link had been further loosened when Benevento was subsumed under the Frankish sphere of authority. Similarly, the Duchy of Naples also belonged to the realm of the Rhomaioi; at least, the Byzantines laid claim to it, although its last two bishops, who had inclined toward the cult of images, had opted for consecration in Rome. The younger of them, Stephen, had risen through the ranks of the Holy See as a duke and consul and thus appeared, like the bishop of Rome, to have set foot on the path to a kind of spiritual princedom.

Even the very first envoys sent to Byzantium by Pepin the Short must have returned with contrasting impressions. The language and the courtly ceremony and ritual must have struck them as very alien. Byzantine diplomacy in general remained a mystery to the Franks, and the longer they were exposed to it, the more clearly it struck them as devious mendacity. They accused the "Greeks" of arrogance and the most malevolent machinations; this was compounded by the well-known differences regarding their faith, above all with regard to the question of images. The pope also complained about having been dispossessed of extensive landed estates (*latifundia*) in Sicily and southern Italy by the *basileus*. All this fomented deep mistrust. Yet Byzantium was regarded as the foremost Christian power, bar none, in the

Mediterranean, and so its recognition of the Carolingian kingship must have been considered a major success in the West.

News of the death of Emperor Constantine V in September 775 reached Charlemagne in the spring of 776 via Rome.[138] The Frankish king evidently had no informants of his own in Constantinople. The succession in the Eastern Roman Empire was played out against the backdrop of political upheaval, but Constantine's son and successor, Leon IV, remained a firm opponent of the cult of images. The turmoil was repeated when Leon died just five years later. Only under his successors did the prevailing mood of iconoclasm in Constantinople yield to a renewed veneration of images. The Byzantine Empire, or certainly Constantinople, swung from one extreme to the other. The Franks were out of sympathy with both. They valued images as educational tools but did not venerate them.

Leon's widow, Irene, vied for power as the coregent with her ten-year-old son, Constantine. Insurrections accompanied the start of his reign and jeopardized the authority of the boy emperor and his mother, especially when the governor of Sicily, Elpidios, rose up and proclaimed himself emperor. Empress Irene sought Charlemagne's help and offered the Frankish ruler an alliance, which would be sealed by a marriage agreement. The chronicler Theophanes reported this development for the year AM 6274 (781/782 CE). The young Constantine would wed Charlemagne's "redheaded" daughter Rotrude (Erythro). In the event, Irene withstood the crisis; Elpidios fled to Africa, where he continued to style himself as the *basileus*.[139] But ultimately, rather than act a regent, Irene reigned as an independent empress in Constantinople—the first such occurrence in the Byzantine Empire. For five years, from 797 to 802, she basked in absolute power there until a revolt toppled her; she died shortly thereafter. Her golden solidi coins bore the legend *Eirini Basilisse* (Empress Irene), while on the contemporaneous *Pala d'Oro,* the lavishly gilded and enameled high altar retable in St. Mark's Cathedral in Venice, she is even accorded the title *eusebestate auguste* (most pious empress).

The engagement of the two royal children was agreed in 781, a fact noted briefly in the *Lorsch Annals*.[140] A Greek teacher for the bride-to-be was installed at Charlemagne's court; Paul the Deacon may also have given Rotrude language lessons. It seemed, then, that Charlemagne really did pursue this marriage plan; he may well have calculated that it would ensure Byzantium's recognition of his authority in Italy. Yet for the pope, the Greek-Frankish alliance posed more of a threat.

But then, in Capua in 787, a new delegation of Greek envoys appeared before Charlemagne; according to the entry for the year 786 in the revised *Royal Frankish Annals* some years later, our sole Western source, they begged him to allow Rotrude to become the wife of the *basileus*.[141] Admittedly, the account given by this annalist, which should be read in conjunction with another note from the following year, is somewhat cryptic, but it does give the distinct impression that at this juncture, the king withheld his assent to the long-agreed union, whereupon the jilted bridegroom, Constantine VI, reacted with fury by sending troops to invade Italy the following year.

The reasons for this obfuscation on the part of the annalist are unclear. Did this unknown author manipulate his report at the king's behest? Or was the actual course of events no longer known by the time the annalist took up his pen just a few years later,[142] forcing him to draw his own conclusions? In any event, the texts from the Carolingian period—the *Royal Frankish Annals* and the *Metz Annals*—passed over the whole episode of the Frankish-Greek betrothal without comment. Half-consciously and half-unconsciously, they manipulated the earlier event and created an official version of how the past was to be remembered.

The Greek chronicler Theophanes, meanwhile, made the plausible claim in his entry for the year AM 6281 (788/789) that the basilissa was the one who, much to the annoyance of her son, dissolved the agreement with Charlemagne and selected another bride for Constantine, the Armenian princess Maria of Amnia; it emerges from the context that she was under threat from a new phase of attacks by Arab forces at the time. Later Western annals also date the breaking of the alliance to 788 but appear to ascribe it to Charlemagne;[143] in light of this, our original annalist may not just have been covering up a foreign policy failure by Charlemagne but also hiding the fact that Frankish pride was wounded by Irene and Constantine's rejection of the bride, a daughter of their king—a rebuff that justified a new round of hostilities against the Greeks. The faculty of memory, including cultural memory, selects and manipulates the event that is being recalled by actualizing these recollections. By the time the younger imperial annalist sharpened his quill to record past events, then, a state of high tension existed once more between the two Christian empires.

Indeed, the history of the Monastery of St. Wandrille—an institution far removed from political events of the period—reveals that Charlemagne dispatched one of his palace clergy, the chaplain Witbold, to Constantinople to negotiate the marriage in 786–787, so it is evident that he was still expecting it to take place. The envoy returned fully eighteen months after he had set out, a remarkable testament to the duration of the journey to Constantinople and the protracted nature of the discussions.[144] Charlemagne rewarded Witbold with an abbey; he was clearly pleased with his efforts. Irene's refusal the following year must have come as a bitter blow. The king, who was himself well practiced in refusing the hand of kings' daughters, would doubtless have found it hard to get over the humiliation of his own personage, his people, and his daughter, the rejected bride. Nor could he take revenge for this slight. Never again would he offer one of his daughters for a marriage; he preferred—as with King Offa of Mercia[145]—to take the risk that friendly relations would be broken off. Instead, he gave his daughters—these "crowned doves," as Alcuin later called them—free rein and did not, as one might have expected, immure them in a convent, although he did deny them the chance to enter into legally valid marriages. He kept them by his side at court, where they could flirt with men, even seduce them, and give free expression to their feelings and desires.

The king shied away from a military showdown with the Byzantine Greeks, as they did with him. No expansion of his empire toward Byzantium ever proved lasting, nor, in all likelihood, was this his ultimate aim. Even so, the broken engagement put a total stop to this brief phase of harmony between the two empires, and Charlemagne was not invited to the Second Council of Nicaea, the seventh ecumenical council of the Church, which primarily grappled with the question of the cult of images. Peace was once again in danger. It was 797 before a tentative rapprochement came about. But the deep mistrust of Greek arrogance remained.

Conflict Grows with Bavaria and Pannonia

Charlemagne's expedition to southern Italy must be regarded as more of a misfire than a success. It was accompanied by ill omens: mysterious crosses appeared on people's clothes; blood seeped out of the ground and fell from the skies; fear spread among the people; and the Grim Reaper's yield increased, with Archbishop Lull of Mainz among the dead. Charlemagne, though, continued to advance on Rome.[146] The king himself must have recognized his failure in the south, for quite unexpectedly and clearly in an attempt to manipulate the historical record, the author of the original *Royal Frankish Annals* abruptly changes the subject.

The chronicler goes on to give the following account: No sooner had Charlemagne arrived in Rome than Bishop Arn of Salzburg and Abbot Hunrich of Mondsee—envoys from Duke Tassilo of Bavaria—appeared, before the Easter celebration was even over, and implored the pope to broker peace between their master and Charlemagne. The Frankish king's response was that this was indeed his most ardent wish, but the envoys did not want to decide anything without first consulting the duke. Hadrian, the annalist reports, saw the Bavarian offer as nothing more than a tissue of lies and reacted by immediately excommunicating the duke and his confederates while at the same time reminding them of the loyalty they had once pledged to King Pepin the Short, and he went on to fully absolve Charlemagne and his army in advance, when they invaded Bavaria, "of the danger of committing any sin, be it through burning, murder, or any other wrongdoing" (*Royal Frankish Annals*). This looked very much as though the pope was giving Charlemagne carte blanche to wage war. Once again, as on the occasion of Pepin's ascent to the throne, papal authority was striving to legitimize questionable, even subversive, actions on the part of a Carolingian monarch.

In all likelihood, this account is not an accurate reflection of what actually happened. Rather, the annalist was almost certainly obeying the king's wishes in following a retrospective reinterpretation of events that was directed against Tassilo. We will never know what was really negotiated in Rome between Charlemagne and his loyal servant Arn of Salzburg. Yet no sooner had the Easter celebration come to an end than Charlemagne assembled his forces for the long march back to Francia. His return journey to Worms took him via Ravenna, a place he now visited for the first time, and Pavia.

A curious tale concerning Charlemagne's visit was current for a long time in Ravenna. The city's bishop, Gratiosus, is said to have invited the king to a banquet but to have been warned by his entourage, given his lack of sophistication, not to be too quick to address the king. He promised to heed their advice: "No, my sons, no, rest assured I shall hold my tongue." At dinner, however, he turned to Charlemagne and said, "*Pappa, pappa,* my lord King." Amazed, Charlemagne asked, "What is this word *pappa, pappa,* which the holy man is saying?" Some of the other priests reassured the king: "Please don't concern yourself, my lord King. This man your servant is a simple soul. He is acting like a concerned mother, who soothes her sons and persuades them to eat something; likewise, he is asking your clemency that you might eat and be merry." Whereupon Charlemagne commanded all present to be silent and announced (quoting the Gospel of St. John, 1:47):

FIGURE 17 The Tassilo Chalice, a gift from Duke Tassilo III of Bavaria and his wife, Liutperga, to Kremsmünster Abbey in Austria ca. 770, is still kept at the abbey. The inscription around its foot reads TASSILO DUX FORTIS + LIUTPIRC VIRGA REGALIS (Brave Duke Tassilo + Liutperga royal scion).

"Behold the true Israelite indeed, in whom there is no deceit." "After this, the bishop obtained whatever he asked of him."[147]

Perhaps the converse was also true, for Charlemagne's sojourn in Ravenna, however brief, was not without its consequences. The king took home powerful impressions; as the archbishop's guest, he would no doubt have visited the great churches there—the cathedral, Sant'Apollinare Nuovo, and above all the marvel that was the Basilica of San Vitale. He must surely have been overwhelmed at the sight of them. In San Vitale, this ruler from the north found the model for the way he wanted his palace church in Aix to appear. Like San Vitale, it would be organized around a main central building with an apse, two rows of columns one on top of the other, and sumptuous mosaic work. Without more ado, Charlemagne asked Hadrian's permission to transport marble blocks and finished columns—precious ancient artifacts, some made of imperial red and green porphyry—from Ravenna, and possibly also from Rome, to the Frankish Empire. Hadrian agreed to this. Demolition work must have begun immediately—perhaps in the ruins of the old emperor's and exarch's palace—with the massively heavy pillars being loaded onto oxcarts, and perhaps even barges, to begin their arduous journey to Aix either across the Alps or along the coasts.

In Ravenna, the old residence of the emperor and former seat of the exarch, the only contemporary inscription mentioning Charlemagne—the "king of the Franks and Lombards and patricius of the Romans" (*[Ca]roli regi francorum et langobardorum ac patricio Ro[manorum]*)—has survived to the present day (on the edge of a circular stone tablet now in the city's Museo Archivescovile). This must be connected somehow with Charlemagne's stay in the city in 787 because his next appearance there, in 801, occurred only after he had already been crowned emperor. Was the city's conqueror perhaps trying to make amends for the impending demolition and plundering of ancient buildings by founding new institutions and ordering the construction of new buildings by Frankish master builders?[148]

Charlemagne was reunited with his wife, Fastrada, in Worms; the *Royal Frankish Annals* noted this "private" encounter: "Both were overjoyed to see each other again and praised God for his mercy." This unusual entry, sandwiched between a justification of the attack on Tassilo and a description of the military advance on Bavaria that same year, poses some riddles. It may simply hint at the fact that, during the king's absence, Fastrada assumed certain sovereign rights. But this striking, indeed, uniquely informal insertion into the history of Tassilo's demise may signify something more—it could be that the spouses' joy at their reunion and their praise of God was for a very tangible reason, namely, that Fastrada had become pregnant[149] and was hoping for a son, for whom—since the king had already divided his realm up among Hildegard's sons—another kingdom would have to be conquered. Bavaria? In any event, the king lost no time in marching against Tassilo;[150] later, Fastrada—who was no doubt still hoping for a son of her own (she bore the king two daughters)—would become involved in court intriguing and in her "wickedness" would drive Charlemagne's eldest son, Pepin "the Hunchback," to rebellion and damnation.[151]

The first adversary to be neutralized was Charlemagne's cousin Tassilo III, the son of his father's sister.[152] According to the *Royal Frankish Annals,* Charlemagne's father, King Pepin, supposedly secured his nephew, who was then still a boy, the succession to his father, Duke Odilo, by supporting him against his (i.e., Pepin's) own half brother Grifo, the son of the Agilolfing princess Swanahild, when he attempted to seize the ducal throne of Bavaria. This may indeed have been the case, despite the fact that the reports in the *Annals,* which propagandized against Tassilo, must in general be evaluated as a retrospective construct designed to defame this "ungrateful" vassal. In 756, Tassilo and Pepin had joined forces against the Lombard king Aistulf and had marched on Italy together. The Agilolfing duke reigned unchallenged in his domain, entered into alliances with foreign powers, and led the Bavarian Church through synods that he personally convened and chaired. The Bavarian duke wielded an authority that was almost royal.[153] Yet Charlemagne overran this realm virtually without a striking a blow; his principal weapon, rather, was subterfuge. It was a prize well worth the effort; Bavaria was richly blessed with wine, iron, gold, and silver and even with bees and honey (and hence with the very precious commodity of beeswax) and was replete with "men of great stature and strength," as the contemporary *Life of St. Emmeram* by Arbeo of Freising (750) put it.[154]

Bavaria's destiny, along with its dioceses and monasteries, was energetically directed first by the infant Tassilo and his mother Hiltrud, acting as his regent, and later, from around 754–757 on, by Tassilo alone, who was a good ten years older than Charlemagne.[155] The duke promoted the mission to the Slavs in his realm, won a celebrated victory over the heathen Carantanians (or Alpine Slavs) in 772, and founded the monasteries of Weltenburg on the river Danube, Mattsee, Innichen, Kremsmünster, Frauenchiemsee, and perhaps several more besides, as well as taking control of aristocratic foundations such as Metten.[156] Measures agreed at the Synod of Dingolfing, which Tassilo convened in 776–777, and at which all the bishops of Bavaria were present, included an injunction mandating Sunday observance and resolutions on marriage law and the law of inheritance; in addition, an agreement was reached that bishops and monasteries should come together for prayers.[157] Some years before this, the Synod of Neuching had ordered that priests be permitted to lecture and run schools and that they should be able to understand the Holy Scriptures and sing the canonical hours, the psalms, and other liturgical prayers; these measures corresponded closely to the reform efforts of his cousin Charlemagne in the Frankish Empire, which were instituted soon after. Soon, Bavarian churches would be filled with song, delighting the faithful. Steps were also taken to ease tensions, such as those that existed between the bishops and the monasteries.[158]

The Synod of Neuching provided for the founding of a school in every Bavarian bishop's see—in Neuburg, Säben, Salzburg, Passau, Regensburg, and Freising.[159] Latin was taught in these institutions, as in the following primer entry for the adjective *stultus* (stupid), for example: "Stultus: Stulti sunt Romani, sapienti sunt Paioari / Tole sint Uualhâ, spâhe sint peigira" (The Romans are stupid, the Bavarians are clever).[160] At that time, there was probably a considerable group of "Latins"—as indeed there are still today in a few Alpine valleys in the South Tyrol—living in isolated pockets of settlement in the country. Missionary activity was further encouraged and continued its triumphant onward march, a process that began when St. Boniface instituted the first reforms in the country during the reign of Odilo, Tassilo's father. So, the founding of monasteries, spreading as it now did into remote Alpine valleys, served not only to open up more areas of the country but at the same time to promulgate and consolidate the Christian faith, the education that was required for this, and the institutions associated with both entities.

Tassilo tried to form an alliance with the Lombards and their king, Desiderius, whose daughter Liutberga he married in 763; he also entered into negotiations with the Avars, his unbaptized neighbors to the east. Last but not least, he maintained good relations with Rome. In 772, the same year he triumphed over the Carantanians, Tassilo's eldest son, Theodo, was baptized by Pope Hadrian I. This ruler appeared to be more than just a duke of the kind that the Frankish kings had once installed. Tassilo reigned over his land as a *princeps*. Certainly, the synods hailed him as such: "We thank God for raising you up as our prince at this time."[161]

Was it perhaps the splendor of this principality, as well as its urge to gain independence, that turned Charlemagne against Tassilo? Had the duke overestimated his power? And did Queen Fastrada plot against him? Whatever the case, Tassilo stumbled blindly into catastrophe. Lack of evidence means that we cannot know what the lead-up was to the conflict between the two cousins and what caused it to escalate. When Charlemagne had invaded Spain, a Bavarian contingent had accompanied him (*Royal Frankish Annals*). Yet just three years later, we are told that Charlemagne, through Pope Hadrian, reminded the duke of his oath of loyalty to the Frankish king, and that Tassilo had come to Worms in order to renew the oath that he had once sworn in favor of Pepin, Charlemagne, and the Franks in general; in addition, to guarantee the pledge, twelve Bavarian hostages had been handed over by Bishop Simpert of Augsburg. Apparently, though, Tassilo did not keep his pledge for long (*Royal Frankish Annals*). The collapse of Agilolfing power, at first gradual and then rapid, suggests that there was little solidarity between the region's nobility and their duke. For example, Arn of Salzburg, who began his career under Tassilo, soon enjoyed the confidence of the Carolingian king.

However, the elimination of the Agilolfing ruler by Charlemagne was not simply intended to secure Bavaria for the Frankish realm. The campaign was engineered at the same time as a Lombard uprising threatened Charlemagne's authority in Italy. At that time, many Lombard hostages were deported to Francia.[162] But Tassilo's sons Theodo and Theodbert, legitimate grandsons of the deposed Lombard king Desiderius, came into consideration as principal aspirants to the throne in Pavia after Tassilo's defeat.

The campaign against Tassilo from 787 onward was therefore also designed to secure Carolingian authority south of the Alps. At that time, it would seem, Pope Hadrian withdrew his support for the duke, presumably under pressure from Charlemagne.[163] But Tassilo was now obliged to pay homage to the king—who had just returned from Benevento and now, at the head of an army consisting of three columns of troops, had pushed forward toward Bavaria, as far as the Lech River—and to hand over his land and swear fealty.[164] Moreover, the widow of Prince Arichis of Benevento, Liutprand's daughter Adelperga, seems to have feared that Charlemagne might seize her two daughters, while, as Einhard reported, her son Grimoald was forcibly detained as a hostage at the court of the Frankish king until Charlemagne was sure of his good conduct.[165]

The Agilolfing duke did not just have to pay homage, either; the following year he was either summoned or lured to a synod at Ingelheim, where renegade, pro-Frankish Bavarians accused him of breaking his oath and of forming an alliance with the Avars. He is reported to have announced defiantly: "If I had ten sons, I would let them all perish before I observed the terms of those treaties and honored my pledge"; he would rather die, he maintained, than live as a vassal (*Royal Frankish Annals*). In the end, he was put on trial in Ingelheim on the capital charge of desertion (*harisliz*). This crime must have been committed, if indeed it ever occurred at all, many years earlier, during Pepin's campaigns against Aquitaine in 763. His supposed offense, which had never been mentioned before, was now, a quarter of a century after the war in question, being cited as a result of the "recollections" of "Franks and Bavarians, Lombards and Saxons alike, along with anyone else who had come to the synod from other provinces" (*Royal Frankish Annals*). There was not a shred of credibility to all this; a malicious show trial robbed the Agilolfing duke of his former status, his freedom, and his power. And anyhow, it remains a complete mystery how any Lombards or Saxons could possibly have had any recollection of the alleged crime.

And so—here, as always, we are reliant on the account given in the *Royal Frankish Annals*—the magnates of all the peoples assembled in Ingelheim unanimously condemned Tassilo to death. Only his royal cousin, in a gesture of magnanimity and in response to a personal plea by the duke, commuted his sentence to committal to a monastery. Accordingly, "to save his soul," Duke Tassilo was tonsured and entered the monastery at St. Goar, while his son Theodo was sent to St. Maximin in Trier. Duchess Liutperga and her daughters were forced to take the veil; one was sent to Chelles Abbey to live under the supervision of Charlemagne's sister Gisela, while the other went to the convent in Laon.[166]

The depiction of events in the *Royal Frankish Annals* represents a distorted record of results, which Charlemagne wanted widely publicized. Rather than recording real events, it set in place a particular construction of them that would serve as a chastening reminder to other Franks, Bavarians, Lombards, Saxons, and all other peoples. Manipulated by the king's will, the *Annals* fabricated a recollection that was thoroughly sanitized and airbrushed, designed to gloss over and legitimize the violent elimination of a Christian ruler by the victorious Carolingian. The whole period of history it treated was retrospectively distorted and misrepresented—a clear indication of how scandalous Charlemagne's contemporaries around 790 found the actions he had undertaken against his own cousin.[167]

Only certain isolated references in earlier, hidden testimonies, independent of the *Royal Frankish Annals*—in particular the annals of Murbach monastery in Alsace, plus a handful of letters—reveal the whole devious course of action undertaken by the king.[168] These show that Charlemagne somehow enticed Tassilo's wife and children to come to Ingelheim or had them taken there forcibly, and that he also managed to seize the duke's treasure. When Tassilo duly arrived in Ingelheim of his own volition (admittedly, his eldest son, Theodo, had been in Charlemagne's hands as a hostage since the previous year), he was stripped of his weapons and brought before the king, who proceeded to publicly berate his cousin for persecuting him and for attempting to hatch plots with foreign peoples against his king. The sources report that Tassilo was unable to deny these charges and that he was ultimately tonsured and forced to become a monk "against his will." So as not to dishonor the royal court with such a humiliating procedure, this last act was, it was reported, carried out at the neighboring monastery of St. Goar, at the duke's own request. Thereafter, Tassilo was taken to Jumièges. His two sons were also forcibly shorn and banished, while his wife and daughters suffered the same fate.[169]

And so the Duchy of the Agilolfings in Bavaria, which had been in existence for a century and a half, was brought to an end. Trickery and subterfuge divested this dynasty of power for all time, an outcome justified by Tassilo's consultations with the enemies of Christianity, which he freely admitted to engaging in. Indeed, the Avars tried to exploit this situation by launching another invasion of Bavaria and Italy. "Accordingly, this all redounded to the glory and honor of the lord king," mused the Murbach annalist, "and to the irritation and detriment of his enemies, since the Creator of All Things ordained that he should forever be triumphant." In other words, the Bavarian catastrophe was in accordance with God's will. Heaven itself legitimized this use of force against the Christian duke.

The questionable *Royal Frankish Annals* goes on to recount that the duchy was handed over to Charlemagne's brother-in-law Gerold, who was to act as its "prefect." In all likelihood, however, it was initially meant to be an endowment for Charlemagne's firstborn son, Pepin the Hunchback, before the intriguing of Queen Fastrada prevented this and drove Himiltrud's son into open revolt. Once again, the *Royal Frankish Annals* passed over this episode in silence.[170] Gerold must have taken the region over only somewhat later as prefect; even so, the king by no means had a completely free hand in his choice of governor, for although his brother-in-law was a Frank, on his mother's side—just like Queen Hildegard—he was related to the old Alemannic ducal family. At the same time, this genealogical connection also made him—or so it would seem—a distant cousin of Tassilo, since the Alemannic ducal house, as already noted, had to be counted as a side branch of the Agilolfing dynasty.[171] Gerold's appointment was clearly intended to quell the virulent anti-Frankish mood in the region after the toppling of the duke of Bavaria.

Even manuscripts became caught up in Charlemagne's war in Bavaria, as the case of the so-called Montpellier Psalter (Ms. H409; Plate I) demonstrates. This work is lavishly adorned with gold, silver, and colorful illuminated letters, and with its strikingly small format was designed for a prince to carry around on his travels. Paleographic details reveal that it was produced in the monastery at Mondsee and was probably made for Tassilo III. It subsequently fell into the hands of the victors, along with the rest of the duke's treasure. No sooner had this happened, though, than the final five pages of the manuscript were removed and destroyed, since they almost certainly contained liturgical acclamations of the duke and his family, resembling the *laudes regiae* (the "royal praises," liturgical chants at pontifical high mass for the king and his relatives), which were now supplanted by Carolingian *laudes*. This must have occurred sometime before 792, for the texts still commemorate Charlemagne's eldest son Pepin alongside his brothers (it was in 792 that Pepin embarked on his ill-fated rebellion). In this instance, then, mutilating a book was clearly a way of asserting authority.

The various local saints from Soissons mentioned in the litany—Bantaridus, Drauscius, Vodoaldus, Leodardus, and Medrisma—lead us to deduce that the psalter eventually found a home there at the nunnery of Notre-Dame,[172] where Charlemagne's sister Gisela was abbess, and the leadership of which his daughter Rotrude—the bride the *basileus* had spurned and the future lover of Count Rorico—may well have assumed after her aunt's death. But Rotrude herself died only a few months after Gisela in 810. Before this, a short litany was added after the *laudes,* written in a more recent hand and in Latin that was less than impeccable, and including the following closing prayer: "O Christ, grant that your sister Rotrude may be blessed [*esse beatam* was a formula used to ask for the forgiveness of sins], so that she may serve you for evermore." Evidently, then, the psalter seized from her uncle was given to her when she entered the convent at Soissons.[173] Later, the manuscript found its way to Auxerre.[174]

Gerold did not have long to enjoy his new position; in 799, he was killed while fighting the Avars. He was a benefactor of the monastery at St. Gallen and a patron of the island monastery at Reichenau—the site where he was eventually buried—and would have been assured of heavenly delights, according to Abbot Wetti's visions of Heaven and Hell, because he died while fighting the heathens.[175] Meanwhile, as soon as Tassilo had been neutralized, Charlemagne hurried to Regensburg to "organize the borderlands and the marches against the Avars" (*Royal Frankish Annals*) and shortly thereafter, in 791 and 792, celebrated Christmas in the old ducal city. After six years, however, Tassilo was summoned once more from his monastery and put before the synod in Frankfurt so that he might publicly confess his "guilt" anew and renounce his and his sons' claims on Bavaria for all time. Charlemagne's rule of iron required confession and ecclesiastical blessing, and that acts of closure such as this be staged for all to see.

Signs of the momentous change that had taken place are preserved in documents relating to the unfortunate duke. Tassilo's many privileges for the city of Salzburg have come down to us in copies of original charters. These reveal how the power of the victorious ruler could radically deform the past. Two transcripts have survived, separated by only ten years—but ten years that were decisive, changed everything, and reevaluated the entire past. The older of the two transcripts, the *Indiculus Arnonis*, comes from before Tassilo's overthrow, while the later one, the so-called *Breves notitiae*, was created soon after his downfall and reflects the sad fate of the Bavarian duke. Whereas before, only Tassilo's name would appear as the originator of a document—or during his minority, his and that of his mother as regent—by this stage the explicit approval of King Pepin had crept into the equation.[176] Memories could be manipulated: after the overthrow of the Agilolfing ruler, it seemed that confirmation by a Carolingian was now required, even in the case of earlier pieces of legislation, for the future to be assured. Once again, we can see Charlemagne's present power distorting the past.

Success brought new struggles in its wake. With the conquest of Bavaria, Charlemagne's empire now bordered on Avar territory. This race of mounted warriors from the steppes of central Asia, who in the mid-sixth century had irrupted into eastern and central Europe, had mobilized one last time in 788 for an advance on Italy. Once there, their horsemen plundered large areas before turning their attention to Bavaria, where they were repelled. Now the Frankish king mobilized his forces against them. Although they had once been the terror of Romans, Slavs, and Lombards alike and had pushed forward as far as Pannonia, their power was now on the wane.[177] In 626, they had even reached Constantinople. "Their life is war," wrote Theodor Synkellos, a Greek writer of the early seventh century, in allusion to the Maccabees of the Bible. Their weaponry was terrifying; neither Romans nor Greeks nor any other Western people had anything to match it. A war manual from the reign of the Byzantine emperor Maurice (582–602) was clearly in awe of their equipment: stirrups, heavy armor for both men and horses, composite bows, a spear, and a sword, combined with tactics that were utterly unknown in the West, made the Avars seemingly invincible. The Rhomaioi, who were well versed in the art of war themselves, rushed to imitate whatever they could of the Avars' armory.

Now the Carolingian king girded his loins against the once-unconquerable Avars.[178] All the peoples of his empire supplied contingents of troops, who assembled in Regensburg. In the late summer of 791, the signal horns sounded for the first campaign against the Avars. North and south of the Danube, Charlemagne's divided army swept into Avar territory. In relief, he wrote to his wife that his son Pepin had contacted him to reassure him that he and the pope were safe and unharmed, the frontiers were secure, and the force that had invaded the Avars' lands had just recorded its first victory; this force had been under the command of a bishop, a duke, and two counts. They took 150 enemy soldiers prisoner. However, Charlemagne went on to express his astonishment that Fastrada had not sent a messenger or a letter to let him know how she was and to report on any other events back home; he told her that he wanted to hear from her more frequently—in the midst of war, a moving testimony of loving concern and devotion on his part.[179] He also mentioned in this same letter that three days of fasting and prayer had served to prepare his own forces for the fight. The king proceeded to push on beyond the river Enns. But the enemy constantly retreated, refusing to engage in a pitched battle with the Franks. Charlemagne and his army eventually returned to Bavaria disappointed.

The following year saw the Carolingian ruler launch a second campaign against the Avars, for which he employed all the technological means at his disposal. A readily transportable pontoon bridge enabled his forces to swiftly cross and recross the Danube time and again, and a start was made on digging a canal between the river Main and the Danube, which would further enhance the king's mobility in future conflicts, allowing him to move rapidly from the centers of power to the outer fringes of the empire. Perhaps the bridge over the Rhine that Einhard mentions, whose period of construction is not known exactly, was already in operation too by this stage, helping the Frankish army mobilize against the distant adversary. Yet even the most elaborate tactics did not bring success; instead, Slavs along the Elbe and Saxons exploited the fact that the Frankish armed forces were tied down in the southeast to stage a series of new attacks.

The Avars were divided among themselves, with many wanting to sue for peace with the Franks. Finally, in 795, the Frankish duke Eric of Friuli dispatched a small but powerful force from Italy to Pannonia, commanded by a Slav called Voynimir. The "ring," the seat of the khan there, was sacked and in the following year completely overrun and captured by the Italian king Pepin. The khan was killed in this action, and his treasure, an immense hoard of booty, was divided up among the victors. Theodulf wrote a paean of praise for this victory: God, he claimed, had granted Charlemagne the rich treasures of Pannonia, and the Avars would now come to submit themselves to the rule of Christ; the formerly fierce Hun, he continued, was now a loyal adherent of the faith: "Estque humilis fidei, qui fuit ante ferox."[180] Even the tombs of the apostles received their share of the booty: "Out of gratitude to God, the dispenser of all graces," this donation was handed over by "Angilbert, his [i.e., Charlemagne's] beloved abbot" (*Royal Frankish Annals*). Pannonia was annexed to Charlemagne's realm; missionary work began immediately after the conquest, and henceforth the immeasurably expanded Frankish Empire vied with Byzantium.

The Results of Charlemagne's Wars

What objective, then, was the king pursuing with the wars he waged? Was it solely the expansion of Christendom at the End of Days? For all the king's undoubted piety, this is scarcely credible. Worldly concerns also played a part in his motivation. Like all early medieval monarchs, and in common with his father and all the Lombard rulers, Charlemagne was a warring king. Waging war was an integral part of his upbringing and was in accordance with the obligatory ideal of kingship. Martial success was to be unequivocal and was intended to make people forget the Carolingian revolts against the Merovingians and their acts of violence toward their closest relatives and to consolidate their own rule. Initially, as, for instance, the *Clausula de unctione Pippini* of 767 indicates, this rule was by no means as secure as comparatively later testimonies in court-approved historiography might pretend. The young Charlemagne was positively condemned to engage in conquest; he had to expand his empire in order to prove himself as king and to offer his retinue the appropriate rewards. And so, year after year, he set off on campaign. However, with every triumph, he was drawn ever deeper into the web of power politics in the Mediterranean region.

It is fair to say, though, that it was never Charlemagne's intention to impose a leveling uniformity across the whole of his realm. Saxons and Bavarians remained their own peoples within their own countries, and the Lombards retained their kingdom. Meanwhile, Aquitaine seemed even to be in the process of forming itself into a separate nation. As before, different peoples continued to be divided by languages, citizens' rights, ways of life and customs, and, not least, inheritance law and marriage law. Victorious wars merely added foreign lands and peoples to the empire rather than merging them all into some homogeneous Carolingian body politic. Nevertheless, there were still certain moves toward integration, which must have been ordered by Charlemagne himself. Even before the subjugation of the conquered lands was complete, he dispatched his advisers to the areas that had been overrun to establish his authority there. This transfer of personnel remained a feature over the succeeding centuries.

For example, in the eleventh and even in some isolated cases the twelfth century in Italy, we encounter a so-called *lege vivente* formula, stipulating which code of citizens' rights the person in question was governed by. These indicated that there were Franks, Alemanni, and Bavarians resident south of the Alps. Franks also moved to Saxony, in the same way as Saxons were conversely not only deported to Frankish regions but also gravitated there in the service of the king or the Church. Marriages, too, could be entered into across national borders. Yet it was not the case that a homogeneous population within the empire resulted from these measures, which really affected only certain echelons of free men and of the nobility. In administrative terms, the feudal system (insofar as it had developed by that stage) and the concept of division into counties were introduced by the individuals involved (though not solely by them) into the newly conquered territories. Subordination of the Church to Rome and the pope, which Charlemagne demanded should be consistently observed, also had a long-lasting effect on these regions.

Certainly, this did not all coalesce into a unified system. Divisive elements still predominated. There could be no such thing as "loyalty to the empire," since the empire, if indeed it meant anything beyond the spatial extent of the area under Charlemagne's sway, was assigned to the personal sphere of the king. Moreover—since God had given Charlemagne four, or three, sons—his mind-set was very much one of division rather than unification, notwithstanding the fact that he sought to divide his realm in a very different way than his predecessors had. And so—leaving aside the four factors already mentioned: the dispatch of personnel, the feudal system, the establishment of counties, and commitment to the papacy—a common binding element, a logical factor that would bring it all together, was missing.

Even ecclesiastical practices diverged from one another depending on location. For instance, the Roman Church with the pope at its head even recited the creed differently from the Franks. Thus, alongside various other deviations, in the Spanish-Visigoth and the Anglo-Saxon Churches, as well as in several of the Latin creeds that have come down to us from the early medieval

FIGURE 18 Detail of an eighth-century fresco at the Benedictine Abbey of Marienburg in Mals, in the South Tyrol region of Italy, showing a secular benefactor in customary Frankish garb.

Frankish Empire, a small, dogmatically unimportant addition had been inserted, producing the creed (the so-called Nicaeno-Constantinopolitanum) announced at the Second Council of Constantinople in 381. According to this, the Holy Ghost proceeded not just "from the Father" but from "the Father and the Son" (*a patre filioque*).[181] Admittedly, those versions in the vernacular that have been preserved, such as the Frankish or the Alemmanic creed, omitted the passage in question.

Meanwhile, Charlemagne was keen to impose unity where questions of faith were concerned; accordingly, he pressed to have the *filioque* included in the creed—a decision that was to be the catalyst for ongoing controversy and fierce argument with the Byzantine Greeks. However, even Pope Leo III set his face against this change, despite insistent urging to the contrary by the Franks, and gave everyone a visual demonstration of the difference by ordering the creed without the *filoque* (or the *et filio*) to be engraved on silver plaques and set next to the entrance to the tomb of the apostles and over the entrance to the tomb of St. Paul—in Latin and Greek in the former location, but just in Latin in the latter—as well as at all the most popular pilgrimage sites of Latin Christendom. Only many centuries later, under Pope Benedict VIII, did this change gain acceptance into the Roman liturgy. And so the fact remained: not even the Church could manage to engender an atmosphere of unity; rather, colorful diversity was to characterize the multiethnic Carolingian Empire, which had been brought together through conflict.

Yet Charlemagne was not merely the victim of the belligerent ethos of his age. He cherished his own objectives. He instigated wars against the Saxons and the Lombards in this same period. Was his thought already focused on Rome, which he visited in the middle of the Lombard war, but specifically in a quite profane sense? Gallia Narbonensis, Italy, Rome, Spain, Bavaria, and Pannonia had all without exception been ancient Roman provinces. This fact was not lost on Charlemagne. Even Saxony fitted into this concept of Roman revival, if one is justified in taking Suetonius's *Life of Augustus* as the model for Einhard's *Life of Charlemagne* (one need only think here of the Battle of Teutoburg Forest). One historian of the period was certainly confident enough to claim that he, Charlemagne, already had Rome and the imperial cities of the West (i.e., Trier, Arles, Milan, and Ravenna) within his grasp.[182] Was it this, then, that the conqueror had been aiming at all along right from the outset? We must ultimately, however, cast a doubtful eye on this explanation too, although the king must surely have entertained such thoughts with every new victory.

It is certainly the case that the cause of religion legitimized each of his wars—not least in Charlemagne's own eyes. Every war he entered into was either accompanied or followed by measures paying homage to God and His saints. People were meant to gain the greatest benefit from his conflicts: future salvation and a hope of eternal bliss. The reorganization of a conquered country's land and Church, measures of "reparation" and reform—all these were nothing but good deeds, according to the value judgments of the time. None of the former Carolingian monarchs had ever gone to war to champion such ideals before. Only Charlemagne was in pursuit of higher aims. In Italy, he strove to the best of his ability to bring about peace in the country and secured the independence of the Roman Church. He halted and pushed back the advance of Islam in southern Gaul and northern Spain. His invasion of Bavaria appears to have been carried out with the pope's agreement. Pannonia was regained for Christendom. Where Saxony was concerned, the Frankish king and his confederates succeeded in their quite deliberate and focused objective of bringing culture to regions that had hitherto scarcely been touched by the advanced civilizations of the Mediterranean. Christianity introduced literacy and methodically controlled rationality into countries that until then had not had any form of written culture.

The king was concerned to have the clergy alongside him in this endeavor. First and foremost, he sought their advice on how to clearly formulate the content of his capitularies (legislative and administrative acts). He offered the clergy an exchange of gifts on the grandest scale. The pope reminded Charlemagne at an early stage of the importance of this barter deal. The victorious power of St. Peter that he, Pope Hadrian, with his arms raised in supplication toward Heaven, would call down on the emperor was a ubiquitous source of strength for Charlemagne.[183] In return, the Frankish king and *patricius* of the Romans donated large territories and patrimonies to the heir and successor of St. Peter and to the Roman Church and guaranteed them his powerful protection. After Charlemagne left Rome, the pope ordered that three hundred *kyrie eleison*s be sung every day in all the churches and deaconries within the city and prayed to the Lord God that he might "pardon you [i.e., the Frankish king] all your sins and send down from Heaven to you the great joy of good fortune and many victories"—a jubilant song that filled the entire city. Hadrian informed the young king about this intercession on his behalf as early as 774.[184] In return, Charlemagne attached the Frankish Church to Rome and the pope. He had no desire for the Church in his realm to pursue its own separate path, such as that taken centuries before by the Visigoths or the Irish. This "exchange of gifts" continued to operate for centuries thereafter, right up the present day.

Charlemagne conducted his own idiosyncratic retrospective review of his wars, as evidenced by the account given of them, and no doubt approved by him, in the *Royal Frankish Annals*. This review was meant to proclaim the legitimacy of his actions. Therefore, it glossed over, distorted, or drew a veil over certain events, in the process, not only ignoring unpleasant occurrences or setbacks like that in Spain in 778, the failed marriage of Charlemagne's daughter Rotrude in 788, or the use of force against Tassilo of Bavaria but also exaggerating successes such as the victories over the Saxons before 782. Indeed, these much-vaunted victories were supposed to mask the defeats that had preceded them: the victory over the Saxons versus the defeat in Spain, and the triumph over Tassilo versus the failed campaign in southern Italy.

Independent of this kind of idealized portrayal, though, a clear relocation of authority became apparent. Whereas under Pepin the Short, the great preponderance of power in the Carolingian realm still centered on Paris and Compiègne, the places where Charlemagne's decrees were issued and received indicate that during the course of the war against the Saxons and the incorporation of Bavaria into the empire, this center had shifted northward and eastward. The course of the Rhine now emerged as the principal axis, placing Cologne, Mainz, Worms, Frankfurt, Paderborn, and above all Aachen in the epicenter of things.[185]

Did Charlemagne learn from his wars? From his defeats and victories? Or from the setbacks he suffered? Certainly, it seemed that it was advisable to be mistrustful toward the "Greeks" and the "Saracens." In any event, in Spain the Frankish king henceforth relied much more on force than on treaties, while even against Byzantium, his first recourse was to arms before entering into any fresh round of negotiations. Did the brutality of the first years of war against the Saxons have to switch to moderation to ultimately ensure victory? Did the king and emperor perhaps fear that he might not be able to contain the violence he had summoned forth? It seemed as though this use of force required a counterweight, which Charlemagne hoped to find in the Church, faith, and learning, and in the strengthening of his own authority according to the norms of Christendom at that time.

4

POWER STRUCTURES

CHARLEMAGNE'S ENDLESS WARRING consumed a fortune; there was no cheaper way to secure peace. Charlemagne understood full well, though, that a successful king had to run a successful economy too. Yet how could he afford both war and peace? How might they be financed? There was plenty of money, for sure, in the form of pure silver coinage. But it was never enough to pay all his fighting men, or even his administrators, estate managers, or noblemen.[1] As a result, other instruments of remuneration had to be deployed. So how, then, were revenues generated and the costs of a standing army met? A king had many mouths to feed, including not just his own royal household but also the clergy, guests at court, foreign legations, and countless others, all in a manner befitting both their station and his own royal rank. He was expected to put on a display of grandeur, power, and wealth and to exude an air of splendor through bounteous generosity and conspicuous expenditure. None of this came cheaply. He also had to pay homage to God, in accordance with his status. Who paid for that? Indeed, where did the king's wealth come from? Who generated it? And how was it protected and multiplied? Who was involved in this undertaking? The answer to these questions leads us inevitably to the vast landholdings the king had at his disposal throughout his realm, which needed to be managed efficiently.

"We desire that our estates, which we have selected to cater to our needs, shall serve us exclusively and no one else."[2] The aim was clear: it was the place of commercial enterprises to accord with the king's interests and only those, however much others might covet their services. Charlemagne nurtured business and commerce like few other monarchs. The accounts that have come down to us afford revealing insights into contemporary economic activities, into the organization of the royal landholdings, into how the king's dependents were provided for, and into the king's schemes and desire for order.[3] There is only one thing they do not reveal: how large the population of the Frankish Empire was. For the period in which he lived, the king and emperor pursued a highly successful and effective economic policy that can still be seen today, in its basic outlines, as having been geared toward steadily increasing growth. Nor was it simply confined to agriculture and animal husbandry; it also included mining, manufacturing, and trading, and it availed itself, wherever possible, of money. Charlemagne was familiar with markets. Increasingly, economic activity in his realm was organized and managed along rational lines.

Although urban settlements were not unknown, especially in former Roman territory, economic activity centered primarily on the manorial system, that is, within large complexes of landholdings, which were sometimes farmed by independently operating or unfree, requisitioned small enterprises, and sometimes in-house by so-called *mancipes,* farm laborers who had no land of their own. Churches and wars and peace could all be financed, even if not exclusively by the king. Despite the fact that Charlemagne's biographer Einhard had large estates of his own, this aspect of the king's reign eluded him entirely, largely because his model, Suetonius, said nothing about it either in his *Life of Augustus.* No poet lauded Charlemagne the successful economist. The ruler's acts of profligate indulgence garnered him much praise from contemporaries, whereas his prudent management of the economy did not.

The monarch's immense sovereign estates were supplemented by the old personal landholdings of the royal family, namely, the former king's estates acquired through the overthrow of the Merovingians, as well as by more recently confiscated land; ownerless land also devolved to the king. Furthermore, conquests in Aquitaine, Italy, Saxony, and Bavaria or in the campaigns against the Avars steadily augmented these landholdings. The hereditary family estates comprised a number of connected complexes principally in the Metz region, on the central reaches of the river Moselle, and from Trier via Echternach as far as Prüm, as well as in the area around Nivelles and Stablo. The old royal estates of the Merovingians were distributed throughout the whole of Francia. However, the precise extent and density of those royal

FIGURE 19 Figure of a plowman in a miniature painting from the Stuttgart Psalter (ca. 830). The advent of heavy moldboard plows drawn by two oxen necessitated cooperation between tenant farmers and promoted the rise of the manorial system.

estates became clear only through the practice of dividing them up among offspring, in other words, through a process of steady reduction.

The huge extent of this property portfolio, which steadily increased over the decades, together with the land seized through conflict against the Saxons, Lombards, and Avars, may well have made the king magnanimous and openhanded. War turned out to be a profitable enterprise for those who took part. Charlemagne rewarded his followers, secular magnates, dioceses, and monasteries with generous donations of land; he also never neglected to bestow new territory on the Roman papacy. These institutions all received a share of the booty, even the vicar of Christ. This kind of generosity and indulgence revealed Charlemagne's greatness; the donations scarcely appeared to diminish his own wealth, although in the long term they must have jeopardized the sovereign estates. Yet the principle of reciprocity ingrained in the ruling order and demanded by the system of authority required that such donations be made. Even so, Charlemagne's successors were soon to realize the disadvantages of this kind of exchange of gifts.

All in all, the Carolingian ruling dynasty of the eighth and ninth centuries represented an economic superpower against which no other lord or church in the Carolingian empire could hope to compete. Charlemagne made sure that he catered to their economic interests. However keen he was to gaze upward to Heaven and follow the course of the stars,[4] however devoutly he ascribed his successes to God's good grace, it was the material yield of the earth that formed the vital foundation of his reign and that he was resolved never to neglect. He took a constant and very personal interest in this key aspect of his reign.

Charlemagne undoubtedly took over the structure and bases of the organization of the royal estates from his predecessors, but it was during his reign that they came more clearly to prominence. Thanks to the survival of various documents, these organizational principles can be more or less precisely summarized.[5] Their most striking feature was the innovative structural measures employed. In all likelihood, Charlemagne considerably expanded his control over the way in which work was organized and various tasks were apportioned; he would surely also have taken steps to prevent profits from trickling away. In addition, he would have raised productivity and yield by instituting a more efficient system of supervision. Advisers, such as Abbot Adalhard of Corbie, might well have assisted him in this task, with their aptitude for medium-term planning, careful calculation of requirements, and accumulating reserves (all of which Adalhard displayed in his organization of monastic life).[6]

Forest clearance and colonization, agriculture in all its aspects, animal husbandry and horse breeding, viticulture, beekeeping, wax production and soap manufacture, salt mining, and mining in general, but also manufacturing, arms production, wool and linen weaving, plus local and long-distance trade, financial services, and social welfare—in sum, everything that was within the ambit of Charlemagne's power was interconnected and organized according to the principles of the manorial system. This overarching structure set performance targets for any particular enterprise. Wax (for the many altar candles), salt (for conserving food), and cloth of all types were the major export goods of this period, alongside swords and suits of armor.

At this time, because the cities of Gaul, of Francia, or of the lands on the right bank of the Rhine were simply agglomerations of settlement and nothing more, they had no jurisdiction of their own but rather were either incorporated into royal or episcopal manors or subject to the local count and the common law in force in his domain. Nevertheless, merchants, goods, money, and markets all gathered in these settlements. Occasionally, one of the merchants would be granted a customs privilege.[7] Exemptions from tax had already existed under the Merovingians and now continued under Carolingian rule.[8] The toll-free market on St. Dionysius's Day in St. Denis was protected.[9] Certainly, Charlemagne did not grant any new special market dispensations; even so, there was a capitulary titled *On the Market within Our Palatinate*, namely, Aix-la-Chapelle, which makes it clear that the merchants who resided there—at least during the reign of Louis the Pious— enjoyed tax exemption across the whole empire, with the exception of one or two border posts.[10]

CHARLEMAGNE

New towns beyond the former borders of the Roman Empire developed only very slowly, under the shadow of royal palatinates like Frankfurt or of one or another of the major abbeys, such as Fulda or Werden. They also evolved from various trading places on the coast like Hamburg or Bremen, or above all from episcopal sees, such as Paderborn or Münster. Despite the fact that merchants were basically under the protection of the king, there is nothing to suggest that Charlemagne particularly promoted this trend toward city formation, except in the case of the bishoprics.

The measures Charlemagne put in place are reflected in a relatively extensive series of revealing documents. The *Capitulare de villis* (*CdV*)—a capitulary concerning farmyards—is noteworthy for its unusual content and provenance. Capitularies were royal ordinances, administrative edicts, and legal injunctions drawn up and issued by the king (or emperor) in consultation with his magnates; they derived their name from their division into chapters (*capitulae*). Recent studies have revealed that although they had a stable normative content, they had no hard-and-fast form.[11] As a rule, they were promulgated as the succession to individual sections, each with its own content (*capitula*), and only occasionally in a formal way, similar to a diploma (but without actually being one). Far more often, though, they were transmitted in informal, possibly private, lists. In these documents, the king spoke in either the first person singular or plural; equally, though, the sense could be captured in generalizing sentences with or without a reference to the king's will. In any event, the normative validity of the capitularies lay in the oral consensus between the king and his magnates; the written document had to be seen more as a simple aide-mémoire than as a formal requirement. These capitularies form the most vivid reflection of Charlemagne's reign in practice.[12]

The *Capitulare de villis* related either to the royal estates in general or specifically to those farmsteads whose priority or sole occupation it was to provide food (so-called table goods) to the itinerant court (*discus,* chap. 24, or *ad opus nostrum,* chap. 30); it is a matter of contention whether this edict was formulated during the reign of Charlemagne or of Louis the Pious (the manuscript we have definitely dates from this later period). Researchers have so far been unable to reach a consensus on this point. Whatever the case, the *Capitulare de villis* illustrates the general bases of the organization of the royal estates and their prudent economic management, which certainly did not begin only under or at the instigation of Louis the Pious. As a result, the capitulary may also legitimately be adduced as documentary evidence for the reign of Charlemagne.[13]

Similarly, the *Lorscher Reichsurbar,* preserved for posterity in the twelfth-century Codex Laureshamensis, has as its subject the royal landholdings, and where its content is concerned, it does belong at least in part to the era of Charlemagne.[14] Also, from late in his reign, a fragment of another decree with economic relevance has been preserved in Milan; this originally belonged to the Abbey of St. Denis and documents, for example, the mostly monetary levies due from free men on royal land, which entitled them to cultivate this land on the basis of a loan agreement, or so-called *precarium* contract. It likewise reveals a great deal about the administration of royal estates in general.[15]

An *Urbar* (land register) was a list of sovereign estates in the possession of a particular lord and the income they generated. The *Lorscher Reichsurbar,* together with the somewhat later land register from the Alpine province of Raetia Curiensis, which also concerned royal estates, completes the texts pointing to the organization and the economic potential of Carolingian estate management.[16] In all the documents named here, the same organizational and administrative structures appear time and again, just as they were taking effect under Charlemagne's rule.

These records are further supplemented by various forms on how to render accounts (compiled from instructions that were actually used) that have survived the passage of time,[17] occasional notes in capitularies, and a few later land registers (such as the *Urbar* of the monastery at Prüm, dating from the late ninth century)—all of which may, with due caution, be enlisted as evidence for the reign of Charlemagne. Although the well-known *Plan of St. Gall,* which almost certainly was created and drafted on the model of Reichenau as an ideal monastery ground plan, belongs to the reign of Louis the Pious, where its content is concerned—and specifically as regards the central commercial institutions it depicts on the monastery site—it undoubtedly points back to the age of Charlemagne and can be used to elucidate identical conditions in both the royal and other monastic estates.[18] The aforementioned land registers from Francia or central Europe do not differ greatly from one another, except for the fact that estates in the south of Gallia or in Italy were on a smaller scale and less centrally organized, in accordance with their origins.

Royal estates were distributed across the entire region under Charlemagne's control, sometimes finding themselves in conflict with properties belonging to the Church or the aristocracy, but in the main they were embedded within large interlinked land complexes and were not divided into individual *villae*—royal farmsteads comprising several small tenanted plots

(*Hufen*, or "hides")—but rather into large demesnes. For instance, the complex around Frankfurt took in many villages in the Wetterau, as well as in the Dreieich Forest to the south, which stretched as far as the outskirts of the modern city of Darmstadt. The administrative districts, known as *ministeria* or *fisci*, were run by their own stewards (*iudices* or *actores*), who in many cases came from the ranks of the local nobility. This situation was predisposed to alienate those living under such jurisdiction, as would be demonstrated only too clearly after the end of Charlemagne's reign. How far these terms were interchangeable and in fact related to identical circumstances will be discussed presently.

The queen stood by the king's side in the running of the realm's economy. Indeed, a particular royal privilege has been preserved that Charlemagne granted himself and his wife, Hildegard.[19] Although their estates were scattered across the whole of Gallia and Germania, they still formed part of the royal household and fell within its legal sphere. The lady of the house was in control here, and the *Capitulare de villis* addressed her role directly. The table goods were under her jurisdiction.[20] In addition to supplying the itinerant royal court, these commodities also sustained the resident royal household and sometimes even victualled the army (chaps. 30 and 64). Any surpluses were to be sold on the open market (chap. 33). Even the tithe and the "ninth part" (i.e., a second tithe) were levied in the manorial estates (chap. 6); this was meant to be paid exclusively to the king's own churches and not to any "external" churches. Every royal estate (*villa*) was supposed to keep the following amenities ready in the store-room (in the event, say, of a royal visit): beds; mattresses; feather beds; bedsheets; tablecloths; benches; brass, lead, iron, and wooden receptacles; braziers; chains; and generally all the necessary utensils, "so there is no need to purchase or borrow them from elsewhere" (chap. 42). If he had to stay overnight anywhere in the winter, the king wanted to be sure that he would be comfortable and warm and sleep in a soft bed.

The districts administered by stewards (*maiores*) were not to be so extensive that the official could not ride around one or oversee it within a single day (chap. 26). Under no circumstances were the stewards to be appointed from the ranks of the ruling class (*potentiores*); instead, they "were to be recruited from among the middle class [*mediocres*], whose members are steadfast and loyal" (chap. 60)—a sign of constant worry in the back of the king's mind about the constant threat of rivalry he faced from his own magnates. Accordingly, the organization of the estates was to be clear and simple to monitor, so as to ensure their security. Likewise, the post of steward was to be arranged in such a way that it presented no competition to the bailiffs (*iudices*).

The bailiffs were responsible for directing the activities of foresters, plowmen, cellarers, and tax collectors and other specialists (chap. 6). When ordered to do so by the queen, the seneschal, or the royal cupbearer, they were expected to make their way to the court without delay to give an account of their work (chap. 16). They were forbidden to enlist the king's bondsmen for their own service and to accept any gifts from them, "no horse, no ox, no cow, no hog, no ram, no piglet, no lamb, or indeed livestock or gifts of any kind, except for a bottle [of wine], vegetables, fruit, chickens, and eggs" (chap. 3); nor were they to let their packs of hunting hounds be fed by the king's men (chap. 11). Clearly, the worst kind of oppression was anticipated. Was it the case that the king could not always prevail in his domains with his directives against the bailiffs? Complaints by his bondsmen or by the overseers (*iuniores*) against the *iudices* were indeed supposed to be passed directly to the king (chap. 57), but did this ever happen in practice?

Every Christmas, each bailiff was required to give an account of his activities over the year—in writing, we must assume. Detailed information was demanded about the services they had rendered, the tributes they had collected and the interest earned, the damage caused by poachers, the tax revenues raised, the harvest yields from fields, woods, and meadows, the work that had been carried out repairing bridges and ferries, and the income or profit accruing from selling at market, or the sale of firewood and construction timber, or of vegetables, honey, and wax; also how much wine had been pressed and how much beer brewed, along with details of what had been manufactured—in short, a full report on everything that lay within the ambit of their responsibility, with all items "accurate, and separately accounted for, and neatly organized," "so that we might know what we have at Our disposal" (chap. 62). Literacy was by no means a matter of course; Charlemagne had already decreed that administrators should be able to read and write, but his edict had not been universally followed.[21] A correspondingly detailed balance-sheet of such goods and services has not survived, but at least model surveys such as the fortunately preserved *Brevium exempla* demonstrate that individual invoices must have been submitted.[22] The counts had nothing to do with the administration of the royal estates; they were deliberately excluded from any involvement. Monitoring was carried out by royal messengers (*missi*) sent out to inspect estates on a case-by-case basis.[23] Did the king have a good instinct for fluctuations in yields or even for changes in the economy? No reports to this effect have been preserved from the Carolingian court; the only indications of this are found in certain remarks to this effect made by Charlemagne's cousin and adviser Adalhard of Corbie, to which I will return.

The language of the aforementioned documents differed fundamentally from the records that concerned the reform of the Frankish monarchy and the Church. In the former, verbs of asking were heavily deployed, with the king acting as supplicant to his magnates. In the latter, by contrast, the ruler was in command mode; he "wished" that certain things be done and told his subjects that they "should" do this or that; here, he required obedience to himself and his queen alone. In these documents, the king was acting as landlord; he used language from the sphere of domestic law. "We require that Our farmsteads, which we have earmarked to supply Us, should furnish Our needs alone and not those of anyone else"; "It is Our wish that they plant all available herbs in the garden." Thus ran the opening and closing sentences of the *Capitulare de villis*. The opening sentence continued, "So that no bailiff [*iudex*] might venture to take Our servants into his employ."

Commerce naturally tends toward growth, and so it was back then. Despite regular famines, the growing population alone—a factor contemporaries could scarcely hope to register—demanded a significant increase in crop yields and the performance of the estates. Charlemagne appears to have tried a novel method to achieve a more particularized monitoring of efficiency: dividing the large estates that were accessible to his supervision into individual "hides" (*hubae*, also *mansi*).[24] He proceeded to institute this land reform wherever the remit of his authority ran, both in the royal estates and in the monasteries under his control. The work of these new operational units was recorded in corresponding directories, land registers, and polyptychs.

The land registers recorded, in order of size, the landholdings, the crops they grew, and the tributes paid by the tenants of every one of the hides on a particular estate. No polyptych has survived from the reign of Charlemagne; the earliest that has come down to us dates from the ninth century. The structure of the Church estates was in all likelihood reformed by Charlemagne in close conjunction with the royal domain, as is evident from model surveys that have been preserved, such as the *Brevium exempla*.[25] The polyptych compiled by Abbot Irminon of St-Germain-des-Prés in the Île de France during the reign of Louis the Pious gives a rough idea of the result of such reorganization; likewise, although they date only from the period around 900, the land register of Prüm, a monastery under the direct control of the Crown, and the earliest land register from the monastery at Werden

FIGURE 20 The hoe was one of the most widely used tools for tilling fields. Miniature painting from the Stuttgart Psalter.

on the Ruhr (now part of the city of Essen), a foundation of St. Liudger, reveal a corresponding organization. Werden was situated on the Westphalian "Hellweg," the important main route from Duisburg via Dortmund to Paderborn and then on to Saxony—a route Charlemagne often used. These land registers were, as far as we can tell, drafted only a single time in each case and were not updated. As a result, the dynamism of economic change, which was also present in the eighth and ninth centuries, was not apparent here and hence did not become a prime motive for action on the part of the major landowners, despite the king's best efforts to the contrary.

The precise size of a hide is not recorded; moreover, it could vary according to the kind of estate management and the type of terrain. In regions where vines were grown, they must have been smaller than in regular arable farming or livestock rearing. Modern research sometimes cites an area of around ten hectares.[26] Whatever the case, the size of these farms was calculated so as to ensure that a small tenant farmer's family—comprising a man, his wife, one servant at most, and several children—could run it on their own, and that the crop yield would not only provide subsistence for the whole family but might even generate some surplus. On this reckoning, then, a hide cannot have been much larger than ten hectares. Parceling out land in this way helped make manorial estates more manageable and enabled the size of their harvest and hence their usefulness for the king and the magnates to be assessed more accurately. Charlemagne called for this change precisely for that reason, "so that we might know what resources, and how much of them, we have at Our disposal."[27]

The landholdings' forms of dependency on the king varied. Certain properties were run as self-sufficient enterprises (*Salgut*), feudal tenures were enfeoffed to a vassal, and land was given to free farmers against interest payment. In Francia, a bipartite form of land usage predominated. A *villa* with its estates was often worked by hundreds of farmhands (*mancipes*), while other land, in the form of numerous hides, was granted either to free men or to tied tenant farmers. These hides were required to pay higher tributes, while serfs were recruited to perform menial tasks and only had to generate smaller tributes. The liability for such payments lay with the farm, not the individual person.

The *Capitulare de villis* shows that the king acted like a solicitous squire or landlord, but with a keen eye for the military application of agriculture. For example, it was decreed that breeding stallions should always be put out to graze on the best pastures; it was to be reported to the king if any of these animals was somehow unsuitable or had grown too old for service (chap. 13). Stallion foals were to be separated from the herd at the correct time, and if the number of stud foals increased, they were to be kept in their own paddocks (chap. 14). Such measures were important for the war effort because the Frankish army increasingly became a mounted force. There are numerous mentions of military requirements in the sources. Thus, for instance, bailiffs were supposed to ensure that sturdy barrels reinforced with iron hoops were supplied "to the army and to the Royal Palatinate" (chap. 68).

Charlemagne's solicitude extended even to the smallest details. Flour mills were instructed to keep hens and geese (chap. 18), while barns were expected to have a flock of at least one hundred chickens and thirty geese (chap. 19). Every villa was required to have pens and stalls for cows, hogs, sheep, goats, and rams; there were to be plentiful numbers of healthy cows and oxen to provide a supply of meat (chap. 23). Any foods destined for the royal table had to be "good and top quality and prepared to the highest standard" (chap. 24). The tributes paid by the *iudices* in the form of wax were considerable, a hint at extensive beekeeping (chap. 59). Each villa was expected to employ its own beekeeper (chap. 17). To be sure, honey was the only sweetener available at the time, but the prime mover here was the constant demand for wax by the Church and also—less commonly—for illuminating domestic dwellings, as well as to meet the king's personal requirements. The appearance of wolves was to be reported to the king, and if they were killed, their pelts were to be sent to him; every May, one key task was to search out the wolves' lairs and kill the cubs (chap. 69). Although a wolf-skin cape did not look very impressive, it was ideally suited to keeping out the rain and snow.

Woods and forests were to be kept well maintained; people were expected to undertake felling and clearance work where they were able, and thereafter to prevent woods from reclaiming newly cleared fields. Equally, "Where there should be woodland, felling trees or otherwise damaging them shall not be permitted there." Big game was also to be preserved. Hunting with goshawks and sparrowhawks was to be conducted only "for the benefit of the king," in other words, upon payment of a fee. The estate manager, stewards, and their farmhands were expected to set an example by paying their tithe to the king whenever they turned their hogs out into the royal forest for fattening up, "so that other people might duly pay their tithe in full" (chap. 36). These protections and payment requirements were commensurate with the silviculture industry in the Frankish Empire, which was extensive by the standards of the time. The construction of every domestic dwelling and of palaces and their outbuildings (including regular improvements and renovation), the foundations of churches, plus their roofs and roof trusses—all required valuable timber of the highest quality, especially oak (see Plate VI). For example, the foundations of the Royal Church of St. Mary at Aix (Aachen Cathedral) were shored up by driving piles of decades-old oak into the damp subsoil.[28] The clearance of forests in the empire proceeded apace.

The surpluses of farm produce generated by the major estates must have been considerable. At most, it was only during regional famines that sale of the surplus benefited the populace at large. Serfs were expected to "work diligently and not cavort at the market" (chap. 54). Austerity and poverty must have characterized their lives, with hunger and going without the order of the day. For the ninth century, the extreme disparity in the number of men over women we encounter everywhere in the records at certain locations in the Île de France points to the common practice of killing baby girls—out of sheer desperation, we must assume. Time and again, Charlemagne called for welfare and protection measures for the poor, which leads us to surmise that even during his reign, demographically effective interventions were being undertaken to lower the birth rate. Despite this, the population continued to increase; slowly, too, the number of (exclusively Church) institutions that were able and willing to take in foundlings also grew.

Despite the clear preponderance of agricultural production, the Frankish Empire did not have a purely agrarian economy or even a barter economy. This also emerges from the *Capitulare de villis* and other documents, which mention wine purchasing or bans imposed on the working population to prevent them from visiting markets (chap. 54). Surpluses were actually offered for sale.[29] The fragment from St. Denis concerned tolls on bridges and ferries, markets, and long-distance trade.[30] Many taxes were payable in cash,

FIGURE 21 This scene from the Utrecht Psalter (ca. 820–830) depicts at its center women in a *genitium* (women's workshop) winding yarn and weaving cloth on a vertical weighted loom.

although this did not exclude payment in kind. Manufacturing, market trading, and long-distance commerce were also conducted by the large estates. Manorial estates at the very least participated in the trade in long-distance goods. Spices, incense, and probably also silk and other luxury items found their way into the Frankish Empire. The coinage reform of 794 underlined the importance of the monetary system.[31] It culminated in the increase in the weight of a penny, which now had to contain around 1.7 grams of silver. The forty or so mints in the empire were all situated on the left bank of the Rhine. This reform not only was destined to lay the foundations of the monetary system in France and Germany but also ushered in a financial reform that remained in force for several centuries, and with which even the Anglo-Saxons fell in line. Money, in the form of minted silver, evidently played a vital role in Charlemagne's economic order.

Not only agricultural yields were regulated, but also manufacturing production. Every villa was required to have workshops for the most diverse trades, not least for armorers. Yet there is no evidence of free enterprise at this time. All manufacturing was in some way bound up with estates and organized accordingly. This facilitated the division of labor. Special women's workshops (*genicia,* or genitia) housing some twenty to thirty or more women were used for weaving. Charlemagne decreed that women should be able to ply their trade in solid houses heated with ovens, which allowed them to work even during the winter (*CdV,* chap. 49).

Sunday, though, was observed as a rest day. On the Lord's Day, women were banned from undertaking any "menial tasks" (*opera servilia*)—weaving, cutting cloth, sewing, embroidering, carding wool, scutching flax, doing washing outdoors, or shearing sheep. These proscriptions were contained in the *Admonitio generalis*.[32] Instead, they were expected to attend Holy Mass, which in cases where there was a lengthy journey to and from church could easily take the whole day. Of course, the embroidering and weaving activities of the king's daughters, which Einhard mentions, were exempted from this ban.

Simple vertical looms made every piece of woven cloth—nine cubits long, five cubits wide—every length of linen, every coat and shirt a laborious and extensive piece of work. Wool and flax were the two fibers used. The more comfortable treadle-operated loom becomes evident only from the tenth century onward. Nevertheless, gathering women workers together under one roof in this way helped these workshops achieve remarkable productivity. Bolts of cloth became export articles. For instance, when Charlemagne sent gifts to the Abbasid caliph Harun al-Rashid, particular mention was made of cloth. In the mid-ninth century, in some instances Lorsch Abbey replaced payment in pieces of cloth with monetary payments.[33] This measure does not indicate a fall in demand but rather points to factors such as the concentration of cloth production in workshops.

But for all these individual provisions, there was no all-embracing concept for the interlinking of all measures relevant to the economy, or for any kind of "national economy." Each estate was an independent, self-sufficient economic unit, with every lord, including the king, solely responsible for its administration. There is not even anything to suggest that the royal *ministeria* cooperated systematically on central planning, which happened only to a very limited degree at best. All the same, Charlemagne's economic planning was geared to growth. Yields and production were to be steadily increased for the benefit of the king, the army, the Church, and the general populace.

Information on the overland routes and roads is absent from the *Capitulare de villis*. The old road network had largely deteriorated, although the occasional Roman road was still usable. The ancient "street maintenance depots," responsible for the upkeep of the roads, no longer existed. Ancient roads without cobblestones were more easily traveled in winter than in the damp spring or summer. Regional and local connecting paths played a major role in the carrying of messages. Transport services for widespread economic distribution or for moving materiel and men in wartime are attested only in the context of the major estates. With the exception of the building of the bridge over the Rhine at Mainz, there is no evidence of empire-wide transport planning.

The shadow of war loomed over all economic activity. Every free man with a certain minimum of wealth at his disposal was required to keep a coat of chain mail ready to do war service. Each warrior was expected to meet his own costs in this regard. A miniature in the Golden Psalter from St. Gall (Plate VII) gives us a clear idea what Frankish armor looked like. The illumination shows "shirts," but rather than being woven from linen, they consist of interlinked iron rings. These iron shirts were anything but comfortable. If a conflict went on for longer than expected, the king was expected to recompense his soldiers. War materiel had to be manufactured in the estates, and a stockpile of weapons, draft oxen, and horses had to be kept ready.[34] Chain mail, helmets, shields, lances, swords, bows, saddles, and tack were all produced by the estates.

All the trades necessary for this, and more besides, are well attested on the estates.[35] The king demanded that various skilled workers be present in all of his *ministeria,* including ironworkers, gold- and silversmiths, cobblers, wood turners, cartwrights, shield makers, fishermen, falconers, soap makers, beer brewers and spirit distillers, bakers ("to bake rolls for Our use"), net makers for fishing and bird catching, and many other trades (*CdV,* chap. 45). Blacksmiths and armorers (*fabri ferramentorum*), unlike goldsmiths, are mentioned by name on the evidently idealized St. Gall monastery plan. These artisans—particularly those detailed to work for monasteries that performed war service, such as Fleury, Ferrières, Corbie, Lorsch, or Tegernsee—would not just have manufactured plowshares, knives, nails, horseshoes, metal wheel rims, and millrinds, especially since on the monastery plan their workshops are shown next to those of sword burnishers (*emundatores vel politores gladiorum*) and shield makers (*scutarii*). Manorial estates belonging to noblemen would surely have been no less comprehensively equipped.

We do not find any armorers working as freelancers, which is surely not the result of a lack of documentary evidence. After all, where could they have got the necessary raw materials when the mining rights to them—as was also the case with salt—were the sole preserve of the landed nobility? There is no record of specialized centers of production, although they must have been close to deposits of iron ore. So, did a Frankish free man who was obliged to do war service and who had no great manorial estate to supply his needs simply acquire his weapons on the open market? In other words, was there a trade in arms? Certainly, we know that Charlemagne banned the export of swords or suits of chain mail to the Slavs and the Avars.[36] Clearly, production capacity and quality were sufficiently high, and merchants could equip themselves with the requisite goods. Or was it rather the case that the king was trying to retain control over the possession of arms? One of the duties of his officials was to ensure and monitor the upkeep of iron weapons; "on being brought back [from war], they are to be deposited in the storeroom" (*CdV*, chap. 42). Moreover, it is significant that Charlemagne makes specific reference to his weapons and saddles in his will.

There is much talk of signal fires that had to be maintained and sentry duties that had to be carried out; evidently, even the king's estates in his own realm were not totally secure (*CdV*, chap. 27). These orders in no way simply related to the border to the south, then, with the enemy territory of Muslim Spain, but instead must have held for the defense of every border. Fences were to be erected to protect individual farmsteads. In order to prevent farms from being overexploited, king's messengers and envoys—even if they were hurrying to the royal court—were banned from staying overnight there without the express permission of the king or queen (chap. 27). Regulations were also issued on the internal jurisdiction of the individual *ministeria*.

How Were the Estates Managed?

The manors of the landed nobility were beyond the king's sphere of influence. Yet the king would undoubtedly have concerned himself to a limited degree with the landholdings of the Church. They enjoyed extensive royal protection and multiplied as a result of land donations to the various monasteries. These gifts occurred regularly, as recompense for the monks to remember the monarch in their prayers, but they also must have been intended to meet the need of the economically weaker freemen. These so-called precarists were people who gifted their land to the monastery in order to guarantee themselves its protection; they were given it back in the form of a *precarium* and were permitted to enjoy its fruits for the duration of their lives. This form of land tenure was akin to a kind of annuity agreement.

Charlemagne now required certainty concerning the extent and potential of royal and ecclesiastical estates. Directives such as those in the so-called *Brevium exempla* foreshadow this.[37] These "letters" provided model examples of reports the king had called for, namely, records of the ownership and yield of various types of manor. The church at Staffelsee in Augsburg served to illustrate the features of a bishop's estate,[38] while Wissembourg in Alsace was cited as an example of a royal monastery, and those associated with it holding precarial tenure in the diocese of Worms exemplified the traditions and benefices that evolved there. The royal *fiscus* (manor) of Annappes (in the present-day Nord *département* of France), the *fiscus Treola* southwest of Annappes, and various other unnamed royal estates served as examples of a royal manor and its facilities.[39] The submitted reports were used as models, as chapters 23 and 24 of the *Brevium exempla* indicate, with instructions to the royal emissary conducting the survey: "You should record the remainder correspondingly," and "The livestock are to be recorded in exactly the same way." These models convey the individual inventories of the central estates that have survived from the reign of Charlemagne up to the time the document was compiled, and must be seen as exemplary here. They reveal circumspection, solicitude, and the expectation of profit. The people who compiled the reports were specially dispatched royal messengers.

At Staffelsee, St. Michael's Monastery with its furnishings was singled out for comment: "The altar decorated with gold and silver, five gilded reliquaries studded with translucent jewels and crystals, in addition to one made of copper and partially gilded, a reliquary cross made of gilded silver leaf and fitted with a latch, another smaller reliquary cross of gold and glass, and a larger cross of gold and silver with translucent precious stones. Above the altar hangs a partially gilded silver crown." Lavish wall hangings (*paraments*) and altar accoutrements were listed, and all the church's books were meticulously cataloged. They were predominately biblical and New Testament texts but also included a manuscript containing homilies by Pope Gregory the Great, a *liber canon excerptus*—that is, a canon-law collection—an anonymous commentary on the Psalms, two antiphonaries, a commentary on St. Matthew's Gospel by St. Jerome, and a manuscript of the *Benedictine Rule*. This kind of inventory laid bare the material facilities of the estate in question.

The report of one set of royal monitors runs thus: "Then we came across the farmstead and the manor house and the other buildings that belong to the Church. This farm has 740 yokes [the area that could be plowed in a day with a team of oxen] of arable land, together with meadows that produced 610 cartloads of hay. All we found of the harvest was 30 cartloads, which we gave to the 72 prebendaries . . . and in addition a broken-in horse, 26 oxen, 20 cows, 1 bull, 61 pieces of small livestock, 5 calves, 87 sheep, 14 lambs, 17 wethers, 58 goats, 12 goat kids, 40 hogs, 50 piglets, 63 geese, and 50 chickens." "A *genitium* is also situated there, with 24 women," presumably employed in weaving at twelve looms; the workshop's warehouse stock was ascertained to be five bolts of light wool, four of linen, and five completed shirts. A mill was also recorded, with an annual output of twelve bushels of flour. This, then, was the sum total of the central farmstead's equipment and production, but it did not include the output of the estate's tenant farmers.

Twenty-three occupied free farmsteads were attached to this manor, and their tributes, along with the services they rendered in plowing, harvesting, or other special duties, were painstakingly registered. In addition, there were another nineteen farms run by serfs, which alongside their negligible yields were also required to undertake corvée labor three days a week throughout the year, and whose women each had to provide a linen shirt or a length of spun cloth. Around a quarter of the free men also had to perform messenger duties, usually on foot. If they needed a horse, they had to keep and feed it themselves. At least half of the free men on an estate did military service, while the remainder were permitted to join with another man to fulfill the duty, although each had to provide one or two draft oxen. All others provided the army with two oxen annually; tenant farmers were expected to fatten them up throughout the year. Augsburg had a total of seven manorial estates, which were not listed individually. Only the total of all farmstead federations (villications) was presented by way of example: "1,006 occupied free farms, unoccupied 35, 421 occupied bondsmen's farms, unoccupied 45, making a total of 1,427 occupied and 80 unoccupied farmsteads"; living and working on these properties would have been some 7,000 to 8,000 people, not counting the "homeless" *mancipes*.

With its forty-two farmsteads clustered around the central manor and around two hundred to three hundred people working the land, Staffelsee was a relatively small estate. The number of serf farms here was far less than that of free farms, whose inhabitants were liable for military service, although in some cases this could be fulfilled by turns. Was there a trend toward the abandonment of serf farms? In any event, the number of unoccupied serf farms exceeded that of unoccupied free farms. Free farmers had to feed the oxen destined for war service, without doubt a considerable burden. If one assumes that the other estates in the Diocese of Augsburg were more or less similarly equipped, the bishop would have provided around four hundred or more men for Charlemagne's campaigns, together with almost as many oxen. Very few horses were stabled at Staffelsee, most likely for courier services; yet surprisingly, a comparatively large number of messengers lived there. Around a third of the women were required to provide at least one linen shirt per year. Some 150 or more women housed in eight or more *genitia* may have supplied the bishop with woolen and linen cloth; as the inventory taken at Staffelsee appears to show, part of this stock may then have been used for trade. Baking and brewing were also women's work, as were gardening and harvesting, as well as foraging for food in the forest.[40]

Traditions observed at the monastery of Wissembourg, which was situated within the bishopric of Worms, served as examples of free men holding precarial tenure and prebendaries (*benificiarii*). The manor, along with the numerically recorded dependent serf farms and vineyards, plus the fiefdoms of the monastery, were handed over to the control of the precarists, along with their own church on occasion. These "beneficiaries" occasionally received more extensive lands in fee, with a manor house, dependent occupied and unoccupied free and serf farms, meadows, vineyards, and forestry rights; mills and livestock could also be allocated. Everything would be carefully recorded.

Alongside their farming activities, the royal estates also sought prestigious furnishings. These estates would then subsequently find their way into the records (plus their farmsteads, their livestock, and their yields, although these were not listed in the model surveys) with all their facilities noted. So, in the case of Annappes, we find the stone-built "Royal Hall" plus three other rooms and discover that the whole building was ringed with balconies and had eleven ladies' chambers and seventeen wooden outbuildings belonging to the royal farmstead, with a stable, a kitchen, and other utilities, all protected by a solid fence and a stone gatehouse that had a guardhouse or living quarters on the first floor. Other facilities listed were a bed, a tablecloth, various receptacles, and two bronze coal scuttles and one iron, along with other tools, scythes and sickles, and wooden implements. On one occasion, the inspectors recorded that in a particular (unnamed) location, there were no gold-, silver-, or blacksmiths and no facilities for hunting. Another time, the inventories cite a stone-built manor house whose interior was completely paneled in wood.

Then it was the turn of the number of barns and storehouses and the stock of farm animals to be listed. The following were registered at Annappes: 51 older mares, 5 three-year-olds, 7 two-year-olds, and the same number of yearlings, 10 two-year-old and 8 one-year-old foals, 3 breeding stallions, 16 oxen, 2 donkeys, 50 cows with calves, 20 sucklings, 38 one-year-old calves, 3 bulls, 260 full-grown hogs, 100 piglets, and other sundry livestock. Annappes and, generally speaking, all the other royal estates mentioned were extraordinarily well appointed and bred horses for a large surrounding area. On one of the farmsteads, no fewer than 79 older, 24 three-year-old, 12 two-year-old, and 13 yearling fillies were counted, along with 6 two-year-old and 12 yearling colts and 4 stud horses, in addition to other large livestock. The directives relating to this activity in the *Capitulare de villis* had clearly been followed. Yet where were the many warhorses in the

Frankish Empire stabled? Were they distributed among the free men who were liable for military service, and who were not in a position to breed horses themselves, or were they sent to another royal estate in a central location? The royal estate of Annappes was capable of accommodating the king and his retinue for some time without more ado; indeed, it is thought that Charlemagne visited the estate in 800 when he and his entourage traveled from Aix up to the North Sea coast and on to St-Riquier on a tour of inspection.[41]

The king wanted to know what resources he had at his command. But did he also appreciate the efforts and the sheer sweat, hunger, and hardship—indeed, the endless suffering—that lay behind statistics such as these? Did he stop to think of the toiling masses whenever he took delivery of the reports? What kind of accounts did he keep? For instance, did he attempt to review the earnings from his estate with an eye, say, to upcoming plans? Or to alleviate periods of hardship? Did he collate all the reports he received in order that he might compare them year-to-year, or possibly also in order to be able to monitor his inspectors?

Although none of this has come down to us in the sources, it is hard to imagine that people back then simply lived some hand-to-mouth economic existence. The decrees issued by the Synod of Frankfurt in 794 display more forethought than that and give clear indications of instituting welfare provisions. How were these provisions put into practice? Just a few of the measures instituted by Adalhard of Corbie, whose monastery was sufficiently large to make it liable for war service, give evidence of a degree of contemporary fiscal calculation where estate management, planning, and welfare were concerned. Corbie is second to none in providing us with comprehensive information about monastery life during the Carolingian period.

As the abbot and lord of the manor, Charlemagne's cousin Adalhard was deeply concerned with the organization of the abbey's landholdings—or, to be more precise, their reorganization. The relevant statutes date only from the year 822, namely, from the period after Adalhard returned from the forced exile into which Louis the Pious had banished him after the death of Charlemagne.[42] But the terms in which these statutes are couched do not provide any evidence of any serious divergence from the period before. They reveal a strong, efficient estate administration that clearly follows the practices adopted in royal record keeping. Could it be the case that Adalhard had once worked on these? At that time, in 822, there were barely 350 monks living at Corbie, although generally the complement of this monastery was reckoned to be 400 brothers.[43]

Documents that have been preserved, however, include resolutions concerning the prebendaries, the paupers' hospital, the year's harvest yield, the monastery gardens, the refectory and the monks' kitchen, the monastery gateway, and the way in which the tithe was administered. As an addendum, we also find a directive about the cellaring arrangements, namely, that 600 hogs were to be slaughtered annually, of which 60 were to go to the gatehouse guards, 370 to the cellar master (i.e., one a day, plus five extras), 120 for the prebendaries, and 50 for the abbot to dispose of as he wished. The 370 hogs sent to the cellar—many of which were turned into salt pork and sausages—were meant to meet the requirements of those who were sick, the monastery's vassals, and all the other recipients of food within the monastery who neither belonged to the gatehouse nor were prebendaries. The prebendaries' 120 hogs were also processed in the cellar. There were precise instructions on how the cellar master was to handle the slaughtered animals, how the prebendaries' share was to be distributed to them, and how the gatehouse's portion was to be used.[44] The cellar master was required to keep a written record of all these transactions.

The running of an estate was conducted by servants such as chamberlains, cellarers, gatekeepers, or seneschals, and an official known as the *actor villarum* oversaw the operations of all the various farms, while the hospital and the garden were also administered by specially designated officials. These functionaries were responsible, for example, for supervising the exactly 150 clerical or lay prebendaries—no more and no fewer—with each prebendary being apportioned four-fifths of a hog for himself and his family each year. Just like other landlords, the monastery employed these people to perform duties both within and outside the estate, for instance, in the individual workshops (say, for blacksmithing or goldsmithing, or for the manufacture of shields or parchment), or engaged them in specialist tasks (such as horse rearing or in the hospital); their number also included three brass founders (*fusarii*) and two physicians. Precise accounts were kept of how much bread, beer, fruit wine, or wine each prebendary should receive and when, and what outer and undergarments or caps were due to them, plus what special rations they were entitled to on the Church's thirteen annual feast days.[45]

The other services were similarly regulated. Every night, twelve paupers were put up at the almshouse, while others in need were given a meal. Secondhand clothes and shoes were handed out. Were there corresponding arrangements at Charlemagne's court? The annual receipt of cereals, the daily distribution of which was supervised by the provost, was precisely determined. But because the harvest could sometimes be better and sometimes worse, with higher or lower yields accordingly, averages were calculated according to a smaller unit of weight than at the royal court in such a way that a certain quantity of yield might always form the basis of the calculation. The amount of bread to be handed out each day was specified exactly, and estimates were made of what the lowest, the average, and the largest weight of bread required might be in order to monitor what quantity should be apportioned to the serfs, monks, vassals, guests, school pupils, and prebendaries, respectively. The tithe was to be applied to each crop and each field separately, given that the quality of the produce from each individual field would not be the same;[46] the tithe on livestock was also governed very precisely.

As a result, Adalhard's concerns were focused on a number of areas: the redistribution of harvests; making sure that the monastery's dependents were catered for; providing for guests, the sick, and the poor; and, not least, increasing annual yields and performance. He was at pains to emphasize the importance of this last responsibility, noting that everyone wished that each harvest "might grow and not dwindle."[47] Abbot Adalhard always factored in reserves. Money was not an alien concept to him; bondsmen could also be recompensed with cash. In principle, the king's estate may have been administered according to the same rules, although it is undoubtedly true that the provisions on tributes would have been complicated by the size of the estates, the large number of palaces, the organization of the table goods, and the peripatetic royal court.

The objective for both ecclesiastical and royal estates was to increase yield. Improved methods of cultivation were one way to achieve this, but extensive forest clearance played a major role here. This was completed or initiated across a wide area. The sacrifice of vast tracts of virgin forest—such as the Ardennes, the Eifel, the Taunus Mountains, the Odenwald, the Westerwald, or the Alps—to the expansion of farmland by the king, the churches, and the magnates began in this period, not in the following centuries, as is often assumed. Monasteries were at the forefront of this endeavor. Lorsch Abbey, to cite just one instance, which was transferred to the king's control soon after its foundation, may serve as an example. Its rich landholdings soon saw the monastery obliged to engage in military service.

The Heppenheim Marches region, which Charlemagne assigned to Lorsch soon after he acquired control of it, and which stretched as far as the border with the Maingau and hence extended from the present-day Bergstrasse (Mountain Road) in Hesse far into the Odenwald (as a borders report compiled in 795 by order of the king clearly indicated), provides evidence not only of early attempts in this period to describe a tract of land but also first and foremost of the imposition placed on the monasteries to exploit the land. Effectively, half of the Odenwald as far as Michelstadt, a piece of land at that time largely untouched primeval forest, now lay open to the monks to colonize.[48] In addition, there is the description of the boundaries of the parish of the Church of St. Peter in Heppenheim, which also points back to Charlemagne: "This is the perimeter [*terminatio*] of this Church"; there follows the description of a boundary about forty kilometers long, listing all the individual localities along its route in order. "This boundary description was conducted in the year 805 by the Holy Roman emperor Charlemagne"—so runs the inscription on the twelfth-century stone plaque now located in the basement of the church tower; the spelling of the Old High German place names in the text of this inscription may actually point back to the Carolingian period.[49] This parish also extended into the Odenwald and is documentary proof of the early success of the Lorsch monks in colonizing the region.

By way of recompense, new forests came into being, that is, managed woodland areas such as those in the Ardennes, not far from Aix. Charlemagne himself had given his estate managers similar instructions: "Our woods and forests are to be well protected. Whenever a suitable site for clearing appears, they should clear the ground and make sure that the fields they create do not get overgrown by wood again. Where there is meant to be wood, they are forbidden from felling or damaging trees. They should also nurture the game that lives in our forests."[50] The king wanted to be able to hunt.

Above all, though, forest clearance created new farmland that could be put under the plow, thus helping the food situation. An increasing number of people were thus able to feed themselves. Hand in hand with this came an increase in the cultivation of cereals; it was around this time too that the three-field system, with its compulsory crop rotation, appears to have been introduced, although this development was by no means universal and definitely did not occur in places with extensive grazing. The heavy soils now opened up for farming could be worked only by using the heavy moldboard plow but produced a much higher yield. This wheeled plow required a draft team of at least two oxen, a major outlay that none of the small subsistence farmers could afford, but that was perfectly feasible on the large estates. Charlemagne profited here from a technological development that he was not responsible for instigating.

Even so, the Frankish Empire remained highly susceptible to periods of famine. Adalhard, though, disregarded this threat—the centers of the manorial system, it seems, were less badly affected by this scourge. With a ratio of seed corn to harvested grain in bread cereals of just 1:3 or at best 1:4 (nowadays the ratio is 1:16 or even better), the yield had to fall by only one grain per ear of wheat for a third or a quarter of the harvest to be lost. The populace lived largely on porridge, bread, cheese, and—depending on social class—different meats. Only the nobility, for instance, were entitled to hunt large game; often, all that ordinary people got to eat in a year apart from cereals was a fattened hog, some poultry and eggs, and possibly a hare they had trapped. Hog rearing was practiced intensively by the Franks. Einhard recalled that Charlemagne's favorite dish was venison (chap. 24), a delicacy poor people were precluded from eating.

Famines were a regular occurrence, hitting some places every three to five years; this can be seen from people's bone growth and corroborated by exhuming bodies from the period. Time and again, Charlemagne tried to alleviate the effects of famine by lowering the price of grain and bread and by selling off surpluses generated by his estates cheaply. He was prompted to do this both by religious ethics and by good economic sense, inasmuch as he needed to sustain his workforce. In fact, sufficient food stocks that could be used as "intervention cereals" existed only on the central farms of the major estates, not with the individual tenant farmers. Frequently during times of famine, these stocks were released only at extortionate prices—even by bishops and abbots and in defiance of directives by the king and the synods. It was economically relevant to implement religious commandments. In any event, extensive interregional transportation of grain was possible only in areas with navigable rivers. Accordingly, the king's opportunities for intervention were confined to inadequate measures, such as the aforementioned edicts on prices and the willingness to sell off surpluses.

The king relied especially heavily on the free men to bear the costs of waging war. The burden imposed on them by making them perform regular military service grew over the years. Ultimately, the situation required that the king intervene. Fragmentary traces of social legislation from this period have been preserved. For example, church vassals and royal bondsmen from the Le Mans region complained about their workload, prompting Charlemagne to decree that anyone who owned a specified, small tract of land and a healthy draft animal should be required to plow for one day per week for his master, and no more. If he did not have all the necessary equipment, then he should join forces with others to fulfill his duty. But anyone who was simply unable to perform such a task should do manual work for his master for three days a week, from morning to evening. But these tasks were to be organized in such a way, the king decreed, that some people had to work the whole week, others half a week, and still others just two days a week. The bondsmen were not to interfere with these arrangements. Clearly the three days were an average for the group of the poorest bondsmen. Certainly, more work time was not to be demanded from them.[51] For the remaining days of the week, they could look after their own affairs.

The numerous *precarium* contracts associated with the monastery at Wissembourg reveal a trend among free men to enter into enduring relationships of dependence on patrons such as monasteries (expressed through the payment of interest). Such contracts did not, however, lead to serfdom on their part. That class of free men, who were now cared for by Charlemagne, was to be prevented at all costs from renouncing their independence, making themselves bondsmen of foreign masters, and so evading their obligation to do ruinous war service. So it was that Charlemagne's solicitude also served to maintain the king's military strength.

The military service that weighed so heavily on the "poor" free men now clearly required proper regulation, while the burdens it placed on those required to do it needed to be reduced. But the pursuit of justice ran up against an uncontrolled system of weights and measures and a chaotic coinage. The Synod of Frankfurt called for reform; the Christian commandment of love demanded it. And so a coinage reform was instituted. Henceforth, all money, including the pure silver that was minted into denarii, was to have a fixed relation to measure of capacity and bulk weight.[52] Everything had to be fair, easily understandable, verifiable, and rationally ordered. Charlemagne became a king of organization.

However, famine continued to rage unabated. The Synod of Frankfurt reported, "Our most devout master, our king, determined, with the agreement of the synod, that no man, whether he be of ecclesiastical or secular rank, should sell the harvest at a higher price than the tariff set by this synod in 794, either during times of plenty or in a period of general price increases."[53] This stipulation was placed at the head of a list of further edicts for the benefit of the Church and the king. Yet without the magnates or the participation of the bishops and influential abbots, such an undertaking was doomed to failure right from the outset. It was essential that the powerful and rich should be involved. Admonished by the terrors of the Day of Judgment and Hell, they were obligated to observe the Christian commandment of love; Christian charity was to actively bring succor to the poor and needy.

"Whosoever holds a fiefdom from Us [the king] should take urgent care with God's help to ensure that no bondsman beholden to that fiefdom should die of hunger; and anything that goes beyond his own requirements for feeding his own servants shall be sold as instructed."[54] This demand was included in the same Frankfurt capitulary. Chapters 33 and 34 of this edict run as follows: "So that the Catholic faith in the Holy Trinity and in the Lord's Prayer and the creed might be proclaimed to everyone. And in order that greed and avarice might be vanquished." Proclamations of faith and the economic order, royal power, and church reform went hand in hand or were certainly intended to. Submission to religious commandments and to God and economic activity were all aspects of one and the same royal authority. Charlemagne wanted to implement them all among his magnates and all his subjects. Christian social ethics were to be espoused and put into practice. Such an undertaking required comprehensive reforms. Would the magnates comply with their king's wishes?

Center and Periphery

I am mindful of your request and my promise to write you a
few words of exhortation for your occupation, which—I am
fully aware—requires you to engage in armed conflict, in order
that you might continually have to hand some words of paternal
admonition. You should always bear them in mind, and be
encouraged by them to strive for eternal bliss. I will gladly assent
to your laudable request, and trust that my words might serve to
bring you perpetual salvation. I know that many worldly matters
occupy your thoughts. That is precisely why I am imploring you
that concern for your own redemption might lead you to read this
missive regularly, so that your soul, when it is worn out by
external cares, might return to a state of quiet self-contemplation
and recognize wherein it finds true contentment and the goal
toward which it should strive. I therefore exhort you to be tireless
in your desire to prepare for yourself a place of glory in Heaven
through generous almsgiving, through ensuring that your judges
pass just sentences, and through constant acts of mercy.

Alcuin wrote these words to Count Wido (Guy) of Brittany, one of the great noblemen in the entourage of the Carolingians and the founding father of a dynasty that would in time ascend to imperial status, after Wido had asked the scholar to compile a moral treatise for him.[55] In 802, Wido was the imperial *missus* in the Touraine region, close to where Alcuin lived; it was around this time that the small treatise containing this passage was probably written, and before long it was widely disseminated. To be sure, Alcuin's *De virtutibus et vitiis* was an example of paraenesis (moral advice), but it had been requested by the count to enable him to discharge his new secular role in a just way, that is, in a manner that accorded with the tenets of Christianity. In making this request, Wido was not obeying any orders to do so or even simply complying with the wishes of the emperor, although he was following his example. The kind of attitude displayed by Wido was entirely in keeping with Charlemagne's intentions; the king's aims were shared by his magnates.

The religious author was not discussing any real power relations or hinting at the antagonistic interests of aristocratic society in his tract. Rather, a belief in the power of goodness and trust in faith that could move mountains were the guiding principles of Alcuin's admonitions. Institutional and structural perspectives were entirely lacking in this code of ethics, which focused on practice. No other contemporary piece of writing filled this gap. According to Alcuin, real life should follow the commandments of the Church and organized religion.

To start with, Alcuin claimed at the beginning of his exposition, people had to recognize "what true knowledge and genuine wisdom" were. There followed a series of brief, tightly formulated commentaries on the Christian virtues, on wisdom, faith, love, and hope, encouragement to read the Holy Scriptures regularly and zealously (Alcuin was, after all, instructing a layperson here), and homilies on peace, mercy, clemency, patience, humility, and compunction of the heart, as well as on confession, repentance, conversion, fear of God, almsgiving, chastity, and avoiding fraud, on the sort of judges who should be appointed and the fair justice they should dispense, on bearing false witness, on envy as a socially destructive force, and on pride and proneness to anger. Alcuin then went on to treat the seven deadly sins and the four cardinal virtues (prudence, justice, fortitude, and temperance). He concluded by exhorting the count once more to study this little manual regularly and telling him, "Let neither the habit of a layman nor the quality of a secular way of life frighten you, as if in this habit of life you might not be able to enter the doors of Heaven." The entrance to the kingdom of God, Alcuin maintained, was open equally to "every sex, age, and person, according to dignity of merits."

Granted, the gap between the ideal and reality was wide. Even a ruler of Charlemagne's stature could do nothing about it. The Reichenau schoolmaster Wetti claimed that an angel appeared to him on his deathbed and confided in him that Frankish noblemen, who were repeatedly accused of greed, were "no avengers of injustice, but friends of Satan."[56] They condemned the righteous, vindicated the guilty, and made common cause with thieves and criminals.[57] Before long came an endless stream of complaints. The reality of aristocratic society made for ongoing conflict between the magnates and the churches and also dragged noblemen's bondsmen into the quarrels as well. The richer these magnates were, the more greedily they behaved, it seemed. In these circumstances, then, the ethics of rulership all too easily fell by the wayside.

For example, on one occasion, a count summarily deprived some free men of their liberty, but they succeeded in bringing a grievance before the emperor (Louis the Pious). Louis sent a royal emissary to investigate the matter, who was able to corroborate their claim. As a result, the emperor used his imperial mandate to free the men from the "yoke of serfdom and gave them and their relatives, who had also been forced into servitude, their former liberty back," and in perpetuity, no less. The official wording of a document from the imperial chancellery, which kept the relevant mandate ready to be enacted, suggests that similar cases arose repeatedly.[58] The situation would scarcely have been any better under Charlemagne. Greed and avarice were impossible to stamp out, either in society's upper or lower echelons. The king's spiritual advisers were convinced that this malaise arose when people, incited by the Devil, showed a blatant disregard for the Church's commandments. These vices inevitably ran counter to every rapid success in the reform of the realm.

This made the reorganization of royal power and the Church all the more urgent—far beyond any individual estate. It also explains the urgency of Alcuin's admonition to Count Wido. Everything was to be adapted to the demands of divine worship and those commandments and values designed to strengthen and protect the kingdom and maintain peace among the populace. To be sure, the nobility had to be won over to Charlemagne's objectives; indeed, more than that, it needed to embrace them wholeheartedly of its own accord. Wido did so with Alcuin's help.

Although it may not have been the violent actions of certain counts that first brought it to light, the necessity of better cooperation between the king and the aristocracy became clear when plots to attack Charlemagne were uncovered. The repercussions of the uprising by the Thuringian count Hardrat in 786 turned out to be long lasting. Reports state that treacherous people had fomented "great unrest in the empire of our master and king

Charlemagne."[59] The insurrectionists were said to have calmly justified their actions by claiming that they had not sworn fealty to the king. This situation had to be remedied. The king's messengers were dispatched, presumably in 789, with orders to extract oaths of loyalty from bishops, abbots, counts, and royal vassals wherever the writ of Charlemagne's authority ran, as had been the custom "since ancient times," as the official obfuscating justification for this action claimed. Did more than just a handful of Thuringians dare to defy the king?

Everyone over the age of twelve was required to attend court hearings—be they reeves and vicars, "centenarians" (i.e., the heads of alliances each numbering one hundred heads of Frankish families), or members of the population at large. Everyone was included: the inhabitants of the regions (*Gaue*), villeins, serfs, foreign vassals (*in bassallatico honorati* or *commendati*). Anyone who tried to take flight to avoid swearing the oath was to be reported to the king.[60] Charlemagne demanded the oaths of allegiance both for himself and for his sons; there was even a prescribed wording for the act: "I the undersigned thus pledge that I am loyal to my lord King Charlemagne and his sons and will remain loyal for my entire life without any trickery or malicious intent."[61] The oath committed the person making it to loyalty, not to service; therefore, it differed from the oath of allegiance a vassal made to his master. The "messengers," *missi dominici,* who had to oversee the swearing of these oaths were also expected to ensure that everyone without exception obeyed the call-up to join the army as ordered whenever a general mobilization was announced. Those affected, however, had to inform one another by letter when and where they could assemble.[62]

The note about the *vassi* (vassals), who had to swear allegiance like everyone else, reveals that "loyal followers" and "vassals" were not identical despite the fact that both had to take the oath. A vassal, rather, was a man who owed his master certain services. He might be a simple war servant, endowed with royal or other land held in fee, in return for which he had to provide services, usually of the martial kind. Usually, he would be supplied only with his own equipment and weapons: a horse, a shield, a spear, and a long or short sword;[63] but equally, a vassal could be an abbot, a count, or—at least under Louis the Pious—a king's son.[64] The term did not refer to any legal status but merely to a reciprocal arrangement between a "man" and his master. Vassalage was entered into by means of an oral contract, made visible through symbolic acts such as paying homage and the oath of allegiance.

The "empire," that is, the king's political system of rule, presented itself in the quoted or comparable statements as a ruling or peace association instigated by the king, constituted through the nobility's personal connections to the monarch, and held together by an obligating Christian set of ruling ethics. Certainly, institutional factors were not entirely lacking; one need only think of the aforementioned institution of vassalage or of the legal system mentioned in the same capitulary and its organization within the counties. But apart from the king and his court, these factors in no way concerned the empire as an institution; at that stage, nobody had any conception of an "imperial constitution" or any notion of how all the organizational factors connected with one another. Royal power was too permeated by aristocratic power.

Fundamentally, the counts and their areas of activity (*ministeria*) were subordinate to the king, notwithstanding the fact that pre-Carolingian conditions continued to have an effect, frequently tying the king's hands. Estimations of the number of counties in the Frankish Empire vary between 250 and 300, or even considerably fewer.[65] There is no evidence of a closed network of counties. We know only very few counts by name; they appear very infrequently in the contemporary annals, and in the absence of documents or memorial entries in books of the dead, the class that they represented—the upper echelon of the Carolingian nobility—remains completely obscure.[66] It was by no means the rule that their areas of competence were passed down from father to son, even though the sons of counts stood the greatest chance of also taking control of a county (though seldom their father's). Likewise, there was no bureaucracy to speak of, nor any general body of people predisposed to serve the empire by virtue of their birth, still less any specific imperial institutions, merely individual "servants" (*ministri*) of the king and the concept of "serving" him. Certainly, this kind of "servitude" may well have been more in tune with the Carolingian ideology of power than it was with social or political reality.

Nevertheless, in the case of Charlemagne, for the first time since Roman times a king was concerning himself with the protection of the realm's borders; it was during this period, then, that a concept of the empire's border as an external frontier of the entire Frankish Empire (*fines vel marcae; Royal Frankish Annals* for 788) first came into being, that is, the notion of a territorial limited sphere of power within which the Frankish king held sway. Some border march areas were established, although there was no closed fringe of marches surrounding the whole empire.[67] This period saw the creation of the first "margraves" (*marchiones*), who governed more than a single county and were responsible for guarding their region's frontier. The Breton margrave Roland has become famous through legend and poetry, while Eric of Friuli won renown for his successes against the Avars on the southeastern borders of the empire.

The self-organization of the magnates on their allodial (i.e., freely held) estates and fiefs was accorded constitutive significance. The king could and had to influence them and try to direct them without driving them in an undesired direction; but he took care not to intervene in the running of aristocratic property. He was dependent on the allegiance and loyalty of his "strongmen" or "magnates." Repeated royal "donations" were designed to reinforce their allegiance and secure their support in the long term. In this way, the king's followers also profited from each lucrative military success he recorded. This practice also gave rise to widely distributed, though unconnected, complexes of landholdings belonging to the "imperial nobility," extending in some instances from the North Sea or the Atlantic coast as far as Italy. A certain Cadolah, for example, who was himself the son of a count and the father of another, a member of the Berthold clan (still recalled today in the name of the Baar region in southwestern Germany), appears from 790 onward in the records of St. Gall Monastery. Cadolah served under Charlemagne as a royal inspector of estates in Italy; later, under Louis the Pious, he was made duke of Friuli.[68] The interests of this "imperial" aristocracy were correspondingly extensive.[69]

The consort of a king who was chosen from an influential family likewise helped strengthen the bonds among the country's elites. Not least for this reason, Charlemagne may have chosen for his third wife a bride who would assure him a large following among the Bavarian and Alemannic aristocracy. Similar considerations may also have prompted him to marry the East Frankish Fastrada, although there is no way of verifying this. As was the case with the nobility in general, royal spouses were involved in the political system. The oath of allegiance Charlemagne made his subjects swear did not include the queen, though; nor was there any question of gender equality. Charlemagne and his contemporaries followed the old doctrine based on the letters of St. Paul the Apostle, which stated that women must be subservient to men "since their mind is smaller and more inclined to temptation."[70] Even so, royal authority under Charlemagne, in which the queen also played a part, was characterized by consensual rule and reciprocity of power.

How assertive was the royal command, the *verbum regis*, under such personal conditions? Who heeded it? The *Capitulare missorum* of 789 hints at the answer to this question. It reports that complaints had come to the king's attention, indicating that "many people" feared for their rights (and that the counts had not been fulfilling their duties in the expected manner). However, it was the king's stated will that the rights of every one of his subjects should remain inviolate. The aim of this was not to establish any kind of general equality under the law, but to maintain the prevailing inequality between "free" and "unfree" men and between the "powerful" and the "poor." Yet the "subjective," "personal" sense of justice that acted as a yardstick in everyone's life was to be protected. This principle helped preserve peace among the populace, even if it did hamper social change. But if a count or royal messenger, including representatives of the king himself, infringed on this right, it was to be reported to the king: "For he desires to fundamentally improve this situation."[71]

Abuses were a frequent occurrence, conditioned by the personal system of rule. This was not lost on a perceptive observer like Alcuin. Courts met infrequently and at preordained locations. It was customary for evidence to be taken on oath; false witness and perjury were the order of the day. Plaintiffs frequently had to travel to the court from far afield. Who could afford to do so? And if they did, could they find enough compurgators? It is therefore open to question how far the king's stated wish to improve matters was actually crowned with success. Even in the final years of his reign, the emperor was bemoaning the illegal oppression of the poor by his "strongmen," and it was for good reason that Alcuin admonished Count Wido to exercise mercy and to respect judges and the verdicts they reached.

Those who suffered oppression were by no means bondsmen, but rather free men. Many of them, another document claims, were driven by sheer hardship to become swindlers, thieves, and criminals.[72] Robbery—whether out of desperation or on other grounds—was widespread in the Frankish Empire. And it was the same poor people who were its victims—a cycle that the poor in general were forced to pay for through increasing dependence on regional rulers. Charlemagne sought in vain to find a lasting solution to this problem.[73] He was just as unsuccessful in this endeavor as any of his successors. Mindful of the physical distance that separated them from the center of power, strongmen obeyed the king only when there was something in it for them in return—in the form of gifts, grace and favor, greater prestige, honor, or advancement in rank.

The difficulties began with establishing the royal writ of authority universally. The "empire" held sway, and the "king's word" was law, only in the place where he happened to be at any given time. There, he was able to impose his will and his authority. But the farther from the center of the empire the magnates operated, the more they took it on themselves to act independently, and the more the king had to rely on their loyalty. Who learned what Charlemagne had ordered, or when he had proclaimed his capitularies, or where the royal messengers had announced their content, or what these documents commanded, or to whom the king was extending his protection? The surviving documentary material is far too scanty for us nowadays to be able to monitor how efficient the king's edicts were, although the example of the *Admonitio generalis* does at least reveal the channels by which they were disseminated.[74]

The methods employed to govern particular areas appear primitive by modern standards, but they were the most efficient at the time. They included regular court assemblies at which bishops, abbots, and counts gathered; written royal decrees; a functioning network of messengers; royal coercive envoys with supervisory and other special powers; communication between magnates in accordance with the king's will; the co-opting of each magnate's own military authority to the service of the kingdom as a whole; and, above all, decentralization. Charlemagne's "empire" was in actual fact multicentered. From an early date, Charlemagne established dependent satellite realms and put his underage sons in charge of them; in 781, he created the kingdoms of Italy and Aquitaine for Carloman (Pepin) and Louis the Pious, followed by Francia as a potential bequest to his second son, Charles, who in the interim was given control of the "Duchy of Le Mans" (*ducatus Cenomannicus*), also known as the "empire west of the Seine" (*regnum ultra Segona*).[75] Later, he also set up Bavaria, possibly for the son he hoped Fastrada would bear him, and then (in 791–792) for Pepin the Hunchback.[76]

In all likelihood, the groundwork for this particular measure was laid as early as 780; the annals of the Benedictine monastery at St-Amand-les-Eaux note for that year: "King Charlemagne divided his kingdoms up among his sons."[77] Communications between the monarchs took place through royal messengers and through regular visits by the sons to their father's court. In this way, the power Charlemagne's sons wielded was never able to disengage itself from the firm direction of the "grand king," and they and their realms became just intermediate stations of central royal authority. The margravates also formed regional centers of power.

Indeed, Charlemagne's rule by direct edict also extended to Italy and Aquitaine. Thus, in 801, Charlemagne dispatched Charles to Aquitaine at the head of an army to assist his brothers at the siege of Barcelona. Likewise, Louis the Pious was expected to come to his brother Pepin's aid in Italy. First and foremost, and in the absence of any other orders, the capitularies applied throughout the whole of Charlemagne's sphere of power, in-

cluding the subordinate kingdoms. Only in the case of Italy may some capitularies have been issued that appear to have been written by Charlemagne's
son Pepin;[78] no such documentary evidence exists for Aquitaine, however.[79]

Then again, in commissioning the royal envoys, from around the 780s,
Charlemagne effectively created an instrument of power tailored to the personal circumstances of his royal power. In doing so, he could rely on earlier
precedents; after the imperial coronation in 800, the institution of the "royal
messengers" would be organized with even greater efficiency.[80] These *missi*
were intended to oversee subordinate officeholders, such as bishops and
abbots, counts and royal vassals, in well-defined areas of jurisdiction, and
sometimes also to ensure communication with the king's sons. Therefore,
they presided over spheres of competence clearly defined both spatially and
functionally. They were assigned responsibility for distributing the capitularies and other edicts, for administration and jurisprudence, and occasionally even for certain military operations. Thus, in 787, an abbot and a count
were charged with inspecting the estate of the Monastery of St-Wandrille,[81]
while six years later a count and a cleric were empowered to assign certain
palaces in Aquitaine, namely, Doué, Chasseneuil, Angeac, and Ebreuil, as
residences to the young king Louis the Pious during the winter months on a
four-year cycle, and hence to intervene directly in the organization of royal
authority in Aquitaine.[82]

The *missi* were dispatched with instructions (undoubtedly written), often
in the form of short aides-mémoires, which read like memos: "On Thieves
and Robbers. On False Witnesses. On Perjurers. On Fugitives. On People
Who Have Been Incarcerated for Minor Transgressions. On Coinage."[83]
Whether succinctly formulated or expounded on at greater length, such instructions on monitoring a region imposed a restrictive ubiquity of royal
authority wherever they were applied. Fortunate coincidences in the survival
of sources to the present day, such as those outlined in the widely distributed *Admonitio generalis* of 789, reveal that the decrees were disseminated
by various different paths; in the case of the *Admonitio generalis*, we can
identify at least seven different transmission routes from the eighth century.[84]
These mirror the activities of the messengers, who fanned out from the royal
court, each carrying his copy of the original example of the edict created in
the palace at Aix and transmitting it to the appropriate regional center, be it
a monastery, a bishop's see, or a secular center of power. There, they had
them copied anew, thus ensuring a comprehensive dissemination of the decree in question. Whether the situation outlined here was the normal practice or just a special case must remain a matter of speculation, however.

The transmission of the *Admonitio generalis* in fact reveals even more about Charlemagne's exercise of power if we consider the example of a manuscript now housed in Leiden in the Netherlands (Voss. Lat. Q. 119). This manuscript shows signs of having been part of a book containing a number of legal texts the messenger carried with him, and by means of which the *missi* informed and monitored the parishes they had been sent to inspect.[85] Shortly after 805, this volume was incorporated into a larger collection in Tours. It concerned Aquitaine and the messengers who had been sent there, Bishop Mancio of Toulouse and Count Palatine Eugerius. It was their task to accept the general populace's oath of allegiance, which had just been made compulsory in 789. These two emissaries were equipped with a "breviary" containing at least four capitularies: the Herstal capitulary of 779 and, alongside the *Admonitio generalis,* two further decrees dating from 789.[86] Charlemagne governed his growing "empire" with the aid of written edicts, coercive emissaries he dispatched personally, and both written and oral publication of the decrees at their intended destination. The reports his envoys brought back kept him abreast of situations and apprised him of the necessity to intervene at this or that location.

Repeatedly, and on a regular basis from 802 onward, it became the practice for a bishop or abbot and a count to undertake the mission for their region together in order to ensure that ecclesiastical and secular issues were properly investigated. It appears that in the heartland of the Frankish empire—that is, in Francia proper and Burgundy—fixed parishes were established at this time to facilitate the monitoring functions of the royal emissaries, whereas before they had been sent out only on an ad hoc basis.[87] Both men, the clerical envoy and the secular one, did not as a rule, or at least not invariably, come from the aristocracy of the region in question. Rather, their authority resided in the royal assignment they were called on to carry out. For the duration of Charlemagne's reign and for the first few years of Louis the Pious's, there is no doubt that this instrument of power had a certain efficiency about it. But equally, some limitations became apparent. Passive resistance to the royal orders would likely have been widespread; moreover, it is a moot point whether the *missi* always acted in the king's best interests. After all, who or what could compel them to adhere to Alcuin's doctrine of virtue, unless it was the threat of divine anger and of the torments of Hell and eternal damnation? The Anglo-Saxon writer did not omit to mention these in his tract. Or did the risk of losing the king's grace and favor exert greater influence on them?

The counts acted as the king's representatives in their counties. Regular "unbidden" and extraordinary "bidden" court hearings brought together the judicial communities of free men to determine legal cases and to receive notification of the king's rulings. As required, the counts had to account for their actions at court assemblies and potentially also in front of the *missi;* it was therefore possible to bring them to book. Instances of unlawful use of force and unjust rulings on the part of the counts had to be brought before the king for judgment.

Every lord who could muster armed men, every bishop, every abbot, every count, and every magnate had the potential to become a political force. These men's positions were reinforced by friends and relatives, bonded together in clan-like groupings. It was quite possible for tensions—triggered by envy, anger, revenge, violence, false testimony, perjury, or other vices that no court could control—to erupt between the counts and the regional magnates from either the laity or the clergy, even to the extent of a blood feud. Not least among the king's duties was preventing these from occurring in the first place and quelling them if they did arise.

As the justifications for his marriages showed, Charlemagne also had to take influential aristocratic groups into account and attempt to win them over to his cause. Repeated bans on any sworn alliances—which failed to have any decisive success—were meant to prevent the growth of concentrations of power independent of the king. The king could allow himself to get into conflict with aristocratic groups only in exceptional cases. Nevertheless, Count Wido's request and Alcuin's pledge at least revealed that some of the magnates identified the need for action and strove to find ways of operating correctly and justly. The ethical code of the ruler began to take effect.

Alcuin worked from the presumption that secular magnates would be literate and know Latin. Charlemagne would also have expected this. And it is certainly true that literacy among the ruling elite experienced a noticeable increase under his rule. Above all, this became possible because the churches established schools on a grand scale and became an integral part of the royal exercise of power. The scribes, chaplains, and literate administrators who formed a vital part of the burgeoning major empire were all educated—at least north of the Alps—among the ranks of the clergy. In Italy, meanwhile, a comparable elevated system of lay education, geared precisely toward training pupils in the law, had existed since classical antiquity.

As a general rule, the Carolingian king acted reactively rather than proactively. Further inquiries were often necessary. A record of answers to queries of this nature that had been posed by a "coercive envoy" has survived.[88] "You asked whether a count should receive payment of a shilling for the transcript of a verdict, along with the lay assessors and the notary. Read the book of Roman law and act according to what you find there; but if the case has to do with the Lex Salica [namely, Frankish law] and you find nothing relevant there, then raise the matter at our court assembly" (chap. 2). Key factors concerning the efficiency and structure of power are implicit in the formulation "You asked." If no one inquired, then no pronouncement came from the king. Roman law, which operated only in the south of Gallia and in parts of Italy, still enshrined certain general norms to which the king could refer. Frankish law, on the other hand, relied on the oral tradition and on ad hoc verdicts. Individual verdicts were arrived at repeatedly; these did not add up to an overall norm or a ruling that was valid throughout the empire, still less to any imperial statute book. All too often, expediency guided the framing of the law, which accordingly proceeded from error to error, and from one individual correction to the next.

The *missus* had the power to impose the king's ban on any bishops and abbots and others in the king's inner circle who refused to appear at the envoy's court; this meant that they forfeited a fine of sixty shillings. If they still refused to attend, their names would be reported to the royal court (chap. 5). Bridge toll was to be collected only at the officially appointed customs stations. "We instructed you by word of mouth to do this, but you have not done it" (chap. 6). Also, no unfree man was allowed to independently present his certificate of emancipation (*carta*); rather, his former master was required to scrutinize it and, "if he is able so to do," to reject it as fake (chap. 7). The king's rule was unstable; therefore, it had to assert itself with every new instance, and the farther away from the center of power it had to prove itself, the more tentatively this occurred. These examples amply demonstrate the enormous difficulties Charlemagne was confronted with.

How long, then, did it take for the king's answer to arrive, even when the messenger system was functioning properly? Was it still of topical relevance when it did? Charlemagne's letter to his wife Fastrada may once again serve as an example.[89] In it, he cites important information that must have been of decisive significance for the imminent campaign against the Avars, and that Charlemagne's son Pepin had just sent to him from Italy via a messenger. This news implies that a messenger had also been dispatched beforehand from the father to his son, imparting information that ensured that the military operations of the two kings could be coordinated over long distances. Information in Charlemagne's letter to Fastrada that related to the business of ruling, and that was conveyed to the queen for her to implement, was supplemented by personal messages. But in the same communication, Charlemagne complained about messengers from his spouse who had failed to arrive. This single piece of documentary evidence thus gives us an insight into both the efficiency and the shortcomings of the messenger system. Both were to be expected.

The army played a key role in establishing the might of Charlemagne's Frankish kingdom. Only the king was empowered to issue the military draft order; he must surely have also decided where the troops were to be raised. Not every free man had to report for duty by any means.[90] Basically, raising the forces necessary for a war required the agreement of the magnates. All too frequently—as in the first wars against the Lombards—they were at loggerheads. In such cases, it was left to the king to deal with the question of how he might assemble a force and with all the other circumstances, such as what sanctions he ought or was in a position to enact against draft dodgers. The lure of potential war booty or actual favors offered by the king usually facilitated the magnates' decisions.

Vassals of the king and of the magnates increasingly came to form the backbone of the army. Each was granted his own property, in return for which he was expected to supply his own weapons, horse, and other equipment, such as an expensive coat of chain mail, in times of war. This military-oriented vassalage was a characteristic feature of the Frankish Empire. "King's vassals," *vassi dominici,* had at their disposal at least twelve farmsteads and in some cases considerably more. Even though it had not yet evolved into a full-fledged feudal system, this practice of land held in fee had already spread to the Carolingian fighting forces. Increasingly, this development drove the majority of free men out of the army. The situation reflected their growing poverty and social decline; many free men now preferred a sheltered state of bondage to a freedom fraught with risk and so submitted to a foreign master. In the final years of his reign, Charlemagne began to consider the consequences of this development by restricting the obligation to military service for the poor according to their assets.[91] Even so, this could not halt the social decline of those concerned; in actual fact, a sweeping process of mediatization of free people was under way, which saw them enter into a state of increasing dependency on local magnates— counts, bishops, and other lords, whose protection they were forced to seek. Under Charlemagne, this development was still barely perceptible, but over the long term the regions became ever more independent of the royal center of power.

Orientation in a Vast Space

Charlemagne ruled over a vast empire. What conception did he have of it, of the huge expanse between the North Sea and Campania and across to the Pyrenees and the river Ebro, or the land between the Atlantic and the river Elbe—over all of which he had dominion—and of the regional powers that governed the various localities? We cannot know the answer to this. However frequently Charlemagne's edicts may have addressed different aspects of the ethics of rulership, they seldom discussed any real circumstances, such as the conditions in this or that region, the difficulties of communication, journey times, or any other practical details. So, to what extent did Charlemagne mentally combine the various parts—kingdom, duchy, county, ecclesiastical province, a diocese here and there—into a whole? He had no special means of help at his disposal. The Church's division of space, from the ecclesiastical province to the parishes, still represented the most highly developed and at the same time most stable administrative network extending over the whole of the empire, but this could be really understood only on the ground. In an ideal case, the king's instructions could be handed down through this network from above to below and put into practice among the populace. But no one had a complete understanding of the internal structure of the empire.

We do not know how Charlemagne oriented himself. The size of his empire could only approximately be guessed at, and royal orders took a correspondingly long time to be transmitted. Speed was not a familiar dimension. Distances were measured in concrete terms of the number of days it took to complete a journey, not in miles or kilometers. Charlemagne, too, knew from experience how far the route was from Francia to, say, Rome or Regensburg. The efficient postal system of the Roman period had long since collapsed. A substitute arrangement comprising a plethora of messengers had supplanted it, as outlined in the description of the monastery at Staffelsee in Augsburg.[92] The king's messenger network must also have been highly developed by this stage; we may presume that in this case particular messengers were assigned to specific palaces, and that their local knowledge enabled them to quickly pass on orders and information.

There were no abstract maps at this time; ancient geographers had mostly used Greek, which by now was more or less (apart from certain exceptions such as Rome) a defunct language in the Latin West. With few exceptions, like the famous *Tabula Peutingeriana*, Roman maps had all been lost;[93] there is nothing to indicate that any of them were in use any longer. This one surviving panel, discovered by the German humanist Conrad Celtes in the late fifteenth century and bequeathed to Konrad Peutinger, was a twelfth-century copy (possibly via a Carolingian interim stage?) of an original fourth-century map. The cities of Mainz, Cologne, Xanten, and Tongeren are clearly marked on it, but Aix (Aachen), Echternach, Prüm, and Lorsch are missing. We may speculate whether an early medieval landowner could have successfully got his bearings using it.

Popular knowledge was on a small scale, geared strictly to the immediate vicinity or at most the local region; only the imperial nobility had broader horizons. But everyone's conception of space was conditioned by a number of factors: the lack of any geographical maps, with people navigating just by the points of the compass; the hardships of travel, involving interminable riding along roads and long-distance tracks and tented encampments. Only in the heartland of Francia did Charlemagne move easily from palace to palace; on his campaigns to Aquitaine, Saxony, or Bavaria, as well as Lombardy, he had to make do with sleeping under canvas.

The route to Rome, for instance, involved proceeding from one staging post to the next, strung out like pearls on a string, along the roads that led across the Alps to the south; the journey was captured in brief reports by those who undertook it. Even in Charlemagne's time, the road from Pavia to Rome followed a route that later became known as the Frankish Way, the Via Francigena, namely, the great military and pilgrimage road that ran to Rome via Lucca, Florence, Siena, and Acquapendente; in parts, this route used the ancient Roman consular road known as the Via Cassia.[94] Charlemagne will doubtless have traveled this route. But even in Italy, the old Roman roads were by now not in the best state of repair. Even so, the Via Amerina, another former consular route, formed the backbone of connections between the Exarchate of Ravenna and the Duchy of Rome, and therefore with the evolving Papal States. Charlemagne surely knew this road too; from Rome, it ran east of the Via Cassia and west of the Via Flaminia to Ameria (the present-day town of Amelia in Umbria).[95]

Otherwise, wherever one ventured, there was a distinct absence of any serviceable road infrastructure. The ancient postal and way stations had not handed down their former functions to posterity. Grass, scrub, and woodland had overrun many of the old routes, and they had crumbled into ruin. East of the Rhine, the situation was even worse than in the area occupied by the former Roman province of Gallia. Mobility and transport facilities were correspondingly restricted. In the main, the only vehicles using the roads were two-wheeled oxcarts. There is no way of ascertaining to what extent four-wheeled wagons, as used in antiquity and in the Merovingian period, were still being employed. All in all, communications were hampered by technological difficulties.

The locations of the rivers Rhine, Rezat, Altmühl, and Danube were so vividly described to Charlemagne "by those who maintained that they had experienced them firsthand"[96] that during the war against the Avars in 793, he was able to plan a navigable connecting canal—the Fossa Carolina, a three-kilometer stretch of which still exists today and has water in it—and begin getting it excavated. Its ultimate failure was due to technical problems rather than any lack of topographical know-how; the ground, softened by days of incessant rain, kept slipping back into the canal. But even under these circumstances, by steering through the most favorable stretches of the canal, ships still found themselves repeatedly able to transfer from one river to the other.[97]

The outstanding importance of Mainz, Worms, and Frankfurt in the heart of the territories he ruled persuaded Charlemagne to build a wooden bridge "500 paces long" across the Rhine at Mainz; however, within a year of its construction, it fell victim to a fire. The plan was to replace it with a stone structure, but this was prevented by Charlemagne's death.[98] The king found ways to attack Saxony alternately from the south and the west, from Frankfurt and Duisburg; in all likelihood, he was able to call on the help of local leaders—an ideal combination of wide-ranging and local knowledge that facilitated long-distance communication, although it was still not possible to swiftly enact urgent resolutions and measures.

Not all regions of the burgeoning Carolingian Empire were affected equally intensively by the king's reform plans or by his concern for their welfare. Once again, the heartland regions formed the focus of his attention. The king could not be everywhere at once. Although he traveled regularly—in the early years of his reign, at least—through Francia, the extensive heartland of his empire, Neustria (the western part of his realm, west of the Seine) and Alemannia saw little of him, while at times he visited Bavaria relatively frequently. He went to Aquitaine only very occasionally, despite the fact that the route to Spain ran through this region. Charlemagne visited Italy on five occasions, though. In both Aquitaine and Italy, he left the exercise of royal authority in the hands of his sons: in the former, Louis, in the latter, Pepin.

On his journeys through the empire, Charlemagne had the luxury of basing himself in royal palaces only in certain regions. They afforded him lodgings and were equipped to cater to the needs of the itinerant royal court. These buildings were thick on the ground in Francia, with only a few days' journey between them; but, as already noted, the picture was different in Aquitaine and Italy, and still more so in Saxony. There, the palace at Paderborn, at the confluence of the Pader and Lippe Rivers, was for a long time the only such institution in the region. All too often, the king and the royal entourage simply had to make the best of what was available. For example, on his return from Regensburg to Frankfurt in 793, he set up camp between the rivers Altmühl and Rezat, and it was at this tented encampment that he received a papal legation, which came bearing "great gifts."[99] In 801, Charlemagne met the delegation sent by Caliph Harun al-Rashid at the armed encampment between Pavia and Vercelli. Even though he had a particularly pressing need for a palace at this location, none could be placed at his disposal.

Catering for the traveling royal court was an onerous business and required foreknowledge about the king's itinerary. After all, it has emerged that a retinue of up to two thousand people traveled with the king.[100] In theory, hospitality was the sole responsibility of the palaces, but monasteries and bishops also found themselves co-opted into providing this service. Excusing oneself from extending hospitality to the king was not an option. A royal visit to this or that location was certainly a point of great honor and undoubtedly brought with it some expression of grace and favor, but it involved considerable expense on the host's part. Feeding two thousand mouths, even for a day, in addition to supplying fodder for the horses and other draft animals, was a massive drain on resources that saw countless oxen and sheep slaughtered and hay supplies exhausted. The monastery at Novalese in Lombardy got to experience this firsthand during the young Frankish ruler's first campaign to Italy; the king allegedly remained there until all the storerooms and pantries were emptied.[101] Privileges were granted to compensate for the losses incurred, but over time, paying for these was to cost the kingdom dear.

In exercising his rule, Charlemagne was able in part to take his cue from practices dating from his father's reign, which were still upheld in the centers of power in Francia. Yet the constant expansion of the borders of the realm made a partial reorganization of protocol inevitable. New counties were created not just in Saxony but also in Italy, since the Lombard Empire had not had any counts. In Gallia, meanwhile, many of the *civitates* from late antiquity—large or smaller settlements with an urban center and a delimited hinterland—had survived the cultural shifts that had occurred since the end of the Roman Empire. East of the Rhine, however, and north of the Danube, no cities existed.

Even within the territory of the former Roman Empire south of the Danube or in the former *Agri Decumates* area identified by Tacitus (i.e., east of the Rhine and north of the Danube, in the southwestern corner of what is now Baden-Württemberg), circumstances had changed fundamentally. Passau, Regensburg, Salzburg, and Augsburg had shrunk or lay in ruins; furthermore, no trace of the fabric of civic society had survived since the withdrawal of Roman troops from the region. Salzburg (*Iuvavum*), Regensburg (*Castra Regina*), and Augsburg (*Augusta Vindelicorum*) had at least retained their Roman names, a fact that speaks to the continuity of a Roman populace in these places in the face of a growing Bavarianization. Sometimes, the newly created counties in these regions based themselves on older *Gaue* (geographical districts). However, it was only long after the reign of Charlemagne that more hard-and-fast borders became apparent.

Occasionally, surviving letters, such as those of Einhard, give us an insight into how the magnates, and by analogy the king too, communicated with estate administrators. We see orders being issued and reprimands and chastisement being dished out. "We want you firstly to send a few men to Aix to renovate and put our dwelling in order and secondly to ensure that everything we might have need of there, namely, flour, beer, wine, cheese, and other provisions, arrives there in good time as usual."[102] "We are astonished to find that everything we had instructed you to deal with is still in the same state as before. You have not sent the materials to Mühlheim that you should have. . . . We now have only thirty hogs, and they are not even good ones, just average quality. . . . If you cannot send me anything better from there [i.e., Fritzlar] than what you have supplied me with, then what use is there in my having a fiefdom there?"[103] "We hereby give notice that we require wax for our use. We cannot obtain any here, because the honey yield has been bad over the past two years."[104] Of course, in his letters to bishops, counts, or the emperor, Einhard's tone was friendly and humble.

All in all, though, the measures adopted by Charlemagne—in some cases confirming, in others renewing, and in yet others innovative—proved to be highly effective. The Church constitution, which was taken from late antiquity—the time of the Church Fathers—and was revived and firmly set in place, has endured to the present day. Basically, "counts" existed only within the bounds of the Carolingian Empire and the structure of rule pertaining there; by the late Middle Ages, counties had shifted or had been dissolved altogether. But the institution of counts and counties spilled over into those new polities that derived directly or indirectly from the old Carolingian Empire, such as Norman England, the Norman Kingdom of Sicily, or the crusader states established in the Holy Land. The same is true of the institution of vassalage, which likewise is encountered only in regions with Carolingian roots and which actually laid the foundations for the feudal system of the late Middle Ages. As one of the pillars on which Charlemagne's power rested, only the manorial system underwent a radical change after his reign and therefore behaved no differently from modern business.

Italy—A Special Case

Everything in Italy was different from Francia: the Mediterranean climate, the survival of ancient traditions, the language, the social structure, the legal system, the organization of production, relations with the pope, religious observance, education, and knowledge in general—in short, nothing was the same. There the old city culture had not been entirely extinguished, although, as elsewhere, the area occupied by towns had shrunk, leaving them surrounded by fields of rubble. Everywhere, preserved or restored buildings testified to the former glory of the settlements. The urban center, the *civitas,* the see of a bishop and since the Carolingian period also the seat of a count, was encircled by a more or less extensive surrounding area, the *comitatus.* Occasionally these urban-centered counties turned out to be exceedingly small scale. Yet the Franks' encounter with Italy and its people, their confrontation with this alien world after the conquest of Pavia, and their first experience of an ancient civilization still in evidence sent intellectual shock waves rippling northward. Over time, Charlemagne gradually became ever more conscious of the backwardness of his own Frankish Empire. He felt gripped by a powerful urge to undertake reform. This insight coincided with the first attempts at restructuring the realm, which had already begun under Charlemagne's father, Pepin the Short.

The Lombards never overran the whole of Italy; large tracts of the country remained imperial, that is, Roman. The center of this latter region was Ravenna, the seat of the exarch, the emperor's representative in Italy. Even when the Lombard king Liutprand advanced southeast along the Via Emilia, capturing Bologna in 728, and his successor Aistulf took Ravenna twenty-three years later, these successes did not lead to any blanket imposition of the Lombard systems of rule or the law. Southeast of Modena, in the Romagna, it was Roman law and not Lombard law that was in force; very different conditions pertained than in the west and the north of the country. The army, a person's marital status, the judiciary, and many other aspects of life differed greatly from region to region.

Occupying the center of the peninsula was the Lombard Duchy of Spoleto; it was more or less independent of the kingdom in Pavia but was ultimately under the control of the Frankish king. Farther south, the embryonic polity later known as the Papal States, the *Patrimonium Petri,* was slowly taking shape. Still farther south, toward the *mezzogiorno,* the duke of Benevento held sway; he too was a Lombard who had recently gained independence from the king in Pavia. Maneuvering between the two fronts, he was able for a long time to successfully resist the Carolingians. Apulia and Calabria were still uncontested as part of the empire of the Rhomaioi, the Byzantine Greeks. Therefore, the Apennine Peninsula presented anything but a unified picture. Even a Charlemagne could achieve nothing here except by military conquest; he found it impossible to unify the country in terms of either the law or its culture.

Pavia was distinguished by the presence there of a series of central institutions. The king's palace (*palatium*) was the center of power and the home of the royal treasury, where all the tributes (*exactiones*) were collected. It was also the site of the king's court, where "palace judges" (*judices palatii*) who were not only conversant with the law but also literate operated, alongside court notaries. Charlemagne's endowments of estates in Italy referred repeatedly to the donations that flowed from them to the *palatium.*[105] Pavia may also have housed a law school, at which judges taught students how to administer Lombard law. The so-called *Honorantiae civitatis,* a collection of official documents describing the royal chambers and the palace, gives some idea of the efficiency of the organization of royal power in the early Middle Ages. In the form in which they have come down to us, these documents come only from late Ottonian and early Salian times, although they presumably had much older roots reaching back several centuries into the period of Lombard rule.

The very first chapter of the *Honorantiae civitatis* indicates this: "All of you who are imbued with love for the realm of Lombardy and the urge to serve and honor it, be of good cheer to learn that all the offices assigned to the king's chamber and the palace and all the essential rights of the Lombard people were established in ancient times."[106] Admittedly, the only monarchs named in this document were from the tenth century, with no mention of a single Carolingian or even a Lombard king. Trade tariffs and coinage were regulated, and the taxes payable by gold panners and other trades were fixed, together with the wardship for rich ladies who had no guardian. One or more schools at which members of the laity both taught and were educated flourished in the city and were sanctioned by the royal

FIGURE 22 Bernard of Italy (ruler of the Lombards, 810–818) as king and lawgiver, from an early ninth-century capitulary manuscript. Benedictine Abbey of Saint Paul in Lavanttal, Carinthia, Austria (Cod. 4/1, f. 1v).

court; these institutions, which undoubtedly went back at least as far as the Lombard period, provided a literary education still worthy of note. Charlemagne would benefit from their existence, despite the fact that the traditions of the Frankish Empire and the personality principle of the law prevented a takeover of these institutions.

Education of the laity certainly flourished in Pavia and elsewhere. The teaching of grammar and instruction in Latin (including poetry) were held in high regard. The scholar Peter of Pisa taught in Pavia before moving north with Charlemagne. Paul the Deacon too had been schooled as a layperson in the city and also later taught there from time to time before accompanying Princess Adalperga to Benevento and subsequently, after the demise of the Lombard Empire, moving back to the monastery at Monte Cassino. Meanwhile, Paulinus, whose exceptional learning first prompted Charlemagne to summon him to court and whom he then made archbishop of Aquileia, had been a teacher in Cividale, the seat of power in Friuli, a city distinguished by its unique Tempietto Lombardo (Lombard Temple), which still exists as the Oratorio di Santa Maria in Valle. It is possible that some colleges for craftsmen and other vocations also survived—say, in Pavia or Milan—the creeping decline of classical antiquity.

The Carolingian kings of Italy, however, did not make their residence in Pavia, preferring—perhaps as a result of its proximity to the border with the Avars—to site their palace initially in Verona instead. There Charlemagne's son Pepin (and possibly Charlemagne too) gathered together a wealth of ancient manuscripts and texts. It may indeed be the case, although this is by no means certain, that a manuscript held in the Berlin State Library and known as Diez B Sant. 66 contains an inventory of these works from Verona (although admittedly this document can also be connected to Charlemagne's court in Aix).[107] The remarkable thing that emerges from this list, a unique survival from the eighth century, is the many works of pagan authors that may have been in the library in question, but of which there is no record at the court of the Frankish king: the poets and playwrights Lucan, Statius, Terence, Juvenal, Tibullus, Horace, Claudian, and Martial, the two prose writers Sallust and Cicero, and the three grammarians Gaius Julius Victor, Servius, and Arusianus Messius. To whichever institution this list may belong, it provides incontrovertible evidence of a more secular educational outlook than existed elsewhere in the Frankish Empire before 800.

In general, alongside Pavia, Verona, or Ravenna, other centers of Carolingian authority and pre-Carolingian learning also came to prominence.

Unquestionably, one such location was the Irish monastery foundation in Bobbio. Even Rome—notwithstanding the Donation of Pepin—was included. Much to the annoyance of the pope, Charlemagne convened court there as emperor. Apart from among the Irish, the last vestiges of knowledge of Greek in the Latin world were to be found in northern Italy, the city of Rome, and Benevento, as well as in the environs of Byzantium. Charlemagne made no attempt to revive it.

The individual regions of Italy all had their own peculiar social conditions and their own legal systems. Lombard law was effective in the Lombards' sphere of authority, while vulgar Roman law applied in the Romagna region; however, the Franks, Bavarians, and Alemanni whom Charlemagne sent to Italy brought their own laws with them, which they continued to live by up to the High Middle Ages. Henceforth, the first question posed in every court in Italy was which legal system those involved in the trial observed. Once more, the originally Lombard Duchy of Spoleto was a law unto itself in political, legal, and cultural terms. After Charlemagne's conquest and incorporation of Italy into his realm, all these different systems coexisted cheek by jowl, not to mention the whole of southern Italy, which remained rooted in either Lombard or Byzantine traditions.

The law pertaining to capitularies certainly reached Italy, but generally speaking, the Carolingian kings there issued capitularies specifically and solely relating to their realm there. Such edicts began even before the conquest of Pavia with a decree that Charlemagne apparently issued in his encampment; in it, the king ordered that those free men who had sold themselves into bondage out of desperation were to be granted their freedom once more, that unlawful sales of personal property were to be revoked, and that all future sales and donations were to be conducted according to the law.[108] It seemed that the arrival of the Frankish army had caused a degree of anxiety among the indigenous populace.

Only the most important decrees issued in the north penetrated as far as the south. This is attested, for example, by a comparatively early collection that must have been written shortly after 789 and that has come down to us in a "small manuscript for practical usage" presumably copied in St. Gall in the early ninth century (St. Gall Monastery Library 733).[109] This collection combines the expanded Herstal capitulary (779)[110] and the famous *Admonitio generalis* of 789[111] with some older Italian capitularies issued by Charlemagne and his son Pepin. It may be that this manuscript was intended for the use of the latter, whose inheritance was to include Alemannia with St. Gall, or possibly for his son Bernard, the young king of Italy.

Among the texts in this collection, there is also a missive by Charlemagne to the secular Italian magnates.[112] Even the opening address, with its plethora of named officeholders, makes clear the contrast to the Frankish Empire: "To our beloved counts and judges, to our vassals, vicars, centenarians, and all our messengers and appointees." In this letter, Charlemagne chided those he was addressing that it had been brought to his attention that they were not obeying their bishops and priests as ecclesiastical law required, inasmuch as they were not introducing their priests to the bishops and were attracting foreign clerics and installing them in their churches, and in addition were taking the tithes and the ninth parts for themselves, refusing to remit interest payments and generally hampering attempts to renew the Church. This missive, sealed with the royal seal, which in all likelihood was dispatched from the court sometime before 789, emphasizes not least the difficulties encountered in trying to carry through the reform objectives throughout the length and breadth of the Carolingian Empire, and hence the necessity of sending a separate monarch—Charlemagne's son Pepin—to rule over Italy. Thereafter, the capitularies and royal edicts were issued in the name of both father and son.

However effective the system of rule within the Frankish Empire was in stabilizing the monarch's hold on power, without Italy Charlemagne would not have attained the pinnacle of renown he did. Italy was home to three former imperial residence cities, Milan, Ravenna, and Rome, and was also the center of ancient learning and scholarship; moreover, the head of the Church resided there. Charlemagne sent his most trusted advisers to Italy to lend support to his son. Ancient "Roman" knowledge flowed north from there. And Italy supplied the crown that was soon to adorn his brow.

5

THE RULER

"IT IS OUR ROLE TO DEFEND by force of arms the Holy Church of Christ everywhere from the attacks of pagans and the devastation of infidels without, and to enforce the acceptance of the Catholic faith within." If any sentence in Charlemagne's correspondence with the bishops of Rome can be said to encapsulate a general program of kingship, then it is this brief excerpt from a letter to Leo III, who had just been consecrated as pope in December 795.[1] At the time he wrote these words, Charlemagne was forty-eight years old and at the height of his powers. He was a tireless warrior in his defense of the faith, and his objectives were clear. He was aiming to establish a religiosity that was Catholic and followed the dictates of his own soul in its devotion to God.[2] What he was striving for might be said to be a form of religion that merged seamlessly with secular royal authority, a political religion, so to speak, although such a term risks sounding like an anachronism.

Charlemagne was raised from an early age in the bosom of the Church, following to the letter the eternally valid message of the faith. It did not countenance any alteration; it was complete and perfect as it stood, and it could only be threatened, falsified by heretics, and lost forever. It was the fundamental duty of the king to protect the faith; after all, it had been formulated for all eternity and was binding on all. A few personal testimonies, at their pinnacle the confession of faith, the creed, concealed its fundamental message, although this was encapsulated in terse phrases that were hard to fathom. The blessed Church Fathers had elucidated their secrets. No disruption of this scheme of things was to be permitted; people needed to return to the roots of their faith. The writings of the Church Fathers proclaimed the correct norm. This may well have been how Charlemagne saw religious matters, and he acted accordingly. He viewed it as his most pressing duty to propagate this faith and to consolidate it.

And so, wherever the conquering king advanced on his campaigns, he was accompanied or closely followed by those who proclaimed the faith. This strategy placed Charlemagne in a long tradition of Christian rulers. Yet this was not enough for him; he went further than this, surpassing any previous boundaries. He set himself up as the guardian of the correct understanding of the faith and of canonical knowledge about it. He saw the pope's role as one simply of intercession: "It is for you, Holy Father, to aid our force of arms [*nostram adiuvare militiam*] with your hands upraised to God like Moses, so that while you are praying, Christians may, with guidance and succor from God, emerge always and everywhere victorious against the enemies of His holy name, and so that the name of our Lord Jesus Christ might be glorified throughout the world." God, the Church, and the One True Faith were all encompassed within this concept of "His holy name." Thus strengthened by the intercession of St. Peter's vicar on Earth, Charlemagne's principal purpose was to glorify Christ's name. He had ascended to the pinnacle of power. Wherever he was victorious, God shared in his triumph.

The letter to Leo III was the work of the Anglo-Saxon scholar Alcuin, who had recently arrived at the Frankish court, and who was to live the rest of his life in the Frankish Empire. The programmatic sentences it contained do not reveal a specifically Anglo-Saxon position, however. What he took down in dictation must in fact have been fully in accordance with Charlemagne's conceptions, wishes, and aims. Alcuin's opponent, the Visigoth Theodulf, who at this time was either already the bishop of Orléans or was about to be appointed to this post, hastened to give an even clearer definition of sacred and secular duties: "You [i.e., Charlemagne] hold the keys of the Church, but he [Leo] holds the keys of Heaven. You direct the pope's powers and lead the clergy and the people. He will lead you to the heavenly choirs."[3]

Others took a similar view. In his pastoral letters, the Irish cleric Cathuulf drew the distinction (theologically and in terms of canon law not unproblematic) that the king was a "representative of God, whereas a bishop was only a representative of Christ,"[4] while in 794 the bishops of Italy lauded him as "master and father, king and priest, most temperate ruler of all Christians."[5] "King and priest": this designation indicates that his rule was here being construed as far more than any mere protectorate, since it intervened in the organization of the Church, kept watch over the faith, and did not shy away from taking on spiritual duties. Leo or even Hadrian before him could scarcely have approved of such interference but had to put up with it all the same. Every war Charlemagne waged, every court Charlemagne convened, every punitive action he ordered, and in particular every intervention of his in theological disputes—of which there were many—derived from his role as leader of the Church.

Charlemagne took his cue from the experiences of the foregoing centuries. The churches of the Frankish Empire, their priests, and their landholdings all suffered greatly in the aftermath of the unsettled and warlike conditions that blighted the early eighth century. Reform was clearly called for here. Yet people at that time understood the Church as embracing much more than simply the clergy. The Church transcended all earthly things; it was the mystical Body of Christ and in the view of the apostle St. Paul represented the only model of corporate order available to his contemporaries: a spiritual body with a head and limbs, with eyes, ears, and other organs (see St. Paul's Epistle to the Romans, 12:4, and the First Letter to the Corinthians, 12:12–28)—in other words, it was a sacred unit. This conception of a mystical body hallowed by the apostle must have had the effect of symbolically transforming the kaleidoscopic, fragmented world of everyday experience into a clear, Christian-oriented social and institutional whole.

The king saw himself as being at the center of this Church, organizing and leading it as its defender of the faith. In its earthly manifestation, the sacred unit was in need of his welfare and protection: protection for the many churches and their parish priests, as well as for the property that belonged to them, for monasteries and monks, for the true faith and the education that was required to foster it, and for all Christians and their worship, as well as protection for the pope and the Apostolic Church in Rome. Charlemagne was determined to bring about the reign of peace that was vital for the salvation of the Church; as a result, building peace became his most pressing priority. There thus accrued to the king a directing authority that was designed to harmonize the Church and the outside world; or, to be more precise, obeying the exigencies of the time, he arrogated such authority to himself.

Charlemagne did not recognize any sharp distinction between temporal and spiritual matters, between the monarchy and the Church; such a division was automatically precluded at that time. Accordingly, his "kingship" (*regnum*) was intrinsically bound up with the Church, whose head was Christ. Historians of the period, trapped as they were in the traditions of

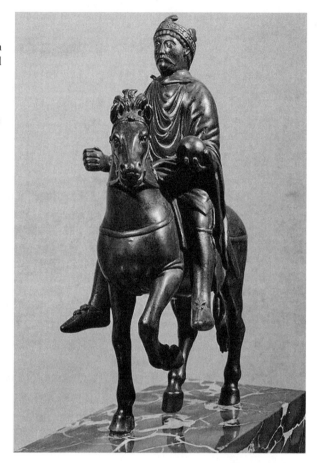

FIGURE 23 This famous bronze equestrian statuette, dating from the ninth century and now in the Louvre in Paris, depicts either Charlemagne or his grandson Charles the Bald.

annals that merely enumerated events, had nothing to say on religious faith worlds or the objectives that they stimulated. But Charlemagne's capitularies and the canons of his synods referred repeatedly to such matters; for example, the letter to Pope Leo cited above expressly interpreted the king's rule and the exercise of royal military power as service to God. Such "military service" (*militia*) united war and peace and legitimized the campaigns against the heathens and unbelievers, against the enemies of St. Peter, as well as justifying the use of force against each and every troublemaker and perjurer within his own realm. Thus, kingship as a service to God justified—indeed, even hallowed—Charlemagne's use of violence against the Saxons and the Lombards and against his cousin Tassilio, for "the Creator of All Things had chosen him [Charlemagne] to be a conqueror forever."[6]

Set alongside this "Church," of which Charlemagne and Theodulf both spoke, the three or four other facets of imperial order—the royal household with the king's landholdings and their management, along with the army and the court system—all tended to recede into relative unimportance, although Charlemagne by no means neglected them. That may be the fault of the historical record, which, despite being relatively favorable in this instance, is still generally very poor; record keeping focused rather one-sidedly on ecclesiastical legacies, whereas secular matters had a chance of being passed down to posterity only if they ended up being recorded in good time in ecclesiastical, or especially monastic, archives.[7]

At that time, however, a specifically political mode of thought did not yet exist (or perhaps no longer existed)—in other words, a way of thinking that differentiated between society's divergent interests. The "empire" was not a subject, "politics" was not a considered category of activity, and "imperial policy" was still some far-off, future, and, for the time being, inconceivable grand phenomenon. Centuries would have to elapse before this situation changed. In the meantime, the Church, as an overarching, God-created entity, and the "royal house" (*palatium, aula, domus regis*) as the organizing epicenter of "royal authority" and of its sphere of influence (*regnum*), along with the Frankish and other "peoples," all formed the semantic framework within which Charlemagne oriented himself, together with his contemporaries, and ordered his world.[8] For them, the Church was an indivisible unity of redemption and the exercise of authority.

Behind Alcuin's phraseology when he was writing to Leo III lay Charlemagne's tried and tested resolve to put into practice the concept outlined in this letter. The newly appointed pope was not to be greeted by mere empty diplomatic platitudes but instead by a list of vital duties that the king was busy fulfilling all the time, and that Leo still had to fulfill. The most demanding and highest aim of royal dominion, which kings had long been pursuing, was conveyed to the earthly representative of St. Peter for information and in the hope of a new blessing, by way of offering protection and support for the Church and the faith. The letter from the king to Pope Leo continued: "Your Holiness, let us entrust ourselves and all our followers to God's blessed grace and proclaim the peacemaking unity of our whole realm according to God's will." Charlemagne urged the pope to daily implore the apostolic princes to grant the Church stability and the king and his followers well-being, and to request that they might bring good fortune to the whole of the empire that had been entrusted to his care by God. In closing, though, Charlemagne admonished the pope to "abide by the canonical law in all things and always obey the precepts [*statuta*] of the Holy Fathers." Was the king here monitoring the way in which the pontiff discharged his duties? Had the newly elected pope somehow given cause for concern?

In his concern to uphold the true faith, Charlemagne did not spare even the bishop of Rome. The programmatic sentences that Alcuin had lent his pen to formulating not only reminded the new pope of his pontifical duties but also were at the same time a kind of stocktaking of Charlemagne's own rule up to that point. The Carolingian ruler had actually to deliver on the claims that Alcuin made in writing. No matter how much his greatness rested on the point of the sword, the king had long since realized that force alone was not enough to keep any empire together. Royal authority, and hence the realm as a whole, required internal order, and this in turn called for God's blessing. But God's grace had to be earned and secured through service. Success revealed divine benevolence, but failure was construed as a warning from Heaven, requiring improvement and redoubled effort. Charlemagne followed this simple reasoning, submitting himself to the same code of ethics that he expected of his magnates.

Charlemagne's solicitude toward the Church thus proved to be a means of exercising dominion over his realm. Faith and authority complemented each other, cooperated, and provided mutual strength. Not that Charlemagne would have sacrificed the mysteries of faith to his ambitions to extend his power. He was all too aware of the threat posed by the Last Judgment and the fast-approaching End of Days. His actions were intended to prepare for this event, promoting as they did peace, unity, and justice in his realm.[9] The king would have gleaned more information on this subject from popular tracts that were circulated in the Frankish Empire. News of the last trumpet was couched precisely in the vernacular. For instance, in the Old High German stave rhyme known as the "Muspilli" (v. 65), it is claimed that anyone called on to pass judgment in a court of law (*mahale*) should act justly (*rahano . . . rehto arteile*): "*Denne ni darf er sorgen, denne er ze deru suonu quimit*" (Then he need have no fear himself when he is called to face the Last Judgment).

The tract on the twelve failings of the world (*De duodecim abusivis saeculi*) was even more forceful in its critique. It is thought to have originated in the seventh century in Ireland before being widely disseminated in Charlemagne's kingdom.[10] The fifth failing was the shamelessness of women, while the sixth was "the master without virtue, whose rule is in vain"; the ninth, meanwhile, was "the unjust king" (*rex iniquus*), and the twelfth "a lawless people." "The throne is exalted through the justness of the king,"

"Yet the king's justness resides in oppressing no one unjustly with his power." On Judgment Day, an unjust king would find that the evil deeds of all the sinners in his realm would come to rest on his shoulders. This was a massive threat, and Charlemagne was at pains not to saddle himself with such a heavy burden of sin.[11] He punished people, to be sure, but imposed a regime of "gentle terror," as Charlemagne's grandson and Frankish historian Nithard would later describe his reign in his *Four Books of Histories* (1.I). He exercised brutal force on occasion, but his actions were always dictated by a sense of "rectitude." Anyhow, miscreants and opponents were punished and neutralized but not murdered, as in previous centuries.

Armed conflict must have struck Charlemagne as relatively straightforward compared with the tribulations that stood in the way of recognition of the Catholic faith and the internal peace and security of his realm. Obstacle after obstacle mounted up; no sooner was one overcome than the next appeared, even more insurmountable than before and requiring more knowledge and skill for it to be resolved. And with every new challenge, intellectual doubt would set in, along with the temptation to think and question and an inquisitiveness that sought to break existing boundaries. Once it had been laboriously raised aloft, the boulder of knowledge gained unstoppable momentum, plummeting into the bottomless abyss. Over the course of his long reign, Charlemagne also had this experience. The letter he got Alcuin to write to the pope was a summary of his successes, but at the same time it was a plan for a labor of Sisyphus: to strengthen Christ's church through recognition of the Christian faith.

"Restitution" and "Renovation"

In the foregoing centuries, social upheaval had changed everything—everyday life, learning, and the Church. The Roman West of late antiquity had tottered and succumbed to a cultural decline such as had never been experienced in the East; Christians, with apocalyptic expectations in mind, had found themselves unable to halt this collapse. Slowly and imperceptibly, many losses had been suffered; no one had seen them coming, and no one had warned of them. A far-reaching descent into barbarism had swept culture away with it. Charlemagne had gained an inkling of the damage that had been caused ever since he had encountered the rituals of the papacy, the most prominent and only surviving mirror of the ancient Roman tradition—a papacy that had only just begun its rise to the position of representative of the *res publica Romana* (the Roman state) after the downfall of the

Ravenna Exarchate. And when he first met Alcuin or Italian scholars, he also began to appreciate the terrible loss of knowledge and skill that had occurred since the age of the Church Fathers.

But how might this steady decline be halted and a new renaissance initiated? The example of biblical and historical figures, such as King Josiah and the Visigothic ruler Athaulf, encouraged Charlemagne to pursue a path of renewal. But how to actually bring this about? Centuries ago, cultural development had faltered and ground to a halt, ever since Rome had been sacked by Goths and Vandals and finally pushed to the margins of the Byzantine Empire by the victorious Rhomaioi. Athaulf, the successor of King Alaric, who had sacked Rome in 410 and had died and been laid to rest in the bed of the Busento River later that same year, had browbeaten the Roman emperor into offering him his daughter Gallia Placidia's hand in marriage in 414. This noble Roman lady thus found herself in a misalliance with a barbarian. Athaulf boasted that his intention was to fashion a Gothic Empire from the remains of the Roman imperium.

Yet Gallia Placidia, whose magnificent sarcophagus can still be seen in Ravenna today, ended up taming the barbarian. No laws, it seemed, could constrain the boundless wildness of his Goth warriors. And so it was to keep them in check that Athaulf sought to revive the title of Roman emperor. "Restitution" and revival became his agenda.[12] The historian Orosius, who had formerly worked alongside St. Augustine of Hippo, recorded Athaulf's joyously optimistic wedding speech for posterity. This speech represented the first expression of a desire to bring about "renewal" (renovare, renovatio) and "renaissance," a yearning that would remain unquenchable for centuries to come. The blessing of a fresh start. And the Visigothic Empire did indeed become one of the last repositories of ancient learning in the West, which was dying out. Charlemagne and his Franks were to reap their rewards from Athaulf's realm; the seed that the Roman emperor's daughter had sown finally germinated in the Carolingian Empire.

For a thousand years from the time of this Visigothic-Roman union onward, we encounter this Rome-fixated thirst for renewal as a regularly recurring, repeatedly rekindled cultural urge that brought in its wake a series of attempts at renovation and renaissance. Aside from the Latin West, no other civilization displayed such a seamless and repeatedly revived need for renewal. But looking back like this did not stimulate any reactionary plans to restore the Roman Empire; on the contrary, the aim was to search out the old in order to assimilate it and transform it. The result was constantly something new. But as is the case with every mountain, the act of reascending it was far more onerous and took far longer than the descent. Setbacks and collapses were inevitable. Centuries were to elapse before a genuinely new civilization, a Latin culture that was on a par with classical antiquity, emerged in the form of the High Middle Ages of the twelfth and thirteenth centuries. But it was Charlemagne who instigated this definitive change.[13] What made this possible?

The earlier decline of classical civilization had affected virtually every sphere of life, by no means just the Church. The old Roman roads now lay neglected and unusable, the *Gesta municipalia*—the document registers of the principal legal transactions that took place in towns—were closed and forgotten, and the education of laypeople had tailed off. Only very few people in the early Middle Ages could read and write. The highly literate society of classical antiquity, to which the Church Fathers had contributed in no small way, had been supplanted by a culture that largely (to a greater extent in the north and east of the Frankish Empire than in the south) made do with orality and was defined by it. The spoken language determined the way life was lived, communications, and social practices; and last but not least, it shaped the prevailing mode of thought.

In such circumstances, then, long-winded description rather than analysis was the order of the day, while facts were amassed and strung together instead of being systematically arranged, and cause and effect were not always distinguished from each other; indeed, sometimes they were even reversed. It was not common practice to reach logical decisions or to differentiate between facts. Mental constructs such as "the whole and its parts" still lay far in the future. Likewise, not only were abstractions like "society," "the body politic," "feudalism," or the "manorial system" as yet unknown, but such concepts would have been wholly unintelligible; even "empire" did not at this stage appear as a subject, but only as the object of royal rule or even merely as a pure description of physical space.[14] Concepts such as "association," "federation," or "imperial law" would find their way into public discourse only at a much later date.

Charlemagne's Frankish native tongue, and presumably also the Romanic that was spoken in the west and south of Gallia, could not have embraced such concepts. Every renewal of religion and theology, every kind of scholarship required Latin. Yet this language, too, was no longer the one that Cicero, St. Augustine, or Pope Gregory the Great had used. It had long since begun the long journey of transformation into vernacular Romance languages, and in places where it was still used conversationally, it had become "wild" and "barbarized." Yet in those cases where peoples who spoke a foreign tongue sought for various reasons to acquire the learning of the ancients, it had to be specially preserved and taught in schools, whether this be among the Anglo-Saxons and the Irish, the Lombards or the Visigoths, and now among the Franks as well. In imitation of the ancient language, there arose a "New Latin" as the language of narrow clerical educated elites, to which the lay ruling elites gained only individual and exceptional access.

The Christian faith and the organization of the Church now found themselves confronted by almost insurmountable linguistic barriers. Who, for instance, could comprehend the concept of the God who was Three in One? In the west of the former Roman Empire, this doctrine had been promulgated exclusively in Latin, a language understood by an increasingly dwindling number of people, and especially not by the inhabitants of the lands that lay beyond the borders of the old Roman Empire. Charlemagne must have been concerned about the situation. How might the faith reach the general populace outside the literate elites? Neither the Old nor the New Testament nor a single work of any of the Church Fathers was translated into a vernacular language in the decades around 800. The task undertaken by the Gothic bishop Ulfilas (ca. 311–383) and his successors of translating the Bible into the vernacular was not replicated in Charlemagne's realm, although it is possible that the king transferred the famous Codex argenteus (now kept at Uppsala in Sweden, with one page in Speyer) from Ravenna to the library at his court, from where, in the ninth century, it is thought to have been taken subsequently to the monastery at Werden.[15] All biblical exegesis at this time, indeed, the entire discourse surrounding the faith, was the preserve of a tiny scholarly elite schooled in Latin.

Similarly, Charlemagne set great store by converting the illiterate mass of the population. Not least, this would contribute to his own redemption. He remained committed to this endeavor right to the end of his life. No sooner had he quit Italy than the first systematic attempts were begun to make at least the central texts of the Christian faith—the Lord's Prayer and the Nicene Creed—accessible to the common people by translating them into their language.[16] In the early ninth century, these efforts were followed by the *Heliand*, a recounting of the life of Jesus in Old Saxon stave-rhyme form, and the gospel harmony in rhyming couplets (*Evangelienbuch*) by the Frankish poet Otfrid of Wissembourg.[17] This last work was dedicated to Charlemagne's grandson Louis the German, a sure indication of the high-ranking aristocratic audience for such works. Both of these writers were content to create more or less free adaptations of their source material, embellishing their verses with imaginative renderings of their own present-day world; what they produced, then, were emphatically not translations of the Gospels but rather had the feel of tentative rehearsals in an unfamiliar religion.

Charlemagne knew about the "mysteries of the faith,"[18] and that they must remain hidden from the common people. Were they too profound to be understood in Frankish or Alemannic? Or did the Church authorities perhaps fear that people might begin to misuse the sacred but odd-sounding texts for the purposes of magic and as formulas for incantations if they were simply presented in the vernacular? And was a translation of the Bible inevitably marked by the stigma of the Arian heresy? In particular, the rites of Christianity, such as the celebration of Holy Mass, were conducted in Latin. Only the priest's sermon (which around 800 was little more than a brief paraphrase of a pericope—a reading from Scripture—or of the Lord's Prayer) was given in the vernacular.

The king was tireless in his issuing of edicts and prohibitions. The people were to be led toward redemption through the recitation of formulaic prayers, not through an independent understanding of the Bible; the other pillars of faith would be belief in the power of the saints and in the efficacy of confession and atonement. All the "foulness of paganism" was to be cast off and washed away, together with all the old rituals, sacrifices, auguries, amulets, every kind of use of occult symbols or charms, and "the performing of magic with the Host and the invocation of saints, holy martyrs, and confessors, as practiced by simple people in a heathen rite that mimicked church liturgy." Such acts only awakened God's wrath. Edicts like this were issued as early as the reign of Charles Martel.[19] His grandson reiterated the proscription.

Abuses would certainly not have changed over the brief period separating their reigns, just as the enforced sexual abstinence of clerics, monks, and nuns took widespread root only very gradually, under the threat of whippings and long-term incarceration with just bread and water as sustenance. Elsewhere, namely, in Bavaria, as it was now expressly called, the Church took steps against the "scourge of drunkenness," since it provoked conflict and strife, discord and murder.[20] This campaign was of little avail. The people clung to their customs. It was essential that these be challenged if the faith was to be consolidated and spread among the populace. Then learning could follow in its wake.

The real-world ways of life that had been handed down from the forefathers persisted tenaciously. These were for the most part narrow, clear, and determined by a few individuals. Society was regulated by practical rules. House and home, relatives and friends, parish church and law court, tributes and services, conflict and consensus constituted the way of life of both masters and servants. Only the ruling elites clustered around the king and the counts and around bishops and abbots owned books and had broad cultural horizons. It was now incumbent on them to bring about the "restoration" and the "renewal" of the faith and the Church.

This "imperial aristocracy," as it has been called,[21] numbered only a handful of individuals, perhaps a few thousand in total. Their actions were permeated by a deep-seated rivalry that could sometimes be murderous. Everyone envied the next man his success, his closeness to the king and his paladins. In this competitive society, violence was the order of the day—and by no means just as a result of drunkenness or solely among laypeople. Even the kings and their relatives were in danger, as Charlemagne himself proved only too clearly. Monarchs had to buy the magnates' assent to their rule and its longevity with grace and favor and generosity; sometimes, they must have feared for their lives. Maintaining this vital consensus between the king and his elites meant donating a constant stream of gifts.

Frankish society demanded that the king be a warring monarch. Yet Charlemagne wanted something more, and something different. His love of the sciences, astronomy, calendrical calculation and mathematics, and dialectics and rhetoric, along with his awareness of his society's need for redemption, points far beyond mere martial concerns. Was Charlemagne really a scholar at heart? Or a man of science? Is that why he promoted such activities to the extent he did? Or were there more elevated reasons for his interest in them? Did they also, or precisely they, form part of the program of protecting the Church and strengthening the faith, if not among the populace at large, then at least among their spiritual shepherds? Whatever the answer may be, the fact remains that Charlemagne felt duty bound to exalt the "Name of Jesus Christ" in the Vale of Tears that was his contemporary age. The knowledge-based society that Charlemagne wanted to revive for the sake of the faith came into being against the backdrop of war, jealousy, conflict, and violence wherever one looked.

The king and his advisers could very well have known about that early Visigothic-Roman marriage. The histories of Orosius, where the subject was treated, were well known at the Frankish court, and the potential for taking their message and applying it to the Frankish Empire was clear.[22] This piece of historiography was effectively a declaration of war against the heathens and a battle cry for the true faith against those who, as Orosius put it, "know only temporal things and, since they do not keep their eyes on what is to come, forget the past and pay it no heed."

Orosius's apologia discussed the downfall of the pagan Roman Empire and the many punishments God had visited on it, right up to the latest conquest of Rome by the Goths. He proclaimed the necessity of serving the one true God and of safeguarding and praising His Church in order to free oneself from the power of death. As long as news of the true religion remained unknown and unheeded, death reigned supreme, a premonition of greater terrors to come; this form of death was evil, akin to the Devil, who would triumph once again at the End of Days, before the Antichrist appeared and the Last Judgment loomed (1, prologue 9–16). Seen in the light of this interpretation of the world in a Christian apologia, the renaissance of Rome, Roman knowledge, and Roman scholarship appeared as a vital task for the salvation of souls.

Charlemagne understood this message and endeavored to follow it. He may well have construed it as his destiny. In his own realm, he had discovered a whole series of shortcomings; his condemnation of them as "wild barbarianism" signaled his desire for reform. Indeed, despite a multitude of reforms instigated by his father, Pepin, the organization of the Church was in a parlous state. The expansion of the faith was in a state of stagnation when Charlemagne ascended the throne; superstition and faithlessness spread unopposed, heresies were rife, and the education system that was an essential element in combating these failings was in a truly sorry state. Charlemagne was adamant, though, that religion should be brought to the various peoples of his realm. It was equally necessary for the redemption of their souls and of his. To strengthen religion, scholarship needed to be renewed and the seed of knowledge that might lead people once more to heed the message of the Christian Fathers replanted. For the Carolingian ruler, renewal on many levels became a principal aim, with far-reaching implications.

The Fascination of Rome

Yet where to begin on this bold venture? No programmatic utterances of Charlemagne have come down to us from the early years of his reign. Only his actions, which were always in close concert with the needs of the Church, speak for themselves. Charlemagne's oldest attested charter was issued to St. Denis, the burial site of his father, where he also wished to be interred. The monastery, however, of which Abbot Fulrad was the head, lay in the portion of the empire controlled by his brother. Charlemagne now transferred to the abbey's control (from his own family's landholdings) the small monastery of St. Dié in the Vosges Mountains, so that the ten or fifteen monks there might hold a prayer vigil for himself, Charlemagne, and for his dead father—an intercession for the living and the dead that would never cease "day or night" and was meant to remain potent even beyond death.[23] St. Dié also lay in the part of the realm controlled by Carloman. Undoubtedly, this donation was intended to win over Fulrad, his father's former chancellor, to Charlemagne's side, but it may also at the same time have been construed as a snub to Carloman, who was apparently not included in the monks' prayers. To whom would God show himself merciful?

The war against the Saxons—which at the same time was intended to be a campaign against heathens and hence a war to spread the dominion of Christ, as well as securing extensive gains for the Church—began auspiciously in 772 with the destruction of the Saxon shrine, the Irminsul.[24] Thereafter, baptism, proclamation of the faith, priests, and parishes followed the troops into Saxony, organizing the territory according to the norms of the Catholic Church. Bishop Lull of Mainz may have advised the king on this matter. Only complete subjugation could force this uncomprehending, defiant, pagan people to accept God's grace. Those who were bringing the gift of salvation did not shy away from using force, but this was directed against pagan cults, not against those people whom they were attempting to save.

The experiences that Charlemagne had undergone during the long months of his first Italian campaign had served only to deepen his conviction that he needed to redouble his efforts to spread Christianity. Military success over the Lombards was not the only result of these experiences. This period also saw Charlemagne's second encounter with Rome—that is, the ecclesiastical, visible, and cultural Rome. This Rome provided certain guidelines—Catholic, oriented toward virtue, and commensurate with his own religiosity—that Charlemagne was able to use as moral yardsticks for his actions.

This became clear at Easter in 774, when the Frankish ruler was received in the Eternal City by St. Peter's earthly representative[25] and moreover in the same manner as the former exarch of Ravenna, the envoy of the Byzantine emperor, the *basileus*. This was of enormous symbolic significance, indicating as it did that the Frankish king had, in terms of protocol, now taken the position once occupied by the Rhomaioi, the "Greeks," the "Byzantines"— though not entirely, for the exarch still lived in Rome at that time, on the Palatine Hill, inside the Aurelian Walls; Charlemagne, though, had taken up quarters in Santa Petronilla, outside the precincts of the city.[26] Yet henceforth, he styled himself with the title *patricius Romanorum,* which the Carolingians hitherto had not used; with this act, he signaled that he felt bound to Rome in his role as its temporal ruler/guardian.[27] Einhard (chap. 27) reported that Charlemagne had no more fervent desire than to revitalize the authority of Rome through his efforts and to safeguard and endow with lavish decoration the Church of the apostolic princes.

Charlemagne pledged himself to the service of St. Peter, his vicar on Earth, and the Roman Church. He wanted to be a friend to their friends and an implacable enemy to those who wished them harm. He had taken this vow when he was still a boy, along with his father; Pope Stephen III reminded him of this when he indicted Charlemagne for his marriage to the Lombard princess.[28] In essence, the young king kept his pledge. In return, he demanded the blessing and protection of the apostolic prince and the intercession of his vicar, and this in turn required compliance with the commandments of the Church—a spiritual exchange of gifts as a prerequisite of successful rule. Pope Hadrian I admonished him repeatedly on this score. Popes were especially wont to remind Charlemagne of this exchange whenever they saw his leadership of the Church encroaching too far on spiritual matters and when they were concerned to keep the royal defender of the faith in check. Ultimately, they also did this in order to erect a symbolic defensive wall against the direct authority of the Frankish king over the *res publica Romanorum*, namely, the surviving ruins of the Byzantine-Roman sphere of control around the city of Rome.

The first steps toward renewal were indeed introduced at that time in Rome. During his visit there, Charlemagne asked Hadrian to let him have a compendium of ecclesiastical law, as used by the Roman Church. The pope was keen to fulfill this request and so ordered that a copy of the *Dionysiana*, a chronologically organized collection of canon law compiled by the Roman abbot Dionysius Exiguus some centuries earlier, be prepared, including a number of newly written supplements, and sent to Charlemagne. This became known as the *Collectio Dionysio-Hadriana*. It combined the canon law promulgated by the Vatican councils with papal decretals and in so doing placed the pontifical legal pronouncements on a par with resolutions of the councils. "If you observe these commandments, you will never deviate from the faith" (*A lege numquam discedi haec observans statuta*): With this verse as a dedication, the pope duly handed over the collection to the Carolingian ruler.

The original (*codex authenticus*) of the new collection, that is, the copy sent from Rome, was housed in the royal library. All transcripts were made from this original. These spread, albeit rather slowly, across the whole of the Frankish Empire. Was it that Charlemagne wished to establish Roman canon law as the general norm? If so, such a plan could never have been realized, for in practice by no means all ecclesiastical law followed the papal collection.

FIGURE 24 Byzantine fresco from the Church of Santa Maria Antiqua at the foot of the Palatine Hill in Rome. Today the church is in ruins, but in Charlemagne's day it was one of the most important places of worship in the city.

Inconsistency was inevitable. Older collections of canon law were not simply supplanted by the *Dionysiana,* not even in Rome itself. Uniformity of canon-law norms lay far in the future and was in no way achieved during Charlemagne's reign. So who decided in any given location which collection should be used as the basis for actual legal verdicts? Whatever the answer, Charlemagne's actions clearly reveal a desire to impose regulation, whereas "truly primitive and dirty dealings characterized the lowlands of the Church's daily life."[29]

When the *Collectio Dionysio-Hadriana* was sent to Charlemagne, it was accompanied by a series of programmatic verses. These maintained that Charlemagne had, in his triumph over the Lombards, fully embraced the faith to which he had been receptive from childhood on; thereafter, full of joy and with auspicious dispatch, he had hurried to the threshold of the apostle, where he had demanded that he be absolved of the sins of his youth through the pope's prayers and had assured his "teacher" (*magistro*), the pontiff, that he, Charlemagne, would "forever protect the Holy Roman Church" and would "safeguard the law of the exalted St. Peter for his patron." The verses urged that he follow the teachings of the Apostolic See, restore its possessions, and thereby earn his place in Heaven; on Earth, he would triumph over all his foes. All this made the law appear to be less a juristic norm than a directive of the sacred order.

Thus, in the accompanying verses, Charlemagne could read the following injunction: "Honor the Lord, constantly love God's commandments, keep the true faith, safeguard the spiritual life, and keep St. Peter by your side as your helper in your triumphs," and further, "Follow the light of Church doctrine, and the faith of the Apostolic See." As the context suggests, these words may well be an echo of Charlemagne's own statements in the pope's presence, though not simply this. The first five maxims informed his actions; as far as he was able and without adhering slavishly to them, he turned them into the basis of his renewal program. The last two maxims, however, reminded the king of the spiritual authority wielded by the successor of St. Peter. Hadrian must have hoped that the commandments of the pope would act as a bulwark against the Frankish king's suzerainty over Rome.[30]

Charlemagne had overrun the fortifications of the Lombards, the verses claimed, "with the help of God and St. Peter," while in reference to the king's actions at Pavia, which he finally took after a ten-month-long siege, the text has the following comment: "With God's help and through the agency of the apostolic princes Pater and Paul, the glorious king returned from Rome to Pavia." The *Liber pontificalis* hailed him as *magnus, christianissimus rex* (great, most Christian king), *a Deo protectus* (protected by God). And in the hymns of praise that the pope, following recent Frankish tradition, commanded should be sung for the king, he was accorded such imperial attributes as *a Deo coronatus, magnus,* and *pacificus* ("crowned by God," "great," and "peacemaking"):[31] "Christus vincit, Christus regnat, Christus imperat. / Exaudi Christe. / Adriano summo pontifici et universali papae vita / Redemptor mundi. Tu lo iuva. / Sancte Patre. Tu lo iuva. . . . Exaudi Christe. / Karolo excellentissimo et a Deo coronato magno et pacifico rege Francorum [et Langobardum] ac Patricio Romanorum vita et victoria / Salvator mundi. Tu lo iuva. /Sancte Iohannis. Tu lo iuva."[32] (Christ conquers, Christ reigns, Christ commands. / Hear, O Christ. / Savior of the world, / Give succor to the life of the greatest pontiff and universal pope Hadrian. / Blessed Father / Give succor to him. / Hear, O Christ. Savior of the world, / Come to the aid of the most excellent Charles, king of the Franks [and the Lombards], the great and peacemaking ruler crowned by God. Grant him long life and triumph, Savior of the world, / Come to his aid. St John, / Come to his aid.). At the end, together with the king, "all judges [that is, the great and the powerful] and the whole Frankish army" were wished "long life and triumph." The threefold invocation of Christ at the beginning was repeated at the end, concluding the laudation: "Kyrie eleison, Christe eleison." The concordance of Frankish rule with the divine world order and Christianity's objective of salvation emerges clearly from this hymn of praise. *Gloriosus rex* (the glorious king)—this particular formulation was first used of Charlemagne in the *Chronicon Anianse* (or *Chronicon Moissiacense*),[33] while the *Royal Frankish Annals* for 774 repeats the phrase three times.[34]

New challenges now faced the ruler in Italy. Hadrian repeatedly reminded the king of that exchange of gifts and at the same time took the opportunity to accuse the archbishop of Ravenna, who "with a tyrannical and presumptuous demeanor has set himself in opposition to St. Peter and ourselves" and who had also, he claimed, unilaterally revoked papal suzerainty and in doing so cited the example of Charlemagne. "Those who envy both yourself and us" had dared, the pope claimed, to seize for themselves whatever territory they happened to have unrestricted control over during the rule of the Lombards. None of the promises made by the Franks had come to fruition; as a result, these "godless and impertinent people" were flaunting their own power. Hadrian urged Charlemagne to take steps against these upstarts, to the greater glory of God's holy and universal Church and in order that he, the king, with the help of the apostles St. Peter and St. Paul, might enjoy boundless triumphs and thereby deserve to hold the reins of power for a long time.[35]

This was the first letter from Hadrian to the Frankish king that Charlemagne ordered to be put on record; many others were to follow. Hadrian knew what motivated the king: he was concerned that the blessing of the apostolic princes should be upon him in both peace and war—a religion not of inwardness, then, but consisting rather of ritualistic acts and the exchange of gifts. Under the protection of this blessing and of the Lord's power, Charlemagne wanted to renew his realm as the "legitimate patron of the Holy Church," as the pope had already exhorted him to be.[36] A new exchange of gifts was staged: the king's protection by force of arms in return for the pope according the monarch the safeguard of prayer.[37] This exchange was founded on a sworn bond of friendship, but it was also meant to prevent the king from jeopardizing his protection by the apostolic princes by attempting to extend his sovereignty to include Rome.

Charlemagne thus concluded a pact of "friendship" with Hadrian; seven years later—just as had happened earlier with his father, Pepin—this was enhanced by a spiritual alliance when the pope agreed to become godfather to Charlemagne's son Carloman-Pepin on the occasion of his baptism. Mutual oaths sworn before the confessional of the apostolic prince on Good Friday 774 had already paved the way for this friendship and had created the precondition for Charlemagne to be able to enter the city of Rome.[38] This was followed a few days later by Charlemagne's pledge to donate extensive estates to the Church, that is, the confirmation that the exarchate and other regions in the center of Italy would be restored to the Apostolic See.[39] In subsequent correspondence with Hadrian's successor, Leo III, the king variously described this exchange of oaths as a "pact" (*pactum*) and an "inviolable alliance [*foedus*] of loyalty and love."[40] It is possible that the two partners in the pact understood the concepts of "friendship" (*amicitia*), "loyalty" (*fides*), and "love" (*caritas*) differently. Nevertheless, the signing of this *pactum* reinforced a development that had begun under Pepin in 754 and that would endure until the eleventh century. Undoubtedly the agreement also included Charlemagne's promise of protection for the Roman Church; in return, the pope undertook to intercede for the king.

As Einhard (chap. 19) was to mention many years later, Charlemagne really did regard Hadrian as a "friend." This friendship was to last until the pope's death. This event is said to have wrung tears from the king, as though a brother or a beloved son who had passed away. And with good reason.

The Frankish ruler had much to thank this particular successor of St. Peter for, not least the legitimizing of his Lombard crown and ecclesiastical help in his campaign to win Bavaria. And so he organized an impressive program of mourning for Hadrian. Charlemagne testified to his love for the deceased pontiff in many ways, one of which was an epitaph in verse on a commemorative plaque of expensive black marble. The Anglo-Saxon scholar Alcuin of York and the Visigothic poet Theodulf of Orléans both submitted drafts for this inscription.[41] The plaque can be seen today in the portico of the Church of St. Peter in the Vatican, commemorating both the pope and the king.

In the event, the Anglo-Saxon was more successful in conveying the king's grief than the Visigothic writer. Alcuin gained Charlemagne's approval for his formulation of the epitaph, not just because his poem imagined the king in person speaking the words of lament but first and foremost because of the immediacy with which this associated the king with the commemoration of the deceased pontiff:

> *Nomina iungo simul titulis, clarissime, nostra:*
> *"Hadrianus Carolus," rex ego tuque pater.*
> *Quisquis legas versus, devoto pectore supplex:*
> *"Amborum mitis," dic, "miserere deus."*

> (Most illustrious of men, I link your names and titles with my own.
> I, Charles the King, you, Hadrian the Holy Father.
> Whosoever may chance to read these lines, say, with devout and suppliant heart:
> "Have pity on them both, O Merciful God!")

So it is that Charlemagne's name still greets any visitor to the Apostolic Church who can manage to decipher the inscription (it is set very high up on the wall of the portico).

Theodulf's elegiac verses were more sophisticated in their sentiments, but it was only through sheer luck that they escaped being lost into oblivion. In them, Charlemagne laments the dead pope with a mixture of love and pain (with the king referring to himself as *me tuus,* "I who am yours"; he also praises Hadrian and finds that his death revives memories of the grief he felt at the death of his parents, Pepin and Bertrada. But the main thrust of Theodulf's epitaph was that of a *memento mori* admonishing each and every

FIGURE 25 Commemorative plaque of black marble from the portico of St. Peter's Basilica in Rome, inscribed with an epitaph dedicated by Charlemagne to Pope Hadrian I. Alcuin, the Anglo-Saxon scholar and adviser to Charlemagne, composed these verses.

reader, whoever he or she was, to be mindful of his or her own death. At that time, this was not to Charlemagne's taste.

> *Sexus uterque, senex, iuvenis, puer, advena, civis,*
> *Quisquis est, "Hadriano," dic, "sit amoena quies."*
> *En est quod fuerat: pulvis de pulvere sumptus.*
> *Sed putres cineres tu [deus] reparare vales.*
> *Hos apices quicumque legis, te nosce futurum*
> *Hoc quid hic est, omnis hoc caro pergit iter.*

(Man or woman, old man, youth, boy, foreigner, citizen.
Whoever you are, say, "Let there be a delightful rest for Hadrian."
So he is now what he once was, dust from dust.
But you are capable of reviving the putrid ashes.
You who read these words, be mindful that you
Will be just the same as this man; all flesh passes this way.)

This testament of Charlemagne's love for the deceased pontiff was to form the prelude to a lifelong enmity between the two poets—something that no one could have foreseen.[42] Both men, Alcuin and Theodulf, were head and shoulders above the rest of courtly society at that time in their knowledge and aptitude and vied for first place in the ruler's favor.[43] In this context, the poems not only portrayed the court as a haven of learning but also testified to a far greater extent to the highly competitive mood among the ruling elite in Frankish society, which was dominated by rivalry; this mood was especially prevalent among the clergy. Charlemagne, though, ordered "all Christian people" to hold commemorative prayer services "for the soul of our blessed Father Hadrian," services that also included prayers for himself and his realm.[44]

The safeguarding of the Church and the spreading of the message of peace were therefore the order of the day. They were expected to embrace and permeate all aspects of life, royal authority and the organization of the Church alike, education and economic activity, and the actions of the powerful, as well as the protection of the poor, encompassing the whole of society but above all the people at court, especially the prime movers there. Yet Charlemagne's epitaph for Hadrian was not just directed at the deceased but was also intended to sing the praises of the living king, and moreover to do so in Rome, the capital of the world.

Teachers from Foreign Climes

Alignment to Rome through renewal: that was the policy that Charlemagne pursued for decades. The Frankish poet Angilbert praised Charlemagne for cultivating knowledge at his court: "David [as Charlemagne liked to style himself in Aix] wishes to gather around him at court teachers, wise in spirit, for the adornment and glory of each and every branch of learning, in order that he might diligently revive [*renovet*] the wisdom of the ancients."[45] Again, it must be reiterated that such an objective could not be attained through conquests. The Frankish king who, after months of hard fighting, had just conquered the kingdom of the Lombards in northern Italy—and thereby incorporated one of the last isolated pockets of ancient learning into his realm—must have been shocked at the lack of such education in his Frankish kingdom. He acknowledged the "sense of superiority with which the Italians felt endowed by their high standard of intellectual education" and "therefore resolved to free his Frankish people from the yoke of ignorance."[46]

He may have had in mind the error-ridden Latin of his monks, as evidenced in many of the rogations they wrote for him, which must have made him fear for the efficacy of these prayers. Centuries before, St. Boniface had been annoyed when he had come across a priest in Bavaria who was wont to baptize people with an idiosyncratic version of the Trinitarian formula that had been mutilated so severely as to be unrecognizable: "In the Name of the Fatherland, the Daughter, and the Holy Spirit" (*In nomine patria et filia et spiritus sancti*). What did it matter, as long as no one understood Latin? Yet these formulas possessed magical qualities. They had to be right in order to achieve the right effect. Only in Rome did people pay more attention to the purpose than to the words. Yet it was a different situation north of the Alps. There, it was expected that correct knowledge should precede correct observance. Charlemagne required it—a monarch who was soon more familiar with all forms of scholarship than any other ruler and who set about promoting them more assiduously than had hitherto been the case among the Franks.

Correct learning, though, required the capacity to speak properly (*recte loquendi*) and to understand correctly the words that were being uttered in prayer, read, or spoken. Charlemagne later reproached the monks of Fulda and other monasteries with this in an attempt to get them to improve their knowledge of Latin, which had been found wanting.[47] He did this, as the king himself was at pains to stress, in his capacity as the "protector and humble helper of the Holy Church." He reported that he had received letters full of incorrect Latin, and that this had caused him great concern over whether people were understanding the Scriptures properly. This situation could not be tolerated. Errors in the spoken language were dangerous enough, but far more perilous were those in understanding. Make an effort, he urged them, so that you might more easily and properly penetrate the mysteries of the Holy Scriptures. In your heart of hearts, he went on, you should be humble, while outwardly you should be studious and lead a chaste life, and when you speak you should sound educated, in order that your listeners might learn from you. This is broadly what the king urged the monks to be: *interius devotos et exterius doctos*. The correct faith and the protection of the Church called for a root-and-branch revitalization of the education system, learning and skills, schools, and the internal organization of the Church—and this renewal was meant to further the eternal aim of salvation. Charlemagne did not exclude himself from this program. No lesser tutor than Alcuin taught the king to recognize the order-bringing branches of scholarship as a series of steps leading to salvation, "for the defense of the true faith and for the proclaimers of the truth."[48]

Such a program of correction could come to fruition only in stages. Yet in the kingdom of the Lombards and among the Romans, Charlemagne discovered erudition and artistry of a kind that was still lacking among his compatriots despite the best efforts of his father. There, in the south, laypeople could still read and write, knew Latin, and could recite poetry. The foreign land of Italy opened the young ruler's eyes to his own realm's pressing need to catch up; although the scholarship of late antiquity had not completely evaporated there, it had long since ceased to be of any great quality or significance or at all widespread. Indeed, in large parts of the kingdom it had sunk without trace. There were simply too few teachers among the Franks, too few schools, and scarcely any pupils or libraries. Very few manuscripts of the Bible existed in the country. Only a few people learned Latin, the key to a scholarly education, to the sources of the true faith and learning. No poet or artist came to the fore. Everything was in need of revival.

Even before Charlemagne's reign, the Anglo-Saxon monk Winfrid, who took the name "Boniface" when he was consecrated as a bishop in Rome around 716 by Pope Gregory II, had begun to plant the seeds of scholarship in the "barbarian" east of the Frankish kingdom. There he was able to establish three dioceses—Erfurt, Büraberg (near Marburg), and Würzburg—

as well as the monastery at Fulda, and to preach the true faith. Charlemagne was only six or seven years old when Boniface, whose last position was as bishop of Mainz, was slain by the Frisians as he was trying to preach the word of Christ to them and became the Church's most recent martyr.

Even after he became king, Charlemagne often liked to recall the life of St. Boniface. His father, Pepin, had, almost certainly at Boniface's instigation, sent a number of clerics to Rome to be initiated into the mysteries of Gregorian plainchant. Canon law and church discipline were in need of reform. Bishops' synods were convened at the behest of the king. The beginnings of a new push to advance education become apparent in this period, but at this early stage it still lacked any real momentum, a unifying vision, general support, and suitable helpers to make it happen. Even so, a school for plainsong on the Roman model was opened in Metz, possibly at Pepin's urging. However, that was not enough for Charlemagne.

The monarchy, the Church, and the realm all required a highly educated elite. This was to consist, first and foremost, of Franks, Alemanni, or Bavarians rather than of foreigners. The task that Charlemagne had to set himself was clearly defined: to revive education, learning, and skills and the organization of the church and the realm. The first decrees he issued tied in with those promulgated by his father's administration. But Charlemagne's renewal plans soon began to go much further. The teachers he required were not to be found among his own populace, who still lacked the necessary education at this time. Accordingly, the king looked for scholars from abroad. The very fact that he was able, even after just a few years, to chide the monks at Fulda and others for the shortcomings in their learning testifies to the first fruits of his success in this endeavor. And the reforming program really did begin in the very center of power, at the royal court and in various monasteries that were close to it.

Shortly after his return from Italy, as early as 776, Charlemagne summoned the Lombard scholar Paulinus, a teacher in Cividale del Friuli, to his court; ten years later he promoted him to patriarch (archbishop) of Aquileia. This proved to be a good decision; Paulinus was a key figure in supporting the Frankish king's reform measures in Italy. Likewise, the grammarian Petrus Pisanus, formerly a teacher in Pavia, heeded Charlemagne's call; the king himself is reputed to have received instruction from him. In 781, Charlemagne encountered the great Anglo-Saxon scholar Alcuin for the second time; at this stage he was head of the cathedral school in York and had an especially profound knowledge of the trivium, the three basic disciplines of the canon of classical education, namely, grammar (i.e., Latin), rhetoric (i.e., oratory informed by reasoned argument), and dialectics (i.e., thinking in terms of argument and counterargument). Alcuin was also versed in the discipline of *computus*, the complex calculation of time and calendars, which was of fundamental importance for the Church with its principal movable feast of Easter. Yet this man did not delve to an obsessive degree into the "treadmills of the calculators and the sweatshops of the mathematicians."[49] To assist him with the calendar reform that he planned during the later years of his reign, Charlemagne was obliged to consult other scholars.[50]

The following year, 782, saw Alcuin take up permanent residence at the Frankish court—albeit with a break of several years between 789 and 794— where he took over the running of the court scriptorium. There ensued a lifelong dialogue between the king and the Anglo-Saxon tutor, as evidenced by the many letters that Alcuin wrote to, and for, Charlemagne.[51] Later, in 797, the king placed this learned man in charge of the monastery at Tours, which under Alcuin's leadership developed into perhaps one of the most important educational establishments in the Frankish Empire. The chronicler and monk Notker the Stammerer, the "Monk of St. Gall," later eulogized Alcuin in the following terms: "His erudition bore such rich fruit that the Gauls and Franks of modern times may be said to be on a par with the ancient Romans or Athenians."[52]

An increasing number of scholars began flooding to the court at Aix. They were lured there by Charlemagne's widely renowned thirst for knowledge, his reforming zeal, and not least the career opportunities promised by being in the king's service. In 781, Charlemagne personally brought back with him from Italy the Lombard monk Paul the Deacon (also known as Paulus Warnefred), who was likewise an outstanding grammarian.[53] He had already made a name for himself as a historian, had served as tutor to the Lombard king Desiderius's daughter Adalperga in Pavia or Benevento, and knew and taught Greek. He was the scion of one of the Lombard aristocratic families that had formerly, in the sixth century, emigrated to Italy from Pannonia with King Alboin.

During Charlemagne's sojourn in Italy in 780–781, Paul the Deacon appeared before the mighty ruler to plead for the release of his brother Arichis, whom Charlemagne had imprisoned. The king refused to let him leave. Paul duly spent four or five years at the Frankish court, wracked with grief and homesickness, but still managed to function effectively there as a historian and a teacher before Charlemagne finally allowed him to return to his homeland and his monastery. During his time in Aix, he instructed Charlemagne's daughter Rotrude, who was betrothed to the young emperor Constantine

VI of Byzantium, and also wrote a history of the bishops of Metz, which included a paean of praise for the Carolingian dynasty. Once he had returned to Italy, he withdrew once more to far-off Benevento, home of the last Lombard principality that was still at least partially free. He had been a monk at the Benedictine monastery of Monte Cassino, where he is thought to have taken the monastic name of Paulus and to have been consecrated as a deacon. Before this great scholar left Aix, Charlemagne asked him to compile a collection of sermons by the Church Fathers, which were subsequently used as models for preaching sermons throughout the Frankish Empire.

At the same time, around 780, the Visigoth Theodulf also found his way to the court of Charlemagne, having fled his native Spain. Theodulf, who was an expert in Aristotelian dialectics, was an astute theologian with a keen appreciation of irony. Charlemagne was later to entrust him with the difficult task of refuting Greek misconceptions during the iconoclastic controversy. The complete Vulgate, the Latin translation of the Bible, which hitherto had been available only in manuscripts of individual books, was brought together by Theodulf, using a tiny script, in a single codex for handy use. These "Theodulf Bibles" were the first single-volume Scriptures in history and were a marvel of critical sense and organization. One modern commentator has observed, "He tirelessly scrutinized the exact wording, using primarily manuscripts of the Vulgate from northern Italy for the purpose of comparison, kept a working copy that he constantly corrected, and on occasion would even refer back to the Hebrew text by having a baptized Jew check through St. Jerome's original translation into Latin."[54] At the end of the book he "signed" his work with two distichs (and not without a hint of pride): "*Vive deo felix per plurima tempora lector / Theodulfi nec sis inmemor oro tui. / finis adest operi. His, quibus est peragentibus actum, / sit pax vita salus et tibi lector ave.*"[55] (Reader, may you have a long and happy life in the care of God, / But please do not forget to pray for Theodulf, / Now you are approaching the end of this work. To those who have got this far, / I wish you peace, a happy life, and good health. Farewell to you, dear reader.)

This Visigothic scholar, then, was highly educated but in addition was capable of writing verses full of corrosive mockery. Charlemagne held him in high regard and, perhaps in gratitude for writing the *Libri Carolini,* made him abbot of the Benedictine monastery at Fleury (St-Benoît-sur-Loire) and various other religious institutions; sometime before 798 he then promoted him to bishop of Orléans. The preferred target of Theodulf's bitter scorn was the Irish, who had gained access to Charlemagne's court, where their strange habits and customs and their idiosyncratic form of Christian education had irritated many people.

Amusing stories circulated about them, for example, how two of these "Scots" had landed on Frankish soil as part of the retinue of Breton merchants and had immediately begun peddling their knowledge, both secular and spiritual, like some commodity to visitors to a market, calling out to the assembled crowd, "Anyone who wants wisdom, come to us! You'll get it here! Going cheap!" Charlemagne got to hear of their antics, summoned them to appear before him, and after testing their theological knowledge, appointed one of them, Clemens by name, to a teaching post in a monastery in Gallia, while the other was sent to the Monastery of St. Augustine in Pavia. Notker of St. Gall (1.1) tells this famous story, although there is no way of knowing whether it is true or apocryphal. Yet even in Notker's retelling, we catch a hint of the envy that Charlemagne's generosity toward these strangers engendered in many Franks.

So it was that an "international" community of scholars comprising Lombards, Anglo-Saxons, Irish, and Visigoths, which was convened and funded by the king, assembled at Aix; such a gathering of fine minds was not to be found at any other princely court of the time, not even in Rome. Of course, tensions and animosities were not lacking. These foreigners, reliant as they were on the good grace of the king, were deeply suspicious of one another, begrudged one another their successes, and spent their time feuding among themselves with barbed words and poems. Yet it was precisely this rivalry among them that made for such a lively intellectual atmosphere and generated a fresh new spirit of enquiry that had not been seen for centuries in the Latin West. This was the energizing by-product of a deeply competitive society.

Schools, Scriptoria, and Prayers

It was these very foreigners at Charlemagne's court who went on to found schools in his realm. It was for this reason that religious foundations and monasteries were placed in their charge. Charlemagne entrusted the monasteries above all, but also monastery schools like the one in Tours, with the vitally urgent task of root-and-branch renewal of the educational system. They were expected to redress the widespread lack of learning. This was by no means a straightforward proposition, for monks were supposed to live apart from the world, leading a hermit-like existence and praying for their own salvation and that of their benefactors rather than slaving away for the benefit of others. Schools had existed hitherto only to meet the internal needs of the monasteries. Comparatively little breadth or depth of learning had sufficed for this purpose, however.

Now, though, the more significant monastery schools transformed themselves into general schools, with a genuine remit to serve the entire clergy, the Church, and society as a whole; one key task, for instance, was to transcribe the books that the clergy urgently needed.[56] The costs of the Carolingian educational revolution were huge. Meeting them required special economic measures in order to set up schools, to build up libraries, and to acquire the original texts that were to be copied. Furthermore, money was needed to fund benefices for teachers and pupils alike.

Only the very wealthiest patrons had the wherewithal to fund an entire school. Foremost among these was the king himself; the great monasteries and religious foundations and—albeit after some delay, though with all the more success thereafter—the episcopal churches were also drawn into this grand project. Parish churches, meanwhile, were involved only in a quite rudimentary fashion in providing a basic Christian education.[57] Measured against the economic potential of society at that period and its productivity, namely, the gross national product (if one can speak of such a concept at this stage), the sums involved were certainly no lower and in all likelihood higher than a modern state's education budget. However, in the Carolingian era, the cost was spread across several shoulders, particularly the major churches and monasteries with their large incomes.

Writing workshops, or scriptoria, were initially to be found only here and there, predominantly at the larger monasteries, while "studios" for book illumination were even scarcer. At first, this massively limited the spread and the speed of dissemination of knowledge, although this situation soon improved thanks to the efforts made during Charlemagne's reign. The king wanted to intensify the monasteries' involvement in copying and collecting texts and to reproduce elsewhere the endeavors of this kind that were already under way. As a result, many new scriptoria came into being, specialized workshops for the production of books, involving all the relevant trades, from parchment makers to scribes and illuminators.

This too saddled the monasteries concerned with unimaginable costs while also lending them cultural significance. According to its layout and extent, the production of each book cost a greater or lesser fortune. It took a small flock of goats or sheep, or several calves, to make a single work on vellum (parchment). Large-format luxury volumes required correspondingly larger herds, not to mention the enormously expensive pigments for the illuminations, which made lavish use of gold, silver, and purple and other colors made from ground or pulverized semiprecious stones. The manuscripts dating from after 780 that have survived give evidence of increased copying activity at this time; this seems to have been instigated by the royal court and to have swiftly caught on in the large monasteries or canons' foundations.[58] Even by the early years of Louis the Pious's reign, these institutions each had libraries containing several hundred manuscripts. Historians have calculated that a total of around ten thousand manuscripts were produced during Charlemagne's reign.

Those involved were proud of this achievement and were keen to proclaim it. For example, around 800, a scribe in Verona, who may perhaps have just prepared the costly vellum for a book he was about to transcribe, left a little self-congratulatory riddle in the form of the following four lines of verse on the first page of his codex: "*Se pareba boves / alba pratalia araba / et albo versorio teneba / et negro semen seminaba*" (I harnessed the oxen / tilled white fields / and held the white plowshare / and sowed black seed). In other words, the writer had first smoothed out his piece of vellum, had covered it with a layer of chalk in preparation for writing, had then taken up his goose-feather quill ready to write, and had penned black letters on the page. These verses were no longer in Latin (which the scribe would have had a very good command of) but instead were written in a form of Romanic, a dialect just in the process of embarking on the long journey that would culminate in the language of Dante's *Divine Comedy*.[59]

Criticism of the demands that Charlemagne made on the monasteries was not long in coming. It raised its head, in fact, just a few years after his death, in the reign of Louis the Pious. The aim of the monastic reform that Louis commissioned the Visigoth Benedict of Aniane to undertake was to allow schools henceforth to operate only for the internal benefit of the monasteries once more. However, a determined opposition, which soon came to predominate and was led by the likes of Adalhard of Corbie, halted this retrograde step. The monasteries' commitment to more general education was upheld and for the time being saved the new culture of learning from an untimely demise.

The Frankish king was not acting without any precedents in his promotion of education. The Irish and the Anglo-Saxons had long provided relevant models of school education systems. Monastery schools were a widespread phenomenon in their communities. Almost every Anglo-Saxon episcopal church had a cathedral monastery with a school. Some—like Alcuin's former place of employment, York, Canterbury, or Jarrow (once under the leadership of the Venerable Bede)—were notable for their outstanding libraries, teachers, and pupils. The first Irish scholars to reach Charlemagne's court were Raefgot and Jonas, sometime before 780, although nothing more is known about them; Alcuin greeted them on their arrival in Aix.[60]

The organization of the Church under which these Irishmen worshipped differed fundamentally from that of all other Western churches.[61] Its most important institutions were monasteries, each of which was under the control of an abbot; under the abbots were priests and bishops, all of them monks too, who had taken the appropriate vows. Unlike in the continental churches, Irish bishops exercised authority only in liturgical matters, not in questions of jurisdiction. Several of these monasteries offered instruction in Latin, and some even in Greek as well. The rules and customs of these monasteries appeared strange in comparison to those of the continental mainland. Penance became a central theme of the Irish way of life. Subject to the gravity of the transgression, these penances were done according on a scale of fixed "tariffs" that were stipulated in penance books.

These Irish monks practiced an itinerant form of faith. They called it "holy pilgrimage," in other words, a constant peregrination, whose precise itinerary was ordained by God. So they would simply set off to foreign climes, seeking out the misery of the world, without any clear objective. Time and again since the Merovingian era, this mode of existence had scattered learned monks far and wide, from uninhabited islands in the far north to the Frankish Empire or to Italy. They did missionary work, founded monasteries, and, following the practice of such institutions in their homeland, established monastery schools too. Luxeuil in the western Vosges, St. Gall in Switzerland, and Bobbio in Emilia-Romagna may be cited as examples.[62] These Irishmen or Scots were responsible for introducing two new genres of religious book, the admonishing treatise and penance books, into the Frankish empire. Several of these monks knew Greek, but all too often they found themselves the object of envy, mockery, and derision because of their unorthodox practices.

One courtier was outspoken in his criticism of one of the Irish monks, a man named Cadac-Andreas: "You rabid creature, cease your drinking, so that you might regain your senses in eternal slumber."[63] Did the Irish really drink more than other people? And did they go around boasting of their knowledge of Greek, a skill otherwise totally absent at the court of Charlemagne? Did their unfamiliar expressions of sorrow on someone's death cause offense among native Franks? The writer of the scathing words above

FIGURES 26 AND 27 Ivory front and back covers of the Lorsch Gospels, carved around 810 in the court scriptorium of Charlemagne in Aix. The left (back) cover, showing Christ, is in the Vatican Museums, while the right (front) cover, showing the Virgin Mary and Jesus, is in the Victoria and Albert Museum in London.

was not a great poet nor a great scholar; he came from the lands on the far side of the Rhine. Many of his audience would have blanched with anger on hearing such uncouth, xenophobic insults, but equally, others would have grown pale with envy that they had not penned such verses: the king welcomed this kind of polemic and repaid it with favors.

So what did these Irish or, for that matter, the many foreigners of all nationalities hope to achieve among the Franks? The irksome Visigoths, the supercilious Lombards, the arrogant Greeks? Or even the barbarians from the far side of the river Enns? Even Einhard, himself a Germanic Frank, found himself shocked and muttered something about foreign infiltration, which was threatening to become a burden on the court and the realm at large. Yet even he was careful not to voice these opinions in public. Several decades later, he would advise Charlemagne's successor to be wary of foreigners.[64]

Charlemagne, though, was very fond of the foreigners in his kingdom. He eagerly adopted the suggestions even of those who had come from far afield. The king supported episcopal churches, monasteries, and religious houses, be they long-established foundations or recently created ones, and he put several foreigners in charge of such institutions. An abundance of centers of culture and learning came into being as a result. New schools, whose importance soon transcended their local region, began to flourish, and the first episcopal schools were founded at this time. In the ensuing decades, the length and breadth of the Frankish Empire, from north to south and west to east, was covered with a network of educational institutions.

To name just a few of these, in the west the outstanding seats of learning included the monasteries of St-Denis and Corbie, Marmoutier Abbey in Tours (founded by St. Martin and under the care of Alcuin from 796 to his death in 804), Fleury Monastery under Theodulf of Orléans, and the convent of Notre-Dame in Chelles, where Charlemagne's sister was abbess. In the east, the major institutions were to be found in Mainz and Würzburg, together with the monasteries at Fulda and Lorsch, as well as Wissembourg in Alsace, the Swabian monasteries on the island of Reichenau and at St. Gall, the Bavarian episcopal schools in Freising, the Monastery of St. Emmeram in Regensburg, and also the Monastery of St. Peter in Salzburg. Scriptoria were established, manuscripts were produced, and libraries were founded; some of these centers also became famed for book illumination. Not least Louis the Pious's reign was to reap the benefits of this development.

Literally hundreds of monasteries were spread across the entire realm. The prosperity of many of them obliged them to undertake services for the empire, which were by no means restricted to supporting schools. Under Louis the Pious, they were divided into three categories according to their economic potential: those that were required to pay tributes to the king and had to provide military assistance in times of war; those that only had to pay contributions; and finally the great majority of institutions, which were expected only to offer up prayers for the well-being of the ruler, his sons, and the realm in general. The first category was headed by the monastery at Fleury, along with Corbie, Lorsch, Mondsee, and Tegernsee, while the second category was represented by Fulda and Hersfeld, and the third by Wessobrunn, for example.[65]

Charlemagne had already presumably placed similar burdens on the monasteries. Schools and scriptoria were among the achievements of monasteries in the third category. Convents were no exception, either. For example, the convent at Chelles, where daughters of the Carolingian dynasty were repeatedly appointed abbess, seems to have been distinguished by history writing and the production of manuscripts.[66] Laypeople also participated in Charlemagne's revival of education. Einhard, for instance, the biographer of Charlemagne, belonged to the laity, as did Charlemagne's grandson, the Frankish historian Nithard. Around 780 or shortly before, this effort to promote education bore its first fruit when Abbot Adam of Masmünster in Alsace copied the treatise *Ars grammatica* by Diomedes and prefaced it with a dedication to the king in verse, not forgetting in the process to include a verbose and rather inelegant passage begging the king's favor.[67]

Corbie in Picardy soon became an outstanding seat of learning. A Merovingian foundation dating from the seventh century, this monastery combined material wealth, a body of highly educated monks, and a wonderfully appointed library, containing valuable tomes of canon law and literature. There is documentary evidence that St. Boniface had connections to Corbie. With the change of dynasty, it was not long before the monastery was receiving support from the Carolingians. The movement to create prayer confraternities brought monasteries and bishops from different regions into contact with one another. Corbie, for instance, belonged to the Attigny prayer league, which was formed in 762 by twenty-two bishops, five abbot-bishops, and seventeen abbots "to promote the cause of religion and the salvation of souls." On the death of any of its members, it undertook to have a hundred psalms and a hundred masses sung; for clerics, thirty masses were said by each participating bishop personally, and any abbot who was not also a bishop could formally request that his bishop hold these services.

In this way, the abbot of Corbie, say, found himself in league with the bishops of Metz or Mainz and the abbots of St-Denis, St-Germain-des-Prés, St-Wandrille, and many others.[68]

Corbie experienced its first golden age under the leadership of Abbot Maudramnus, who died in 780. The Bible that was completed there during his tenure became famous and epoch making both for its text and for its illuminations. Furthermore, in the scriptorium attached to the monastery, rare texts were copied, further enhancing the stock of the library. They were a major factor in the Picardy monastery's rise to become one of the most important educational centers in the Frankish Empire. Charlemagne's cousins Adalhard and Wala were both abbots of Corbie.

It may have been in Corbie that a writing reform began that was subsequently to have worldwide impact, namely, the invention of the script form known as Carolingian minuscule. This script had clear characters and placed upper- and lowercase letters with their ascenders and descenders within a framework of four equally measured lines; individual words were thereby clearly separated from one another—an immensely valuable aid for reading and understanding any text, from the Holy Scriptures to any speech that was written down in the script, while in addition offering an aesthetically pleasing access to the text in question. Maudramnus's Bible is a prime example of Carolingian minuscule, although the first traces of this new script can be found in works copied under his predecessor Leutcharius.[69] It made the layout of a manuscript and the internal organization of its texts and pages easy to understand and enhanced the graphic attractiveness of every page; decorative scripts such as uncial, semiuncial, and canonical capitals, plus initials with or without pictorial decoration, the use of gold and silver inks, purple vellum, and illuminations, lent manuscripts an opulence they had not displayed for centuries. This enterprise was conducted both to the glory of God and at the behest of the royal court.

So it was that a new book art came into being under the king's supervision. As an early example, which was produced for the king, we may cite the Dagulf Psalter. Yet the truly outstanding, epochal manuscript of the Carolingian period is the evangelistary (a book of excerpts from the Gospels) that bears the name of the Frankish scribe Godescalc, written "with golden letters on purple sheets of vellum." Its magnificent illuminations still have the power to captivate anyone who sees it. Its creator, who may have been a deacon in the church at Liège, lavishly decorated it with gold and silver; in addition, exquisite miniatures, elaborate marginal illustrations around the texts, and the appearance of gold and silver ink on purple parchment gave

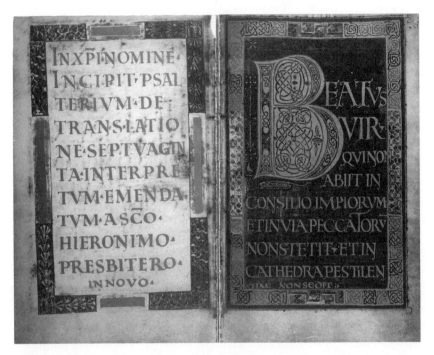

FIGURE 28 Opening page of the Dagulf Psalter, an illuminated manuscript commissioned by Charlemagne sometime between 783 and 795 as a gift for Pope Hadrian I. In the seventeenth century, the psalter was taken from the cathedral treasury at Aachen/Aix and found its way to Vienna, where it remains to this day. Austrian National Library (Cod. 1861).

the whole work an exemplary quality that was much imitated. This masterpiece was created for the king and his wife Hildegard in 781–783, when the royal couple traveled to Rome, where their son Carloman was baptized by Pope Hadrian I with the name Pepin, an occasion that the evangelistary's attached calendar highlighted in gold ink.[70] Both of the manuscripts noted here are attributed to the so-called court school at Aix, which had just been founded at this time. Moreover, the evangelistary is the first book that can be verified as having been commissioned by a Frankish ruler. It provides tangible and exceptional evidence of Charlemagne's program of educational and ecclesiastical reform. Its script, text, images, and materials all combined to form a piece of representational art so splendid that Charlemagne's court no longer needed to fear comparison with other cultural centers.

East of the Rhine, however, circumstances were by no means as favorable as in Corbie, or in the West in general, for that matter. In this region, which

Roman civilization had never reached or at best had only fleetingly touched, intensive instruction and remedial work were required. Many institutions had to be created from the beginning: dioceses and monasteries, religious foundations, and schools. A great deal was achieved within just a few generations. The first teachers to arrive there were brought over from England by St. Boniface; the first scribes we can identify in Freising and at other schools came from the British Isles. The Bavarian monasteries and bishoprics, which had already been founded under the rule of the Agilolfing dynasty and which had been supported by Tassilo III, also enjoyed royal patronage under Charlemagne.[71]

In the east of Francia, the dioceses of Würzburg and Eichstätt had been established. Boniface's monastic foundation at Fulda, situated at the crossroads of two vital long-distance routes to Thuringia and Saxony and now under the leadership of Abbot Sturmi, had already been lent support by Charlemagne's uncle Carloman. Even at the turn of the eighth century, to judge from the oldest surviving register of books, it was still an anchoritic community of several hundred monks with rather deficient knowledge of Latin and negligible educational facilities.[72] Only under pressure from Charlemagne, with the active assistance of a former pupil of Alcuin, Hrabanus Maurus, the *magister* (head of the monastery school) there and later abbot, did things begin to change at Fulda. Before long, it was numbered among the outstanding centers of learning in the Frankish Empire; as early as the mid-ninth century, its library housed several hundred manuscripts, representing the life's work of numerous literate monks. Hersfeld, Fulda's sister institution, located in the far north of Old Franconia, close to the border with Saxony, was developed from a hermitage at the instigation of Bishop Lull of Mainz in 769.

Yet despite all such efforts, it took centuries for the new thinking to establish itself across a broad front. One key prerequisite was a comprehensive availability of ancient knowledge. Certainly, some manuscripts from classical antiquity with relevant texts could still be found during Charlemagne's reign, but any scholar had to search extensively to locate this or that example, and it required painstaking transcription to save the found text and disseminate it.[73] As a rule, the material used in the ancient books was comparatively cheap but fragile papyrus, and only rarely more expensive vellum. With the subsequent decline in both writing activity and papyrus production, the consequences were catastrophic. The situation is starkly portrayed when one considers the numbers: nothing survived of the renowned libraries of antiquity, some of which were vast, and which were estimated to have held up to a million volumes. Not one single ancient papyrus roll with a scholarly text survived the passage of time.

With very few exceptions, scarcely a trace of ancient learning and literature would still be extant, not even the works of the Latin Church Fathers, if the scribes and scholars employed by monarchs from Charlemagne onward had not used vellum for their transcriptions. Their diligence and zeal have preserved for posterity all manner of texts, from those presenting the ancient program of the seven liberal arts to handbooks on the "mechanical arts," together with Cicero's speeches, Seneca's treatises, and the magic of classical Latin verse and drama, as exemplified by Horace, Ovid, and Plautus. To their contemporary world, though, they imparted the very first inklings of art and poetry. Although no one was conscious of it at the time, their endeavors set in train an important process whereby texts that were threatened with destruction were saved.

Yet the process went beyond this, for Charlemagne's court also witnessed the rebirth of a mode of thought that was subject to logical, verifiable rules. Like all newborns, it was tiny at first, reliant on the help of outsiders, but most definitely alive and kicking. Fostered by the king, it grew up and thrived. As a result, a distinct "Western" style of thought was able to develop and spread. It was to change the world in a way that could never have been anticipated. The miracle of this birth is inseparable from the name of Aristotle and his translators, but also from the name of Charlemagne and his court, for the first sign that the logical works of Aristotle were being reclaimed came from there. Admittedly, no one could have known what a huge effect this would have and what a broad and ever-widening path with endless branchings this development would initiate.[74]

Reforms Are Long Overdue, but Where to Begin?

Reforms were overdue; even the bishops would now have to be accountable before God for the way they conducted themselves in office. Yet it was not merely corrections in behavior that were being called for; instead, what was required was a revival of the sort of knowledge that had become submerged under previous Frankish rulers and their priests, and that had only very occasionally resurfaced. Even as late as 800, Theodulf of Orléans's first and widely disseminated capitulary on bishops opened a window on a parlous state of affairs. Reading and manual work were suggested as remedies. Whether they helped is a moot point. Theodulf found that the bread, wine, and water for the ritual sacrifice of animals were not always clean, and that women were allowed to approach the celebrant or even lived under the same roof with priests; in some places, churches were used as storehouses for grain and hay, or people congregated there simply to chat, while clergymen got drunk in alehouses, and some of them barely knew the Holy Scriptures or misused the sacred altar sacraments for profane purposes; meanwhile, there was a sad lack of parish schools. At least twice a day ordinary people were supposed to recite the Nicene Creed and the Lord's Prayer as a form of self-discipline, so to speak; this practice, it seems, had fallen into abeyance. And so the list of abuses went on—a shocking litany of shortcomings despite the fact that reform attempts had long since been introduced. This all testified to the fact that the long march to become a Christian civilization had a very sluggish start.[75]

What might the situation have looked like twenty years earlier, though, when Charlemagne's reform program first began to take shape? Certainly no better. It was at this stage, some ten years after he had ascended the Frankish throne, that the surviving records indicate that the ongoing succession of capitularies commenced—royal decrees, administrative edicts, and legal directives, all originating from the royal court. These were all aimed at fulfilling the reform program that Charlemagne had gradually begun to flesh out.[76] We do not know what was to blame for Charlemagne's delay in instituting this program. Was this new start now perhaps intended to expunge memories of the ill-fated Spanish campaign and the disastrous Saxon invasion that followed? Might God's wrath, which was revealed in these defeats, be pacified by reforms or deflected, and might the unrest that was becoming apparent among the magnates be effectively quelled by them? Had the pope's admonitions had an effect? Or was it the case that Charlemagne had only now managed to find the helpers he needed in order to put such a comprehensive reform plan into action?

Charlemagne was not acting alone; who, then, were his confederates? We know by name hardly any of the clerics in his inner circle, the members of the court chapel, or his closest confidants. Indeed, the only people who are known from this early period are the archchaplain, the aged Fulrad of St-Denis, and the chancellor Rado, along with various notaries. It is possible that Charlemagne was by this stage already placing greater reliance on Angilram of Metz, who took over Fulrad's position after his death in 784, as an adviser. Around 780, we begin to encounter in the records the names of the count palatine Worad, the chamberlain Adalgis, the marshal Geilo, and the cupbearer Eberhard;[77] also Gerold, the brother of Queen Hildegard, could well have been found frequently at court. Otherwise, the dignitaries were specially summoned to attend court meetings and synods. A fleeting spotlight is thrown on Charlemagne's advisers and the courtly society of this period by a poem written in a letter or a circular by a visitor to the court, Alcuin, in salutation to Charlemagne and his magnates on his return to England after a journey to the continent in 778–780. The Anglo-Saxon scholar had already paid a courtesy call on Charlemagne during his stay in Rome in 774[78] and on this occasion had visited him again,[79] although this time he did not, as finally happened after his third encounter with the king in Pavia in 781, remain for a protracted period at the royal court in Aix.

Alcuin's letter-poem is presented as an "emissary" sent by the writer to his friends on the Continent, extending formal greetings to them: Bishop Alberic of Utrecht and his prior Hadda, who, since Frisia had no oil or wine to offer, were kind enough to serve their guests honey and butter. Go on, letter, Alcuin urges his emissary, but avoid the town of Dorestad, where an uncouth, greedy merchant by the name of Black Hrotberct refuses to provide a "hospitable roof" (hospita tecta). Going upstream along the Rhine, Alcuin instructs his letter to visit Bishof Ricvulf of Cologne and, farther on, down the river Moselle, the abbot of Echternach Monastery and Samuhel-Beornrad, bishop of Sens, a cousin and possibly also a former pupil of Alcuin. Then hasten to Aix to the court of the ruler—"My salutations, dear king!"—and while you are there, do not forget to flatter Magister Paulinus of Aquileia and give him a quiet warning (Alcuin had already known Paulinus for some time) about Peter of Pisa, who, "look out! . . . sets about his opponents with a club of Hercules," and greet the courtiers Ricvulf, Raefgot, Jonas, two Irishmen, and the chancellor Rado; then proceed to Mainz to see Bishop Lull, to Speyer and Bishop Basinus, and finally to visit Fulrad of St-Denis, the archchaplain of the court.[80] In this poem, then, Alcuin mentioned certain bishops and abbots by name and exposed a single layman (the merchant) to ridicule but said nothing about the queen or the king's sons.

Preparations for the court meetings, at which key decisions were made, undoubtedly lay in the hands of the court chaplains, the notaries, and the chancellor. Yet specially invited clerical and secular magnates also played a part in the proceedings.[81] It is not known, though, who edited the texts of the meetings; the senior chaplain would have exerted some influence over this, while the chancellor's sole responsibility was to notarize them. The oldest indisputably genuine capitulary of the great king was probably concluded in agreement with the king in March 779 at an assembly of bishops, abbots, and counts in Herstal.[82] Their consent with the ruler was stressed in the introduction to the document, but not one of the magnates who had attended the meeting was cited by name. Charlemagne's actions showed themselves to be in concert with the magnates of his realm and in the service of God: the capitulary expressly addressed "current tasks that must be done in accordance with God's will" (*secundum Dei voluntatem pro causis opportunis*) and was directed at ecclesiastical order and discipline. Both God's and the king's will ordained that the bishops should be subject to their metropolitans, and that they should reform whatever was in need of reform; further, that bishops should be promoted to take over vacant dioceses without delay; that monks should abide by their order's rules and abbesses should reside permanently in their convents; that priests and other clerics were subordinate to their diocesan bishops, and only them; and finally, that tithes were to be paid.

Concealed in these terse sentences is one of the most momentous steps taken by Charlemagne, namely, the revival in the Frankish Empire of the metropolitan constitution of late antiquity, which during the early Middle Ages had fallen into disuse. In this system, an archbishop presided over an ecclesiastical province comprising several dioceses.[83] In his time, St. Boniface had criticized the lack of any effective church organization, claiming that in over eighty years the Franks had not convened a synod or appointed a single archbishop.[84] This situation was about to change. The synod in Herstal revived the ancient principle that ecclesiastical boundaries should follow those of the state. As far as we can tell, the synod approved their restoration at Charlemagne's urging and with the approval of Pope Hadrian I. In order to redress this situation, Charlemagne now adopted as his guide the *Notitia Galliarum*,[85] an ancient register of all state provinces with their metropolises (*metropoles*) and other towns (*civitates*), which dated from the period around 400. Hadrian had sent him a copy of this work. Taking its cue from the example of Gregory the Great, the new organizing principle of the church consciously and avowedly sought to replicate the hierarchical structure of the Roman imperial constitution of late antiquity.[86] As a result, church provinces and archbishoprics were now newly established or restored. It is probable that Reims, a former metropolis, took the lead in this, followed by Mainz, a newly created one, whose province extended deep into Saxony as far as the town of Verden on the river Aller, while to the south, it stretched as far as Konstanz and Chur. As a consequence of the Saxon wars, the Church had expanded greatly to take in formerly pagan regions; this new administrative development confirmed this expansion for all the world to see. But the regions that had been subjugated were also to reap benefit from the church's reorganization; Saxony too was divided into ecclesiastical provinces. This process, then, intensified and formalized the incorporation of the former barbarian lands into the advanced civilization of the Mediterranean region.

Whatever the former situation may have been, henceforth the archbishop acquired a jurisdictional leadership function within his church province. This meant that he was empowered to convoke regular provincial synods and thereby assume some measure of control over the episcopacy, which in its turn was responsible for supervising the priesthood and other clergy within its diocese. The effect of this decision of Charlemagne's has endured to the present day. At that time, though, not all metropolitan regions were restored simultaneously; the business of implementing the program took at least two decades. In 798, again at Charlemagne's behest, Salzburg was promoted by Pope Leo III to the Archepiscopate of Bavaria. Later Holy Roman emperors, such as Louis the Pious and Otto (I) the Great, were to follow in Charlemagne's footsteps in this matter.

Secular measures to complement these developments were also announced in Herstal; for instance, one provision stipulated that thieves who came from areas that enjoyed immunity—that is, from estates that the count could not legally set foot in—could nevertheless be summoned to appear before the count's court (chap. 9). Other clauses regulated how perjurers were to be dealt with, decreed that counts were to formulate their judgments on the basis of "true justice" rather than hatred and malice, and proclaimed that private retinues (*trustis,* chap. 14) or sworn conspiracies (*sacramenta per gildonia,* chap. 16) were outlawed. Furthermore, it was forbidden to waylay anyone traveling to the king's palace to hand over tributes (*cum collecta,* chap. 17). No illegal new tolls were to be levied, suits of chain mail were not to be sold outside the borders of the empire, and it was required that "Wehrgeld," a penalty payment for inflicting death or injury, should be both paid and accepted; otherwise the distant royal court would become involved. Unfree servants (*manzipien*) could be sold only under the supervision of an ecclesiastical or a secular judge and on no account were to be traded beyond the frontiers of their native marchlands. Counts and royal vassals who did not fulfill their judicial duties were to be publicly compelled to do so (chap. 21). A first-time offender who stole goods would lose an eye; if he committed a second offense, he would lose his nose; the third time, he would forfeit his life (chap. 23)—in other words, draconian sentences to try to confront a danger that would not go away.

These, then, were the miseries of day-to-day existence in both the Church and secular life, which ran counter to godly order and prompted the king to act in order to try to eliminate these abuses. They reveal what uncertain circumstances, often even confusing and ruled by violence, prevailed among the clergy and the people, how ordinary citizens were oppressed, and what dangers lurked everywhere. Yet they also tell us that the king and his followers were placed under great pressure by aristocratic powers that could bring to bear their own armed retinues, and show what an enormous effort it took to make changes or improve conditions. Finally, they reveal the simple additive thinking that was needed to get control of the chaos and overcome it: making one improvement here and another there, and then a third and a fourth, and so on, anchored in and subservient to God's will. Monarchical power was construed as a service to God, was meant to impose order on the populace and the Church, as well as creating consensus among the ruling elite, and was a vital element in achieving redemption. But to a large extent, all this was just piecemeal effort, without any systematic guiding principle behind it.

Ten years later saw the issuing of the next capitulary to have survived, the famous *General Admonition (Admonitio generalis)*, which I will examine in greater detail presently.[87] It was compiled over several years and—coordinated by the king—in conjunction with all the scholars who were then presiding at the court. Not least among them was Paul the Deacon, although by the time the *Admonitio* was proclaimed, he had long since returned to live at his monastery after giving Charlemagne strong support in the planning of his educational reforms. He appears to have helped draft this admonition, which, as far as we can tell, was addressed to Bishop Lull of Mainz, urging him to give his clergy education in literacy. In it, Charlemagne professed himself astonished that the archbishop had not given this matter greater attention despite being a learned man himself. The gloom of ignorance was spreading in the hearts of Lull's subordinates (*subditi*), the king maintained. He demanded that the situation be remedied. If they resisted, he advised Lull that they should be "enthused for the light of education"[88] either with gentle words or, if need be, harsh ones.

A second, somewhat later communication, known as the *Epistola generalis,*[89] was sent by Charlemagne to all "readers" among the clergy. The king told them that he wanted to ensure "that the state [*status*] of our churches constantly improves." Accordingly, he claimed, those things that "the negligence of our predecessors" had omitted to do would now have to be put right. He, the king, intended to study the liberal arts himself in order that others might follow his example. He had already made sure that certain texts ruined by bad transcribers had been corrected. Liturgical readings would continue to be improved henceforth. He announced that he had instructed his confidant Paul the Deacon to compile an anthology of sermons from the *Dicta of the Catholic Fathers,* in two volumes, which presented them "error-free" (*absque vitiis*) and organized according to the succession of feast days in the cycle of the Church year. He, the king, endorsed these volumes with the seal of his authority and presented them to the Christian churches for their use. This epistle, then, with its invaluable personal testimony of the ruler, was the covering letter for the dispatch of Paul the Deacon's collection of homilies, which Charlemagne had brought back with him to the North from Monte Cassino in 787.

The aims of the educational reform, whose next high point was reached with the publication of the *Admonitio generalis,* matured over a number of years. The *Admonitio* began with sixty introductory chapters summarizing the essential parts of the *Dionysio-Hadriana* but then proceeded to supplement these independently, using impressive phrases to elucidate the very God-given impulse to reform and renew that prompted its own creation, and also to display that same point-by-point approach already noted. The divine protection for Charlemagne's royal authority, as well as the dictates of his own soul, required strict church discipline: "We are sending our emissaries to you, whom We have endowed with Our authority to work with you to improve what requires improvement." Directives were issued—carried by the *missi dominici* (king's messengers)—to bishops, priests, monks, veiled virgins, and all laypeople, indeed, to the populace at large. The pent-up urgency for reform came to a head at the synod that was convened at Aix on 23 March 789 and the accompanying court assembly.

The *Admonitio,* though, which was now distributed to the four corners of the Carolingian Empire, surely cannot have come about by chance (or, to be more precise, the time when it was published cannot have been mere coincidence). Once again, it was imperative to counteract the effects of a revolt, this time the one staged by the Thuringian count Hardrat and his friends in 786, and no doubt also to announce something positive to divert attention from the scandalous actions against Tassilo of Bavaria in 788. Such crisis situations, which had come to public attention, could not simply be passed over in silence when recalling the past; instead, it was necessary to consign them to oblivion primarily through actions aimed at reforming the church, expanding royal authority, and strengthening the faith. In other words, the organization of the church was to prove itself as an instrument of power.

The Thuringian rebels of 786 were reputed to have planned to seize and murder the king. If they failed in this, they intended at the very least to renounce their allegiance to him. The *Royal Frankish Annals* contains no mention of this insurrection or its suppression; only when it was revised by Louis the Pious was this incident recalled, albeit very briefly. The strong impression is still that Charlemagne wanted there to be no record of this terrible event. Once again, it was only the annals believed to have come from the monastery of Murbach in Alsace, which also provided more information on what happened to Tassilo, that recorded details of this incident for posterity.

These reported that Charlemagne got to know about the rebels' plans very early on but initially did nothing. But when one of those involved, almost certainly Hardrat himself, refused to release his daughter, who was married to a Frank in proper accordance with Frankish law, and despite a direct order from the king to do so, the conspiracy exploded into open insurrection. The rebels clearly understood this refusal to be a signal to rise up.

Enraged, the king had the property of the insurrectionists razed to the ground; in the hope of being shown clemency, the rebels were able to flee to Fulda, to the sanctuary of the abbey there, where St. Boniface's remains were interred. Charlemagne then summoned them to appear before him; he had them brought to him, he claimed, "in peace," where he questioned them in person. He apparently asked them whether it was true that they intended to kill him or to refuse to obey his commands. Innocently, even recklessly, one of the rebels got carried away and freely confessed that if his comrades had followed his advice, the king would not have crossed the Rhine alive. Charlemagne, however, "the most lenient of all Frankish kings," supposedly sent a few of their number to Rome to seek guidance from St. Peter and dispatched others to the shrines of saints in the West and in Aquitaine. There, they were expected to swear allegiance to the king and his sons, which they duly did, the Murbach annals report. But on the homeward journey, some of them were captured and blinded, while others, who made it as far as Worms, were taken prisoner there, dragged off, and also blinded, while their property was seized and allocated to the royal *fiscus* (privy purse).[90]

Charlemagne, therefore, had the insurrectionists punished only after he had got them to swear allegiance to him in the presence of godly witnesses. The temporal sequence of these acts was irrelevant; cause and effect were inverted here. But the breach of an oath remained just that, come what may, and demanded fitting punishment. Concern that the peace be maintained legitimized the use of violence against disloyal and violent criminals. Admittedly, the real cause of the revolt, or so it was commonly believed, was the cruelty shown by Queen Fastrada; in any event, Charlemagne's biographer

Einhard (chap. 20) retrospectively attempted to exonerate his king on these grounds. The argument is unconvincing. The whole situation of securing peace, anger, subterfuge, and revenge needed no queen to direct it. In his customary contemplative manner, the author of the Murbach annals concluded his account of the deadly cunning shown by his master in the following way: "Yet the king continued to govern the realm of the Franks, the Lombards, and the Romans, safe and unscathed, since the king of Heaven proved to be his guardian."

Even a King Has Worries

The reason that Charlemagne demanded that the whole Frankish populace swear allegiance to him—from the highest bishop down to the lowliest servant—was surely that disloyal vassals would have brought down trouble on the realm and threatened the king's life. Only monks were exempted; because the *Rule of St. Benedict* forbade them to swear any oaths, they were allowed simply to give a "promise" of fidelity. Even unfree people—or more specifically those who possessed "horses, weapons, a shield, a spear, and a long or a short sword" and had been assigned administrative or military duties by their masters—were expected to swear allegiance.[91] In other words, loyalty was required for the sake of peace.

Indeed, Charlemagne was greatly concerned about "the blissful state of eternal peace and eternal happiness"; he was, after all, living in a period that was commonly held to be approaching the End of Days. Once the storms of insurrection and court proceedings had been weathered, both the clergy and laypeople were urged to promote peace. The *Admonitio generalis,* which was promulgated to this end in 789, called for unity and unanimity throughout the realm. These principles had been jeopardized and ought now to be revived. A common theme of sermons was "Love thy neighbor as thyself" (Leviticus 19:18; chap. 62). This love was no doubt also extended to the Thuringian rebels who had "only" been blinded, and to the king's cousin Tassilo of Bavaria, who had "only" been dishonored. One long chapter (chap. 64) of the *Admonitio* dealing with perjury might well have been written with the "broken oaths" of both the revolutionaries and the Bavarian duke in mind.

> Reflecting with dutiful and calm consideration, together with
> our priests and councilors, on the abundant mercy shown by
> Christ the King toward us and our people, we have considered
> how vital it is, not only with our own heart and voice to offer

thanks unceasingly for His goodness but also to persist in
the continuous exercise of good works in His praise so that He
who has given our kingdom such honors may deign to preserve
and protect us and our kingdom forever. Accordingly it has
pleased us to solicit your efforts, O priests of the churches of
Christ and leaders of His flock and bright beacons of the world,
to strive to lead the people of God to the pastures of eternal life
by watchful care and urgent advice and stir yourselves to bring
back the wandering sheep within the walls of ecclesiastical
constancy on the shoulders of good example or exhortation, lest
the wolf, plotting against anyone who transgresses the canonical laws or violates the fatherly traditions of the ecumenical
councils—which God forbid!—find him and devour him.

Charlemagne's unusually comprehensive introduction to the collection, that
is, the foreword of the *Admonitio,* announced the rationale and the aims of
the king's actions. Therefore, it was a royal address, which took its rhetoric
from biblical models and was remarkably graphic in its expression. The king's
objectives were couched in terms of metaphors rather than abstractions.

"I, Charles, by the grace of God and the gift of His mercy, king and ruler
of the kingdom of the Franks and devout defender and humble supporter of
the Holy Church": Charlemagne used this programmatic enumeration of his
titles to open his programmatic edict, a text that one historian has described
as having "the authority of a charter, the courtesy of a letter, and the persua-
sive power of a sermon."[92] In the *Admonitio,* Charlemagne assumed the
tone of the self-confident but humble lawgiver, thus consciously echoing certain of his predecessors, notably his father and his uncle, but probably also
Justinian.[93] "I, Charles": the people were to be led to eternal life in the spirit
of Christian love, wrongs were to be righted, superfluous matters swept
aside, and rectitude established.[94] Charlemagne was following the example
of the "saintly Josiah," the biblical king who traveled the length and breadth
of the realm that God had given him in order to correct and admonish his
subjects to revive the veneration of the one True God. Charlemagne was at
pains to stress that he was not comparing himself to this holy man, but at
the same time he was clearly aligning himself with King Josiah and the other
saints because he was keen wherever he could to follow their example and
apply himself to leading a good life in the praise and glory of Jesus Christ.

Charlemagne acted in accordance with the prompts that he believed that
the biblical king was giving him: bypass, improve, admonish, renew. The

opening words of the *Admonitio generalis* of 789 quoted above succinctly summed up the king's aims. Albeit through the mouthpiece of the synods, this was Charlemagne speaking, the defender of the faith and the supreme lawgiver, for the Church as well as for his realm. Those whom he was addressing were urged not to disregard anything that might be of benefit to God's people. They were to assemble all necessary and useful things in order that Almighty God might reward the diligence of the ecclesiastical classes and the secular authorities, as well as the obedience of their subjects, with eternal happiness. It was for this reason that the king had summoned his bishops, abbots, and counts to come to Aix in 789. This was the first great court assembly, the first imperial synod, that he convened at the site where he would soon establish his permanent residence.

The king compiled a list of reform requirements that was more comprehensive than any seen hitherto, a catalog comprising more than eighty chapters.[95] As far as we can tell, the final editing of the work was done by Alcuin. Certainly the choice of vocabulary, the style, and the content all indicate this. The Anglo-Saxon scholar had only just recently come to the Frankish Empire and the royal court, in 786, possibly precisely for this reason; his task was to assist the king in his long-planned reforms of the empire and the Church. The very next year, after the forthcoming issue of the *Admonitio* had been announced, he returned to his homeland before entering the service of the Frankish king for good three years later. Alcuin produced a unique text, one that was undoubtedly shaped according to Charlemagne's instructions and after intensive consultation with all the king's advisers. The text was finally issued on 23 March 789. The fact that surviving copies of the *Admonitio* come from right across the empire, including Italy, in addition to what we know for sure about the history of its reception, suggests that this capitulary, whose content was dictated by an awareness of the impending apocalypse, should be seen as a kind of basic law of the Frankish Empire under Charlemagne.[96] Although the pope was not mentioned in person, his influence was present in the text by dint of the inclusion of Hadrian's *Collectio*, from which many legal norms were taken.

The contents of the capitulary can be briefly summarized as follows: the organization of the Church, the fight against ignorance, heresy, and superstition, and the Christianization of the people. To make this a reality, the king required the collaboration of all the magnates of his realm, the bishops as well as the counts and the manciples of estates. It is therefore fair to assume that there were regional differences in how this was achieved in practice. The oldest surviving manuscript of the Aix capitulary, a slim codex

FIGURE 29 Image from the inside front cover of the Fulda codex of the Aix capitulary, now held at the Herzog August Library in Wolfenbüttel, Germany. This quick sketch is thought to be of Charlemagne.

from Fulda, concludes with transcriptions of the sermons of St. Augustine and an explanation of the Lord's Prayer; because it may have been intended for use in missionary work in Saxony, this codex was therefore already complying with the requirements set forth in the text.[97] This manuscript was almost certainly written before 800 and on the inside of the front cover contains a contemporary though incomplete line drawing—surely not intended to be seen by the king—showing a church building and next to it a male figure holding in his right hand a shield that is resting on the ground, and with his left hand held aloft as if clutching a spear—not shown, but given the presence of the shield, a more likely surmise than a papal ferula (a pastoral staff surmounted by a cross). Comparisons with other images allow us to interpret it as a sketch of an ancient emperor or king, or even of Charlemagne himself. However sketchy and unaccomplished the drawing is, its message and its moral could not be clearer: the ruler appears here as a powerful protector, guarding the Church with his weapons and—as the following text emphasizes—restoring it according to the dictates of the faith and the Church Fathers in preparation for the impending end time.

Throughout his realm, this ruler now proceeded to take steps against the many abuses occurring both within the Church and in the world outside. He strove after a body politic that was to be Christian to the core, right down to people's innermost thoughts and feelings. Old canon law, taken from a number of traditions but in particular from the *Dionysio-Hadriana,* was called to mind, and new ecclesiastical and secular commandments were promulgated in preparation for what was coming. Uniquely among all the capitularies issued by the king, these were directed first at the bishops, priests, and the clergy, then at monks, and finally at "everyone." No chapter was aimed specifically at the nobility, although the king's messengers who journeyed throughout the land distributing the *Admonitio* would doubtless have been required also to instruct those counts who had not been present in Aix.

Since it was based on an accumulation of historical models, the *Admonitio* was not totally devoid of any systematic organization, although the reasons for renewing this or that norm in preference to others were not explained. The material was organized according to the tripartite division into matters that were "necessary," "useful," and (unusual for capitularies) "proclamations of faith." Was it perhaps compiled in response to concrete individual grievances, the details of which have been lost in time? Certainly, in one instance (chap. 74) the text begins, "It has come to our attention." Had Charlemagne's advisers gathered together a list of abuses and presented them to the king en bloc for correction? Was there thus a reactive aspect to the decrees? It was all about establishing a new order of salvation. A great deal of discussion took place before Alcuin embarked on the final edit. The individual chapters did not follow any overarching lawmaker's plan but rather promulgated commandments that were taken from the redemptive realm of canon law and were intended to satisfy the needs of the moment. As a result, contemporaries referred time and again to this admonitory decree.

The section issuing directives began by listing indispensable matters (*necessaria;* chaps. 1–59). The rhetoric here changed from the first person of the foreword and the conclusion to the third person of general norms. Thus, the series of chapters in this section began with the statement that anyone who was excommunicated by his bishop was not permitted to take Communion with anyone else. The primary aim here was to strengthen the episcopal power of jurisdiction. Another clause stipulated that before any candidate could be ordained as a priest, his bishop was required to test his faith and scrutinize his way of life. Similarly, peripatetic and foreign clerics could not be ordained in the Frankish lands without written permission from their superiors. Furthermore, it was forbidden to ordain a bishop or a priest in return for payment. Priests and clerics were not allowed to share dwellings with women, unless it was with their mother or sister or other respectable persons. Lending money for interest (usury) was forbidden to all. Casting bad-weather spells, harmful spells, or even healing spells was to be outlawed and condemned. The struggle against paganism was still far from won. Neither monks nor clerics should indulge in worldly business affairs, nor should they frequent taverns to partake of food and drink. In this way, a code of ethics was revived by which the Church as a whole could orient itself. Edicts concerning sexual purity were part and parcel of this code, although it was true that only very few clerics adhered to them. As servants of God, priests were expected to discharge their sacred duties with a clean body.

An unfree man could be tonsured to become a cleric or a monk only with the consent of his master. Everyone was to be taught in sermons to believe in the Holy Trinity, the Incarnation of the Son of God, and Christ's Passion, Resurrection, and Ascension. After a divorce, it was forbidden to enter into a new relationship while one's former partner was still alive. Sodomy and homosexuality among priests were to be punished with the greatest severity. Priests who repeatedly transgressed against the decretals and refused to mend their ways were to be defrocked. All this and more should constantly be borne in mind; these rules were to be observed lest one fall victim to anathema, the dreaded ecclesiastical verdict of damnation. Yet despite such threats, this code never permeated the Church organization, at least not completely; some clauses have remained unobserved to the present day. Even Charlemagne did not always behave with total probity, given that he transgressed against the passage on divorce (chap. 43) when he took a third wife even though his previous two spouses were still living. Was the king, then, above the law?

In the *Admonitio*, there then followed—in accordance with Charlemagne's express wishes—the enumeration of a series of "beneficial" norms for practical living (*utilia*) (chaps. 60–79), which were in part adopted from older civic rights or early capitularies. A number of these provisions, though, exceeded any human capacity. Religious belief was to be preached to the people by bishops and priests. "There is but one God . . . and we should worship Him with all our heart, and with all our mind, from the depths of our soul and with all the power at our disposal." The *Admonitio* went on to voice the wish "that peace, unity, and unanimity may reign throughout Christianity, among bishops, abbots, noblemen, judges, and all people, be they high-born or lowly, and wherever they may be; for without peace, nothing pleases God" (chap. 61). At the time, even priests were at loggerheads and setting their vassals on one another. This call for peace was repeated time and again over the following decades—but with no ultimate success. What was just would need to be determined by legal norms. Judges needed to acknowledge the body of common law that wise men had assembled for the people. But what was justice exactly, and who was empowered to assess it? People should be very fearful of committing perjury, for every oath would have to be accounted for at the Day of Judgment. Pagan practices clung on tenaciously. Action was still being taken to combat them even toward the end of Charlemagne's reign. In the *Admonitio,* soothsaying, white and black magic, and the worship of trees, rocks, and springs were forbidden.[98] Furthermore, the capitulary urged priests to preach against envy, hatred, and greed, as well as against avarice, the evil that lay at the root of all human wickedness.

It was not just through these proscriptions of all manner of magic that the *Admonitio* broached social questions. Murder, theft, unlawful marriage, and bearing false witness were all punishable offenses. Anyone who had killed another person would be brought before the judge appointed by the king but could be executed only if the law demanded it. This measure was directed against blood feuds and private vendettas and was aimed at maintaining peace within the realm, as was the following passage, which stated that theft, illegitimate concubinage, and false witness ought, as the king had warned many times before, to be prosecuted and eradicated. The bishops should take care to ensure that their priests understood the litany of the Mass, sang the psalms properly, and knew the meaning of the Lord's Prayer well enough to be able to interpret it correctly for their parishioners. Many of these priests had only a rudimentary grasp of the Latin that they sang during Mass. Moreover, priests and deacons were not permitted to carry weapons; rather, their defense should be their trust in the Lord. How far was the opposite the case, however?

Identical measurements and correct weights were to be used in cities and monasteries alike; this was another key measure for keeping the peace. "Everyone" was encouraged to maintain hospices, in accordance with canon law, to accommodate foreigners, pilgrims, and the poor, "for in the retribution that will be meted out on the day of reckoning [at the End of Days], the

Lord himself will announce: 'I was a stranger, and you took me not in' "
(chap. 73). Apocryphal writings, alleged "Heaven's letters," and the like were
to be consigned to the flames. Sunday was to be sanctified, and no one was
to undertake "servant's work" on it, be it working in the fields, tending the
vines, clearing woods and felling trees, breaking rocks, building a house,
hunting, weaving, sewing, embroidering, spinning, beating flax, or washing
clothes in public—all these activities were forbidden as a way of honoring
the Lord's Day. Only the transporting of war materiel, foodstuffs, and the
dead was permitted. Despite being almost at the end of this long capitulary,
it was at this point that the nonecclesiastical requirements of the Frankish
Empire were mentioned. Evidently, Charlemagne had not forgotten them.
However, aside from imposing rigid norms on the newly Christianized
Saxons, Charlemagne did not dare to reform, or even simply supplement,
citizens' rights—that is, the rights of various peoples like the Franks, the
Burgundians, the Goths, the Alemanni, the Bavarians, or the Lombards—until
after his coronation as emperor.[99]

Some of the more important chapters of the *Admonitio* concerned education (chap. 70). Literacy and the organization of the Church and the question of redemption went hand in hand. School pupils were expected to
know the psalms, to be able to read and write letters (*notae*), and to learn
the cantus (ecclesiastical singing, including liturgical chanting), and were
also required to master the discipline of the *computus* (the complicated calculation of time and the calendar, which was of crucial importance for celebrating the Crucifixion, the Resurrection, and the Ascension of Christ) and
grammar (i.e., Latin). Because all too often Mass was celebrated wrongly
because of inaccurate transcription, henceforth the texts of liturgical books
were to be corrected. From now on, the Gospels, psalters, and missals were
to be copied with the greatest care only by grown-ups, not by schoolboys. It
was deemed vital that prayers during Mass and in the psalter should be sung
intelligibly and in a dignified manner (chap. 68). In order to promote unity
with the Apostolic See and peaceful concord within the Church as a whole,
the Frankish clergy were now to have control over the *cantus Romanus,* that
is, the way in which Holy Mass was sung (chap. 78). In addition to the renewal of the hierarchical and jurisdictional structure of the Church, these
provisions were to have the most enduring influence; indeed, one might reasonably claim that their effect is still felt today.

The numerous edicts concluded with a long, sermon-like chapter
(chap. 80), the central theme of which was the profession of faith. Here it
was stipulated that preachers should not spread their own personal doc-

trines but stick rigidly to what the Holy Scriptures proclaimed: namely, practical, admirable, righteous lessons and the fact that the Father, the Son, and the Holy Ghost were all manifestations of the one Almighty God who created Heaven and Earth, and that the three separate entities of the Trinity together formed a godhead, a single substance, and a heavenly majesty. The whole doctrine of the Christian faith was set forth here, including the damnation of the godless "into the eternal flames of Hell, along with the Devil," and conversely, the assumption of the righteous "together with Christ to eternal life." So that preachers and others responsible for educating the common people might know what they were fighting against, the whole catalog of human vices was recalled at this point: fornication, baseness, debauchery, idolatry, sorcery, enmity leading to murder, drunkenness, and excesses of all kinds. The things that were needed to bring salvation were also listed: humility, patience, chastity, tolerance, mercy, the giving of alms and confession of sins, and the pardoning of the guilt of "culprits." This lesson culminated in a warning about the End of Days, a time when false prophets would appear: "Therefore, O Beloved Ones, let us prepare ourselves in full knowledge of the truth, in order that we might resist the enemies of Truth and so that the Word of God might grow." This change back to the first person once again included the king. "Peace to the preachers, blessings upon the obedient, and all glory to Our Lord Jesus Christ. Amen!"

The *Admonitio* urged that a simple faith should be proclaimed and called to mind the basic requirements of the Church, its constitution, and its hierarchical structure, as well as everyday Christian needs. Yet everything ultimately led to anticipation of the end time. All canon law and all the Church's organization were geared toward approaching the Day of Judgment in the right way. A refrain here is "We must prepare ourselves." In light of this, the earthly realm of the Frankish king was to be ordered, improved, revitalized, and transformed into a secular rulership agreeable to God. The route to the Kingdom of Heaven began with the establishment of a Christian world order, as Pope Hadrian had hinted to the king in sending him his collection of canon law. Yet who could possibly find his or her way around this welter of individual decrees, this hodgepodge of old and new social edicts? Not only the illiterate populace would have had trouble doing so.

Certainly by this stage, in 789, the king was looking at matters much more profoundly than before and, aside from seeing the pressing need for reform, was recognizing more clearly than previously that one of the most important reasons for the decline was the lack of literacy, knowledge, and practical aptitude. His intention was to right previous wrongs, to make his court, his reign, and the people, religion, and the Church in his realm a beacon, to excise everything that was superfluous and corrupt, and to enforce a move toward rectitude. Beneficial actions required proper knowledge. "Right action," Charlemagne warned his clergy and monks, "is better than mere knowledge; but in order to do what is right, we must first know what is right" (*Quamvis enim melius sit benefacere quam nosse, prius tamen est nosse quam facere*). What a simple but wise sentiment, which any politician nowadays would do well to take to heart.[100] Charlemagne's decisive impulse for reform could scarcely be expressed more succinctly but comprehensively. The king's agenda was to renew the whole of society according to the principles of the Church Fathers and the directives of the pope and also, mindful of his own sense of God-ordained destiny, to act as the defender of the Church, to strengthen the faith, to promote peace, and to impose order on the world. Yet the overriding priority was to reform learning.

"Restore the Wisdom of the Ancients"

"Despite the fact that all knowledge and study of the various individual academic disciplines can be accessed only through speech [*oratio*], no one thus far, my son, in whatever discipline he may be versed, has chosen to treat the origins and foundations of speech. Therefore, we may wonder at the scrupulousness of the philosopher Aristotle, who, eager to investigate all fields of knowledge, began with an enquiry into speech, a subject he was aware everyone ignored but which was the key to everything." Thus ran the opening sentences of a little treatise on categories and predications that was widely read around Charlemagne's court and its environs. This work had been written in late antiquity and became known at the Carolingian court from an early stage. Had Alcuin perhaps brought it with him, or the Visigoth Theodulf? As was so often the case with ancient works whose authorship was unknown, it was ascribed to St. Augustine of Hippo, although it retained an easily comprehensible paraphrase of the Greek philosopher Themistius (or an author from his circle) from the fourth century CE, possibly in the Latin translation by Vettius Agorius Praetextatus.[101]

This text, the *Categoriae decem* (Ten categories) is found in the oldest preserved manuscript in the world found to date that contains a work by Aristotle. The manuscript, which is held today at the Marist monastery in Rome, was transcribed in 795 for Archbishop Leidrad, presumably as a copy of another that was already available at the king's court. The scholar Theodulf had already consulted this treatise on categories when he was writing his *Libri Carolini* in 793–794.[102] The *Categoriae decem* treated such concepts as "noun," "verb," "substance," and "accident" (i.e., the coincidental property of an object, such as the color of a dress) and expounded the doctrine of Aristotle's ten categories; there was also mention of the "antipodes," those people who dwelt on the far side of the globe and were believed to have feet facing the opposite way. At the end of the work, the author pompously reassured his readers: "We have omitted nothing in this work that might edify the educated or even more certainly instruct the uneducated." The treatise raised an abundance of questions, but who could answer them?

An alert contemporary would surely have registered many shortcomings in the argumentation of the *Categoriae decem,* but this only served to pique Charlemagne's curiosity. The task for which he consulted his foreign scholar Alcuin was obvious. The gaps in learning were revealing themselves all too clearly; too much had been lost over the preceding centuries. This was becoming ever more obvious with the advance of knowledge and skills. The young king realized this early on in his reign, and at the end of his life, after forty years on the throne, the worldly-wise emperor was still bemoaning this situation and devoting even more of his energy to his unfinished reform program.

It was essential that the ancient academic disciplines be revived in order to gain a connection to the doctrine of the Christian Church Fathers. The extensive field of the culture of reason, which had lain fallow for centuries, had to be tilled once more. To achieve this, it was first necessary to learn a wholly unfamiliar vocabulary of philosophical terminology; indeed, a whole new mode of expression had to be learned, or rather relearned, and dialectical thought patterns had to be practiced anew that had long lain dormant but that followed the Aristotelian laws of logic. St. Augustine himself had shown the way with his *De doctrina christiana* (On Christian doctrine). Charlemagne held this work in just as high regard as he did the same Church Father's great apologia *De civitate Dei* (The city of God), which closed with visions of the end of the world and the Day of Judgment, so underscoring the urgency of all reforming activity.

Between sections discussing the love of God and philanthropy (1) and the fear of God and faith (3), a passage in this famous didactic work by St. Augustine that stressed the need for biblical exegesis (2.42–60) also included a defense of the pagan academic disciplines—history, computistics, and astronomy, dialectics and rhetoric, and mathematics and ethics. In particular, the science of drawing inferences, definitions, and divisions, including logic, and, indeed, the "liberal arts" (and only them) in general were, the saint maintained, of incontrovertible use for understanding the truth, even though they did not represent the truth themselves. Charlemagne and his court scholars could not help but interpret this as a program to be put into action.

The difficulties that stood in the way of success were considerably greater some twelve hundred years ago than they would be in the twentieth or twenty-first centuries. They began—something that Augustine could not have foreseen—with the language, Latin. Charlemagne's mother tongue, an earthy form of Frankish, was hardly suitable for academic, scholarly, philosophical, or theological flights of fancy. Likewise, it could not cope with dialectics. Conversely, Frankish had a positively inexhaustible wealth of words at its disposal to describe the various life stages of the domestic pig and the wild boar, which, after the horse, was the most important animal for the country's nobility; Latin could not hope to match this. Frankish was characterized by a simple pictorial expressiveness in place of rational argumentation, enumerative lists in place of subordination, and situational thought in place of abstraction and redundancy.[103]

The primitive native languages of the Franks, the Alemanni, and the Bavarians, which dispensed with any technical terminology, could not possibly have formulated the simplest philosophical or theological thought or any consistent syllogism. They lacked the necessary concepts and their corresponding patterns of expression. But the various fields of learning needed Latin, a language that, beyond the "Germanic" world, had itself long since been subject to a transformation into the Romance vernaculars, which had in no way retained the language's ancient clarity.

Notwithstanding the last remnants of the knowledge of Latin on the Continent, the onward march of the vulgarization of the language—that is, the ancient tongue's development into the regional Romance colloquial languages—was unstoppable, and as it did so, a distinct loss of expressive force and the capacity to differentiate became evident. In other words, Charlemagne's renaissance had to begin with the language, with Latin. In order to relearn it, schools first had to be established. And, as the *Admonitio generalis* of 789 demanded, these schools needed to have copies of the Psalms, the liturgical texts, the *computus,* and grammars readily available in corrected manuscripts.[104] Admittedly, this was still not enough.

Insofar as they were common practice at all, the sermons preached by most of the clergy, the means by which ordinary people received a religious education, sounded coarse and clumsy. But how might the people be instructed properly if the preachers themselves did not understand what they were talking about? The collection of homilies by Paul the Deacon, which Charlemagne had requested in Monte Cassino, could do little to rectify this situation, let alone do so in the space of just a few years. The very first explicit piece of evidence for the linguistic change that was taking place, a canon of the synod that was convened at Tours in 813, made this lack of comprehension very clear. There, "in order that everyone might more easily understand what is being said," the synod demanded that the bishops translate the content of their sermons into the "Romance vernacular," the *rustica Romana lingua*, and into its "German" counterpart, the Thiodisca.[105]

Sometimes, even "Romance" peoples did not understand Latin anymore, and so they too had to learn it afresh. The kinds of sermons that needed translating persisted in displaying a naïve comprehensibility in their expression and audience-friendly simplicity in the religious practices and doctrines they expounded. Yet bishops preached primarily at their diocesan synods, in front of their clergy rather than to the common people. And it was precisely the clergy who therefore experienced difficulty with Latin and now needed to go back to school.

Charlemagne led by example; at least, this is what the propaganda claimed. He was the most prominent student in his realm. As the son of a king, he had already been educated in literacy; now he set about deepening his knowledge. As chapter 25 of Einhard's *Life of Charlemagne* reveals, "He was not satisfied with speaking his native tongue and so turned his attention to learning foreign languages. He became so fluent in Latin that he could speak it as well as his mother tongue. However, where Greek was concerned, he could understand it better than he could speak it. He was so eloquent, indeed, that he might have passed for a teacher of eloquence." Even as a boy, this royal scion must have studied Latin, but whether his knowledge of Greek—possibly learned through study with Paul the Deacon—went beyond a few scraps of the language is a moot point. Writing some fifteen years after the emperor's death, his biographer retrospectively created a role model to remind Charlemagne's son and grandson of their illustrious forebear. During the lifetime of the great king, commentators were even more uninhibited: "The magical power of his speech outshines even the great Cicero, and his oratory surpasses the eloquent Homer, while in dialectics he outdoes the ancient masters of the art." An anonymous poet lavished praise on his lord and master.[106] This was unquestionably a panegyric, but it was also using the example of the ruler to announce an educational program and to celebrate its first successes. Therefore, it was at the same time a piece of propaganda for learning.

Indeed, we know that little jests were staged and jokes told in Latin in Charlemagne's hearing. No one, however, would have dared to laugh unless the king could also understand the witticisms and laugh along with them. We might also speculate whether mathematical problems were also posed in the royal audience hall. For example, "A house-father provides for twenty families. He wants to distribute twenty bushels of grain from the harvest in such a way that the men of the household will receive three bushels, the women two, and the children one half-measure each. From this, work out, if you can, how many men, women, and children there are living in the household." Charlemagne may well have been the recipient of the collection of problems containing this example; he would not have been bothered about the preferential treatment it gave men. The author of this notional bread-distribution problem, most probably Alcuin, provided the answer immediately below: one man, five women, and fourteen children.[107]

Oratory was an instrument of power in a society that was characterized by the spoken language—in Latin for the scholars and ecclesiastical figures and in the vernacular for the army. Charlemagne managed it accordingly. "He was," Einhard reported (also in chapter 25), "an articulate and captivating speaker who could express whatever he wanted to say with the utmost clarity." But although we can assume that he made them, none of his speeches have survived. He called for a major expansion in the ability to speak Latin. Granted, the teachers would themselves first have to take on board the unfamiliar modes of thought and expression that they found in the old texts, with their complex layers of meaning, before they were able to pass them on to their students.

The first Latin–Old High German dictionaries were created at this time but only partially achieved their goal of fostering a proper understanding of the language. The oldest of these, the so-called *Abrogans,* named for its first headword, was probably produced, as far as we can tell, in Bavaria in the mid-eighth century, possibly for the purpose of missionary work. It was a thoroughly error-strewn translation of a Latin glossary for reading the Bible, originally written in late antiquity. However, this text was transcribed several times during Charlemagne's reign. The oldest preserved copy (though once again far from error free), now housed in the abbey library of St. Gall in Switzerland, was written sometime before 800, presumably in a monastery in Alemannia, which had not yet been caught up in the great renewal movement.[108] Therefore, it is a particularly powerful reflection of the linguistic obstacles that at that time stood in the way of any deeper understanding of texts. It starts as follows: "Here begin the glosses from the Old

Testament": *Abrogans—dheomodi* (modest), *Humilis—samftmoati* (gentle), *abba—faterlih* (fatherly) ... *aehomet—ihha* (I), *ego ipse—ih selbo* (myself), *ego inquid—ich hquad* (I say), *ego dixi—ih quidu* (I said); and so it continued, listing a total of more than 3,600 terms.[109]

The mysteries of religious faith called for subtler forms of expression than the Frankish or Alemannic tongue could offer. The "wild thinking" of these barbarian peoples had to be "tamed," in other words, fundamentally re-formed, transformed from an enumerative, iterative, paratactic way of speaking into a subordinating, hypotactic one. In every respect, the renewal had to begin with language. The barbarian colloquial languages were wholly un-suitable for the liturgy, since they would not have been able to do its rich-ness justice. Only the two or three most important prayers of the liturgy were translated into "Germanic" vernaculars; no contemporaneous versions of the Our Father are known from the Romance-language regions of the Frankish Empire. The Gothic translation of the New Testament remained unknown in the country. Worship and the Eucharist, fitting veneration of the Almighty, called for Latin. Who could possibly hope to follow the Church's commandments if no one actually understood them properly or was in a position to interpret them correctly?

The revival of language tuition for the intellectual elite concentrated ini-tially on the Latin of the Church Fathers and the ancient grammarians, and later on the work of pagan writers and the standard language of the Roman poets. Frankish educators made a conscious effort to imitate them as best they could. However, Alcuin was at pains to warn his students about Virgil, supposedly admonishing them—to no avail—in the following terms: "Do not taint yourselves with the unbridled garrulousness of Virgil; the poets of the divine should be enough for you."[110] We can only imagine what he would have had to say about Ovid's *Ars amatoria* (The art of love).

Any form of "poetic" effortlessness was alien to the serious writing style of the Anglo-Saxon scholar. Also, this new acquaintance with Latin burned itself out, expending too much time and effort in imitation. Only after Char-lemagne's reign did the odd writer, though very rarely, find his own creative and virtuosic voice. Attempts at imitation focused on certain idioms and figures of speech used in phrases that their authors thought sounded like classical statements. Yet at least at first, in many such instances the semantic content of the originals fell by the wayside. The language needed to reflect an objective, social, and literary context for which the time was not yet ripe.

Only intensive language tuition, that is, instruction in grammar, and patience could remedy this situation. The king gave repeated and express orders that this teaching should take place. Moreover, it was not conducted in isolation but instead followed the classical tradition of being taught in conjunction with rhetoric and dialectics, thus giving students the capacity to systematically pose questions that had to be answered according to the rules of logic. Reading, comprehension, and oration thus came to form a new whole, which at first intellectuals attempted to master but which in time, over the ensuing centuries, also took hold of the vernacular languages, causing them to increasingly model themselves on Latin and its patterns of expression.

Yet what any individual in the Frankish Empire got to read was often a matter of chance. The full range of classical literature was by no means still available in its entirety. Much had disappeared and had been lost forever. Because of lack of knowledge of the language, almost everything in ancient Greek had by now vanished from the educational canon of the Latin peoples, insofar as these works had not been translated or popularized in Latin in the classical period or late antiquity. Indeed, the image we have of ancient Roman literature has to this day been fundamentally shaped by the Carolingian age's eagerness to read such works. Every piece of Latin literature that this period managed to get hold of and save has been preserved for posterity; conversely, the works it shunned or never got to know have been lost forever.[111]

The effort involved in acquiring these texts was enormous. The material for study lay strewn all over the place; it first had to be tracked down and made available to the public. Impatience was out of place here. Anyone who wanted to read had to travel far and wide, unearth texts, amass knowledge, and copy whatever he discovered that appealed to him, book by book. Many unfamiliar works that were hard to understand were among this material. The first study aid came in the form of a kind of encyclopedic dictionary known as the *Liber glossarum*. Organized according to a series of alphabetical entries, it provided definitions and synonyms for every headword; it is thought to have been compiled in Corbie under Charlemagne's cousin Abbot Adalhard around the turn of the ninth century, perhaps at the behest of the king himself and under his supervision.[112]

This extensive volume was based on the writings of numerous ancient authors and on works of grammar, patristics, and medicine, as well as on the *Etymologies* of Isidore of Seville. The result was an enormous tome: the oldest manuscript, in Corbie, totaled 368 pages in folio format, each page was written in three columns, and the whole work was bound in two volumes. Around two hundred sheep or goats were slaughtered to provide the necessary vellum. Only wealthy scriptoria or patrons could afford such a grand work. But its spread in the ninth century indicates that it was actually used.

In former times, extensive treatises or the contents of entire books and libraries, which nowadays can be transmitted around the world by e-mail within seconds, or minutes at most, took many decades or even whole centuries to stand even a chance of being widely disseminated or preserved, and even widespread distribution was by no means guaranteed. So it was that only a chance piece of good fortune preserved the minor works of Tacitus, including the *Germania,* when, at the last minute, the only extant manuscript—dating from the ninth century—was quite literally saved from being fed to pigs by a diligent humanist in the fifteenth century. The shelves of even the best-endowed libraries rarely or never held the entire oeuvre of any particular classical author. So-called florilegia, or compilations of excerpts from various works, came into vogue. In the period around 800 or shortly thereafter, it is fair to assume that not a single cathedral library possessed the complete works of St. Augustine or any other Church Father, however valuable any individual manuscript in its collection may have been.

Charlemagne became the most important patron and the most distinguished collector in his realm. His library contained many unusual, marvelous, and as yet sometimes barely understood works. The rarest texts—for example, a manuscript of the Roman *agrimensores,* authors who wrote on the art of land surveying,[113] are thought to have been among his holdings. Admittedly, it is virtually impossible to gain an overview of what titles there were in his library since no catalog or inventory exists. However, we may assume that our knowledge of many an author, along with his works, was saved as a result of this royal collection.

Charlemagne sought private assistance where he identified shortcomings and rewarded successes by dispensing appointments, thus making his knowledge-hungry court into an exemplary model for the subjects of his empire—lords and the common people alike—along with those of future rulers. The Carolingian court became a center of learning and at the same time the nerve center of the educational organization of his realm.[114] "He most zealously cultivated the liberal arts, held those who taught them in great esteem, and conferred great honors on them."[115] The king and emperor kept a close supervisory eye on the quality of both students and teachers in his kingdom.

Pious endowments and additional economic assets and revenues were essential if the vital revolution in education was to succeed, embrace the whole of the Carolingian Empire, and endure down the ages. If the monarchy had not existed, everything would have proceeded much more slowly, if it had even happened at all; without the pressure that Charlemagne in person exerted on the churches and monasteries, things would have been far more difficult. As it was, this period saw the embryonic beginnings of Western scholarship and technical skill, on which all subsequent science and technology were able to draw. Collecting, understanding, and thinking things through became a fundamental requirement—and all of this in a language that first had to be learned, with a technical terminology that had to be discovered step-by-step, and with a methodology that at first no one could master.

It took considerable staying power to hand on the knowledge that had first been gleaned in antiquity to future generations and allow them to absorb and mentally assimilate it. A literary education was a privilege even for the nobility, and one that only very few people could enjoy. The first significant supraregional schools developed around the teachers that Charlemagne had recruited from abroad. Subsequently, the most gifted graduates of these institutions were expected in their turn, in a kind of chain reaction, to become tutors in their own home monasteries or churches and to establish schools there. Thus, the young Einhard, and shortly afterward the boy Hrabanus Maurus, were both sent by Baugulf, abbot of Fulda, to study under Alcuin; subsequently, Einhard would go on to found the court school at Aix, while the younger Hrabanus took over control of the monastery school at his home abbey of Fulda.[116]

The three basic disciplines of grammar, dialectics, and rhetoric (the trivium, literally "three ways") were now supplemented by four mathematically oriented fields of study: arithmetic, geometry, music, and astronomy (the quadrivium). St. Augustine's *De doctrina christiana* or the *Institutiones* of Cassiodorus provided the canon for this program of the seven liberal arts, Alcuin taught them, although he never completed his handbook on this subject,[117] and Theodulf propagandized for them in verse.[118] The king himself needed a knowledge of mathematics and astronomy, in particular, in order to be able to work out time and the course of the world, as well as for calendrical calculations and to determine the age of the earth, a vital piece of information with regard to the impending apocalypse. Charlemagne took special pleasure in astronomy, and the *computus* played a major role in his correspondence with Alcuin.[119] The king found himself drawn night and day by his curiosity to gazing at the heavens.

At this early stage, there was still no fixed canon of reading, such as later existed in schools during the tenth and eleventh centuries—certainly not for grammar, and still less for any of the disciplines of the quadrivium. Schools filled their libraries only very gradually. When he arrived at the Frankish court, however, the Visigothic scholar Theodulf of Orléans certainly brought a reading list with him in the form of a poem noting the Christian and pagan authors he read most often: these included Gregory the Great, St. Jerome, St. Ambrose, Isidore of Seville, St. John Chrysostom, St. Cyprian, and many others, in addition to a number of heathen "philosophers," such as the grammarians Pompeius and Aelius Donatus, as well as the "garrulous" Virgil. His citing of this Roman poet was a deliberate dig at Alcuin, who, as we have seen, warned his pupils off the author of the *Aeneid*. Theodulf, though, justified reading his works on the grounds that they were susceptible to a "mystical" (i.e., allegorical) interpretation if they were read alongside those of the philosophers, who were wont to reveal the truth beneath the fables of classical poetry (*fabulae poetarum a philosophis mystice pertractentur*).[120]

Even so, people at this time did not always understand the works they read in an appropriate manner; things that looked alike were by no means the same. In terms of its social, religious, and educational significance, the meaning of classical works existed constantly within an alien context, something that the scholars of the eighth and ninth century were still unable to appreciate. Accordingly, they were able to provide an allegorical exegesis of Ovid's *Ars amatoria* that turned it into something spiritual, like the biblical Song of Songs. Likewise, the *res publica* of ancient Roman authors and that of Carolingian authors were in no way the same. The *utilitas publica* did not equate to the "public good" but rather to the benefit of the magnates concerned. And St. Peter was presented as some sword-wielding warrior. Nevertheless, the business of becoming versed in and imitating classical works saw Frankish society make remarkable advances.

The most fully developed example of such imitation was Einhard's *Life of Charlemagne*, which can be said to have revived the defunct literary genre of the secular biography. The author took his inspiration from Suetonius's *Lives of the Twelve Caesars*, in particular (though not exclusively) his life of Augustus. "Here then, dear reader, you have a book that commits to paper the memory of a truly renowned and great man. There is nothing in it to wonder at except for his deeds—and perhaps also the fact that I, who am a barbarian and very little versed in the Roman language, have had the temerity to imagine myself capable of writing elegantly in Latin."[121] Einhard was evidently more than a little proud of the resulting achievement. Yet however remarkable the *Vita Karoli Magni* may be in many respects, it was incapable of re-creating the very particular excitement and sense of authority conveyed by Suetonius's work. Nor did other biographers follow in Einhard's footsteps. Even so, here was firm evidence that the "barbarians" had revived the knowledge and the presentational style of the Romans. "The Roman language," in other words, the language of Cicero, as Einhard himself emphasized and contemporary readers also remarked, was paving the way for a new literate culture. Thus, for all its limitations, Einhard's *Life of Charlemagne* occupies a unique historical position.

Once it was in regular use by the ruling elites of the Carolingian age, the Latin of this period sloughed off its vulgarization, experienced a revival, and in so doing gave access once more to classical literature, rhetoric, philosophy, and theology. But renovation also stimulated innovation, giving rise to the first stirrings of independent Frankish scholarship. The green shoots that began to appear in the Frankish Empire were still tender plants that could as yet hardly hope to compete with the blossoming civilizations of the Byzantines or the Arab world, but they were original, and they would one day bear abundant fruit. The intellectual elites of the Frankish Empire learned to think in Latin once more. The trivium of grammar, rhetoric, and dialectics, which were taught in basically the same way in all schools and therefore were consistently learned and practiced over several succeeding generations, became the intellectual tool kit for the resurgence of Latin culture—indeed, of Western culture in general. Admittedly, this process was greatly aided by the rediscovery of the works of Aristotle, a process that occurred in stages but yielded more and more material over time.

King Charles the Wise

"Charlemagne, our guiding light, adored by the people, you pious king and wise leader, renowned for your virtues and your feats of arms, most deserving of all the praise that the world heaps on you." With these words, the scribe Dagulf, author of one of the first books written for the Carolingians, namely, the first psalter to be produced in Aix during Charlemagne's reign (Figure 28), celebrated its dedicatee and expressed the fervent wish that he might henceforth "find his place in the choir of King David." The term Dagulf used for the biblical psalmist, *doctiloquax,* "wisdom-proclaiming king," was a subtle allusion to his own monarch, the gifted orator and "David" of the court at Aix.[122]

Charlemagne was pleased with this comparison. He was characterized by a thirst for knowledge. As a "wise leader" and "sagacious ruler," as the king of scholarship, he did not fit the customary mold of monarchs during this period. In truth, this ruler was keen to learn and grew ever more inquisitive in his search for enlightenment. Alcuin was to aid him in this quest: "I want to ask you about the art of oratory and its rules. It would be absurd not to pay heed to this skill in the royal palace of all places." In this way, Charlemagne encouraged the Anglo-Saxon scholar to engage in a rhetorical dialogue that at the same time touched on problems of logic. This heralded the first true dialectical works of the Middle Ages: Alcuin's *On Rhetoric* and *Dialectics*, which expounded the two fundamental disciplines behind every higher, reason-oriented kind of Western scholarship. Both these works were written for Charlemagne, both were couched in the form of a dialogue, and both—however indirectly—owed a great deal to Aristotle. The broad distribution of the manuscripts of these works that have come down to us proves that the king did not just want these treatises for himself but instead to benefit his entire realm. As a monarch who set great store by wisdom and guidance, he was determined that the intellectual elite of his empire should read these works too. Nothing emphasizes more clearly how vigorously Charlemagne pursued this goal of reviving intellectual endeavor. His intention was for dialectical thought and reason to permeate his entire sphere of control.

"God has enlightened you, my master King Charles," Alcuin's *On Rhetoric* began, "with the light of total wisdom and marked you out with a special clarity of learning. Yet in order that no one might accuse me of disobedience, I shall here endeavor to answer what you asked of me: 'Tell me about the discovery of rhetoric!'" "There was a time, I have been told, when men lived like wild animals in the field, and had no capacity for reason but could only utilize their physical strength. Similarly, they performed nothing by way of divine worship or any truly human task. Instead, ruled as they were by blind, thoughtless lust, they misused their powers. But then one important and clever man recognized what a remarkable base material and what great aptitude lay dormant in the human intellect, if only someone were able to tease it out and direct it toward higher things."[123] Charlemagne listened attentively. *Oratio*, in other words, the practice of classical rhetoric, was education and the beginning and foundation of all scholarship. Not only did it attest the capacity for reason, but also, much more than that, it represented humanity, a rationality-bound human dignity wrested from an animal-like existence. Therefore, it also went to the heart of the duties of kingship and the spiritual core of Charlemagne's own being. Charlemagne was determined to act in accordance with this principle; court assemblies and the administration of his empire would be the beneficiaries.

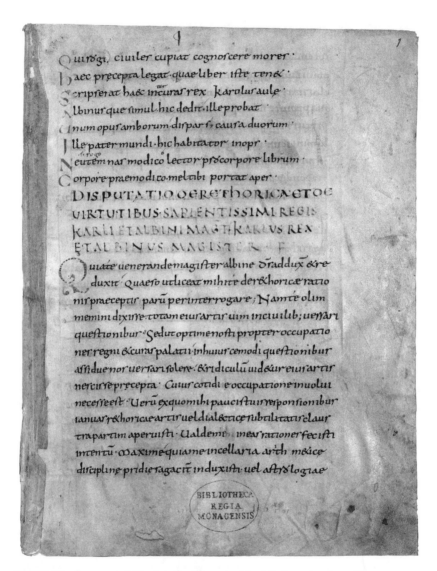

FIGURE 30 The first page of Alcuin's *On Rhetoric*. Munich, Bavarian State Library.

Alcuin followed his classical models in his two works. Yet despite this, it is striking how modern and characteristic of our contemporary age the arguments of this early medieval Anglo-Saxon appear; the notion of man's ascent from an animal-like state to the employment of reason as a result of increasing knowledge is more reminiscent of Darwin than of Kant, who thought in categories of progress rather than evolution. Alcuin's treatise makes no mention of self-inflicted immaturity. Rather, he presents a grandiose vision of man progressing from a bestial state to one of human dignity through the awakening of his capacity for reason. Certainly, though, Alcuin's fable implies that different levels of education exist in different human societies. Within Charlemagne's realm it was clear, however, that the intellect was to be awakened, divine worship observed, and people led toward higher things—even if at the outset this would apply only to the country's elites.

The beginning of Alcuin's treatise consisted of various simple exercises. "What is sophistic discourse?" Charlemagne wanted to know. Alcuin hesitated to cite an example to his king because it seemed too disrespectful. And so he tried a different approach, asking Charlemagne, "Am I permitted to ask you a question?" "Why not?" the king replied. "What are you, then?" asked Alcuin. "I am a man [*homo*]." "So, if you say that I am not the same as you, and that I am a man, then it follows that you are not a man." "It does indeed." "But how many syllables does *homo* have?" "Two." "So are you then those two syllables?" "What kind of nonsense is this?" "Well, you did ask to see through the trickery of sophism."[124] But rhetoric could also appear in a far more useful guise: "Induction is a form of oratory, which reveals uncertain facts through certain [statements] and compels a person who is reluctant to accept them to agree." Charlemagne could hardly believe that such a thing was possible. "It strikes me as impossible that a person can get an opponent to agree just by means of oratory."[125] The king was accustomed to coercion and force, and to deception and lies.

Alcuin's *Dialectics*, meanwhile, broached unfamiliar rather than challenging subjects. Readily understandable and once again written in the form of a dialogue, it was designed to introduce the Carolingian court to Aristotle's doctrine of categories, and in particular his *Peri hermeneias* (On interpretation), which contained his doctrine of propositions. "Alcuin: Aristotle's treatise on understanding, so to speak, is called the *Peri hermeneias*.—Charlemagne: How do you mean understanding?—A: Every fact that is a fact and can be represented by means of a word is expressed in the form of either a noun or a verb.—C: So how do these two categories function?—A: Nouns are used to convey the substance of each and every thing, say, a 'person.' Actions or sufferings are indicated by verbs, say: 'The person runs,' or 'The person is being tormented.' These two elements of speech represent the entirety of what human reason can create by way of a proposition." And so Alcuin's treatise continued, following more or less directly the fourth-century CE philosopher Themistius's commentary on Aristotle's text. This way of presenting an argument offered anything but high philosophy, but for all that it was unfamiliar, needed to be specially practiced, and over time changed the way people perceived and expressed things.

The king as student: nothing helped propagandize the desire for renewal more clearly than this kind of conceit, which soon became widespread. Anyone who read Alcuin's *Dialectics* could and should follow the king's example. Moreover, the Anglo-Saxon's *On Rhetoric*, which was disseminated in similar fashion, was not just intended to help people embellish and polish their dazzling oratorical skills. Rather, it had been used as a practical tool by the opposing parties in court in ancient times, and to hone their argumentation when confronting one another in a trial. In this capacity, it required that people develop the techniques of systematic cross-questioning, memory training, formulating practical definitions and distinctions, and logical argumentation. Last but not least, it helped foster the art of persuasion.

This discipline was akin to that of dialectics and gave rise to the doctrine of circumstances, that is, the doctrine of facts, illuminated through persistent questioning, and their "circumstances," which systematically inquired after the "who" and "what," the "where" and "when," the "why" and "with what" and the "in what way" of any given subject—in other words, the categories of Aristotle, which the Greek philosopher believed were the means by which everything could be expressed. These small steps toward a manageable use of reason and a perception guided by rationality were practiced at the Carolingian court and in the schools; and with them, a new style of thinking imperceptibly found its way into Frankish society and permeated its elite groups. The king wanted to introduce his country's elite to a rational conception of their world, and his way of urging them to adopt this mind-set was to make himself the model to emulate.

With a little practice, this doctrine also enabled people to understand complex social, manorial, and organizational relation appropriately and to see them both in their constituent elements and as a coherent whole. An analytical sense for predicates was formed; at the same time, rationally guided modes of perception and patterns of questioning were taught and practiced, in order that the faculty of perception might be schooled in the same manner and a sense of curiosity might be implanted in people's minds, an inquisitiveness that—as would presently become apparent—stopped at nothing in its quest for truth. As a result, this rhetoric revealed itself to be a science of enlightenment, which worked hand-in-glove with dialectics.

The few rudimentary basic disciplines, which were soon being practiced in all schools—in the East and West of the realm, as well as among the Anglo-Saxons and in Italy; indeed, everywhere the Latin language held sway—and which derived from a handful of texts from late antiquity that had been edited and reedited, not only led over time to a growing mastery of the dialectical method and to an ever-firmer trust in modes of thought dictated by the rules of reason, but also at the same time culminated in the West gradually taking on a particular uniform intellectual character that was to distinguish it from both Byzantium and the Arabic-speaking world. This development was not, however, to the exclusion of "national" variations and "international" competition. Yet the basic fact remains: from Charlemagne's time onward, an Aristotelian form of intellectualism spread throughout all the schools of the West in fundamentally the same way.

This renaissance in knowledge and aptitude was not sought for its own sake, nor was competence in Latin revived just for the purposes of logic. The purpose of both, as the Church Father St. Augustine had stressed in his writings, was to promote the soul's redemption, the true faith, the correct observance of sacred rites, and the understanding of the Holy Scriptures and of the world order ordained by God, and thereby to support a form of rule that was pleasing to God and included welfare provision for the poor and disadvantaged, another key requirement of religion. Religious motives really did drive Charlemagne's concern for education, and along with this his desire to establish the first step in the rationalization of European intellectual culture. At this stage, no one had an inkling that rationality might one day pose a fundamental danger to religion.

Petrus Pisanus, one of the first teachers of grammar whom Charlemagne summoned to attend his court, reminded his master of these higher aims: anyone who wished to follow his instruction should desist from fostering childish ignorance and from stirring up discord with his words. Instead, he should peaceably embrace the message of the Scriptures: "For Christ the King himself is the bringer of peace." This was the inner peacefulness of the soul that only knowledge could bring, peace at the heart of the realm of Christ, not merely an absence of war against external enemies or against heretics or heathens. What a blissful vision!

Academic pursuits obeyed God's will; their purpose was everywhere to search out this will, to which He had made His creation subject. "Philosophers were not the creators of the sciences, merely their discoverers. For the Creator of All Things has determined the nature of everything according to His desire. The wise men of this world were the discoverers of these sciences inherent in the nature of things." Alcuin wrote these words to the king while teaching him about the sun's course along the ecliptic.[126] Each and every science strove for concordance with God's will. "For what do we contemplate and marvel at other than the wisdom of the creator evident in the natural course of the sun, moon, and stars?"

This culture of learning was meant to shape every aspect of life, including divine worship, the Church in general, and even the decisions taken by the royal council. The defense of the faith, resistance to heresy, and order within the realm all cried out for it; grammar was needed for prayer, rhetoric for ruling, and dialectics for faith, while the sum total of knowledge was required to maintain the divine order of the world. These arts provided a theoretical grounding for real life, for the philosophy and exercise of power, and for Charlemagne's Frankish Empire as a whole. Accordingly, the king ensured their dissemination throughout his realm; on no account were they to be restricted to his court. Education has always required a broad base to thrive; conversely, it withers away if the foundations begin to crumble. Charlemagne was well aware of this from the centuries of Frankish history that had gone before.

Admittedly, the entire *Organon* of Aristotle—in addition to the *Categories* and the work on propositions (*On Interpretation*), this body of work by the Greek philosopher on logic also included four further treatises: the *Prior Analytics* (on deductive reasoning and the theory of the syllogism), the *Posterior Analytics, Topics* (on the art of dialectic), and finally *Sophistical Refutations*—was introduced only in stages into the Frankish educational canon; the final three or four works became available to the Latin world only from the twelfth century onward. In the meantime, a partial substitute appeared in the form of Boethius's *De divisione,* a small work on logic that treats all kinds of division, for example, the division of a whole into its constituent parts. Its key proposition was that the essential defining characteristic of a "thing" (*proprium*) had to be distinguished from its accidental features (*accidens*). Thus, a person remains a person regardless of whether he is tall or short, fat or thin, learned or stupid. The difference between various objects, the key feature that distinguished them from each other (for instance, a person's girth), had to be determined. Yet the business of differentiating was made easier by applying an organizing principle, in other words, the classification according to genus and species and thence into further subspecies. "The whole is divided into parts until we have laid bare each and every element of which it is composed," for example, like dividing a house into its roof, walls, and foundations.[127]

The period before the twelfth century was spent in practicing this skill of thinking in categories, agonizing over such concepts as *proprium, accidens,* distinction, and division, and relating these factors to circumstances, which in their turn called for categorical classifications. So it was that, over the course of three centuries, a technique of rational thinking according to fixed rules and in controllable stages developed and spread to all schools throughout the West. Concepts, categories, modes of expression, rules, classifications of differences, and the like were basically all learned and practiced in the same way from Scotland to southern Italy and Sicily and from Poland to Portugal until, in the High Middle Ages, the great breakthrough finally occurred, which was of such momentous significance for world history. This was the most important move toward modernization to be instigated in the early Middle Ages, and its effects can be felt right up to the present day. And it was at the court of Charlemagne that this development began. Alcuin provided the decisive impetus. The modest pride with which Einhard, a student of the eminent Anglo-Saxon scholar, presented his *Vita Karoli Magni* already shows the influence of these intellectual developments: it was a "book" (essence, not just any book) (the need for differentiation), but one that recounted (the category of action) "remarkable deeds" (*proprium*) in "elegant Latin" (*accidens*).

The king besieged Alcuin with a barrage of questions about astronomy, inquiring about the age of the moon and leap months, the planets, the transit of the moon through the meridian, the significance of the fact that Mars had become visible once more, and many other matters. Alcuin referred him to the work of Pliny the Elder and even quoted his Natural History albeit almost certainly from the Venerable Bede's study of the Roman writer. In September 798, Charlemagne professed himself especially fascinated by the reappearance of Mars in the sky, an event that had occurred in the preceding July/August (when the sun was in Leo): "Our thoughts have long been preoccupied with investigation of this planet; not even its reappearance can satisfy our curiosity."[128] Charlemagne was tireless in his questioning. He wanted to know, for instance, whether Mars had its own orbit or whether its course was influenced by the sun. After all, he had observed the recent ascent of Mars with his own eyes: "Did this occur as a result of its [the sun's] power or as a portent that the planet was about to complete an orbit of two years in just one? If it was accompanying the sun, then how could such a swift passage be possible?" These "distortions" of Mars's orbit unsettled the king.

Alcuin gave him an evasive answer. Although he assured him that the planet's course was following its "natural order," the scholar did not venture to provide an explanation for this. Nevertheless, he did challenge the idea that the phenomenon might be interpreted as a portent. Was Charlemagne prone to astrological superstitions, or was the king trying to grasp the connection between the cosmos and the earth? Whatever the truth of the matter, his question about Mars remained a perfectly good one for the next eight hundred years. Only when mathematicians were equipped with the requisite knowledge did Tycho Brahe make a systematic collection of data on the orbit of Mars; in his will, Brahe bequeathed his tables of calculations to his colleague at the court of the Holy Roman emperor Rudolf II in Prague, Johannes Kepler, who used them to formulate the four planetary laws that bear his name and govern the courses and the movements of the planets around the sun.

In the age of Charlemagne, neither astronomy nor astrology was based on a large body of source material. Nor was grammar or didactics of any help in understanding them. They required a knowledge of the natural world that during Charlemagne's reign was even more scanty in the Latin West than information on the disciplines of the trivium. Only a few, generally rather poor textbooks dealing with such topics had been passed down from antiquity, foremost among them Cassiodorus's *Institutiones,* which contained hints and allusions rather than any real expositions.

It was from the educational theories of the Greeks and Romans that the West inherited the traditional division of human aptitudes into the "liberal arts" and the "mechanical arts." The former category denoted those disciplines that did not involve any manual labor and did not require a day job to pursue. As a rule, they were premised on a free, prosperous citizen whose livelihood relied on the hard work of an army of people dependent on him to a greater or lesser degree. The designation "mechanical," meanwhile, embraced all those activities that required the use of hands, such as surgery or medicine, hunting, seafaring, trade, and all kinds of handicrafts. Accordingly, these skills were not taught in schools, a situation that would change only in the age of the university.

For their part, the liberal arts were subdivided into the trivium and the quadrivium. The ancient educational program of these seven liberal arts was never officially abandoned. Among the Irish and the Anglo-Saxons, it endured, in some cases in an expanded form, longer than in the Frankish Empire; this classical form of education also continued to flourish among the Visigoths and the Lombards. In the Frankish realm, the effectiveness of studies dwindled during the dark centuries of the early Middle Ages, although even the kings of the Merovingian dynasty were able to speak Latin and read, while many an educated man was still to be found among the clergy. But considered as a whole, learning and skills declined markedly for a number of reasons. It was only now, under the first Carolingian kings, tentatively at first under Pepin but then with full force under his son Charlemagne, that a counterreaction set in.

The study of the arts was set to rise again. The canon of seven disciplines became firmly established once more, not least as a result of a brief introduction by Alcuin to an unfinished, encyclopedically arranged study on the subject of precisely these liberal arts, a dialogue he titled *Disputatio de vera philosophia* (Disputation on True Philosophy). In the logical succession of his writings, Alcuin placed this work before his *Grammar,* which was based principally on the work of the grammarian Donatius but also on Boethius's

De interpretatione. His *Rhetoric* and *Dialectic* then followed the *Disputatio.* This disputation—once again couched in the form of a dialogue between a "master" and his "pupils" (a questioning Frank and a shrewd Saxon)—blossomed into a concise Neoplatonic introduction to the liberal arts. Charlemagne too would doubtless have taken great pleasure in this treatise.[129] "Your curiosity knows no bounds. You are eager to go beyond the confines of a little textbook," the master tells his students approvingly.[130]

Philosophy, literally the "love of knowledge," the learned teacher in Alcuin's text explains, is the mistress of all virtues, and anyone who has acquired an understanding of it should take care never to lose it. The light of learning, he continues, is innately at the disposal of the human intellect, but without proper instruction it remains nothing but a trapped spark. It is simple to point out the path of wisdom to a person if he is seeking it for the sake of God, for the cleansing of his soul, and to learn the truth, indeed, even just for its own sake rather than in pursuit of praise from others or worldly honors and riches. It is a natural tendency of the human mind to strive after what is good and true. Yet it is essential to maintain a sense of moderation, the master warns; the key watchword is "nothing to excess." Wisdom is an eternal treasure of the soul, and the path to it proceeds via the seven pillars or steps of the liberal arts: grammar, rhetoric, dialectics, arithmetic, geometry, music, and astrology (i.e., astronomy), along with the pillars of the seven gifts of the Holy Ghost (Isaiah 11:2–3)); through these a person may come to see the pure beatific vision.[131] Grammar as the first step toward a vision of God—this was Charlemagne's agenda. Learning demanded that humans be shaped according to the measure of their souls. In his lifetime, though, Alcuin never got around to discussing the disciplines of the quadrivium.

The success of Charlemagne's educational program did not occur in giant strides, but it was not long in coming either. To have a whole society make the "ascent to wisdom" was not a matter of just a few decades' work. Instead, it took several generations to accomplish, although over time this long process made for a truly unified Western intellectual culture. The decisive factor, then, was not rapid progress but the permanence of the theoretical aim and the consistent way in which it was put into practice. These factors were responsible for the sense of durability that pervaded the entire culture and gave rise to a common way of thinking.

Aristotelian propaedeutics created a springboard for the golden age of medieval Scholasticism—a point of departure that actually never ended but kept pressing forward into the future. These foundations enabled the beginnings of Western theology—penetrating intellectual investigation of the mysteries of faith—to unfold; this was followed by rationalist philosophy, which became increasingly beset by religious doubts, and by the secular sciences. Both areas of inquiry soon became indispensable, not least in their analysis of actual and imagined heresies, and experienced a revival such as they had not seen for centuries even as early as Charlemagne's reign, at least where the West was concerned. Henceforth, scholarship and learning were to set early medieval society, which at this stage was still rooted in the oral tradition, on the long march toward a culture of reason, which was to begin with the principles of methodically controlled thinking and would proceed via the techniques of rational argumentation toward cosmology and the empirical sciences.

Such advances were not achieved through casual discussions in bathhouses or in the royal court; patient practice of these new aptitudes was called for. Enacting this program needed to proceed on many fronts. It was not war but rather the question of the organization of the Church and his realm that commanded Charlemagne's greatest attention, and these goals were not to be realized without learning. The empire and the Church needed the protection of the army externally, but internally they required order and faithful observance of the commandments of God and the Church Fathers, along with correct education of the clergy and the laity, a revival of skill in Latin, rhetoric, and dialectics, and an overhaul of schools, books, and the justice system. The material cost of all this called for royal patronage and careful management by the king of both his own farms and the Church's estates, and hence an efficient economic system in general, insofar as this lay within the king's grasp. A pressing need for reform was evident throughout his realm, and Charlemagne was well aware of it.

Notwithstanding his position as a mighty king and conqueror, Charlemagne was not above taking instruction, and he graciously thanked his tutor Alcuin: "I confess that my thirst for knowledge led me to question things, and I am grateful to you that you did not object to this."[132] This was more than a magnanimous gesture on the part of the great man; the king was all too conscious of the urgent need to reform the education system. Indeed, he expressly ordered and promoted this course of action, but at the same time he intuited that knowledge and learning constituted their own realm, a domain that not everyone, not even the most victorious conqueror, was destined to inhabit. It was in this spirit that Charlemagne the king—an inquisitive, questioning, and grateful king—thanked the scholar Alcuin.

Diversity within Church Law

The organization of the Church, which during the final decades of Merovingian rule had been severely disrupted, was in dire need of renewal, consolidation, and protection. Charlemagne, though, required learning in order to strengthen the Church through "awareness of the faith," hold the "keys of the Church" in the correct way, revive its organization, and implement canon law. He even warned Pope Leo "to obey the sacred canons and follow the commandments [*statuta*] of the Church Fathers." Yet at this stage, the Church was far from having a set of uniform legal norms at its disposal. The situation was deeply confusing. Despite this, the king resumed his father's efforts to establish legal concordance with Rome. After all, as early as 774, when he had hurried from Pavia to Rome, he had requested from Pope Hadrian I a compendium of all the canon laws that were in force in the Eternal City. These then became the basis for the chapters of the *Admonitio generalis*.[133] Yet this tome that the pope sent Charlemagne, the *Collectio Dionysio-Hadriana*, did not guarantee uniformity of canon law within his realm either.[134]

Alongside this volume, other chronologically organized collections continued to be copied and remained in circulation. The so-called *Quesnelliana*, the *Concordia canonum* of Cresconius Africanus, and various other minor collections contained old canonical norms.[135] Systematic collections also continued to circulate in the Frankish Empire, such as the older *Collectio vetus Gallica* or the *Collectio Hispana;* there was also an Irish collection of canons. Their contents by no means always agreed with one another and could even be full of contradictions. In consequence, there was a continual need for clarification. It was frequently the case that different norms came into force in all four corners of the realm, for none of these collections—in most cases, their present names derive from jurists of the early modern period who edited and published them—was binding, and none was more or less valid than the others. There was no central regulating instance for canonical norms. Charlemagne could do little to alter this situation.

Yet the king or his advisers were not prepared to let matters rest at this. They were intent on creating greater clarity. "Anything that isn't useful is superfluous; and anything that is superfluous is invalid," ran Theodulf's dictum; Charlemagne was impressed by this syllogism.[136] Perhaps it chimed in with the maxims that guided his actions? Around the turn of the century, a systematically organized collection of canons duly appeared, based on the *Dionysio-Hadriana*, a small step forward underlining the way in which all this earlier legal material had permeated intellectual debate, and a sign of the first successes of the effort to revive education. The legal norms that were relevant in any particular case could be found far more easily in this work than in the earlier collections. The new collection may have been produced in the episcopal city of Lyons, or it may have been edited under Visigothic influence, since this reworked *Dionysio-Hadriana* also included canon law from Visigothic regions. This new undertaking, the so-called *Collectio Dacheriana,* was extremely successful, but once again it was not without competition or universally valid.

The oldest surviving manuscript (Cologne, Cathedral Library 122) was written in 805 and has traditionally been associated with Charlemagne's "court bishop" Hildebald of Cologne and through him almost certainly with the actual king's or emperor's court itself. It appeared alongside similar older collections like the *Collectio vetus Gallica* (from the period around 600), which likewise remained in use, but its success was immeasurably greater than that of all those earlier works. The *Dacheriana* organized the material into three books, the first of which (thanks to its relevance to the matter of salvation) concerned penitence, while the second covered criminal law, and the third the ecclesiastical hierarchy. As stated at the end of the introduction, the decisions reached at universal church councils ranked higher than those of the provincial synods and most definitely above any individual judgment. This work provides clear evidence of a desire to systematize things and place them within a hierarchy. Even if it did not have its origins in Charlemagne's court, it would surely have been totally in accord with it.

How completely unsystematic the framing or revising of laws was at that time may be judged from an example that is inextricably bound up with the question of the Christian way of life.[137] As a result of papal intervention, Charlemagne's father, Pepin, had outlawed incest, together with marriage between blood relations (see, for instance, Leviticus 18:1–18). In doing this, he was falling back on a long tradition in Gallia, but the brand-new element was the broad swathe of relatives to whom the incest proscription now applied. Thus, everyone right back to the common forebears of both spouses was included. The counting method was adopted from Roman law, for example, from a husband up through his father and grandfather to his great-grandfather and, if this last was the common ancestor, back up the various branches of the family tree via the grandfather and father of the wife. This method of counting yielded the yardstick of six stages of kinship, three on each side of the marriage (3:3).

Merovingian synods had repeatedly sought to define such limits, but their stipulations had all been at variance with one another. Different norms therefore applied among the Visigoths, Burgundians, Franks, and Anglo-Saxons. A relationship that was perfectly legal in one place was banned in another. Pope Gregory the Great's decretal *Libellus responsionum* of 601, written to the Anglo-Saxons, outlawed marriage only between siblings, a proscription in line with what is said on this subject in the Book of Deuteronomy (27.22). In other words, here the demarcation line was located at the second degree of kinship (2:2). The most influential penitentials (handbooks for confessors, listing sins and their appropriate penances) of the time adopted this norm, especially the penitential of Bishop Theodore of Canterbury from the late seventh century, which gained widespread currency, even in the Frankish Empire, not least through having been cited in Bede's *Ecclesiastical History of the English People* (1.27).

But ever since Gregory II in the early eighth century, Roman pontiffs had required that their flocks observe new and stricter rules that originated in Constantinople. The Carolingians were keen to adhere to these rules. The first capitulary issued by King Pepin (751/755) determined the limit—in accord with the penitentials and Gregory the Great—as still being siblings. But Rome, after the Byzantine model, now extended the proscription as far as the fourth generation.[138] And so, as a result of closer relations between Pepin and the papacy, the synods of Compiègne (756) and Verberie (757) adopted this new ruling, thereby tightening the legal norm in force in the Frankish Empire. The first step (756) was to rigorously apply the fourth canonical degree as an impediment to marriage, while correspondingly a decree was issued ordering the dissolution of "incestuous" marriages. This position was then modified the following year, when 4:4 marriages were permitted, and only unions between great-nephews and great-nieces (3:3) and 4:3 marriages were declared illegitimate.[139] The ways in which such relations were calculated were not clear to everyone. At first, people evidently understood the fourth degree of kinship as indicating the furthest limit at which marriages were forbidden, not at which they were allowed.

Nevertheless, Pepin's proposed new order did not come to fruition. The populace and the Frankish Church failed to observe the royal and synodal legal decrees or at best did so to only a limited extent. The low level of literacy among the laity and the lower ranks of the clergy and poor communication did the rest. Pepin's first capitulary with the strict limit on incestuous relationships[140] was disseminated during his son's reign in various different collections of legal documents, either separately or together with either one or both of his later capitularies, which set broader limitations. As a result, marriage laws in the Frankish Empire were characterized by a coexistence of mutually contradictory norms. No attempt was made to resolve these contradictions, nor was the earlier edict rescinded by the later one. As yet, there was no hierarchy of legal source material according to which earlier rulings were automatically annulled by more recent ones.

It appears, then, that the tightening of the incest limitation was merely an integral part of Pepin's ascent to the throne and thus of the special relations between the newly crowned king and the pope, that it was probably proclaimed only very halfheartedly, and that after all this initial activity no one paid a great deal of attention to the question of incest any longer. It was now virtually impossible to work out what rules were actually practiced, which ones priests were expected to respect, and to what extent any transgressions were punished by the bishops. This would remain the case for the next fifty years.

Although Charlemagne also expressly proscribed incest in his very first capitulary, there is no extant act of law passed by this king specifying where the boundaries lay.[141] The new Roman-canonical norm was brought back into play—and then only tentatively—only from 798 onward, when Charlemagne's ambitions to revive the Western emperorship first became clear.[142] The older implementations of laws, such as Gregory the Great's *Libellus responsionum,* the penitential of Theodore, and other similar decretals, also remained in force. Marriage between cousins (2:2) was therefore widespread and well established as a legal act. What were the king and his advisers using as a yardstick here, though? Certainly the recent papal norm did not seem to be particularly important to them.

In order to monitor implementation of the ban on incest, Charlemagne now demanded the collaboration of the bishops and the secular lords. It seems that the bishops were to be responsible for the jurisdiction of the new laws, while the counts were empowered to use coercive measures to implement them.[143] Yet it is unclear what limitations the king wanted to see observed here. Was he perhaps leaving the decision about where to draw the lines to the diocesan bishops? Even when the emperor Charlemagne convened a major Frankish imperial synod at five separate locations in 813 with the express intent of promoting the standardization of canon law, the norms still varied widely between the second (2:2) and the fourth (4:4) degree of kinship. Indeed, the boundaries regarding incest remained an open question until far into the ninth century and even beyond. What guidelines was an ecclesiastical judge supposed to follow? Moreover, this confusion over the question of legal norms for incest was also repeated where other norms were concerned. The age of Charlemagne was far from possessing a standard system of canon law.

Centuries would elapse before the effort to introduce a uniform, systematically organized system of canon law finally took permanent root. Even then, the availability of the law and agreed norms did not mean that people adhered to them in real life. Charlemagne himself violated the precepts of the marriage law when he divorced his lawful Lombard wife (Einhard used the Latin term *uxor* to describe her) and married again in her lifetime—"illegitimate nuptials," in the harsh posthumous judgment of the historian Paschasius Radbertus, a fierce critic of Louis the Pious and the Carolingians. Radbertus's attack began with a dig aimed at Louis that no contemporary could have failed to recognize—Louis, the youngest son of Charlemagne's second and canonically illegitimate union. Despite all efforts, uniformity of canon law was never achieved. Indeed, it was the High Middle Ages before the full force of canon law could be unleashed.

Even so, the steady increase in the decretals issued by Charlemagne testifies to a growing familiarity on the part of the king and his advisers with the practical business of reform, as well as their increasing urge to enact these reforms. At the same time, though, it accentuated the seemingly chaotic conditions that existed within this multiethnic empire and its lack of homogeneity. Contradictory legal standards made for confusion, meaning that order, peace, and security were by no means guaranteed. This moribund aristocratic society, which also permeated the Church and which no royal edict seemed capable of subduing, represented a constant threat to the stability of the empire.

Diversity of Forms of Worship

When he announced his program of reform, the Frankish king found himself faced with difficulties similar to those encountered by the Visigothic king Athaulf. However, he had the advantage of far more time than the barbarian had had to put it into practice. The peoples of his realm had either all been baptized or, in the case of the Saxons, were about to be. This entailed further problems that no canon law could solve at the drop of a hat. No amount of baptism could entirely supplant the old cult practices, and no prayers could completely efface the old observances; even the *Admonitio generalis*, for all its threats of punishment, did not manage to eradicate them. At best, pagan practices mingled with Christian innovations. Popular culture was characterized by a more or less syncretistic religious observance. This becomes clear if we consider the so-called "Wessobrunn Prayer," which is the oldest surviving prayer in the German language from the period before 814 and is named for the Bavarian Benedictine monastery in whose library it was held for centuries:

> *Dat gafregin ih mit firahim firiuuizzo meista,*
> *Dat ero ni uuas noh ûfhimil,*
> *noh paum nihheinîg noh pereg ni uuas,*
> *ni suigli sterro nohheinîg noh sunna ni scein,*
> *noh mâno ni liuhta noh der mârẹo sêo.*
> *Do dar niuuiht ni uuas enteo ni uuenteo,*
> *enti dô uuas der eino almahtîco cot,*
> *manno miltisto, enti dar uuârun auh manake mit inan*
> *cootlîhhe geistâ. enti cot heilac.*

(This I learned among mortal men as the greatest wonder:
That there was neither the earth nor the heaven above.
Nor was there any tree nor mountain.
Neither any star at all, nor did the sun shine,
Nor the moon gleam, nor was there the glorious sea.
When there was nothing, no ending and no limits,
There was the One Almighty God,
Of all beings the greatest in grace, and many with him:
Good spirits, and the holy God.)
(see Figure 3)

Many pre-Christian elements are in evidence here. Right at the beginning of the poem—which furthermore is prefaced by the title *De poeta* (On the Creator) in the manuscript—certain features reflect the language and idiom of Old German oral epics, such as the alliterative verse, introductory formulas, and repetition used in the Anglo-Saxon and Old Saxon traditions. The creation myth it evokes is reminiscent of the *Völuspá*, the first poem of the Icelandic *Prose Edda*, and although its origins may be Anglo-Saxon, it has been recast with distinct Bavarian overtones, notably the mention of "Almighty God," the "good spirits," and above all the concept of "no ending and no limits." These elements are joined together with Christian content.[144] Just as the *Merseburg Incantations* recall the pagan gods Phol and Wotan as earlier healers, so here is the Creation invoked in order—as if by magic—to stimulate faith within the person praying. This form of Christianity, which was also that of most Franks, was celebrated less through deep devotion and more through the exercise of a prescribed ritual, the observance of numerous ecclesiastical commandments and proscriptions in obedience and subjugation to the church hierarchy and to secular authority, and the recitation of formulaic prayers.

And it was precisely such elements that the king concerned himself with in the long term. The purity and beauty of the liturgy, fitting celebration of the Eucharist, incantation, the melodiousness of prayers, and the ornamentation of the church all revealed God's majesty and omnipotence. They were an essential requirement for proper worship,[145] as stipulated in the *Admonitio generalis*. Each time the Eucharist was celebrated in this way, it served to remind people of the fact that Christ died for our salvation. Charlemagne observed them at every opportunity, but the illiterate populace did not understand them. All the same, nothing unworthy or impure was to defile the service of divine worship. Einhard (chap. 26) recounts how his lord and master applied these aims specifically to the Royal Church of St. Mary at Aix (Aachen Cathedral); it was through the solemnity of the sacred rite, along with fasting, chanting the litany, and doing penance, that humans submitted to God's omnipotence.

Charlemagne asked to be sent a copy of the liturgy of the Roman missal, the sacramentary known as the Sacramentarium Hadrianum, which had been transcribed from a codex of the (papal?) *cubiculum* (private library) and, after the addition of supplements (possibly by Benedict of Aniane), became the standard text for the Mass in the Frankish Empire. Paul the Deacon most likely conveyed Charlemagne's request to the pope in 784–785; certainly, the manuscript arrived at the court in the following year.[146] The constituent parts of this Mass already basically corresponded to those of the Tridentine Mass, which was in force until the Second Vatican Council of 1962: the Introit, the Kyrie eleison, the Gloria, the Collects, the Epistles, the Graduals, the Gospels, the Offertory, the *Praefatio communis* (the Preface of the Mass), the Sanctus, the *Te igitur* (the beginning of the Canon of the Mass), the Lord's Prayer, the *Pax Domini*, and the Agnus Dei.

Whenever danger threatened or in times of great hardship, the king ordered periods of fasting in the army, in the kingdom at large, and in his palace; and when thanks were due to God after the danger had passed, he commanded that prayers be said throughout the realm. Such forms of worship were not mentioned in the *Admonitio generalis*. Nevertheless, they are well attested, for example, in the letter that Charlemagne sent to his queen, Fastrada, during his first campaign against the Avars in 791.[147] In fact, this is the only letter to one of his spouses to have survived, and this came about only because it was reworked into a model piece of correspondence, a template to be used repeatedly. Fasting and prayer, often accompanied by processions, unified the people in worship.

On three set days, Charlemagne told Fastrada in his letter, the queen was to ensure that she prayed for God's mercy "in order that He might grant us peace and good health, victory, and a campaign free from danger, and so that He might in His compassion and clemency be our helper and adviser and protector in all our travails." On these days of intercession, only the sick, the old, and the very young were to consume meat. Rich citizens should donate a shilling for alms, while the poor should give what they could afford. Every priest was expected to personally hold a sung mass unless he was prevented by illness, and each cleric was to sing fifty psalms, intone litanies, and go barefoot. "On campaign, we have all followed these principles and achieved this with God's help." Now, with the assistance of suitable helpers, it was up to the queen to ensure that she did the same. War and power, victory and health were all intrinsically bound up with worship and ritual observance. Charlemagne was mindful of this at all times; he too went barefoot on these occasions.

The kind of worship he espoused became visible, tangible, and a model to others. The magnificence of the churches in his realm was designed to overwhelm the observer. No royal palace in Franconia was furnished more lavishly than the great places of worship, with their pillars, ambulatories, apses, mosaic and fresco decorations, and their sacred altar vessels of gold and silver and ivory. The sole exception to this general rule was the palace at Aix (Aachen), which Charlemagne increasingly favored with visits from 794–795 onward and which for a long time he had, through the addition of costly buildings, been expanding into the most imposing palace in his kingdom; only the royal palace at Ingelheim near Mainz came close in the lavishness of its decoration.[148] Even today, Theodulf of Orléans's church at Germigny-des-Prés, the layout of which supposedly echoed the cathedral at Aix, still conveys an impression of the mosaic interior decorative idiom of that period.

The king expected the other magnates of his realm to show the same degree of solicitude for correct forms of worship that he himself practiced. This manifested itself especially in the establishment of religious institutions and in support for monasteries. The buildings of this period, together with their decoration and liturgical practices, bear witness to the success of this program. Many monasteries revived the ritual known as "eternal praise of God" (*laus perennis*), last practiced in late antiquity, a form of antiphony involving several choirs. Its roots lay in Greek Christianity; however, the practice was introduced into northern Europe and Franconia at an early stage via the monastery of canons regular (Augustinians) at St. Maurice d'Agaune in the Burgundian-controlled Swiss region of Valais, which was founded in the sixth century and lay on one of the most important passes into Italy.[149] Those foundations that adopted this form of worship included the royal-affiliated Abbey of St-Denis, the monastery at St-Germain-des-Prés in Paris, and the monastic community at Aniane near Montpellier, which was founded by the Visigothic monk Benedict (born Witiza). St-Denis was the first major construction project undertaken by the new Carolingian dynasty; it was completed in Charlemagne's reign. It was followed by Lorsch Abbey and St. Emmeram's Abbey in Regensburg; the legend later spread that the church at the last institution was built at the express behest and with the permission of Charlemagne himself.

In this regard, the testimony of Angilbert, on whom the king conferred the title of lay abbot of Centula (St-Riquier, northwest of Amiens) in 790, is especially impressive. The new abbot expanded the monastery into a magnificent institution housing three hundred monks and boasting no fewer than six bell towers and a rich treasury, where Angilbert displayed his precious collection of holy relics. These included a fragment of the stone that Christ stepped on to ascend the Cross, soil from Calvary, a fragment of the rock onto which the spear wound in Christ's side dripped blood, relics of the tomb where Jesus was laid to rest and of the stone that was rolled in front of it, a splinter from the True Cross, a strip of leather from his sandals, a piece of wood from Jesus's crib, water from the place where Jesus was baptized in the river Jordan, some earth from the Mount of Olives, a fragment of the whipping post and sections of the ropes used to bind Christ, drops of Mary's breast milk, a hair from the beard of St. Peter the Apostle, a splinter from the Cross of St. Andrew, and so on. This collection of relics of martyrs, confessors, and virgins had been assembled from gifts donated by Popes Hadrian I and Leo III, from places as far afield as Constantinople and Jerusalem, and from Italy, Germania, Aquitania, Burgundy, and Gallia, as well as from the emperor's court.[150] As he did with his precious relics, Angilbert also kept a meticulous record of the abbey's many altars, ciboria, and other sacred vessels and treasures; only the monastery's holdings of manuscripts were recorded en bloc: two copies of the Gospels and two hundred "other" volumes.

Abbot Angilbert, who enjoyed staging elaborate religious ceremonies, formed three choirs of monks, who moved around like small armies of God in an endless procession through the abbey church and between the smaller

FIGURE 32 The Abbey of St. Riquier (Centula) in Picardy, northern France. Engraving by Paul Pétau, 1612.

churches within the complex, crisscrossing the entire monastery grounds and alternately singing praises to the Almighty—a truly uplifting spectacle. In symbolic acknowledgment of the Holy Trinity, Centula had three main churches and a series of subsidiary churches: the central basilica, dedicated to the Savior (west) and St. Richarius (east), and churches of St. Mary and St. Benedict, which the processions of monks visited via an arcaded passageway in uninterrupted alternation. Their chanting rang out day and night, after vespers and before matins, while even more elaborate processions were held on the major church festivals. It seems that the ceremony practiced at St-Riquier was retained until at least the eleventh century. A description and a map of the entire complex from this period have survived (albeit in a seventeenth-century copy) to the present day, although nowadays the only one of the buildings still standing is the main church (not the Carolingian original but a later construction from the High Gothic period).

In fact, Angilbert enjoyed such intimate relations with the royal and imperial court that Charlemagne's daughter Bertha married him and bore him two sons, Hartnid and the future chronicler Nithard, two grandsons of the great Charlemagne. As a close confidant of the king, Angilbert was seen at court as a contemporary Homer, who delighted the court society with his verses. When Charlemagne visited the Abbey of St-Riquier to celebrate Easter in 800, he had occasion to see the monastery and its impressive buildings and hear the songs of praise. Alcuin was also attached to the court by this time; during the king's visit, Angilbert took the opportunity to ask the Anglo-Saxon scholar to write a brief life of the monastery's patron saint, Richarius, giving a somewhat more complex picture of the holy man than the tales of miracles that people had had to make do with hitherto.

Alcuin acceded to Angilbert's request and dedicated the finished work, which he called "a constant friend for your salvation," to the emperor; he added the following note: "When in your piety, o sublime Master, you sojourned at the sacred and justly renowned site of Centula, and when I, your Majesty's servant, followed in your devoted footsteps and stayed a while there, the great lord and venerable abbot Angilbert asked my humble self to write a little book about the holiest and truly outstanding confessor Richarius."[151] Although Alcuin's address to the emperor followed standard formulas in the adulatory epithets it applied, the writer nevertheless adopted a more subservient attitude than in his earlier writings for the king or in his early letters to him. Did the highly esteemed scholar perhaps write these words to try to fend off a growing sense of alienation from the emperor— *gratia Dei semper augusto* (by the Grace of the ever sacred God)? Whatever the case, he had complied with his ruler's demand in portraying his subject "as though it were something intended for a wise man's ears."[152] The monastery at St-Riquier witnessed a coming together of ritual and prayer, wealth and power, education, music and poetry, stagecraft, an abbot with ambition and a strong self-image, deference to the ruling emperor, and eternal praise to God. The impetus that Charlemagne had provided was beginning to produce some far-reaching and diverse effects.

Organization Requires a Hierarchy

This ruler was accustomed to being in command; he issued orders with a clear and constant voice. Despite being accredited as a skilled orator, he was not given to verbosity, preferring to use terse and precise interjections and terms of approbation and judgment like "good," "outstanding," "sensible," "shrewd," and "extraordinary." He almost always uttered just a single word, and by no means only on the central theological issues of the day. We know this thanks to the painstakingly meticulous record kept by a scribe in the margin of the *codex authenticus* of the "work of King Charles against the Synod," namely, the so-called *Libri Carolini;* this comprises a total of eighty entries, eighty authentic words of the great king.[153] Evidently, the manuscript of this work, compiled by Theodulf, was read aloud to the king for him to give his blessing to the content, despite the fact that in all probability he did not remotely understand the theological subtleties of the text. When all was said and done, Charlemagne was a layman, not a theologian. Nevertheless, this contentious text would never have attained wider publication without the express approval of the king, who wielded the highest authority where questions of faith were concerned.

Other texts received similar treatment. After Alcuin's criticism of the position of Bishop Felix of Urgell had been presented to the king, the scholar wrote to him as follows: "I thank your most revered piety that you have had my pamphlet read out before the ears of your great wisdom and have ordered errors to be noted and sent back to me for correction."[154] The opinion of experts, the king's confidants, was also adduced in these matters,[155] meaning that works were subject to a twofold monitoring. Because they relied on his grace and favor, the king's advisers—sometimes Theodulf, sometimes Alcuin—went in fear of him and vied with each other for his approval. The great man Alcuin was circumspect in offering his recommendations where the dignity of the office of emperor was at stake. It was vital to approach powerful people at an opportune moment; too early or too late could fatally harm one's case. The magnates of Charlemagne's court would wait patiently, customarily from very early in the morning, until he deigned to give them an audience, either outside his bedchamber on the upper floor of the palace or elsewhere, biding their time until the right moment seemed to have arrived. While they waited, they would also come to agreements with one another.[156] Anyone who had an audience with the king, or any historian recounting his deeds, would always experience some anxiety or timidity. He reportedly instilled "fear" or "a mild terror" in his interlocutors, according to his grandson Nithard (1.1). Only very few people were able to suppress fear in his presence and hold a mirror up to the all-powerful monarch or even go so far as to admonish him, like the Irishman Cathuulf.

Charlemagne was a king who set great store by order while at the same time being a devout Christian. He demanded rationally structured thought; the order of the world permitted such a mindset. Charlemagne had come to this realization at the latest after discussions with Alcuin and Theodulf. He who, as Theodulf once wrote, "held the keys of the Church"[157] convened the imperial synods and had their resolutions published and disseminated. In these forums, his voice was heard and his word held sway, although he did not act without spiritual helpers. At the royal court, the king's chapel, headed by the senior chaplain,[158] was the source of knowledge and in-depth advice about all aspects of canon law, both old and new. The archchaplain (as he later became known) coordinated reform measures and advised the ruler on their objectives, on the requirements of the new culture of learning that was to be established, on the setting up of schools and the minimum ecclesiastical knowledge required of pupils, and most probably also on the internal personal politics of the Frankish Church. Even so, it was Charlemagne's decisions that played a key role in directing and organizing the Church and controlling its activities.

One factor that was urgently needed to strengthen the faith among the general populace was a stabilizing of the Church's different levels of organization on the ground.[159] The cooperation between the king and the pope represented just the uppermost tier of this edifice and did nothing to ensure religious observance among the lowest echelons of society. The organization of the Church could be understood as a logical division: from the royal synods via the archdioceses and dioceses down to the parish churches in which the common people worshipped. Each authority had its own tasks, its own domain of responsibility, so to speak, and its own peculiarities. A bishop's see could be established only in a "town" (*civitas*) and required the preexisting presence there of other religious institutions, such as a monastery or a convent. These came under the aegis of the bishop. Tithes were allocated to the parish church. The restoration of the hierarchical structure of the Church was thus closely bound up with the spatial organization of the empire as a whole and with questions of urbanization, for example, concerning the relationship between the towns and the countryside. These touched not least on questions of economic organization and were premised on the demarcation of boundaries, namely, of church provinces, dioceses, parishes, and judicial districts. In those areas that had once been part of the Roman Empire, these boundaries could be based on the situation that had existed in late antiquity; but in regions east of the Rhine, urban life had first to be initiated before this could take place.

After taking the claims of various noblemen into account, Charlemagne appointed archbishops and bishops, along with abbots of monasteries under his jurisdiction. These appointees traveled to the synods that the king convened. The Lombards and the Irish, as well as the Anglo-Saxon scholar Alcuin and the Visigoth Theodulf, the outstanding theologians at the royal court, were almost certainly not members of the court chapel. Nor would these foreigners have exerted much influence on personal politics in Franconia. Conversely, this meant that their advice was free of family bias. It is unclear how they and others like them were integrated into Frankish courtly society. In Alcuin's case, we know that Charlemagne personally asked whether he could bring him to the synod held in Frankfurt in 794 (Einhard, chap. 56); in individual cases, others may also have become involved with the Frankish court in the same way. These foreigners' breadth of learning and skill commended them to the king, who furnished them with lucrative offices—leading positions in monasteries and convents, occasionally even a bishopric.

Charlemagne began his program of renewal in the churches, with the service of worship. They were an integral part of his system of rule. The first aspects he concentrated on were practical concerns like the hierarchical structure of the Church and ecclesiastical discipline, the lifestyle of clerics, and the basic knowledge required for the religious education of the people; deep theological questions took a back seat for the time being. Charlemagne used the clergy and the monasteries as an instrument of power, something he was able and entitled to do because he was at the same time the means by which they attained wealth and influence. In return, he relied on their ability to bring salvation through the power of prayer.

Instituting Practical Measures

Over the course of the turbulent period that had gone before, many norms of canon law had fallen into desuetude and no longer appeared to be valid. It was vital that they be renewed. The churches benefited directly from the revival of the culture of learning that was now taking place. Their reorganization followed patterns set in late antiquity, as revealed by records of legal convocations and historical traditions. Model texts like the *Dionysio-Hadriana*, which Charlemagne had requested in Rome in 774, the *Rule of St. Benedict* from Monte Cassino, and Paul the Deacon's collected sermons were kept safe in Charlemagne's court library and were transcribed there. These texts indicated the path that was to be followed. Although the king did not found any monasteries, he created numerous dioceses and established church provinces, taking the ancient models as his template. Charlemagne's intervention even went as far as tending to the upkeep and restoration of church buildings; he also naturally took steps against priests who had gone astray.[160] Overall, he pressed for the revival of the Church according to the principles laid down by the Church Fathers and insisted that their standards be imposed within his realm.

The objective was for the correct form of reverence before God to become established among the Frankish people. To achieve this, it was first necessary to impose justice and peace, as Charlemagne repeatedly proclaimed. With very few exceptions, the precise stage at which particular measures were taken, or how exactly they were implemented, is lost in the mist of time thanks to the lack of detailed historical records. Only isolated documents such as the capitulary of Herstal (779), the *Admonitio generalis* (789), and the capitulary of Frankfurt (794) are extant from the period of the king's reign. Penitentials became more widespread over time, and Roman law, alongside the collections of canon law, was of some significance in the reorganization of the Church, while, of course, the proscriptions noted in the Book of Deuteronomy (on marriage) were also binding on Christians. The occasional capitulary by a bishop that has survived down the ages—such as that written by Theodulf of Orléans—affords only rare insights into this or that diocese. The actual circumstances that pertained on the ground can barely be reconstructed.

What we can be sure of, though, is that no peace could prevail without justice. The sheer hardship, hunger, and poverty suffered by ordinary people cried out for it. To alleviate the situation, Charlemagne resorted to extraordinary measures: currency reform and an edict fixing the price of goods. Even money, then, was to serve the cause of peace. The reform that Charlemagne announced at the Synod of Frankfurt in 794 would, as it turned out, remain in force for centuries to come.[161] The new denarii, or pennies, broke with tradition in being heavier than earlier such coins. But they were designed to be used throughout the length and breadth of the empire, and over time this did indeed come about. As the report from the synod stated: "They carry our [i.e., Charlemagne's] name and are of pure silver and a good weight, and should anyone refuse to accept them in any shop, then he will be required to pay the necessary fine." Twelve of these denarii or pennies made a shilling, which became and remained a standard unit of accounting. Numerous finds of coins from this period indicate that the weight of the new denarius was set at around 1.7 grams of pure silver; before this, the penny was around 0.4 grams lighter. On this basis, throughout the empire regional weights and measures were aligned with the royal standard measure, and even arrangements involving paying in kind could now be standardized. Thus, in Saxony a one-year-old ox would henceforth "cost" as much as three bushels of wheat elsewhere, that is, twelve denarii or one shilling. The ratio of the value of silver to that of gold was 1:12.

One key aim of the monetary reform was to try to combat a famine that was raging at the time, as well as to forestall future such crises. It fixed the bulk weight of the most important types of grain in relation to one another via the common denominator of monetary value and regulated the maximum price for each. From now on, no one—either in times of plenty or in times of want—was allowed to sell grain for more than the set price per bushel. A bushel of wheat was expected to yield twelve wheat loaves, each weighing two pounds, which were to be sold for one penny apiece, a bushel of rye fifteen loaves, of barley twenty, and of oats twenty-five. Furthermore, cereals sold from royal estates were to be a third cheaper than otherwise. On the other hand, only what was not needed for the internal use of the estate would end up on the open market. The watchwords of the time, as noted in Einhard's biography, were "No one should die of hunger in Franconia," "Greed and avarice are to be suppressed," and "Avidity and greed must be stamped out" (chap. 34). The economic order and Christian commandments to love one's neighbor and observe the faith were to be brought into line with each other.

The king also turned his attention to the monastic system. Although this was hardly mentioned in the two capitularies of 779 and 789, it was not entirely ignored either. Those assembled in Frankfurt needed to address this issue in greater depth. The synod there issued the following resolutions: "Monks are not permitted to leave their monastery either to engage in secular legal proceedings or to attend court sittings, except in the manner prescribed by the *Rule of St. Benedict*" (chap. 11). "No one may become a hermit without the agreement of the appropriate bishop and abbot" (chap. 12). "According to the *Rule of St. Benedict,* the abbot should share sleeping quarters with the monks in his charge" (chap. 13). "We have heard that, driven by sheer greed, some abbots are demanding money from anyone entering their monastery"; the synod strictly forbade this practice (chap. 16). Where the king required it, an abbot should be appointed only with the express agreement of the relevant bishop (chap. 17). No abbot was permitted for whatever reason to blind or maim any of his monks; rather, he was to punish him in strict accordance with the *Benedictine Rule* (chap. 18). Not only monks but also clerics of all kinds were strictly forbidden to visit taverns (chap. 19).

Despite the central role the monasteries played in the religious life of early medieval Europe in commending people to God in their prayers, and the fact that the first "prayer confraternities," like the one established at Attigny[162] (to which the king did not belong, however), brought together bishops and abbots, no special rules governing monasteries were promulgated under Charlemagne. Even so, the privileges that the king handed down indicate the strong support and protection he gave the monasteries.

Yet many contradictory regulations were in circulation, a situation that demanded some clarification. In many cases, a monastery would find itself challenging the diocesan authority of the bishop who was responsible for it. The key question was to what extent monasteries, even in cases where they did not enjoy special exemption, were actually under the control of the diocesan bishop. Over time, many usages had been relaxed. The question does not appear to have been settled conclusively. Certainly the resolution passed at the Synod of Frankfurt in 794 (chap. 17), at which Charlemagne presided, namely, that each bishop had to agree to the appointment of an abbot by the king, tended to consolidate the power of the bishops.[163] Yet it seems that this demand was never implemented in practice, at least not under Charlemagne, leaving a situation where divergent practices coexisted.

Nevertheless, the king wished to see the monasteries adopt a regulated way of life without, it seems, expecting or requiring that any particular rule should be imposed on them. The capitulary of Herstal (779) and the *Admonitio generalis* (789) included only a very general call for the lives of monks to conform to a set of rules.[164] The manuscript of monastic rules that the king had requested from Abbot Theodemar of Monte Cassino in 787, which had supposedly been transcribed from the copy that St. Benedict was said to have written with his own hand,[165] may suggest a change in this matter. It was the only monastic rule we can definitely prove was known at the court of Charlemagne, while in Frankfurt the only talk was of the *Rule of St. Benedict*.

The king evidently longed for authenticity. However, the particular version of the *Benedictine Rule* that at that time was attributed to Monte Cassino and was subsequently accepted in Charlemagne's Aix was not the one that ultimately prevailed. It was characterized by a peculiar form of Vulgar Latin, which with the passage of time an increasing number of better-educated monks began to take issue with. Instead, a linguistically smoother version ultimately became the one that was generally adopted. This, the so-called *Textus receptus*, quickly became widespread.[166] But it was only after Charlemagne's investiture as emperor that the *Benedictine Rule* began to gain official precedence over other monastic rules in Carolingian legislation. Henceforth the domestic lives of monks in Charlemagne's realm were regulated primarily by this set of precepts, although this did not come about everywhere in the same way or at the same time.

The *Rule of St. Benedict* finally became the standard rule of monasticism in the reign of Louis the Pious. In bringing this about, Louis's spiritual adviser Benedict of Aniane ("the second Benedict") expressly did not refer back to the Aix specimen copy from Monte Cassino, with its partially offbeat Latin, but instead relied on the fruits of his own research. This culminated in the generally accepted and linguistically clean text of the *Benedictine Rule*. In addition, the abbot of Aniane and, following him, Emperor Louis demanded that when the rule was applied to the daily lives of monks, other common usages, insofar as they were widely observed, should also be taken into account.

The fruits of this particular aspect of Charlemagne's reform program soon became apparent. From the late 780s onward, reports of synods and capitularies revealed a new single-mindedness and scope in the measures enacted by the king. Fundamental questions of law and organization were addressed, although these ultimately never resulted in any coherent, self-contained body of legislation. Such systematic institutional thinking was as yet too unfamiliar. Moreover, the mass of tasks that needed to be taken in hand was simply too complex. Last but not least, despite increasing schooling in dialectics, there was still a lack of adequate conceptual categories for a comprehensive analytical analysis and differentiation of the ecclesiastical, social, and lordly spheres of existence. Those that were available operated primarily on a personal level. Even so, under Charlemagne we can observe an attempt to impose order that went far beyond any earlier such initiatives. This must be counted as a personal initiative on the part of the king, which harbored considerable future potential for modernization.

Opposition to and pitfalls inherent in this initiative soon became evident. Charlemagne's appeals for people to maintain the peace commenced at a remarkably early stage. They were aimed specifically at the major churches, leading to the surmise that these institutions must have lived in a state of repeatedly erupting conflict. Evidently the same deadly rivalry that kept the lay nobility in a state of high tension was also rife among bishops, abbots, and the secular clergy. The *Admonitio generalis* of 789 contained just such an appeal: "May peace, unity, and unanimity with the whole of the Christian communion reign among bishops, abbots, counts, stewards [*iudices*], and all people wherever they may be, great or small" (chap. 62); even the last decrees issued by Charlemagne were still repeating this message. The magnates who surrounded the king were to embody the principle of peace, while a general compact among the ordinary people was to safeguard it.[167]

With such readiness for conflict in evidence, protection for the Church was urgently called for, and Charlemagne duly granted it. This protection took the form of ensuring that the rule of law was upheld rather than that of any armed intervention. The churches concerned, especially the episcopal churches, were responsible for their own military protection, having as they all did vassals and armed men at their disposal. Rather, insofar as a conflict affected secular matters, the jurisdiction of the churches was protected against the king's intervention, including its internal organization in both spiritual and property-law terms. Then again, it was incumbent on the churches to assert their rights themselves. Charlemagne the warrior-king had never literally taken up arms in defense of a church—leaving aside Rome, that is. Generally, he was content to dispense the full grace of his royal privileges.

Despite significant losses, the monasteries and the convents actually retained the bulk of their holdings of historical documents. These institutions were of two kinds: on the one hand, royal convents and monasteries, and on the other, either aristocratic or episcopal foundations. The latter group could receive special royal privileges guaranteeing protection or immunity. Immunity was meant to prevent "public" (that is, royal) officeholders, including counts, from entering the property of the person who had been granted it, who took on sole responsibility for the tasks of internal jurisdiction and law enforcement. This ban was designed primarily to keep the peace; only the *missi dominici* were exempted from it. The royal monasteries—regardless of whether they were foundations of the royal family like, say, Prüm or Echternach, ones that had been bequeathed to the ruler (Lorsch, for example), or ones confiscated by him, like those in Bavaria after Duke Tassilo had been deposed—received royal protection. This was a clear expression of authority by the ruler, an intertwining of keeping the peace and exercising power. The founder of a religious institution and his heirs enjoyed the assurance of remembrance in the prayers of its monks and canons. But it was the master of the institution, namely, the king, who appointed the abbots, and who, as recompense for furnishing it with extensive and lavish material assistance, demanded various services for the king and tributes to him, the *servitium regis,* and generally that the monastery participate in some of the duties of royal authority.

This all demanded a constant monitoring of Church property, both that belonging to the monasteries and that of the convents and dioceses, along with its economic exploitation by the king. Charlemagne seems to have suggested or commanded that the organization and acquisition of Church property should proceed according to "Hufen" (*hobae;* standard tenements), that is, the basic operating unit of the smallholding (*mansus*), including a "division into tenements" (*Verhufung*) of the extensive Church manors according to the model of the royal estates. This process may be characterized as a bipartite production process, in which dependent operating units of differing legal status and differing economic potential were distinguished from land under the direct personal management of the landowner. Admittedly, this kind of schematism was never fully realized.[168] But the king did dispatch a number of messengers to take possession of the appropriate properties on the spot.

An indication of how this was enacted has been preserved, concerning the monastery of Fontanelle (at St-Wandrille in Normandy) and relating to the year 787: "This is the sum total of property of this monastery, which by order of the invincible King Charlemagne, in the twentieth year of his reign, the same year as the death of Abbot Wido, has been appropriated by Abbot Landric of Jumièges and Count Richard. To start with, there is the property that appears to be for the personal use of the monks and their accommodation: 1,326 undivided manses, 238 half-manses, 18 trade manses, making a total of 1,569 [*sic*]; in addition, there are 158 uncultivated manses and 39 mills. Property held in fee is as follows: 2,120 undivided manses, 40 half-manses, 235 trade manses, making a total of 2,395, plus 156 uncultivated, and 24 mills unoccupied. The grand total therefore amounts to 4,264 [*sic*] manses, not counting those that the lay abbot Wido allocated for use by the king's men or others."[169] The property assigned to the monks, which amounted to around two-fifths of the monastery's landholdings, could not be touched by outsiders, while a larger portion, fully half, of the property was at the disposal of the abbot, not least in order that he might be in a position to fulfill the monastery's duty of service to the Crown. If disputes arose, the king's decision was final.

The tracts of farmland called "hides" (*Hufen*) were not all equal. A "free hide" (*mansus ingenualis*) had to pay higher tributes to the landlord than a "servant's hide" (*mansus servilis*), although the latter was conversely obliged to provide compulsory labor, as a rule three days per week. The personal legal status of the hide owner remained fundamentally unaffected by this. An unfree person could till a "free hide," and vice versa. Alongside this property dispensed to tenant farmers, the landowner would also farm a large area himself, often as much as half his land, employing for the purpose unfree laborers with no land of their own (*mancipes*). This type of division into tenements—the second advantage that such an arrangement afforded the king—enabled the monarch to gain an overview of the complete inventory of an ecclesiastical manor, which was then recorded in the form of land registers. Listings of this kind allowed the productive capacity and organization of the land to be gauged—not least its economic potential for the Crown, the *servitium regis*. It may be for this very reason that Charlemagne strove so hard to implement the policy of division into tenements.

Bishops, and even secular magnates (the so-called lay abbots), could take on an abbacy without the monastery thereby leaving the royal sphere of control. This generally happened in recompense for services rendered to the king. Thus it was that Archchaplain Angilram, archbishop of Mainz, was at the same time abbot of the monasteries at Senones and St-Trond, while after Charlemagne's annexation of Bavaria he also took control of the abbey at Chiemsee. His successor as archchaplain, Archbishop Hildebald of Cologne, ran the foundation of Saints Cassius and Florentius in Koblenz and Mondsee Abbey in Bavaria.[170] Bishop Theodulf of Orléans, meanwhile, had control of several monasteries, including St-Benoît sur Loire (Fleury), which prided itself on having the true relics of St. Benedict of Nursia, while Theodulf's opponent, the deacon Alcuin, was head of the religious institution at Tours, as well as the abbeys at Ferrières and St. Lupus in Troyes.[171] As we have seen, Wido was lay abbot of St-Wandrille. Moreover, Angilbert of St-Riquier, who was a confidant and son-in-law of the king, was neither a cleric nor a monk. He also served Charlemagne in the capacity of envoy to Rome. Finally, Charlemagne's biographer Einhard, another layman, ran a number of abbeys from Ghent to Pavia, albeit only after Charlemagne's death and probably not all at the same time.[172]

The king assigned important functions within his system of rule not only to the bishops but also to the royal monasteries. Clerics served as royal messengers at their own expense. The abbots of the larger monasteries and the bishops were required to provide men for military service, as well as to perform the task of securing the empire's borders militarily (*wactae*). Above all, though, monks had to prepare themselves for missionary work. Numerous monasteries were pressed into service as rearward mission stations because they had all that was needed for this role: ample material and personnel resources, the necessary knowledge and skills—for which in turn the monastery schools were responsible—and plenty of experience in administration. Once again, Corbie must be cited in this context, a key institution, like Fulda, in the Christianization of Saxony. The first outstanding Saxon monastery, Corvey on the River Weser, or New Corbie (Nova Corbeia), was, as its name indicates, founded by monks from Corbie during the abbacy of Adalhard and in collaboration with his brother Wala, who was the son of a Saxon woman, although this came about only after Charlemagne's death and the resulting rehabilitation of these two cousins of his by his son Louis the Pious (822). This foundation, though, accorded completely with the intentions of Charlemagne in his reform program.[173]

Even Priests Clash

It must be conceded, though, that no injunction to keep the peace or any form of protection of the Church could prevent the nobility from warring among themselves. And the upper echelons of the clergy showed themselves to be no less ready to engage in conflict than the lay aristocracy, from whose ranks most clerics came anyhow. Dissent about Church constitutions and monastic practices, as well as about laws, status, and proximity to the king, were all the order of the day. Experience taught Alcuin, for example, a sad lesson: "There is so much envy and dishonesty among people! You can always find plenty of friends around the dinner table, but few in a crisis." The Anglo-Saxon advised a young pupil of his who was about to travel to Italy that he should always act in a straightforward and truthful way. God's blessing would grow from such obedience to Christian values; otherwise perdition threatened. Peter and Judas, both apostles of the Lord, received diametrically opposed deserts. While Peter was raised to prince of the apostles, Judas was damned to Hell and the Prince of Demons.[174] Alcuin's bitter realization was that only a small degree separated good and evil.

Yet how was peace to inhabit the land when the magnates of the realm, scorning all the dangers of the afterlife, were locked in deadly conflict with one another? Intense rivalry, envy of each other's property, and the stress of vying for the king's approval led to constant clashes between the counts and other important secular figures, as well as between senior clerics. The most infamous such clash was the ugly rivalry between the two outstanding foreign scholars at Charlemagne's court, Alcuin of York (latterly of Tours) and Theodulf of Orléans.[175] Their conflict dragged on for years as they competed for the king's grace and favor. They even deployed poetry as a weapon, vying to compose an epitaph for Charlemagne's "friend" Pope Hadrian.[176] Whose verses would ultimately be immortalized on the pontiff's tomb at St. Peter's Basilica in Rome? On that occasion, Alcuin emerged victorious.

Charlemagne had declared the winner, but the animosity between the two scholars continued to grow. With bitter irony, Theodulf taunted his rival, portraying Alcuin sitting at the king's table, eagerly grasping "with mouth and hand" at the regal dishes laid out before him: "*Aut si, Bacche, tui, aut Cerealis pocla liquoris / Porgere praecipiat, fors et utrumque volet . . . / Quo melius doceat, melius sua fistula cantet*" (If he [Alcuin] calls for cups of thy liquor [wine] to be brought forth, O Bacchus, or cups of the liquor of corn [beer] / And perhaps partakes of both . . . / It is in order that he might teach better, or play a sweeter tune on his pipe); "*Este procul pultes, et lactis massa coacti, / Sed pigmentati sis prope mensa cibi*" (Take away this porridge and these curds of soured milk, / And bring some well-spiced meat to the table!).[177] Maybe Theodulf was accusing the aging Anglo-Saxon here of being toothless, or of habitually overindulging in alcohol, like the Irish. Whatever the case, the Visigothic writer's ridicule was deeply unpleasant.

Alcuin also scored a significant victory in the contest over the "whole" Bible, that is, the collection of all the books of the Bible into a single edition. Although the distant future would come to value Theodulf's small codex and critical text of the Bible more highly, for now the heavy tome edited by Alcuin won the day.[178] Before long, this dispute between these two leading figures would erupt into a major scandal. In 802, two years before Alcuin's death, a cleric who had been convicted of a criminal offense in Orléans managed to escape from prison and, on the justified assumption that he would find a warm welcome there, took refuge with Alcuin, seeking sanctuary in the church of the Abbey of St. Martin. Once there, the man is said to have demanded reconciliation and called on the king's court of justice to hear his plea.

Theodulf reacted by dispatching armed men to Tours, the city's arch-bishop intervened, and unrest broke out. Through his friends at the king's court, the Anglo-Saxon scholar now lobbied to have Charlemagne preside over a hearing to determine whether it would be right and proper if the accused were to be abducted by force from the church and taken back to jail. Charlemagne's response was as unequivocal as it was unfavorable: he berated Alcuin, the eminent scholar, and the canons of Tours for defying orders and not immediately sending the wrongdoer back to Orléans; he commanded that they were to do precisely that without more ado: "He is to be sent back to the judge before whom he was accused, who sentenced him and sent him to jail, and from whose prison he absconded." However, the monks and clerics who had defied the emperor's express orders were now to appear before him, Charlemagne, in person and answer for their ac-tions.[179] Exactly what the guilty man had done was not reported; it was ir-relevant. Rather, the crucial thing was to arbitrate between the ecclesiastical right of asylum and the proper jurisdiction of the diocesan bishop. Charle-magne came down in favor of the Church hierarchy; order took precedence over asylum.

Rivalry of this kind between clerics also held potential danger for the king or emperor. It threatened the cohesion of the empire, as indeed would later become clear during the reign of Louis the Pious.

A conflict between abbots could be no less dangerous. The role of the largest monasteries was not confined just to praying for peace and for the salvation of their founders and the emperor; at the same time, they were also major landowners and were required to supply troops. Their abbots joined military campaigns and took part in consultations at the royal court. Dis-sent within their ranks affected the decisions made by the king, the synods, and the meetings of the king with his chief princes. Disputes could break out over questions of property ownership or personal matters or arise from disagreements about divergent practices or different religious observances or how the *Rule of St. Benedict* was to be squared with the practical de-mands of everyday life.

It was on this last question that Adalhard of Corbie and Benedict of Aniane clashed at the Synod of Aix in November 802. Adalhard was a close confidant of Charlemagne and had become one of his principal advisers, while Benedict had served the king's son Louis during his time as king of Aquitaine, where he had emerged as a staunch reformer of the monasteries within the territory. It was said that Charlemagne's cousin Adalhard incited him to take action against Benedict, threatening to have him deposed and exiled. But Charlemagne supposedly confirmed Benedict in his office, gave him the "kiss of peace," and passed him a goblet of wine with his own hands. This son of a Visigothic count also had a powerful champion at court in the margrave William of Gellone, one of Charlemagne's most successful military commanders.[180]

Both of these high-profile conflicts reveal that Frankish monasteries too were part and parcel of the agonal society of the age, which was riven with bitter rivalries. Conflicts between religious institutions inevitably spilled over into the wider society, something that Charlemagne could not always prevent through prudent intervention. Initially, the conflict between Adalhard and Benedict ended with no real damage, but after the emperor's death, it erupted far more devastatingly than ever before, sending Adalhard into years of banishment, his brother Wala into a monastery, and their nephew Bernard, Charlemagne's grandson, to his death, not to mention driving the empire as a whole to the brink of catastrophe.

These two abbots had fallen out over the customs that monasteries should be observing, for instance, the question of how long the probationary period should be before novices were permitted to take their vows, be tonsured, and be received into holy orders. In strict accordance with the *Benedictine Rule,* the abbot of Aniane called for it to be one year, while his colleague from Corbie argued in favor of an unspecified shorter period, perhaps as short as two months.[181] Furthermore, the refectory rules at the renowned Picardy monastery, which permitted paupers and strangers—but not rich noblemen—to eat with the monks did not correspond with the expectations of the Visigothic abbot, who came from a closed order. When high-ranking guests visited Corbie, Adalhard would dine separately with them in the abbot's house. Moreover, under Adalhard's regime, in contrast to what happened elsewhere, monks who had fled the monastery for fear of punishment only to return were required to do penance before they were allowed to take their place among the brothers once more. This rigorous exercise of discipline was reminiscent of Charlemagne's aforementioned decision against Alcuin. Various other differences of this kind further stoked the controversy. Charlemagne's cousin did not fundamentally question the validity of the *Benedictine Rule* but simply called for greater autonomy for individual monasteries—that is, for abbots—in determining the precise way in which the rule would be implemented. Ultimately, the exegetical differences and the various differing customs for which both abbots agitated may well have been emblematic of other such conflicts, that is, the deadly rivalry between two high-aristocratic kinship groups that were jostling for decisive power and influence.

At the synod at Aix, which actually met as two separate partial synods for lay clergy and monks, respectively, Charlemagne had the canonical statutes, papal decretals, and the *Benedictine Rule* read out for clarification. After all, the court library contained the manuscripts of these works that Charlemagne had once acquired at Monte Cassino, which were widely regarded as a direct transcription of the *codex authenticus* St. Benedict had supposedly written in his own hand.[182] It was decreed that whatever had been done formerly that was against the *Rule* should now be made good according to its precepts. The *Chronicle of Moissac* even went so far— no doubt under Benedict of Aniane's instruction—as to maintain that the emperor had decreed that throughout the empire, and in imitation of the model established by the Roman Church, the Liturgy of Hours should now be sung in the way prescribed in those monasteries that observed the *Benedictine Rule*.[183]

The two conflicts of Alcuin versus Theodulf and Adalhard versus Benedict, each involving the participation of confidants close to the emperor, shows how Charlemagne exercised his ecclesiastical authority in practice. He gave precedence to the legal norm of episcopal disciplinary power against individual clerics over the rights of a foreign church. In this way, the emperor reinforced the legislative power of episcopal judicial authority. But Charlemagne was no less adept at reining in the conflicting forces within the aristocratic society of his age. A gracious gesture on the emperor's part saved Benedict of Aniane from humiliation, insofar as the public reading and affirmation of the *Benedictine Rule*—if this did indeed happen in the way the Moissac annalist described it—appeared to accommodate his views without actually diminishing or even decisively weakening Adalhard's position. In the case of both disputes, Charlemagne exploited the rivalry between his magnates to consolidate his own position of power. Sometimes he would play people off against each other without jeopardizing their loyalty, while at others he would placate them without actually taking sides.

Events in the wider realm were concentrated and intensified at the royal court. In consequence, the call for peace, unity, and love that presently began to issue year in and year out from the synods and the imperial assemblies became all the more insistent. Even at the court, indeed, particularly there, envy and competition were rife among the magnates of the realm, provoking violent clashes. The court was where they had to come to arrangements with the king's closest family, the queen's relatives, and the trusted allies of the king's sons and was the place where offices, honors, and gifts were bestowed. It was where they had to account for their actions and where judgment was passed, but all too often the prevailing atmosphere there was one of mutual and potentially violent mistrust.

The teachings of the Church Fathers came to be held up as a model for the king, the clergy, secular magnates, and the people alike. In particular, the capitularies, the first mirrors of princes, and other contemporary writings abounded with references to the reading of St. Augustine's *City of God,* with its powerful advocacy of justice and peace. After all, in the absence of justice, kingdoms would become nothing but large, organized bands of robbers. But enunciation of the concept of justice was not confined to abstract theories. Instead, its advocates traced the interrelationship among life, actions, knowledge, and faith and demanded that rulers take ultimate responsibility for all these spheres. They expressly called for rulers who would "make their power the handmaid of God's majesty by using it for the greatest possible extension of His worship" (*Dei cultum*) and who would "fear, love, and worship God."[184] Of course, this was far from being common practice at the time. But where such core values did become established as principles of kingship, they did at least manage to curb despotism and violence without, of course, eradicating them entirely.

Despite these high-minded intentions, there would doubtless have been many occasions on which opponents of Charlemagne returned to their quarters or houses angry, upset, and plotting revenge after being granted furlough by the king. Many of them—as Einhard is thought to have done at that time—would already have acquired their own property in the palace city of Aix-la-Chapelle.[185] This was a wise move, since with advancing age Charlemagne left the city with its hot thermal springs less and less, obliging his advisers to increasingly come and visit him there. Aix became *the* royal palace for the king and for his magnates alike. It was there that they met, exchanged experiences, and planned concerted action. And this made it essential that peace be maintained there.

6

THE ROYAL COURT

CHARLEMAGNE WAS RELAXING in his bathing pool, as he was so fond of doing. After swimming a couple of lengths, he was now leaning on the poolside. He was not alone; several courtiers were also bathing with him. He beckoned Alcuin over: "Revered Master Alcuin, God has seen fit to bring you back to us. Allow me to ask you a few questions. If I remember correctly, you once said . . ." A doctrinal discussion then ensued between the two men, in the year 796/797, which the Anglo-Saxon scholar later worked up into an instructional dialogue. Charlemagne loved the relaxed mood, the conviviality around the bathing pool, and the learned conversation. And in general, he loved the warm water that flowed up out of the ground from thermal springs. He loved this place, which gave him so much pleasure, in that special way that is only ever reserved for one particular location. In his case, it was Aix-la-Chapelle (Aachen), the site of his palace. He enjoyed the way it nestled in its gently undulating valley, its mild climate all year round, the favorable location of his palace among the properties of his immediate family, its proximity to well-stocked hunting grounds nearby, and the possibilities it afforded for horse breeding. He spent time here as often as he could. Plagued by gout, he sought relief after hunting, campaigning, or long arduous journeys on horseback in the warm water of the pool, where he would relax and engage in conversation.

The warm water did him good. His sons, his courtiers, his friends, and even his bodyguard all bathed alongside him. The king invited them specially to indulge in this pleasure. It is said that more than one hundred people at a time would sometimes splash about there. But Charlemagne was the master of them all at swimming. It must have been quite a spectacle. Einhard, who reported it (chap. 22), may well have attended the bathing parties now and then; he was a man of small stature, and perhaps the others teased him about his short limbs. There was no mention in the biography of the king's daughters or of the other ladies at court. Did they not bathe? Or was there a dedicated ladies' bathing day? Or a separate pool for them? We may speculate whether the princesses cast stolen glances at the men as they bathed. Whatever the case, we do know that Charlemagne thoroughly enjoyed bathing.

Alcuin recalled sitting alongside his master "in a warm bath of fresh water" and explaining biblical numerology to him. The tutor wrote this as a reminder to another of his pupils, who had apparently witnessed the scene.[1] There was policy consultation during the royal ablutions. Did Charlemagne rule his kingdom from his bath? As a rule, did he have his closest advisers convey their most urgent announcements to him while he was luxuriating in the steam of the hot springs? Ensconced in the warm water, did he reach important decisions on what was right and wrong, on war and peace, and on the fate of the peoples within his realm? Lying back, did he listen contentedly to the male singers (again, there was no mention of female singers) and revel in the idea of the courtly role-playing game that declared him to be King David? The original David, the monarch who delighted in playing the harp, also looked down from the roof of his palace onto a pool and, finding himself enthralled by the sight of the beautiful Bathsheba bathing, fell instantly in love with her, thereby bringing ruin down on his kingdom (2 Samuel 11). The new David was more circumspect, but he still loved beautiful women, bathing, and songs:

Surge, meo domino dulces fac, fistula, versus.
David amat versus, surge et fac, fistula, versus![2]

(Go to it, then, pipes, play sweet music for my master.
David loves songs, so go to it, pipes, play your music!)

Charlemagne's friends were allowed to take part in the courtly entertainments. Gratitude for this came in the form of this homage from afar in verse form. It also contained a veiled homage to Charlemagne's daughter Bertha, "who deserves all the muses' songs." Who would have suspected that these few words harbored a declaration of love? Certainly, there was no further mention of it in the rest of the song. No personal or confidential message for the distant sweetheart, who would ultimately bear the poet Angilbert—known at the Carolingian court as "Homer"—two sons. In any event, she would not have been allowed to participate in activities around the bathing pool; nor was there any song about bathing. Praise of the ruler and of the sublime life at court took a highly ritualized, ossified form. All intimacy, everything mundane, and all proximity to real life appeared to have been banished.

There were many poems that were composed for the court, and that were doubtless also recited and sung there, but not one single set of verses committed to parchment treated the topic of friendship, or love, or the proclivities that change a person's innermost being and have the power to bind together a man and a woman. Such expressions of emotion still lay dormant at this stage, to awaken only in the distant future. Not even the most pretentious pseudonym could enable a poet to broach such subjects. How different things were at the courts of Córdoba and Baghdad, where poems boldly signed with their creators' names were not only widely disseminated but also precisely captured human emotions and sang openly of love. By contrast, the tone of works presented at Charlemagne's court was one of lofty praise of the ruler teamed with proof of the new learning. The hexametric verses sent by Angilbert culminated in praise of God. "David loves Christ, Christ is the glory of David" (*David amat Christum, Christus est gloria David*). Just as, when bathing, Charlemagne was still intent on gaining serious insight into religious symbolism, so he expected even the most panegyrical poetry to reflect his own God-fearing piety.

But not just that. The court was characterized by strangely erotic and homoerotic goings-on. After all, David was not merely the victor over Goliath, a hero and monarch, the conqueror of Jerusalem, the unifier of kingdoms, and the progenitor of Jesus, nor was he just the king with the harp; he was also the sinner who consorted with Bathsheba and the guilt-ridden adulterer who sent her husband to his death. If one counted up, one could find the names of eight women in the books of the Bible with whom King David had relations; Charlemagne also indulged in such pleasures and even, according to Einhard (chap. 18), had two more "concubines" than his biblical counterpart. The notion of the powerful king of the Franks as the new King David combined praise with covert criticism, the sayable with the unsayable, the image of the great illustrious ruler with that of a womanizer who faced atonement and punishment for his deeds, whose son rose up against him, and who was not permitted by God to construct a temple (1 Chronicles 28:3). Likewise, beneath the praise of the Frankish David there also lurked much fear and worry.

Charlemagne, then, loved women, including his daughters. And they in turn loved life. The king had a total of five wives, whom he married in succession and who at least temporarily were regarded as legitimate. These were, in chronological order, Himiltrud; the unnamed daughter of the Lombard king Desiderius; Hildegard; Fastrada; and finally Liutgard. After the last's death on 4 June 800, he made do with a succession of concubines, according to Einhard. He mentions four of these by name in chapter 18 of his biography; he almost certainly knew these women personally, whereas a fifth woman he mentions, who undoubtedly enjoyed the king's favor before his time at court, he knew only as the mother of Hruodhaid.

Charlemagne's emotional relationship with his spouses is obscured by a distinct lack of information. None of his wives was the subject of any major eulogy; Theodulf devoted just a handful of verses to Liutgard in the great courtly poetry he wrote in 796 (*Carmen* 25, verses 83–90), where he refers to her as *virago* (courageous woman) rather than *regina* (queen). There, he portrays her as generous, indulgent, friendly, willing to learn (she was evidently very young), and innately gifted (*ingenuae artes mentis*).[3] At no point is there any talk or hint of romantic love. And not a word was written about any mistresses Charlemagne may have kept alongside his official marriages. Perhaps they never existed? Or was Einhard ill-informed on this point?[4] Every aristocratic marriage at this time was entered into with an eye to the social advantages it might bring. The ladies chosen were expected to expand the king's entourage and broaden and consolidate his power base; in short, they were intended to add more supporters to the royal entourage. Therefore, every new marriage slightly altered the mix of courtly society and the network of power relationships.

Charlemagne shared his camp with these women. We may speculate whether he loved any of them or, conversely, whether any of them loved him, that is, loved in a life-transforming way. Indeed, did he even expect this? There is nothing about this in the records, but we must seriously doubt it. Even the posthumous forms of address like "most beloved" or "dearest wife"—which appear in the document endowing the monastery of St. Arnulf in Metz, the burial place of Charlemagne's third wife, Hildegard (who later was the first to be seen as legitimate, although in strict canon-law terms she was not)—must be seen as formulaic and reveal nothing. "Dear" (*cara*) and "sweet" (*dulcis*) were stock courtly attributes, not instances of personal, emotionally charged language.[5] Even Charlemagne's concerned inquiry in a letter about the health of his "beloved and most adorable wife" Fastrada loses its private character when the letter goes on in precisely the same vein to send "aside from the queen, to our most sweet daughters and the rest of our followers who are with you, our most heartfelt wishes for good health."[6] Subjective emotional ties within court society vanished behind the objective obligations of Christian love of kith and kin or friends. As a result—aside from the repercussions of jealousy and mutual envy among the emperor's paladins—these remain more or less hidden from us. No love song in either Latin or Old High German survives from this period. Even if such songs existed, they were not deemed worthy of being consigned to parchment. The language of liturgy and prayer, the language of reason, and the language of laudatory address were all nurtured and practiced at court, but not the language of human love.

The king selected his women without respecting ecclesiastical marriage law but rather with power-political considerations in mind. He dismissed them when it seemed opportune to do so and circumstances allowed. Nor did they all die prematurely by any means. The first, Himiltrud, the mother of his eldest son, Pepin, may well have still been alive when he married his second wife, the daughter of the Lombard king Desiderius. Growing tired of her, in turn, after just a year, in an act tantamount to a declaration of war, he sent her back to her father in order to be able to marry his third spouse; Himiltrud may even have outlived this wife, Hildegard. Hildegard and her successor, Fastrada, were in fact the only two wives of Charlemagne to die before he moved on to the next. Could it have been the case that the unnamed Lombard princess was still living in some Frankish convent when these two successive wives married the king, and was required in each case to pray for the new queen?

Besides, Charlemagne the lord and master required a wife as a homemaker in order to give his court a center as an institution. We know from capitularies—decrees issued by the king—and from Hincmar of Reims's *De ordine palatii* (On the governance of the palace, a treatise on systems of government and the duties of a sovereign written in 882) what a high position the queen occupied there, and how much responsibility devolved to her in, say, the administration of the royal estates as a whole. Similarly, on the estates of the imperial nobility, wives, as mistresses of the household, had far-reaching authority. Charlemagne expressly stipulated, "It is our wish that whatever we or the queen may order any of our stewards [*iudices*] to do, they shall carry out in full in accordance with our instructions [*placitum*]. And whoever falls short in this task through negligence, let him abstain from drinking wine from the moment he is told to do so until he comes into our presence or the presence of the queen and seeks forgiveness from us." This directive formed part of the *Capitulare de villis*.[7]

In this capitulary, the king makes it clear that he shares power with his consort within the household. Only after his coronation as emperor did Charlemagne go without a homemaker-wife and content himself with mistresses instead. Einhard knew them all by name. Yet who in this case was the "first lady" of the court and controlled the administration of the estates can no longer be determined by modern historians. Perhaps Charlemagne's sister Gisela, or his cousin Gundrada—Adalhard's sister, who was resident at the court—or even one of his own daughters assumed the role of homemaker. Whoever she was, she was faced with a task that was anything but leisurely. Even when she was heavily pregnant, the queen would travel throughout the realm with her husband; the daughters also accompanied them, while the sons were raised and educated in the duties of kingship from a very early age outside the confines of the court.

The queen was always apt to exert influence in political affairs. Such interventions were a way of manifesting the rank and status of her clan, but only occasional evidence survives of them. Charlemagne's mother, Bertrada, intervened repeatedly in the decisions of her two sons, with varying degrees of success. Charlemagne's wives also had their say. There is a remarkable appreciation of Queen Hildegard, who came from the family of the dukes of Alemannia, in the epitaph composed by Paul the Deacon on her death (783). It maintains that she was the only person worthy of holding the golden scepters of multiple monarchy in her hands: "*Tu sola inventa es, fueris quae digna tenere / Multiplicis regni aurea sceptra manu*."[8] With these verses, the Lombard scholar went beyond customary panegyrics to queens. This queen, who wielded the scepter, was in some measure a ruler too, or at least ought to be and deserved to be. Her successor at Charlemagne's side, Queen Fastrada, would have been unlikely to have demanded any less of a right to intervene or to have held fewer scepters than her predecessor. Quite the contrary, in fact: her husband empowered her with a number of individual assignments over which she had sovereign authority.[9] The fact that she seems to have exercised considerable power hints at influential kinship, although this is untraceable nowadays.

A memorable scandal in Charlemagne's closest family is associated with the name of Fastrada. This took place in 792 and was remembered for many decades thereafter. It was said that the "cruelty" of Queen Fastrada had driven Charlemagne's eldest son, Pepin, who supposedly was hunchbacked, to rebel. The background details of this "conspiracy" are somewhat confused. Even as late as 780, Pepin was being spoken of by the annalist of Lorsch Abbey (who had close ties to the throne) as a legitimate son of the king, and hence as the heir apparent.[10] The insurrection saw Pepin the Hunchback form an alliance with an influential group of "young and old Franks."

The biblical comparison the Lorsch annalist makes between the seditious prince and the figure of Abimelech (Judges 8–9) alludes to the role played by the relatives and brothers of Pepin's mother, Himiltrud, as confederates of the rebellious king's son.[11] Just before the uprising, in 791–792, in Freising—in other words, in the territory of Bavaria only recently subjugated by the Carolingian Empire—the young Pepin was actually being celebrated as "rex Pippinus."[12] At that time, then, after the toppling of the Agilolfing dynasty, might it have been Charlemagne's intention to make the unfortunate Pepin a subsidiary ruler in Bavaria? Or had a portion of Francia, the heartland of Charlemagne's realm, already been set aside for him? And did the "cruel" Fastrada, who hailed from the eastern territories of the Frankish kingdom, perhaps find herself bitterly opposed to such a plan in the vain hope that she might one day bear the king a son? After all, she would not have been the first stepmother in history to react in such a way.

Such an explanation is by no means wholly implausible, but the details of this incident are sadly lacking. The queen's implacable "cruelty" supposedly warped Charlemagne's customary leniency; in any event, three decades after these occurrences and in a time of growing tension among members of the Carolingian dynasty, this was how the elderly Einhard (chap. 20) chose to defend his hero's course of action. The rebel Pepin was quickly defeated, forcibly tonsured, and incarcerated in Prüm Abbey to spent the rest of his days as a monk; he died there eighteen years later. Never before, according to Einhard, had the king responded with such brutality. Charlemagne's biographer evidently had a deep dislike of his fellow East Frank Fastrada. Granted, she had died in 794 and had been buried in Mainz; she did not, as it happened, bring a son into the world, and Einhard presumably owed her nothing. But was personal animosity alone enough to explain why Einhard might sharpen his pen to write this indictment of the queen? And was the dead Fastrada the real target of this censure?

For, just then, history appeared to be repeating itself. Conspiracy, thoughts of murder, civil war among the Franks, and a stepmother's provocative cruelty to the son of a former wife of her husband—the same constellation of events that had blighted 792 was also present in the years leading up to 830, when Einhard was sharpening his quills and preparing to direct his Charlemagne biography as a warning from history at the Carolingian court of his day, where the beautiful Judith of Bavaria was pressuring her husband, Louis the Pious, to favor her son to the detriment of her stepsons. Einhard anticipated what the consequences of this would be and warned about them with a historical example that would have been well known at court. In the event, he would be proved right. This time, too, insurrection and civil war were not long in coming; once again, sons rose up against their father, although on this occasion their revolt was to usher in the end of the Carolingian Empire. Disillusioned, Einhard withdrew from the court.

Fastrada's "cruelty"—as everyone knew—was cut short by her death soon after Pepin's revolt. Moreover, Charlemagne's biographer was able to summon up the courage to lambast Fastrada only because she was not the mother of the reigning emperor, and even then only long after her husband, Charlemagne, had departed this life. Even the earlier revolt by the Thuringian warlord Hardrat reportedly met with a harsh response from Fastrada. This broke out, as I have already noted, in 786, a few years after her marriage to Charlemagne.[13] Its causes appear to be even more mysterious than those of Pepin's revolt against his father, but this much is clear: the nobility and princes did not lead a tranquil life; there were pitfalls and dangers at every turn, and queens could decide their fate.

In some cases, at a tender age Charlemagne's sons were sent away to the royal domains assigned to them, where they were brought up, far removed from their father and his court at Aix. Initially, the only male offspring to remain in close proximity to the king were the elder Pepin, Charlemagne's son by Himiltrud (subsequently, as we have seen, rumors began to spread that he was hunchbacked, in other words, unfit to rule), and the second-born, the eldest son of Queen Hildegard, who bore the king's own name. We have already seen what became of Pepin. As for Charles the Younger, he was admonished and warned by Theodulf of Orléans in various satirical verses disguised as panegyrics.[14] Lampooning Alcuin, Theodulf wrote a parody of the Roman poet Virgil's *Second Eclogue,* which had as its subject the love of the shepherd Corydon for the young boy Alexis. In Theodulf's ironic portrayal, the prince was now depicted playing Corydon's flute, wooing his lover with laments of "*Ah Mochanaz, Mochanaz,*" and showering him with gifts of barley, salt, hay, and colorful clothes. But as the Visigothic scholar knew only too well, the name *Mochanaz* was derived from the Arabic *muhannat,* a term for a sodomite, in a Christian context a lover in a homoerotic relationship. This figure may possibly be identified with Osulf, a pupil of Alcuin, whom his tutor had already reprimanded for his "boyish faults"[15] and who was frequently to be seen around the court of Charlemagne and in the retinue of Charles the Younger.[16]

Homoerotic relationships were not uncommon, then, within the closest circle of the king's son (including Charles himself) and the royal court in Aix. It was an open secret of which everyone was fully aware, and the reputation of Alcuin's pupil was well known. It appears that Charlemagne, who took a liberal attitude where love affairs were concerned, was not offended by his son's proclivities. Or was it rather the case that his concerns over the feared failure of his eldest son to produce an heir prompted him to commission Theodulf's poem as a way of reining Charles in? Whatever the case, homoerotic experiences were very familiar at this court, which fostered all manner of friendships between scholars. Alcuin himself, the revered cleric, may have spoken from experience in his criticism of Osulf. In late 790, he wrote ecstatically to his friend Bishop Arn of Salzburg: "Oh, I am yearning for the time when I might put my longing arms around your neck and caress it with my fingers. . . . How eagerly I would kiss not only your eyes, ears, and mouth but also each finger and toe not once but many times."[17]

The younger Pepin, who had been granted Italy as a kingdom, and his brother Louis, who had sovereignty over Aquitaine, were raised in those regions, far from their father's court. Pepin lived mostly in Verona, from where he could easily cross the Alps; Louis, meanwhile, moved annually among his four palaces. These two sons of Charlemagne were required to present themselves as kings even in childhood and boyhood. Charlemagne's cousin Adalhard of Corbie accompanied Pepin across the Alps and, as his brother Wala also did subsequently, remained in Italy alongside Pepin for some time, acting as his adviser. Louis found an influential aide in the figure of Benedict, the son of a Visigothic count and later abbot of Aniane, who became a rival of Adalhard and who was responsible for the revival of the *Benedictine Rule.* No one could have anticipated that these appointments would set future conflicts in train.

This atmosphere was not calculated to foster any kind of parental love; instead, what was inculcated was fear of the emperor. Louis's decades-long absence from his father's court, to which he was summoned at best only infrequently to give a "report" of his realm, really did succeed in alienating him from his father, who was more interested in indulging in love affairs. For his part, after 778 Charlemagne gave Aquitaine, the territory south of the Loire, and in particular the far south of Gallia a wide berth. The leading aristocrats of the region appear to have reoriented themselves toward the court of the young Louis, although the precise nature of their allegiance is unclear.[18] The two contemporary descriptions of the life of this son of Charlemagne almost completely pass over Louis's early years, and apart from a handful of documents and various isolated bits of information, other accounts of his life are simply not available. All the same, it appears that under Louis's rule, a kind of Aquitainian national consciousness began to develop, which manifested itself more clearly over the course of the ninth century. This was, as far as we can tell, not focused on the personality of the king but rather on the institution of the royal court of Aquitaine.

The three youngest sons of Charlemagne—Hugo, Drogo, and Theodoric—who were all born after 800, remained at the court in Aix until their father's death. After their mistrustful brother with the irritating soubriquet "the Pious" became emperor, he initially allowed them to stay at the court and even made them his "table companions," as his nephew Nithard (1.2) reported. But after a brief time—barely three years—out of fear of unrest after the violent death of King Bernard of Italy, the boys were forcibly tonsured and sent to monasteries in order to exclude them permanently from any future struggles over the succession.[19] In the light of this, might the name Louis the Cruel have been more fitting?

At least seven daughters were born to Charlemagne; renowned for their vivacity and the teasing games they played around the court, they became known as the "little crowned doves." Alcuin warned one Nathanael, a young cleric of his acquaintance, about them: "My beloved son, may your life remain blameless in the eyes of God and men, inasmuch as this is possible. Let not the crowned doves that flit about in the chambers of the palace come to your windows, nor allow them, like wild horses, to break in at the door of your chamber. Do not occupy yourself with dancing bears, but instead pay attention to psalm-singing priests."[20] According to Alcuin's experience, newcomers at court were evidently given a once-over with a view to erotic adventures. Around the same time, Alcuin also encouraged Gundrada, Adalhard of Corbie's sister, who lived at court and had taken the veil, to act as a model of chastity to the virgins there, namely, the king's daughters, so they might become as noble in their behavior as they were noble by birth, and not give themselves over to the pleasures of the flesh but instead devote themselves to the teachings of Christ, doing penance for their earlier sins and avoiding committing any future transgressions. God could also look into our innermost thoughts, he told her.[21] This admonitory plea by Alcuin was, it appeared, of the utmost urgency. Had Gundrada perhaps assumed the role of mother to these very young girls after the death of Queen Liutgard? Yet this was all to no avail, as it turned out. One after the other, the princesses became pregnant, although none of them was betrothed.

Indeed, these daughters of Charlemagne were so alluring, young, and vivacious that the king, in the wake of the failed betrothal of Rotrude to Constantine VI, was determined not to give them to any other foreign princes or even to any of his own magnates as wives, but rather always to keep them close at hand; but for precisely this reason, they were to bring him dreadful misfortune. Einhard (chap. 19) alludes to these problems but does not go into detail. Even so, his most illustrious reader, Emperor Louis, would have known full well what the paladin was talking about. Two of these "crowned doves" bore sons. One of the girls, Bertha, was made pregnant by the lay abbot Angilbert, who was a member of the court chapel and who may possibly have taken minor holy orders,[22] while the other, Rotrude, was impregnated by Count Rorico. A third man, a certain Hodoin, who was also almost certainly a lover of a royal princess, was put to death in 814 when the new emperor Louis set about reforming his father's court, and a suspected fourth was blinded. A fifth man, who may have gone by the name of Richwin and was one of the royal entourage who signed and witnessed the emperor's last will and testament, sired another illegitimate grandson of Charlemagne called Richbod.[23] So, once they reached the age of sexual maturity, all these young ladies took lovers; their father must have tolerated this, for he did not lock them away.[24] Charlemagne's court was thus at the same time devout and full of erotic intrigue, as well as being intellectual but thoroughly human. A court, perhaps, made in the emperor's own innermost image?

The Royal Center of Power

The royal court did not just bring the king's family together in one place. It was also the center of power, and initially, it was not confined to one location. Anyone entitled to participate in any shape or form in upholding royal authority congregated there. Rumors, information, and learning were disseminated from there, and it was also the epicenter of intrigues. At various times, all the leading players of the Carolingian Empire made an appearance: Petrus Pisanus, Paul the Deacon, Alcuin, Theodulf, Hildebald, Adalhard, Arn, Einhard, the young Hrabanus Maurus, and all the many others—eminent clerics and secular magnates alike, although on some occasions, they would have been seen clad only in underpants or a loincloth, luxuriating in the communal baths. "He is more righteous and more powerful than them all. Exhibiting great grace and favor, he dubs them dukes or counts" was how one anonymous epic poet characterized the court of Charlemagne.[25] Theodulf, meanwhile, listed the lords and ladies at court in 796 in more or less hierarchical order: first and foremost the king, his sons and daughters, then his queen, followed by the chamberlain Meginfrid, Archbishop Hildebald, Alcuin, Archbishop Riculf, and the chancellor Ercambald. Even Einhard, bustling around like an ant on his short legs, got a mention, while fun was poked at the *Scotulus* (Cadac-Andreas). Finally, the writer devoted a few verses to the seneschal Audulf and the cupbearer Eppinus.[26] Young and old alike were praised, teased, or openly mocked—in the king's hearing.

Charlemagne's so-called testament containing the bequest of all his riches, which he had had drawn up in 811, possibly by Einhard—certainly, his biographer was the only person to record it (chap. 33)—was signed by eleven bishops, four abbots, and fifteen counts, all listed by name—a roll call of all his most trusted followers. They included Hildebald of Cologne, Riculf of Mainz, Arn of Salzburg, Theodulf of Orléans, and Bishop Heito of Basel, Fredegisus (a pupil of Alcuin and his successor as abbot of Tours); the list of the counts was headed by Charlemagne's cousin Count Palatinate Wala and also included Unruoch of Friuli, Gerold (prefect of Bavaria), Bera of Barcelona, and sundry other members of the upper echelons of the Frankish nobility; Einhard himself, though, was not among them. No doubt a court assembly in Aix provided the opportunity for having the document countersigned by these magnates.

At first, the court was located wherever the monarch happened to find himself. But over time, for various reasons, a list of certain preferred palaces for such assemblies begins to emerge, including winter palaces, hunting lodges, and ceremonial palaces.[27] The general designation "palace" (*palatium publicum*) was used as a catchall term to denote variously the gathering of magnates; the occasion of the assembly; and the entire physical complex of palace buildings and their furnishings that were capable of catering to the king and his immediate family with their retinue—men, women, and children, vassals, staff, servants, and maids—for several weeks, including all the workshops, storehouses, and barns, and the stables and pens for horses, cows, hogs, and draft oxen.[28] The country's underdeveloped infrastructure and the ensuing difficulties experienced in obtaining supplies precluded a fixed royal residence. At this stage, only the first moves toward establishing such an institution are apparent. Worms and Ingelheim, with

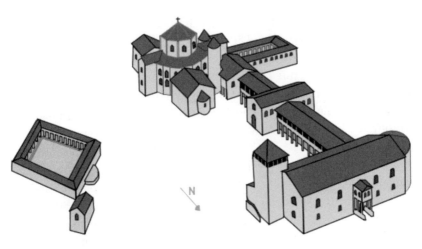

FIGURE 33 Model of Charlemagne's palace complex at Aix (Aachen).

their favorable location on the Rhine, were visited repeatedly,[29] but in the end it was Aix-la-Chapelle (Aachen) that stood out as the ideal spot.[30]

A "palace"—*domus, palatium, aula, curia regis*—was therefore to be thought of in spatial, personal, institutional, and communicative terms. It also served, so to speak, in a paraenetic way, to embody and make manifest the doctrine of rulership. It was everything rolled into one: a location, sometimes here, sometimes there, a group of people with the king at its center, the fixed epicenter of power, a treasure trove of ecclesiastical and cultural knowledge, a meeting place and a communication community, and a focus for the renaissance of the culture of learning and of the practice of religion. Aside from the immediate royal family and the aforementioned functionaries, there was no fixed courtly society. The court was a magnet for hundreds of people, perhaps as many as one or two thousand all told: men, women, even small children, advisers, visitors, people who had been summoned there, foreigners, the king's relatives, his wife, lady's maids, sons, daughters, nurses, servants and menial staff and cooks, the entire retinue. Many armed men accompanied the court wherever it went. From time to time, this whole huge train of people would journey throughout the realm, moving from one palace to the next. Consequently, it is self-evident that the concept *palatium* primarily denoted the totality of people at the court and not merely the built environment of the palace.[31] Yet, despite the fact that this traveling around was a vital element in the personal system of rule, over time it became extremely onerous.

The journeys around the realm were arranged by the court itself. People at all the central palaces—say, in Worms, Ingelheim, or Aix—knew where the king was staying at any given time. The route had to be decided in good time in order to be able to accommodate and feed the large numbers of horses, draft oxen, and people traveling overland in the king's retinue. In 797, when Alcuin wished to know when the king would be returning from Saxony and in which palace he was planning to spend the winter, he turned to Queen Liutgard.[32] After all, in accordance with the provisions of the *Capitulare de villis*, the queen was responsible for large areas of the economic management of the royal household. The seneschal, the cupbearer, and the officers of the stable (*comes stabuli*) also played a large part in organizing the king's travels around his realm and making arrangements to ensure that sufficient supplies of grain, meat, and fodder for the horses and oxen were available wherever they stopped.[33] Sometimes stocks of wine had to be brought from far away, once the king had announced his impending arrival. Entire villages were responsible for providing transport services. The king's retinue often had to make do with tents for their accommodation. This whole enterprise was a triumph of organization and control and spoke to the allure exerted by the personage of the monarch.

The royal estates scattered throughout the empire varied considerably in size and amenities, as they doubtless also did in function, being arranged as ceremonial palaces or hunting lodges and variously suitable just for overnight stay as the king was passing through or for longer sojourns. We gain an impression of the facilities they offered from the *Brevium exempla* and the *Capitulare de villis*, regardless of whether this latter treatise related to the rule of Charlemagne or that of his son Louis. The endless military campaigns also required a high degree of mobility on the part of the king. Only very few places could boast the extensive resources needed to feed and water the king and his entourage for any length of time. The furnishings of the royal palaces were determined by the requirements of the traveling court. As we have seen,[34] Charlemagne took a personal interest in the facilities at these palaces and, in particular, in the economic performance of those supplying the "table goods," which were specially reserved for the use of the traveling royal court, for the *discus* or the *mensa regis* (the plate or the table of the king). For instance, there was a standing order that a tablecloth should always be laid on the king's table and no other.

At the court, the king, as head of the household, would appear in the midst of his people dressed in simple Frankish garb in the manner Einhard describes (chap. 23), namely, in a linen shirt, linen trousers, and over these a silk-trimmed tunic with the inevitable sword belt and scabbard.[35] Only in winter would Charlemagne wear a pelt made of otters' or pine martens' fur draped around his shoulders, with a coat beneath to protect his limbs from the cold. The sword with the golden hilt and the highly decorated scabbard was a constant feature. Because the court traveled around with the king, it always found itself at the focal point of the empire and in the early years of his reign crisscrossed the country tirelessly with him, especially within the more limited area of Francia, convening meetings at a succession of local venues. It was only in the last two decades of Charlemagne's reign, and under his immediate successor, that the court came to be increasingly restricted to Aix, at least during the winter. With the passage of time, the formerly itinerant court changed fundamentally as the palace at Aix was made into a kind of permanent residence during the emperor's final years.

The Rules of the Court

No contemporary witness described exactly how Charlemagne's court operated; the only near contemporary to do so, Charlemagne's cousin Adalhard of Corbie, evidently put pen to paper after the king's death—possibly as a response to the reorganization prompted by the changes introduced under the influence of Benedict of Aniane. But even his account has been lost to posterity. We know of it because the young Hincmar, who later became archbishop of Reims, got hold of it in good time and recalled it in his writings. He states that he became familiar with Adalhard's works when he was still a very young man; indeed, he had read and copied Adalhard's small treatise *De ordine palatii*. Now, in the final months of 882, he produced a work of his own on the subject.[36] The treatise by the metropolitan of Reims followed the guidelines laid down by Charlemagne's cousin, although precisely how closely it corresponds with the earlier work can no longer be determined.[37] So long as we exercise some degree of caution, then, we may rely on the archbishop of Reims's description of the court of Charlemagne and, via his account, also on the abbot of Corbie. Even so, it still remains uncertain to what extent the structure of the court can be attributed to Charlemagne, or how much he simply took over from his father, or indeed how much these accounts merely reflect the circumstances at the court of Louis the Pious. But a comparison between them and the capitularies that concern the organization of the royal estates might well suggest an increase in regular control and written administration and hence a growing degree of rationalization.

Hincmar's *De ordine palatii* therefore gives us only an impression of how things might really have been under Charlemagne's rule. The archbishop's work is in two distinct parts. It begins with several chapters that resemble mirrors of princes; these are Hincmar's work alone and do not concern us here. In introducing the second, more extensive section, the author makes specific reference to a treatise of the same name by Adalhard of Corbie, "the relative of Lord Charles, the great emperor, and the foremost of his chief advisers." The following point stands out: there was no specific court protocol in Aix like that of Byzantium,[38] in fact quite the opposite. When Theodulf, for example, read out the following sentence from his work opposing the cult of images: "If the mob, in their untamed exuberance, in their addiction to splendor and love of flattery, or even out of fear of officers of the law, should lavish vain, ruinous praise on images of the emperor—what does that matter to us, who only measure our worth when set against the fact that Our Lord Jesus Christ died on the Cross for us?" Charlemagne was heard to enthusiastically respond, "Good!"[39]

The few surviving contemporary sources corroborate this lack of ceremony. The itinerant Frankish monarchy and the aristocratic society within which the monarchy had to assert itself precluded the development of any fixed ceremonial. Indeed, how could such a thing arise when the king or emperor was in the habit of inviting his retinue to join him in communal bathing and to dine at his table after hunts? At no stage do we find any description of a ritual ascent of the throne. Einhard mentioned the modest, normal clothing worn by his hero; Charlemagne decked himself out in royal finery only on feast days (chap. 23). And Notker of St. Gall told an anecdote about the reception of Greek envoys at the Frankish court, who repeatedly knelt down before a series of people who turned out not to be the king before Charlemagne, standing at the window and dressed in simple clothes, revealed his identity and gave them an audience. On another occasion, this time dressed in lavish garb, he allowed the "Persian" ambassador and his sons to look around every room in the palace and inspect everything.[40] A reception of a foreign delegation could scarcely have been conducted with less formal ritual.

When the king was present at synods, he sat among the bishops and abbots; in this face-to-face society, a specially raised chair was not required for everyone to know who was sitting there in their midst. The anonymous author of the so-called *Carolingian Epic of Aachen* dwelt extensively on the magnificent clothing sported by the king and his family for the hunt but gave only a very brief account of the royal party's return to their tents and the banquet that followed; there is absolutely no mention of any great cere-monial gathering in the King's Hall. All the writer says is that the king "sits on his high chair" (*sedet solio in alto*), nothing more.[41] Although the palace at Ingelheim had a spacious hall with a broad apse, which scholarly re-search assumes must have housed the throne, nothing of this nature has been excavated at Aachen to date. As ever, the Frankish court cannot be compared either with the Roman-Byzantine ritual observed in Constan-tinople or with the ceremonial of the caliph's court in Baghdad. Everything in Aix was comparatively simple, in keeping with the general tone of the dynastic house from which royal rule had developed.

There were two heads of administration at the palace, responsible for re-ligious and secular matters, respectively. According to Hincmar, an official called the "apocrisiary," namely, the highest court chaplain (*palacii capel-lanus*), directed and regulated all religious affairs. He organized masses at and for the court and everything that had to do with this holy office. Under Charlemagne, this post was filled first by Fulrad, the abbot of St-Denis, who had come to court when he was still a young man under his father's tute-lage, then from 784 onward by Archbishop Angilram of Metz, and finally, from 791/794, by Archbishop Hildebald of Cologne. The entire court clergy was subordinate to them. There had been chaplains at court since the Mer-ovingians. They were responsible—and Charlemagne did nothing to disrupt this—for the safekeeping of the king's collection of religious relics, and, as they always had been, for performing special liturgical services at the court and at the churches on the royal estates, which could at the same time be parish churches. They got their name from the object that for a long time had been the most precious relic of the Frankish kings, namely, the *cappa*, or cloak, of St. Martin of Tours. A "chaplain" was thus originally a guardian of the *cappa*.

But it was only under Pepin and particularly Charlemagne that the royal court chapel became an institution intimately linked to the king's court (*sancta capella palatii*)[42] and staffed by a fixed group of clerics under the leadership of the apocrisiary, who later become known as the "archchap-lain." This institution brought together talented young clerics, many of whom would later be destined to fill high-ranking posts, such as that of bishop, archbishop, or abbot; moreover, these people were also leading rep-resentatives of the new revival in learning and skills. Notker claims that Charlemagne would pick them out when he made occasional visits to the country's best schools.[43] Foreigners, too, could be attached to the royal chapel. Under the leadership of the archchaplain, whom they assisted, the clerics who formed the chapel were thus the keepers of the entire body of religious, ecclesiastical, and canon-law knowledge at the court; at least in spiritual matters, they constituted the king's administrative staff. This was to remain the case for many centuries. Many of the chaplains were chosen to lead diplomatic missions or were recruited as librarians, while others laid the groundwork for the ecclesiastical decisions to be taken at the court assemblies.[44]

The apocrisiary's right-hand man was the chancellor, himself a chaplain, who headed a team of notaries (also members of the court chapel) and was responsible for the production of official documents. Under Charlemagne, the first person to occupy this post, as he had under Pepin, was Hitherius; he was succeeded by a man named Maginarius and others. But under Charlemagne there was no fixed institution of a chancery, or office dealing with all the written documents of state. When used of the Frankish Empire, the term simply denoted an area of responsibility.[45] The documents of state, which nevertheless were underpinned by a very rigid formalized style, were dictated by chaplains, a small group of whom were constantly in attendance at the king's side. One of the innovations introduced by the Carolingians was to restrict the drafting of documents to clerics.[46] The chancellor or, more frequently, his representative would prepare diplomas, append the king's monogram to them, and seal them with a seal decorated with an antique cameo. Even under Charlemagne, these diplomas were probably distributed in the course of a formal assembly—an opportunity to present a communicative ritual of authority, with the commission and the solemn reading out of the document.[47]

The orders issued by the apocrisiary to individual members of the court chapel can still occasionally be made out in the form of Tironian notes, a kind of Roman shorthand, written in the margins of some documents that have been preserved in the original.[48] It is not clear who wrote these documents, since the notaries did not always identify themselves; but it is evident that they were required to master a special form of "document cursive" script. A whole series of scribes would have been active at Charlemagne's court, although we know nothing about their organization or hierarchy. The notaries of the king's messengers no doubt made multiple copies of the capitularies they wished to disseminate around the realm.[49]

Secular matters at the court were managed by a count palatinate, who at the same time was one of the king's key advisers; he was expected to pass judgment on all the disputes brought before the royal court of justice. Cases in which he felt unable to make a ruling were referred upward to the king to resolve. During the final years of Charlemagne's reign, this task was performed by his cousin Wala, who after the emperor's death was forced to take holy orders.

Alongside the count palatinate, there were a host of other offices associated with the court; these were doubtless first listed by Adalhard and are not Hincmar's addition: the chamberlain, the seneschal, the cupbearer, the officers of the stable, the mansionary (quartermaster), the head huntsman and falconer, and beneath them a whole string of other servants like doorkeepers, cellar masters, or dog drivers. They all had more or less strictly circumscribed areas of responsibility; in addition, they were, if possible, to be chosen from all regions of the realm so that people from those areas would have trusted contacts at court. On the other hand, all the most important roles were firmly in the hands of leading noblemen. So it was that Charlemagne's testament was signed in 811 by the seneschal Count Otulf and the marshal Burchard. Only the office of mayor of the palace was never filled again because this was the role the Carolingians had traditionally occupied before their ascent to the throne. The queen and the chamberlain were in charge of the annual tributes paid to the court, as well as gifts from foreign legations, and were also responsible for keeping the court supplied with provisions. The key principle informing Charlemagne's organization of his court was that there should never at any time be a shortage of advisers, sundry personnel, and essential provisions.

The court assemblies (*placita*), which were convened twice a year by the king, usually though not exclusively during the winter months, discussed and settled pending affairs of state. These assemblies were meant to be a forum where the clerical and secular magnates could meet. The magnates were empowered to draft resolutions, while the rest of those assembled were expected to listen to them, discuss them if necessary, and "approve them, not on the basis of a command, but through the exercise of their own reason and judgment. They were also required to offer their tributes."[50] *Ex proprio mentis intellectu et sententia*—the revival of the culture of knowledge was also to be exploited for the benefit of royal authority. Not least, it had the capacity to create a common ground of mutual understanding, which could only facilitate "rational," appropriate decisions.

Yet alongside these wider assemblies, another far smaller council also met, composed solely of the king's most trusted advisers. This group, which brought together the king's closest counselors, planned for the future, deciding when wars should be waged and against whom, when and where truces were to be concluded, and when hostilities should be commenced. The participants in these meetings were sworn to say nothing about their decisions until the next court assembly. Then their resolutions were to be announced in such a way as to make them seem as though they had just been reached "through divine inspiration" and in conjunction with those who had gathered to attend the assembly.[51] But in the event that these decisions that had been taken in camera were made known prematurely, this still would not "nullify them or render them useless, or make them harder to implement due to any kind of rancor."

The members of the inner council were required to place uppermost in their thoughts their everlasting bond of loyalty to the king and his authority and were expected to act "neither as friends, nor foes, nor relatives of the king, nor should they give the king presents or shower him with flattery, or indulge in any diatribes against him, or argue in devious manner," but instead to allow "that wisdom and reason" to prevail that silenced all cunning.[52] Indeed, this last assertion was reminiscent of Charlemagne, who in a letter to Hildebald of Cologne had once enthusiastically stressed the indispensable and indissoluble, natural unity of "wisdom and reason."[53] "Who can possibly know something without first understanding it, and conversely, how can anyone who is not knowledgeable understand anything?" he wrote at that time. "Who could possibly search his own soul or advise others without wisdom and reason?" The requirements of both the Church and the kingdom coalesced in the revival of learning, and the court assemblies were to take advantage of this convergence.

The decisions of the inner council were reached in a kind of conclave. The apocrisiary and the chamberlain were always present at these meetings. Initially the clerics and the lay members held separate discussions before sitting down together, always in the company of the king. Charlemagne would also, though, take representations in the form of reports and complaints from the various regions of his empire into account. There is no mention of the queen ever attending these meetings.

Knowledge Concentrates at the Court

First and foremost, however, the court was the place where scholars gathered to exchange information, knowledge, and ideas and to pursue their scientific studies or creative writing. The court comprised a unique communication community of power and knowledge, which messengers and letters then expanded beyond its physical confines. Alcuin called Aix, which at that time had just been promoted to the king's permanent residence, a new

Athens in the land of the Franks (letter 170). The royal hall in Charlemagne's palace rang with praise of the ruler, a eulogy written in dignified hexameters and possibly performed to the accompaniment of the lyre:

Illum aliquando tegunt nimboso nubila tractu,
Hunc ullae numquam possunt variare procellae;
Ille caret proprio bissenis lumine horis,
Iste suam aeterno conservat sidere lucem.
Pace nitet leata, pariter pietate redundans
Nescit habere pio lapsurum lumine casum.

(Sometimes rain-heavy chains of clouds obscure the sun,
Yet no storm can ever change him [Charlemagne].
The sun does not have its own light for twelve hours a day
But he retains his radiance throughout, a constant star.
He beams in joyous peace, he is lavish in his grace,
And the starlight of his goodness never wanes.)[54]

The poets at court—in this case the anonymous author of an epic poem about Pope Leo and King Charles—together with Alcuin, Theodulf of Orléans, the king's quasi-son-in-law Angilbert, and many others, all competed with one another to write poems in praise of the king and win his favor. The court basked in the presence of these muses. Frankish writers imitated the praise of rulers and panegyrics from classical antiquity. *Maximus armis, ensipotens, omnipotens,* and *bellipotens* (the greatest warrior, mighty with the sword, a master of arms, and powerful in war)— Charlemagne, the great king, *Karolus magnus rex,* loved to hear warlike scenes presented in artful metric form. He was fond of being compared to King David, a trope possibly invented by Alcuin. Common variants on this theme are *dulcis David, David dulcissimus* (sweet David, David the sweetest). But he also greatly valued biting irony and caustic ridicule. Were these, then, a true measure of his soul?

Activities of this kind at court were especially geared toward entertainment. Yet even in the context of a courtly pastime, who would dare to make jokes about the king? This was a dangerous step, and no one took it. The rivalry among the writers at court was intense. Particularly the Irish, or at least one of their number, fell victim to this competitive atmosphere. His name was Cadac-Andreas, and he aroused particular antipathy in Theodulf.[55] This incident may have been typical of the febrile, tension-laden atmosphere at the court of Charlemagne and among his intellectuals. After one performance of his work, Cadac came forward, with tousled hair and unshaven, to receive the kisses of those present, adulation, as one commentator described it, "like that which the fierce wolf [i.e., Theodulf] shows to the long-eared ass. Sooner would a hunting dog suckle leverets, or the evil wolf lambs, sooner would a cat turn its back on a trembling mouse than the Visigoth would make peace with the Scotsman." Theodulf then proceeded to lay into the poor fellow Cadac, "this little Scotsman, this wildly raging thing, this horrible specimen, this terrible enemy, this dull-witted horror, this bitter pestilence, this quarrelsome disease, this wild man, this great sin, this abomination of Nature, this dilatory and despicable creature."

The dazzling scholarship of this brilliant Irishman (or Scotsman?), who knew Greek, did not sit well with the Visigoths or the Lombards and the Franks who had been taught by them.[56] One of the last group now joined in the tirade of insults: "O benign king, most benign of rulers," he addressed the king, "we implore you to expunge the disgrace brought on this court by the stupid Cadac having the temerity, like some blasphemer, to bestow on himself the name of the holy apostle [Andreas; St. Andrew]. . . . He should be incarcerated in a bleak jail until he learns that he will never be a master.— Tell us, you heavy drinker, you raving Irishman, you glutton, . . . tell us, you blind man, you stinking asses' sputum, why did Apollo never grow a beard? Tell us, you bovine dullard, you horned goat, what letters the Greeks read first? Tell us, you insane skull, what is a diapsalma and where in the psalms does one encounter a synpsalma? You most stupid of poets. And finally, o godless man and deluded defrauder of learning, please tell us who was the first among the Irish to paint his face at a funeral?" Charlemagne would have laughed uproariously at this, relishing the sight of his schoolmasters, abbots, and bishops growing ever more quarrelsome as they tried to advance their own careers. Perhaps he was just waiting for signs of mutual antipathy; such knowledge could sometimes make the business of ruling easier.

Charlemagne also expected his court to perform duties beyond the exercise of royal authority, tasks hardly any imperial or royal court had tackled hitherto. To this end, he surrounded himself with scholars, placed them in charge of institutions of learning far and wide, and from his central position at court then monitored how successfully they achieved the reforms he charged them with instituting. The literacy of the court, which steadily increased over the long decades of Charlemagne's reign, served as an example and model for many others, above all, monastic and ecclesiastical educational centers throughout the empire. Yet above and beyond this, the king

1 Image of Christ from the Psalter of Tassilo III of Bavaria. This work was produced at Mondsee Abbey in Austria sometime before 788 and is now held at the library of the University of Montpellier, France. Ms. H409.

II AND III The Godescalc Evangelistary, created in the court scriptorium of Charlemagne around 781–783. These elaborately illuminated pages contain images of the fountain of life (left) and a pericope for the Christmas vigil (right). Paris, Bibliothèque nationale (Nouv. acq. lat. 1203).

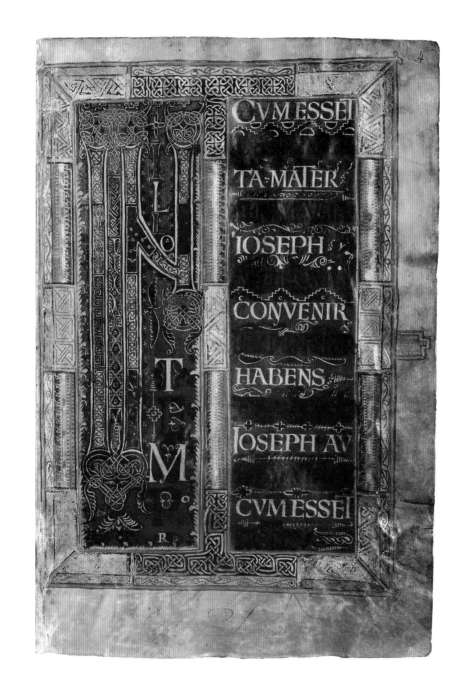

CVM ESSEI

TA·MATER

IOSEPH

CONVENIR

HABENS

IOSEPH AV

CVM ESSEI

IV Portrait of St. John the Evangelist from the Coronation Gospels, a liturgical manuscript transcribed at Charlemagne's court in Aix before 800. Vienna, Imperial Treasury of the Hofburg Palace (Inv. XIII 18).

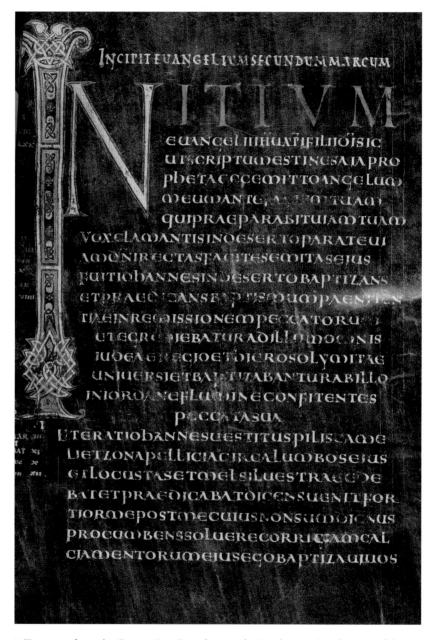

INCIPIT EUANGELIUM SECUNDUM MARCUM

INITIUM

EUANGELII IHU XPI FILII DI SIC
UT SCRIPTUM EST IN ESAIA PRO
PHETA ECCE MITTO ANGELUM
MEUM ANTE FACIEM TUAM
QUI PRAEPARABIT UIAM TUAM
VOX CLAMANTIS IN DESERTO PARATE UI
AM DNI RECTAS FACITE SEMITAS EIUS
FUIT IOHANNES IN DESERTO BAPTIZANS
ET PRAEDICANS BAPTISMUM PAENITEN
TIAE IN REMISSIONEM PECCATORUM
ET EGREDIEBATUR AD ILLUM OMNIS
IUDEA REGIO ET HIEROSOLYMITAE
UNIUERSI ET BAPTIZABANTUR AB ILLO
IN IORDANE FLUMINE CONFITENTES
PECCATA SUA
ET ERAT IOHANNES UESTITUS PILIS CAME
LI ET ZONA PELLICIA CIRCA LUMBOS EIUS
ET LOCUSTAS ET MEL SILUESTRE EDE
BAT ET PRAEDICABAT DICENS UENIT FOR
TIOR ME POST ME CUIUS NON SUM DIGNUS
PROCUMBENS SOLUERE CORRIGIAM CAL
CIAMENTORUM EIUS EGO BAPTIZAUIUOS

V Text page from the Coronation Gospels reproducing the opening chapters of the Gospel according to St. Mark.

PSALMVS DAVID. INCONSVM
MATIONE TABERNACVLI·

VI Building a house, from the Golden Psalter of St. Gall. Switzerland, St. Gall Abbey Library (Cod. 22).

VII Warriors and an army besieging a city, from the Golden Psalter of St. Gall.

VIII Engravings (1533–1536) by the Dutch artist Maarten van Heemskerck of the Papal Palace (above) and the Campus Lateranensis (below) in Rome. Berlin, Print Room of the Prussian Cultural Heritage Foundation.

and his court called for the revival of ancient learning and its dissemination so that the Frankish kingdom might become a beacon of educational renaissance—just as, on the political level, Charlemagne's imperial seal proudly proclaimed, *Renovatio imperii Romanorum* (renewal of the empire of the Romans).

This ushered in a new era for the Frankish Empire, one no longer merely content with the long-term institutionalization of the royal court; rather, in a quite general sense, it now became a school, notwithstanding the fact that the actual "court school" mentioned in the sources was not an academy and probably served only the children of distinguished courtiers plus a few ordinary pupils who were sent there.[57] For all that, in the winter of 796/797, just after he had taken control of the abbey in Tours, Alcuin urged the king "to encourage the young boys at the court of your excellency" (*in palatio excellentiae vestrae*)—which could only mean in the palace at Aix—"to study wisdom and to practice it, in order that they might become worthy citizens, developed from callow youths into adults, and so that through wisdom they might attain eternal bliss."[58] As Alcuin had already stated in the foreword to his *Grammar*, the kind of wisdom he had in mind, which could be studied and practiced, attained its ultimate goal via the steps provided by the seven liberal arts.[59]

First and foremost, the program required books. Alcuin complained to Charlemagne about the situation he encountered in Tours: "I, your insignificant servant [*servulo*], am lacking here the most important books of scholarly learning, which thanks to the great and humble diligence of my teacher and through my own efforts I had at my disposal at home." Accordingly, he asked for permission to send a group of his students to Britain to acquire books there.[60] Charlemagne tried to make up for the shortfall as best he could. He set himself and his followers the task of being constantly on the lookout for books and for knowledge that had got buried over time. His retinue obeyed these instructions, searching out manuscripts and sending them to Aix or having them copied. Charlemagne's court became home to a library whose treasures are praised to the skies by modern historians. A list of books contained in the manuscript Berlin Diez. B. Sant. 66, which is thought to have originated in Verona, does give us insight into the sheer collecting zeal that made the assembly of this court library possible in the first place. Originally thought to relate solely to Charlemagne's court library, it somehow, although the details are now lost, came to link the court of Charlemagne's son Pepin, the king of Italy, with the Aix court; ultimately, though, scholars do not regard it any longer as being the catalog of a real library.[61]

Undoubtedly, though, valuable manuscripts and rare works were avidly collected at Charlemagne's court.[62] Grammars from ancient times, including treatises on the teaching of Latin, were an essential component, as was Augustine's *City of God,* Cassiodorus's *Institutions,* the canon-law tome the *Collectio Dionysio-Hadriana,* the *Gregorian Sacramentary,* and the *Rule of St. Benedict,* while it is most likely that a *Liber pontificalis,* a history of the popes, also found its way there from Italy or Rome, along with an illustrated manuscript of the *agrimensores* (authors of handbooks on Roman land surveying), the *Ten Categories* (*Categoriae decem;* a brief paraphrase of Aristotle's doctrine of categories), a bundle of writings on logic, which Alcuin may well have been respnsible for procuring for the library, and Pliny the Elder's *Natural History.* Charlemagne's library at Aix is also thought to have held a copy of Plato's dialogue *Timaios* in the Latin translation and with a commentary by Calcidius, although the oldest verifiable manuscript (Paris, Bibl. nat. lat. 2164) belonged to Helisachar, Louis the Pious's chancellor. However, it seems entirely possible that he acquired this from Charlemagne's library. Indeed, even the *Codex Argenteus* (Silver book), the only surviving manuscript of the Gothic Bible, may well have been held there too.[63] This selection of works indicates not only an appreciation of theoretical texts; Charlemagne was equally interested in practical matters and the realization and application of knowledge. He saw it as his duty as ruler to open the portals of the royal court to all manner of learning.

Nevertheless, the Aix court did not possess its own scriptorium, an essential facility for producing books; others were responsible for transcribing the volumes deposited there. It seems fair to assume that the nuns at Chelles Abbey, for example, where Charlemagne's sister Gisela was the mother superior, copied books for the king's library.[64] The court school at Aix, which art historians often mention, and to which they ascribe the exquisitely illuminated manuscripts in Charlemagne's collection, was not actually located at the court itself, as far as we can tell. Charlemagne commissioned these masterpieces, no doubt financed them as well, and kept them in his library. After the emperor's death, the library was dissolved, and its former holdings were dispersed far and wide. Even so, it is thought that it was responsible for handing down a whole series of ancient texts to posterity. The precise location of the library in the palace complex is not known, although the fact that Charlemagne bequeathed all his books in his will to the poor and other recipients indicates that the library did not form an integral part of the cathedral chapter of the Royal Church of St. Mary.[65]

The various impulses that had their origins in Charlemagne's court played a decisive role in shaping history, not least the way in which the culture of learning was directed and spread from here, and in which the king himself was instrumental in promoting the revival of writing and the art of book illumination, and of the culture of books in general. The court at Aix instigated a transfer of knowledge that transcended time and space, and it was thanks to this institution—and the king's own receptiveness to learning, which led him to breathe new life into the program of the seven liberal arts—that standardized curricula gained a foothold in all schools in the Frankish Empire and hence across the whole of "Latin Europe," with grammar, rhetoric, and dialectics acting both as the trivium of basic disciplines and as publishing aids, say, for sermons and for the religious education of the people.

Charlemagne set great store by the reacquisition of Latin—in other words, ecclesiastical and academic—language skills, the collection of exemplary texts, the reading and critiquing of both Christian and pagan authors from classical antiquity, the setting up of schools, and the appointment of competent teachers. In many cases, wealthy monasteries and ecclesiastical foundations were required to take on these tasks and establish schools and scriptoria of their own. At least in the case of the former, this represented an unreasonable demand and was met with considerable opposition,[66] for a monastery was, by its very nature, a hermitage, a place that was supposed to be detached from the hustle and bustle of life and left free to devote itself solely to the worship of God and prayer.

Secular music was presumably performed at court, although there is scarcely any mention of it in the sources. The richly illustrated Utrecht Psalter, made in 825 and possibly modeled on a work from late antiquity, pictured a wide range of instruments, although it gave no indication to what extent they were actually played at the Carolingian court. The lute, harp, lyre, and organ are all depicted, along with trumpets and horns, hourglass drums, and shawms. Admittedly, the musicians in the psalter are all angels, shown flying toward Christ or playing in front of him. Secular instrumental music is not portrayed here.[67] However, the courtier Angilbert could often be heard playing his flute, and a (water) organ, like the one Charlemagne's father had once been given as a diplomatic present by envoys from Byzantium in 757 and very similar to the one pictured in the psalter, could actually have been played at the court.

Not least because of the presence of the court chapel, the royal court also became over time a center of learning, a center for the organization and dissemination of knowledge, and, as such, in a way no ancient imperial court had ever managed, a model for all the royal courts of the Western world that followed it. Anyone who wanted to be seen as significant in Charlemagne's eyes had to bring with him learning and aptitude and show distinction in them. The revival of ancient culture was not, however, confined to the court alone. Foreigners were therefore welcome, so long as they met the necessary requirements. Xenophobia was alien to the court of Charlemagne, even though individual Franks may have regarded the many successful foreigners at court with more than a touch of envy. Charlemagne's realm was meant to learn from these outsiders. With his library, which held the most precious ancient texts, and with the archives, which preserved all the edicts issued by the king, together with treaties and the letters of various popes to the Carolingians, and with the whole enterprise of education orchestrated by the mechanism of the palace, the royal court constituted not only a center of organization and learning unique in early medieval history but also, and more important, one that was wholly innovative. The supervision that modern states exercise by means of ministries of culture and science over schools and places of higher learning, as well as over scientific academies and societies, can be seen as a distant echo of these early endeavors of Charlemagne.

All art at the court was representational, yet hardly a single image of Charlemagne as ruler has survived, despite the fact that images are known to have existed. Even the mosaics of Pope Leo III, which also included portrayals of the Frankish king, are now lost and are known to us only through Baroque sketches or copies. The only depiction thought to have survived from Charlemagne's kingdom itself was the aforementioned sketchy line drawing made in Fulda, but this was hardly intended for the court.[68] In addition, a small arch-reliquary made of embossed silver and no doubt originally intended to carry a cross showed two riders armed with lances (these have occasionally been interpreted as images of the emperor, or of St. George), plus various other figures, which might likewise be images of rulers, although no one can be sure. As the inscription on the back of the triumphal arch reveals, Einhard made this reliquary at an unknown date and "dedicated it to God"; but the dedicatory inscription says nothing about the king or emperor ("Einhard, a sinner, strove to set up and dedicate to God this arch to support the cross of eternal victory").[69] We know about this artifact thanks to a drawing of it made by an antiquarian in Paris in the seventeenth century. Lapidary art also experienced a revival during the reign of Charlemagne; this particular art form was responsible for producing a

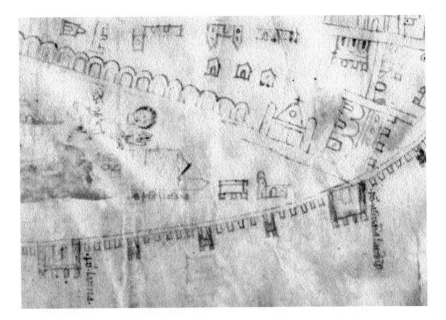

FIGURE 34 Map of Rome (1346) by Fra Paolino da Venezia. This detail shows the buildings of the Lateran, with (from right to left) the papal palace, the Basilica of St. John Lateran, fragments of the colossal statue of Constantine, the *Caballus Constantini*, and, in the far left bottom corner, the palatium Neronis Lateranense (Nero's Lateran Palace). Venice, Biblioteca Marciana.

crystal seal of Charlemagne (now lost), in which a stylized image of the ruler was said to have been engraved.[70] Like so much else from the king's palace, the original has been lost.

The only images to have been preserved are a few likenesses on coins. These portraits, done in the classical style, bring the emperor vividly to life, showing him garlanded with a laurel wreath, wearing an imperial cloak with a clasp, and sporting a heavy mustache. We encounter this stylized depiction once more on the famous equestrian statuette now housed in the Louvre in Paris (Figure 23).[71] This artifact is commonly interpreted as a commemorative image from the reign of Charlemagne's grandson Charles (II) the Bald, although there is no other evidence to suggest that this monarch had any interest in equestrian statuary (unlike Charlemagne, as evidenced by his efforts to have the statue of the Ostrogothic king Theodoric brought from Ravenna to Aix). Might the Louvre statuette in actual fact somehow be more closely associated with Charlemagne himself or with his court? Is it in fact the image of a king who is mounted on horseback like an emperor? The tradition of Metz Cathedral, where the statuette is known to have been used for liturgical purposes in services from the sixteenth century onward, suggests that this may be so.[72] As such, therefore, the equestrian statuette points beyond Charlemagne's period as king toward his assumption of the title of emperor.

The Palace in Aix Recalls the Palace of Constantine the Great

Before long, Aix was being hailed as a new Rome. The Frankish poet Moduin of Autun eulogized the city and its ruler in his work *Egloga:* "My Palaemon [Charlemagne] looks out from the lofty citadel of the new Rome and sees all the kingdoms forged into an empire through his victories. . . . Golden Rome is reborn and restored anew to the world. . . . The place where the head of the world resides may justly be called Rome."[73] Before this, soon after Charlemagne's investiture as emperor, the anonymous poet of the panegyric epic poem about Pope Leo and King Charles, who may possibly have been Einhard, celebrated Aix as a "second Rome," an allusion to the Roman poet Virgil's description of Carthage.[74] Charlemagne was happy to have such praise lavished on him. His Aix was testament to "a great renaissance,"[75] a revival of Rome, and an imitation of Rome, not just in a cultural or architectural sense but, most important, in a religious sense too. The things that had been revived in emulation of Rome were permeated by the spirit of Christianity as Charlemagne understood it, for it was not pagan Rome but ecclesiastical Rome and in particular the first Christian emperor, Constantine the Great, that the Frankish king visualized when he planned the "sublime citadel" of the new Rome.

In the last twenty years of Charlemagne's reign, the palace on the upper reaches of the river Wurm came to be regarded as his "royal seat," whose "architecture" revealed the religious attitude of its master, the "measure of his soul," so to speak. Attaining this status required that the king spend long spells in residence there. The royal court consolidated its presence at Aix at first over the winter months, but later on a regular basis. In their time, the Romans had established Aix as a thriving spa settlement. Warm springs with water that could reach temperatures as hot as 60°C enabled the recreation of bathing to be enjoyed even in winter.[76] King Pepin, Charlemagne's father, appreciated the place and began to develop it as a palace. In 765/766, he was able to celebrate his first Christmas and first Easter there, facts that tell us that suitable buildings such as a church and various utilities must already have been built by that stage.[77] Pepin may well also have taken over control

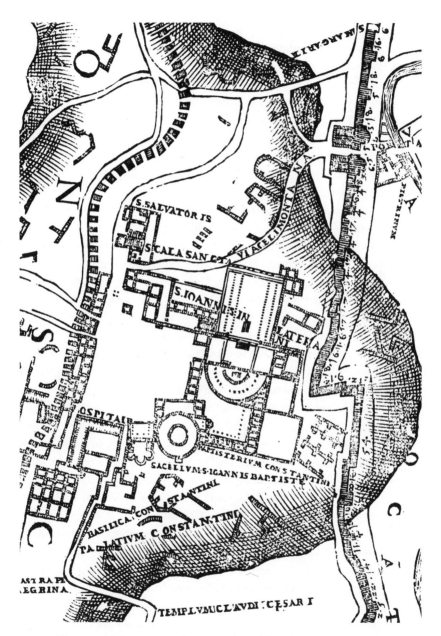

FIGURE 35 This map of Rome (1551) by Leonardo Bufalini clearly locates and labels the site of Constantine's former church and palace (Basilica Constantiana/Palatium Constantini) below that of St. John Lateran and the octagon of the Baptistery.

of one or more of the thermal springs.[78] The new palace was situated at the center of an extensive estate, a *fiscus,* the management of which was placed in the hands of an official known as an *actor,*[79] who would have belonged to one of the leading aristocratic families. The *Capitulare de villis* gave a thorough account of this form of administration.[80]

Likewise, Pepin's son experienced his first Christmas celebration as king in Aix.[81] From 775 onward, an increasing number of decrees were issued from the ruler's palace (*palacio nostro*) in the town; the use of the possessive pronoun refers to the building, not to any assembly. The location had found great favor with Charlemagne.[82] He liked spending winters there because of the warm waters, and because he could celebrate Mass here in surroundings of great splendor. In 789, he ordered the imperial synod to convene in Aix, the body that was ultimately to promulgate the *Admonitio generalis.* Thereafter, though, he avoided visiting the palace for the next five and a half years; this was evidently the period in which the original palace was extended and converted into the new showcase royal residence.[83] The aforementioned poem about Pope Leo and King Charles, taking the spring of 799 in Aix as its point of reference, praised the palace's spacious layout and mentioned the construction of a harbor, a marketplace, and the "senate, where the people are to have law and justice and spiritual guidance dispensed to them."[84] It lauded the building of a large theater and the impressive vaulted halls in domestic dwellings (*atria*) and spoke of a "magnificent temple of the eternal king" (*aeterni regis amoenum templum*).[85] Other royal palaces—such as Nijmegen, Ingelheim, or Paderborn—correspondingly also had care expended on them by the king. Yet he lavished his attention on Aix like nowhere else.

Both on top of and among the ruins of the ancient Roman settlement, Charlemagne erected his new palace complex, including the great Council Hall, with generous interior dimensions measuring seventeen meters wide by forty-four meters long, a southerly extension facing the large palace courtyard (might this have been the "theater" referred to?), and a series of other buildings. A few years later, the Granus Tower was added, which is still standing today (as part of Aachen city hall). The Council Hall was almost certainly in use from 794, although it still may not have been fully finished by this date. A wooden passageway connected it to the church to the south; it is thought that Louis the Pious replaced this structure with a stone gallery. Further dwelling and utility buildings extended the palace complex over the ensuing years, turning it into an impressive ensemble. The king also erected new baths. This facility, with a pool measuring fourteen meters by

FIGURE 36 Albrecht Dürer, view of Aachen Cathedral and the adjoining section of the Katschhof, seen from the town hall, 1520. British Museum.

nine meters and incorporating three central pillars, lay not far to the north-east of the main palace complex, close to the later so-called imperial spring; Charlemagne's living quarters must have been somewhere in the vicinity of this. The epic poem about Pope Leo and King Charles praised the stone-built pool and did not omit to mention the "marble seats" around its edge, or that the warm water was piped around the entire facility through little channels.[86] Charlemagne was proud of his "new Rome," which he built on the site of ruins. He may even have provided Aix with a small port, served by a canal he ordered to be constructed.[87]

The rebuilding of the palace complex with its unique church was a major undertaking, and Charlemagne was keen to see the project completed. All the monasteries and bishoprics surrounding Aix were called on to provide services to aid the construction of both edifices, a fact recalled by Notker of St. Gall in his *De Carlo Magno*.[88] The churches were required to send lab-orers, who—in Notker's account—worked incredibly hard on the palace; it was also incumbent on the churches, not the court, to feed the men, supply draft oxen, and provide considerable amounts of capital and building mate-rials. These obligations were still being met long after Charlemagne's death.[89]

The author of the epic on Pope Leo and King Charles announced, "The wagons creak along, and a constant roar of noise ascends to heaven."[90] The extensive cooperation that took place, especially in the building of the Palatine Chapel, explains the rapid completion of the work within just a few years. Although the anonymous epic poet mentions the construction of several *atria*, none of these is emphasized in a way that might lead us to believe that the *aula regia*, the Council Hall, is the building in question.[91] It would appear, then, that this structure was already standing by the time he presented his work.

The palace complex in its entirety disappeared over time; the only evidence of what the buildings still occupying the site in the late Middle Ages looked like comes from an early sixteenth-century drawing by Albrecht Dürer, which gives some impression of the great variety of buildings that once lay in the shadow of the Palace Church of St. Mary. One final indication hinting at the sheer extent and size of the ensemble of buildings that constituted the central palace comes in the form of the later additions—the Gothic town hall and the Katschhof, the open space between the town hall and the cathedral—beside the church and the Granus Tower to replace the former Council Hall, which still exist to this day. We know nothing, though, of the location and appearance of the living quarters occupied by the king and his family, or the chambers of the ladies-in-waiting (the *atria*?), or the subsidiary buildings housing the servants and other staff. The last presumably lived in wooden huts, not in (half-timbered) buildings with foundations. It seems unlikely that these structures would have clustered closely around the cathedral, as in Dürer's drawing, or around the connecting gallery that led from the church to the Council Hall.

Like the imperial residences of antiquity, the palace as a whole was an open complex with no perimeter wall, as far as we can tell, even though the Council Hall itself was built within the ruins of an ancient fortress and incorporated some of this former structure into its fabric. The palace at Aix must have put Charlemagne in mind of the imperial buildings he had seen on the Caelian Hill in Rome. As a palace site and the center of the Aix domain—that is, the royal estate attached to the palace with its various close and far-flung villages—Aix quickly developed into an early urban settlement, with facilities for the clergy, secular magnates, and court servants and with a market, artisans, and a mercantile class, which included Jews.[92] Aix must also have been home to large barns and stables, at least for horses and draft oxen but probably also for hogs and cows, and have supported a correspondingly thriving agricultural economy. No doubt the king would often have been woken from his slumbers by the whinnying of horses and the bellowing of oxen. The town continued to be home to servants and common people even when the king was absent. When Charlemagne's son Louis the Pious took over the reins of power after his father's death, he even referred to alleged harlots in the town whom he would no longer tolerate and whom, if they should transgress, he would have publicly flogged on the market square.[93] Was he referring to his own sisters, perhaps? Or to their maids?

In planning his new palace, Charlemagne recalled Rome, the city of the apostolic princes and of the vicar of Christ. Yet in his imitation of the Eternal City, he was not content with simply adopting Roman liturgy and Roman law. Roman buildings had captivated him, and now he demanded the same kind of architecture in Aix. Not least, the new Palatine Church would be the equal of imperial buildings in Rome. Did the *cantus Romanus,* the church music of Rome, require "Roman" architecture as its setting? Charlemagne was adamant that it did, and to this end he asked Pope Hadrian to send him—from Rome and Ravenna, the two foremost imperial residences in Italy—all manner of ancient classical decorative features: mosaics, pillars and capitals, floors, marble slabs, and sundry other items. Charlemagne's biographer Einhard (chap. 26) mentions this specifically in the case of Aix. A corresponding letter from Hadrian, thought to date from 787 or shortly thereafter, that accedes to the king's request and authorizes transfer of the items was incorporated by Charlemagne into his *Codex Carolinus.*[94] The plans to expand Aix into the primary imperial residence date from this period at the latest.

The details of which architectural elements the king helped himself to here and there, which buildings were ransacked, and where the spoils were taken have been lost in the mists of time. The former palace of the exarch in Ravenna, the representative of the Byzantine emperor in the West, is one obvious place we might think of. But Charlemagne's request to the pope reveals that he had not simply passed by the ancient walls and works of art unmoved when he had been in Italy, but rather that he recognized them as important symbols of Rome and emperorship, and that he chose them as the model for his own building program and as a way of projecting his own authority. As a result, he himself specially selected what features he wanted and had them delivered to his realm in order that he might, insofar as this was possible, compete with Rome. Charlemagne's buildings therefore quite deliberately remind the onlooker of Rome. The city's religious topography combined everything he required in Aix.

Now Charlemagne was able to re-create in his adopted city the scene he had formerly witnessed as a young king on several occasions when he had stood on top of the Caelian Hill, at Constantine the Great's supposed seat of power, and had surveyed the scene before him: in the east the *patriar-chium* (the residence in the Lateran Palace), to the south the Church of the Redeemer and the baptistery, with the Aurelian Walls in the background, and in the west—presumably in the midst of ruins—Constantine's (supposed) palace and in the middle of the square in front of it the imposing equestrian statue of "Constantine."[95] Albeit with certain variations conditioned by the new surroundings—the overall layout was smaller in its dimensions and was rotated through 90°—this basic arrangement also dictated the building program for the palace at Aix. Its ground plan therefore followed the model of Constantine, the first Christian emperor.

The central square of the palace complex was flanked to the north by the Council Hall, which was surrounded by ancient fortifications and which, on the side facing the square, had a low building (the theater?) in front of it, while to the south stood the Palace Church of St. Mary and the Redeemer, along with various buildings for the use of the clergy. The western side of the square, meanwhile, was occupied by a wooden gallery (later rebuilt in stone) leading from the hall to the church, while on its east side were the baths and various other buildings (see Figure 33). The bronze, gilded equestrian statue of Theodoric, with a shield slung over its left shoulder and its right hand raised, clutching a spear, was sited in the center of the square. Charlemagne ordered it to be brought there from Ravenna after his investiture as emperor and installed in such a way that the statue faced the palace—in exactly the same way as the statue of "Constantine" in Rome faced the Lateran Palace (see Plate VIII and Figure 10).[96] In both locations, Rome and Aix, the Church of the Redeemer was located behind the bronze statue of the ruler. Water also flowed past the statue, as it did in Rome, where the Aqua Claudia was channeled past "Constantine." In defiance of all the imprecations heaped on the dead Visigothic king by historians at that time, Charlemagne gave his youngest son (born in 807) the name Theodoric.[97] However, under Louis the Pious, increased learning began to have an effect, condemning the precious statue to removal and destruction.

Even the name of the Constantine-inspired palace (although it was in use for only a short time) consciously recalled Rome. According to the oldest written report on the expansion of the palace, the *Chronicle of Moissac*,[98] the ensemble of palace buildings at Aix followed the Roman model entirely by calling itself the *Lateranis;* likewise, a capitulary issued by Louis the Pious in 816 refers to what was almost certainly a single building as "ad Lat-eranis."[99] Just as the *Actus b. Silvestri* expressly noted on Constantine that this Roman ruler had "erected a Church for Christ within the precincts of his palace" and had thrown it open to public use,[100] so the Frankish king designated his Palatine Chapel as a parish church for the people. Thus it cannot be a coincidence that during Charlemagne's reign the designation "ad Lateranis" came to apply to the palace at Aix. Charlemagne's center of power was designed to imitate the complex of Constantine's Palatium Lat-eranense, as described in the *Actus b. Silvestri* and as witnessed firsthand by Charlemagne himself during his repeated visits to Rome.[101]

Yet this highly educated and devout Carolingian monarch was not content with mere ornamentation or with styling himself as a Roman emperor. His palace was intended to be emblematic of his commitment to spread the Chris-tian faith and of his concern for the Church and proper observance of the faith, as well as being a symbol of his anticipation of his own salvation. And so it was that, alongside the great Council Hall, another even more magnifi-cent building soared "heavenward to the stars" to grace the skyline of Aix, a masterpiece that embodied all the intellectual and technical abilities Charle-magne's contemporaries could muster: namely, the Church of the Redeemer, dedicated to "the eternal king." With its foundations, galleries, and octagonal tambour, it was the tallest domed building of its time north of the Alps.

This edifice rose up majestically from the center of the new palace build-ings. It was constructed on the site of an earlier building that had been within the bounds of a cemetery and was thus regarded as the parish church of the relevant district. An impression of the former architecture can be gleaned from the model commissioned by the donor of Charlemagne's shrine from the period around 1200. The "smoothed walls" were rendered on the outside with striking red plaster (made with the addition of crushed brick), while the capitals of the tambour shone brightly. A man called Odo of Metz was recorded as the supervisor of building works. He may well have been the same person as the courtier whom court society at Aix gave the biblical name Hiram, and whom Theodulf praises as the master builder of the church (cf. 1 Kings 5:18).[102] Hiram of Tyre was the man who helped Solomon build the first temple in Jerusalem. Did this courtly nickname reveal Charlemagne's intentions? In other words, was Aix conceived not merely as a new Rome but also in an anagogical sense as a likeness of Jerusalem, leading to eternal salvation? Did Odo also factor this into his plans?

As the central edifice of the palace complex, this Palatine Chapel pri-marily echoed the imperial Basilica of San Vitale in Ravenna, the church

FIGURE 37 This panel from the Shrine of the Virgin Mary in Aachen Cathedral portrays
Charlemagne kneeling and dedicating the church to its patron saint (late twelfth to
early thirteenth century).

whose mosaic decoration suggested a strong association with Emperor
Justinian and in which Charlemagne may well have prayed a few years
earlier, during his fourth Italian campaign in 787. An inner octagon was
surrounded by a broad sixteen-sided ambulatory of low groin vaults.[103]
The octagon quoted not only Ravenna but also other buildings of the
Byzantine imperial tradition, including the far-off Church of Hagia Sophia in Constantinople (the latticework decoration of the pillars also
recalls this building), as well as other octagonal churches like the chapel
in the Lombard palace at Pavia and perhaps even the octagon at the
Dome of the Rock in Jerusalem as well, which in those days may have
been mistakenly seen as the temple of Solomon. By erecting this church
in his palace, the king was reviving an imperial concept, known to him at
least through reports from Constantinople and brought to life by his own
firsthand observations in Rome and Ravenna. But he fleshed out and
completed this concept according to the requirements of Western cathe-
drals. Could there be any more apposite characterization of the building's
gestation?

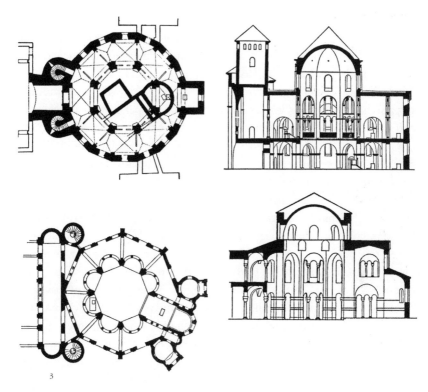

Ground plan and elevation of Aachen Cathedral (above) and the Church of San Vitale in Ravenna (below). From *Aachen im Bild IX*, Burg Frankenburg Museum, Aachen, Germany.

The decoration of the church came in the form of the ancient columns, marble features, and floor slabs that had been cannibalized from Ravenna and possibly also from Cologne and Trier. Where there was a shortfall of these original salvaged elements, stonemasons were set to work imitating ancient patterns—a task they performed with considerable skill. The bronze work for the cathedral—the doors and the railings of the upper church—were technical masterpieces; the craftsmen who made them are unknown, although traces of their smelting furnaces have been found in the middle of the Katschhof (the square outside the church). Einhard (whose nickname was Bezaleel, after Exodus 35:30–33) is thought to have been in charge of all smelting and casting activities and goldsmithing.[104] (The biblical figure Bezaleel was the person responsible, during the flight of the Jews from Egypt to the Promised Land, for creating and furnishing the tabernacles.) Sculptures of ivory provided a touch of royal magnificence during the religious observances.[105]

Like the late antique Church of San Vitale in Ravenna, the church at Aix also had an upper story, the "high church" (*Hochmünster*), whose main altar—like the Basilica Constantiniana in Rome or the chapel in the palace at Pavia—was dedicated to the Redeemer and to the Holy Cross, while the lower church was consecrated in the name of the Virgin Mary and undoubtedly also had St. Peter as its patron saint.[106] This upper story was decorated with two lines of sixteen columns each, a feature that distinguished it architectonically from the lower story. This detail may also have been a deliberate allusion, for thirty-two columns, sixteen on each side, also supported the clerestory of the Lateran Basilica in Rome.[107]

By 796, the church in Aix was nearing completion and may well—albeit only partially—have been consecrated on either 17 July or 8 September of that year, both days being feast days of the Virgin Mary. No chronicler invented this date or cited any celebration of dedication. Rather, it is confirmed by poems written by Theodulf in the spring of 796, which had as their subject prayers of thanks offered for Charlemagne's victory over the Avars "with eyes, spirit, and hands raised to heaven," and which maintain that these took place *in aula,* that is, in the church, which is praised as being "a beautiful building that soars up in a series of magnificent arches," *qua miris surgit fabrica pulchra tholis.* After the service of thanksgiving, the congregation walked across to the Council Hall, *palatina sedes.*[108]

A similar picture emerges from a letter written by Alcuin. In 798, he had occasion to admire the capital decorations (no doubt recently installed) for the columns in the church and celebrated vespers in the building in the company of a lady of the court.[109] The ancient salvaged columns were delicate and expensive, some of them being made of the "imperial" red porphyry. They had no structural function but merely served as symbolic elements and decorative features. The foundations of the sixteen-sided ambulatory on the upper story show some signs of earthquake damage, however; the floor pavement installed at the time of building was also affected. This damage is said to have been sustained in 803 (*Royal Frankish Annals*) but may have happened before or after this date. Work on the cathedral was basically completed by the early ninth century, a date suggested by the epic poem on Pope Leo and King Charles, where it is stated that the church was finished in 799.[110] In January 814, Charlemagne was laid to rest in the church; thereafter, an order of canons was dedicated to observing his memory.

The liturgical manuscripts required for use in the church at Aix were specially created on-site. Like the marble and columns for the fabric of the

FIGURE 39 View looking down from the cupola of Aachen Cathedral on the throne of Charlemagne, situated on the church's upper level, the "high church" or *Hochmünster*. From *Die karolingische Pfalzkapelle in Aachen,* p. 248.

building, their illuminators or even the original texts may have come from Italy. These exquisite creations, including the Coronation Gospels (see Plates IV and V)—possibly transcribed before 800, kept in Aix until 1816, and now held in Vienna—and the only slightly younger Treasury Gospels, which still form part of the treasure of Aachen Cathedral, took their inspiration from the late antique, in other words, "Roman," tradition of illumination.[111] Here, too, then, we find echoes of an imperial past. Was one of these sets of Gospels perhaps intended for the higher church and the other for the lower? Whatever the truth of the matter, it is clear that the Church of St. Mary and the Redeemer at Aix was to present as magnificent a spectacle as the ancient imperial basilicas within Charlemagne's sphere of control and as the temple in Jerusalem.

Although the Marian dedication of the Palatine Chapel after the death of Charlemagne is well attested (Einhard, chaps. 17 and 31), there is nothing to suggest that Charlemagne was particularly devoted to the Virgin Mary. Charlemagne's synods and councils, his capitularies and edicts, and the letters addressed to him did not refer specially to the Mother of God. Christ, the apostolic prince St. Peter, and even the apostle to the Gentiles St. Paul were prominent, but no cult of the Blessed Virgin Mary was evident.[112] Yet the church in Aix had little choice but to follow the example of the Basilica Constantiniana; although it cannot be directly attested, this church is believed to have been designated by its founder as a collegiate church with twelve canons and its own independent revenue, dedicated in honor of Christ the Redeemer, the Virgin Mary, and St. Peter and devoted to intercession for the king and the nurturing of his and his family's memory. This institution was founded under one roof alongside the old parish church. But when? Charlemagne's testament of 811, as recorded by Einhard (chap. 33), bestowed gifts on the episcopal churches of his kingdom, his children, the poor, and the servants of the royal palace at Aix but omitted any mention of the palatine collegiate church. This strongly suggests that it was founded only after his death.

The oldest surviving imperial edict from Aix, a diploma issued by Lothar I in 855, would appear to bear out this fact. This document relates that Charlemagne and his son Louis, Lothar's father, built the "church [*capella*] at Aix from the foundations up, furnished it at their own expense, and lavishly decorated it" in order that "Mass might be celebrated there in perpetuity." There is no mention in the diploma of the old parish church, despite the fact that it continued to exist as an institution. The assignment of ownership and the duty of memorialization point to a clerical society, and hence to the collegiate church.[113] Admittedly, the foundation and construction of the church were due to Charlemagne alone, meaning that the further establishment of the collegiate church was primarily to be attributed to Louis the Pious; its official date of foundation in 814 bears this out.

The construction program and the inscriptions of the founders of the Palatine Chapel that have been preserved all point in this same direction.[114] At no point is the Virgin Mary mentioned. Theodulf claimed that Hiram/Odo dedicated the church (*aedes*) to "the Almighty enthroned on high."[115] Did he mean the image of Christ as the triumphant lord of the world that originally adorned the interior of the cupola? If so, this image, which was almost certainly painted rather than a mosaic, could then definitely be dated to before the end of 800.[116] Its apocalyptic theme (after the book of Revelation 4:2) was based on Roman models (say, on the facade of St. Peter's or on the triumphal arch of the Basilica of St. Paul outside the Walls [San Paolo fuori le mura]), although the execution would have been in the vernacular Frankish style.[117] The figure of Christ enthroned shown in the cupola may even be preserved in a contemporary illustration in a manuscript originally held at the monastery in St. Gall.[118] Similarly, a preliminary sketch in red chalk, depicting a standing Madonna with Child, a hybrid of a Virgin Hodegetria and a Maestà or Maria Regina (depictions, respectively, of the Virgin Mary holding the infant Jesus and pointing to him, and the Virgin Mary and the Christ Child enthroned) in the southeastern segment of the cupola also harks back to Roman iconographic antecedents, unknown in northern Europe, but was nevertheless rejected in favor of the apocalyptic imagery.[119] Only the supervisor of building works can have authorized such a step.

The Church of the Redeemer was incorporated directly into the palace complex; it was a work of imperial architecture and in keeping with this grand aspiration was magnificently appointed. From the very beginning—and in this, too, it bore a remarkable resemblance to Constantine the Great's Lateran Basilica in Rome—it also served as the parish church for the palace city and for the financial center (*fiscus*) of Aix/Aachen.[120] In this church, the king devoted himself in a special way to the service and worship of God, and it was here, before the Altar of the Redeemer, that the emperor Charlemagne celebrated the "Christian religion" and in a liturgical context also his recognition by the Byzantine *basileus*. It was here, too, that Louis the Pious was crowned emperor.[121] Yet this imperial ambition was inextricably bound up with a foreboding of the Apocalypse.

A Prayer in Stone

Charlemagne's "temple" was a symbol in stone of his faith and was genuinely more than simply a magnificent showpiece building projecting his power. A predetermined numerical symbolism lay behind the construction of the octagon and the sixteen-sided ambulatory.[122] The proportions of both were determined by the perfect number six and by eight, the numeral relating to the resurrection of Christ and of the dead.[123] Charlemagne was well versed in the meaning of this kind of symbolism, as a letter of Alcuin to the king attests.[124] The diameter of the octagon was 48 feet (six times eight), while that of the sixteen-sided ambulatory was twice that. The total length of the two constructions was three times 48 or 144 feet; 144 was a significant number in numerology, being the number of cubits that St. John ascribed to the periphery of the Holy City of Jerusalem in the book of Revelation (21:17). The circumference of the octagon, measured between the internal corners, was also 144 feet.

Three rows of arches drew people's gaze upward 31 meters (once again, 48 feet). There, at the top of the cupola, the Apocalyptic Christ sat enthroned in judgment (Revelation 4:2–4) amid 144 stars, no doubt a symbol of the 144,000 souls saved at the Apocalypse (Revelation 7:4–8 and 14:1), a figure that, according to the conception of contemporaries, was synonymous with the total number of people saved at the End of the World.[125] In addition to the perfect number six and eight—in the form of the eight columns of the octagon and the two rows of sixteen columns—another important number in the numerology of the cathedral was three, significant in terms of the Trinity and the history of salvation, and represented here by the three rows of arches that led the viewer's eye up to the enthroned Christ. The apocalyptic measurement of 144 also results from multiplying these three numbers, 6 times 8 times 3. In other words, the entire building from top to bottom was proportioned and executed according to figures that related to the End of Days. Charlemagne was no doubt fully aware of this symbolism.[126]

The dedicatory inscription of the cathedral confirms this interpretation. Comprising four elegiac distichs, in other words, eight lines of verse, it ran "around the edge of the cornice between the upper and the lower arches" of the octagon; there was no mention of the Virgin Mary. In the form in which we now see them, they may well be the work of Alcuin, but they borrow the first three distichs from the poet Prosper of Aquitaine, who in his turn reworked ideas broached by St. Augustine, especially in his commentary on the Apocalypse of St. John:

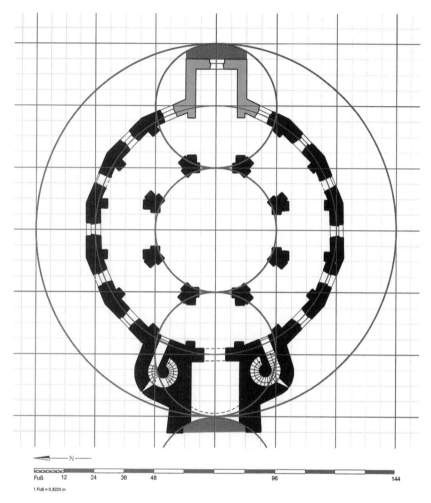

FIGURE 40 Ground plan of the octagon of Aachen Cathedral (after the architectural historian Ulrike Heckner); the inner circle has a diameter of 48 "Carolingian feet," the middle circle 96, and the outer circle 144 (1 Carolingian foot = about 13 inches).

Cum lapides vivi pacis conpage ligantur,
inque pares numeros omnia conveniunt,
Claret opus domini, totam qui construit aulam,
Effectusque piis dat studiis hominum,
Quorum perpetui decoris structura manebit,
Si perfecta auctor protegat atque regat:
Sic deus hoc tutum stabili fundamine templum,
Quod Carolus princeps condidit, esse velit.

(Once the living stones have been joined together in peaceful
    union,
And all the measurements and numbers are in agreement
    throughout,
The works of the lord who created this great hall shall shine
    forth brightly.
The completed edifice crowns the pious efforts of the people,
Whose work shall stand as a monument of eternal beauty
If the Almighty protects and rules over it.
May it therefore please God to watch over this temple,
Which Charles our emperor has established on solid
    ground.)[127]

This great hall, as the church is called here, proclaimed a theological message with its construction dimensions and its dedicatory inscription. Did Alcuin really draft them, or was it the "court bishop" and expert in the *computus* Hildebald? According to the terminology of the New Testament and patristic authors, the phrase "living stones" could mean the faithful and, by extension, these believers in their union constituting the whole Church, the heavenly city of Jerusalem, and indeed, even Christ himself. The "lord" and "almighty" praised by the inscription could denote God as well as the church's founder, namely, the king or emperor. The only figures that counted as whole numbers were those that could repeatedly be divided into two equal parts—the eight and sixteen corners and the two sets of eight pairs of columns that decorated the upper part of the octagon; only the one signified indivisible unity and represented the hidden presence of the creator of the world among the other numbers.

The church building reveals itself to be a complex symbol. Eight lines of verse praised the lord who had constructed the church, Charlemagne had received eight blessings from God when he had ascended the throne, and—as Cathuulf had reminded the king[128]—the "fortress of the Lord" was also supported by eight "pillars," namely, eight royal virtues, and eight columns carried the roof of the fountain of life, from which Christ would give those who had been saved at the End of Days a drink of water (Revelation 21:6). This scene was the subject of an illumination in the Godescalc Gospels, which was commissioned personally by Charlemagne and his wife, Hildegard, sometime in 781 (see Plate II).[129] Eight was also the number of beatitudes (Matthew 5:3–10), the number of souls saved in the ark built by Noah (1 Peter 3:20 and 2 Peter 2:5), the embodiment of the new covenant, and the promise of the eternal day of the Lord. Moreover, according to the second epistle of St. Peter (1:5–10), eight efforts (*curae*) would lead the faithful to an understanding of the divine nature of Jesus Christ and protect them from sin: "Add to your faith virtue; and to virtue knowledge; and to knowledge temperance; and to temperance patience; and to patience godliness; and to godliness brotherly love; and to brotherly love charity." Yet according to St. Paul, love possessed sixteen qualities (1 Corinthians 13:4–8);[130] and in the teachings of St. John the Evangelist, God was love (1 John 4:16). Thus every element of Charlemagne's temple building pointed beyond itself, acting as an anagogical symbol with apocalyptic overtones.

An old hymn from the breviary reinforced these messages. This may possibly have been written before 700, although it is more likely to date from shortly before 800; the oldest manuscript of the work also points to this later period. Some hymnologists believe that it originated from Visigothic Spain. Was the text or subject matter perhaps brought to Aix by Theodulf of Orléans? Nothing is certain in this regard. In its eight stanzas, the hymn also used the image of the "living stones" and their "joining together" in a wall (*compago parietis*); by the time the hymn reached Aix, this had become "joined together in peaceful union" (*compago pacis*). In addition, the first six strophes also contain numerous eschatological allusions to the Apocalypse, to Isaiah, to Daniel, and to Gregory the Great's commentary on the book of Ezekiel—all highly relevant references that fitted in perfectly with the mosaic in the cupola at Aix.[131]

Irrespective of whether there were originally eight or six stanzas in this hymn, both numbers recur in the church in Aix. Had this hymn, which was sung at the church's consecration, been specially composed for this ceremony or just used on this occasion? As far as is known, the image of the "living stones" is encountered only once more in the period around 800, in another poem by Alcuin, albeit in a totally different and purely Anglo-Saxon context.[132] But this only makes the connection between the hymn and the Palatine Church at Aix all the more striking.

The hymn begins as follows:[133] "*Urbs beata Jerusalem, dicta pacis visio, / Quae construiter in coelis vivis ex lapidibus*" (verses 1–2). Later verses turn toward Christ: "*Angularis fundamentum lapis Christus missus est, / Qui compago parietis in utroque nectitur*" (verses 15–16). The "living stones" are a reference to the heavenly city of Jerusalem; the foundation stone and the union of stones are Christ. This is precisely the same thought that is expressed in the dedicatory inscription in the Palatine Church in Aix; accordingly, was this church of his, above and beyond its imperial significance, at

FIGURE 41 Sketch by Giovanni Giustino Ciampini of the cupola mosaic in the octagon of Aachen Cathedral, *Vetera Monimenta I*, Rome, 1690.

the same time a symbol of the eternal city of Jerusalem for Charlemagne? The throne room of the Redeemer, as it were? The program of dedicating the church to various patron saints also accorded with the hymn insofar as its sixth stanza, which reads like a doxology, refers to the Trinity: "*Omnis illa sacra et dilecta civitas, . . . Trinum Deum unicumque cum favore praedicat.*" These verses proclaim the God who is Three in One: the Father, the Son, and the Holy Ghost, who proceeds from both. An altar consecrated in the name of the Trinity stood in the center of the octagon in Aix.[134]

Beyond all sensory allegory, this building was a promise made real in terms of space and visual imagery, a prayer in stone and furthermore an avowal of faith and a personal mirror of princes. Its proportions followed the apocalyptic measurement of 144 feet. And the image in the cupola, spanning a roof supported by two sets of sixteen columns (restored in the nineteenth century), depicted the *Maiestas Domini* (Christ Enthroned in Majesty) surrounded by the twenty-four elders, an apocalyptic motif deriving from the book of Revelation: "And behold, a throne was set in heaven, and one sat on the throne. And he that sat was to look upon like a jasper and a carnelian: And round about the throne were four and twenty seats; and upon the seats I saw four and twenty elders sitting" (4:2–4).[135]

Einhard, who reveled in the church's beauty, mentioned the (ancient) columns and the marble and spoke about the gold and the silver, the chandeliers, and the bronze work of the doors and railings (for which he may himself have been responsible) but said nothing about the pictorial decoration of the church and its theological symbolism. After all, was he not the person who devised this symbolic program? Charlemagne, though, under Alcuin's tutelage, was well versed in the theory of religious numerology and the revelations of the Apocalypse and was constantly exhorted to focus his thoughts on the End of Days. Moreover, it was precisely the first great reform program, the *Admonitio generalis,* conceived in Aix, that had imbued the clergy and people with this admonition about the Apocalypse.[136]

Another neighboring church in Aix that lay within sight of the Romanesque Church of the Redeemer was the institution commonly known at the time as Hierusalem; this church was dedicated to the Holy Cross. Charlemagne also subsumed its patronal dedication into the palace complex and in so doing unified what in Rome had been separate entities, for the king elected to consecrate the upper story of the two-story Palatine Church to the Redeemer and the Holy Cross. Here, in the heart of the palace of the king or emperor, the people would gather to celebrate Communion. As was the case in Rome on the Caelian Hill, so in Aix access to the church was via two flights of winding stairs.

It is probable that Charlemagne—like his quasi-son-in-law Angilbert—possessed a splinter of the True Cross. Yet in all likelihood the analogy went even further than this. Alcuin, for example, once referred to Aix as Charlemagne's *Jerusalem optatae patriae,* that is, the "Jerusalem of the homeland he yearned for," in which he erected the temple of Solomon, namely, the Palatine Church. Was that just a metaphor designed to flatter the king? Yet it is true that the Lateran Baptistery also had a chapel of the Holy Cross, built under Pope Honorius I, while the Lateran Church had a relic of the True Cross, endowed by Sergius I and carried in the procession to the stational Church of Santa Croce, every Good Friday.[137] In other words, the Lateran complex in Rome also provided a model for the cultic association of the Redeemer and the Cross. Charlemagne must have been mindful of this.

Indeed, the king demanded sensory evidence of the promised "fatherland" and was not content merely to use the splinter of the Cross to this end. Instead, doubtless shortly after his investiture as emperor, he ordered the construction in the upper story of the building, the high church, of a throne of ancient marble slabs, which in all probability had been brought to Aix from Jerusalem, presumably from the Church of the Holy Sepulchre. These would serve as relics in their own right. After all, Angilbert had amassed a personal collection of precious relics from around the Holy Sepulchre as a result of his master's mediation.[138] The king and emperor would doubtless have received even more valuable relics. Yet Einhard described the treasures in the Church at Aix relatively extensively (chap. 26) but mentioned the gifts of relics from the Holy Land only en masse without going into detail and said absolutely nothing about the marble throne or the rich pictorial imagery in the church, despite the fact that this formed part of the original decoration of the building.[139]

The right flank of the throne, the display side that faced the sun, and its backrest still show traces of ancient carvings in the stone, some highly profane and others religious, including a game of nine men's morris and a quick sketch of a crucifixion. These engravings could easily have been sanded off or hidden by turning them to face the inside of the throne. Yet they were evidently intended to be seen clearly, attesting for Charlemagne's contemporaries the authenticity of the artifact's provenance—its provenance, that is, from Calvary (where Roman soldiers once whiled away their time playing dice beneath the Cross) and from the Church of the Holy Sepulchre. Likewise, the floor on which the throne came to be placed was covered with ancient slabs matching the preciousness of the relics, including pieces of green and red porphyry, no doubt imported from Ravenna or Rome.[140]

This throne may well have originally been very simple in form, with a trapezoid-shaped backrest, lower than it is today. It was positioned close to the edge of the upper story "between two marble pillars."[141] Nowadays, the throne has been moved back to the middle of the ambulatory and, like King Solomon's throne (1 Kings 10:18–20), mounted on a dais of six steps. Since 1305, the so-called Nicasius Altar has been propped up against the backrest of the throne. This may well have had a Carolingian predecessor. Under the seat of the throne there is a cavity that at least at some time during its history appears to have housed another valuable relic, namely, the golden purse containing earth soaked with the blood of the early Christian martyr St. Stephen, which was later to become part of the imperial treasure.[142]

This sacred artifact may have come into Charlemagne's possession from Leo III, who was elected to the papacy on St. Stephen's Day in 795. According to tradition, the bones of the saint had been housed in the church of San Lorenzo fuori le mura, the great funerary church of Rome. Equally, though, the king's relic of the True Cross (since lost) may have been depos-

FIGURE 42 The Nicasius Altar and behind it the rear side of the backrest of Charlemagne's throne in Aachen Cathedral.

ited in the hollow space under the throne. Both relics pointed to Jerusalem. Accordingly, the throne was both a relic in its own right and a reliquary. There is no evidence to suggest that Charlemagne ever sat on this throne, however. It was only in the reign of Otto the Great—on the occasion of either his own or his son's coronation, in 936 or 961, respectively—that the throne, now pushed back into the middle of the ambulatory and raised up on its plinth, first became the seat of a monarch.[143]

But what significance attached to an empty throne? An answer may be provided by the liturgy, which knows this symbolic image by the term *Hetoimasia* (or *Etimasia*). The final chapter of the book of Revelation (22:1–4), alludes to this phenomenon: "But the throne of God and of the Lamb shall

FIGURES 43 AND 44 *St. Stephen's Purse* (front and back), a ninth-century reliquary containing earth soaked with the blood of the martyr. Vienna, Kunsthistorisches Museum.

FIGURE 45 Mosaic of the *Hetoimasia* (Preparation of the empty throne) in the Baptistery of the Arians, Basilica of San Vitale, Ravenna.

be in it; and his servants shall serve him," while Psalm 89:14 relates the image to the Second Coming of the Messiah and expectation of the Day of Judgment: "Justice and judgment are the habitation of thy throne."[144] This kind of interpretation accords closely with what we already know about the church at Aix, the apocalyptic dimensions of its construction, the image in its cupola, and its supposed hymn of consecration.

In the early Middle Ages, the motif of the preparation of the throne for the judge of the world became a familiar piece of iconography in the West through a series of mosaics and the liturgy of the Second Mass at Daybreak on Christmas Day (the Offertory, Psalm 93:1–2: "God hath made the round world so sure, that it cannot be moved; ever since the world began hath thy seat, O God, been prepared"). Charlemagne may well have heard this psalm immediately before his coronation as emperor and could also have marveled with his own eyes at depictions of the act, say, during his coronation in the confessional in St. Peter's in Rome,[145] or in the mosaic on the triumphal arch of the great Marian church in Rome, Santa Maria ad Praesepe, and elsewhere. The other "actors" involved in the preparation of the throne, angels and the apostles

Peter and Paul, may conceivably have been depicted in the form of frescoes on the pillars flanking the throne in its original position in the church at Aix.[146]

The theme of the "preparation" was widespread in the Eastern Church. Although there is no record of the original pictorial decoration of Hagia Sophia in Constantinople, a portrayal of the empty throne may well have stood there and served Charlemagne as a model. Similarly, the ivory throne of Archbishop Maximian of Ravenna, which may have been a gift from the Byzantine emperor Justinian and was decorated with scenes from the life of Jesus but was actually too small to serve as a real seat, can also be interpreted as a symbol of the Etimasia. Charlemagne may have regarded "his" throne as essential for the anagogical meaning of his institution in Aix, symbolizing the ascent to the heavenly Jerusalem. The priest who celebrated Mass at the throne altar could look up and see the judge who would come at the End of Days. In any event, in this church of his, Charlemagne could feel himself to be not only the successor to Justinian but also the king and emperor waiting in anticipation of the new era and of the coming Day of Judgment.

Everything was in harmony here. Charlemagne's palace, the Council Hall, the apocalyptic measurements of the church building, the "Roman" columns and capitals, the imperial symbolism, the dedications to patron saints, the reliquary throne and the Etimasia, the judge of the world and the Redeemer seated on high in the cupola with its 144 stars, the broad square separating the Council Hall and the church, and the statue of Theodoric on the square—these elements all belonged together and formed a whole, whose name ad Lateranis reveals where the model for Charlemagne's palace complex was to be found: in Rome, in the Palatium of Constantine the Great. Charlemagne's palace took its cue from Constantine's seat of power, as disclosed to him by the *Actus b. Silvestri* and the evidence of his own eyes on his repeated trips to Rome, and even outstripped it, insofar as—unlike the first Christian emperor—the royal and imperial client and head of the household in Aix remained true to his faith right up to his death, battled against heresy, and was able to anticipate redemption.

This last factor was also proclaimed (but from when?) by an altar in the emperor's church; this altar stood in the center of the octagon, directly beneath the enthroned Judge of the World, and was consecrated to the Trinity, whose proper worship Charlemagne had stoutly defended against adoptianism and against the Greeks who, regardless of whether they venerated images or were iconoclasts, all rejected the *filioque*;[147] this was the epitome of Charlemagne's faith and rule. But like Constantine in the Church of the

Redeemer that he constructed in his palace, Charlemagne was also keen that "the Christian congregation should assemble together with us and give thanks to our Lord Jesus Christ," and what is more, should do so in the Palatine Church.[148] So it was that, right from the outset, this place of worship with its imperial "high church" was at the same time also the parish and baptismal church for the people of Aix/Aachen.

With all these symbols, with its imperial architecture, which directly recalled the Church of the Holy Sepulchre and the Chapel of the Ascension on the Mount of Olives,[149] with its apocalyptic measurements and the apocalyptic cupola image, with the Etimasia, with the programmatic assemblage of patron saints, with the symbol of the 144,000 who had "the name of the Lamb and that of his Father written on their foreheads" (Revelation 14:1), with the supposed consecratory hymn *Urbs beata Jerusalem,* which lauded the heavenly city of Jerusalem, with all these symbols, Charlemagne's "temple" called to mind at the same time the city of the Holy Sepulchre, the Ascension, and Christ's Second Coming to sit in judgment on the world. The Church of the Redeemer was an embodiment in stone of its patron's hope of salvation. Rulership and awareness of redemption, the Roman liturgy and avowal of the one true faith combined with the "joining together in a wall" and the "living stones" to create a prayer in stone and a reflection of the ruler's innermost being. In the Palatine Church at Aix, the mystery of the Christian faith was revealed anew here to the king and emperor and to all the faithful.

Charlemagne's Other Palace Buildings

Aix was only the most prominent palace in the later years of Charlemagne's reign. We are in a position to describe the church there in detail because it established itself from 936 onward (or possibly only from 961) as the coronation church of the German kings and in this capacity—as well as being the burial church of Charlemagne and Otto III and the memorial site for Emperor Charles IV—was basically able to withstand all the storms of the ensuing millennium. The other palaces of Charlemagne—at Nijmegen, say, or Ingelheim near Mainz on the Rhine, or Paderborn[150] in the Saxon region, where Charlemagne convened court assemblies on several occasions and where he received Pope Leo III—have all more or less completely vanished. We have no idea how they were furnished. Einhard describes the first two of these palaces as "ornaments of the kingdom" (chap. 17, *ad regni decorem*). But there were no thermal springs at these sites. Recent excavations have

FIGURE 46 Model of Charlemagne's palace at Ingelheim. The royal Council Hall is the large separate building on the far left.

enabled archaeologists to make a relatively accurate reconstruction of the Council Hall at Ingelheim, at least as regards its basic dimensions. We may even be able to get some idea of its decorative elements, thanks to a poetic description by Ermoldus Nigellus, who was writing around 830.[151] The images he describes are of various scenes that loosely reference the doctrine of four successive world empires, as expounded by the biblical prophet Daniel and as enlarged on especially by the Christian historian Orosius (fourth–fifthth centuries).

The frescoes Ermold describes—or were they tapestries?—depicted, along one side of the great meeting hall, a historical cycle of world domination, beginning with Cyrus the Great of Persia and Ninus/Nimrod, the founder of Nineveh in Mesopotamia, and proceeding via a series of rulers to Alexander the Great and possibly to the Roman emperor Augustus too. In this way, then, it outlined the history of violent and despotic pagan rulers at key turning points in world history. On the opposite wall, Christian rulers were shown, from Constantine and Theodosius up to the contemporary era, including the heroes of the Carolingian dynasty, such as Charles Martel, the victor over the pagan Frisians, Pepin the Short, who regained the whole of Aquitaine from the Muslims, and Charlemagne himself, who was portrayed twice, as the ruler of Italy and as the conqueror of heathen Saxony. There may also have been captions beneath the frescoes explaining the significance of the scenes. The theme of the decoration at Ingelheim may be summarized as follows: the expansion of the Christian Church and the return of the world to God.

It is a moot point whether the Palatine Church at Ingelheim was also decorated, as Ermold claimed. This assertion of his may have arisen from a confusion with the Church of St. Alban in Mainz. The fresco cycle there is said to have featured, on the left-hand side, the story of Man's Fall from Grace up to the building of Solomon's temple, while the right-hand wall of the church was devoted to Christ's life on Earth, from the Annunciation to the Ascension and the Glory of Christ Pantocrator.[152]

The Council Hall at Aix may also have been covered with corresponding religious or historical picture cycles; in any event, we can be sure that its walls would have been as richly decorated as those of the Church of St. Mary.[153] The royal court and the palaces at various locations were all projections of power. Their murals manifested the monarchy's self-image, but also far more than this: by virtue of their layout and their furnishings, as well as in the programmatic intent behind their construction and various other symbolic elements—such as the equestrian statue of Theodoric or even an organ—the palace complexes were designed as imperial signifiers, as proclamations of a Christian monarchy that regarded itself as being on a par with the emperors of Rome. As such, then, Charlemagne's palace buildings, which he began construction of in the final decade of the eighth century, addressed themselves to a public audience that assembled in the palace precincts from time to time when summoned there by the king. The people marveled at what they saw, and they learned and imitated. It furnished them with clear evidence of the status of their lord and master and made them willing to follow him "to Rome," to the pinnacle of imperial power.

7

REVIVING THE TITLE OF EMPEROR

"**W**E ARE AWARE** that in the Last Days false prophets have arisen, as Our Lord himself foretold in the Gospels and as St. Paul also attests in his Epistle to Timothy." The *Admonitio generalis* concluded with this warning of danger. What is more, the warning was justified. It did not take long for the first reports of heresies to arrive from Spain, while the Byzantine "Greeks" seemed constantly to be on the verge of idolatry. The signs of danger increased. "And so, dearly beloved, arm yourselves wholeheartedly in full knowledge of the truth, in order that we might combat those who deny it." Charlemagne—clearly concerned about recent developments—set himself up as the guardian of the faith.

The king's own words confirmed his eschatological forebodings. When Theodulf, in refuting the Greek cult of images, gave an eschatological reading of certain lines of Psalm 30 (v. 5: "Weeping may endure for a night, but joy cometh in the morning"), interpreting the night as "our era, in which the End of Days and the Last Judgment may fall," whereas the morning was the time for resurrection and for the saints to be given their rewards, the king was enthusiastic in his praise, calling out *"eleganter"* (elegantly put!).[1]

Nor did Charlemagne remain silent when Isaiah's prophecy about the last days (2:2–3) came up for discussion.[2] The End of Days and the Last Judgment preoccupied him all the while, even more in his later years than in his youth. Perhaps it was precisely the final books of St. Augustine's *City of God* that he held in especially high regard.

It is certainly the case that many contemporaries at Charlemagne's court, like Alcuin, saw the emergence of heresies as a sign of the impending end of the world, and the worship of idols as the cult of the Antichrist. Everything was in a state of flux. Paul had also been at pains to warn Timothy about the "perilous times" of the last days (2 Timothy 3:1).[3] Eschatological expectations had always been at the very heart of the Christian faith. The doctrine was taught in Holy Scripture and spread with the practice of baptism in the Greek East, as well as in the Latin West. Its message was unequivocal. The Apostle Paul had warned about "false brethren" (Galatians 2:4) and "false apostles" (2 Corinthians 11:13), while Peter had spoken about "false prophets" (2 Peter 2:1). Charlemagne was well versed in scripture. Jesus himself had issued this same warning about the End of Days (Matthew 24:5), although he did not suggest that the appearance of these false prophets was in and of itself a harbinger of the Apocalypse. Beyond a doubt, though, it was an irrefutable sign that the end was nigh.

So people needed to be vigilant. But the terrors that these last days were supposed to bring about spread as anticipatory knowledge among the general populace and the elites alike. People prepared themselves through prayer, and Charlemagne was no exception in this regard. Alcuin insistently admonished him "in these last days of the world [*his novissimis mundi*] to make good all things that have been corrupted" and to "lead those souls that have been blinded by dark ignorance toward the light of the true faith." Doing this would, Alcuin assured Charlemagne, bring him praise and rewards "when judgment falls on the great day of reckoning." The nearness of the Last Judgment required that people make supreme efforts, for "the era of earthly existence is rushing swiftly past and will never return."

> Cot *almahtîco, dû himil enti erda gauuorrhatôs*
> *Enti du mannun sô manac coot forgâpi,*
> *forgip mir in dîno ganâda rehta galaupa*
> *enti côtan uuilleon, uuîstôm enti spâhida enti craft,*
> *tiuflon za uuidarstantanne enti arc za piuuîsanne*
> *enti dînan uuilleon za gauurchanne.*

(Almighty God, who hath made Heaven and Earth and hath
     done so much good for Man,
give me in Thy Grace true faith and good will, wisdom,
     cleverness, and strength to
withstand the devils and to avoid evil and to do Thy will.)
(See Figure 3)

This was no poor contemporary whose prayer in Wessobrunn was recorded for posterity. Charlemagne could well have implored God in much the same manner. He owed his wealth and power to God, and he loyally followed the divine commandments, spreading Christianity among the pagans, persecuting heretics, and supporting the Church. He ruled his empire with force, shrewdness, and wisdom and directed ecclesiastical affairs; and all the while his magnificent "temple" was taking shape in Aix. The devils, though, were arming themselves to do battle for people's souls and when the day came for them to die. Immediately, a fierce battle would ensue between the armies of Heaven and Hell. To which army would a person's soul be carried after death? That of Satan or that of the angels? In Hell, the vat of pitch was already boiling, into which the damned would be cast. Many of the powerful men in the land feared for their chances of salvation.

Indeed, fear, even mortal dread, of the Last Judgment seized poor and rich alike. The terrors of the End of Days cast a long shadow, and it was by no means only the simple, uneducated populace that began to feel anxious. Even a saint like Augustine, the man whom Charlemagne admired so much, had, as he conceded in his *Confessions*, spent his whole life in fear of death and God's judgment (*Confessions* 6.16.26). He could not insist on God's grace but merely allow himself to hope that he might be granted it. A powerful figure like Charlemagne knew this feeling only too well and was careful to follow as best he could the teachings of the saints.

Death and judgment came together and threatened each and every person. As the epic poem the "*Muspilli*" proclaimed: "This is what I heard those versed in the law of the world relate: / That Elijah will be wounded in battle against the Antichrist, / That when the blood of Elijah drips onto the soil / The mountains will burn, no tree will stand, Not any on earth, water dries up, the marshland will swallow itself up, the sky will be aflame with fire." Then, the poem went on to foretell, the Day of Judgment would draw nigh, when no lies or perjury would help a person. Charlemagne personally spread the message of the End of Days and the Last Judgment. The *Admonitio generalis* of 789 came to a climax and ended with a dire warning on this subject. It was a way of keeping discipline among the populace.

Images of the conflagration that would consume the entire world, as in the verses cited above from the *"Muspilli,"* were common currency in Charlemagne's realm. They required book learning to be fully understood and reflected the beliefs of preachers and the literate elites. Study of the Apocalypse was a subject for experts and presupposed a scholarly education. Knowledge of the Apocalypse was spread, and fear of it stoked up, precisely by scribes rather than by the uneducated populace. Charlemagne, the king and emperor, would have awaited his own fate and the end of the world beset by the same visions. But when would this come to pass? Would it occur during his lifetime? Or soon after? Or sometime later? Who could possibly know? Could one ever be certain on this score?

The king and his scholars gave absolutely no indication of how near at hand or far off this final phase in the history of salvation was. Yet alarming news began to come from Spain, and events in Constantinople appeared to confirm it. Was the end now nigh? Anyone who consulted the history books or who read the works of the Church Fathers came across a whole series of mutually contradictory authorities on the subject. The voices of heretics were included in this choir, but it was saints like Jerome, the translator of the Vulgate—in other words, someone who knew the Bible in its entirety—who set the tone. Others tried to calm those who had been disquieted, although even they did not dispute that the End of Days was approaching. With every passing year, the time grew shorter as the term of six thousand years that had been granted to the world as its span of existence steadily ebbed away; and this required careful consideration.

"A span of 5,199 years separates the creation of the world from the second coming of the Lord . . . and it is 789 years from the time when God became incarnate to King Charles's twentieth year on the throne." Thus ran the calculations of the monks at Lorsch Abbey, the creators of the prototype of the Carolingian imperial calendar, a work that was produced in the aforementioned year, supposedly the 5,988th year since the creation of the world.[4] This reckoning followed the calculation of St. Jerome and revealed an unsettling proximity to a date that had particular relevance for the history of salvation, namely, the end of the sixth millennium. In much the same way, in 763 Paul the Deacon had calculated the passage of time for his mistress, the king's daughter Adelperga. He also worked out that only thirty-eight years still remained until the completion of the sixth millennium. At this stage, the kingdom and the Duchy of Benevento were still enjoying peaceful times. Yet his warning ended thus: "The heavenly judge comes like a bolt of lightning from the blue. The day and the hour are hidden from mortals. Those whom the Lord finds prepared will be fortunate. When Arechis, the merciful prince, stands before your throne, O righteous judge, with his illustrious wife, may you grant them eternal joy along with the chosen ones."[5] These were highly dangerous times to be living through. If the calculations of the saints were correct, then Christmas Day 800—actually the first day of the year 801 according to Carolingian calendrical reckoning—would see the current epoch draw to a close, for according to the convictions of rabbinical scholars and the beliefs of the Church Fathers, the world was due to survive for just six thousand years.[6]

Elsewhere too, say, in the monastery of Liébana in northern Spain, similar calculations were also being made. There, the abbot Beatus made a particularly precise calculation in his commentary on the Apocalypse.[7] He had written this work in 786 (or 776 according to another manuscript) while he was in great fear of the Moors and anticipating the imminent advent of the day when the people would be raised from the dead to attend the Last Judgment. Thus, only fourteen (or twenty-four) years remained before the final millennium was at an end and before the second coming of Him who would judge the world; God had reserved for himself only the knowledge of the exact day and hour, not of the year, when this would come to pass.[8] The *Mozarabic Chronicle* of 754 calculated the date in the same way.[9] Only the Greek East—Byzantium and the Orthodox Church—followed another set of calculations, which took its point of reference from the Septuagint, not the Vulgate.

Yet knowledge of the Apocalypse related to the universal Church. Up to this point, Charlemagne had fought wars on the borders of his royal domain and had also widened these frontiers, as well as consolidating his rule internally as none of his forebears or predecessors had done; he had aligned his authority with the aims of the Church, expanding Christianity eastward, offering those under his rule peace and justice, and organizing and strengthening the churches under his jurisdiction, and had ultimately bowed his head in humility before the successor of the apostolic princes in Rome. Now it was up to him to protect the universal Church worldwide and Christianity as a whole. Now Charlemagne found himself faced with universal obligations that pointed far beyond the narrow horizons of a Frankish ruler.

"Opposing the Enemies of Truth"

The apocalyptic reflections of Beatus of Liébana were accompanied by a spreading heresy. The abbot was writing with regard to and in opposition to a rising tide of false doctrine that had its origin in the Muslim lands; he corresponded specially on this subject with Alcuin, who by this time had himself either already written a commentary on the Apocalypse or was about to.[10] This heresy had its seat at Mozarabic Toledo, in other words, among Christians who were living under Muslim control, but it had already spread as far as the Diocese of Urgell in the Pyrenees. The leading representatives of this new doctrine were Archbishop Elipand of Toledo and Bishop Felix of Urgell. Invoking St. Paul, and in total opposition to the Apostles' Creed (which was widespread in the Frankish kingdom and had been translated into the Frankish language), they declared Christ to be not simply God's "only begotten" son (*filium unicum* or, in Frankish, *suno sinan einagon*);[11] instead, they taught that whereas Christ was indeed the only begotten son of God where his divine nature was concerned, his human nature meant that he had merely been taken by God as his son. Accordingly, to put it in simplified terms, they declared Jesus the man to be God's "adopted son."[12]

This flew in the face of Catholic teaching. In alarm, the pope addressed an admonishing encyclical to the Spanish, which he promptly forwarded to the king as well.[13] It has come down to us from the royal archive. The doctrine of adoptionism may possibly have come into being under the influence of Islam, and specifically the Prophet Muhammad's pronouncement that Allah had no son. Furthermore, the "Meshiah" (Messiah) of the Jews, despite being chosen by God, was not God's son. But the Christological and dogmatic discourse of previous ages also left its traces behind.

In Toledo, then, Christians made a distinction between "God [i.e., Christ] the son of God, Light from Light, true God from true God, the only begotten of the Father without adoption" (*Deum Dei filium, lumen de lumine, Deum verum ex Deo vero, ex patre unigenitum sine adobtione*) and the "firstborn [son] at the end of time," "the true man through conception by the Virgin and assumption of the flesh" (*primogenitum vero in fine temporis, verum hominem adsumendo de virgine in carnis adobtione*), who was "begotten of nature, and the firstborn by adoption and grace" (*unigenitum in natura, primogenitum in adobtione et gratia*).[14] It was in these terms that the Spanish bishops confessed their faith in a missive to the Frankish king. The only begotten Son of God was bodiless and consubstantial with the Father, whereas the firstborn was corporeal, sprung from the womb of Mary, became God's son through adoption, and in this way was both truly divine and truly human. At the End of Days, "we" too (the true Christians, that is) would become like him, Christ, "in becoming flesh and not in his divinity" (*similes utique in carnis adobtione, non similes ei in divinitate*).

The Spanish invoked the holy archbishops of Toledo—Eugene, Ildefonsus, and Julian—and the Mozarabic Maundy Thursday Mass (*missa in coena domini;* Mass of the Lord's Supper).[15] Yet what they taught was heretical. The oneness of both of Christ's natures was in danger, and this old Christological question was too explosive for its settlement to be put off any longer.[16] It threatened the whole doctrine of salvation. Charlemagne became worried; no sooner had he been informed about it than he immediately took charge of the matter, putting it on the agenda of a synod that was due to be held in Regensburg in 792. Bishop Felix was duty bound to attend this meeting, and at its conclusion he was escorted to Rome by Charlemagne's confidant Angilbert, where he was questioned by the pope. Meanwhile, Alcuin and other scholars were charged with writing refutations of adoptionism.

The Spaniards were sternly rebuked (794): they were informed that it was better to trust the testimony of God the Father rather than Ildefonsus and the liturgy he devised. "Your Ildefonsus may well call Christ adopted [*adoptivum*], but our St. Gregory, the pontiff of the Roman See, the teacher who enlightens the entire Earth, never hesitated to call Him only-begotten [*unigenitum*] in his prayers."[17] Given the large population of displaced Visigoths, especially in the south of Gallia, the conflict of Rome versus Toledo was bound to spill over into the Frankish kingdom.

A growing number of disconcerting reports began to arrive in Rome and at Charlemagne's court from Spain. A missionary bishop named Egila, who was almost certainly a Visigoth, and whom Archbishop Wilcharius of Sens ordained and dispatched to Spain to spread the true Word—surely with Charlemagne's approval—appears to have fallen under the spell of the "new heresy" of Mingentius (or Migetius), who spread a curiously confused doctrine of the Trinity—he identified the divine Trinity as King David, Jesus, and St. Paul—and who first and foremost called for Christians to reject out of hand any communication whatsoever with Muslims. In addition, he maintained contact with Elipand of Toledo. Egila was easily able to demonstrate the orthodoxy of his beliefs, but even so, it must have seemed to the pope and the king that the true faith was in grave danger of demise among the Mozarabic Christian community.[18] There, Easter was not celebrated with Rome, people were encouraged to partake of "things strangled and blood"

(Acts 15:20; i.e., halal meat), marriages between Christians and Jews or Christians and Muslims were allowed, and an inappropriate doctrine on predestination was promulgated.[19]

Renewed attacks by Arab forces under 'Abd-al-Malik in 792/793, threatening Aquitaine, placed Christianity in peril once more. These attacks were perhaps intended to divert attention from internal divisions among the Umayyad rulers of Spain, which were also known about in the Frankish kingdom, and exploited the fact that Charlemagne was tied up fighting the Avars in the east of his realm. Carcassonne and Narbonne held out, but only just, but a heavy defeat at the battle of Orbiel of border forces under the valiant Count Guillaume of Toulouse by the Muslim invaders revealed clear weaknesses in the Franks' frontier security.[20] Even so, the case of Egila does show that Charlemagne also had clear aspirations to send missionaries to Spain, that is, into territories under the sway of Islam.

Royal land had meanwhile been appropriated, especially in the south of the country. Visigothic *aprisionares,* that is, refugees from Moorish Spain, who were both landowners and free farmers and to whom Charlemagne had apportioned land some years previously in return for military service and forest clearance, were probably even at this early stage put under pressure by the relevant local noblemen and had at least in part had their estates annexed by them. They also obeyed no common, overall command.[21] The distant royal authority could assert itself only to a very limited degree. Might any relief be forthcoming for these people? It was precisely the case of these "Spaniards" that saw the emergence of regional authority; however, although this new development took place in defense of Frankish power, it did not always necessarily follow the king's wishes.[22] Many landowners who controlled particular estates did not heed the call to participate in military campaigns. Everything hints at difficult times for Carolingian rule during this period. Louis of Aquitaine was in no position to render gifts befitting his status to his father at this time.[23]

Charlemagne decided to intervene. He sent two royal messengers to the south, Count Richard and a cleric called Willibert, who would presently become archbishop of Rouen, who were charged with the task of regaining the royal estates (*villae*) for the crown. In a three-year reversal of fortune, the king's fifteen-year-old son Louis had no fewer than four palaces assigned to him as "winter residences"; these all lay in the north of the kingdom of Aquitaine: Doué in Anjou, Chasseneuil, Angeac in Angoulême, and Ebreuil in Berry. The military watch duties, which were also expected of bishops and the larger abbeys, needed to become more efficient and were duly improved.

We have no record of the further changes Charlemagne implemented at this time, but we know that Louis ordered the payment of tributes to be relaxed at various locations, made contact with Muslim rebels, and restored the defense installations at Vich, Cardona, and a number of other strongholds.[24] Indeed, the situation on the border with Muslim Spain improved markedly over the course of the following years.

However, developments in Spain called for the utmost ongoing vigilance. Two years after the Synod of Regensburg, the Christological question was debated once more in Frankfurt. Felix of Urgell had traveled to attend the synod once more but was unable to justify his adoptionism on this occasion as well. Instead, he was defrocked and banished to Lyons, where he died twenty-five years later. In addition, two or three years after the Synod of Frankfurt, Alcuin, from his base in Tours, once again attacked Elipand and Felix in writing. "Rise up, you elect of God, rise up, you child of the Lord, you warrior of Christ, and defend the bride of the Lord your God!" he exhorted Charlemagne. The king was meant to protect the church—the bride of Christ, "with whose protection and guidance your God entrusted you"[25]—from this false doctrine. A third synod, which was convened in Aix in 799, reaffirmed the verdict against the Toledo doctrine and was finally confirmed in Rome. Charlemagne, the "warrior of Christ" who transcended all earthly boundaries of power and the guardian of the "Lord's bride"—did this characterization of Alcuin's really get to the heart and soul of the ruler? Whatever the case, Charlemagne willingly took on the task with which he had been charged.

But to fulfill his allotted role, the king desired the express approval of the Apostolic See. The Synod of Frankfurt of 794 had been convened in the presence of the papal legates Theophylact (of Todi?) and Stephen (of Naples?); representatives of the Catholic Church from England and Italy were also in attendance. The synod had been well prepared.[26] Pope Hadrian's encyclical to Elipand, the response of the Italians under the leadership of Paul of Aquileia, and the statement issued by the Frankish bishops have all been preserved. Charlemagne personally had them dispatched to Elipand with his own accompanying note. The Spanish, including Felix, judged the situation correctly and sent their defense of their position directly to the king.[27]

It was with a "fervent heart" that Charlemagne urged those present at the synod to fight against all forms of heresy. Paul of Aquileia praised the king's intervention. Every schism within the church could only endanger the kingdom. The guests invited to the synod began to assemble under the king's eyes: Charlemagne attended the Frankfurt synod in person, fulfilling the roles of "listener" and "judge" (*auditor* and *arbiter*); it was he who decided the outcome of the Inquisition.[28] Elipand and his supporters were cautioned in the following terms: "With the help of God's grace, we shall be your companions in joy as soon as you signal your willingness to join us in becoming preachers of the one true Catholic faith." Otherwise, if they chose to cling to their false belief, Charlemagne the layman threatened them, the Spanish bishops, with anathema. His missive to Toledo ended with an (expanded) declaration of faith in which he confessed his belief in Jesus Christ, "God's only begotten son, born of the Father before all the world and for all eternity, light of light, very God of very God, begotten, not made, by his very nature, not adopted . . . being at one and of one substance with the Father."[29]

The *Opus Caroli regis*

Adoptionism was not the only heresy threatening the Church that the Synod of Frankfurt had to deal with. A second heresy arrived from the East. There, the debate about imagery in Christianity inevitably provoked a controversy about the cult of images and sacred icons. The shock waves of this argument reverberated as far as Rome and the kingdom of the Franks.[30] The iconoclastic controversy had been dragging on since the early eighth century and a few decades after the end of Charlemagne's reign was destined to flare up again and engage the attention of Western intellectuals once more. Those who abhorred images stirred up hatred against those who revered them, a clash of the "iconoclasts" versus the "iconodules."

Since the eighth century, the wide-ranging (though never total) scorning of imagery in both Judaism and Islam also influenced the debate going on in Byzantium; the fear of idolatry even prompted occasional, though admittedly never very strictly enforced, bans on religious imagery. The precise magnitude of the controversy in the East is uncertain and was presumably deliberately exaggerated by the political propaganda spread by the iconodules. Powerfully eloquent Christian preachers like the Church Father John of Damascus (d. 754)—who was given the sobriquet Chrysorrhoas (literally "streaming with gold") and who spent the final years of his life at the Saba monastery in Jerusalem, where he went by the Arabic name of Yahya ibn-Mansur—defended the practice of worshipping images.[31] Platonic philosophy may have played a role here, with its clear differentiation of the "archetype" and the "image"; in any event, a distinction was sometimes drawn in the debate between "adoration" or "worship" ("latreia"; προσκύνησις τῆς λατρείας) and "veneration" ("proskynesis"; προσκύνησις τῆς τιμῆς); the first was due exclusively to God and the saints, while the second, the act of prostrating oneself, was performed in front of a secular authority like the emperor; it also described the kind of devotion shown to sacred icons. This meant that there could be no question of adoration of images and idolatry.

The Eastern Roman emperors Michael II and Theophilos later described the traditional practice of veneration to Louis the Pious: the faithful would banish the cross from churches and replace it with icons, before which they lit candles and incense, and to which they would pray, imploring the saints depicted for their help. They would wrap the icons in cloths that they would subsequently use to lift their child out of the font after baptism; in addition, those who were tonsured for the monastic life would allow their cut hair to fall on an icon and leave it there like some votive offering, while it was not uncommon for priests and other clerics to scrape flakes of paint off icons, mix them with wine, and pass it to those who wanted to receive Communion after hearing Mass. Others, meanwhile, would place the Host in the hands of the figure painted on the icon in order that the faithful might ostensibly receive the Body of Christ directly from the saint. Some people even set up icons to use as altars in their own houses.[32] Bishop Freculf of Lisieux, who was sent to Rome to negotiate with Pope Eugene II on the question of veneration of images in 824, confirmed this particular abuse but explained on his return that the pope had expressly sanctioned such veneration.[33]

The cult of images in Rome, where religious practice was still very strongly influenced by Greece, would have observed a similar practice. Admittedly, though, the scholars around Pepin and Charlemagne may well have been only partially familiar with this practice. Icons were most definitely venerated as sacred, such as the icon of Christ in the Sancta Sanctorum, the private papal chapel in the Lateran Palace; the icon has survived to this day, but the image is barely recognizable anymore. Every Maundy Thursday, the stigmata depicted on this icon were ritually anointed.[34] Charlemagne must have experienced the liturgical practice surrounding this icon, or others like it, in person during his visits to Rome, not to mention the mosaic decoration he must have marveled at in the great churches of the patriarchate. Comparable icons, however—that is, portable painted panels—are not documented as having existed in Charlemagne's Frankish kingdom, nor even during the reign of Louis the Pious. The king, who feared idolatry, must have been astonished by the cult surrounding them; indeed, the whole enterprise may well have struck him as strange and deeply alarming.

Now, in the final years of the eighth century, the Eastern Roman Empire was still feeling the aftershocks of the iconoclastic controversy. The argument

FIGURE 47 The icon known as the *Maria Advocata* (or *Madonna of San Sisto*) is in the Church of Santa Maria del Rosario in Rome. This picture has been dated to the sixth century and is thought to have been brought to Rome from Syria.

had been raging for many decades and had been a constant source of tension in Constantinople, fomenting clashes that verged on civil war and flaring up repeatedly. Ultimately, at the Second Council of Nicaea in 787, the seventh in a series of such ecumenical councils, the Byzantine empress Irene, who since 780 had been acting as regent for her underage son Constantine VI, reaffirmed her support for the veneration of images, together with the Eastern patriarch Tarasios. This success greatly increased her power. When Constantine reached the age of majority, he was barely able to assert his authority against his mother; the ensuing power struggle between them effectively crippled Byzantium.

The power of the Frankish king also grew over this period. After Charlemagne's victory over the Lombards and his entry into Rome, all the old imperial residences of the West were now in his hands. His son Pepin of Italy's decisive defeat of the Avars in 796 extended the boundaries of his empire far to the southeast. The former Roman province of Pannonia was now under Carolingian control;[35] the result of this was that the kingdom of the Franks now had the Byzantine Empire as its immediate neighbor. "Have the Frank for your friend but not for your neighbor" was soon the exasperated cry in Constantinople.[36] Einhard quoted this Byzantine proverb in the original Greek in his biography of Charlemagne; it was the product of bitter experience, with the Byzantines now coming under pressure from the Franks in both southern Italy and the Balkans.

With this growth in power, however, the responsibility of the Frankish king for the whole of Christendom also increased. Charlemagne found himself forced to act. "On occasion, our Mother Church finds herself beset by attacks from unbelievers or heretics, and on others disturbed by the hostility of schismatics or presumptuous mistaken beliefs." "Yet she is the Holy Mother, the Immaculate, the Brightly Shining and Spotless One, she is the fertile Mother who cannot lose her virginity and yet never ceases to bear children . . . the Mother who becomes ever more exalted the more she finds herself beset by troubles." "God has placed direction of the Mother Church in the bosom of our kingdom. It is therefore essential that we fight with all our might and with Christ's help to safeguard her and to raise her up, so that we might earn her praise for being a good and faithful servant." "Anyone who is not with her is against her. . . . These circumstances compel us to speak up now, something we do with great dismay since, to paraphrase the words of St. Paul the Apostle [2 Corinthians 11:29], we are 'weak along with the weak.' "[37] These sentiments were expressed by the scholar Theodulf, writing in 794 in Charlemagne's name and at his behest. Indeed, this was how the king regarded himself: as the guide and guardian of the Mother Church, raising her up and strengthening her and monitoring her adherence to orthodoxy and the correct form of liturgical practice.

The repercussions of the iconoclastic controversy really did reach the Frankish kingdom and force the king to take action, all the more because the narrow theological controversy was compounded by disturbing political reports from the Bosphorus and the extremely ill-tempered ecumenical council that was convened in Nicaea in 787. No sooner had Constantine VI attained autocracy in 790 on reaching the age of majority than he promoted his mother, Irene, who until then had governed only as regent for her son, to the status of co-empress (792)—the first woman to sit on the throne of the Caesars. Disorder heaped on disorder! Besides, Frankish pride had been wounded. The Franks and the Anglo-Saxons had not been invited to the Second Council of Nicaea by the "arrogant Greeks." Yet it was they who found themselves outraged by the council's most important decision. As they understood it, sacred images were henceforth to be venerated as though they were the Holy Trinity. In their eyes, this was nothing short of heresy. It was essential that Charlemagne, the guardian of the faith, take steps against this ruling.

In addition, some irritating deviations in the creed became apparent at this time. It was rumored that the patriarch of Constantinople, Tarasios, had issued a proclamation in which he erroneously and in contradiction of the creed announced that the Holy Spirit proceeded "from the Father through the Son" (*ex patre per filium*). This opened up a second front in the controversy: according to the Franks, the Second Council of Nicaea had promulgated an idolatrous heresy and was spreading a false doctrine of the Trinity and a cult of image veneration with more than a hint of paganism about it. Both were to be condemned outright and vigorously opposed. This was why, in 792, Charlemagne sent his trusted courtier Angilbert to Rome with the purpose not only of presenting the schismatic Felix of Urgell to Pope Hadrian I but also of handing over to the pontiff a collection of particularly scandalous pronouncements by the Second Council of Nicaea that needed to be refuted; this compendium was known as the *Capitulary against the Council* (*Capitulare contra Synodum*).[38]

Yet mere protest of this order was not enough for Charlemagne in his self-appointed role as guardian of the faith. It was incumbent on his court to issue a fundamental refutation of the Greeks' false beliefs—both the erroneous doctrine of the Trinity and the quasi-idolatrous cult of images. The Visigothic scholar Theodulf, who later became the bishop of Orléans, was

FIGURE 48 This image of Empress Irene of Byzantium was made during her reign (797–802); it was plundered by Venetian crusaders during the sack of Constantinople during the Fourth Crusade in 1204. In Venice, it was incorporated along with other booty into the *Pala d'Oro*, the high altar retable in St. Mark's Basilica, where it can still be seen today. In English, the Greek inscription reads "Irene, most pious ruler."

entrusted with this theologically audacious task. And so he set about sharpening his quills in preparation for writing the so-called *Libri Carolini*, namely, the *Work of Charles, King of the Franks, and of Gallia, Germania, and Italy, against the Synod* (*Opus Caroli regis contra synodum*).[39] The original manuscript with addenda and brief annotations inserted by the king himself has been preserved (Vaticanus latinus 7207). In completing his four-volume work, or rather the "work of King Charles," which contains a total of 120 chapters, Theodulf astutely deployed all the available theories of categories and predication espoused by Aristotle and others in the interpretation of the Bible and other Christian writings, as well as numerous quotations from the Church Fathers. It is certainly the case that the king, thanks to his self-image as the guiding influence of the Church, played a very direct part in refuting the ideas of the "Greeks." He ordered that Theodulf's exposition be read aloud to him, sentence by sentence, so that he might give his approval.

The Visigoth, who appears to have spent three years—from around 790–791 to 793 inclusive—working on the *Libri*, did not shrink from using caustic and occasionally ironic language. He accused the Greeks of displaying casual arrogance and of shunning the true Christian doctrine. At the very beginning of his text, he castigated the "madness" of the Byzantine emperor and his mother, who claimed that God was their coregent in Constantinople. "Since our being is so far removed from that of God, and likewise our life from his life and our mode of rule from his, their [i.e., the Byzantine emperors'] delusion is more lamentable than it is astonishing, they who in their confusion have the temerity to call God their coregent. Their being comprehends existence only in the here and now and knows nothing of a past or future existence; it does not participate in eternity." Moreover, Theodulf was able to use the logical differentiation between category and type to corroborate his argument against the idolatrous banishment of all images from churches; God had commanded that this be done only in regard to graven images of false deities. They were evidently unaware, Theodulf accused the Greeks, "that an image [*imago*] represents a category [*genus*], whereas an idol [*idolum*] is a type [*species*], and that a type can be reduced to a category, but not vice versa. For despite the fact that almost every idol is also an image, conversely, it is not the case that every image is an idol. . . . An image always signifies something other than itself, while an idol never denotes anything but itself."[40]

Even in Rome, clear magical practices had been identified in conjunction with the veneration of icons, for example, scraping paint from pictures of the Madonna and the saints and mixing it into medical potions. Bishop Freculf of Lisieux described this practice among Romans around 825. The icons embodied the Mother of God and the other saints, and particles of paint from such a picture were supposed to guarantee the presence of the saint in question at the sickbed of the person to whom the potion was administered. In this, it was not unlike the cult of relics, which was also just gaining a foothold during this period. We may speculate whether Charlemagne and his advisers also participated in these practices. In any event, the essential thing was to rid sacred images of any form of cult or hint of adoration. "Whether or not they were placed in churches to commemorate some miraculous event or merely for decoration, they could not generate any 'prejudice' against the Catholic faith, since it is well known that they have no function in the actual execution of sacred mysteries." Charlemagne gave his express assent to these words of Theodulf.[41] In his realm, little tolerance would be shown to the idea that paint dust might be used to cure the sick.

Images were therefore neither to be worshipped nor to be destroyed. Rather, a middle course was to be pursued. Charlemagne let it be known that this was the "perfect" solution. In this way, he formulated a new and independent position. It diverged as much from Roman liturgical practice, in the form that Frankish bishops appear to have accepted even as early as the Synod of Rome in 769, as it did from iconoclasm, which had just been overcome at the time. God in his eternality was beyond our ken and remained so in the time of Charlemagne, but this was emphatically not the case with the historical Jesus Christ, who had been made flesh as a human being. Thus images served as decoration in Frankish churches (*in ornamentis ecclesiae*), while at the same time, following Gregory the Great, their function was also seen as being the "instruction of the ignorant." Images, which were created "for the instruction [or edification] of the unknowing populace, in order that the illiterate might gain an understanding of history and comprehend what was being said during services," were permitted for the purposes of "instruction," but on no account—as artifacts that had been fashioned by the hand of man—were they to be worshipped. Emphasis was therefore placed on the didactic nature of images for the uneducated, which could be conveyed only through words; a historical sense could and ought to be imparted to images, and the moral and anagogical meaning duly emerged from them. Charlemagne expressly approved this approach. It was permissible to use images as a form of aide-mémoire. "The eyes should be flattered by images; for it is through them, acting as it were like messengers, that recollections of past events are confided to a person's heart."[42] Scholarly learning thus regulated a naïve faith. At the Synod of Frankfurt (794), which was meant to discuss the "cult of images" and to which papal legates were also invited, the intention was for the *Opus Caroli* to be generally accepted before the work was subsequently handed over to the pope.

But suddenly, like a bolt from the blue, Pope Hadrian's response to the *Capitulare contra Synodum* arrived at the Frankish court, containing the scarcely believable news that he himself, St. Peter's successor, had approved the decisions reached at the Council of Nicaea through the presence there of his legate.[43] A poor translation had led Theodulf and the Franks (who did not know Greek) astray. This translation had not drawn any distinction between "veneration" of images and "adoration," the latter of which was owed solely to the Holy Trinity; in consequence, the scholars at the Carolingian court were misled into identifying idolatry among Orthodox Christians and agitating for steps to be taken to combat it. And although Theodulf forbore to allude to it, even the Romans did not make a clear distinction between "adoration" (*adorare*) and "veneration" (*venerare*).[44]

The Greeks, however, had done precisely that: "For the more the images are contemplated, the more they move those looking at them to fervent recollection of their prototypes. Therefore, it is proper to accord to them a fervent and reverent veneration, not, however, the veritable adoration that, according to our faith, belongs to the Divine Being alone."[45] Lack of linguistic knowledge, misunderstanding arising from ignorance of an alien culture, and insufficient scholarship thus paved the way for catastrophe. In these circumstances, the great effort expended on the logic, argumentative acuity, and political irony of the *Opus Caroli* and the resolution of the Synod of Frankfurt were all in vain.

Indeed, the matter-of-fact explanation from Rome caused the proud work of scholarship that was the *Opus Caroli regis* to simply disappear into oblivion, but at the same time this obscurity saved the original manuscript—that is, the working copy drafted by the Carolingian court—for posterity, preserving it to the present day as Codex Vaticanus latinus 7207. It is clearly identifiable as such from all the many deletions, erasures, additions, and amendments, all of them carried out in the most meticulous way, apart from certain exceptions toward the end of the work. Aside from this, only three traces of copies of this work survived: one fragment from Corbie, which consists of only a single sheet; another that was transcribed in Reims under the supervision of the great archbishop Hincmar (now similarly mutilated); and a third copy that has been lost entirely and that we know about only through a library catalog.

It was only in the era of humanism that the original codex of the *Opus Caroli* (likewise now mutilated, with its beginning and end missing) was re-discovered. It had somehow found its way to Marienfeld (in the Diocese of Münster) and from there had been taken to Italy in the sixteenth century, where it eventually ended up in the papal library. The first printed edition appeared in 1549. Since then, scholars have been engaged in studying this outstanding work, which testifies to the intellectual culture that pervaded the Carolingian court. Yet it was only from the early twentieth century onward, largely thanks to the efforts of the scholar Wolfram von den Steinen, an associate of the poet Stefan George, that the unique status of this Vatican codex was fully appreciated: Steinen discovered that the manuscript contained a series of approving exclamations written by the king, authentic words from the great man himself, in the form of Tironian notes (a system of shorthand) in the margin. These represent the only writings by a medieval ruler to have been preserved anywhere.[46]

Charlemagne did not dare to argue with the successor to St. Peter; he was precluded from doing so by the high esteem in which he held the office of pontiff. At the very beginning of his letter to the Frankish court, Hadrian, presumably drawing inspiration from older memoranda issued by the Roman See,[47] and with barely disguised criticism of this monarch who was presuming to posture as a theologian, reminded Charlemagne of Christ's injunction to St. Peter, "Feed my sheep!" (John 21:17), and above all of the words of institution from the Gospel According to St. Matthew (16:18–19), whose meaning he lost no time in explaining to the king: "You see, St. Peter was entrusted by Christ with the keys of the Kingdom of Heaven and responsibility for the entire Church; and as we well know, Peter in turn duly handed down this responsibility to his representatives, the popes."[48] Hadrian then went on to elucidate, sentence by sentence, the resolutions of the council that Charlemagne had unjustly discredited. He explained that the Council of Nicaea had approved the reverential raising up (*erectio*) of images of saints; in doing so, it had adhered strictly to the "orthodox tradition of faith."[49] Furthermore, the pope continued, the council's critics did not have a proper understanding of the tradition of the Church Fathers, since this also justified *per filium procedere,* that is, the notion of the Holy Spirit proceeding "through the son."

Charlemagne deferred to this doctrinal decision by Rome. No sooner had the pope's refutation arrived in Aix than all work on the *Opus Caroli regis* was immediately stopped; the manuscript today still reflects this radical break, inasmuch as the text up to chapter 13 of book 3 is written and corrected with the utmost care, but thereafter the entire fourth book of the work shows every sign of being a rough working draft, with crossings-out and hasty corrections with no evidence of careful transcription.[50] But surely Charlemagne still harbored some doubts? The king was not content with the answer he had received from the pope. His theologians would come back to the *filioque* question time and again over the ensuing years; this doctrinal issue was debated repeatedly in Charlemagne's realm, for the final time at a synod held in Aix in 809. And time and again the reigning pope of the time— first Hadrian, then Leo III—was urged to incorporate the *filioque* that was so familiar to the Franks into the creed of the Roman Church.[51] All, however, to no avail.

A Hidden Failure: The Synod of Frankfurt

Charlemagne did not allow the pope's doctrinal dressing-down to cramp the brilliant demonstration of his guardianship of the Church that he had planned. His disagreements with the Spanish and the Greeks would proclaim to the whole world how fruitful the Frankish king's efforts to bring about a thoroughgoing revival of education had been, how astutely his scholars were able to engage in debate, and what a diligent defender of the faith he himself was. He was determined to present himself as the protector of Christendom. Indeed, the confrontation with heretics acted as a stimulus for intellectual schooling and methodical progress and a mode of thinking guided by formalized reason. These advances represented the first tentative beginnings of a Western theology.

The king did not stop at simply refuting heresies. Rather, he set in motion a comprehensive program of reform, which also found its way onto the agenda at Frankfurt in 794. This synod in particular reveals the enormous extent to which the Church, meanwhile, had come to serve as an instrument of power for the king. Alongside questions of dogma and ecclesiastical procedure, those attending the meeting were also expected to deal with purely secular matters, as the capitulary adopted at Frankfurt makes clear. In other words, they were required to tackle an extensive agenda.[52]

Once the dispute over adoptionism had been settled and the cult of images had been rejected,[53] the synod turned its attention to the final verdict against Tassilo of Bavaria. The meeting then went on to impose various regulations and decrees concerning fixed market prices for cereals like oats, barley, rye, and wheat before discussing coinage reform and finally concluding by passing a series of ecclesiastical provisions, some of which were borrowed from the *Admonitio generalis* and now received synodal approval. These provisions related, for instance, to such matters as episcopal jurisdiction within the dioceses, the old dispute between the archbishops of Vienne and Arles, the oath of cleansing proposed by Bishop Petrus of Verdun for those suspected of having conspired against the king, how to depose any bishop who was found to be questionable, and various other ecclesiastical and monastic regulations. For example, the synod decreed that all bishops should have a full knowledge of canon law and the *Benedictine Rule*, that Sundays should be observed as the holy day from the preceding evening to the evening of the day itself (like the Jewish Sabbath), that no episcopal sees could be established in villages, that churches were to be decorated in a fitting manner and that those who entered God's House should be instructed in how to behave appropriately, that cabals and conspiracies were forbidden, that no new saints were to be venerated, that (pagan) sacred trees and groves were to be felled, that small children should not be required to swear oaths, that God could be prayed to in any language (not just Hebrew, Greek, or Latin), and that Bishop Hildebald (of Cologne) might, with papal approval, continue to reside at the royal court "for the benefit of the church."

The last phase of the trial of Duke Tassilo of Bavaria was played out in Frankfurt. Evidently, the king welcomed the public forum of a synod for this procedure, and moreover one at which he had just shown himself to be the guardian of religious orthodoxy. What ensued was a form of show trial. The Agilolfing nobleman had, after all, already been sentenced and stripped of his ducal title and had been in Charlemagne's custody for some time. Now he was summoned from the Monastery of St. Goar, where he had been tonsured and accepted into holy orders, and was made to publicly renounce all claims to the duchy by both himself and his sons before withdrawing once again to the monastery to which he had long since been banished.

Had criticism of Charlemagne's brutal behavior toward his cousin stung him into taking action, perhaps? Or had the uprising staged two years previously by his own outcast son Pepin the Hunchback, who had originally, it seems, been chosen as the future king of Bavaria, stirred things up? Was this new trial actually less about the aging duke himself and much more about his sons Theodo and Theudebert, who as grandsons of the Lombard king Desiderius could be regarded as a latent threat to Charlemagne's reign in Italy? Einhard certainly hinted at such concerns when he accused Duchess Liutperga, Desiderius's daughter, of fomenting opposition to Charlemagne within Bavaria in chapter 11 of his biography of the emperor. Whether or not this was the case, Tassilo's entire family had already been enticed to travel to Ingelheim in 788, where they had promptly been taken into custody and spirited away forever behind dismal convent walls—Tassilo was incarcerated in St. Goar and Theodo in St. Maximin, while the duke's daughters were sent to the convents of Chelles and Laon.[54] Father and son are thought ultimately to have ended up in Jumièges, where their feet may have been mutilated to prevent them from staging any return to power.

New grain prices (Frankfurt capitulary, chap. 4) and a coinage reform (chaps. 4 and 5) may well reflect the results of a famine that affected large parts of the Frankish kingdom. "Our pious king stipulated, in accord with the holy synod, that no cleric and no layperson may ever sell their grain harvest at inflated prices, be it in times of plenty or in times of want." The prices were brought into a fixed relationship with those set out in the following chapter of the capitulary and in relation to the older (now heavier) denarius (penny), which had a weight of 1.7 grams of silver, and the repercussions of this were reflected in reasonable regulated bread prices.[55] In every region, every town, and every marketplace, coins were henceforth to be worth the same amount. In conjunction with this step, all the various different measures of capacity and weight that were to be found around the kingdom of the Franks were to be brought into line with one another.

A *solidus* (shilling), which was nothing but a notional denomination, was fixed at a value of twelve (silver) denarii, the only currency that was actually minted; twenty shillings made one pound. In consequence, a pound weighed 408 grams of pure silver. A shilling corresponded in Saxony, say, to an ox, while in the north of the empire it bought thirty bushels of oats or fifteen bushels of rye. Grain was always scarce in spring, just before the harvest. The populace was hit regularly by famine, especially the poorer sectors of society. There is documentary evidence to suggest that during such periods of crisis, moneylenders charged an extortionate interest rate of several hundred percent. And it was by no means exclusively laypeople who acted as usurers; the largest grain stores were in church hands.

A fixed relationship was established among grain prices: a bushel of oats was set at 1 denarius, a bushel of barley was 2 denarii, while a bushel of rye was 3 and a bushel of wheat 4. Grain and bread from the royal estates was to be sold more cheaply than on the open market; the so-called king's grain stood in the ratio of 1:1:2:3. Following the same sequence of cereal types listed above, a bushel of each was meant to yield, respectively, 50, 80, 90, and 96 (Carolingian) pounds of bread. The Frankfurt coinage reform was also to have some far-reaching consequences. This formed the basis of the entire monetary system over the following centuries; even the Anglo-Saxons fell in line with Charlemagne's system of coinage. One denarius in their country also had a weight of around 1.7 grams of pure silver. The impressions on Carolingian coins were very plain and simple; often they showed only the name of the ruler. It was only after the coronation of Charlemagne as emperor (800) that a few mintings of certain coins—perhaps not even intended as currency within the empire—showed a portrait of the emperor on the obverse and various different designs on the reverse, in imitation of ancient imperial Roman coinage.[56] The coinage reform did not instantly catch on throughout the realm and had to be reaffirmed later.[57] Royal envoys (*missi*) had to monitor public acceptance of the new money, and decrees ordering its introduction were issued time and again by the king (and later emperor).[58] Counterfeiting appears to have been a widespread problem. To combat it, Charlemagne repeatedly decreed that coins—with a few authorized exceptions—were allowed to be struck only *in palatio*—that is, in one or other of the royal palaces. *Missi* were instructed to monitor and enforce public compliance with this directive.[59] The totality of these measures certainly testifies to a degree of economic interest in asserting this reform, but not least of all it was designed—indeed, this was arguably its primary objective—to protect the poor, implement justice, and maintain peace among the populace.

The Frankfurt synod also addressed the question of church building (chapters 26 and 54 of the capitulary). The design of a church should both be imposing and follow the requirements of the liturgy. On many occasions, churches were constructed with a nave but with no transept, and with one or more apses on the eastern side or in addition an east and a west choir (e.g., the abbey church at Lorsch). The archetype for this style of church was the Roman basilica. The monastery at St-Denis, meanwhile, whose abbot anyhow had maintained close ties with the Apostolic See since Pope Stephen II's visit to the Frankish kingdom,[60] was the first, as far as we can determine, to mimic the architectural concept of St. Peter's in Rome, a style later repeated in Fulda and Cologne: a nave with a western transept and in front of this a circular apse. Important churches had several altars, each of which was designed to hold relics. The huge demand for sacred relics was an open invitation to swindlers. In this regard, the decrees concerning new saints issued by the Synod of Frankfurt were meant to curb the widespread fraud in religious relics.

The acrimonious dispute that had been going on since late antiquity between the archdioceses of Vienne and Arles was brought to an end in Frankfurt with the adoption of a compromise (chap. 8): Vienne was assigned four suffragan dioceses, while Arles was given nine. It was left to the pope to decide to which of these archbishoprics the dioceses of Tarantaise, Embrun, and Aix (en Provence) should be assigned. Finally, the last two pieces of ecclesiastical legislation passed by the synod entailed important provisions for Charlemagne personally. First, "in the interest of the Church" but in contravention of general canon law, it was decided that subject to the approval of the pope and the agreement of the synod, Archbishop Hildebald of Cologne should, like his predecessor as archchaplain, Angilram of Metz, be permitted to reside permanently at the royal palace. And finally, the king "requested" that the synod members induct Alcuin into their numbers and remember him in their prayers, "since he is so well versed in the disciplines of the Church."

Angilram did not find a successor in Metz, however. The archbishop's throne there was to remain unoccupied for at least twenty-four years. In this period, Charlemagne not only exploited the property of this diocese but also broke it up. In this way, the king managed to contain the individual power of an independent prelate. This situation in Metz finally changed only when Louis the Pious installed Charlemagne's son Drogo as archbishop there in 834.[61] Yet despite the fact that Hildebald became very close to Charlemagne, the historical record reveals nothing about his personality. He came to prominence for commissioning and funding many precious manuscripts of works of patristics, canon law, and rhetoric and in particular treatises on the calculation of calendrical time (*computus*) and astronomy. His interest in these last subjects was shared by Charlemagne. The king commissioned a metal (presumably gilded) altar cover for the western altar, which was dedicated to St. Peter, in the cathedral in Cologne, Hildebald's episcopal church.[62]

The king's presence was called for simultaneously on many different fronts, requiring him to divide his attention among a number of tasks. Everywhere, far-reaching changes and radical upheavals were becoming apparent in rapid succession. The struggle against heresies, as enacted by the Synod of Frankfurt, was a vital requirement in the achievement of salvation. According to the teachings of the apostles, "false prophets" would appear at the End of Days. The Spanish had warned the king about this end time,[63] and Charlemagne himself had taken their admonishment to heart.[64] This made attaining the ultimate goal all the more urgent, namely, "the renewal of the Church" (*renovare . . . ecclesiae statum*).[65]

No sooner had the Avars been conquered than Spain once more—albeit this time for a different reason—required Charlemagne's presence, or at least his intervention.[66] His first appearance south of the Pyrenees had not been forgotten. Charlemagne's letter to Elipand of Toledo, sent in the wake of the

Synod of Frankfurt, appeared to recall this incident.[67] Yet despite his earlier failure there, which had emboldened the Saxons to launch a new attack on his kingdom, he now doggedly continued to pursue his goal of extending Frankish rule to the banks of the river Ebro. The Muslim rulers of al-Andalus clearly recognized his intention, as evidenced by 'Abd al-Malik's relief attack on Aquitaine, which was successfully carried out, though not without heavy losses, in 792–793. Only a change of ruler in Córdoba in 796 and the ensuing power struggle in the emirate there turned the tables in favor of the Franks, just as victory over the Avars delivered the decisive liberating blow on the kingdom's eastern frontiers. East and West, the concluding phase of the war against Saxony and the death of Hadrian I on Christmas Day in 795, an ongoing need for reform within Charlemagne's realm, and the first reports of internal conflicts in Rome between the new pontiff, Leo III, and the old ruling elite around Hadrian I—all these factors combined to demand efficient coordination and extreme vigilance on a number of different levels.

The disagreements with Elipand of Toledo and Felix of Urgell, who both expounded their views at length at a synod held in Aix (Aachen) in 799, came at precisely the same time as new shifts in the balance of power within the Emirate of Córdoba and its border with the Frankish kingdom began to make themselves apparent. In 797, Zeid, the Arab governor of Barcelona, presented himself before Charlemagne, though presumably without any real intention of showing him fealty; Zaid is said to have guaranteed that his city would be handed over to the Franks as soon as the first Frankish troops set foot in the country (*Royal Frankish Annals*). This all sounded fatefully like the situation two decades earlier. As a result, Charlemagne was immediately on his guard.

Zeid was not the only "Moor" to make an appearance at the court in Aix at that time. When the Umayyad prince Abdallah, a son of 'Abd-ar-Rahman, found his hopes of rulership dashed by the son of the emir Hisham, al-Hakam I, who had usurped 'Abd-ar-Rahman's line of succession, he lost no time in coming to see Charlemagne in Aix and giving vent to his disillusionment. Claiming that he was being persecuted by his cruel nephew, he tried to encourage the Frankish king to embark on a military campaign to take Gerona and Barcelona. We may fairly presume that the Carolingian court possessed a certain amount of internal intelligence about al-Andalus, but unfortunately no writer from the kingdom of the Franks ever committed this to paper. Certainly, such information was never gathered in any systematic way or expanded. In the fall of that year, Charlemagne sent Prince Abdallah back to Spain in the company of his son Louis (*Annals* for the year 797).

However, mindful of his earlier defeat, he avoided instigating a war. It was only in 800 that he finally ordered his son to advance against the cities of Lérida, which was razed to the ground, and Huesca, whose environs were laid waste, while Barcelona actually remained under Muslim control, albeit not for long.

At this time, new, alarming news began to arrive from Constantinople. There, on the shores of the Bosphorus, after seven years of turbulent power sharing with her son, Empress Irene had finally emerged victorious in 797. After deposing Constantine VI, she gave ample evidence of what a splendid mother she was by having his eyes put out; he died of his injuries five years later. The Frankish annalists (not necessarily writing contemporaneously) took a keen interest in Constantine's fall but drew a veil over its exact cause, confining themselves simply to complaining about the "regiment of women" (*femineum imperium*) that now held sway over the Rhomaioi. Did they perhaps suppress the truth in an attempt to retrospectively legitimize their own king and the momentous changes that he had in the meantime set in train? Alcuin, at least, saw Irene's cruelty as nothing other than cold godlessness and a sign of the advancing apocalyptic threat,[68] thus placing her actions on a par with the rise of the heretics.

The Prelude to Imperial Rule

These were dangerous times indeed. Anyone examining the present could see the need for salvation, "for," as Alcuin wrote to his friend Arn of Salzburg, "we read in the Holy Scriptures that the time which was foretold is now upon us." Traces of knowledge and research regarding the impending Apocalypse led via a computistic-astronomical manuscript written by Bishop Hildebald of Cologne, the king's archchaplain, directly to the royal court (Ms. 83 II).[69] In 798, the resident scholars there, or those in his wider circle, juxtaposed several different calculations of the age of the world. Some of these corresponded with those worked out in Spain by the monk and geographer Beatus of Liébana or by the group of scholars around the Lombard Paul the Deacon; both predicted that the year 800 would witness the resurrection of the dead or other momentous changes. In the same way, Hildebald's collection also drew from the calculations made by St. Jerome and Orosius and regarded the eight hundredth year after the birth of Christ as the conclusion of the sixth and final millennium since the creation of the world—in other words, the end of the "sixth eon" (*sexta mundi aetas*). So, were there just two years remaining before the Apocalypse?

And would a seventh eon then commence, consisting of the last day of the world's existence, at the end of which Christ would return to sit in judgment?[70] Yet Hildebald's manuscript followed other sets of calculations, which maintained that the year 6000 had already passed and that it was now—as per the Septuagint—the year 6268 of the world era. Still others preferred to follow the calculations of the Jewish calendar.[71] According to the Jews, the year AM 6000 still lay almost one and a half millennia in the future. One contemporary scholar who followed this line remarked in exasperation that anyone who did not believe it should toil over the numbers and work it out for himself. In the light of such a contradictory body of knowledge, nobody who turned his mind to eschatological questions and received no clear answers could have any certainty whatsoever. As a result, such questions became all the more pressing.

The juxtaposition of putative ages of the world that Hildebald recorded was presented in the context of questions concerning "the end of the world" and the Antichrist. The inception, duration, and end of the world all belonged together; anyone who thought about one aspect could not help but consider the others. To be sure, the date of Judgment Day remained hidden from men, angels, and the "son of man" alike; only "God the Father" knew when it would be.[72] Hildebald's collection of dates also recalled this fact. The "son of man" referred to here was not equated with Christ but—in rejection of adoptionism—more generally, and in accordance with Mark 13:32—with Christ as a child of God. But the Antichrist would supposedly insist that people worship idols (even pictures could be deemed such), demand circumcision, masquerade as Christ, and finally erect his own statue in the temple at Jerusalem so that it could be venerated. He would, it was claimed, reveal himself at some unspecified time before the Day of Judgment and rampage for three and a half years before his end finally came. In other words, there was danger wherever one looked.

We can no longer know but only guess at what Charlemagne believed in this regard. At this time, he sought clarification from his scholars about the concept of time and the meaning of the words associated with it, asking what the semantic difference was among *aeternum, sempiternum, perpetuum,* and *immortale*—all terms that denoted "eternity" and described things that were lasting and immortal—and what the time terms *saeculum, aevum,* and *tempus* meant.[73] The doctrine of *proprium* and *differentia* was clearly bearing fruit.[74] Now the king was keen to know more about the movement of the sun and the zodiac and about the return to visibility of the planet Mars, as well as information on the planets in general and the moon.[75]

Did astrology and futurology find their way into Charlemagne's court at this time? In a Christian context, they could easily have served to corroborate eschatological speculations.[76] Presumably Charlemagne's anxiety about the impending end time, which he had harbored for many years, prompted him to get Alcuin and Paul the Deacon and others to conduct meticulous measurements of time and to investigate the way in which time was calculated and the calendar. In other words, he was seeking enlightenment about his own position in the history of salvation, even if he had to forgo ultimate knowledge about the End of Days and God's Last Judgment.[77] Is this perhaps the reason that the king wanted to be kept informed so punctiliously about the situation in Jerusalem?[78] Admittedly, though, none of Charlemagne's own writings about the Antichrist have come down to us.

Be that as it may, dangers were clearly looming for Christendom, and Charlemagne had to ward them off. But how was he to go about this task? Didn't this larger crisis far outstrip the remit of a Frankish ruler? Was it perhaps incumbent on him to act like an emperor, now that the Eastern emperor in Constantinople had clearly failed in his duties? He was, after all—as Alcuin wrote—the only person in whom the salvation of Christianity resided.[79] Exactly what Charlemagne was planning at that time, he who held sway over all the other imperial residences in the West, was shrouded in a secrecy preserved by all those involved. No one at this stage in history formulated governmental programs, but certainly Charlemagne would not have acted aimlessly either. Aided by his team of advisers, he had been ruminating for the best part of a decade on the question of royal "authority" (*potestas* or *res*) and the appropriate "name" (*vocari* or *nomen*) by which it should be known,[80] and it would presently have struck him that his existing title of *patricius Romanorum* no longer matched his actual power. Was he searching for a unifying basis for legitimizing his disparate realms of power, including the former Lombard lands, the Exarchate of Ravenna, the Pentapolis, Rome, and the Duchy of Benevento? Or was he casting his eyes beyond these regions?

Some evidence of serious planning has been preserved for posterity. For the year 797 and the next four years the *Royal Frankish Annals* registered a remarkable increase in the number of diplomatic missions, such as had never been recorded before. Frankish delegations visited Jerusalem, Constantinople, and Raqqa in Syria, where the caliph at that time mostly resided;[81] conversely, the foreigners who came from far and wide to Charlemagne's court hailed from such diverse places as Muslim Africa, the Christian kingdom of Asturias, Muslim-controlled Huesca, and the disputed city of

Barcelona. As we have seen, a son of ʿAbd-ar-Rahman, the emir of Córdoba, even came to visit the court in Aix. It is quite evident that the annals wished or were intended to convey the impression that the kingdom of the Franks was open to the world and enjoyed considerable international standing.

Charlemagne himself may have taken the initiative and followed earlier Byzantine Christian emperors from Justinian to Heraclius in sending his envoys to meet the "king of the Persians," that is, the caliph Harun al-Rashid.[82] Indeed, it was precisely at this time, in 798, that the first signs began to appear hinting at a revival of the emperorship in the West. Over the coming years, five delegations, the first of which embarked in 797, were sent to the East by the Carolingian king, to Jerusalem, Raqqa, or Baghdad.[83] The first of these missions was made up of two men by the name of Lantfrid and Sigismund, about whom we have no other information, accompanied by a Jew called Isaac,[84] who was there presumably not just as an interpreter who knew the region but also in order to facilitate trade contacts. This delegation of Charlemagne's is all the more remarkable for the fact that we do not know any particular reason or motives behind their journey.

Surprising and exceptional archaeological finds of several Arab *fulus* (a copper substitute coin for small change, with a currency value that was not matched by the value of the metal it contained) from the time of Harun al-Rashid point to the existence of dedicated trade contacts between the caliphate and the Frankish Empire.[85] The coins in question were discovered at the site of the ancient settlement of Reric, a trade center on the southern coast of the Baltic (which later relocated to Haithabu) within Charlemagne's sphere of influence, and elsewhere. As worthless token coins, they had no place in the Frankish realm's long-distance trade with other regions but instead provide clear evidence of trade in cheap "copper scrap" with the caliphate.

These finds have prompted new interpretations of long-familiar Arab texts by Abu l'Arab Muhammad ibn Ahmad at Tamimi (d. 944/945 CE) and Abul-Fadl Iyadh (d. 1149 CE), which shed new light on this trade link. Both authors, who wrote quite independently of each other, used old historical accounts to describe the shipments of weapons, "iron" (in fact, steel), and copper from the Tunisian city of Kairouan to a "tyrant," which must have been an allusion to none other than Charlemagne. This highly controversial shipment remained alive in folk memory because the friendly relations that Emir al-ʾAkki maintained with Charlemagne stirred up religious opposition in Kairouan and sparked a rebellion against his rule. Al-ʾAkki was acting on behalf of Harun al-Rashid but died shortly after the uprising was put down in 799 by Ibrahim ibn al-Aghlab.

The story was somewhat different in the Latin West. According to this version, as recounted by Einhard thirty years after the event (chap. 16), the Frankish king is said to have asked the caliph to send him an elephant—the only one, in fact, at the latter's disposal. As Charlemagne's biographer himself appeared to assume, this bizarre wish could hardly have been the only reason, let alone the most important one, for sending a delegation to the caliph. Accordingly, Einhard did not cite it as a motivating factor. Was Charlemagne even the supplicant in this case? Instead, the biographer chose to concentrate on the pilgrimage destination of Jerusalem, to which another delegation from the future emperor set off at around the same time. Yet even the desire to make a pilgrimage may not have been the prime motive behind this visit. As Einhard reveals elsewhere (chap. 27), albeit without mentioning specific dates, these envoys certainly devoted part of their trip to supplying funds to poor Syrian, Egyptian, and African Christians living under Muslim rule in Jerusalem, Alexandria, and Carthage, respectively. Charlemagne sanctioned this in expectation of gaining the "friendship of overseas rulers." All Western commentators either failed to mention or left unclear the real political and mercantile context of this delegation, but the fact remains that it may well have resulted in the two rulers, the Western king and the Eastern caliph, adopting a policy of united opposition to al-Andalus and Byzantium, as well as being the practical catalyst for the arms shipments (whatever these may have comprised). This delegation was therefore groundbreaking, representing as it did the first trade contact between a Latin ruler and the Muslim East.[86] This relationship appears to have run extremely successfully.

Alemannic pilgrims would no doubt have sailed alongside Charlemagne's envoys from Venice to Jerusalem, where they hoped to acquire relics of St. Genesius. A brief report of their activities has survived. For all its brevity, however, it has a great deal to say about the difficulties of transferring these relics from Italy, where they had fortuitously ended up, to Alemannia. Yet the Alemannic monk who wrote this account did not dwell on the king's aims nor even bother with a description of the relics' place of provenance, Jerusalem. A short time later, Charlemagne's quasi-son-in-law Angilbert likewise boasted about having acquired sacred relics from Jerusalem, recounting that Charlemagne's envoy had brought them back.[87] Neither of these writers, or others, said anything about the actual journey to the Holy Land. Not a single Muslim religious rite was described, nor did the authors see fit to even mention the coexistence of the three great Abrahamic religions in the Holy City or the Muslim observance of praying five times daily. They did, however, find space to impute idolatry to Islam, while for their part Muslim commentators of the time accused Christians of idol worship thanks to their veneration of the Cross. Unfamiliarity has a habit of distorting and skewing things.

Four years after the dispatch of Lantfrid and Sigismund, who both died on the journey, and just a few weeks after his coronation as emperor, Charlemagne found himself receiving a reciprocal delegation from Harun, the "king of the Persians," in Italy; this mission was accompanied by a delegation from the Aghlabid emir Ibrahim, a "Saracen from Africa," who likewise now resided in Kairouan. Harun's envoys announced that their gift would be an elephant called Abul Abaz, which Isaac then sent from Africa to Aix (*Royal Frankish Annals* for 801); it duly arrived the following year (*Annales Laureshamenses*, chap. 35). The animal died nine years later (*Royal Frankish Annals* for 810). This mighty elephant excited everyone's attention. Later accounts preferred to concentrate on this and other "precious gifts" brought by the delegation, without revealing anything of substance about the mission, including what it discussed with whom and its observations on the Franks.[88] In particular, they said absolutely nothing about the controversial shipment of weapons and metals, which Arab sources claimed that Charlemagne requested, which the elephant may have accompanied, and which almost certainly came about through Isaac's mediation. In those days, it was not appropriate to talk about the trade in arms, especially when—as seems to have been the case here—it pitted Christians against their coreligionists.

At this stage, then, the attention of travelers and the recipients of gifts focused on external things, on spectacular show, rather than on people's intentions, the substance of what they said, or any subtler concerns, let alone any curiosity toward foreigners. The Latin Christians did not disclose their views on the liturgical practices of the Christians they encountered in Jerusalem, which diverged wildly from those of the West, and they said absolutely nothing about the practice of Islam within the Holy City.[89] All that happened was that when Latin monks got to learn about the Orthodox Christian creed, which was intoned without the *filioque*, they complained about it in the West, thus sparking a new theological dispute there.[90]

Even the delegations to Aix of the patriarch of Jerusalem and the delegations Charlemagne sent in return—for example, the one led by the palace priest Zacharias in 800—served only to awaken an interest in the relics and other treasure that were to be had in the Holy Land. Some of the most striking of these found a mention in the historical records in the context of the delegation from Jerusalem that arrived at Charlemagne's court in 800, bringing with it the keys to the Holy Sepulchre and to Calvary, along with the keys of the city and a flag (*Royal Frankish Annals*). It was probably also on this occasion that the marble slabs that made up "Charlemagne's throne" were brought from Jerusalem to the West.

As I have noted, the initiative for this exchange with the East came from Charlemagne himself, while the timing of this contact, at least superficially, was dictated by Umayyad activity in Spain. Nevertheless, the designation of Harun al-Rashid as "king of the Persians"—Einhard and even Notker employ this formulation—is significant and warrants our attention. It shows that the Franks considered Harun a "Persian" (*Persa*) through and through, as opposed to being a "Saracen" (*Sarracenus*) like his predecessor as caliph, al-Mansur; unlike the emir of Africa and the other Muslims from that continent, who had invaded Corsica in 806, he was no "Moor" (*Maurus*) either.[91] The designation they gave him quite clearly concealed a deliberate Frankish interpretation of world history, for the "Persians" had been both the military adversaries and the treaty partners of Roman emperors from Justinian to Heraclius, as scholars at Charlemagne's court would have been able to ascertain from the chronicles of the so-called Fredegar.[92] In the same way as this chronicler hailed Heraclius as the "new David" as a result of his victory over the Persians, so Charlemagne was happy to be flattered as "David" at his court. It was only around 810, when relations with the Abbasids had deteriorated, that we find Harun posthumously being referred to as the "king of the Saracens" (*Royal Frankish Annals*).[93]

Accordingly, the Persians were the opponents and treaty partners of Christian Roman emperors from Justinian onward. Their rulers were thus treated in diplomatic protocol as "brothers" of the *basileus*, the Byzantine ruler. Likewise, according to the tradition of the Franks, anyone who exchanged diplomatic missions and concluded treaties with them was regarded as their "brother" and of equal rank with the Eastern Roman emperor. Charlemagne was aware of the rank of the "Persians";[94] he made sure that all the missions he sent to Raqqa were recorded in the *Annals*.[95] Under these circumstances, his legations to a "king of the Persians," especially when they were aimed at ensuring the security and welfare of Eastern Christianity in general and of Jerusalem in particular, can be seen as a sign of long-term preparation on Charlemagne's part for assuming the "imperial title" (*nomen imperatoris*) and for reviving the Western empire. These objectives were to become clearly evident from the second half of the following year.[96]

Indeed, in parallel with the exchange of diplomatic missions with Harun al-Rashid, the years 799 and 800 saw two legations sent to the patriarch of Jerusalem.[97] These point in the same direction as the legations to the caliph, namely, to nascent plans to revive the office of Western emperor. The response of the patriarch arrived promptly, with the aforementioned gifts of relics, in December 800, when Charlemagne was already staying in Rome, preparing to assume the title of emperor. The guests from Jerusalem must surely have witnessed Charlemagne's coronation by the pope. Such timing was no coincidence; everything points to Charlemagne's single-minded determination to attain one goal: his elevation to emperor. This came about as a result of his own efforts and was not driven, as is often assumed, by the chance outbreak of a revolt by the Roman nobility.

The new emperor engaged openly in public negotiations with the envoys of the Abbasid caliph (among whom there may possibly have been some Christians), but any more specific recognition of the "Persian" religion would have entailed—as, say, Fredegar's earlier reference in his chronicle to the case of the Byzantine emperor Maurice demonstrated—liturgical defilement. Rather, in place of religion, history and the historically justifiable imperial claim of the Frankish ruler were put at the forefront of the encounters between the two sides and the reporting of them. The cultural effect of this exchange has come down to us only indirectly, through later accounts, which were no doubt already embellished by myth by the time they were written. Charlemagne may have sensed the intellectual superiority of the Byzantines and the Arabs, but he never expressly acknowledged it, even though the West steadily drew lessons from these foreign cultures with the passage of time. Presumably, though, he greatly admired the steel that they supplied to his armorers.

As regards Charlemagne's coronation as emperor, another less well-known piece of evidence from the period just preceding the epochal year 800 may provide further testimony concerning his own self-image, which focused expectantly on "Rome" (provided, that is, that this evidence does not prove to be spurious—a question that scholars are still debating). The artifacts in question are the images thought to have adorned the walls of the King's Hall at the palace in Ingelheim, as described by the poet Ermoldus Nigellus.[98] This picture cycle—which was in the form either of paintings or of tapestries[99] and took its inspiration from Orosius's theory of four successive world empires—was created (assuming that it really did exist, a view to which I subscribe)[100] at precisely this same time, namely, just before 800.[101] It is inconceivable that Charlemagne would not have had a decisive influence on its content.[102]

The images embodied a historical construct that accorded a central significance to Rome in world historical and universal terms. One wall at Ingelheim depicted pagan rulers from Cyrus and Ninus, the founding of Rome by Romulus and Remus, and then Hannibal and the appearance of Alexander the Great through to a possible portrayal of Caesar Augustus, "showing how Roman power reached its zenith," *ut Romana manus crevit et usque ad polum*.[103] The other side of the hall was devoted to Christian rulers and "brought together the exploits of Roman Caesars with those of the Franks."[104] It commenced with Constantine the Great, who left Rome "for love" of the wondrously beautiful maiden Constantinopolis,[105] founding the eponymous city there, and proceeded via Emperor Theodosius to Charles Martel in his role as victor over the Frisians, then on to Pepin the Short as the conqueror of Aquitaine, and finally culminated in Charlemagne, "the Wise" (*sapiens*), who was almost certainly shown in a double portrait: first as the ruler of Italy resplendent in his crown and second as the subduer of the Saxons, a king in both cases (4.279–282).

According to the verses accompanying the relevant mural at Ingelheim, then, Constantine had "left for love" the city of "Rome, where the Caesars were wont to reside" (as the Lorsch annalist, a court insider, noted). The same city, however, along with the other imperial residences in the West, had been placed by God "under Charlemagne's authority"—another formulation from the *Lorsch Annals* (for the year 801), this time in justification of Charlemagne's coronation as emperor the previous year.[106] The meaning of the historical painting cycle can only be construed as follows: fulfilling his allotted role in the history of salvation, the Carolingian monarch had returned to Rome as the conqueror and proselytizer of the heathens and as the future emperor—to the Rome that Constantine had abandoned. Roman history in the Christian era therefore flowed inexorably into the history of the Franks, merging with it in the process; this history thus led directly from Constantine to Charlemagne, the protector of the Roman Church and—according to Alcuin—the sole protector of Christendom.

If the office of emperor on which Charlemagne had so firmly fixed his sights was to be of any lasting duration, it was essential that it be recognized by the emperor in Constantinople. This aspect could not be left to chance, but making it a reality required years of careful preparation. The Rhomaioi had somehow to be brought on board. Empress Irene, the loveless mother who sat on the imperial throne in Constantinople, and who had just imprisoned her son Constantine VI and blinded him, would no doubt have feared internal opposition. To many Greeks, a basilissa seemed a scandalous idea. Irene needed peace on the frontiers of her empire, which were threatened not only by the Franks but to an even greater extent by the

Bulgars and the Arabs. Did she perhaps learn about Charlemagne's relations with Harun al-Rashid and with the patriarch in Jerusalem? If so, the news must have filled her with dread. Accordingly, she entered into negotiations with Charlemagne, although no Greek source recorded them. We should not be surprised at this. If Irene really was, as those in the West saw it, holding out the possibility of recognizing Charlemagne as Western emperor, she was taking a huge risk. There, in Byzantium, the emperorship was not some bargaining chip to be negotiated away. Were the talks with Charlemagne therefore possibly held *in camera*?

Two independent reports from the Frankish royal court may well indicate that this was the case. Admittedly, they sound so curious that historians have hitherto either mistrusted them or ignored them out of hand. Yet one of them, at least—which has come down to us in materials concerning the *computus*—is more reliable than any collection of annals from either the East or the West, produced as they were retrospectively and not infrequently sanitized of anything controversial.[107] This news was transmitted contemporaneously in 798 by Charlemagne's archchaplain Archbishop Hildebald of Cologne, who recorded it in his aforementioned sumptuous manuscript on history and astronomy.[108] His note reports briefly how envoys had arrived in Aix in that year "from Greece . . . in order to transmit imperial power to Charlemagne" (*ut traderent ei imperium*).

The second note appears in the *Annals of Northumbria* for the year 800; in other words, it was transmitted outside Charlemagne's immediate sphere of influence and hence far removed from any retrospective official portrayal of events. It maintains that "around the time" at which Charlemagne was endowed by Pope Leo III with all the accoutrements of emperorship—the purple cloak, the golden crown, and the imperial scepter—"envoys of the Greeks also came to him, having been sent from Constantinople laden with lavish gifts," and entreated him "to accept their office of kingship and emperorship" (*rogantes ut illorum susciperet regnum et imperium*).[109]

Even though these annals or the messages contained in them have come down to us only from the twelfth century, they nevertheless convey—with only a mild degree of distortion: Irene would certainly never have requested that the Frankish ruler take over her own office of "basileia"—current or contemporaneous information. The report they give of the coronation was in all likelihood transmitted by the circle of scholars around Alcuin to his former homeland via a number of way stations that skewed the facts. Around 798, the abbot of Tours maintained close contact with the Frankish court and, even before Charlemagne did so, lobbied for an *imperium christianum* (a Christian empire).[110] Furthermore, we should not set too much store by the phrase "around the time" (*eo quoque tempore*). All it tells us is that the Greek invitation arrived sometime around the same period in which the actual coronation took place. But in actual fact, in the months before and after the coronation—that is, for the whole of 800 and 801— there is no record of any Greek legation having visited Charlemagne in either Aix or Rome.[111] Yet it is true that in terms of its content, the news in the *Annals of Northumbria* does tally with the Cologne note from the royal court mentioned above.[112] In truth, then, it must also come from that same source.

The interpretation of both of these messages is a matter of dispute. Only this much is certain: they did not by any means record the original wording of the Byzantine proclamations but instead reflected the way in which the messages were understood by the Frankish court or those around it. What was to be reported clearly happened before the coronation of the emperor in 800, and quite independently of the revolutionary events in Rome that preceded it. Whatever it was that the Byzantine diplomats put forward, in Aix it was interpreted as an offer, indeed, as open consent to the coming assumption of the title of emperor by the Frankish king. This offer was answered with a goodwill gesture on the part of Charlemagne: Sisinnius, the brother of the patriarch Tarasios, who had been held captive as a prisoner of war in the West for a good ten years, was allowed to return home.[113]

Thus, Charlemagne had been planning the revival of the emperorship in the West since 798 at the latest, if not somewhat earlier. He evidently laid the groundwork for this step by sending a legation to Harun al-Rashid and by purchasing arms from the caliph before subsequently negotiating with the Byzantine empress Irene about taking the title of emperor. Under pressure both in Constantinople itself and from the foreign powers ranged against her, the basilissa may have found herself amenable to making concessions, although she may also—as she had done earlier over the question of the marriage of her son[114]—have been attempting to stall the Frankish king. Just the year before, in 797, a letter from Constantine VI—clearly written before he was blinded—arrived at Charlemagne's court; its contents were kept as secret as those of a diplomatic note from the *patrikios* (military governor) of Sicily that was brought to Aix the following year (*Royal Frankish Annals* for 799); its bearers were received with honor and in the same spirit sent back whence they had come.[115]

Charlemagne was well aware of the significance of the year 801, which was fast approaching. Could this be why he ordered a new assault against the Muslims in Spain? Did he perhaps already envisage it as an outstanding symbolic act to mark the first day of this new era, the first day of the seventh millennium after the creation of the world, according to St. Jerome? The day in question fell on 25 December of that same year 801 (800 in the modern Julian calendar). This was an apocalyptically significant date, which Charlemagne's scholars had calculated. In 800, for instance, Alcuin had taken the words of St. Paul's Second Letter to Timothy (2 Timothy 3:1: "Perilous times shall come") as the basis for his repeated warnings about the "turbulence of the end times."[116]

Here the question of salvation intersected with the fight against heresies. Rome too was fully aware of the calculation of the age of the world that could be traced back to the Bible translator St. Jerome. Yet the Anglo-Saxon scholar the Venerable Bede had made a different calculation—familiar among his compatriots, as well as in the kingdom of the Franks—that postponed the ominous end of the sixth millennium for several centuries. So when would the world's final hour toll? Charlemagne never forgot this question; calendrical calculation thus became both an indispensable element in formulating policy for the here and now and a kind of futurology focused on salvation.[117]

The Enemies of the Pope Stage a Rebellion in Rome

Meanwhile, the situation in Rome became very unclear because the city on the Tiber was rocked by chaotic fighting between opposing factions. The new pope Leo III, who did not come from one of the old established aristocratic Roman families, had many enemies as well as friends. The old struggles for supremacy that had dogged Hadrian I's reign followed the new pontiff from the outset. It is now impossible to say how much truth there was in the accusations of gross moral turpitude that were leveled at him. But various changes from the way Hadrian had run the papacy were clearly evident.[118] The social climber Leo did not, for example, follow the practice of his aristocratic predecessor in having his portrait stamped on the obverse of the coins he minted, but one of the apostolic prince St. Peter; his papal name appeared, as the authority minting the coin, only on the reverse and in the genitive form: *Domini Leonis papae*. Also, in a departure from earlier usage, the dating of the papal documents Leo issued added the regnal year of Charlemagne, albeit after the pope's own.

First and foremost, however—sometime after 797/798, possibly in 799/800—Leo III commissioned two mosaic images of great symbolic importance. One of these adorned his former cardinal's church of Santa Susanna, now rebuilt. On it, Leo was depicted alongside saints as one of the patrons of the church, while opposite him, on Christ's left hand, Charlemagne was portrayed as a king in Frankish traditional garb.[119] Such a thing was unheard of: a picture in a public space of a foreign ruler, a Frank, a barbarian, who was neither a founder of the church nor a city dignitary, who, furthermore, was not mentioned in the inscription to the patrons,[120] and whose sole justification for appearing here was as a partner of the controversial new pope. Conservative forces within Rome were bound to construe this mosaic as a provocation and a threat. Was this perhaps the reason that Leo asked the king and future emperor (as Hadrian had once done before him) to don Roman costume on his visit to the city in 800? Einhard (chap. 23) registers surprise when recording this change of clothes.

The second commission was even more challenging. It was located (both mosaics have since vanished and are known to us only through rough sketches made in the Baroque period) in the triclinium, a state room with three apses in a cloverleaf shape (*triconchos*) that Leo commissioned to be built around this time in the Latin *patriarchium*. The room's main apse was occupied by a portrayal, laden with meaning and painted in a novel compositional style, of the sending out of the apostles by Christ; in it, the figure of St. Peter—the heavenly representative of the earthly papacy—was specially emphasized. The associated end wall of the *triconchos* (in iconographic terms, on the left-hand side) featured a second portrayal of the apostolic prince seated on his throne and handing a pallium (an ecclesiastical vestment) to Pope Leo and a pennant to the Frankish king Charlemagne.[121]

This mosaic picture—its dating strikes me as very uncertain[122]—is open to a number of different interpretations. The pope is shown occupying the place of honor on St. Peter's right hand. The images of the pallium and the pennant indicate a clear division of responsibilities between the two men: the power of leadership of the Church was vested in the successor to the apostolic prince, whereas the protection of his Church was the king's duty. This division could hardly have satisfied the expectations of the powerful Carolingian ruler. The inscription below the mosaic was highly controversial, for here too the pope was given clear precedence over the king: "*beate petre donas vitam leoni papae et bictoriam carvlo regi donas*" (Blessed St. Peter, grant life to Pope Leo and to King Charles bring victory). The status of the king thus appeared to have been reduced to a mere provider of protection to the Apostolic Church. Nevertheless, at least Charlemagne was—as he had never been under Hadrian I—present here for the first time

FIGURE 49 Sketch from the Baroque period of the mosaic commissioned by Pope Leo III for the Church of Santa Susanna in Rome, showing the pontiff in his first triclinium (sometime before 800). The mosaic was destroyed in the sixteenth century.

in the *patriarchium,* in the very heart of papal church leadership. This fact alone must have greatly displeased the former ruling clique around Hadrian.

From the spring of 798 onward, Leo was accused of heinous lapses by his opponents. Before long, talk of revolt was in the air. News of this reached the kingdom of the Franks. Charlemagne immediately dispatched Archbishop Arn of Salzburg and Abbot Wirund of Stavelot to Rome to investigate how matters stood; military protection for them was to be provided by Duke Winigis of Spoleto. Suddenly, just before their arrival, things came to a head. Leo's enemies were determined to fight. Dire reports soon began to reach the Carolingian court,[123] claiming that dreadful atrocities had taken place. On the occasion of the great annual procession on St. Mark's Day (25 April)—the so-called *Letania major,* which led from the church of San Lorenzo in Lucina along the Via Flaminia and across the Milvian Bridge on its way to St. Peter's, the populace of Rome had allegedly attacked the pope, cut out his tongue, and gouged out his eyes before throwing the maimed pontiff in jail; there, they stripped him of his robes and declared him deposed. This catalog of horrors seemed only to presage even greater evil and to herald the End of Days, the cleansing of the world through fire, and the Apocalypse depicted in the "*Muspilli*"—the Last Judgment and the unquenchable, eternal burning of the damned in the maw of chaos.[124]

But almost at the same time rumors of a miraculous recovery by the pope began to filter across the Alps. The pontiff's supporters were overjoyed: "Blessed be the Lord, the God of Israel, who alone can perform great miracles and who never forsakes those who believe in him. The Lord is my light [*inluminatio*] and my salvation: whom then should I fear? The Lord is the great guardian of my life: of whom should I be afraid?"[125] Many people did indeed believe in the miracle announced by the Romans.

Charlemagne, who for all his propensity for violence remained a devout Christian, must have been extremely surprised, alarmed, and profoundly shocked when he read the reports from Rome. What did all this portend? What was to be done? Answers to these questions were urgently required if the king was to act justly and in a manner pleasing to God. But what kind of criteria were to be used to interpret the situation, and what were the king's ultimate objectives? Master Alcuin regarded the events taking place in Rome as an apocalyptic sign, too; he saw the imminent onset of the end of the world. The proliferation of such signs in both the East and the West and the heretics in Spain were further proof of what was happening. The end was nigh; Charlemagne recognized this too. Yet did the Last Judgment await mankind, or rather was a new Sabbath dawning for the world, a new eon? How long would the reprieve last? The king had been tireless in seeking advice from the greatest sages in his realm, so that when the time came, he might rule with justice and be prepared for anything; in the process, he had grown wise himself.

Action was now called for. The pope had been toppled from the apostolic throne, the *basileus* had been impiously deposed by his own people, and he, Charlemagne, was the only one left who could be called on to direct the affairs of Christendom. "See, the salvation of Christ's Church has been entrusted to you and you alone," his old teacher from Tours reminded him.[126] Should Charlemagne take on this mantle of emperor for the End of Days? Indeed, "perilous times shall come," as God had once predicted; and, as Alcuin had once warned him in the words of Jesus foretelling the Apocalypse in St. Matthew's Gospel, "The love of many shall wax cold" (Matthew 24:12).[127] The redemption of Christianity now lay entirely in his, Charlemagne's, hands.[128] These desperate times required him to restore order. Yet Charlemagne knew the ringleaders of the Roman rebellion personally and may well have regarded them, who after all had been the envoys whom Pope Hadrian had once sent to him, no less highly than the former pope himself. Their word had once carried great weight, and the message they had conveyed had been cordial.

This only made the question of what was to be done all the more urgent. Had these rebel leaders perhaps been dissimulating? Should he make haste to Rome himself? Alcuin certainly urged him to do so; Charlemagne considered his advice for a moment.[129] This course of action would be unavoidable; but, as Alcuin had also written to him, "the king must take care not to disregard his own safety in this enterprise."[130] First, though, Charlemagne needed to bring to a conclusion an affair that was even more pressing for him, namely, to convert the Saxons, who were still pagan, to Christianity.[131] This mission was also a form of preparation for the Last Judgment and promised to call down blessings on the ruler who achieved it, as St. Augustine had once taught.[132] Charlemagne had harkened attentively to Augustine's message and adhered strictly to his teachings.[133] Accordingly, he advanced on Saxony at the head of his army; he camped at Paderborn to await further developments, while his son Charles marched north to engage the enemy.

These were dangerous times indeed. "False prophets" in the form of heretics abounded. "Justice is enslaved, there is a surfeit of injustice, love grows cold, and infidelity creeps up on us like poison and will not desist from destroying the limbs of Christ like some cancerous growth." Deeply shocked, the great teacher of the Frankish kingdom, Alcuin, interpreted the apocalyptic signs that the Lord had proclaimed in the Gospel (Matthew 24:12) and that he could see coming to pass in the here and now. Alcuin's own experience confirmed his sense of foreboding. At the very moment when the appalling news from Rome began to take shape in May 799, the Anglo-Saxon scholar found himself engaged in debate with Bishop Felix of Urgell, the leading Spanish heretic and adherent of adoptionism.[134] Everything appeared to be racing toward a conclusion.

Before long, more detailed information from Rome reached Charlemagne's ears. It conveyed some bad news about the pope—so bad, in fact, that the correspondent could scarcely bring himself to put pen to paper. Alcuin burned the letter containing this dreadful intelligence, which had been written by his friend Arn of Salzburg, the man whom the king had sent to investigate the situation in Rome just before the attempt on Pope Leo's life. Now the apostolic father found himself accused of grave moral transgressions; there was talk of fornication and perjury.[135] These were common-enough accusations, but in these circumstances they took on a terrifying aspect. Nor was this the worst of it. The ringleaders of the revolt had planned the pontiff's overthrow, an act of sacrilege directed against the rightful successor to St. Peter. Charlemagne could not and would not turn a blind eye to this outrage.

The basic facts of what happened on St. Mark's Day are undisputed. It was certainly true that the pope had been the victim of an attack at the start of the procession. His assailants had taken him to San Silvestro in Capite, a monastery of Greek monks that was firmly in rebel hands; there, they had attempted to render him unfit for office by mutilating his tongue and eyes. His blood-soaked body was dragged before the altar, where he was stripped of his papal vestments and formally deposed.[136] The accounts of Roman and Frankish eyewitnesses record solely these acts of violence, however; only Frankish authors mention the pope being deposed, and even then in a somewhat casual and covert manner. Leo, though, was able to get away while he was in transit to another monastery; presumably he had helpers among his assailants or their servants. Under the protection of the Frankish envoys, Abbot Wirund and Duke Winigis, and probably also Archbishop Arn, he made good his escape.[137] Charlemagne then ordered Leo to be brought to his court at Paderborn.

There, Theodulf of Orléans wrote a commentary on the events, couched in sometimes ironic verses mocking the credulity of certain contemporary observers for believing in miracles: "The furious mob tore out your [i.e.,

Leo's] tongue and stripped you of your pontiff's robes and your office. St. Peter restored it all to you. . . . Meanwhile, the mob spread the lie . . . that nothing had actually been taken from you, and that they were only planning to take it. Restored to you—how miraculous; and how miraculous that they weren't able to deprive you of anything. I ask myself which of these two facts I am more astonished by."[138] Theodulf evidently saw the "miracle" as having been fabricated to fool the general populace. Was his mockery intended to warn the king not to place too much credence in the reports emanating from Rome? It is certainly the case that none of the subsequent reports of the incident originating from the Carolingian court made any mention of the supposed miracle.

The signs of impending horror continued and multiplied. The patriarch of Grado in Spain was murdered. Charlemagne sent Arn of Salzburg there too to investigate the crime, although he was soon instructed to hurry on to Rome to escort Pope Leo to the Frankish kingdom. Throughout September, Charlemagne awaited Leo's arrival in Paderborn, in darkest Saxony, a place to which the ruler could legitimately and proudly claim that he had brought the Christian faith. Alcuin, whose advice Charlemagne had sought, reminded the king of the tenets of ecclesiastical law: whatever the charges against Leo might be, "the Apostolic See sits in judgment; no one sits in judgment over it."[139] The king thus came to a decision; the question of how the havoc that had been wreaked in Rome might be healed would remain open for the present. In the meantime, he sent his archchaplain, Archbishop Hildebald, Count Ascherius, and his son Charles to form a fitting reception committee for the pope.[140] Accompanied by an impressive retinue, the pope duly arrived at the palace at the confluence of the rivers Pader and Lippe, ready to submit himself to the "just verdict" of the king and to ask for his support.[141] What the two men discussed is not known. The historians are silent on this matter. The epic poem *Karolus magnus et Leo papa* (the *Paderborn Epic*) confines itself to saying the following: "The king, the father of Europe, and Leo, the highest priest on Earth, met and held discussions on a variety of topics."[142]

At the very least, the two men would have agreed on the Frankish king's upcoming fourth visit to Rome and surely must also have sketched out what would happen thereafter. Leo, though, whom the rebels had declared divested of his office, was allowed to return in the company of Frankish royal messengers to occupy the apostolic throne once more. No matter which city he passed through on his return journey, he was received as the reigning pope. When he reached Rome, the populace greeted him and his accompanying contingent of foreign troops, comprising Franks, Frisians, Saxons, and Lombards; brandishing crosses and flags and singing hymns, they accompanied him to St. Peter's, where he celebrated Mass. The *Liber pontificalis* recorded all this in detail[143]—a clear sign of how very real the ritual deposing him had been.

The revolt in Rome had created a whole new landscape. Frankish envoys, working in conjunction with archbishops, bishops, and counts, conducted an initial, provisional investigation. "Barbarians" were now sitting in judgment on the most senior Roman officeholders, and what is more, in Rome. The situation could not have been worse for the city's old ruling elite. The thing above all that Hadrian and his predecessors had striven hard to achieve, the independence of Rome, was now a thing of the past. The ringleaders of the revolt, the *primicerius* (head of bureaucracy) Paschalis and the *sacellarius* (chief treasurer) Campulus, were deported to the Frankish kingdom but were required to return to Rome during the year to hear the charges against them and to ultimately stand trial.[144]

Before Charlemagne made his own way south, he set off on a long detour through the northwest of Francia, visiting St-Bertin and Centula/St-Riquier, the monastery run by his quasi-son-in-law Angilbert; his route took him on through Rouen, close to the barely subdued region of Brittany and on to Tours. He planned to pray at the Basilica of St. Martin, the patron saint of the empire, and also wanted to lament the recent death of his consort, Liutgard.[145] But the initial purpose of this detour was to inspect the coastal defenses along the English Channel. Farsightedly, Charlemagne had ordered them to be constructed to guard against the threat of seaborne attacks by northern pirates. They were designed to protect the river estuaries and also included a plan to construct a naval fleet;[146] whether this latter objective ever came to fruition, and if so, to what extent, is not known. Later developments, however, raise doubts on this score.

Aside from Charlemagne's desire to pray at Tours, the real reason for this grand detour remains something of a mystery, however.[147] Did the king perhaps wish to show his face once more in certain regions of his realm that were under threat before absenting himself from his kingdom for a long while and before implementing the great changes he was planning in Rome? Did he want to prepare the groups of noblemen, who had begun to coalesce around his sons, for the period of his absence and thereby secure peace for the realm in general and for his sons in particular? He likely paid special attention to the groups within the future kingdom of his son Charles, who was to be crowned in Rome on this visit. In any event, while he was in Tours, the king took the opportunity to revisit the question of how best to arrange his succession. The documentary evidence for this—which points to the court as its source—is succinct and clear but very skimpy in terms of its content. Its subject matter was unequivocally, as one commentator emphasized, the organization of the kingdom, *de utilitate regni Francorum*—this phrase appears in the annals that were almost certainly compiled under the supervision of Charlemagne's sister Gisela.[148] For now, though, actual developments on the ground eclipsed resolutions for the future. At the Basilica of St. Martin in Tours, Charlemagne met his sons Charles, Pepin, and Louis and "divided up his realm among them" (*disposuit regnum filiis suis*).[149] In doing so, he corrected an old plan for partition, which appears to have been drawn up in 781, and which still recognized Himiltrud's son as an eligible heir.[150]

Finally, in the early spring of 800, after Charlemagne had returned to Aix via Orléans (Theodulf's seat), Paris, and Laon and had announced his intention to march to Italy at a meeting in Mainz,[151] the king set off on his journey south. Theodulf, a Visigoth who remained somewhat aloof from the doctrine of the papacy, gave Charlemagne some fundamental advice before he departed: "St. Peter holds the keys of Heaven; he summoned you to take them. You now hold the keys of the Church, while he retains those of Heaven" (*Caeli habet hic claves, proprias te iussit habere. / Tu regis ecclesiae, nam regit illi poli*).[152] In the eyes of the Visigothic scholar, the pope was just a bit player.

Charlemagne spent seven days en route in Ravenna, where he gave his son Pepin orders to march with a contingent of troops on the Duchy of Benevento and lay waste that territory while he himself marched on Rome.[153] At the city of Nomentum (modern Mentana) in Lazio, a small episcopal see just twelve miles from Rome, he was met by the pope. After they dined together, the pope went back to Rome ahead of the king—though clearly with his express approval, since if Leo had escorted Charlemagne into the city in a formal procession, this would have looked as though the outcome of the planned court case to establish Leo's legitimacy had been settled in advance. The following day in Rome, 24 November, Leo, having not long got back himself, somewhat breathlessly staged a formal reception for the Frankish king on the steps of St. Peter's, while the assembled ranks of both citizens and foreign newcomers greeted Charlemagne with a rousing chorus of Laudes.[154] Albeit in truncated form, this was the imperial reception ceremony that was played out here and was recorded in the *Royal Frankish Annals*. Traditionally, the pope had ever gone out of the city only to meet the

Roman emperor—and even then only to a distance of six miles, not twelve as he had done in the case of Charlemagne.[155]

Leo had made careful preparations for Charlemagne's appearance in Rome; after all, he had had the best part of a year to do so. Henceforth two pictorial representations in the city were to portray the Frankish king.[156] The mosaic on the end wall of the newly built reception and dining room of the papal residence—the triclinium with its three niches (*triconchos*) mentioned previously—may even have been constructed specially to host the king.[157] The mosaic was not integrated into any total composition covering the wall in question. Yet it does still appear to have been the pope's "response" to the dangerous attitude at Charlemagne's court, which—as exemplified by the verses of the Visigoth Theodulf cited above—virtually declared the king to be the representative of the apostolic prince.

"Life" for the pope and "victory" for the king—the inscription below the mosaic could not have summed up any more succinctly the actual situation after the attempted assassination and the "survival miracle." Prevailing circumstances effectively divided the upcoming acclamation of Charlemagne as emperor, distributed the honor equally, so to speak, between the pope and the Frankish king, and did so with the utmost care. St. Peter's giving of the pallium to Leo put the Church hierarchy back on an even keel once more. The mosaic's symbolism was therefore politically explosive. The image could not fail to remind the Carolingian monarch not only of the mercy of St. Peter but also at the same time of the fact that his royal office owed its entire foundation to St. Peter and his earthly representative, the pope. Was Charlemagne pleased by the picture? Did the investiture scene it depicted strike him as appropriate as he stepped forward to be crowned emperor? Might it have actually have been concealed from him? Unfortunately, we have no answers to any of these questions.

One week after Charlemagne's entry into Rome, a great assembly of Frankish and Roman clerics took place in St. Peter's, to which laymen were also invited.[158] It was not only ecclesiastical matters that were on the agenda. The assembly sat for three weeks, discussing the causes and actions that had led to the attempted assassination. There were many questions to be settled: whether Leo should remain pope, how his damaged reputation might be restored, whether he should formally be deposed, and what was to be done with the assailants and their helpers, plus various concerns over Charlemagne's elevation to emperor and other matters. Verdicts were even passed on some regional disputes. But the most important decision must have been taken behind closed doors and only submitted to the full assembly for approval, as indeed was the usual procedure at the royal court.[159] This matter concerned the Frankish king in person.

The delegates agreed, albeit not without some pressure from the king, not to bring any charges against the pope; in reaching this decision, they relied on the old legal principle deriving from the so-called Symmachian Forgeries of 501: "*Papa a nemine iudicatur*" (The pope cannot be judged by anyone). Instead, on 23 December—"voluntarily" and "condemned and compelled by no one so to do"—Leo purged himself of his sins by swearing an oath on the Bible "before God and all His angels" from the pulpit of St. Peter's maintaining that he was innocent of the crimes of which he was accused: "As God is my witness."[160] The heavens were not rent asunder after Leo swore his oath, so he was deemed to have told the truth. The bishops present intoned the Te Deum, and Charlemagne supposedly sang along.[161] Over the coming feast days, Leo was allowed to conduct all his sacred offices unimpeded. Charlemagne had saved St. Peter's successor from any judgment—and, moreover, in perpetuity. Henceforth, no pope who had been legally elected would ever be brought before a secular judge unless it was by the use of malicious, illegal force.

Thereafter, Charlemagne celebrated Christmas with Leo. Yet what took place during the third Christmas Mass bemused historians on both this and the far side of the Alps, dividing them in their opinions and leading them to record radically divergent facts. No contemporary documents about the events have survived, only retrospective recollections. These are all the more confusing since the reports they give are contradictory. Four such accounts are regarded by modern historians as authoritative: the *Royal Frankish Annals*, the so-called *Lorsch Annals*, the *Liber pontificalis*, and Einhard's *Life of Charlemagne*. These sources differ wildly in the legally relevant details they provide; why this should be so is by no means self-evident and needs to be the subject of a critical analysis. The fact remains, though, that something unique was to occur on that Christmas Day—a turning point, a performance that (although no one could have guessed it at the time and despite many subsequent alterations) would endure for the next thousand years. It blended Roman-Byzantine features with elements of a completely new creation and discrepant recollections, which would embed themselves highly selectively as a precedent in the collective cultural consciousness, and which still confront any historical analysis with unresolved challenges.[162]

The Coronation—Supposedly Repudiated

It was Christmas Day, 25 December 801 according to the Carolingian calendar, and the eschatologically significant first day of the seventh millennium since the creation of the world, according to the calculations of St. Jerome. Charlemagne attended Mass in the Basilica of St. Peter, close to his palace in Rome, and when he rose from prayer before the confession, the pope placed a crown on his head. Before the assembled Roman congregation, he was feted as emperor: "May life and victory be granted unto Charles, the Augustus, the great God-crowned and peace-bringing emperor of the Romans!'" *Vita et victoria*. Then the Laudes were sung.[163] Thereafter, "the pope paid homage to Charlemagne in the manner of the ancient emperors [i.e., through the act of 'proskynesis,' or prostrating himself] and named him, who had now cast off the title of *patricius, imperator* and Augustus."

At least, this was how the *Royal Frankish Annals* recorded the coronation. This remained the orthodox version of proceedings accepted at the Carolingian court in the years immediately after this unique event. Shortly thereafter, the *Metz Annals* repeated what was recorded in the *Royal Frankish Annals*, without changing a word.[164] According to this account, then, it was Romans who had performed the constitutive acts of coronation— namely, the crowning by the pope and the proclamation of Charlemagne as emperor. But did this represent a full account of what actually happened? The coronation and the acclamation were noticeably more briefly covered in these annals than the subsequent trial of the leaders of the revolt and the other ways in which the new emperor asserted his authority in the city of the apostolic princes. In other words, the annals that were closest to the royal court offer not the slightest indication that doubts may have been raised in some quarters over the legitimacy of this coronation.

Indeed, why should such misgivings have been recorded for posterity? Charlemagne was now master in and over Rome, as the pope's proskynesis clearly demonstrated. Admittedly, no pope or patriarch had ever played such a prominent role in the coronation of any former Roman or Byzantine emperor as the highly controversial Leo had done on this occasion. The liturgist appeared, as it were, to have acted as a master of ceremonies at the coronation of Charlemagne. It may be that he even anointed the new Caesar, although this is not likely. Only the Byzantine chronicler Theophanes (in his *Chronographia*) mockingly caricatured the proceedings, claiming that Leo had repaid the Frankish ruler for punishing his would-be assassins by "anointing him all over with olive oil, from head to toe, and bedecking him

FIGURE 50 This fresco in the Roman church of Santi Silvestro e Martino ai Monti is a seventeenth-century reconstruction of the interior of the Old St. Peter's Basilica in Rome, begun by Constantine. It was demolished in the early sixteenth century and replaced by the current building.

with the accoutrements of emperorship and a crown"; no Western observer had anything to say on this score. Whether or not this is true, the pope would not have been able to conduct the service without Charlemagne's approval. But were Leo's actions truly constitutive or merely validating?

Another version of events also made the rounds north of the Alps, one that accorded the pope and the Romans a noticeably less prominent—or at least a very different—role in the proceedings. Did this portrayal perhaps give voice to a certain dissatisfaction among the Franks with the events in

Rome? Its origins are unclear, although the only surviving representative example, the so-called *Lorsch Annals,* was also closely associated with the royal court. At the conclusion of its account of the great assembly in St. Peter's, the *Lorsch Annals* explains that because at that time the "imperial name" was vacant among the Byzantine Greeks, and because they had a (potentially scandalous) "female emperorship" (*femineum imperium*), it seemed to Pope Leo, all participants in the synod, and the rest of the Christian people (*reliquo christiano populo*) only right and proper "to name the Frankish king Charles "emperor [*imperator*]." For he had dominion over Rome, where the Caesars had always resided, as well as over the other seats of imperial power in Italy, Gallia, and Germania. Since Almighty God had placed these realms under his control, it seemed only right to them that, with the Lord's help and at the urging of the whole of Christendom, he should bear this name." Charlemagne reportedly acceded to this request—it must have been on 23 or 24 December—and on Christmas Day duly "with Pope Leo's blessing" (*cum consecratione domni Leonis papae*) accpted the "name of *imperator.*"

Here, then, the king and *princeps* was acting in concert with the parties named; indeed, this was the decisive act after or during the December synod, for which essentially all the bishops in Charlemagne's empire had gathered. It entailed all of the kingdom's magnates, even those who were laymen, consenting in the king's assumption of the "name of emperor," in other words, the restoration of the proper and God-ordained order of things, which required that power (*res*) and nomenclature (*nomen*) should match each other.[165] The Romans played at best a subordinate role; there was no mention here of a "Roman emperor." Rome, the ancient head of the world, was instead placed on a par with the other "seats of imperial power" and thus devalued. Did this version of events accord with Charlemagne's own view of his elevation to emperor? And did its mention of the "whole of Christendom" correspond to the concept of the *imperium christianum* Alcuin had urged Charlemagne to establish?[166] Was it also Charlemagne's plan to create such an entity? Was, then, the Lorsch portrayal of events in fact less a reflection of retrospective criticism than of calculated planning—plans that had been laid, say, in Paderborn in 799 or subsequently?

The Lorsch annalist is alone in claiming that the assignment of the title of emperor came about as a result of the Christian people's urging and Charlemagne's compliance; however, this should not give us cause to doubt this claim, but quite the opposite. No imperial coronation could have taken place without Charlemagne's explicit agreement. This chronicler was well informed. He accorded the office of emperor political legitimacy, discounted the Romans, and presented the assumption of the title of emperor as a consensual act involving the pope, the synod, the magnates, the Christian people, and the Frankish king, followed by a confirmatory "benediction" by the Roman pontiff. This chronicler chose to gloss over the details of the ritual: here, there were no public acclamation and no Laudes, indeed, not even a formal coronation ceremony.

The staging of the coronation recalled the accession of Pepin the Short and his sons as kings almost fifty years before, particularly as described in the first edition of the *Royal Frankish Annals,* which had appeared around a decade earlier. Indeed, Charlemagne may well have had intentions very similar to those of his father: to independently fashion a consensual emperorship of the kind that had been in preparation since 797/798, one that was designed to give leadership to the whole of "Christendom"; to assume a proper imperial title that accorded with the real extent of his power (in Charlemagne's case it was the title of emperor, whereas for Pepin it had been that of king); and to impose a rational and essential order, as his study of dialectics dictated and as confirmed by a papal coronation.[167] As Alcuin had taught the king and his son Pepin the Hunchback,[168] "The essence of a name resides in the fact that it denotes substance, quality, and quantity." In this instance, it was the substance of real power, the quality of dominion over kings, and the quantity of all imperial seats of power in the West.

Did this idea displease the Roman pontiff? Certainly, the *Liber pontificalis* presented the event in a fundamentally different way. Its portrayal only superficially tallies with that found in the *Royal Frankish Annals.* The observance of Christmas in Rome was characterized by no fewer than four stational masses, at all of which the pope was expected to officiate: the Vigil in Santa Maria Maggiore on the Esquiline Hill; the nighttime mass held at the hour when the cockerel crowed "at the crib," that is, in the cave of the Nativity in that same church; the second Christmas Mass in the church of Santa Anastasia at the foot of the Palatine Hill, to the west of the city near the Circus Maximus; and finally, the third Christmas Mass at St. Peter's.[169] This involved an enormous procession passing through the entire inner city of Rome during the night before Christmas, Charlemagne presumably attended all four masses, yet the coronation took place only during the third Christmas Mass. And all the accounts of Charlemagne's ascent to emperor talk only about this mass.

The *Liber pontificalis,* which waxed lyrical about Leo's return to Rome from Saxony, and which had reported extensively on the episcopal court hearing against the would-be assassins Paschalis and Campulus and the purging oath taken by the pope, saw fit to include only a few extremely brief sentences on Charlemagne's coronation, noting that the pope had crowned "him" in St. Peter's with a valuable crown, and that "afterward all devout Romans" proclaimed him emperor "thanks to his protection and the love that he has shown toward the Holy Roman Church and its *vicarius,* according to the will of God and his blessed guardian of the keys St. Peter," and that Charlemagne had thus been installed as the "emperor of the Romans." "*Karolo, piissimo Augusto, a Deo coronato, magno et pacifico imperatori, vita et victoria.*" Here, then, in the papal account of events, Charlemagne and the Franks were not the prime movers, but rather the people of Rome and their pontiff, who were doing nothing other than implementing the will of God and his apostle. There was therefore no talk here of a "designation" (just as there was none in the *Royal Frankish Annals*); the coronation had preceded the transfer of the "title" and was a coronation as "emperor of the Romans." Had it thereby become a constitutive act? At once, Leo anointed Charlemagne's son Charles as king with holy oil.[170] Then again, this act must have required the new emperor's volition and active instruction.

After celebrating Mass, the emperor Augustus and his sons and daughters endowed St. Peter's Basilica with precious gifts, which once again were listed in detail. There was certainly no hidden message of resentment toward Leo in this catalog. The Church of St. Paul and the Church of St. Savior, the pope's episcopal church, were also given donations. This may perhaps indicate that Charlemagne attended Mass in these two churches, which were the stational churches of the day, on the Feast of the Holy Innocents (or Childermas; 28 December) and on the first Sunday of Lent. The donation to the Church of St. Savior was mentioned in Leo IV's entry in the *Liber pontificalis*—namely, a *crux gemmata* fashioned from pure gold and studded with precious stones, which was henceforth carried at the head of the *Letania* procession in front of the pope until it was stolen during the reign of Pope Paschal I (817–824).[171] But gemstone crosses traditionally allude to the Second Coming of Christ to judge the world and represent the future, heavenly Jerusalem.[172] Thus, on the occasion of his coronation on the first day of the apocalyptic eon, Charlemagne was clearly intending the gift of the cross as a symbolic admonition.

Yet the Frankish king is said to have been dissatisfied by his church visits in Rome at Christmas, even to the point of being thoroughly dismissive (*aversatus*). If he, Charlemagne, had guessed what the pope had planned (*pontificis consilium*), he would never have set foot in St. Peter's Basilica, even though it was Christmas—at least, this was the story peddled by his biographer Einhard (chap. 28). Since time immemorial, and even up to the present day, historians have puzzled over this sentence. Was it the way in which the pope had drawn attention to himself that irritated Charlemagne? Certainly, when he made his own son Louis emperor in 813, there was no papal involvement, nor any mention of Rome and its *imperium*. Was this the Frankish king's response to Leo's III's unwelcome actions? Or was he simply, because of the negotiations that were going on at that time with Byzantium, showing some consideration toward the Eastern Roman Empire, which, despite allowing others to bear the title of emperor, reserved that of "emperor of the Romans" exclusively for itself? In 813, was Charlemagne deliberately falling in line with the Byzantine, the true "Roman" custom, according to which the principal emperor (not a pope) crowned a co-emperor?[173] Charlemagne was therefore familiar with the Eastern Roman coronation protocol. Did he possibly consider that it had been violated at his own coronation?

Earlier in his biography (chap. 23), Einhard had already noted that, quite exceptionally, Charlemagne had dressed in Roman garb for his coronation at the express request of the pope (as the king himself had conceded): the long tunic, worn with a Roman cloak and Roman ceremonial shoes. Yet anyone who dressed, or allowed himself to be dressed, in this way knew what to expect; the king, therefore, could not have been remotely surprised at what then took place in St. Peter's. Einhard thus contradicted himself in making his infamous remark. Charlemagne must have been expecting what occurred during the third Christmas Mass and hence must also have wanted it to unfold in the way it did. Every last detail of the coronation ceremony must have been discussed and agreed in advance.

No one, then, could have placed a crown on the Frankish king's head if he had been unwilling, or could have anointed him or paid homage to him. Nor could the succession of ritual acts elevating him to the emperorship possibly have surprised or antagonized the king as he knelt in prayer in St. Peter's; after all, he had long been very well informed about the liturgy of the Mass.[174] His coronation by the pope was only the visible sign of the Roman ceremony of acclaiming someone emperor, in which admittedly, according to the *Liber pontificalis,* no Frank appears to have participated. The acclamation occurred, then, at the "correct" liturgical juncture. Nothing in this procedure vindicates Einhard's misgivings.

Even in Constantinople in the decades under discussion here, a "spontaneous" acclamation as emperor was not customary; during this period, each young emperor was elevated by the principal emperor, his father. Might it then have been the actual wording of the "acclamation as emperor" that displeased Charlemagne, inasmuch as it unequivocally proclaimed the Frankish king "emperor of the Romans"? Charlemagne did not want to be elevated to emperor through their grace and favor, but rather by his own authority and by the grace "of God." Indeed, the transfer of the "imperial title" (albeit with no mention of Rome or the Romans) had been decided some days before in agreement with the "whole of the Christian communion." Yet even this possible explanation of Einhard's cryptic comment remains unconvincing.

The *Royal Frankish Annals* gives us an idea of Charlemagne's preferred view of the coronation ceremony, namely, as an integral part of his elevation to emperor and Augustus. The *Annals* does not indicate whether the actual placing of the crown on Charlemagne's head preceded the acclamation, took place at the same time, or followed it. We may surmise from the fact that the *Royal Frankish Annals* also did not omit the inclusion of the Romans in the imperial acclamation that it was by no means unwelcome to the new emperor.

Furthermore, the succession of ritual acts was of no consequence. Even in Byzantium, whose "Roman" ritual Charlemagne's own coronation ceremony had consciously emulated, investiture with the regalia of emperorship and the actual coronation could precede the acclamation in cases where the Senate, or a combination of the army, the Senate, and the people or their representatives had already proposed a binding nomination of the candidate.[175] The business of raising someone to imperial office in the Eastern Roman Empire had long since become a protracted chain of ritual acts: nomination either by the combined forces of the empire's high lords (*archontes*), the Senate, and the representatives of the army, or just one of these bodies, followed by the coronation and finally the acclamation.

We can identify this, then, as precisely the procedure and the sequence that were followed in the case of Charlemagne's coronation the moment we take into account the declaration of intent by the pope, the members of the synod, and the Christian communion at large, which the *Lorsch Annals* highlights, but which the *Royal Frankish Annals* and the *Liber pontificalis* disregard as not being an integral part of the liturgical confirmation of emperorship.[176] Seen in this light, Charlemagne's coronation as emperor followed its Byzantine model to the letter, including observance of the "proper" Roman ceremonial. Thus, the magnates proposed Charlemagne as emperor (*iustum eis esse videbatur, ut . . . ipsum nomen aberet*), and the

Christian people "requested" that he be appointed to the post (*populo pe-tente*).[177] Such a "request" can only—as in Byzantium—have ensued as a kind of acclamation. On the next day, the pope conducted the coronation and "venerated" the new emperor before the assembled populace acclaimed the newly crowned ruler in St. Peter's. Many such acclamations accompanying a coronation are well attested in the case of Byzantium. The "Rome of the East" was seen as the ultimate yardstick for Rome itself.

Admittedly, all this does not help solve the mysteries of Einhard's statement. Charlemagne had been seeking to become emperor for some years now. Neither the pope's participation nor acclamation as *imperator Romanorum* by the Roman people could have come about without his agreement. There is nothing to suggest that Charlemagne's coronation can be construed as some error of judgment on the pope's part. The reports that have come down to us do not reveal any clash of diametrically opposed views of the form or the nature of the coronation—say, from Frankish and Roman perspectives—even though the accounts do differ to some extent. The account given in the *Royal Frankish Annals* and its repetition in the *Metz Annals* clearly refutes such an idea. Yet retrospective interpretations of the significance of the details that were mentioned or not mentioned, as the case may be, diverge wildly.

We therefore have to assume that Charlemagne's alleged aversion to the title of emperor, which in any case the Frankish ruler by no means shunned, referred to another historical context and not to the events of Christmas Day 800 (801). The biographer proceeded from his puzzling remark about "what the Pope had planned" (*pontificis consilium*) to talk about the patience his hero showed toward "Roman [i.e., Byzantine] emperors" who envied him his imperial title. This was the only occasion on which Einhard referred to the Byzantines—whom he elsewhere consistently called "Greeks"—as "Romans." Now, though, he attested the patience shown by his hero, newly crowned as emperor, to the "Roman emperors" (*Romanis imperatoribus*).

Just before this, in the same chapter (28) of his biography, Einhard had talked about the other "Romans"—namely, those who lived along the banks of the Tiber and who had tried to assassinate Pope Leo after he conceded that the rulers of Constantinople were entitled to use this name. In doing so, Leo was merely falling in line with their own official designation of themselves. This can only be interpreted as a response by Leo to the recognition of Charlemagne as "emperor" by the Byzantine "emperor of the Romans" (βασιλεὺς τῶν Ῥωμαίων) in 812.[178] If Charlemagne's comment as noted by Einhard has any historical truth whatsoever to it, then it is clearly in this context. In order to conclude peace with Byzantium at that time, did the Frankish emperor basically shift the entire blame for his "Roman" imperial title onto the pope and his "irritating" actions? And was this the reason that, in the following year, he established the practice of crowning his son emperor without any involvement from Rome? Or was it that during Louis the Pious's reign, when Einhard wrote his *Vita Karoli*, in 828, criticism had begun to increase against the whole idea of an imperial coronation directed by the pope and focused on Rome and the Romans—a development that the biographer tried to claim his subject had instigated, and thereby to legitimize it?

Whatever the truth of the matter, the reports originating from the Frankish Empire and from Rome diverged in a spectacular and hence very revealing way. The things on which the *Royal Frankish Annals* and the *Liber pontificalis*—and to some extent the *Lorsch Annals* as well—agreed were the venue of St. Peter's as the location of the coronation; the fact that the crowning itself was done with a crown that Charlemagne himself supplied; the almost identical wording of the acclamation by the Romans and the transfer of the "imperial title"; and the fact that Charlemagne was dubbed "emperor of the Romans." The differences, though, are no less significant and cannot be glossed over because it is precisely they that point to another view and a different construction of events and the divergent motivations of the protagonists. They reveal their differing aims and the means that they employed—even if these are only retrospective historiographic ones—to achieve their ends. Over time, though, everything took on historical significance,

The first thing that the *Liber pontificalis* said nothing about was Charlemagne's reception like an emperor by the pope twelve miles outside the city; it also ignored the "veneration" that both the royal and the Lorsch annalists recorded and, along with this last aspect, also the clear, very public subordination of the Roman pontiff to the new "Roman emperor." Instead, the *Liber pontificalis* emphasized the fact that the coronation took place before the acclamation, and it stressed Charlemagne's duty of protection toward the Roman Church and the new emperor's relationship to the holder of the keys of Heaven and the apostolic prince St. Peter and to his vicar on Earth (it mentions this last element not once but twice). In this account, the emperor emerged more as a protector of the Roman Church than as its guiding hand. The Laudes sung by the Franks present at the coronation, with their brief salutation of "*Vita!*" (life!) directed at the pope, as compared to the prolonged cries of "*Vita et victoria!*" (long life and victory!) for the Augustus, his sons, the Frankish magnates, and the Frankish army,[179] were the actual truth behind the *Liber pontificalis*'s phrase "their invocation of many saints"; this anodyne phrase was evidently designed to gloss over these decidedly "political" expressions of praise and turn them instead into an "apolitical" litany to the saints.

All these instances point to Leo III's and his advisers' mastery not of liturgical dramaturgy but rather of the business of retrospective historiographic reinterpretation of events, which managed to transform a situation of distressing dependence into one of liberating superiority. In their account, the pope and not Charlemagne was now master of the proceedings. It was this version that came to hold sway over the ensuing centuries. The *Liber pontificalis* disseminated this interpretation, which was not merely for internal consumption within the Vatican and Rome but for centuries hence, thanks to the extensive distribution of the *Liber pontificalis,* also enjoyed widespread currency in the Frankish Empire and later in France and Germany, and indeed in the Latin Christian world at large. As a supposed "legal precedent," it even came to carry canonical and authoritative legal weight. The life of Leo in this volume may possibly have reached the court in Aix while Charlemagne was still alive;[180] perhaps, then, the contentious statement in Einhard's biography was designed to counter this version of events. Later coronation tradition went even further in placing the endowment of imperial authority even more firmly in papal hands, dispensing entirely as it did with the element of acclamation by the people.

The true significance of this coronation, the precise nature of this momentous historical turning point in the long reign of Charlemagne, therefore lies hidden beneath divergent intentions and contradictory interpretations and recollections of those who participated in it. At least we are in a position to reconstruct an approximate objective timetable of events, beginning with Charlemagne's designation as "emperor" by the pope, the synod, and the whole of Christianity before Christmas, followed by Charlemagne's prayer before his confession with the apostolic prince during the third Christmas Mass, then the ensuing coronation, and finally the acclamation by the Roman people (though probably omitting any anointment). But in adopting this order of events, as we have ascertained, Charlemagne and his papal celebrant were without reservation following the ritual of the Byzantine coronation ceremony.

Whatever Charlemagne may have intended, and however the sequence of the coronation service and its subsequent judgment by posterity may have panned out, the fact remains: this was a Roman emperorship that was being revived on Christmas Day 800 and, moreover, not one that was restricted to "the Romans."[181] The dating on Leo's papal encyclicals henceforth placed Charlemagne's years as emperor before the years of the pope's reign. Money, though, proved to be transient; no one later insisted on taking the testimony offered by coinage into account. Charlemagne and his son Pepin, the king of Italy, on the other hand, would probably have taken great care over the symbolism of the coins they minted.

The new emperor may well have regarded the high office he had just attained as the zenith of his rule and willingly have shouldered the task that had now fallen to him as the universal guardian of the Christian faith, but he could scarcely have imagined the enduring repercussions of his Christmastide coronation. With this act, the Frankish king established a tradition that lasted until the coronation of Frederick II in 1452—indeed, in its basic form, until Charles V and his coronation by Pope Clement VII in the Church of San Petronio in Bologna in 1530. Therefore, it outlived its model, the true office of "emperor of the Romans" among the Byzantine Greeks, whose empire was brought to an end in 1453 by the Ottoman sultan Mehmet the Conqueror's capture of Constantinople. By contrast, the office of Western emperor survived for over a millennium, until 1806 and even, if we take into account the successor "emperors" to the Holy Roman emperor—*l'empereur* in France, the Kaiser of the Austro-Hungarian Empire, *el emperador* in Mexico, the German Kaiser, and the British empress of India—well into the twentieth century.

8

♛

IMPERATOR AUGUSTUS

"**L**OOK HOW THE SUN'S RAYS are streaming down: in the same way, David illuminates the world with the bright light of his grace."[1] Poets (in this case the anonymous author of the *Paderborn Epic*) vied to outdo one another in praise of the king. According to this same writer, the kingdom of the Franks was the "beacon of Europe," from which "King Charles broadcast his magnificent name to the stars," while the monarch himself was "an eternally shining star." The writer clearly had feast days in mind when he wrote these words. On such occasions, the king would wear gold-embroidered robes. But at all other times, as Einhard recalled, Charlemagne made do with a simple tunic, woolen socks held up with garters, a pair of trousers, a linen shirt, and a woolen coat (no doubt the product of much laborious stitching by maidservants). Invariably, he wore his sword by his side, which on high days and holidays would be one with a hilt made of gold and a jewel-encrusted scabbard but was otherwise a plain, functional weapon. Even without any finery, the ruler outshone everything around him. At least, this was the picture painted by contemporary panegyrics of the Frankish king. But did this reflect the real situation? And what of his deeds and his aims?

On 25 December 800 (801 in the Carolingian calendar), Pope Leo III crowned Charlemagne emperor at a ceremony in St. Peter's in Rome. This event appeared to herald the dawn of a new eon, a new universal age: an age that would be ushered in by the first emperor from the Frankish people, and the first whom a successor of the apostolic prince St. Peter had vested with imperial authority. A new empire came into being. "Already, mighty Rome can see her trophies returning to her."[2] This new beginning was accompanied by joyful expectations and hopes, but skepticism was also in the air. The accounts of the coronation originating from the Frankish Empire and from Rome, respectively, contradicted each other, heralding a political power struggle between the person conducting the crowning and the recipient of the crown, the pope and the emperor, which, as things transpired, would come to dominate the centuries that followed.

The revival of the empire in the West changed the world. The events in Rome seemed to send out a message of peace. Like the first Roman emperor, Augustus, whose name his title as ruler would henceforth recall, Charlemagne wanted to go down in history as a peaceful ruler, as well as a devout, orthodox defender of the Christian faith. Peace and justice were to be restored, and peace would reign on Earth. The young poet Moduin, whom Charlemagne dubbed with the courtly sobriquet *Naso* (an allusion to Ovid, whose full name was Publius Ovidius Naso) captured this key aspect of Charlemagne's reign in his implicit imitation of Virgil's fourth *Eclogue*, the quintessential example of Augustinian bucolic verse. In this work, unity and eternal peace spread throughout the land, no one feared for his or her life, poverty was banished from the world, and the earth gave up its bounty without need of a plow.[3] "Charlemagne, the Caesar, brings together peoples and nations under his protection, he guides all the nations on Earth, and his imperial authority holds benevolent sway around the globe."[4] As if to confirm such extravagant praise, no sooner had the coronation taken place than news came of the successful capture of the Saracen-held city of Barcelona. Christ's realm of peace had suddenly grown in size.[5] Charlemagne may even have dared to believe in Moduin's claim of "imperial power around the globe," from Toledo to Rome and on to Constantinople, Raqqa, and Baghdad.

It was not only the young Moduin who hailed the bringer of peace with topical verses. Charlemagne's extensive reading of St. Augustine of Hippo's works bore abundant fruit. He took the yardstick and the model of all his actions from the revered Church Father's famous work *De civitate Dei* (The city of God). It was beneficial for "good people" (*boni*) who venerated the true God to hold power. Simple piety (*pietas*) and righteousness were enough for them, Augustine claimed, to attain true happiness, and it was through this that a person might lead a good life and enter into Heaven. "A good man, though a slave, is free; but a wicked man, though a king, is a slave. For he serves not one man alone, but what is worse, as many masters as he has vices" (4.3). Charlemagne took such sentences as this to heart. Furthermore, Augustine inquired, if justice was removed, what were kingdoms but great bands of robbers (4.4)? Every capitulary that Charlemagne issued bore testimony to his desire to exercise justice, punish injustice, and eradicate iniquity. Augustine's *De civitate Dei* was one of the emperor's favorite books, as Einhard knew full well; his close adviser Alcuin, too, was constantly reminding Charlemagne of the work of the Church Father.[6] Even though it ossified into something of a standard mantra, reference to Charlemagne as the "most pious" (*piissimus*) Caesar was commonplace among correspondents of this time.

The Bible insistently proclaimed the close bond that existed between peace and justice. The book of Psalms (85:10) exulted, "Righteousness and peace have kissed each other." Without justice, then, there could be no peace. In his exegesis of the Psalms, the Venerable Bede had already declared the two to be sisters: "Peace will not come unless justice goes before it."[7] All these texts would likely have been familiar to the new emperor, who from his childhood had been raised in a Christian and highly literate household. And he acted accordingly; his questions regarding the interpretation of Holy Scripture, for which he sought answers from Pope Leo, are well known.[8] Were these prompted by a profound spirituality on his part? Certainly, after his coronation in Rome, the number of admonitory decrees he issued increased, and their tone became more insistent. He was adamant that the Gospel should be proclaimed to everyone. Before the last trumpet sounded, all men should, Charlemagne believed, come to know the mysteries of the Christian faith. This was the message that the emperor's envoys, Bishop Bernar of Worms and Bishop Jesse of Amiens, conveyed to the pope; its urgency was, they explained, "consonant with the extraordinary times we live in" (*secundum huius temporis qualitatem*).[9] By way of preparation for the end times, the evangelist St. Matthew exhorted all believers to pray (24:20), watch (24:42), and hold themselves ready (24:44).

A person's faith, though, had to stand the test: "For I was hungry, and you fed me. I was thirsty, and you gave me a drink. I was a stranger, and you invited me into your home. I was naked, and you gave me clothing. I was sick, and you cared for me. I was in prison, and you visited me" (Matthew 25:35–36). Charlemagne also understood and acted on this message. Over the final years of his reign, his concern for the poor, the oppressed, and the weak grew. When he was at the height of his external power, he embarked on the most ambitious program imaginable—nothing less than the internal reorganization of his huge empire according to the parameters of justice and peace. His realm, which extended from the river Eider to the borders of Calabria, from the Atlantic to the river Elbe and even to Pannonia (the Balkans), found itself constantly having to fight against Vikings and Muslims, Greeks and Slavs, and rebellious, power-hungry noblemen within its borders, in addition to combating the plight of the poor and the superstition that was deeply rooted in paganism.

Some historians believe that these anxious late capitularies reveal some indications of a disintegration of the Frankish Empire, of "decomposition" and incipient decline.[10] Yet the difficulties during Charlemagne's reign as emperor were no different from those that he had faced before his Roman coronation. In the interim, however, learning and religious instruction had undoubtedly sharpened his appreciation of social concerns and of the consequences of the agonal society he had grown up in and found himself surrounded by. "Under the royal authority that had been vested in him by God, his aim is to impose order using the norm of rectitude [*ad rectitudinis normam*]. Yet he does not have at his disposal as many helpers to establish justice as there are enemies who would destroy it, nor as many preachers as there are marauders [*nec tantos praedicatores quantos praedatores*]." In this letter, Alcuin praised the emperor and in the same breath warned his friend Arn of Salzburg not to accept any gifts in return for court judgments.[11] Does this imply that the archbishop of Salzburg was also one of the "marauders"? Whatever the case, Charlemagne could see destructive forces operating even within ecclesiastical circles. He was determined to counter them through the application of peace and justice, according to the norm of rectitude. But could he succeed in keeping people's selfishness in check?

Peace was the necessary outcome of a just order of things. Yet all that was required to bring this about was a modification of the laws that were already in force; it did not call for any radical reforms of authority or society. It demanded that everyone should respect the rights of others, but it did not do away with the system of dominion and servitude or the differences in citizen's rights. Masters remained masters, free men remained free men, servants remained servants, and Franks remained Franks; but even a servant had certain rights. The calls for peace followed these basic parameters: they protected masters, free men and servants, and laymen and clerics alike, but each according to his own rights and within his station in life. Any deviation from this principle would mean fomenting injustice. Admonitions therefore confined themselves to questions of form because they did not dare to touch on any matters of substance, let alone challenge and reject them.

FIGURE 51 The bronze main portal (the so-called Wolf's Door) of Aachen Cathedral.

The first measure implemented by the newly crowned emperor clearly reflected this state of affairs. Charlemagne called on "the Holy Roman Church to abandon its discord and return to a state of peace and unanimity"[12] while sitting in judgment on those who had violated the peace on the Tiber and had attempted to assassinate the pope. In doing so, he was intent on strengthening the traditional formal justice system and on avoiding dragging anyone's personal behavior into the light for examination. Even so, the proceedings he instituted there, in the Eternal City, were not universally welcomed, for Charlemagne also laid claim to imperial law. Pope Leo's adversaries had conspired against the Roman people and had risen up—an act of sacrilege—against their master the pope, who could not be judged by any mortal, and even against the majesty of God. The motives for their actions, namely, the grave accusations that they leveled against Leo, were not examined by the court; to this day, we do not know exactly what they were. Yet once Leo had voluntarily sworn an oath and cleared his name at a synod of Frankish and "Roman" bishops before Christmas, the conspirators' guilt was a foregone conclusion even before the start of the trial.

The *quaestio* mentioned in the *Royal Frankish Annals*, therefore, did not denote a forensic investigation as we know it but merely concerned what judgment to pass on the ringleaders. In accordance with Roman law, a fact stressed only by the *Royal Frankish Annals* and deliberately glossed over in the *Liber pontificalis,* the perpetrators, who were former close confidants of the Frankish king, were condemned to death for having committed a "crime against the Crown." After Leo's intervention, however, the verdict was commuted to one of lifelong exile. Charlemagne himself, the emperor, whose team of legal advisers, headed by the Visigothic scholar Theodulf of Orléans, had presumably referred to the *Lex Romana Visigothorum* (5.31.1.2),[13] must have welcomed these proceedings. This was the first occasion on which the offense of "a crime against the Crown" was cited; henceforth, this same charge would be laid repeatedly in the Frankish Empire. The very existence of the office of emperor entailed there being an offense of *crimen laesae majestatis* (high treason). Anyone who in word or deed took up arms against the *imperator* and the *res publica* was liable to be sentenced to death.

Three hundred coconspirators are said to have been beheaded at that time on the Campus Lateranensis. At least, this was what was reported in a small nostalgic tract that was published a century later. Titled *A Pamphlet on Imperial Power in the City of Rome* (*Libellus de imperatoria potestate in urbe Roma*), it focused on Charlemagne's period of rule.[14] The figure given here may be an exaggeration, but the basic facts are not in question, although it is true that no other witness corroborates them, and the *Royal Frankish Annals* appears to claim the opposite. But the location of these events was remarkable. Charlemagne was laying claim to be the successor of Constantine. The legend of St. Sylvester (see Chapter 3) would have led him to believe that it was the site of the former emperor's palace where he was sitting in judgment on the conspirators, and where the verdict and sentence were handed down, in sight of the bronze statue of Constantine, between the former palace of the first Christian emperor and the papal residence, the *patriarchium,* the most symbolic and significant place in early medieval Rome. The new Caesar was thus—at least according to his own conception—presiding over the highest court in the city of Rome. At that time, the *Pamphlet* added, the people of Rome were sworn to loyalty to the emperor. All the leading figures of the city, from the bishops to the lay magnates, were henceforth bondsmen of the emperor.[15] Of course, Leo III would doubtless have wished it otherwise.

In this trial, Charlemagne quite consciously acted like a Roman emperor. The pope, the former master of Rome, feared the consequences that the emperor's appeal to Roman law and the charge of a "crime against the Crown" would inevitably entail. The *Liber pontificalis* thus drew a veil over the whole outcome of the proceedings. "In the presence of the devout emperor," the principal wrongdoers, Paschalis and Campulus, now accused each other of committing the crime; the emperor sentenced them to be banished into exile in the Frankish Empire.[16] Apart from this, the *Liber pontificalis* says nothing about Charlemagne, despite the fact that he spent a further three and a half months in Rome, during which time he was by no means idle. But beyond this, after just six years of his papal reign, all contemporary accounts concerning the life of Pope Leo in the *Liber pontificalis* come to an abrupt end following this obfuscating report about the defendants accusing each other of the assassination attempt and being sent into exile by Charlemagne; on the remaining fifteen years of his pontificate, the *Liber pontificalis* has nothing to report except the endowments he bestowed on various churches in the city.

Yet the record of these endowments, dry though it may be, commemorates an act of donation that was highly political. Almost certainly in the last years of his papacy, Leo had silver tablets put up in both of the city's apostolic churches, which were inscribed, in defiance of Charlemagne's express wishes, with the creed in Greek and Latin, in the traditional form of the so-called Nicaeno-Constantinopolitanum—in other words, without the *filioque* formulation that Charlemagne wanted to see included.[17] Thus, the dispute between the pope and the emperor did not come to an end, even though Rome, as it had done once before under Hadrian I, fell into a state of quiescence once the Carolingian ruler's authority was imposed on the city of the apostles. Instead, the dispute shifted to the spiritual realm, where the decision in the long run devolved on the highest priest and bishop, the successor of the apostolic prince.

As the *Royal Frankish Annals* reported—once again, the only contemporary source to do so—"Charlemagne spent the entire winter organizing secular, ecclesiastical, and 'private' matters" in the city of the apostles.[18] The later *Pamphlet on Imperial Power in the City of Rome* went into greater detail about his activities: Charlemagne or his *missi* supposedly held court "at the home of the Laterani, at a place known as 'at the she-wolf,' as the mother of the Roman people is called."[19] Even relatives of the pope were called to book. The pamphlet's account telescoped the events of 800/801, identifying them (though not implausibly) with conditions at the time when it was written, namely, during the reign of Charlemagne's grandson Lothar I and great-grandson Louis II.[20]

Yet there were also some more harmless court cases to settle. For instance, the bishop of Arezzo had accused his colleague from Siena of having "snatched" a monastery from his rightful jurisdiction; Charlemagne confirmed the judgment that Leo III had already passed at the synod in December in favor of the plaintiff.[21] The first diploma issued after his coronation as emperor to have survived confirms this. But his ruling title "Charlemagne by the grace of God king of the Franks and Romans and Lombards" (*Carolus gratia dei rex Francorum et Romanorum atque Langobardorum*) had always attracted attention, given that it made no reference whatever to his imperial status. Rather, it appeared to indicate some hesitancy regarding his new "name," or even some reservations about the title of emperor of the Romans.

These facts may well be open to a different interpretation, however. The document in question is a supplementary or secondary copy, a reproduction of the original, which was sealed without being examined and which therefore was not countersigned by the chancellor.[22] The basic template may have been drafted while the synod was still going on, namely—as the title of "king" also seems to suggest—before Charlemagne's coronation as emperor, although the copy we have was probably sealed only on 4 March 801. The title as given here was still stressing Charlemagne's dominion over the Franks ahead of that over the Romans even immediately before his investiture as emperor. Around this same time, the *Lorsch Annals*—highly unusually— designated Charlemagne as *princeps*.[23] Be that as it may, the most we can surmise is uncertainty on the part of the chancellery, not any misgiving or "diplomatic" recalcitrance regarding his new office.[24]

The emperor celebrated the Feast of the Resurrection in the company of the pope,[25] sent yet another force under the command of his son Pepin to attack the Duchy of Benevento, and withdrew only at the end of April, alongside the king of Italy, who had by then returned from his campaign, to Spoleto. He set off for that city on St. Mark's Day,[26] the day of the *Letania maior* procession in Rome; shortly after his arrival five days later, Spoleto was hit by an earthquake. The *Royal Frankish Annals* reported heavy damage. Indeed, the whole of Italy was affected; in Rome, the roof of the Basilica of St. Paul collapsed.[27] Was St. Mark avenging himself on the emperor for failing to attend the penitential procession in Rome on his name day? Later that same year, earthquakes hit many places on both sides of the Rhine, in Gallia and Germania alike, while the *Annals* for 801 reported that "pestilence" was visited on the land because the winter had been too mild.

From Spoleto, Charlemagne moved on to Ravenna. This was the first time in thirteen years that he had set eyes on this city, whose ancient buildings had captivated him almost as much as those in Rome. His objective was, likewise, to establish "justice and freedom" in Ravenna.[28] On this occasion, though, he stayed only a few days. Roman emperors had once resided here, as had the Visigothic king Theoderic, whose bronze statue (or was it actually of Emperor Phocas?) Charlemagne now ordered to be relocated to Aix. Here, the first emperor of Frankish stock encountered his Roman predecessor Justinian in mosaic depictions; here, in the episcopal archives, ancient documents of imperial Roman provenance were held. Not far from the city gates, by the old port, stood the imposing Basilica of Sant'Apollinare in Classe, with its inscriptions dating from late antiquity. Could it be the case, then, that the new emperor came up with his future ruling title only after spending time in these surroundings? We shall never know, although it is only from this point on that the series of imperial "diplomas" begins, which provide much of the information we now possess on Charlemagne as emperor.[29]

As a general rule, in their official titles, the earlier Caesars refrained from the "heathen" practice of naming the place over which they held dominion. In Ravenna, though, official documents now came to light clearly expressing, in the formulation *Romanum gubernans imperium* (governing the Roman Empire) the intrinsic connection between the office of emperor and the city of Rome—a fact eagerly seized on by the king of the Franks and the Lombards. He adopted this formulation and henceforth styled himself "Charles, most serene Augustus, crowned by God, great and pacific emperor governing the Roman empire, and who is also by God's mercy king of the Franks and the Lombards" (*Carolus serenissimus augustus a Deo coronatus magnus pacificus imperator Romanum gubernans imperium, qui et per misericordiam Dei rex Francorum et Langobardorum*).[30] This title brought together all the "heathen" bases of the new emperor's power, but significantly the order of the domains listed in the title had changed since the time when Charlemagne had been the *patricius Romanorum*. From now on, the Roman Empire took pride of place. Yet this realm did not arch over the people and the kingdoms of the Franks and the Lombards, subsuming them within it, but instead was ranged alongside them as an independent component. Charlemagne's Roman coronation had not, therefore, brought about any new conception of a rule that had hitherto been seen in very personal terms.

Charlemagne's gaze now turned to Rome and Jerusalem. The new emperor's first proclamation—leaving aside documents directed at subjects of his own empire—was addressed to the "king of the Persians." In it, Charlemagne summoned the envoys of the caliph to an audience with him at his tented encampment, which had been pitched between Vercelli and Ivrea on his homeward journey to Aix—in the midst of his army, in other words. One of them was reputedly a "Persian" from the East, another a "Saracen" from Africa (*Royal Frankish Annals*). They were able to take back with them to the East news of the imminent success of the siege of Barcelona; this must have delighted Harun al-Rashid. The trade contacts that the Franks forged with Muslim Africa also date from this time.[31] Charlemagne responded to the legation sent to him in 802 by the caliph by donating lavish gifts for the Holy Sepulchre.[32]

Attention Turns to the Near East

Eventually, the emperor returned home to the Frankish Empire, to Aix, where a court assembly was convened for the fall of 802 and Christmas was celebrated. Presently, an emissary by the name of Leo arrived from Constantinople; a Sicilian by birth, he had been sent by Empress Irene to negotiate a peace treaty with the Franks. This could only mean—at least in their view—that the empress was now prepared to recognize Charlemagne as emperor despite the fact that she had had no direct involvement in the decision. No special reasons were mentioned for sending this legation. They may well be sought, however, in a new crisis that had recently overtaken the empress; homegrown opposition to her reign was causing her mounting difficulties (*Royal Frankish Annals* for the year 802). For the time being, only good fortune and a show of strength had enabled her to gain the upper hand over her enemies. Yet, as the chronicler Theophanes reported (for the year AM 6291), even her closest confidants had started to plot against her.

Bishop Jesse of Amiens and Count Helmgaud took Charlemagne's answer to Constantinople, but they arrived too late. As their ship lay at anchor in the Bosphorus, Irene was arrested in October 802 and deposed; she died soon after in exile. Wild rumors began to circulate in Constantinople, no doubt generated by Irene's opponents; these claimed that Charlemagne had offered the *basilissa* his hand in marriage in order to unite East and West, and that his envoys had come to make preparations for the marriage. But Irene's closest courtly adviser, Patrikios Aetios, allegedly managed to block it by raising forceful objections. It was rumored that, as a eunuch who was himself disbarred from holding power, Aetios was anticipating Irene's demise in order to help his brother become emperor. However, an opposing faction at the court preempted him and installed Nicephorus on the Byzantine throne instead.[33]

The new emperor, whose envoys had witnessed the coup firsthand, now immediately offered the Carolingian ruler a peace treaty while refusing to acknowledge him as emperor in the West. In 803, Nicephorus's envoys—Bishop Michael of Synnada, Abbot Petrus, and the imperial dignitary (*candidatus*) Callistus—were sent to discuss peace with Charlemagne while he was enjoying some autumn hunting at his palace at Salz on the river Saale in Francia. His answer, which they took back with them to Constantinople via Rome (*Royal Frankish Annals* for 803) would have been in the negative. In any event, for the next nine years the relations between the two powers were hallmarked by tensions and occasional skirmishes.

The caliph also took his time in responding to the Frankish king's second legation. It was only in 807 that Harun's envoys, alongside those sent by the patriarch and the delegation of monks from Jerusalem, finally arrived in Aix. Once again, they brought with them valuable gifts—the *Royal Frankish Annals* lists bolts of silk, a lavishly decorated tent of enormous dimensions, a wondrous water clock (*klepsydra*), a pair of huge brass candlesticks, spices, perfumes, and much more besides. Were these magnificent presents given in thanks for Charlemagne's successes against the rule of the Umayyads in al-Andalus?

In his *Life of Charlemagne* (chap. 16), Einhard recalled that "such unity in friendship" existed between the two rulers that Harun—"heaping on him alone marks of honor and munificence"—even exceeded the Frankish king's wishes by "guaranteeing to assign [*concessit*] to his jurisdiction the most holy sepulchre and place of resurrection." Although it was devoid of any practical substance, this was still a friendly gesture on the part of the caliph and was taken as a sign of respect. But above all (and this was something that may not have been fully understood at the Frankish court), it was intended to ensure that the Frankish king remained hostile to the *basileus* Nicephorus, with whom Harun was at war at that time. For his part, Charlemagne showed his gratitude by sending gifts to the caliph and to the Christians living in the Abbasid Empire.

Yet appearances were deceptive. As it turned out, Harun al-Rashid was embarking on his last campaign against Byzantium. At Hiraqla, ten kilometers west of Raqqa (in modern Syria), he erected a "victory monument" to celebrate his military triumphs. His attacks in this region were accompanied by a wave of unrest among Jews and Christians, which saw synagogues and churches in Jerusalem and elsewhere razed to the ground. The caliph, who may have feared further upheaval and was preparing to launch new campaigns in Iran, transferred his residence back to Baghdad but died there in 809. His death plunged his sons into infighting over the succession, which was to last for many years; this was followed by a new round of harassment against the *dhimmis*, the non-Muslim "Peoples of the Book" (i.e., Christians and Jews living in Muslim-controlled territory); the most trivial of these measures, which may not have been universally observed anyway, was the imposition of a discriminatory dress code requiring them to wear a yellow patch.[34] Once again, churches in Jerusalem were destroyed.[35]

News of these events almost certainly reached the Western emperor via Rome, along with complaints from the Latin monks in the monastery on the Mount of Olives about being accused of heresy by their Greek Orthodox counterparts for having recited the creed with the *filioque*.[36] Charlemagne, the defender of the Holy Sepulchre, saw himself forced to act; he duly did so, but in a surprising way that observed the customs of the Middle East but at the same time implemented measures hitherto unknown in the kingdom of the Franks. A military intervention was out of the question. The only route open to Charlemagne was to try to exert influence through donating arms and money. Indeed, Einhard makes repeated mention of Charlemagne sending funds to the Christians of the Near East, Syria, Egypt, Africa, and particularly the Holy Land and Jerusalem (*mittere solebat,* chap. 27). The emperor's biographer was clear on this point, stressing that it was "money" (*pecuniam*) as opposed to bars of silver or gold, say, that he dispatched; and in turn, in the Near East this money would have clearly drawn attention to the donor in the form of images, inscriptions, and symbols on the coins and made evident the purpose of his generosity.

Are any of the coins in question still to be found—in particular, pennies minted with the portrait of the great emperor? It is extremely rare for such coins to have survived; to date, only thirty examples in total have come to light. Yet they come from at least eleven or twelve different possible places of minting: Worms, Mainz, Cologne, Milan, and possibly Frankfurt have been suggested, along with names specifically mentioned on the reverse side: Dorestad, Quentovic, Rouen, Trier, Lyons, and Arles, along with Melle. This abundance of mints might possibly suggest that these coins were produced in large numbers, although this is not borne out by the very few that have actually been found.[37] But coinage that was intended to be sent to Muslim countries and was minted for only about three years had very limited circulation within the Frankish Empire; this, then, explains the surprising rarity of the "portrait denarii" that have survived.[38]

These coins were designed to spread an imperial agenda. To this end, they combined two different models. Their obverse consciously mimicked ancient coinage of the kind that was still familiar in the east of the former Roman imperium. A solidus of Constantine the Great, of which we still possess an example, may have served as the model for the obverse design. The new coinage issue shows a profile portrait, facing left, of the laurel-wreathed "sublime emperor"—KAROLUS IMP(ERATOR) AUG(USTUS). Various different motifs appear on the reverse. Sometimes this might be a church or mausoleum, stylized to resemble a temple (though without any indication of the place of minting), along with the legend, partially in Greek letters: XPICTIANA RELIGIO (the Christian faith); another, less common, variant had the name of the place of minting in lieu of this legend, plus a symbol like a ship or a city gate.[39] Under Louis the Pious, the *xpictiana religio* type—albeit in a slightly altered form—became a kind of imperial denarius and is well documented.

This kind of combination of images of a ruler and a temple was not unknown on ancient Greek and Roman coins, generally commemorating the consecration of a temple; there was therefore no question of it having been invented by Charlemagne and his master of coinage (Einhard, perhaps?). The coinage that we know about from pagan times depicted the cult figure of a deity in the temple's interior.[40] Charlemagne's *xpictiana religio* denarius, however, replaced this image with a cross, which was repeated on the gable end of the temple building. In this way, through his novel combination of emperor and church, the Frankish king transformed pagan imperial coinage into Christian money and at the same time proclaimed the orthodox Christian devotion of the restored Western Roman imperium. The legend on these coins may have been intended to associate the minting with the building of the Church of the Redeemer (the upper story of the cathedral) in Aix, for according to Einhard (chap. 26), it was there that Charlemagne used to observe the *religio christiana*, which "had been instilled into him from infancy with the greatest fervor and devotion."[41]

Admittedly, this by no means precludes another, more apt interpretation of the new coins. Since the coinage, especially of the *xpictiana religio* type, may not have been designed, at least not principally, for circulation within the Frankish Empire, it might instead have represented that "money" (*elemosina*) that was to be dispatched to Jerusalem and to other Muslim regions to fund the "restoration" of churches and to help support Christians living there. We know for certain that an assembly of the court at Aix in 810 expressly sanctioned this form of aid.[42]

FIGURE 52 The reverse of the coin shown in the frontispiece (Figure 1) includes a schematic image of the Holy Sepulchre in Jerusalem.

The image of the temple with the cross in its center was strongly reminiscent of contemporary Western and particularly also Byzantine portrayal of the Holy Sepulchre;[43] such depictions may well have served as a template for the coins. In the light of this, Charlemagne's coinage publicized the restored Western Christian empire's extensive protection of this most sacred sites. The propagandistic portrait of the emperor on the obverse was thus given an analogous propaganda image on the reverse—an image that would have been instantly recognizable to the intended recipients of the coins in the Near East, and that also had a clearly decipherable legend.[44] In this way, then, Charlemagne was presenting himself as the true protector of Christianity.

Only after Harun's death—in fact, only after 810, when the atrocities being inflicted on Christians in the Holy Land became known—was peace with Byzantium placed on the political agenda once more, and furthermore at the initiative of the *basileus*. He was facing a dire threat from the Bulgars at the time and sensed the enormous danger posed by any understanding between the Franks and the Arabs.[45] The caliph seemed to have used the Carolingian ruler as a pawn in a political power game, both against the Umayyads in Spain and against the Byzantines in the East. The accounts in the *Royal Frankish Annals* indicate that Charlemagne, meanwhile, seems first and foremost to have savored the elevated sense of honor that the gifts

FIGURE 53 Relief image from late antiquity of the Holy Sepulchre in Jerusalem. Dumbarton Oaks Collection.

and gestures of the "king of the Persians" apparently bestowed on him and his people, the "glory of his reign" (*gloria regni*), as Einhard expressed it. Diplomacy and politics versus archaic concepts of honor? In any case, this brief interlude of friendship came to an abrupt end. By 810, the *Annals* was already recalling Harun al-Rashid, the ruler who had once sent Charlemagne an elephant, as a "king of the Saracens," not as a Persian any longer. And thereafter no mention at all is made of the caliph.

What was life for Christians under Muslim rule like at this time? After all, there were still more of them at that stage than their Muslim overlords. Even so, like the Jews, they paid an increased poll tax (*jizya*) and in addition now had to wear a yellow patch marking them out as non-Muslim. Otherwise, in common with the Jews, they had come to terms with their new masters. How much had Charlemagne's envoys seen of the living conditions of Christians in the Holy Land? If we are to believe the scant reports of the legation that circulated in the West, they were escorted through the foreign cities in the Levant with blindfolds over their eyes and their ears blocked. Did they never hear the *muezzin,* then? And did they not see the crowds of Muslim pilgrims in Jerusalem, making their way to the Temple Mount, Islam's "first direction of prayer" with its two holy shrines? Hadn't their Christian hosts there told them anything about the Jews and Muslims and how they all lived cheek by jowl in the city and across the caliphate as a whole? Or about the Dome of the Rock and the al-Aqsa Mosque, which during the reign of Charlemagne, just a few years before his legates arrived in Jerusalem, had been destroyed by a powerful earthquake and then extensively restored by Harun's predecessor, al-Mahdi?[46]

Hadn't Charlemagne just undertaken similar reconstruction works on the cathedral in Aix? Yet the reports of the mission have nothing to say on the subject. The envoys evidently felt not the slightest curiosity to record the alien world they found themselves in, or any mission or urge to compare their world with it, or to delve into things more deeply; not even the sight of unfamiliar ceremonies could stir the Frankish envoys to sharpen their wits and look afresh at their surroundings. Charlemagne, it seems, had no interest in having such things noted and recorded for posterity. Other religions were regarded as delusions and the work of the Devil. They were to be shunned, not studied. This purblindness toward other cultures was counterpointed by an avid commitment to the Church and the Christian faith in a realm where there was still a need to combat pagan practices.

Only one thing in the Holy Land interested the emperor from the Frankish dynasty: the number of monasteries and other churches, how many people they were home to, and what funds they required. He ordered his envoys to ascertain this information and transmit it to him. The results of this survey have survived, albeit in very fragmentary fashion.[47] To give just one example, the Holy Sepulchre was served by 9 priests, 14 deacons, 6 subdeacons, 23 canons, 13 guards "whom they call whip wielders," 41 monks, 12 candle bearers, whose task it was to walk ahead of the patriarch, 17 servants of the patriarch; 2 "provosts," 2 pursers, 2 priests whose sole job it was to oversee the Holy Sepulchre, plus 1 more at Calvary, 2 more to administer the Lord's Chalice at the Eucharist, and 1 to look after the relics of the True Cross and the *sudarium* or "veil of Veronica," together with a further 15 servants; this amounted to a grand total of 160 [*sic*] people! The funds required annually by the patriarch of Jerusalem were correspondingly large, although the information on this score is only very patchy: 700 *solidi* to pay the staff, 500 *solidi* for the patriarch's salary, 30 solidi for needs unknown, 80 *solidi* "for the Saracens" (to pay the *jizya?*), and an unspecified sum for the servants of the Saracens. All in all, it is estimated that around 2,000 *solidi* was required every year, an enormous sum of money. Under these circumstances, Charlemagne's financial donations would have been very welcome.

In addition, a number of whimsical stories concerning the "Saracens" made the rounds in the West at this time. One or two of these were recounted by the chronicler Notker of St. Gall.[48] For instance, one story claimed that the envoys of Harun, the "king of the Persians," were so overwhelmed by the splendor of the court at Aix that they bemusedly announced that they had seen only people made of clay before they arrived there; now, though, the people they saw were of pure gold. The sheer expenditure on clothes and weapons there astonished them, while hunting European bison and aurochs put them in a panic. Their gifts—an elephant, apes, balsam, spikenard, various unguents, spices, and elixirs—were so plentiful that it seemed as though they had emptied the entire Orient and filled up the West. Charlemagne's gifts in return were said to have been bolts of cloth from Frisia and above all hunting dogs that could bring down lions and tigers. Such a disproportion in Westerners' perceptions (whereby their own world was deemed far more remarkable) clung on tenaciously; it seems that even pilgrims to Jerusalem in later centuries had eyes only for what they expected to see, not the unexpected.[49] This situation changed only in the age of the Crusades.

Harun's designation as a "Persian" served to legitimize but at the same time to disguise Charlemagne's friendly dealings with the otherwise demonized "Saracens." These negotiations were almost solely responsible for restoring the relations between Christian Roman emperors and the Persians, which had appeared moribund for over a century. This reception of Harun's legates a few years before the final break in relations thus happened at precisely the right moment and in the right place, namely, at the field encampment in Italy in the midst of the Frankish army just a few months after Charlemagne's coronation, and not, like the reception of the Christian envoys from Jerusalem, before the coronation and in Rome.

No record of the reaction of the "Persian" envoys to that initial meeting has survived; in fact, to date no historical archives in the Arab world have been found that contain any mention whatsoever of the diplomatic exchanges between Charlemagne and Harun al-Rashid.[50] Clearly, it was the new Frankish emperor who was most concerned to underline the "Persian" confirmation of his status—evident not least in the gift of the mighty elephant Abul Abaz[51]—by drawing attention to the links between the two empires. In an addendum to its summary of the year 801, the *Royal Frankish Annals* announced that the cities of Barcelona in al-Andalus and Teate (modern

Chieti) in Italy had fallen, and that their prefects had been brought before the emperor on one and the same day and sent into exile. The exchange of diplomatic missions with the caliph thus climaxed in a signal success against the Saracens in the West. This news would not have been unwelcome in Raqqa.

Internal Order within the Empire

The emperor now set about organizing his empire and the Church. He had restored peace and unity in Rome and had imposed order and calm in Ravenna. Charlemagne emerged from the narrow confines of the earlier kingdom of the Franks as an emperor dedicated to framing legislation and bringing peace. The final decade of Charlemagne's reign was dominated by this urge for peace, justice, and unity. Curiously, the *Royal Frankish Annals* had very little to say on this subject, generally sticking to recording major affairs of state, wars and peace treaties with foreign powers, and diplomatic exchanges with, say, the Anglo-Saxons, Rome, Constantinople, and Jerusalem and describing expensive gifts, hunting parties, or the celebration of the main Church festivals. The only exception to this general pattern is the entry for the year 806, insofar as the succession arrangement concluded in that year and cited by the annalist was at the same time regarded as a division of the empire, Charlemagne's "last will and testament," and a peace constitution.[52] But the capitularies, synod proceedings, letters, and treatises that have survived, along with the fragmentary *Lorsch Annals,* speak a different language.

Charlemagne sensed the lack of consolidation and integration within his enormous empire, as well as the weaknesses of his Church and the increasing hardship being suffered by the free citizens of his realm. Legislation to a degree hitherto unknown was intended to remedy this situation. Supplements to civil-law codes, capitularies, and synodal resolutions all announced Charlemagne's intention. No fewer than fifty-five capitularies were issued in the thirteen years of his reign as emperor, as against just fourteen over his thirty-one years as king.[53] His coronation in Rome resulted in a great impetus to innovation, which affected the ecclesiastical and secular bureaucracies in equal measure. Henceforth the emperor presented himself first and foremost as a lawgiver. The first measure—soon after his coronation, "in the first year of his consulate"—was an amendment to Lombard law, for Charlemagne, as the person "who rules the Roman Empire" (*Romanum regens imperium*), had supposedly spotted some loopholes, which were now closed.

For instance, he decreed that all donations should now be irrevocable; that anyone who was not exempt from army service but refused to perform it should be liable to pay the full military levy of sixty solidi; and that anyone who deserted should be condemned to death for committing a "crime against the Crown"; plus various other measures.[54] Once again, the effect of the coronation as emperor could be seen in the newly formulated offense of a "crime against the Crown," which up to that point had been unheard of in both Lombard and Frankish law.

The traditional civil-law code of the Franks, the *Lex Salica,* was similarly amended at this time. In his *Life of Charlemagne* (chap. 29), Einhard praised the fact that Charlemagne was "determined to add what was wanting, to reconcile the discrepancies, and to correct what was vicious and wrongly cited." The biographer went on to claim that the emperor "caused the unwritten laws of all the tribes that came under his rule to be compiled and reduced to writing"—an exaggeration and distortion attributable to the circumstances prevailing when Einhard wrote his work. In actual fact, only the oral traditions of Frankish, Bavarian, and Alemannic law show any clear and enduring signs of influence by Charlemagne's measures, whereas no such effect is discernible in the case of the Saxons, the Thuringians, and the Frisians.[55] Anyhow, other conditions pertained in those regions where Roman vulgar law held sway, such as in southern Gallia and in the Italian Romagna, as well as among the Lombards.

Certainly, apart from various individual amendments—also to Bavarian law[56]—nothing can be adduced to corroborate Einhard's claim; this means that it is more accurate to regard the imperial court as providing an impulse to the spread of already existing civil-law codes rather than as the source of completely new codes. At most, Thuringian civil law may have been fixed and codified in 802 by the aristocratic assembly in Erfurt, a body that was headed by two emissaries sent by the emperor to the region, Archbishop Riculf of Mainz and Count Werner, the latter of whom was a member of the Guideschi (Widonid) family, whose power base was along the Middle Rhine.[57] A memo relating to Francia that has survived by chance makes clear how new legislation was announced in that region. The new legal provisions were communicated to a local count, who was then expected to promulgate them in the public court sessions of his town; the lay judges appointed by the bishops, the abbot, and the count would then agree to these new measures and countersign them.[58]

Undoubtedly not for the first time, the liberty of many of Charlemagne's free citizens was potentially jeopardized; but the emperor moved swiftly to impose new norms that were designed to nip any feuding or vendettas in the bud: "Should a person consider that his freedom has been compromised and out of fear of falling into servitude murder a relative on whose account he fears becoming enslaved, be it his father, mother, or the brother of either of his parents, then the person who commits that act shall himself be killed, and his children and blood relations shall be taken into servitude. Should he deny the murder, then he must submit to the ordeal of the nine red-hot plowshares."[59] This involved the accused having to walk barefoot over nine red-hot plowshares without the burns he sustained subsequently growing septic. Poverty forced many parents to hand their children over to a life in servitude.

The need to impose order could sometimes even postpone preparations for war. As the author of the *Lorsch Annals* expressly notes, no military campaigns at all were conducted in 802: "The emperor Charlemagne remained quietly in the palace at Aix with his fellow Franks and did not go on campaign."[60] Instead, the business of the law and welfare measures for the poor took precedence. No doubt in the course of a court assembly with an accompanying church synod, the emperor called to mind (as the Lorsch annalist noted) "his sorrow over the misery of the poorer citizens [*pauperiores*] who lived in his realm but were deprived of their full rights." These "paupers" were all free men, not bondsmen. Those in the latter group were subject to the court tribunal of their master, not that of the king or emperor. Charlemagne now took new steps to monitor fair implementation of the law. He opted for a radical reform, or consolidation, of the institution of the royal envoys, the *missi dominici;* this measure, though initially highly effective, was not without dangers for the emperor's authority in the long term. The first bailiwicks were established as areas of jurisdiction for these envoys—an embryonic though not enduring attempt to institutionalize the body politic.[61]

> The Lord Emperor chose from among his most outstanding,
> prudent, and wise men various archbishops and bishops,
> venerable abbots, and devout laymen and sent them
> throughout his kingdom. Through them, the emperor exhorted
> all his subjects to live according to just law by virtue of the
> regulations the envoys were conveying to them. Yet where the
> law acted in a manner that was neither just nor fair, then it
> would be thoroughly scrutinized and reported to him. For he
> wanted to improve the law with God's help. . . . Moreover,
> these *missi* were empowered to diligently investigate any

person's claim that another had done him an injustice and to expedite justice by submitting forthwith a written report on the case in question to the [imperial] court.

Thus ran the Lorsch annalist's summary of the remit of these envoys.

To be sure, *missi* had existed before this, deployed on a case-by-case basis; there was also, within the Carolingian manorial system, a class of "extraordinary commissioners" (*missi discurrentes*) who were employed by every lord of a manor as part of the bureaucratic apparatus of managing his estate. The Carolingians appointed them from the ranks of the court staff and other low-ranking persons, the "poorer vassals of the court." Evidently Charlemagne had also entrusted such people with the kinds of tasks that brought them into contact with the large landowners of any region. Now, however, the institution of royal envoys, which had been in formation since around 780, was ordered not to employ any more poor vassals of the king to monitor implementation of royal decrees for fear that they might be bribable, dispensing justice in return for gifts (*propter munera*). Instead, the envoys should now be elected exclusively from the uppermost echelons of the ecclesiastical and secular hierarchy, and furthermore for a long term. They were to come from the ranks of archbishops, bishops, dukes, and counts, the powerful magnates, the *potentes,* who would not (or at least so it was hopefully assumed) would not accept "gifts" from the poor. And so "Charlemagne sent them throughout his kingdom, so that they might administer justice to the churches, to widows, orphans, and the poor, and to all the people."[62]

As has been said, well-defined bailiwicks were assigned to these envoys, who were expected to perform their duties in teams of two, consisting of a churchman and a secular magnate. One stipulation was that they should be actual or potential property owners within their allotted domain; the laymen among the envoys belonged to the local aristocracy. To cite just one example, in the Middle Rhine region, in 802 the joint *missi dominici* were Riculf of Mainz and Count Werner, followed in the early reign of Louis the Pious by Heistulf, archbishop of Mainz, and Count Ruotprecht (the eponymous ancestor of the powerful Robertian family), who acted in this capacity for many years.[63] The assignment of official positions and land to aristocratic families guaranteed their loyalty to the king or emperor. Endowing a person with the power of a *missus* could—at least in Charlemagne's reign—have a decisive influence on the outcome of clashes between rival local families of noblemen.[64] This system clearly brought considerable benefits for the authority of the king but also harbored future dangers.

Admittedly, to begin with, there was a fair degree of uncertainty about this policy, even (and particularly) among those who were chosen to carry out these kinds of tasks. In 802, for example, Wulfar, the future archbishop of Reims, who had been assigned to conduct a "legation," asked the experienced Abbot Fardulf of St-Denis, who was also charged with similar duties at that time, what he was supposed to do. After all, Wulfar wrote, Fardulf had been instructed in writing how bishops, canons, and monks should be questioned and according to which chapters of the law. Wulfar therefore requested that he, Fardulf, write him as soon as possible with this information and include a copy of the text (*pagina*) that was read out to all *missi* before they were dispatched from the court. These instructions may well have more or less corresponded to the information circulated by the Lorsch annalist. Generally, Wulfar implored Fadulf to let him know anything that might possibly be of use to the legation he was about to lead.[65]

The emperor's urge to impose order soon ran into serious difficulties. Plainly there was a comprehensive program of reform, but there was also a distinct lack of information about its content or execution. This first had to be laboriously extracted, or its details obtained, through internal communication among the magnates; moreover, the amount of information divulged was subject to the wealth of experience of the envoys and the level of information they were allowed to have access to. This was fated not to achieve the central authorities' aim of establishing order throughout the empire in a uniform and evenhanded way. Accordingly, the implementation of norms encountered numerous problems. Too much depended on chance and local conditions, despite many written instructions to the contrary. Even so, the whole enterprise was clearly driven by a desire to establish a better system of control and organization. For that reason alone, Charlemagne would be hailed in the later traditions of the Middle Ages as a great lawgiver.

It was the task of the *missi* to convene and preside over regional assemblies, to monitor how various officeholders discharged their duties, to take steps to promote peace, and above all to inform the emperor of any instances of maladministration, abuse of a person's position, or acts of violence against the poor. Charlemagne had them report back to him on a regular basis. It was through his envoys that the emperor was made aware (or demanded that he be kept informed) of critical situations, a belligerent mood among the populace, or dangerous developments on the ground even in the most remote parts of the empire, even when he was staying in far-off Aix or another of his palaces in central Francia—an invaluable instrument of power. Its deployment soon became apparent and was reflected in the numerous capitularies that were issued in response to the reports submitted to the emperor from 802 onward. It was precisely the *missi* who were required to publish the administrative orders, make them known within their baili-wicks, monitor their implementation, and report back to the court on their impact. This would over time give rise to a tripartite system of monitoring, standardization, and punishment.

Certainly, in the long run the institution of envoys meant a strengthening of the regional authorities at the expense of the central monarchy. But this was not yet the case; at this early stage, it still allowed Charlemagne to ex-ercise greater control over the nobility. Likewise, in these early days—as was evident from the reforming capitularies of 802, which were promulgated in the context of a synod and proclaimed throughout the realm by the en-voys[66]—no flattery or bribery on the part of an individual, no immunity (*defensione*) by virtue of family relationships, and no fear of those in power was to be allowed to block the "right path" of justice. The effect of these capitularies was felt as far afield as Italy.[67] What may have been Charle-magne's final capitulary decreed, "We require that each and every people of our realm should obey our *missi*, counts, and judges and support them in their task of upholding the law [*consentientes ad iusticiam faciendam*]."[68]

The very first task that these *missi* were required to fulfill, in 802, was to get the populace to swear fealty to the emperor. Everyone who had reached the age of twelve, irrespective of whether he was a cleric or a layperson, was expected to swear an oath of allegiance to Charlemagne : "I swear," runs one of the formulas that have come down to us, "that from this day forth I will remain loyal to Charles, the most devout emperor and the son of King Pepin and Queen Bertrada, with a pure mind and without deceit or ill intent, for the honor of his realm [*regnum*], and as it is only right and proper that a man should swear fealty to his lord and master. So help me God and by these saints' relics before me, I do solemnly swear that I will hold to this pledge for all the days of my life so long as God grants me the gift of reason."[69]

The emperor was the master of each and every free man within his realm. The emperorship served—or at least was intended to serve—as a new force under which all the diverse peoples and churches of the Carolingian Em-pire could coalesce. The oath was not merely meant—as expressly stated in one capitulary, and as we might perhaps be tempted to regard it if we see it as just a corollary to the coronation and the ensuing trial for crimes against the Crown[70]—to safeguard the life of the emperor, or to stop any enemy from fomenting hostility against the empire, or to prevent anyone from es-pousing or concealing a disloyal attitude; rather, it was intended to make everyone realize that certain key responsibilities transcended personal concerns [*in se rationem*]. Seven chapters (chaps. 3–9) were specially given over to enumerating these obligations ("These things here mentioned should be observed as being comprised in the oath to the emperor"): No one should abstract the property of another, harbor fugitive fiscaline slaves (i.e., servants from royal estates), or neglect a fief of the emperor. Anyone who was liable for military service might not be released from his obligation by bribing an official. Furthermore, no one should presume to disregard any precept or order issued by the emperor or intervene in the court case of another with an eye to manipulating the outcome; rather, it was incumbent on "each man, with regard to his own case, or tax, or debt, to conduct his own defense." Charlemagne's capitulary of 802 thus outlined key tenets of royal and imperial authority and enjoined the entire populace to abide by them in a way that had never been seen before. These tenets could be gathered together under the umbrella term of "the honor of the royal office" (*honor regni*).

Instructions such as this continued to be of the utmost urgency. It was not just the lay magnates who were spoiling for a fight. The upper echelons of the clergy required no less admonition; indeed, it was they who were primarily instrumental in stirring up unrest. When Leidrad, the archbishop of Lyons, was called on to pronounce on the subject of "renouncing the Devil," he cited greed (*cupiditas*) as one of Satan's works and pointed to the many conflicts between high Church officials and secular bureaucrats that had been caused by this sin; however, he claimed that its worst effect was that it "generates hatred between teachers [*doctores*, i.e., bishops] and those being taught [*auditores*], stirs up enmities, and breeds contempt."[71]

The synod held in the spring of 802 therefore also urged bishops and priests to live their lives according to the precepts of canon law and to teach others to do likewise. Bishops, abbots, abbesses, and other prelates should treat their subordinates with respect and solicitude (*cum veneratione hac diligentia*) and refrain from oppressing them with severe and tyrannical rule (*potentiva dominatione vel tyrannide*) (chap. 11); their bailiffs and sheriffs and judges should be skilled in the law, lovers of justice, and peaceful and merciful, so that, through them, more profit and gain might accrue to the holy Church of God (chap. 13). These edicts echoed the grievances of the provinces. Peace was the guarantor of prosperity.

The high priests should be in accord, exercising the law with charity and unity of purpose in peace, and live according to God's will; they should give the unfortunate and pilgrims consolation and protection. Conflict was also, it seems, resurfacing among the daughters of the nobility in their convents.

Chapter 18 of the 802 capitulary ordained that they should "be firmly ruled, and the nuns shall by no means be permitted to wander about . . . nor should they be permitted to quarrel or contend among themselves." Abbots should show obedience to their bishops in all humility, as required by canon law (chap. 15). In monasteries, bishops or abbots "should not prefer the more worthless men in a monastery to the better ones, nor endeavor, on account of relationship, or through any flattery, to advance them over the better ones"; rather, those who ought to be put forward for ordination should be "men of such kind that, through them, gain and profit [*merces et profectus*] will accrue to us [i.e., the emperor] and to those who recommend them" (chap. 16). In other words, a person's achievement rather than his social rank should be the deciding factor. Furthermore, no bishops, abbots, priests, or deacons—exclusively noblemen, like their worldly relatives—were to be permitted to keep hunting dogs, falcons, or sparrow hawks (chap. 19). The clergy of this period were very fond of falconry and hunting with hounds, but this ran counter to the precepts of a life of piety. The capitulary then went on to proscribe another worldly pleasure, namely, that of the flesh: "Any priest or deacon who . . . shall presume to have women in his house without permission of the canons shall be deprived at once of his position and of his inheritance until he shall be brought into our [i.e., the emperor's] presence" (chap. 24), Even at this early stage, the rule of celibacy claimed several victims.

Judges and their assistants were to act justly and fairly, appoint trustworthy people, and not oppress the poor and were required to provide envoys sent by the emperor with all the care and assistance they needed, "so that they may pass through their districts with all due dispatch" (chap. 28). And the destitute, whom the king in his mercy (*in sua elemosyna*) had absolved of all their outstanding debts, should not be deprived of this relief again by judges, counts, or king's envoys (chap. 29). Perjurers should lose their right hand, the hand by which they swore their false oath (chap. 36). And so it went on. General legal provisions and trusted standards were invoked as yardsticks by which to measure the present. At the same time, these could sometimes thereby reveal their shortcomings.

Charlemagne had called the next court assembly and the next synod for the fall of that same year. Both duly convened at Aix in October 802.[72] The assembled bishops and other clerics were reminded of canon law, and the abbots and monks of the *Rule of St. Benedict,* by recitation of them before the meeting began. They were then called on to make a public commitment to live according to the constitutions of the Church Fathers and the *Benedictine Rule*. What had been lacking among the clergy, the monks, and the general populace was to be made good according to the dictates of canon law. In all churches, whether within the precincts of monasteries or outside in the wider world, Mass was to be sung in accordance with the Roman liturgy. The counts, dukes, and other secular judges (*judices*) were to ensure that ordinary people throughout the empire, and especially the poor, "received justice."[73]

As the reports of the king's envoys came back to the court over time, it became apparent that poverty was on the rise, and that people's suffering was increasing. This was the visible cost of some of the ostensibly successful measures that Charlemagne and the Franks had implemented. Did the emperor make this connection? The next admonitory edict was issued in the following year, 803. Once again, as the Lorsch annalist recorded, Charlemagne "spent the year without campaigning,"[74] while the *Royal Frankish Annals* was silent on the subject, as before. But the capitulary in question has survived.[75] As had been the practice for decades, it persevered in instituting individual measures. Yet these give us some idea of the kind of pressure that secular and ecclesiastical magnates alike exerted on the unprivileged members of Frankish society at this time. The most diverse grounds for conflict emerged, whose victims were precisely poor free men. It is not out of the question that some magnates were simply guilty of conscious and deliberate disregard of imperial decrees;[76] mutual envy between noblemen, snobbery, corruption, and aristocratic rivalry in general and other factors did the rest. Members of the Frankish aristocracy too were under enormous pressure, both from the king and emperor and from within their own class, to prove themselves and to succeed.

Yet Charlemagne was adamant that charity should prevail and was eager that this principle should be observed. But with the best will in the world, this initiative foundered on the lack of a reliable system of transmitting commands across the enormous Frankish Empire, which stretched from the North Sea to Benevento in southern Italy and from the river Elbe in northern Germany to the Bay of Biscay, and in particular on the absence of efficient ways of monitoring implementation of edicts and effective supervision of compliance with imperial orders. Charlemagne was only too well aware of this shortcoming. Some of his last surviving statements reveal his concern on this score: in one, he asked what measures from all the capitularies that he had been sending around the empire for decades had actually been realized and wondered how best to deal with those who had not followed his orders and who had so willfully "ignored God's commandments and our decrees."[77]

As had always been the case, much was left to improvisation. The capitularies show only too clearly how dependent their realization still was on the loyalty of self-regulating bishops or counts, and how limited central control of their activities was. Little by little, virtually unnoticed by the central authorities, powerful magnates were extending their power through the process of making formerly free men dependent on them (mediatization) and thereby forming their own retinues. They exploited to their own advantage poor free men's liability to perform military service by sometimes disregarding it entirely and then suddenly forcing compliance, thus making those affected dependent on their whims. The *missi* were also meant to prosecute such abuses of power, but in practice this rarely, if ever, happened.

A Final Meeting with Pope Leo III

Exceptional occurrences may also have been reported to the emperor. In the summer of 804, rumors reached Charlemagne that the blood of Christ—a relic containing the blood of the Savior—had supposedly been found in Mantua. He asked the pope to investigate the matter for him.

It was the first time since 801 that the emperor had turned to the Apostolic See for help. But quite unexpectedly and without being invited, Leo expressed a wish to have a face-to-face meeting with Charlemagne; he was just on the point of leaving for Aix, he informed the emperor. Charlemagne was surprised and irritated. What did the holy father want with him? The emperor had not planned on any meeting but now found himself unable to avoid one. His reluctance is clearly apparent even in the later report of the events in the *Royal Frankish Annals*.

In keeping with tradition, he sent his son Charles on ahead to St-Maurice to receive the pope; he himself then met the pope in Reims and escorted him to Soissons, where he asked the pontiff to wait while he, Charlemagne, visited his gravely ill sister Gisela at Chelles Abbey. He then invited the pope to come to his memorably lavish palace at Quierzy, where they celebrated Christmas together; from there, they finally departed for Aix. This was to be the first and only time that a pope would be Charlemagne's guest at his palace there. He was permitted to stay for eight days, but no longer (*Royal Frankish Annals*). Leo could now see firsthand the emperor's palace, with its allusions to Rome, such as the bronze equestrian statue, and the magnificent construction of the upper story of Aix Cathedral (the Church of the Redeemer), which he would not have been able to see five years earlier. The buildings of the palace complex in Aix may have surprised him but—since he was accustomed to the imposing surroundings of Rome—would scarcely have enraptured him. It is interesting to speculate whether he recognized the layout in Aix as an imitation of the Lateran palace complex. Admittedly, no sooner had Charlemagne departed from Rome than Leo set about altering the appearance of his episcopal residence anyway, by building, next to the aforementioned triclinium, an even more magnificent hall, which he had decorated with expensive mosaics. At their Aix meeting, Charlemagne was very reserved; after all, there was little to discuss. Even so, the emperor lavished gifts on his guest and had him escorted back to Ravenna via Bavaria.

Although it was obvious what triggered the meeting, the pope's motives in seeking it were anything but clear. Was he attempting to get the Carolingian monarch to march on Rome again? Did the apostolic father see himself as being threatened by his opponents in Rome and by the aristocratic forces in central Italy? Or was he seeking help against the bishops, who were refusing to submit to Charlemagne's and Pepin's "donation"? The pope's face-saving "withdrawal" to Ravenna (which Charlemagne clearly ordered) might suggest that the pontiff had indeed been importuning the emperor. Also, thereafter Leo was constantly making complaints about the insubordination and reluctance to pay tributes of regions that Charlemagne had transferred to the Holy See, as well as about encroachments by imperial *missi,* even to the gates of Rome.

The surviving letters that the pope repeatedly sent north from 808 onward bear witness to this tension.[78] Was he perhaps trying to get the emperor to grant new concessions in favor of papal control over Rome and the Papal States? Charlemagne's responses have been lost; we know, though, that some capitularies were among them. Unlike under Hadrian I, the emperor made no attempt to deepen contacts with Rome. On one occasion, he excused himself from forging closer ties on the grounds that he did not have enough envoys who would be acceptable to the pope—the flimsiest of reasons.

Leo justified his approach by maintaining that those around the emperor had poisoned his mind with "lies and evil machinations." For his part, Leo announced that he would not desist from instructing Charlemagne about good and evil; all he was doing was warning the emperor in a spirit of love and loyalty to consider his soul's salvation and to fear the impending judgment of the Lord. He would, he claimed, call on the Lord's mercy, on the

Mother of God the Virgin Mary, and on the apostolic princes St. Peter and St. Paul to imbue the emperor's heart with "such beneficial advice . . . that the gatekeeper of the Heavenly Kingdom would be able before God's countenance to put him forward for entry into heaven with the offering given by his father King Pepin, which he himself had confirmed (the so-called Donation of Pepin) and in this way Charlemagne would deserve to be granted eternal salvation."[79] This kind of correspondence hints at a cool relationship between this successor to the apostolic prince and his most powerful worshipper; relations would no doubt have grown even frostier after 809, when Leo refused Charlemagne's wish to revise the wording of the Nicene Creed.[80] Nevertheless, the pope knew perfectly well what terminology to use to try to sway the emperor. His invocation of God and the saints reads almost like a listing of the patron saints of the palace church at Aix.

At least tensions between Pepin, king of Italy, and the pope, which may well have had their origin in divergent views over the role of the Papal States and of which Charlemagne must have been fully aware, came to the fore only somewhat later.[81] Time and again, Leo tried to assert full authority over Rome, for instance, by appointing "dukes" (duces) without prior consultation with the emperor.[82] Corsica was another bone of contention between them.[83] In a pointed challenge to Charlemagne, Leo chose to live—the first pope to do so—not as pontiffs had done before him in the patriarchium, the "patriarch's residence," but after 813, and in clear imitation of the imperial court, in a palatium, a "palace," which he proceeded to extend with the addition of two positively imperial prestige buildings. Charlemagne almost certainly did not live to see their completion.

The imposing triclinium with the image of Charlemagne, which dates from before 800, portrayed—as I have already noted—the pope and the emperor at the same height on its facing wall. But the image and the inscription were never updated; therefore, in papal Rome, Charlemagne remained in view only as a king, not as an emperor. The polyconchos, which was begun only in 801/802, in other words, after the imperial coronation and Charlemagne's departure from Rome, was built with the hosting of official papal banquets in mind and had at its center a large dish of red porphyry, from which water flowed.[84] Porphyry was considered an exclusively imperial stone; many archetypes could be seen in Constantinople.

The mosaic in the main apse of the polyconchos depicted the traditio legis (transmission of the law, i.e., Christ as lawgiver). The image on the facing wall of the apse showed the symbols of the four evangelists next to a Christ figure, as well as what were presumably Christian martyrs and on the lowest register the twenty-four elders of the Apocalypse (Revelation 5:8–10), while beneath them were pictured representatives of the 144,000 saved. In other words, the beginnings and end of the Christian Church were shown, and the centerpiece of this tableau was formed by the pontiff who resided in this hall. The side apses portrayed the apostles preaching to the peoples of the earth.[85] We can no longer tell how much Charlemagne knew about this sophisticated building and its decoration. Anyhow, an image of a secular ruler would have been totally out of place here.

After Charlemagne's death, Leo—now freed from any imperial control and in his capacity as secular head of the Papal States—set about prosecuting a capital offense in his court, an action against which Louis the Pious raised only a very ineffectual protest.[86] Charlemagne would have regarded such developments with astonishment, perhaps even concern, and would certainly have taken steps to counter them. He would certainly not have consented to them, in any event. For his part, Leo would presumably never have dared provoke his savior Charlemagne, even though the Frankish ruler had pointedly excluded the pope from all involvement in the coronation of his successor Louis as co-emperor in 813.

A New Enemy Appears: The "Northmen"

Defending the realm was now the chief priority. Dangers were looming on the horizon both externally and internally. Especially in the north, unfamiliar enemies were spreading terror; they were tenacious foes who were difficult to beat off, and Charlemagne attempted to keep them away from the empires' frontiers by signing treaties with them. An uncertain situation also prevailed in the south. Although the city of Barcelona had recently, in 803, been seized from the enemies of Christendom, this had not averted the danger that threatened from Spain and North Africa; intent on revenge, the defeated Moorish forces used their fleets to attack islands in the Mediterranean and the coasts of Gallia. Meanwhile, in Italy, resistance began to grow in the Duchy of Benevento to Charlemagne's rule. And in the southeast of the realm, in Venice and Dalmatia, Byzantine Greeks, who were suspected of heresy, were fighting the Frankish authorities. The question of the dual emperorship in the East and the West, which still awaited resolution, had made for repeated tensions between Charlemagne and the *basileus* ever since Nicephorus had replaced Empress Irene on the throne in Constantinople. The defense of the borders demanded an unremitting readiness for combat, ruinously costly watch duties around the clock, and a constant military frontier presence. All the emperor's vassals, but especially the great churches and monasteries of the empire, felt the strain of this burden.

Unknown "Northmen" now threatened the borders of Saxony and the Frankish Empire: Normans; Danes; pirates known as *vikingr,* hence the term "Vikings"; barbarians; and heathens—and by a variety of other names— plundered the coasts and the monasteries close to the sea. Using their fast longships, which from the eighth century onward were equipped with sails, they would suddenly appear on the horizon, pillage a town or church, and then disappear before local defenses could assemble. The Irish and the Anglo-Saxons were the first to be on the receiving end of their mysterious aggressiveness. In 793, a Viking force attacked the monastery at Lindisfarne (Holy Island) on the coast of Northumberland (northeast England) and returned to their homelands laden with valuable treasures. Their success only spurred them on to plunder more booty. As merchants and marauders rolled into one, they organized themselves into shifting bands. Their unbridled aggression and almost unbelievable daring impelled them to venture forth in ever-larger hordes on ever more audacious voyages across the seas and up the great rivers deep into the European interior. Soon they occupied large tracts of land and began to establish permanent settlements there. Over the following decades, they would circumnavigate the continent and venture as far as Paris, Italy, Constantinople, Aix, Cologne, and Mainz.

For a long while, the Franks did not have any contacts whatsoever with Scandinavia. It was only Charlemagne's campaigns against the Saxons and the ongoing conquest of Saxony that brought them into proximity with the "Danes." They, in turn, were not a written culture, and so their oral poetry, however formally superior it may have been, has scarcely been preserved for posterity. Only very occasional pieces of news from around the Frankish Empire break the otherwise overwhelming silence concerning these strangers and their culture. Little information is therefore to be had about the early history of the "Normans" during Charlemagne's reign. Their ways of life are only hinted at, and in extremely sketchy terms.[87] This much is certain, however: the coastal navigation these peoples had been practicing hitherto did not pose any real threat to the Franks. Yet this situation changed radically hereafter.

The *Royal Frankish Annals* for 777 contains the first brief mention of the "*Nordmannia* region" as a place of refuge for Duke Widukind; only in the revised version of the annals do we read in more detail that the Saxon duke fled and sought shelter with the Danish king Sigfrid. Charlemagne personally evidently felt no need to have the incident recorded any more precisely. Five years later, at the court assembly held in Lippspringe in Saxony, at the height of the Widukind crisis, a person by the name of Halftan appeared as the envoy of the "Norman" king Sigfrid. His presence there is mentioned only as an aside, and any more detailed information is passed over. He apparently arrived in the company of "all" the Saxons except Widukind; envoys of the khan of the Avars also came to the meeting. It would appear that the presence of these legations further enhanced the triumph over the Saxons that the king hoped to be able to score at that time. Only several years later, at Easter 798, do we encounter the next reference to Northmen; on that occasion, "Northern people" (*Nordliuti*) on the far side of the river Elbe, in other words, North Albingian Saxons, were reported to have attacked Frankish envoys who had been sent there to dispense justice. As the later version of the *Annals* noted, a legate of King Gottschalk, who was on his way back from an audience with King Sigfrid of the Danes, was also murdered by the insurrectionists—an obscure, barely decipherable piece of information that serves only to reveal that the Carolingian court had no clear knowledge, nor perhaps even any wish to know, about the Danes, their social order, their authority structures, and their internal power struggles, let alone their religious cults and their centers of worship. Likewise, the *Annals* makes no attempt to distinguish among the various different peoples of Scandinavia.

Indeed, no one in the Frankish Empire seems to have noticed the storm clouds that were gathering in the north. The breakthrough was achieved by the adoption of the sail.[88] The Franks were in no way prepared for the Norman incursions, which began on a large scale shortly after the turn of the eighth century and would endure for over a century thereafter, with devastating consequences. This foreign people remained alien to them. Attempts to send Christian missions among them began only with Louis the Pious, and even these did not meet with any swift or lasting success. In 804, the "Danish" king Gottfrid appeared with his fleet and cavalrymen at Schleswig, where his kingdom bordered on the Saxon lands. He promised to hold a meeting (*colloquium*) with Charlemagne, who was then encamped with his army at Hollenstedt, north of the Elbe; ultimately, though, after being warned off by his own people, he failed to appear and simply instructed an envoy to convey his demands. Charlemagne in turn called for Frankish fugitives to be returned. But what really happened here is unknown. The *Royal Frankish Annals* was eager to cover up failures.

When Gottfrid attacked the Obotrites in 808, Charlemagne's eldest son, Charles, hurried across the Elbe at the head of an army but left nothing except a few ransacked Slavic villages behind him before recrossing the river, while the Danish king went on to destroy the trading center of Reric and forcibly relocated the merchants who had lived there to Schleswig and Haithabu. Gottfrid then ordered a defensive earthwork to be constructed there, on the border with the Saxons, running from an inlet of the Baltic Sea to the river Eider; parts of this famous fortification, the *Danevirke,* can still be seen today.

The year 810 marked a high point of confusion among the Franks. Frisia had been attacked by two hundred longships from "*Normannia,*" and all the offshore islands had been ransacked; chapter 17 of Einhard's biography of Charlemagne also recalls this period. The Danes defeated the Frisians and extorted from them a tribute of one hundred silver marks before withdrawing—a total weight of over fifty kilograms of pure silver. During this attack, however, King Gottfrid had remained at home; it seems questionable whether he was even responsible for this longship assault. Charlemagne duly dispatched an army against the "pirates" and himself led a second army to the Lippe estuary and then on to the river Aller in expectation of engaging King Gottfrid, who had boasted that he would happily engage in a trial of strength with the emperor on the field of combat.

No sooner had Charlemagne reached the Aller than news began to come thick and fast, informing him that Harun al-Rashid's elephant had arrived in Aix-la-Chapelle, that the Danish fleet responsible for the attacks had sailed home, that King Gottfrid had been murdered by one of his own men, that Hohbuoki Castle on the river Elbe (the site of which is unknown to this day) had been destroyed by the Veleti tribe, that the emperor's son Pepin had died in Italy, and that two delegations from Constantinople and Córdoba, respectively, had come to Aix to discuss peace terms. Charlemagne found himself with no choice except to abandon his disastrous campaign against the Danes and hurry back to Aix. Furthermore, during the course of this campaign the countryside had also been ravaged by a terrible disease affecting cattle, which killed the army's entire complement of draft oxen, as well as all the cattle throughout the realm. This was a catastrophe for the poor and formed the prelude to even more serious setbacks to come, notwithstanding the fact that in the following year the Franks were able to conclude a peace settlement with Gottfrid's nephew and successor, King Hemming (*Royal Frankish Annals* for 811).

The fast dragon boats of the Vikings, powered by both sails and oars, versus the sluggish draft oxen of the Frankish army—this was a contest that the Franks could not possibly win. Charlemagne had ordered the construction of a fleet as early as 808,[89] followed by renovation of the lighthouse at Boulogne in 810 (he went there in October 811 to inspect the works in person). At the same time, a capitulary updated the requirements of military service, including watch duties on the empire's borders; this stipulated that no one was to report drunk for duty or incite his comrades to drink; moreover, everyone liable to military service was required to bring provisions for three months with him, along with sufficient clothes and other equipment for a six-month campaign.[90]

These orders were not specifically geared toward fighting off Norman incursions but rather were applied across the length and breadth of the empire, from the Pyrenees to the Elbe and beyond. A Frankish fleet was also stationed at Ghent. The records do not tell us how many ships were involved in this undertaking, how they were equipped, or who financed their construction. There are also no details available concerning the crewing of the ships of the fleet or its deployment. Only one brief provision of the capitulary of Boulogne survives, stipulating that whenever the emperor wanted to dispatch a warship, all other ships' masters (*ipsi seniores*) should put to sea with their vessels and hold themselves in readiness.[91] Evidently, the tasks of construction, fitting out, crewing, and providing for the ships' complements all devolved on noblemen living in the vicinity of the coast and the churches of the region. Einhard (chap. 17) supplied further information on this score, reporting that the emperor "fitted out a fleet for the war with the Northmen; the vessels required for this purpose were built on the rivers that flow from Gaul and Germany into the Northern Ocean. Moreover, since the Northmen continually overran and laid waste the Gallic and German coasts, he caused watch and ward to be kept in all the harbors, and at the mouths of rivers large enough to admit the entrance of vessels, to prevent the enemy from disembarking." This all sounds more like planning than actual execution. The Frankish fleet in the North Sea would at all events not have been a large one; indeed, we hear nothing more on this topic after the accession of Louis the Pious.

Few reports in the various annals testify to any ongoing interest on the part of the Franks in the power struggles among the Danes. Hemming died in 812, and the ensuing battles over the succession claimed many lives, including those of both candidates for the throne. Ultimately, two brothers, Harald and Reginfrid, were able to prevail, who immediately sued for peace with Charlemagne; this was duly signed the following year at the frontier. It was at this juncture that the first reports of internal conflicts among the Danish warrior elites began to trickle through to the Frankish Empire, including the news that the sons of King Gottfrid had fled and sought asylum with the Swedish (*Sueones*) and had then proceeded to lead an army from Sweden against the new kings of the Danes (*Royal Frankish Annals* for 813). Yet even then there was no more precise information provided on the Franks' enemy to the north, on his objectives or motives. Frankish defensive works ground to a halt, and the handful of border strongholds that Charlemagne had built were easily circumvented by the enemy, who simply took sea routes to outflank them. At no stage does a Frankish fleet appear to have put to sea to confront the Vikings. Henceforth, fasting and prayer, rather than any plans for rearmament or gathering intelligence on the enemy, character- ized the struggle against the pirates. We find mention in the records only of sporadic defensive measures rather than any systematic efforts, and no capitulary of this time explicitly addressed the danger posed by the Normans. During his final years as emperor, Charlemagne found himself unable to dispel this particular threat for any sustained period.

Those among the Franks who inquired about the causes of things were inclined to see these defeats as justified punishments meted out to a sinful people, and as warnings of the impending End of Days. A least, this was how this dark period was portrayed by commentators after Charlemagne's reign. The emperor too at the end of his life increasingly resorted to such initiatives as decreeing that fasting should take place throughout the em- pire, along with widespread public displays of atonement and penitential processions.[92] What was to be done when the capitularies did not have the effect the emperor desired, and when the laws of the land were flouted by the counts and bishops alike? Ugly rumors began to circulate that these lords had been bribed to allow injustice to prevail.

Contacts with Foreigners

From Charlemagne's coronation as emperor onward, the *Royal Frankish Annals* bears witness to a remarkable variety of activities. As before, it re- ports a whole succession of military campaigns, often led by Charlemagne's sons, together with numerous legations to both the East and the West and both from and to foreign princes. Yet various capitularies and proceedings of synods show us another Charlemagne. In them, the future salvation of the realm and of the Church came to the fore. Deep anxiety over the future of his empire seared the soul of this powerful man, who was accustomed to successes. He could see all too clearly that the measures he had ordered had not taken hold as quickly as he hoped, despite repeated reminders. He was concerned about maintaining peace, about the realization of an empire-wide reform program that made a genuinely clean break with the hallowed traditions of the Frankish kingdom and its aristocratic society, and about how to secure the peace and welfare of the many different peoples within his realm, of his churches, and of his free and impoverished subjects. He could hardly hope to win the consensus of his magnates on such matters.

Such concerns are not much in evidence in Frankish foreign relations, although they could not remain unaffected by them. The close connections to Britain continued, but they changed in nature. Whereas beforehand missionaries had come from the island to the continent, preaching, founding monasteries, and reforming the institutions of the Church and education, now worldly matters took precedence, especially after the death of King Offa of Mercia and Alcuin of York in 796 and 804, respectively. The largely impenetrable structures of power and authority that existed in the Anglo-Saxon kingdoms now also came to preoccupy the Carolingian court in certain respects.

After being ousted by Offa, the man who would later become King Egbert of Wessex spent several years living under Charlemagne's protection in the kingdom of the Franks. Returning to Britain, from 802 onward he proved himself to be the unifier of England and over the coming years broke the predominance of Mercia. In 808, another Anglo-Saxon emigrant who had been "driven from his realm and homeland," King Eardwulf of Northumbria, found his way to the emperor's court and thence to Rome. With Charlemagne and the pope's help, he was soon able to return to his kingdom. While the papal envoy to Britain was on his way back to Rome, he was seized by "pirates"; Coenwulf, the king of Mercia, paid a ransom to have him released. Leo III, however, wrongly thanked Charlemagne for lending his assistance in this affair, telling him that Eardwulf had always been loyally devoted to him, and that now the whole world would sing the praises of his "imperial power of protection." At the same time, he asked Charlemagne to act as mediator in the long-simmering conflict between Coenwulf and the archbishops of Canterbury and York; he told him that he was enclosing his own pastoral letter to Eanbald of Canterbury for Charlemagne to examine. This has unfortunately not been preserved, but we do at least know from widespread rumors circulating at the time that the letter called on the archbishop to defend his position either to Charlemagne or to the pope directly.[93] Inasmuch as the Anglo-Saxons' route to Rome took them through the kingdom of the Franks, any conflicts on the island tended to reverberate in Charlemagne's realm.

Yet Charlemagne's worries were not solely confined to clashes taking place in Britain. There was also unrest on the borders with the Emirate of Córdoba. Moorish attacks and the row over the adoptionist heresy drew people's attention there. Events in the south of al-Andalus had alarmed Christians and posed a threat to the Frankish Empire for many years now. The weaknesses in frontier defenses that had become apparent in Count Guillaume of Toulouse's defeat by 'Abd al-Malik at the battle of Orbiel in 793, and to an even greater extent Charlemagne's own failed campaign in al-Andalus, dissuaded the emperor from any new attack on the Muslim forces there. He even hesitated when Prince Abdallah urged him to launch an assault on Gerona and Barcelona. His bitter personal experiences from 778 warned him against making any rash decisions. More thoroughgoing preparations than those he had made back then were clearly called for. His ruminations on his score lasted for almost four years, from 797 to 801. In the meantime, Charlemagne ordered his son Louis to besiege Gerona and Huesca.[94] Was this simply a kind of feint by the emperor? Or a test of the young king's martial prowess? In 799, it even seemed as though Huesca might fall, but this came to nothing, as the *Royal Frankish Annals* reported. The city remained a well-fortified outpost of Muslim power right up to the late eleventh century; only during the course of the *Reconquista* did it finally fall to the kingdom of Aragón. Eventually, in 801, Frankish troops under Guillaume of Toulouse advanced to make one final assault on Barcelona.

After a siege lasting two years, the city fell in 803. King Louis, largely absent from the battlefield until then, turned up in good time to witness the great event and so went down in history as the victor of the engagement. Six years later, Tortosa was permanently conquered. The debacle of 778 was redeemed and the objective on that occasion, the banks of the river Ebro, finally reached. However, both Huesca and Zaragoza remained firmly in Moorish hands; it was 1118 before the latter city fell, to the great Aragonese king Alfonso el Batallador ("the Warrior"). But as early as 806, Charlemagne was at least able to found the buffer zone of the Marca Hispánica (or March of Barcelona), which would later form the nucleus of Catalonia. Until the thirteenth century, this region belonged nominally to the Frankish-French kings, before Catalonia seceded from it as part of the confederation forming the Crown of Aragón. These circumstances ensured that a different language from the rest of Spain, a separate legal system, and a distinct cultural identity all developed there, a factor that has important ramifications to this day.

The integration of the Frankish conquests and the formation of the March of Barcelona, which were realized by the Aquitainian ruler King Louis, fundamentally altered the balance of power in the Pyrenean region. Meanwhile, the true victor, Guillaume of Toulouse, became a monk, founding (possibly out of thanks for his success) the monastery of Gellone (St-Guillaume-le-Désert) in 804. Two years later, he took holy orders there himself; nowadays, he is venerated as a saint.

The signing of a peace treaty with the "king of Spain" Abulaz (al-Hakam I) followed in 810. It was fated not to last long; by 815 we hear once more about the resumption of hostilities between the Franks and the Emirate of Córdoba. But it is intriguing to note that only now, after the "victorious" Louis the Pious had succeeded his father on the throne, did chroniclers feel able to write a little more openly than before about Charlemagne's earlier failure in Spain.[95] The son was eager to emerge from his great father's shadow. Thus, remembrance was clearly being shaped by the powers that be, was conditioned by the moment, and was designed to throw light on present circumstances rather than the past.

A glance at the states bordering on the Frankish Empire opened a window on a turbulent world. But internally things were not exactly at their best either. Charlemagne anticipated the troubles that would be visited on his realm after his death. The revolt staged by his eldest son, Pepin the Hunchback, lay only a few years in the past. And his recollections of his early years as king, when he ruthlessly eliminated his brother's sons from the succession, had scarcely dissipated. "How could anyone who killed his own son count on being reconciled with God, and could anyone who had slain his own brother believe that Christ the Lord would be merciful to him?"—royal messengers were sent out to inculcate this warning throughout the entire realm.[96] Recorded for posterity in the *Royal Frankish Annals,* the stories from Charlemagne's childhood about his father's conflict with his uncle and his cousins could no longer be expunged from the collective memory. What emerged was a guilt-laden kingdom.

Organizing the Succession

"In the last days shall come dangerous times," proclaimed St. Paul (2 Timothy 3:1). This apocalyptic message seemed to be coming to pass in the final years of Charlemagne's rule. Anxieties over the end times mounted. Wherever one looked, there were uprisings, disorder, threats to religion, and heresies, among the Greeks, in Spain, in Rome, and in Charlemagne's own realm. The world, it seemed, was rushing headlong toward its demise; unmistakable signs heralded this downfall.[97] Charlemagne, though, the emperor, was approaching high old age by now. From his reading of the seventh-century Irish tract *De duodecim abusivis saeculi* (On the twelve abuses of the world), he would have known that at the Last Judgment, a king was answerable for the sum total of sin that had been accumulated within his realm. It seemed easy to conquer an empire but hard to keep hold of it and even more difficult to govern it in a way that was pleasing to God. So how might he discharge his peoples' debt of sin? And how to save the peace, spread justice, affirm the true faith, and staunchly support the Christian cause, even in the Muslim East? Charlemagne's own experience told him that his death would trigger a series of civil wars. Could things be restored, improved, strengthened, and expanded in time? Answering this in the affirmative entailed the emperor not only implementing reforms in the present but also planning for the future.

And he was truly concerned for the future of his empire. Internally, the continuing infiltration of adoptionist views from Spain called for tireless vigilance. The Greek cult of images, meanwhile, bordered on idolatry. The faith had not yet put down firm-enough roots among his own Frankish people, while the Saxons were still far from being true Christians. Dioceses had only recently been established there and incorporated into the church province of Mainz;[98] but Saxony still had no monasteries or holy relics. The Avars had been vanquished, but the expansion and consolidation of Frankish authority and the dissemination of Christianity in Pannonia were all still very much in their infancy. Missionaries from Aquileia, Salzburg, Passau, and Regensburg vied to have this territory brought under the aegis of their respective dioceses and in the process merely succeeded in hampering one another's work.

The organizational structure of the Church was in a sorry state, and ecclesiastical jurisdiction likewise, not to mention the lifestyle of the priesthood. Reports submitted from all regions by the king's envoys were truly alarming: priests were even, it seemed, neglecting their duty to protect the weak. Not least, the revolts of earlier times, which had fortunately been suppressed but were still fresh in people's memories, sent a warning reminder of hidden threats to law and order. At any time, some magnate or other, or perhaps even one of his sons, might succumb to delusions of grandeur and stage an uprising, which it would be imperative to nip in the bud. The situation required the utmost vigilance and a marshaling of all available resources. Yet the means at the emperor's disposal were also rooted in traditional knowledge; consequently, these in particular needed to be updated, expanded, and made more efficient. But how might experience and learning be augmented and the level of competence raised?

The initial responses to these questions revisited familiar territory. A series of capitularies impressed on the populace the virtues of traditional devotion. Spreading and strengthening the faith and improving the act of worship, the *cultus divinus,* were seen as essential. These were the emperor's first priorities. Over and over, with dogged patience and wearisome monotony, religious standards of behavior and commandments were inculcated, with the injunction that the Church and the people should observe them if they wished to attain salvation. Prelates were instructed not to abuse their authority but rather to live and act in an exemplary manner; anyone who proved himself unworthy of the duties expected of him should be dismissed. Monks should dwell in cloisters, and nuns should live a strictly sheltered existence. Moreover, the rule of law and justice was henceforth to hold sway; the royal envoys were under strict instructions to carry out annual checks to monitor this. Widows and orphans were to be protected at all costs. The poor were not to be exploited, nor should anyone neglect his duties as a vassal. The prospect of being exempted from military service was held out to poorer free men and to vassals with little property to their name.[99] Time and again, the issuing of similar decrees was called to mind; yet with equal frequency the king's *missi* reported back that abuses were continuing unabated.

Incest and other sexual misdemeanors were to be prosecuted, and murderers, especially those who had killed a relative, would face the full force of the law. In times of famine, people were exhorted to offer up prayers asking for God's mercy, but practical measures were also introduced, such as offering grain at much-reduced prices to the neediest. Other measures in the same vein followed. It was vital to bring about peace with God, peace among the magnates, and peace among the people, but it was also imperative that the royal possessions be protected. The *missi* were expressly empowered to investigate whether the emperor's estates were being properly managed or whether they had been neglected and needed to be reorganized.[100]

Continually, and in all aspects of life, the emperor sought to divine the will of God and to fulfill it. Unity, friendship, and love were both the vehicles and the objectives of his program; they were designed to consolidate the monarch's hold on power and to lead to salvation. In spite of all the monitoring that went on, we look in vain for any evidence of institutional reorganizations, reforming structural measures, or new regional policies. Only the twenty-one Church provinces that Charlemagne created, plus the missionary districts, afforded a certain geographical overview of the whole empire.

Implementation of his policies had some personal consequences for the ruler: we may reasonably assume that it was with an eye to preserving the peace and restricting the number of his legitimate heirs that, after the death of his fourth (or fifth) wife, Liutgard, and after his coronation as emperor, rather than take a new empress, Charlemagne consorted only with concubines, four of them all told: Madalgard, the Saxon lady Gerswind, Regina, and Adallind. Although in the process he sired three more sons—Drogo, Hugo, and Theodoric—as well as two daughters, Ruothild and Adaltrud, because they were born out of wedlock, they were excluded from the inheritance and hence from the struggle that would inevitably ensue over dividing the empire. We know about all these consorts and illegitimate children from Einhard's biography (chap. 18).

Christmas of 805, which Charlemagne celebrated at his palace on the river Moselle at Diedenhofen (now Thionville in northeastern France), saw anxiety over the maintenance of peace reach new heights. The emperor summoned his three adult sons who were still deemed eligible to inherit— Charles, Pepin (formerly Carloman), and Louis—to attend him. Once again, capitularies summarized the decisions reached at this meeting and the measures taken to consolidate worship and safeguard peace. Again, royal messengers were called on to make the resolutions known forthwith throughout the realm; a note indicating receipt of such a message by Bishop Jesse of Amiens has survived.

These capitularies did not identify any broad abstract realms in either ecclesiastical or secular life where action was needed; instead, the sources of imminent danger could be pinpointed only individually and cumulatively and so had to be reported by word of mouth, as did the steps taken to neutralize them. But certain standards were now required and placed within the remit of the envoys to monitor: full knowledge of the liturgy, error-free scriptures, proper care and maintenance of churches, correct calculation of time, and medical knowledge.[101] None of this was new, but it seems that these aspects of life and civil order were under threat thanks to neglect and inadequate monitoring.

One particular irritant appears to have been the case of dissemblers, who in an attempt to shirk further service to their masters pretended that they had renounced the world to take holy orders but then neither became priests nor entered a monastery. Now they were to be forced to choose. Furthermore, girls of a very young age (*puellulae*) now could not take the veil and become nuns without being able to make this decision independently (which, according to the conceptions of the time, was after they had turned seven); a later capitulary amended this to the age of twenty-five.[102] Monastery provosts and archdeacons should no longer be laymen and were now required to have made profession in a holy order or to have been ordained as priests. Transgressions of these norms had evidently been reported to the emperor. The same abuses kept recurring in an empire that possessed only a very rudimentary central authority, and in which a whole variety of ecclesiastical and secular powers wielded some degree of authority.

Secular law was also put under the spotlight.[103] For many centuries, brute force had held sway in the kingdom of the Franks. Curbing this abuse called for great tenacity, patience, and determined opposition to long-hallowed practices. Charlemagne's new provisions speak for themselves. Criminals were now subject to the same punishments meted out to rebels (MGH 44.1). It was forbidden to bear any arms, namely, a shield, a spear, or a coat of chain mail, at home. From now on, small-scale warfare in the realm, such as bloody feuding between individual free men, was to be curbed, or its effects at least mitigated. Anyone who owned twelve "hides" of land (in fee from the king?) was expected to have a coat of mail; anyone who turned up to perform his mandatory military service without one would forfeit both his chain mail and his tenure of his fiefdom (44.6). Those who breached the peace—that is, violent criminals—had to appear before the king. Anyone who committed a murder after having signed a peace settlement (including resolutions of minor disputes) or who pursued a vendetta would lose the hand with which he swore his oath and be subject to banishment by the king (44.5). Trade with the Slavs and the Avars was to be conducted and controlled only through certain frontier stations, and under no circumstances were weapons to be exported to these peoples (44.7). Oaths of allegiance could be sworn only to the emperor or—for the ultimate benefit of the emperor—to a person's own master (44.9).

The king's envoys were to ensure that anyone with assets of six pounds of gold or silver or other objects of value, excluding any women's or children's clothing, paid the military levy of three pounds, while those who could not afford such a sum were expected to pay thirty shillings, and those with even fewer assets a correspondingly smaller amount. It was the responsibility of the *missi* to ensure that no one defrauded the king of these taxes (44.19). Wars cost considerable amounts of money, even then, and were funded by levying excises on small and even extremely modest fortunes. These provisions also followed earlier capitularies in invoking the principles of the rule of law and justice and in calling for the poor and vassals without independent means to be protected; once more, there were calls for fugitive clerics and laymen and runaway wives to be brought to book, and for the stamping out of counterfeiting and illegal taxation. Marriages between free men and (unfree) females dependent on the state's finances were also regulated.

The cumulative effect of such individual measures enacted by the central imperial authority would be to permeate the realm with the principle of peace and to consolidate it through law and order, as well as faith and religious observance. However, peace imposed through sovereign authority necessarily brought with it an intensification of royal power. What for its time was a huge concentration of central authority was thus set in motion. After all, there was still no civil service or police force at this stage, only masters and free men, whose propensity for belligerence had to be reined in; the countless servants and maids counted for nothing in these deliberations.

At the same time, the principal business of these final years of Charlemagne's reign needed to be resolved, namely, how best to manage the emperor's succession. By this stage, in 806, Charlemagne was fifty-eight years old and at the very peak of his powers. The empire's borders had been secured as best they could, internal opposition had been silenced, and the restored machinery of imperial power had opened the floodgates of new legislation. Yet how could the realm that the emperor had once inherited, then expanded through numerous wars, and consolidated throughout thirty-seven years of strong rule survive without him in these "dangerous times"? His heirs Charles, Pepin, and Louis were now grown men; even the youngest of them would soon turn thirty. They were busy pursuing their own interests, gathering around them vassals or at least people who wished to become vassals, and in all likelihood preparing themselves to engage in disputes, perhaps even armed conflicts, with their brothers. If peace was to be maintained, urgent measures were called for to stave off such an eventuality. The plan that Charlemagne now enacted reveals a great deal about the remarkable foresight of this powerful man, who saw his end approaching.

A court assembly was convened at Diedenhofen. There, in consultation with his magnates, on 6 February 806 Charlemagne announced a plan to divide the empire among his three sons; intrinsic in this division was a peace constitution.[104] Those present affirmed this decision through an oath. The corresponding charter was given to the emperor's trusted aide Einhard, who may himself have been involved in drafting it, to take to the pope for his agreement and signature.[105] The division and the peace plan formed an indivisible whole. Although he was ostensibly following Frankish tradition in dividing his realm, Charlemagne in fact broke completely new ground with this settlement. The wording of the document as it has come down to us—more a constitution than a charter—presents us with two parts of unequal length: chapters 1 to 5, which consist of a brief announcement of the division, are followed by a series of extensive peace statutes (chapters 6–19) and a concluding chapter. Like a magnifying glass, the document brought together and focused all the emperor's concerns on the succession.

These resolutions were to be proclaimed throughout the realm; although the death of the emperor's two oldest sons ultimately prevented this planned division from coming to fruition, even today traces of three different copies of this document can still be identified. The first points to Adalhard of Corbie, the second also to him or possibly to his brother Count Wala; they were the cousins and most important aides of the aging emperor. The third copy can be traced back through Walahfrid Strabo to the palace archive at Aix. As members of the collateral line of the Carolingian dynasty, his cousins Adalhard and Wala may well have had a decisive influence on Charlemagne's early division of the empire; after all, Pepin of Italy was the husband of their sister Theodrada.[106] However, to date no trace has been found of a Roman manuscript of the document, which must have once existed. The "implementation decree" required that all free men throughout the empire swear an oath consenting to the peace agreement; royal envoys were made responsible for overseeing the implementation and supervising the taking of oaths. This swearing-in process was regarded as the most important peace instrument. In its totality, this whole process—the sons' agreement to take a share of their father's power, the transcription of the agreement, the administration of oaths, and the sending of the succession ordinance to the pope—was highly innovative. It would enable the magnates concerned to accommodate themselves in good time to their future masters.

The constitution was formally addressed to all the faithful adherents of God's Church, the Christian congregation in its entirety among all the peoples living under Charlemagne's imperial sway. The title with which Charlemagne was endowed in the document was equally programmatic: "*Imperator Caesar Karolus rex Francorum invictissimus et Romani rector imperii pius felix victor ac triumphator semper augustus*" (Charles, Emperor Caesar, most invincible king of the Franks and ruler of the Roman Empire, pious and happy victor and ever illustrious conqueror). In its totality, this was not a verbatim copy of any ancient ruler's title but was nevertheless modeled on such titles through its adoption of individual ancient formulas, alongide certain liturgical turns of phrase. Therefore, the title had universal connotations hinting at ancient Roman imperial laws and a correspondingly legitimizing function. Yet copies of the constitution were also circulated with the emperor's familiar title, which had been in use since 801 and was now meant specifically for the consumption of his subjects in the Frankish heartlands and other areas on the right bank of the Rhine. The provisions it decreed were meant to have legal force independent of the civic rights pertaining in each of these regions, as well as in those lands where orality still predominated, and in Lombard and Roman Italy, Southern Gallia, and the former Visigoth areas that were now under Charlemagne's sphere of control, where vulgar Roman law was still in force.

Even the introduction to Charlemagne's charter—its *arenga* (a term denoting a preamble, often lengthy, to a document)—was highly unconventional in the unusual program of continuity it envisaged and in its admonishing appeal to Christian and collective cultural memory. It claimed that God's clemency would, over the course of the succeeding generations, restore to health the current *saecula* (times), which were racing headlong to destruction and downfall.[107] In blessing him, the emperor, with three sons, this divine clemency had, this preamble continued, affirmed his hopes regarding the continuance of royal power and assuaged his fears that it might lapse into oblivion in times to come. Accordingly, the division that he was hereby enacting was intended to counteract this oblivion, to serve the cause of peace, and to be a positive measure against decline. In writing this, Charlemagne was not seeking to dispel his eschatological fears entirely but rather to compel them to succumb to the Christian message of hope. After all, from time immemorial, rulership that was pleasing to God had played a major part in securing the continued existence of the world. Indeed, according to the Church Fathers' interpretation of history, the apostle St. Paul had preached precisely this lesson in his Second Epistle to the Thessalonians.[108]

The arrangement for the succession combined old and new elements. It complemented and completed the earlier edicts concerning peace, brought together the most important forces for peace, and appealed to the traditional Frankish law on the partitioning of property. Yet at the same time, it went beyond this traditional legislation in serving as a kind of domestic or imperial basic law whose validity encompassed all the peoples of the realm. Indicators of this are the title given to the ruler, which was modeled on those of Roman legislators, and the forward-looking terminology of the legal provisions: "authority," "statutes," "decrees," and "agreement," together with the peace statute itself. At the same time, a specifically Frankish-Carolingian memory trace was retained, and with it the cautionary experiences of the emperor and his contemporaries, an ominous recollection of the past. It was Charlemagne's fervent wish not to leave his empire in a state of confusion and disintegration, but to transfer it untroubled by discord and conflict to his three God-given sons.

To achieve this, Charlemagne dared to depart from tradition. Neither the apportioning of an "equal share" of the realm to each son nor the realization of some notional continuing unity of the empire guided Charlemagne's deliberations, as traditional Frankish inheritance law would have demanded. He did not even entertain the possibility of "as even a division of labor as possible" for sons who were on an equal footing, or of a "band of brothers," a *corpus fratrum* acting in concert. Rather, Charlemagne saw an impending division of the kind that was inevitable under Frankish inheritance law as a huge danger for the Church, for peace, and for the subjects of his empire and looked for ways to forestall it. Accordingly, he elevated his three sons to the position of "king's consorts" (*regni consortes*) and ordered the division "of the entire body of the empire" (*totum regni corpus*), so as to clearly preempt any conflict arising among them "on the pretext that he had bequeathed the whole realm to any one of them" (*confuse atque inordinate vel sub totius regni denominatione*). None of his sons, he decreed, was to interfere in the affairs of the portions of the realm ruled by his brothers. As Charlemagne himself put it in his implementation order, he was dividing up his sovereignty in a spirit of concerned foresight and "for the sake of unity in peace." The people were sworn to abide by this same principle.

The clause within the constitution codifying this division, the "*Divisio regnorum*," has survived. It emphatically did not—as might have been expected, judging by the terms of both earlier and later such partitions—envisage three "equal parts" (as described by the formulas *aequa lance* and *aequali sorte* in the *Metz Annals* and chapter 3 of Einhard's biography, respectively) in the way in which both the partitions between Carloman and Pepin (741) and thereafter between Charlemagne and his brother Carloman (768) had done. Instead, each son was enjoined to settle for that portion of his father's realm and inheritance that Charlemagne was now in the process of apportioning to them.

As sometimes occurred in other Frankish families, the three brothers were patently treated quite differently according to the service they had rendered and their seniority. To this end, Charlemagne had taken the precaution of soliciting in advance an "expert opinion" from Alcuin, which had explicitly pronounced the procedure that the ruler now adopted to be legally admissible. Charles, the eldest son, received the largest and richest part, while Louis, the youngest, was placed at a distinct disadvantage by having to settle for the smallest, most insignificant, and least profitable of all the shares of the inheritance. Charlemagne took as his starting point the kingdoms of Italy and Aquitaine, which had already been assigned to the two younger sons in 781; these were later expanded by the addition of more or less extensive parts of Alemannia and Bavaria (to Carloman, later Pepin, of Italy) and Septimania (the area around Carcassonne and Béziers in the south of France), Provence, and parts of Burgundy (to Louis). The "remainder," namely, the largely undivided heartland of Francia, along with a number of adjoining territories—for instance, recently conquered Saxony, the north of Alemannia, and the Nordgau region of Bavaria—was given to Charles.

As far as we can make out, this arrangement represented a radical departure from the previous practice among the Frankish kings, according to which precisely the major heartland of Francia was divided up equally among the legitimate heirs; later, too, in the fratricidal wars among the sons of Louis the Pious, the *casus belli* for the combatants was invariably a proper share of the Frankish heartland with its royal palaces. After Charlemagne's unprecedented break with tradition, the empires that each of these sons of Louis came to rule over were the first not to be divided up in this time-honored "equal" fashion. Yet the collective cultural memory of the Franks taught that this tradition had never at any time been able to safeguard peace; therefore, something new ought to be tried.

A certain amount of preparatory groundwork was laid for this break with tradition. The *Metz Annals* proclaimed its legitimacy. This record was compiled contemporaneously with the "*Divisio regnorum*" in the environs of the emperor's court and may well have reflected the prevailing attitudes there. Yet in an analogous case that had arisen in 741, namely, when Charles Martel had assigned to his "concubine's" son Grifo "within his principality [*in medio principatus sui*] a portion of Neustria and Austrasia and Burgundy" (portions of the lands that would later fall under Charles the Younger's control), the *Metz Annals* reported that "the Franks were thoroughly indignant." They did not wish, the annals explained, "to be divided on the advice of a dishonorable woman [Grifo's mother, Swanahild] and to be separated from their legitimate heirs."

Annals, however, must be read in the context of the period in which they were written; and certainly, at the time when the recollection of these annals was recorded, it had highly topical significance. By citing historic examples, they legitimized the actions of the present. All the sons of Charlemagne born after 800 were regarded as concubines' sons, along with his eldest son, Pepin the Hunchback, who had been banished to a monastery and had been excluded from any share in his father's empire through a retrospectively fabricated illegitimacy.[109] There was no doubt that he would originally have received a portion of Francia and possibly also Bavaria. But Francia was the core of the empire, the land of the Franks, their homeland; the kings of the Franks always returned there after their campaigns. Consequently, the message that the *Metz Annals* conveyed was unequivocal: the Franks of the early ninth century did not wish to see any "division" of their country; their strength resided, as these annals repeatedly demonstrated, in unity, peace, and consensus, which manifested themselves in brotherly fellowship.

Charlemagne acted accordingly when he partitioned his realm. Not some precarious equilibrium but a clear weighting of power and spheres of authority that were clearly separated from one another were what would guarantee peace and unity. Everyone knew that both Aquitaine and Italy had been conquered from the Frankish heartland. The emperor stipulated that conflicts among his sons were to be avoided at all costs; they should settle border disputes amicably (chap. 14). The consensus of the magnates to the partition and the peace constitution—a measure that was made clear here for the first time—had been expressly sought. Charlemagne even had the foresight to specify how a new division should proceed in the event of the death of one or another of his sons; and even his grandsons were included in the succession arrangement (chap. 4). If the people should wish to elect one of the grandsons as the successor to his father, it would require the agreement of both of the father's brothers (chap. 5)

The peace constitution contained detailed provisions on the relations among the brothers. Their father anticipated the causes of potential conflict among them, and so he tried to compel his sons to commit to the cause of peace. No one, he ordered, was to dare to attack or occupy another's realm; to the contrary, each son should pledge to support the others in combating both internal and external enemies (chap. 7); furthermore, none of them should take in refugees from their brothers' territories (chap. 8), while free men were to accept fiefdoms only in the portion of the empire ruled over by their master (chap. 9)—certainly, though, after the death of his master, every free man should have the right to decide whom he wished to serve in the future (chap. 10). None of his sons should acquire, either through purchase or transfer, any estates or "hides" within the realm of another (chap. 11); free women were to be allowed to marry across the frontiers of the subempires, and if the peoples of the different realms formed relationships by marriage with one another, they were to be permitted to retain their property in the part of the empire they had left (chap. 12). In the event of border disputes that could not be settled by legal means, a decision was to be reached by drawing lots (*iudicio crucis Dei*) and on no account through trial by combat (chap. 14). Jointly, the three brothers were enjoined by their father to protect the Roman Church (chap. 15).

The emperor feared the worst for his close family. In great anxiety, he commanded that his daughters should be able to freely decide under which of the brothers' protection they wished to place themselves, or whether they wanted to take the veil or to marry; the brothers were to have no right of refusal in this matter (chap. 17). Charlemagne's provisions for the protection of his grandsons were positively hair-raising in their explicitness: no matter under what pretext they did so, none of his three royal sons had the right to execute, maim, blind, or force into a monastery any of the emperor's grandsons without intensive and proper examination of their case (chap. 18). Here, an emperor was issuing commands who had in his time executed, blinded, maimed, and forced into monasteries many an opponent, a ruler who knew only too well what dire threats a king's offspring faced from their own relatives.

However, ultimately Charlemagne's precautions were to all be in vain. Even the greatest of the Frankish kings was unable to safeguard the peace beyond his own death. His principal heir, Louis, would end up doing precisely what his father had tried to prevent, forcing his sisters into a convent, having their lovers murdered, and in defiance of all oaths ordering the blinding and execution of his brother's son Pepin, as well as having his younger brothers forcibly tonsured and incarcerated in monasteries. No fatherly injunction to honor the principles of peace and love and no consensus on the part of the magnates could guard against the exercise of brutal imperial power; no oath or prayer was of any help here. All too soon Louis, later to become known by the sobriquet "the Pious," would lead the Franks and all their sworn free men and magnates to commit a collective breach of oath and thereby, after the death of the great national hero, plunge the former realm of Charlemagne into chaos, treachery, fratricidal war, dissolution, and downfall.

Signs in the Heavens

For four years after the division of the empire, Charlemagne may have believed that he had put his house in order: four years in which political routines and numerous wars but also concerns over peace within the realm and about how to alleviate the suffering of the poor came to the fore once again. Although Charlemagne now only very seldom engaged in battle against the enemy in person, he increasingly resorted to sending his sons, especially the eldest, on campaign. New opponents appeared at this time in the form of the Slavs, who, after the incorporation of Saxony and Bavaria into Charlemagne's realm, suddenly found themselves, like the Danes, neighbors of the Franks. They too now began to establish some embryonic but enduring foundations of their own empire as the first stirrings of the native nobility in Bohemia and Moravia, as well as among the Slavs along the river Elbe, became apparent.

Even in the year preceding the partitioning, Charlemagne's eldest son, Charles, invaded Bohemia at the head of an army, laying waste the country and killing its "duke," Lech (*Royal Frankish Archives*). The next year the emperor ordered him to march against the Sorbs, west of the Elbe; their "king" or "duke," Miliduoch, also fell in battle, and their fortified towns (*civitates*) were destroyed, while two Frankish strongholds were erected on the Saale and Elbe Rivers, at Halle and Magdeburg, respectively. Later that same year, Charlemagne dispatched a force from Bavaria, Alemannia, and Burgundy against Bohemia.

Its objective was to ward off any attacks and secure the frontier. Saxons too now became liable for military service. If a campaign was launched far afield, say, to Spain or Pannonia, then, as one decree ordered, for every six Saxons it was expected that one armed warrior should join the ranks, whereas in the case of an attack on Bohemia, it was one in every three; for defense of their own region against the Sorbs, every man without exception was called to arms.[110] The establishment of a trade barrier in the East, preventing Franks from going to trade with Slavs and Avars, was also a security measure. It is not recorded to what extent Slavs were permitted to travel to markets in the West. Merchants were subject to trade restrictions and were prohibited, say, from offering for sale weapons or coats of mail. Contravention of this would be punishable by having their entire stock seized and given away, half going to the king and half to the *missi* and the people who denounced the trader in question.[111] Under these conditions, Slavs did, then, trade with Franks and Saxons, and weapons were the most sought-after goods. Accordingly, archaeologists have unearthed numerous Frankish swords in areas east of the Elbe and the Bavarian Forest—clear evidence that trade embargoes were often flouted.

The struggle to establish law and order across the empire continued unabated. Another court assembly was convened at Nijmegen in 806. Draconian instructions were issued to the royal envoys who went out into the country after this meeting.[112] This was hardly surprising, given that it had come to the emperor's attention that both Jewish and Christian merchants (*negotiatores*) had been boasting that they could get hold of anything their clients wanted from Church treasuries—precious stones, Communion vessels, and so on; bishops, abbots, and abbesses were therefore instructed to make sure that their silverware and other treasures were not embezzled by those who had been appointed to guard them.[113] This was the first edict issued by Charlemagne to make reference to the Jews. Was perhaps that same Isaac who had acted so successfully as a middleman for Charlemagne in the East, and who was the only Jew we know about for certain in the emperor's circle of acquaintances, also behind implementation of this successful policy? It certainly would have served the cause of establishing calm within the empire.

At that time, the only significant Jewish communities within the empire were in the south of Gallia, in Aquitaine, in the Marca Hispánica, and in Italy. The task of protecting them, insofar as it was regulated at all, lay in the hands of Charlemagne's son Louis, the king of Aquitaine. The emperor's own capitularies began referring to Jews only now, in 806, when it became necessary to forestall conflict with Christians. In this instance, it seems, no particular effort was made to prosecute merchants for handling stolen church goods. But in cases where merchants were accused of a crime, even at this stage a particular provision, which was recorded in 809, may already have been in force. According to this, if a Jew should bring a lawsuit against a Christian, the plaintiff was required to appear with four, seven, or nine compurgators, depending on the value of the claim, whereas an accused Christian had to adduce only three. Conversely, if the plaintiff was a Christian, then just three compurgators were required on each side to swear the necessary oath on behalf of their party.[114] *Missi* were responsible for ensuring that imperial orders were complied with. This ruling thus combined discrimination with a measure of protection for the Jews, a provision that appeared all the more urgent given that hostile acts toward Jews were highly likely. Indeed, many such anti-Semitic attacks were recorded during the reign of Louis the Pious.[115]

One of the earliest accounts of hostility toward Jews, possibly the first documented in Bavaria, was of a general nature and led directly to the imperial court of Charlemagne's son Louis. When Louis's own son, Louis II "the German," the future king of East Francia, was still a "boy" (*puer*), Archbishop Adalram of Salzburg sent him a work on the subject, namely, a transcript in his own hand of the *Treatise against the Jews, the Heathens, and the Arians*, commonly (and wrongly) attributed to St. Augustine of Hippo.[116] This must have occurred before or around 827, for at that time the boy Louis was crowned king of Bavaria. The author of the tract identified five *genera* of enemies—aside from those mentioned in the title, the Manichaeans and the Sabellians, heretic sects from late antiquity, were also cited—and called for Christians to take up arms against them, but most especially against the Jews. This "sermon" was clearly intended to inform the young ruler in good time about the enemies of the faith. However, the measures implemented by Charlemagne at least afforded the Jews a limited degree of security under the law.

One particular source of irritation for the emperor at this time was the fact that counts and other noblemen were using imperial fiefdoms (*beneficia*) as security to purchase their own property, on which they then employed serfs of the emperor, while the Crown estates were left to go to rack and ruin and neighboring villages suffered great depredations. The second court assembly of 806, at Nijmegen, demanded that this practice cease forthwith (MGH 46.6). Furthermore, people who held land in fee from the emperor were selling their fiefdoms to third parties as if they were their own to dispose of (*in proprietatem*); the profits enabled them in turn to buy their own property (*in alodem*) (46.7). In other words, a whole series of abuses was brought to light affecting the king and the poor under his protection.[117] According to what is believed to be the emperor's final capitulary, such instances of gross misconduct in office continued up to 813.[118]

In particular, monitoring in monasteries and convents would determine whether monks and nuns had, as instructed, made progress in reading, liturgical singing, and other ecclesiastical disciplines. The king's envoys were empowered to take steps to eradicate the Christian sins par excellence of avarice, greed, and usury (46.12–15). There was always famine somewhere in the realm; accordingly, there was a constant need to enforce maximum prices for oats, spelt, wheat, and rye (46.18). Counts were expected to hold regular court sessions and not, as was often found to be the case, to shirk this duty in favor of going hunting.[119]

The *missi* reported back their findings to the emperor and the assembled magnates and also made them aware of further misdemeanors. At least one such report, albeit undated, has survived.[120] It shows how issues were indeed examined with a fine-tooth comb, as-yet-unidentified grievances were uncovered, and the results were conveyed to the ruler in far-off Aix (Aachen). As the system of inspection by king's envoys began to gain traction, it necessitated the introduction of even more sweeping measures against ecclesiastical and secular transgressions and crimes. It required endless patience and tenacity to effect lasting changes. The consequences of a centuries-long lack of a strict central authority and the firm guiding hand of a system of law and order could not be reversed over just a few decades. Every cultural decline is positively precipitate in comparison with the necessarily unhurried process of careful reconstruction.

Welfare for the economically disadvantaged was the order of the day. When famine hit the western region of Francia, west of the Seine, to alleviate suffering, the requirement to perform military service was graded: fief holders were expected to turn out in full, as were those who owned five, four, or even three "hides." However, anyone owning just two hides was permitted to team up with another such person, or even a person with just one to his name; whichever of the pair was more suited to the task would then be fitted out for war service and dispatched to the army encampment on the Rhine. A similar procedure was to be followed for three people owning only one hide each, or five people farming half a hide of their own land; in both cases, only the single most suitable member of the group was required to report for military duty Even people with some money but no land had to get together with five others and decide which of them was to join the draft. Once more, it was the *missi* and the vassals they engaged who were responsible for implementing this program.[121] Over time, abuses of this system became apparent.

As a general rule, decisions on who was required to join the draft were made on a case-by-case basis; it was not uncommon, for instance, for several free men to be permitted to band together and equip just one of their number as a soldier.[122] In this way, Charlemagne attempted to mitigate the worst effects of the endless wars he engaged in. But what he achieved in this regard merely serves to point up the absence of any such relief measures during the reigns of his successors. Under them, the ongoing process of impoverishment and mediatization only gathered pace. Even before this took hold, though, there were the first stirrings of passive resistance. It came to

FIGURE 54 Calendar page from the Carolingian period, with symbolic depictions of the months of the year and the agricultural labors associated with them. The calendar, one of the oldest of its kind, was produced sometime in the ninth century in Salzburg, Austria. Vienna, Austrian National Library (Cod. 387, f. 90v).

Charlemagne's attention that men liable for military service were evading the draft by questioning the authority of bishops, abbots, or counts to issue the call-up order.[123] Some counts complained that the inhabitants of their county would simply refuse to obey the order; many of these men maintained that, as subjects of King Pepin or Louis, they were obliged only to serve them directly. Everyone, it seemed, had a different excuse. The boldest among them voiced their grievances directly, claiming that the magnates were extorting the property of the poor and oppressing them by constantly calling them up to the ranks until they were completely impoverished. Indeed, many contemporaries saw this unfair overburdening of the poor as a glaring injustice. As one example of abuse, bishops, abbots, counts, and abbesses would absolve those among their servants who went in fear of the *missi*—that is, falconers, hunters, tax collectors, provosts, deacons, and others—of their liability for military service, send them home, and in their place call the poor to arms. This exploitation had many faces, and the emperor did not recognize them all in good time.

In 807, the court assembly and synod convened in Ingelheim; no special capitulary seems to have been issued from there, but the general direction of policy to emerge from the meeting is clear nevertheless. Charlemagne ordered the assembled delegates—as the laconic note in the *Chronicon Moissiacense* states—"to ensure that justice was served in his realm." This demand was age old but extremely urgent all the same. Signs in the heavens at that time were said to portend God's wrath. The injunction to establish peace was, as it were, dictated from Heaven. The magnates should thank God for peace and unity.[124]

The following year, 808, saw Charles the Younger led his troops across the Elbe once more to attack the Slavs; he laid waste the region inhabited by the Linones tribe (around the town of Lenzen, in Brandenburg), but losses were heavy on both sides. At around the same time, "Northmen" (Danes) launched pillaging raids against the neighboring Obotrites. The Carolingians' prime concern was securing the border and defense, not conquest. Nor is there any firm evidence to suggest that they enslaved and traded unbaptized Slav prisoners of war, although it is perfectly possible that this did occur. The frontier fighting dragged on for years.

Those heavenly signs, however, drew people's gaze up to the starry firmament, including the emperor's. Einhard reported that Charlemagne loved astronomy and spent much time and labor studying this discipline: "He learned to reckon and used to investigate the motions of the heavenly bodies most curiously, with intelligent scrutiny" (chap. 25). An extraordinary abundance of works and documents on computistics that have survived from this period might serve to corroborate Einhard's claim if only they could be directly linked to the emperor.[125] Sadly, such a link can be demonstrated only in very few instances. To date, apart from one example I will presently discuss, no astronomical manuscripts have been identified that can be positively proved to have come from the court library. An anonymous author does appear, however, to have sent the emperor a treatise *On the Moon and Stars,* a work that describes the fourth day of the Creation. The writer of this work identified the "greater light" mentioned in Genesis 1:16 as being God's love for man, and the "lesser light" as our love for our fellow man; likewise, he associated the seven planets (including the sun and the moon) with the Christian virtues of faith, love, hope, wisdom, justice, courage, and moderation, which he in turn related to the eight beatitudes and thence finally—not without a touch of pagan astrology—to the ages of man.[126]

Also, a showpiece manuscript by the royal chaplain Archbishop Hildebald of Cologne, which still belongs to the library of Cologne Cathedral (Ms. 83 II), hints at how the Carolingian court conceived of Heaven and the cosmos. The courtiers' visual impressions of what Heaven looked like would have been gleaned from Latin authors of late antiquity, particularly Macrobius. The texts in this manuscript began with a chronicle, which can be passed over here,[127] before turning to mathematical-computistic excerpts from Isidore of Seville's *Etymologies* and providing in the form of a dialogue a textbook of computistics, which cited the most diverse texts by Greek, Latin, Irish, Anglo-Saxon, and Frankish authors. Hildebald's compendium then went on to give a concise history of the calculation of time, visualizing this discipline in thirteen diagrams, which through combinations of circles, triangles, and squares enabled scholars to work out such things as the age of the moon, the days of the week, the months, the summer and winter solstices, and the trajectory of planets, as well as offering visualizations of the macrocosm and the microcosm, the cosmos and the world, and solar eclipses and a catalog of constellations with forty-one miniatures of star signs. Finally, there was a transcription of Macrobius's *Saturnalia.* From an early stage, the influence of Irish scholars of computistics made itself felt in Cologne especially.[128]

To be sure, the *Royal Frankish Annals* for this period took note with a precision not seen hitherto of celestial phenomena that must have captivated the emperor's attention—this ruler who looked up to the skies to try to divine there heavenly blessing for what was taking place on Earth. Einhard (chap. 32) would later interpret these phenomena as omens portending the emperor's death. If we are to believe what the surviving records tell us, no specifically astrological expositions of the phenomena were given at the time; even so, the emperor might well have been familiar with such readings. Celestial signs were seen as a kind of heavenly handwriting foretelling the future.

On 2 September 806, the *Royal Frankish Annals* registered a lunar eclipse, recording in the process the precise positions of the sun and the moon; on 31 January 807, Jupiter appeared to cross the moon's path; on 11 February, "around midday" there followed a solar eclipse, while the sun and the moon were in the 24th part of Aquarius; the next lunar eclipse occurred on 26 March, as lines of battle appeared to be drawn up in the sky; the sun was in the 11th part of Pisces, and the moon in the 11th part of Virgo; Mercury appeared on 17 March as a small, black spot on the sun "that we observed for eight days"; on 21–22 August, at "the third hour of the night" (from 21:12 to 0:35 the next morning), the moon darkened once more; the sun was in the 5th part of Virgo and the moon in the 25th part of Pisces. "And so, over the course of the past year, the moon was eclipsed three times and the sun once," stated the *Annals*. This all augured no good, especially when, in 810 and 812, the sun and the moon were eclipsed again.[129] The heavens were speaking in signs to men—was it a threat? These "dangerous times" cried out for interpretation. Seven years later, albeit three days before 31 January, Charlemagne would die. Astronomy took center stage in the emperor's thirst for knowledge during these final years.

A number of unsettling questions obtruded: What is time, and how is it calculated? How might the calendar be organized? A kind of encyclopedia of computistics came into being. And what about the question of creation? And the solar and lunar eclipses? What was the substance of "nothingness" and "darkness"? Charlemagne posed this last question to his court scholars. The answer provided by the deacon Fredegisus of Tours, a former pupil of Alcuin, has survived; Charlemagne in turn is thought to have passed this on to the Irish scholar Dungal to solicit his opinion.[130] The emperor insisted that he not be given the kind of allegorical answers he had long been familiar with but rather "plain speaking, plain knowledge, plain meaning," as he wrote to Dungal. In other words, he was seeking a rational response, which, as it were, would avail itself of the recently introduced techniques of logical thinking. Did this urgency to know more reflect his innermost spiritual yearnings?

The Irishman's answer has been lost. But it is clear that Fredegisus's arguments were composed with the aid of Aristotle's doctrine of categories and propositions. In his work *De substantia nihili et tenebrarum* (*On the Substance of Nothingness and Darkness,* written ca. 800), he came to the conclusion that "nothingness is something great and remarkable, and its magnitude from which so many and such noble things have been produced (e.g., such creations as fire, water, earth, light, angels, and the soul) cannot be grasped. . . . Who could possibly hope to comprehend the substance and nature of such phenomena as light, angels, or the soul?" Yet, he stated, darkness definitely had a place and was spatial and corporeal.[131] It is questionable whether all of Fredegisus's readers could follow his explanations or understand his logical figures.[132] And what about nowadays? Some twelve hundred years after Charlemagne, the German philosopher Martin Heidegger taught that "the nothing negates." Charlemagne would not have been content with this explanation: the nothingness, the void from which everything ultimately sprang, must be "something."

Charlemagne demanded certainty, as evidenced by the works on the imperial calendar that had been produced at Lorsch, Trier, and Cologne since 789 and the *Encyclopedia of Computistics,* which was compiled from 809 onward. Calculations of the age of the world were also on the agenda. The answer was not without eschatological significance. Different answers resulted from the calculations made by the Jews (*Ebraica veritas*), the Septuagint, and the Vulgate of St. Jerome. Charlemagne's team of scholars—most likely led by Hildebald of Cologne, the owner of what still remains the most impressive testimony to the intensive calendrical and astronomical efforts taking place at the Carolingian court, namely, the Cologne manuscript 83 II—initially followed St. Jerome, while in Greek-speaking Byzantium the Septuagint was the preferred text; the Jews, meanwhile, followed their own set of figures. So what year was it, in fact? The principal objective of the calculation of calendrical time was to work out on what days the movable feast of Easter would fall each year. But this discipline was also concerned to try to determine the year when the world had been created, and even the day (a Sunday), and hence was also interested in Christ's lifespan and how many years had elapsed since His birth and therefore, by extension, when the world would end.

Scholars had concerned themselves with the interpretation and measurement of time and the demands that this made on the way Christians lived their lives since Christian late antiquity. In 725, the Venerable Bede had written a treatise concerning the use of the calendar (*De temporum ratione* [On the reckoning of time]), which through the Anglo-Saxon missionary St. Boniface became known to the Carolingian kingdom of the Franks and also, not least thanks to Alcuin, to Charlemagne's court. However, other scholarly opinions were also in circulation, resulting in a situation characterized by disagreement (and differing dates for Easter). Should one merely follow the Christian festivals over the course of the ecclesiastical year or the astronomical markers of time presented in the Julian calendar? And had scholars finally determined the difference between the astronomical and the calendrical start of spring? Charlemagne called for clarification and for an end to all the confusion.

As late as 798, the scholars at the Aix court were still reckoning on the impending year 800 as being the 6,000th year since the creation of the world. Thereafter, though, doubts began to creep in or be expressly raised. In 809, Charlemagne confronted his calendrical experts, whom he had invited to Aix, with a series of terse questions: How many years had elapsed between the birth of Christ and the current day? On what day of which month had Jesus been crucified? How many years had passed between the creation of the world and Christ's birth? When would the vernal equinox fall? And where was it written that Easter could not be celebrated before the spring equinox? And so his questioning continued, lighting on such matters as the age of the moon, the lunar year, and the solar year. The answers the scholars gave were brief and to the point.

Yet estimates of the age of the world still differed considerably.[133] For one East Frankish scholar, the sum of all the lifetimes given in the Bible up to the birth of Christ and from Christ up to the present day, the year 807, gave a total count of 4,759 years. Although they acknowledged the wide divergence that existed in estimates of the age of the world, the scholars who had been faced with Charlemagne's barrage of questions in 809 nevertheless opted—no doubt under the influence of Hildebald of Cologne—for a calculation according to "Hebrew wisdom."[134] One West Frankish author was even more explicit; his calculations, from the time of Adam up to the current year 809, yielded a total of 6,008 years according to Western calendrical reckoning but only 4,762 by the Jewish method. The encyclopedia of 809, relying on the count "according to Hebrew wisdom," decided on a figure of 4,761 years.[135] This final calculation was the one that went on to gain widespread acceptance. In other words, it was thought that there was still a long time to go until the critical year 6000. But all the same, could one be entirely sure?

The calendar that came into existence within the sphere of the Carolingian court responded to these debates; in terms of its intention, its structure, and its success, it may be regarded as archetypal for calendars right up to the present day. With various changes, it remained in use for many centuries. It combined the (Julian) solar cycle with the (Metonic) lunar cycle and the Christian church year with the martyrology. In the sequence of the church year, it added Bible verses at the beginning of every month, gave the hours of light and darkness, the dominical letters and corresponding names of the weekdays, and the Roman count of the days according to the fixed points of the kalends, nones, and ides, named the saints associated with each day in a hierarchy that placed martyrs above confessors and virgins above widows, cited other days of remembrance such as 2 April (as shown in a manuscript from the time of Charlemagne: "Birth of our glorious Lord Charles, emperor and *Augustus* for all time"),[136] and indicated the sun's circuit of the zodiac and the range of the solstices and equinoxes. Therefore, the calendar served as a martyrology and a remembrance book and combined computistic science with expectations for the future, the yearning for salvation, and the certainty of redemption. Although no one could be certain when the End of Days would come, the age of the world and his own advancing years were bearing down on Charlemagne and demanding that he take action geared toward the end times.

The encyclopedia of computistics was completed at exactly the same time as the synod held in Aix in 809, which—for one final time in Charlemagne's reign—clashed with the Byzantines and Pope Leo III over the matter of the *filioque*.[137] The new controversy was triggered by an argument that had broken out between Greek and Latin monks in Jerusalem over the creed.[138] The Western guardians of the faith perceived a heretical threat in the missing *filioque* in the Orthodox creed. They reported this to their emperor, who immediately intervened in the controversy. Once more, he ordered his leading theologians—Adalwin of Regensburg, Arn of Salzburg, the Jerusalem expert Heito of Basel, and Theodulf of Orléans—to prepare reports, convened the aforementioned synod in Aix, and, primarily on the basis of Arn's collation of authoritative statements, wrote to the pope, urging him to include the *filioque* in the creed and to intone the amended version during Holy Mass.

After a lengthy dispute with Charlemagne's envoys in Rome—Bishops Bernar of Worms and Jesse of Amiens, together with Abbot Adalhard of Corbie—Leo refused the emperor's request. Without having any fundamental theological differences with the Franks, he was defending one last bastion against the all-powerful Caesar, namely, the Church's ecumenical unity with the Greeks in the matter of confessional formulas.[139] He had the Roman (and Byzantine) version of the Apostolic Creed (*Symbolum apos-*

tolicum) engraved in silver letters on tablets in both Latin and Greek and displayed prominently in St. Peter's, visible to every pilgrim to Rome as a clear statement of intent; when the tablets were subsequently moved, the Latin version at least found its way to the Basilica of St. Paul outside the Walls.[140]

What were the emperor's motivations? The year 6000 seemed to have been deferred for the present; yet his envoys reminded the pope about the impending End of Days. The calendrical calculations of the *computus* offered no unequivocal answer. So henceforth it would still be vital to be on one's guard: "For the end of the world is nigh. . . . The times are growing dangerous."[141] The End of Days was casting its shadow. Questions of faith above all called for consensus and unity among Christians. Charlemagne did his utmost to bring this about. He did not want to meet his maker and judge empty-handed.

In a letter to Archbishop Magnus of Sens, Charlemagne's close confidant and adviser Theodulf of Orléans wrote that it was his emperor's intention to urge "the bishops to study the Holy Scriptures and to spread a healthy and sober doctrine; the clergy to act in a disciplined way; the learned to an understanding of divine and human affairs; monks to pious observance of religion; the populace in general to holiness; noblemen to good counsel [*consilium*]; judges to dispense justice; soldiers to acquire experience in arms; magnates to act with humility; subjects to obedience; and all in general to prudence, justice, fortitude, temperance, and peace and concord. In this way, this best of all men ceaselessly exalts and intensifies the holy Christian faith; in his remarkable stewardship of both the Church and the state, this most capable of leaders draws from the wellspring of wisdom and achieves his objectives through his patent virtue."[142] This, then, was how the emperor's followers regarded his rule—without any flattering oration, without any flourishes of panegyrical rhetoric, but instead just matter-of-fact and all the more impressive for it: the cardinal virtues as a yardstick for the education of the people. Was this, then, an accurate interpretation of the measure of the emperor's soul?

A Late Peace Agreement with Byzantium

Charlemagne's ceaseless concern for the holy Christian faith and its unity and peace also included believers who lived beyond the frontiers of his realm, especially in the Eastern Roman Empire. The earlier point of contention, namely, the iconoclastic controversy, and the current one concerning the *filioque,* most likely at first lay dormant after Hadrian I and Leo III, respectively, issued their judgments, and despite the fact that for Charlemagne himself, the orthodoxy of the Greeks must have appeared extremely doubtful. But how would the Byzantines now deal with the question of Charlemagne's status as emperor, an issue that had thwarted peace the last time it was discussed? Lasting peace depended on the answer to this question; it would be many years in coming.

The new peace initiative was instigated by Eastern Rome. The *Royal Frankish Annals* initially had nothing to report about Byzantium after 803, but the situation changed suddenly in 805. In December of that year, the doges Willerus and Beatus from Venice, together with Duke Paulus and Bishop Donatus of Zadar (in Croatia), appeared at the Aix court, "whereupon the emperor issued an ordinance concerning the doges and people of Venice and Dalmatia" (*Royal Frankish Annals* for 806); its content is unknown. But both of these regions belonged to the Byzantine Empire. It was quite clearly evident that Charlemagne was seeking to extend his influence over Byzantine territory. He was risking war, and the *basileus,* Nicephorus, responded instantly to this aggression by dispatching a fleet "to retake Dalmatia." Although the prefect in command of this flotilla agreed to a temporary cease-fire with King Pepin of Italy, he promptly sailed back to Constantinople. And so the situation remained in limbo.

Three years later, the Greek fleet reappeared in the northern Adriatic Sea, and an engagement was fought at Comacchio. The Byzantine ships were forced to withdraw to Venice, but the city's doges covertly thwarted negotiations between the prefect of the fleet, Paulos, and Pepin (*Annals* for 809). In 810, the Italian king saw through the Venetians' machinations and overran the city, while the Greek fleet was able only to protect Dalmatia. This was how things stood when the *basileus* put out new peace feelers to the West.

Nicephorus had many enemies within his own country. A looming four-pronged threat to his rule, from internal attempts to usurp him, from the Bulgars in the north, from the Muslims in the south, and now from the Franks in the West—possibly exacerbated by the straitened financial situation of the empire—drove the *basileus* to a change of policy toward the Franks. Might it have been around this time that the phrase "Have the Frank for your friend but not for your neighbor" gained widespread currency? In any event, the *basileus* was looking to reach a settlement with the Latin Christians and was hopeful of signing a peace treaty. This meant that he had to resolve the question of recognizing Charlemagne's emperorship.

As a consequence, envoys were dispatched back and forth between the courts. From the Frankish side, Bishop Heito of Basel and Count Hugo of Tours hastened to Constantinople to settle the diplomatic formalities. Charlemagne was prepared to renounce any claim on Venice (*Annals* for 810). Like Charlemagne's envoys to Empress Irene in 802, Heito and Hugo reached Byzantium just too late and found themselves being kept waiting for months: in October 811, Nicephorus had been killed in battle against Krum the Fearsome, khan of the Bulgars, in one of the heaviest defeats ever suffered by the Byzantines. "Many became widows and orphans on that single day," lamented Theophanes in one of his last entries in his *Chronicle* (AM 6303).

Nicephorus's son and co-emperor, Staurakios, who was himself severely wounded in the battle, was able to cling to power for only a few months. His opponents proclaimed his brother-in-law Michael emperor. Despite being "pious and orthodox," however, he was not fated to have a long reign either. As the *Royal Frankish Annals* for 812 noted, "He received the legates of Emperor Charles and then promptly dismissed them" in order to accompany his own envoys to the Frankish court. Their brief was to confirm the peace agreement that Nicephorus had concluded (*Annals* for 812).

Michael recognized Charlemagne as "emperor and *basileus.*" The Frankish ruler sent Amalhar of Trier and Abbot Petrus of Nonantola to convey his answer to his "sacred brother" on the Bosphorus; by calling him "brother" and giving him his correct title—*imperator et augustus*—Charlemagne was emphasizing that he had the same rank as Michael. His letter to Constantinople went on to announce that he, Charlemagne, gave thanks to Jesus Christ and asked Him to give His blessing to their endeavor to secure a long-sought-after and fervently wished-for peace between the Eastern and Western empires and to unify and bring peace to the holy, Catholic, and immaculate Church.[143]

The patriarch of Constantinople and the pope also corresponded with each other at this time—an easier task, since there was no rift between them.[144] Events in Constantinople than began to develop with breakneck speed. Charlemagne's legates were once again witnesses to the toppling of a ruler. Michael was forced to enter a monastery, and although his successor, Leon, was also ready to make peace, he demanded that a new legation be sent to Byzantium bearing a draft treaty made out in his name rather than in Michael's. Consequently, envoys rushed hither and thither. This delay meant that Charlemagne never got to see the peace deal that was eventually agreed after four years of negotiations; instead, it fell like a ripe fruit into the hands of Louis the Pious (*Annals* for 813–814).

Many malicious stories were put about concerning these peace delegations. These served only to illustrate the willful blindness of the Franks to the desperate situation in Byzantium. After all, two or three changes of leader had happened right under the noses, so to speak, of the Latin West's legates in Constantinople; moreover, all these coups brought considerable upheaval and were staged against the backdrop of dire external threats facing New Rome. Rumors circulated about the disrespectfully shabby and cold reception the Frankish envoys had supposedly received in Constantinople. It was said that the Franks had then, in revenge, led the Byzantine mission to Aix across the Alps over some almost impassable terrain until they were on the verge of exhaustion, only to finally deliver them to the court at Aix, where they were subjected to a vindictively magnificent display of pomp and power by Charlemagne. They were said to have prostrated themselves before the wrong person three times before the emperor finally made himself known to them. Rumors such as these circulated in the Monastery of St. Gall. Might Bishop Heito himself, one of the envoys in 811 and the abbot of the monastery, have been responsible for starting them? That seems highly doubtful. The Franks had never realized what a great debt they owed to the Bulgars in the great power game between empires, or to the Byzantine Greeks in their fending off the Arabs; what is more, in the absence of such an overview of the whole geopolitical picture, when Notker of St. Gall wrote his *Gesta Karoli* (the text that contains these scurrilous stories),[145] he may well have misconstrued and misrepresented the traditional diplomatic protocol of the Rhomaioi. The threefold "proskynesis" would have been wholly out of place at the Frankish court but was the customary diplomatic mark of respect in Byzantium.

Notwithstanding all the diplomatic tensions that existed between them, a lively intellectual exchange had been going on between Byzantium and the kingdom of the Franks for some while and most likely intensified at this time. In the first instance, only scattered and isolated traces of this can be identified. For example, Notker of St. Gall mentions that various Greek instruments were sent as gifts to Charlemagne, including a water organ, which generated air through a system of metal containers, bellows made of cowhide, and iron organ pipes and was capable of producing a rumble like thunder, followed by a sound that mimicked the gentleness of a lyre and then the sweet sound of cymbals. According to the Swiss monk, Charlemagne had his craftsmen copy and reproduce this mechanism.[146] Scholars have also remarked on the likely influence of the Carolingian minuscule on the Greek minuscule calligraphic system that now began to come into use among Byzantine cultural circles.[147] There would have been a great deal of give-and-take on both sides.

The End Is Nigh

Perilous times now loomed, calling for the utmost circumspection. The peace with Byzantium could scarcely mask the impending dangers. Indeed, the year 810 was seared on the memory of those who experienced it as an *annus horribilis*.[148] The military campaign against the Danes, over which Charlemagne had assumed personal command, ended in fiasco. Charlemagne must have seen this as a warning sign. As an indication that God wanted to punish him, it happened in the heart of Saxony, precisely at the same spot where, almost thirty years earlier, Charlemagne was rumored to have executed 4,500 Saxons, at Verden on the river Aller.[149] Even worse, the warning was unmistakably directed at the emperor himself. Charlemagne realized this only too well.

He had slept badly the night before the incident. Were the dead rising from their graves? Were they seeking revenge? And had not the year already begun badly when his sister Gisela, the ever-loyal abbess of Chelles and of the Abbey of Our Lady at Soissons, was laid to rest? And as the year progressed, the emperor was to learn in quick succession of the death of his beloved daughter Rotrude (6 June) and his son Pepin, the very able king of Italy (8 July), who had been his loyal regent in the south and had scored a courageous victory over the Avars. Charlemagne was also informed of the death of the precious elephant given to him by the king of the Persians. Greatly disquieted, the emperor had risen before dawn, left his tent, ordered his horse to be saddled up, and set off across the fields in this utterly flat landscape.

All of a sudden, just before sunrise, a blinding beam of light shot across a cloudless sky like a bolt of lightning. It traveled from right to left. It caused his horse to tumble head over heels, Charlemagne was later to report. The emperor was found prostrate on the ground with his sword belt torn off and the clasp holding his cloak broken in two. The stricken Charlemagne was carried back to the camp. The javelin he had been carrying was found more than twenty feet from where he had fallen. Looking back in his biography, Einhard interpreted the entire incident as an omen of the emperor's impending death and maintained that Charlemagne also construed it as such (chap. 32). This may indeed have been the case; was this perhaps why he was so keen to conclude a peace treaty with the Greeks?

A few months after this dreadful warning sign, Charlemagne divided up his personal estates among his heirs.[150] Neither he himself nor Einhard, the only person to record the wording of the relevant decree (chap. 33), called the document in question a "last will and testament"—in marked contrast to the "Divisio regnorum" of 806. Rather, it was a record, a disposition of his wealth; it referred to Charlemagne in the third person. First and foremost, the churches and particularly the poor were endowed with alms; his children would know what was required of him after his death, but the priests to whom he was now giving donations should pray for his soul.

Two-thirds of the gold, silver, precious stones, and royal ornaments he had amassed was to be split into equal parts and distributed to twenty-one archdioceses (or "metropolitan cities"), which he listed by name: Rome, Ravenna, Milan, Friuli, Grado, Cologne, Mayence (Mainz), Salzburg, Treves, Sens, Besançon, Lyons, Rouen, Reims, Arles, Vienne, Moutiers-en-Tarantaise, Embrun, Bordeaux, Tours, and Bourges. These cities, in turn, were to pass on two-thirds of what they had been given to their suffragan bishops. In this way, each diocese received something. In return, no doubt, all the bishops would have been expected to remember their benefactor in their prayers. The remaining third of Charlemagne's treasure, which included all iron goods such as weapons, along with clothes, blankets, saddles, and the most valuable artifacts produced by the painstaking handicraft skills of maids and servants, was not to be touched until after his death, whereupon it was to be divided into four parts. One quarter was to be given to the metropolitan cities once more for them to redistribute, another to Charlemagne's sons and daughters, and another to the poor, while the final quarter of these goods was to be gifted to the menservants and maidservants of the royal palace. The furnishings of the royal chapel were to remain entire and in situ, but Charlemagne's valuable collection of books was to be sold and the funds thus raised distributed to the poor and needy.

Specific mention was made of three silver tables and one of gold. The silver square table "with a representation of Constantinople" was to be donated to St. Peter's Basilica in Rome, and the round silver table engraved "with a picture of the city of Rome" was to be handed over to the Episcopal Church (*Episcopium*) in Ravenna, while the third silver table, which far surpassed the other two in weight and in beauty of workmanship and was decorated "with a plan of the entire universe," was, along with the fourth, golden table, to be added to the share devoted to Charlemagne's heirs and to alms. The aesthetic quality of these artifacts was of no interest here, merely the material value of the precious metals they were made of. It appears that the way in which this part of emperor's estate was divided was quite deliberate. St. Peter, as it were, took Constantinople, while Ravenna, in all likelihood, rather than feel itself reminded by the donation of its affiliation to Rome, must have considered itself compensated to some degree for what the new Roman Caesar Charlemagne had earlier despoiled it of. Charlemagne's heirs and the poor, meanwhile, would be referred to the wider world.

The document (*constitutio atque ordinatio*) was signed by six archbishops (headed by Hildebald of Cologne), five bishops (led by Theodulf of Orléans), four abbots (Fredegisus of Tours was the first of these to be mentioned, with Charlemagne's quasi-son-in-law Angilbert third), and fifteen counts (with Charlemagne's cousin Wala first and Richwin of Padua—the father of another [illegitimate] grandson of the emperor through his liaison with Charlemagne's daughter Hiltrude—also among them). This made thirty witnesses in total, an impressive collection of people; yet Charlemagne's own signature was missing. Einhard (chap. 33) maintained that it had been his intention to make a will, but that it was begun too late and could not be finished. This remark tells us a lot about the leisurely nature of the exercise of rule at that time, in an age of orality and testimonial evidence with no secretarial services or chancery clerks. Louis the Pious took pains to faithfully fulfill all the conditions of this document after his father's death.

It may possibly have been an epileptic fit that caused Charlemagne to fall from his horse and impelled him to divide up his property. We cannot know for sure.[151] Yet so far as we can tell, after his fall Charlemagne left the palace at Aix on only two further occasions, the first time in 811 for a tour of inspection of the coastal defenses against the Danes at Boulogne and Ghent and the mouths of the rivers Seine and Scheldt, and the second occasion to go hunting for one last time in the nearby Ardennes. But while he was out hunting, "a severe pain in his legs" struck him down again (*Royal Frankish Archives*). Einhard also reports that during the four years before his death, in other words, including the time of his fall from his horse at Verden, "he was subject to frequent fevers; at the last he even limped a little with one foot" (chap. 22).

The great man's old age was plagued with suffering. It was not long before Charlemagne's two eldest sons, Pepin the Hunchback, who had been banished to the monastery at Prüm, and Charles the Younger, also went to their graves. Since his fall, and especially after the death of Charles the Younger (4 December 811), pronouncements of concern regarding the plight of the Church and the people of the realm greatly increased; they might almost be called sermons in the form of capitularies. Was it Charlemagne who was still issuing these? Great hopes had been invested in the forthcoming reform of the empire; never before, while the incumbent monarch was still alive, had the succession been arranged in such a timely fashion. But now all the carefully laid plans were in ruins. Charlemagne was reportedly unable to hold back his tears at the death of his sons and daughters. He cried as a father who had lost his children, and as a ruler who had lost his successor. It was there for all to see that he was imbued not with stoical composure but rather with Christian love, Einhard noted (chap. 19). All too soon, cares were to come knocking at the doors of his palace.

All his former plans were now null and void. Once he had regained his senses, Charlemagne must have been deeply shocked at what had occurred. Had he somehow incurred God's wrath? The emperor and his followers feared the worst. Almost prophetically, they could see this latter-day Caesar's works crumbling under the sheer weight of human sin, insatiable greed, and the "lust" for wealth, power, and dominion of the last of his sons who was entitled to inherit, Louis the Pious, and the aristocratic clique of friends with whom he had surrounded himself. They would presently come to savor their undeserved victory over those magnates who had formerly pledged allegiance to his brothers.

Yet hadn't King Pepin of Italy left behind a son, named Bernard? In defiance of all the tenets of Frankish law, which stated that a grandson should be passed over for inheritance if his father should predecease him before becoming emperor, Charlemagne now took a special interest in promoting the case of this young man, perhaps at the urging of his cousins Adalhard and Wala. The thirteen-year-old Bernard and his sisters were brought to the court at Aix and raised there. Yet this move of Charlemagne's could do little to delay the impending calamity for long. Many of the emperor's closest advisers, doubtless for a variety of different reasons, shared his concerns and sought to fend off the looming chaos they dreaded.

One of these was the emperor's cousin Adalhard of Corbie, another Adalhard's younger brother, Count Wala. Neither of these men was a friend of Louis. Quite the opposite; the two cousins had been advisers to Pepin of Italy and his son Bernard; furthermore, Adalhard had fallen out irreconcilably with Louis the Pious's spiritual counselor Benedict of Aniane,[152] the son of a Visigothic count. The conflict between them was irreparable and lasted into the early years of Louis's reign, until Benedict's death in 821. Their subsequent fate and actions confirmed Charlemagne's fear while also—posthumously—giving us an insight into the wide-ranging plans of the great ruler. A third opponent of Louis may have been Theodulf of Orléans, the eminent theologian, who, having no power base within the ruling family and palace and having relied solely on his great talents, was likewise sent into exile soon after Charlemagne's death. Hildebald of Cologne, who for twenty years had been archchaplain at Charlemagne's court, was stripped of this powerful role and sent back to live the rest of his life in his metropolitan city. New faces now determined the political climate at the court. It is true that Einhard weathered the change of leadership unscathed; he did not reveal how he managed this.

The reforming zeal of the aging emperor and his advisers took on even greater urgency than ever before during the final years of his life. Roman authority, Anglo-Saxon and Visigothic learning, and his own studies of Frankish history and tradition had all fed into his ideas of reform, but their realization had proceeded at a snail's pace. Time was ebbing away for Charlemagne. Many things had not turned out the way he planned. What was to be done? The clerics who were summoned to attend the court assembly at Aix in June 811 found themselves facing a barrage of embarrassing questions and demands.[153]

The bishops and abbots were quizzed separately from the counts: Why, the emperor wanted to know, was none of them prepared to help the other either at home or in wartime? Why did they engage in endless bickering, with one nobleman jealously reproaching another of the same rank in regard to his lands and possessions? And why did they take in the bondsmen of others who had run away from their masters? He also wanted to know in which districts clerics and laypeople were deliberately placing obstacles in each other's way. The bishops were subjected to the most searching interrogation; they were asked whether they knew the meaning of the apostle St. Paul's injunction: "No one serving as a soldier [of Jesus Christ] should get involved in worldly affairs" (2 Timothy 2:4); no one, they were informed, who imagined that he had the right to transgress God's commandments with impunity could possibly be a true believer. "We must take a long, hard look at ourselves and ask whether we are true Christians," Charlemagne admonished them. How could they live as canons and still behave in the way they did? For instance, could a person be a monk without following the *Benedictine Rule?*

This was anything but ironic theatricality;[154] it was an expression of deep concern over the effectiveness of Christian teaching in the empire and the Church. The emperor did not exempt himself from this intensive soul-searching: "*We* must take a long, hard look." Hardship was on the increase, and only God could help. Charlemagne turned repeatedly to Him. Fasting throughout the realm, chanting long litanies, and prayer would, on the one hand, promote peace and, on the other, help fend off such evils as famine, storms, plagues, and enemy attacks. For instance, some years earlier he had issued an implementation order to Bishop Ghaerbald of Liège, instructing him on the timing and the practicalities of how to conduct a series of three three-day fasts. "We all," "Every one of us," the emperor wrote at the time, should take part, proceed to our nearest church to the sound of the litany chant, pray there before returning home and fasting there in the prescribed manner, abase ourselves in contrition for our sins, lament over our transgressions, give alms, and beseech the Lord to have mercy on us.[155] Similar acts of contrition may well have been organized in 810, when the many portents of ill omen heralded impending doom. "We must mend our ways!" may have been the watchword, but in what regard?[156]

"Have the priests and the bishops failed, or have we failed?" Charlemagne must have asked himself. The inquisition of the bishops and abbots continued.[157] They were required to disclose the manner in which they lived, in order that the emperor might determine which aspects of their lifestyle were good and which should be curbed, ascertain to what extent they were mixed up in worldly affairs, and inquire what their true role was, these men who were supposed to be "shepherds of the Church and fathers of the monasteries." These churchmen (*ecclesiastici*) were to be quizzed on whom they imagined St. Paul was addressing when he said, "Be ye followers of me" (1 Corinthians 11:1), and to whom he was referring with his edict "No one serving as a soldier should get involved in worldly affairs." How, then, might one best emulate the apostle and best serve God? And what did the exhortation to "leave behind worldly things" really mean? And could someone who kept amassing more possessions really be said to have left behind worldly things, someone who commended some of his flock to heavenly bliss and threatened others with eternal damnation, but who in both cases was just out to swindle them, rich and poor alike, out of their property? One churchman might be striving to be like St. Paul, while another was busy perjuring himself out of sheer greed. And what was to be said about those who, under the pretense of love for God and the saints, transferred relics, built new churches, and persuaded anyone who would listen to them to make generous endowments? And so it went on—a persistent and pitiless exposé of the practice of greed in the name of religion and the Church.

In what canon, in what set of rules laid down by the Church Fathers was it written, Charlemagne wanted to know, that a person could be tonsured and confined to a monastery against his will? And according to what monastic rule had monks lived before St. Benedict? After all, St. Martin of Tours, who lived over a century before Benedict, had also been a monk and had attracted others to the monastic life. "Because we are called on to follow Christ, the apostles, and their followers, we must in many respects act differently from the way we have done hitherto, and in many regards clean up our habits [*usus*] and customs, something we have omitted to do before now." With these words, Charlemagne ended his address to the assembled clergy.[158] The emperor then left them with this hopeful message: "Be sure to act in a way that befits your office. I place my trust in you, my lord bishops. . . . Farewell, then, in Christ!"[159]

However much Charlemagne may have gained amusement from the deadly rivalry among his courtiers during the early years of his reign, this competitiveness now increasingly alarmed him. He intervened to try to stop it as best he could. He listened carefully to the news and reports submitted by his *missi*. In all likelihood, he gathered them in, scrutinized them, and compared them with one another, looking for signs of change, improvement, or deterioration, and then took the appropriate steps. Peace was what was called for, not conflict, dissent, or enmity, but genuine "love." His worries only increased.

Lately, over forty "Spaniards . . . who trusting in Charlemagne had emigrated from Spain" had brought legal action against the counts who controlled the Pyrenean region. Accordingly, via the archbishop of Arles, Charlemagne summoned eight of their number, headed by Bera of Barcelona, to the court of Louis the Pious to report on and explain their actions. These noblemen were accused of having robbed the "Spaniards" of property granted to them by the king decades before; their intention was to unlawfully expel the rightful owners from their lands, install their own bondsmen there, and then burden them with impossibly high taxes. These noblemen had clearly enriched themselves at the expense of the king's vassals; this rivalry was to cease forthwith. Charlemagne demanded restitution from the counts for the people they had oppressed "if you wish to be party to God's grace and Our favor."[160]

The emperor and his followers attempted with ever-greater urgency to root out discord, injustice, and the bullying of the poor. A late capitulary addresses this subject.[161] Trials and disputes dating from the period of his reign were to be discussed and brought to a conclusion by a reasoned judgment; older disagreements were either to be dropped or submitted to the emperor to investigate and resolve at his discretion (chap. 1). Bishops,

abbots, counts, and other magnates who were at loggerheads with one another and refused to reach a peaceful settlement should appear before the
emperor and no one else and refrain from any exploitation of the poor;
even counts palatinate should not become involved in judging such cases
without the express command of the emperor (chap. 2). Only witnesses of
unimpeachable repute, not swindlers, were to be admitted to give evidence
(chap. 3).

The *missi* were instructed to carefully examine and then record in writing
exactly how much property held in fee (*beneficia*) each person had (this included each and every bishop, abbot, abbess, count, or king's vassal in the
realm, as well as the free men living on their lands) and how economically
burdened these fiefs were, or whether a person had used them to acquire his
own property (*allodia;* chaps. 5–6). The *missi* were to perform these duties
for four months of every year and hold four court sessions every month
(chap. 8). All the taxes and the fines paid by criminals for obtaining pardon
(*freda*) that the envoys collected were to be meticulously recorded and reported to the emperor in order to obtain instructions on what use they
should put these revenues to (chap. 10). The oath of loyalty to the emperor
was to be demanded repeatedly (chap. 13). With the passage of the years
and with the growing reliability of dialectic-analytical education, Charlemagne's insight into the competition-driven nobility of his age had grown
more acute. He could now all the more clearly see through the excesses of
this society, which continued to give him cause for great concern, now more
than ever, and which he was determined to counteract. Yet how could he
change it and in what way? How could he improve it?

Year after year, mindful of the looming end times, Charlemagne (or whoever was advising him at the time) renewed and extended the fiats aimed at
establishing peace. The capitularies that have survived from this time bear
witness to this. Over and over again, Charlemagne's call for peace rang out:
"May peace reign, along with unity and unanimity among all Christian
people, especially men of the cloth, whose sacred example should show
others the way to Heaven!" The emperor was tireless in spreading this message; the *Admonitio generalis* of 789 was not forgotten and was often
quoted in these late capitularies.[162] Was it the case that the court clergy, with
Archbishop Hildebald of Cologne at their head, increasingly guided the
hand of the aging, ailing emperor? Certainly, it must be said that these late
capitularies lapsed increasingly into a sermonizing tone. Above all, members
of the priesthood were exhorted to be of one mind, for the faith was the

way for everyone to attain heavenly bliss, and if it was to be proclaimed effectively, peace and unity were called for. In the absence of peace, no one could serve God in a fitting way or hope to find mercy (*misericordia*) in this world or the hereafter.

In turn, peace and unity sprang from the love of God. And who could teach what he himself had no knowledge of? Who could be a shepherd who did not understand how to tend his flock with the message of salvation? All persons should discover within themselves, in their innermost souls, not in their miserable corporeal being, the likeness of the Trinity: "For as long as he inhabits this physical world, there is nothing more urgent for a person to acknowledge than God and his own soul, for if he acknowledges God, then he has the capacity for love, and if he recognizes that he is created in the image of God, he will cherish his soul all the more dearly." "We exhort and admonish Christ's flock, who have been entrusted to our care, that they should learn and do everything that is necessary for their eternal salvation and shun everything that the Devil provides for their damnation"[163]—the measure of the soul of each and every individual.

The emperor's solicitude was not in vain. The Church was considerably shored up and strengthened in its cultural work. It was around this time, or possibly soon after, that Archbishop Leidrad of Lyons, who was originally a Bavarian, sent the emperor a report on how successfully he had discharged his duties; he had been in his post since 798. Leidrad noted that he had summoned a liturgist from Metz to Lyons so that he might establish a *schola cantorum* there according to the rite practiced at the "sacred palace"; so successful was this, apparently, that most of its choristers were now able to teach others. He had also overseen the training of lectors, who could now give lucid exegeses of the Holy Scriptures, while some of them were even capable of interpreting the spiritual meaning of the Gospels, the Acts of the Apostles, the majority of the prophets, the books of Solomon, the Psalms, and the book of Job. Churches and monasteries within his archdiocese and the city had been restored or built from scratch. Well may Leidrad have exuded self-confidence in giving his report to the emperor. His signal achievements illustrate the outstanding practical successes that the program of renewal that Charlemagne had promoted and overseen in the liturgy, in book production and the churches, and in education and training as a whole could now point to.[164] A proud catalog of success indeed—and a remarkable document of the cultural privations of that period, which Charlemagne was determined to confront with all the powers at his disposal.

Organizing the Succession Revisited

After the provisions he had made for his succession in 800 and 806, Charlemagne now put his house in order for a third time, a house inhabited by his youngest sons, who had barely come of age, his daughters, and the grandsons whom they and their brother Pepin had given him. He did this principally out of concern for his fatherless grandson Bernard. Bernard was a Carolingian on both his mother's and his father's side; his mother is thought to have been Theodrada, a young first cousin of Charlemagne's, the sister of Adalhard of Corbie and his brother Wala.[165] Her marriage to Pepin took place in 796. "Rejoice in the wife of your youth," Alcuin told Pepin when he became a father, quoting the Proverbs of Solomon (5:18), warning him at the same time "not to consort with other women" (cf. 5:17) and to "be chaste."[166] Alcuin regarded the union of Pepin and Theodrada as being blessed by God and wished them many offspring. His wish was duly fulfilled. Pepin's grandsons and great-grandsons survived in the male bloodline to the end of the eleventh century, longer than all the other agnatic Carolingians.[167]

Pepin's marriage lasted for fourteen years and produced six children. The term that the Anglo-Saxon scholar Alcuin used to refer to the king's wife—*mulier*—had a biblical ring to it. Theodrada was the consort whom both God and Charlemagne had ordained for Pepin—like Rebekah and Isaac in the Old Testament—and moreover, she came from the same clan as he (*cognatio*) and was a blood relation of his father (*ad propinquos*) and the daughter of his father's brother. Yet although the relationship between Pepin and his wife was just one or two intermediate stages away from being incestuous, it was actually not so close as to be a problem. Posthumously, Pepin's brother Louis the Pious, who became emperor, deemed this marriage illegitimate and declared it to be concubinage.[168]

Charlemagne cared for Bernard and his sisters in a very special way. He was aware of the tensions among various aristocratic groups around his younger sons. The emperor no doubt recalled the fate of his cousins, the sons of his uncle Grifo, who, after their father was killed in battle, were forcibly consigned to a monastery by Charlemagne's father, Pepin the Short. He also must also have been mindful of his own nephews, whom he had excluded and disinherited. Charlemagne wanted to prevent Bernard from suffering the same fate. Accordingly, after Pepin's untimely death in 810, the emperor went to extraordinary lengths to protect his only son, Bernard, just as previously he had cared for Pepin's widow, Theodrada, by making her abbess of the convent of Notre-Dame-de-Soissons.[169] For the time being, at least, Louis had no option but to put on a brave face concerning this matter.

The emperor was guided in his actions by a sense of familial love that defied the secular inheritance law of the Franks. This excluded the son of a father who died while the grandfather was still alive from the inheritance. Charlemagne responded by endowing his orphaned grandson with the most valuable part of his father's realm, namely, Italy. This was an act of extraordinary piety (*pietas*). The boy's uncles Abbot Adalhard of Corbie and Count Palatine Wala supported the emperor in his departure from tradition. These two men conducted the negotiations on behalf of Bernard to settle the question of the future division of sovereignty with the representatives of Louis the Pious. Even this division gave cause for concern over the maintenance of peace. Monks throughout the country were asked to remember the representatives of both sides in their prayers; we know this thanks to an entry to this effect in the "fraternity book" (monastery register) of St. Gall in Switzerland.

Finally, in 812 Adalhard escorted the young king to Italy and arranged his betrothal there. Meanwhile, Charlemagne had Bernard's sisters brought to his court at Aix, where they were raised alongside his own youngest daughters. At least one portrait of Bernard as king of Italy has, it seems, been preserved. It forms the frontispiece of a legal manuscript that is now housed at the Abbey of St. Paul in Lavanttal, in the southern Austrian state of Carinthia.[170] It shows the young king in 812, without a crown but holding a scepter and poised to eradicate the "vices" of the Church—in other words, depicting him, like his grandfather Charlemagne, as a great defender of the faith. The symbolic content of the image may refer to educational principles practiced at the courts of Charlemagne and Pepin of Italy.

The following year, Charlemagne summoned his son Louis, the king of Aquitaine, to Aix. There, in September and with the support of the magnates, Louis was made co-emperor, while his nephew Bernard's position as king of Italy was acknowledged in an oath sworn by the newly promoted joint ruler.[171] Just a few months later, the great emperor was dead, and Louis straight away began to plot the overthrow of the sworn order and hence the undoing of every measure his father had instituted for the preservation of peace. The clarion calls for peace that had echoed in the court assemblies of Charlemagne's later years had faded away and were henceforth heard no more. The former advisers of the deceased emperor—Adalhard, Wala, Theodulf of Orléans, and others—were sent into exile. Louis, who had been favored by fortune, now deliberately suborned the magnates to break their oath. His royal nephew Bernard was deposed and blinded and died of his injuries. But Louis's position of absolute power in the realm as emperor did not go unchallenged for long. The very disaster that Charlemagne, over-burdened by his struggle to steer the ship of state, had sought to avert now immediately materialized under his successor.

Louis fell prey to warring aristocratic factions. The emperor's second marriage and the death of Benedict of Aniane plunged the court into a state of disarray. Aix now witnessed the return of a "titan," as Louis was forced to rehabilitate his uncle Adalhard. This was the assessment of Adalhard's biographer Paschasius Radbertus, who went on to relate that the "sheer madness" that had been simmering beneath the surface of Louis's court now erupted into full view. The question began to be asked: "Who induced the people's senate to make such a foolish decision [i.e., to confirm Louis's investiture]?"[172] Radbertus, who recorded this, was a monk at Corbie Abbey, where Adalhard was now also reinstated as abbot; he wrote his *Life of St. Adalhard* immediately after his death in 826 and completed it by 828—not only, therefore, daring to air such views while Louis the Pious was still alive but also intending his biography to act as a kind of rallying cry for the increasingly angry and effective opposition that was building against Louis. The leader of this opposition, though, was Adalhard's brother and successor at Corbie, Wala.

The youngest of Charlemagne's first cousins, Wala was still a member of the laity when the old emperor died and Louis assumed the reins of power so disastrously. In 811, he had led the group of twelve counts who had con-cluded a peace agreement with the Danish king Hemming at the river Eider; he was also the first signatory of the emperor's succession provision. As count palatine during the later years of Charlemagne's reign, and as one of his most trusted advisers, he undoubtedly, together with his brother, had a significant influence on the emperor's last efforts at reform, which were so inextricably bound up with concerns to maintain the peace within the royal household and the realm as a whole. Only after the emperor's death was Wala tonsured as a monk in the abbey at Corbie, where his brother had just been dismissed as abbot; later still, he became Adalhard's successor at the abbey. Soon after taking this post, under the assumed name of "Isidor Mer-cator," he was the prime mover behind the publication of a comprehensive and enduringly effective work on ecclesiastical reform, which championed the rights of the bishops and the pope over and against all secular authori-ties, including the emperor.[173] Prompted by developments under Louis the Pious, this work undoubtedly went beyond any of the reform objectives set out by Charlemagne; it presented its case in the form of one hundred fictitious decretals allegedly issued by popes of the early Christian church. The first person to doubt its authenticity was Nicholas of Cusa in the fifteenth century; it took until the sixteenth and seventeenth centuries for it to be definitively unmasked as a forgery, and it was declared completely obsolete only in the nineteenth century, although some of the guidelines it proposed found their way, via various intermediate stages, into the *Codex iuris canonici* of 1917.

Wala, who had learned to fear the emperor's supremacy over the Church—and in whose entourage the legend of Pope Sylvester and Constantine the Great (which demonstrated papal supremacy over all secular rulers) was greatly admired[174]—may also be associated with the second great forgery of this period, the *Constitutum Constantini*. This fictitious text of a constitution supposedly promulgated by the first Christian emperor was more explicit than any other such document in exempting papal authority from the sovereign control of the emperor and from the eleventh and twelfth centuries onward mutated into the notorious *Donation of Constantine*.[175] The synod that met in Paris in 829 was the first to cite the so-called two-powers (or two-swords) doctrine of Pope Gelasius I, according to which the "sacred authority of the bishops" (*sacrata auctoritas pontificum*) not only existed alongside imperial and royal authority but actually exceeded it, "since they [i.e., the bishops] have to render an account for even the kings of men in the divine judgment." It was therefore, Gelasius claimed, "weightier" (*gravius*) than "royal power" (*potestas regalis*).[176] The reformers behind the Pseudo-Isidorian decretals adopted and disseminated this document.

The *Epitaphium Arsenii*,[177] the poignant, long, and exculpatory obituary that Paschasius Radbertus wrote for Wala, his great predecessor as abbot of Corbie, should thus be read not simply as a posthumous criticism of Louis the Pious and his consort, Judith, nor merely as a justification and vindication of the large-scale forgery that went on at Corbie, but at the same time as a flashback to the similar reforming intentions of Charlemagne. These too had to do with the relationship between secular and spiritual authority. Their traces are clearly evident in the final capitularies issued by the emperor.

Charlemagne's Final Decrees and Death

Charlemagne's powers declined rapidly as he neared death; the emperor must have felt this all too keenly. His impending demise was no secret around the court at Aix.[178] Bathing in the warm thermal springs did not relieve the afflictions of old age as it once had whenever he returned home to Aix from campaigning, hunting, and his travels to distant lands. His worries about peace and unity multiplied and did not dissipate even when he bathed. "May peace reign, along with unity and unanimity among all Christian people, especially men of the cloth, whose sacred example should show others the way to Heaven!" As he contemplated the magnificent Cathedral Church of the Redeemer in Aix, the emperor issued this commandment as a remedy against dissent and disunity both within his own family and among the magnates, and as a barrier against disputes over worldly affairs; this edict of his went out to bishops and abbots, counts and judges alike: "For without peace and unity, there is nothing that is pleasing to God." "Love, which is the mother of all virtues, cannot survive without peace and unity."[179]

Faith, justice, peace, compassion, strength of mind, moderation, benevolence, equity, and piety—these were the watchwords that had always guided the emperor's actions. His conception of himself as a ruler shaped and defined by his Christian faith was reflected even in his earliest capitularies. Whereas, many years previously, Charlemagne had begun to rule over a Roman *imperium,* under the aging emperor this polity increasingly changed, as Alcuin had urged that it should, into what was essentially an *imperium christianum,* a "Christian empire," embracing not only the kingdoms and subjects under Charlemagne's dominion but also all the churches within his realm.

The late capitularies adopted a sermonizing tone. The emperor instructed bishops and priests to preach to their congregations "about loving God and their fellow man, faith and hope, humility and forbearance, chastity and abstinence, and goodness and mercy." They were also to proclaim the emperor's good works: his devotion in making offerings and lighting candles, the alms and sustenance for the poor he distributed, his penitence and confession of sins, and his remission of debtors, "so that with God's grace the Word of the Lord may spread far and wide and increase to the honor and glory of the name of our Lord Jesus Christ."[180] Charlemagne expected his archbishops and bishops to report on how they taught their priests and congregations about the sacrament of baptism, explaining, for instance, why people first had to be catechumens before being baptized and why they were required to examine their conscience; candidates also needed to be informed about the creed, renouncing the Devil, exorcism, the use of salt, the act of anointing with oil, and the white robe worn during baptism, and finally about "Communion under both kinds" (the reception of both the Host and the wine during the Eucharist).[181] The emperor demanded precise information on how successful his clergy were in proclaiming the faith. Was he perhaps trying to cast off his own burden of sin in doing this?

Incessantly, the same message was repeated over and over again: "May peace and unity and unanimity reign in our service of God and our love for God [*in servitio et voluntate dei*] throughout the whole of Christendom, among bishops and abbots, counts, and judges and among all people, be they ever so mighty or humble; for without peace, there is nothing that is pleasing to God." Thus began what was almost certainly the great emperor's last capitulary, in which many of the things that he had previously denounced were revisited.[182] A few lines later, we read: "We order that in Church people should give one another the kiss of peace, to show that the peace of Christ is among us" (chap. 11).

This last capitulary ranged far and wide and did not eschew fundamental matters. For example, the second chapter contains the following exhortation: "We call on counts and judges and all the people to show obedience to their bishops insofar as their Christian faith [*ad christianitatem suam*], the doctrine of redemption, and upholding the law in such a way as befits a Christian are concerned." In a later chapter, counts and laypersons were expressly forbidden to appoint, transfer, or dismiss the priests of their church (chap. 4). Never before had the secular regional powers been so curtly, peremptorily, and summarily decreed subject to ecclesiastical authority. Obedience, on the one hand, and consensus in the observance of the law, on the other. Here, then, was an unequivocal statement of the supremacy of religious directives over legal ones. This superiority would continue to make itself felt and would bear fruit a hundred times over in the reign of Louis the Pious.[183]

The obligation to pay tithes was stressed, in accordance with God's directive to Moses (chap. 6); church attendance "with a chaste body and a pure heart" was required on Sundays and fast days (chap. 7); as before, the *missi* and the bishops were to be jointly responsible for ensuring that all church buildings, including the royal chapels, were kept in a good state of repair and were well appointed "so that in all places of worship God might be honored through devotion to our Lord Jesus Christ" (chap. 8); murder and theft were to be severely punished (chap. 12), and drinking sessions that engendered violence were to be clamped down on (chap. 13); bishops and priests were to teach the faith in the correct manner, while laypersons were expected to know the creed, the Lord's Prayer, and the formulas for renouncing the Devil; anyone refusing to obey his or her bishop in these matters would, if he was a nobleman, be compelled to do so by enforced fasting or other penalties, or by floggings in the case of servants or maids (chap. 14). Godparents were expected to instruct their godchildren in the ways of being a good Christian, while their parents were to ensure that they kept to the straight and narrow (chap. 29). No one who had been unable to recite the creed and the Lord's Prayer error-free in the presence of a bishop or priest would be permitted to assist at a baptism (chap. 30).

"We command through God's and Our own word that everyone, be he nobleman or commoner, mighty or humble, poor or rich, be granted full rights under the law; anyone who dares to contravene this shall be answerable before God" (chap. 18), a threatening escalation from royal to divine justice. And so the capitulary went on, treating such matters as perjury (chap. 15); the order in which courts should proceed with their business, with church affairs taking precedence, followed by cases concerning the poor, orphans, and widows (chap. 16); the abusive practice of counts and judges requesting gifts for favors (chap. 17); correct weights and measures (chap. 26); the duty to provide hospitality to strangers and pilgrims (chap. 27); the prohibition of markets on Sundays and feast days (chap. 28); the right way to conduct commercial transactions (chap. 32); the exclusion of secular jurisdiction from all areas of churches, including their porches (chap. 33); the ban on counts and judges acquiring property from the poor (chap. 34); legal intervention by bishops and priests to prevent drunkenness (chap. 37); and many other topics besides. The capitulary concluded with the call for the reporting of persistent offenders "so that we might determine what is to be done with those who for so many years have disobeyed God's commandments and our decrees" (chap. 40). To the very end, then, in concert with God, the emperor was intent on punishing any laxity in the observance of the law.

Phrases like "through God's and Our own word" (*dei verbum et nostrum*) and "God's commandments and our decrees" (*dei praecepta et decretum nostrum*) indicate that right up to his last breath, the emperor construed his actions as being consonant with God's wishes. Whatever the *missi* had improved, or failed to, was to be reported to the emperor "so that, through God's grace and according to His will, that which needs to be amended might be amended, and those things that have already been improved might continue to get better, thus earning us eternal reward in God's eyes and guaranteeing us salvation and renown for evermore."[184] Charlemagne knew that when the Last Judgment came, the king and emperor would be required to shoulder the burden of sins for all his people. The tract *On the Twelve Abuses of the World* had been spreading this message for well over a century. Until the very end, Charlemagne wanted to act in accordance with God's will, *secundum dei voluntatem.*

Charlemagne had scheduled a general council "like those held by former emperors" for May 813, which was intended to assemble all the bishops from across the entire realm. The bishops and abbots assembled at five different locations: Mainz, Reims, Chalon-sur-Saône, Tours, and Arles;[185] they passed more than two hundred resolutions and were meant to meet for a sixth and final grand assembly that would bring them all together. The synod members could thus be sure that the emperor would take notice of their decisions and give them his blessing; everything would then be collated by the forthcoming imperial synod, which was due to take place the next year in Aix. And they knew how Charlemagne conceived of his emperorship and wanted others to regard it.

Accordingly, the bishops who had gathered in Arles prefaced all their decretals with a kind of mirror for princes in shortened form, the full version of which dated from the Sixteenth Council of Toledo in 693: "May the Lord of all the universe . . . strengthen Charlemagne in preserving his faith and arm him with foreknowledge of justice. May He grant him an abundance of peace, enlighten him with the gift of compassion, fortify him with courage, and accord him the right standards in directing the reins of power that have been entrusted to him, in order that he might rule the peoples under his dominion with compassion, lead them righteously, and guide them on the path of godliness."[186] The bishops were plainly reminding their great emperor of the cardinal virtues of a ruler here. His pacific nature and compassion would engender these same qualities, along with others, in the world and throughout the length and breadth of his realm.

Charlemagne heeded these sentiments. Mindful of the fact that the sins of all his peoples were about to be heaped on him, he would no doubt have applauded them; they neatly encapsulated his own self-image as a ruler. But the final synod in Aix never took place, despite the fact that a court assembly was still held there in September 813.[187] It may be that the sheer volume of divergent resolutions passed by the earlier individual synods could not be collated in time. At least a schematic overview of the commonalities and the peculiarities of those five synods, forming a preamble to the most important decisions they conveyed, may already have laid the groundwork for the anticipated imperial synod.[188] This illustrates in any event the quite different ways in which the individual churches applied canon law, and in which they intended to tackle the manifold and diverse difficulties facing the clergy in their respective provinces.

It was precisely these hardships that Charlemagne and his ecclesiastical advisers sought to address to the very end of his reign. The bishops presented him with a concise "collation" of the decisions the synods had taken.[189] At the court assembly, he announced succinctly but decisively how matters were to proceed from there on.[190] First, peace was to prevail between the bishops and the counts (chap. 9). The latter group, along with the other *iudices* (secular judges) and the people at large, were told to obey the bishops, agree among themselves about upholding justice and refuse to accept gifts for dispensing it, and admit no false witnesses (chap. 10). No secular court was to be held on church premises (chap. 21). Counts and other office-holders could henceforth acquire the property of the poor only in a public court hearing with a bishop presiding (chap. 22). It was permissible to use the churches' riches to support the poor (chap. 12). Weights and measures were to be identical everywhere (chap. 13). Godparents were to instruct their godchildren in the one true faith (*catholice*) "so that they might be able to give an account of themselves before God" (chap. 18).

The court assembly yielded a number of other important decisions, for Charlemagne had summoned his son Louis from Aquitaine. By the common consent of the bishops and counts and the other magnates, he was officially adopted as the empire's heir apparent. The poet Ermoldus Nigellus provided a plausible account of how Einhard presented the emperor's wishes to the assembled delegates.[191] The young ruler presently thanked the Anglo-Saxon scholar with lavish gifts. Charlemagne then bade his son place the crown on his head and named him co-emperor.[192] Cries of "Long live Emperor Louis!" rang out. Charlemagne expressly declared that his grandson Bernard, Pepin's son, should be recognized as the rightful king of Italy—an unusual step on his part, since it broke with the conventions of Frankish law, as we have seen. Because of this, Louis would have been specifically required to swear to abide by this ruling before the coronation altar. A few years later, he broke his oath, an act that signaled the prelude to the demise of the Carolingian Empire.

The blessings from Arles and the other metropolitan cities that were now read out in Aix to greet this event sounded at one and the same time like the legacy of the great man, a warning to his son and successor, and a lament to accompany the dying emperor to his rest. For a long time, what was to come had been foretold by omens: solar and lunar eclipses, a blemish on the surface of the sun (a sunspot), collapsing buildings, the bolt of lightning out of a clear sky, the ensuing fall of the emperor from his horse, the shattering of his cloak clasp, the way his sword belt had been torn off and his javelin flung far from where he fell, the disappearance of the word *Princeps* from the inscription in his most exalted church, the Royal Church of St. Mary and the Redeemer in Aix/Aachen (a rumor to this effect went around a few months before he died)—all these things seemed to portend how close at hand his death was. Charlemagne confronted it calmly and resolutely. Einhard recalled this clearly and gave a corresponding account of it when he dictated his *Life of Charlemagne* some fifteen years later.[193]

Where the final "portent" of Charlemagne's death was concerned, here too Suetonius's life of Augustus (in his *Lives of the Twelve Caesars*) served as a model. The Roman author related how, shortly before the celebrated ruler's death, the first letter of the inscription *Caesar* was melted from a statue of the emperor by a flash of lightning. This was interpreted as a sign that Augustus would be deified, since the remaining word *aesar* meant "God" in the Etruscan language. According to Einhard (chap. 32), the name of the new Augustus on the cornice between the upper and lower tiers of arches in Aachen Cathedral, that is, the word *Princeps* in the inscription *Karolus Princeps*, was also effaced, leading people to speculate that Charlemagne would soon die. But the lightning in the account of the Roman emperor was overlaid and outshone by another, expressly Christian story of a flash of light, which Charlemagne's biographer and his first reader, the emperor's son Louis, would surely have known about, even though it was not explicitly mentioned in the biography: namely, the "light from heaven" that suddenly surrounded Saul on the road to Damascus, causing him to fall to the ground, whereupon God spoke to him and he answered: "Lord, what wilt thou have me to do?" (Acts 9:3–7).

The Christian Caesar, the devout *princeps,* could not have failed to imagine being called to account by God. Charlemagne, where is your cousin Tassilo? He betrayed me.—And where is your eldest son, Pepin? He rose up against me.—Charlemagne, where are your brothers' sons? They. . . . Would he come through such a trial? Thou shalt not kill; he knew this only too well. Had he violated God's commandments? "We must take a long, hard look at ourselves and ask whether we are true Christians," Charlemagne had told his clergy in 811.[194] The emperor did not exempt himself from this. Yet he had also done a great deal of good; he had won extensive new territories for Christianity and baptized many heathens; he had brought order to the world, elevated and strengthened the Church, struggled to bring peace, helped the poor, protected strangers, and exercised justice. What would his empire have been without justice? Did he dare hope, then, that he might be saved? Einhard's answer to this, in the image of Charlemagne struck down by the light from heaven, disarmed, and stripped of his title, was comforting: this man spoke henceforth with God.

For the last seven days of Charlemagne's life, when pleurisy and a high fever kept him confined to his winter hunting camp, he was attended by Hildebald, the archbishop of Cologne, who performed the role of archchaplain at the court. Hildebald gave him Communion through the sacrament of the Holy Eucharist. Early on the morning of 28 January, a Saturday, the dying emperor crossed himself, as prescribed in the liturgy, on his forehead, chest, and abdomen, folded his arms across his chest, crossed his legs, closed his eyes, and commended himself to God with a verse from the Psalms on his lips: "Thou hast redeemed me, O Lord God of truth" (Psalms 31:5).[195]

EPILOGUE
Myths and Sainthood

POWER AND PRAYER. Charlemagne had been powerful and had known how to use his power. But had he been happy as well? Would he have even known how to frame such a question? And what of his own feelings of love and his consciousness of others' affection for him? Or were concerns like this still lying dormant, awaiting future intellectual and psychological developments in the West? Would it take another three or four hundred years of spiritual conditioning before such questions could be formulated and posed? And what about friendship? Or trust? Or passion? We search in vain for any clear impression of Charlemagne the human being. Were power and the law the sole parameters of relationships back then? Charlemagne ruled his kingdom for forty-four years, longer than most of his predecessors or successors. Yet his life remains a closed book to us. The handful of definite statements by him that we know of—however exceptional these may be within the totality of material that has come down to us—do not furnish us with enough material to build up a picture of his personality. The very act of remembrance, though, tends to create sinners and saints, heroes and villains. Charlemagne was all those things in the recollection of posterity. But what was the core, the essence of the man?

The fact is, we simply do not know. We scarcely even know when and where he was born or the conditions in which he was raised, and we can deduce or speculate on how things might have been only in a very piecemeal fashion. He was supposedly a handsome man to look at. Einhard referred to his pleasing physical appearance (chap. 22), and two painted likenesses, a number of contemporary "portrait denarii,"[1] and—although this is highly contentious—the equestrian statue originally from Metz (Figure 23) and now housed in the Louvre, which from the sixteenth century onward was attested as being a monument to Charlemagne,[2] would seem to confirm this description: he was large and strong and of a lofty stature, being somewhat over six feet tall; he had a high forehead fringed with some form of pageboy haircut, large and lively eyes, small ears, a long, straight nose, full lips beneath a distinctive mustache, a strong jawline that was showing signs of developing a double chin, a short neck, and a rather prominent belly—in short, an imposing figure of the kind that the period expected any king, not just Charlemagne, to be.

Yet the psychological traits that were of such vital importance in shaping Charlemagne's life, the "measure of his soul," to which he himself alluded,[3] remain a total mystery to us. We know only the deeds that were ascribed to him or that he let be ascribed to him, numerous decrees, and occasional quotations; in addition, we can identify a few of his followers and aides by name, more priests than laymen, although the latter were no less influential. But as regards the development of the ruler's personality from a young king to an old emperor, we are completely in the dark.

The most decisive moments in the ruler's life stand out: the serious setback he suffered in Spain in 778 and its ramifications for the wars against the Saxons and the reforms he planned to make in the Church and Frankish society, his coronation as emperor, and his fall from his horse in the annus horribilis of 810. "What have we done wrong?"—for all such heartfelt exhortations to self-examination, we still find no window into Charlemagne's soul. What he and his helpers wanted to put to the test was nothing less than the "path of righteousness" (*via rectitudinis*). This was the path that in former times, Pope Zachary had, through his missionary St. Boniface, urged the priests and the laity of the kingdom of the Franks to take—namely, implementation of the commandments in their religious observance. If schismatic priests who engaged in warfare and slaughtered and whored were driven from the Church, Zachary stated, then the Franks would surely be victorious over the pagans; clerics who acted in the right way, however, earned their reward in Heaven because in doing so they led the people toward the "true faith" (*recta fides*).[4] Charlemagne strove to attain these goals throughout his whole life; he had been destined to tread this path since childhood.

Yet aside, perhaps, from hunting and a growing fear of the Day of Judgment, Charlemagne's passions remain hidden. How did he deal with the setbacks he suffered? How did he get over his failures? We have no idea. At best, we can identify a certain doggedness in pursuing goals once he had set them; he also seems to have tried to efface defeats by scoring new victories. His anger could sometimes go beyond all measure, and his punishments were rarely lenient.

All the same, unlike his predecessors, he spared the life of most of his adversaries while at the same time eliminating them as a threat. His nephews ended their lives confined in unknown monasteries somewhere (or were they put to death?), King Desiderius of the Lombards and his daughter—the anonymous but lawful wife of Charlemagne—simply disappeared, and his cousin Tassilo of Bavaria, Tassilo's sons and daughters, and his own son Pepin the Hunchback all ended up being tonsured and forced to become monks or nuns; while in the case of the Thuringian rebel Hardrat and his allies, and possibly also Tassilo and Theodo, they were blinded and mutilated. His opponents were effectively silenced forever. No one would ever hear their voices again, and no prayers of remembrance would be dedicated to them. The fact that the historical record has little to say about them should not surprise us. Much more surprisingly, though, the life of Charlemagne—this important figure, this merciless, violent, devout offender, who loved and feared Christ, the incorruptible judge of the end times, and who venerated the guardian of the Pearly Gates, St. Peter, and protected his representatives on Earth, the popes—Charlemagne's life, with all its contradictions, is closed off from us as well.[5]

Certain impressive achievements emerge as highlights of his reign. "Anything that is without benefit is invalid": Theodulf may have won over his lord and master with sentiments like this, but at least Charlemagne could attest to this dictum through his own actions, which certainly were to bring many benefits to his realm.[6] He expanded his empire to the south, east, and north and secured its frontiers.[7] Meanwhile, Byzantium had got into severe difficulties: "Have the Frank for your friend but not for your neighbor!"[8] But Charlemagne's principal concern, which permeated his every action, was for the Christian faith and the Church. Charlemagne had restored Christ's tomb in Jerusalem and extended Christ's realm on Earth. He had converted the Saxons and brought them into the Christian flock. Even Goethe, who had little use for the great Frankish monarch, cited as proof of Charlemagne's significance the relief carving of the Descent from the Cross on the Externsteine ancient rock formation in Westphalia (an artwork he wrongly identified as Carolingian), hailing it as the work of "a monastic artist from among the hordes of priests that the conquering court of Charlemagne brought with it."[9]

In Italy, Charlemagne strengthened St. Peter's successor. He lent the papacy a level of support that it had not enjoyed since the days of Constantine the Great and would not see again after the Frankish emperor's death; he confirmed the Church's primacy of teaching. He was the first ruler to clearly adopt the legal principle that "the pope is judged by no man," not even by a convocation of bishops, let alone by a jury of the common people. Charlemagne's restoration of Church discipline, his creation of ecclesiastical provinces, and his regular convening of synods had great benefits, not least for the king's organization of his secular rule. Conversely, the revival of learning helped the Church as much as it did the ruler's own worldly power. A way of thinking conditioned by a rationality that was schooled in Aristotelian dialectics, in the concepts of *proprium, accidens,* and difference, now began to take root among the intellectual elites. Rationality taught people to see the world in a different light. By the time Charlemagne died, everything had changed.

Indeed, the internal dynamic of dissolution that had been inherent within the society of late antiquity and for several centuries thereafter was now contained and arrested. Yet each act of revival represented at the same time a further development; in each case the different cultural context prevented mere repetition. Reception invariably meant innovation. In this regard, to the very end of his life, the king and emperor was able to rely on some outstanding counselors, such as Petrus Pisanus, Paul the Deacon, Alcuin, Paulinus of Aquileia, Theodulf of Orléans, Angilbert, Adalhard and his brother Wala, Arn of Salzburg, and many others, including his biographer Einhard. Likewise, his consorts, especially Hildegard and Fastrada, gave him invaluable support in his rule; he also had a loyal confederate in his sister Gisela, the abbess of Chelles and Notre-Dame-de-Soissons. All the same, Charlemagne's effective programs of revival catalyzed and hastened radical social changes among a populace that was, generally speaking, on the increase.

The "imperial aristocracy" and the upper echelons of the Church hierarchy were immeasurably strengthened by being assigned fixed areas of jurisdiction and through being granted a role of consensual participation in the king's rule. Meanwhile, the "education" of the great and powerful through Christian paraeneses and models created a hitherto-unknown ideal type of lay officeholder, as characterized in an example of the mirror-of-princes genre of literature from the reign of Louis the Pious, Bishop Jonas of Orléans's work *De institutione laicali,* which he wrote for Matfrid, Count of Orléans.[10] In general, this form of literature, which had died out in antiquity, experienced a revival under the Carolingians. This period witnessed the laying of the foundations (though by no means yet the full formation) of that ethical stance that would, through many changes over time, come to mark out the typical landed squire (*Junker*) of the nineteenth and early twentieth centuries as a solicitous master of those who were in his charge.

External successes—the massive expansion of Charlemagne's empire and the necessary protection of the borderlands that this entailed—came largely at the expense of "little" free men, who performed military service and had to pay for it with their own property. This class of people became more and more dependent on the magnates and in the process were "mediatized" and for all practical purposes thus lost the king as their master. Charlemagne tried to curb this trend, but lack of freedom continued to increase despite the concerns of this farsighted ruler for his poorer subjects' right to life and protection. In the long run, the collective self-interest of the magnates proved stronger. Although some social provisions were certainly implemented, they depended too greatly on the goodwill of these magnates to have any lasting or comprehensive effect. Hardship could only temporarily be held in check.

An economic policy that by the standards of its time was highly successful was intended to alleviate this situation somewhat and indeed managed to do so. The royal estates became more productive as a result of protection of the weak and the poor. In the face of all the military burdens they had to shoulder, they still managed to produce goods for long-distance trade. There is clear evidence that Charlemagne's Frankish kingdom traded as far afield as the Mediterranean and beyond, with goods even being imported from and exported to the Arab world. The king and emperor appear to have actively promoted such initiatives.

Nothing remained unchanged, even if the faith of the Church Fathers, reflected in the dogmatically formalized creed issued by the Councils of Nicaea and Constantinople, was retained word for word. The society of the Carolingian Empire that adopted such standards did not in any way resemble the imperial society of late antiquity, but the understanding of religious formulas had changed. While aiming primarily at renovation and restoration, Charlemagne unintentionally became a champion of innovation.

Commemorating Charlemagne

Yet the world scarcely paused for breath when the great emperor died. Hardly any songs of mourning were heard. There is only one extant lament for Charlemagne, composed in Italy, no doubt at the monastery in Bobbio, which begins: From the rising of the sun to the western shores where it sets, lamentation beats on the hearts of men. Woe is me in my misery! (*A solis ortu usque ad occidua / littora maris planctus pulsat pectora. / Heu mihi misero!*) . . . The Franks, the Romans, and all believers are tormented by grief and great distress. Woe is me in my misery! . . . Alas, poor Rome, poor Roman people, you have lost the most renowned Charlemagne. Woe is me in my misery! . . . May the father of all, Lord of mercy, grant Charlemagne a place of great splendor. Woe is me in my misery! O Lord of the hosts of all mankind and the heavens, Lord over Hell. Woe is me in my misery! O Christ, receive into your holy dwelling in the circle of your apostles the pious Charlemagne! Woe is me in my misery! (*In sancta sede cum tuis apostolis / suscipe pium, o tu Christe, Karolum! Heu mihi misero!*)

This work, which goes by the name of *Planctus de obitu Karoli* (*Lament on the Death of Charlemagne*), expressed both sorrow and hope.[11]

Charlemagne's corpse was washed and anointed and laid to rest in the Basilica of St. Mary in Aix, presumably in the magnificent ancient "Proserpina" sarcophagus, which can still be seen today among the priceless artifacts housed in the treasury at Aachen Cathedral. His final resting place was a tomb with a carved likeness of him recumbent beneath a golden triumphal arch, on which was inscribed the following epitaph in gold letters: SUB HOC CONDITORIO SITUM EST CORPUS KAROLI MAGNI ATQUE ORTHODOXI IMPERATORIS, QUI REGNUM FRANCORUM NOBILITER AMPLIAVIT ET PER ANNOS XLVII FELICITER REXIT. DECESSIT SEPTUAGENARIUS ANNO [DOMINI DCCCXIIII], INDICTIONE [VII], V. KAL. FEBR. (In this tomb lies the body of Charles, the great and orthodox emperor, who gloriously extended the kingdom of the Franks and reigned prosperously for forty-seven years. He died at the age of seventy, in the year of our Lord 814, the 7th indiction, on the 28th day of February). Rome and the Lombard kingdom are not mentioned. Einhard recounted all this (chap. 31) but did not pinpoint the site of the tomb in the cathedral. Only popular tradition locates it in the southeastern wall of the church, right next to the high altar. When the Vikings notoriously turned the cathedral into a stable for their horses after overrunning Aix in 882, the place where the emperor was interred had of necessity to remain hidden. Rediscovered by Otto III in the year 1000, his remains were exhumed in 1165 on the orders of the Holy Roman emperor Frederick Barbarossa; in 1215 Barbarossa's grandson Frederick II drove the last nail home to seal a golden casket containing Charlemagne's mortal remains. However, the old tomb, with its likeness and the sarcophagus, continued to serve as a memorial until 1788, the year before the French Revolution, when it was torn down and the stone effigy of Charlemagne was smashed. The precious sarcophagus was taken to Paris for a few years but was returned to Aix after Napoleon's final defeat.

In St. Peter's Basilica in Rome, too, Charlemagne's name was immortalized by the commissioning of a costly paten bearing his name, KAROLO, while the golden *crux gemmata* (cross studded with precious stones) that he donated to the Church of St. Savior ad Lateranis immediately after his coronation as emperor, and that was carried at the head of the *Letania* major procession in front of the pope, was stolen a few years after his death and vanished forever. Charlemagne's son Drogo, who from 823 until his death in 855 was archbishop of Metz, may likewise have organized a memorial prayer service in his cathedral; the bronze equestrian statuette (Figure 23) plus its now-lost silver companion piece possibly depicting Charlemagne could have been used in Metz for just such a liturgical purpose.[12] Henceforth, the image that later generations formed of Charlemagne was a complex, multilayered one conditioned by a number of different factors: commemorative intercession, more neutral recollection, admiration, rejection, and attempts to use his memory to reflect on and interpret contemporary events or as a vehicle for barely disguised criticism of the present.

From a very early stage, attempts to make him into a hero figure among mortals have distorted remembrance of Charlemagne. This process began after an initial phase of disparagement of his achievements had been overcome as a result of altered circumstances. The first hint of this change of situation is revealed in the name given to Louis the Pious's fourth son, who was baptized in Frankfurt in 823. This occurred after Benedict of Aniane had died, and after Charlemagne's banned former advisers Adalhard of Corbie and his brother Wala had been rehabilitated at court and the emperor had publicly had to make atonement. At this stage, a "Carlist" restoration—evident, say, in Adalhard's *De ordine palatii*—began to put the

FIGURE 55 The Proserpina Sarcophagus is a highly ornate third-century CE Roman marble sarcophagus decorated with high-relief carving showing the rape of Proserpina. Charlemagne is thought to have been interred in this sarcophagus in 814.

errant monarchy back on course and to celebrate the return of the great emperor in people's memories: the boy who was born at this favorable moment was therefore christened "Charles." This was a tangible sign of a change, albeit one that would soon bring further changes and greater irremediable upheavals in its wake.

Even Einhard's *Vita Karoli* could not halt this development. On the contrary, it appealed to the memory of the great emperor precisely in order to admonish the post's present incumbent. Although it was originally intended to counteract worrisome contemporary developments, this shining example of reborn Latin classicism, which drew much of its rhetorical power from the oratory of Cicero, ended up promoting the heroic image of Charlemagne more enduringly than any other work. The biographies of the Caesars by the ancient Roman historian Suetonius, especially his life of Augustus, served as models for Einhard of how to present his material, while the moral tone was set by Cicero's *Tusculan Disputations*. Both these models attest to the increasing standard of education that had been reached in Charlemagne's

realm and the new cultural values that began to spread along with it. Yet at the same time, this piece of literature offered an underlying criticism of the ruling emperor that contemporary readers would no doubt have readily appreciated.

Einhard's little tract probably appeared in 828 or 829, at a time of growing internal tensions within the Frankish Empire, which over time it would find itself unable to withstand.[13] It held a mirror up to Louis the Pious, who, although mentioned only in passing by name, is clearly identifiable as the principal addressee of the *Vita Karoli,* and it did so in a subtle but unequivocal and forceful way. Even the preface, with its reference to Einhard's "friendship with Charlemagne and his children," would have reminded anyone who knew how to read between the lines of the decidedly "unfriendly" way in which Charlemagne's successor had behaved toward the former emperor's daughters and youngest sons. It was for all of them, who had been expelled so unceremoniously from the court by Louis, that Einhard set about preserving the memory of their father for posterity. They would automatically have drawn a comparison between current circumstances and past times.

The first sentence of the first chapter would have set more alarm bells ringing in the ears of a ruler who had a rather frosty relationship with the Apostolic See and who regarded the bishop of Rome hardly less disparagingly than he did his own bishops.[14] This first sentence recounted the following incident: "Childeric [III] was deposed, tonsured, and consigned to a monastery by order of the Roman pontiff Stephen [II]." Einhard was here recalling the founding of the Carolingian royal dynasty and the ascent of the Carolingians to the Frankish throne. Pepin the Short, the first of their line, was "raised by decree of the Roman pontiff from the rank of mayor of the palace to that of king" (chap. 3). These were clear allusions on the biographer's part to Charlemagne's great reverence for the Apostolic See and the potential at any time for the throne to be lost.

This message was understood loud and clear—and not just in the aftermath of the reforming papacy of the eleventh century, when the fall of the Merovingians was repeatedly held up as a precedent for the papal right to depose emperors and kings. On the other hand, Einhard was not simply indulging himself in issuing these warnings. Once more, a few insinuations were enough. Again, they were discreet—it would have been risky to do otherwise—yet unmistakably clear. For instance, Einhard referred to the Lombard wife whom Charlemagne had spurned as an *uxor*, in other words, a lawful spouse. No reader of the *Vita Karoli* at the court of Louis the Pious needed any further explanation; everyone knew what Einhard's simple choice of words meant—in bringing Louis's mother, Hildegard, into the palace as his new wife while his lawful Lombard wife was still alive, Louis's father had acted in a manner that flagrantly violated canon law. Charlemagne was a sinner, and the emperor who was now on the throne had therefore—as Paschasius Radbertus, a spokesman for the opposition to Louis and, as the author of the *Pseudo-Isidorian Decretals,* surely the most eminent scholar of canon law of his age, was not afraid to state openly—been conceived in "illegitimate nuptials" and so, according to canon law, was the son of a concubine.[15] This same criticism of Louis was voiced by the author of the *Constitutum Constantini,* which formed the basis of the *Donation of Constantine.*[16]

At the time when Einhard was writing, this kind of information was explosive. It called to mind once more the death of Bernard of Italy, whose kingship Charlemagne had tried personally to secure, and to which Louis had sworn an oath of assent but later recanted it nonetheless.[17] Moreover, Louis had deprived his nephew of his inheritance on the grounds that his brother had sired Bernard as a "concubine's son." The young king had died a violent death (which Einhard tellingly did not mention) through the terrible injuries sustained when he was blinded, a death that as early as 822 had forced the emperor to do public penance. This act was supposed to give him moral strength but actually formed the prelude to a round of self-destructive conflicts within the Frankish Empire. Here is not the place to discuss this in any greater detail. Disillusioned and feigning illness, Einhard ended up withdrawing from court to his estate near Seligenstadt on the river Main.

The cruelty of Queen Fastrada that Einhard expressly referred to in his biography (chap. 20) and that, in another example of criticism of his hero, he claimed Charlemagne always gave in to, so provoking revolts against his rule, may well have been mirrored at the time Einhard was writing by the role played by Louis's second wife, Judith. Spurred on by her family, Judith had intervened in the succession question with a series of deliberately disruptive demands that caused untold upheaval. Also, as the biographer was at pains to point out (chap. 19), the fact that Charlemagne had shown special *pietas,* the proper attitude to adopt to both men and God, toward the children of his dead son Pepin, and particularly toward his grandson Bernard, for whose death Louis was responsible, was another of those skillfully veiled but unmistakable admonitions to Louis; indeed, citing the good example of Charlemagne was tantamount to a silent accusation leveled at the first reader of the *Vita Karoli.*[18] For Louis was only too keen to have his "godliness" (*pietas*) proclaimed far and wide and to hear himself described by the sobriquet "pious" (*pius*),[19] yet he had been singularly lacking in this quality.

Throughout his entire reign, Charlemagne—as Einhard was keen to stress—had been concerned "to reestablish the ancient authority [*auctoritas*] of the city of Rome under his care and by his influence, and to defend and protect the Church of St. Peter" (chap. 27). Admittedly, Charlemagne's attitude toward the pope and the Roman Church was not quite as straightforward as his biographer painted it. In Hadrian I and—despite his humiliation—the even more successful Leo III, the king and emperor had two outstanding opponents. Leo's strong personality and the coronation of Charlemagne as emperor, which brought about a fundamental recognition of the primacy of papal authority, changed the balance of power. But this was not Einhard's concern at this point. Rather, it was the aim of Louis's adversaries to get him to adopt a very different attitude to the bishop of Rome, one that showed far greater respect to the successor and heir of the apostolic prince and to the city of Rome in general. This emperor, who substituted Frankish revival for Roman, had not followed in his father's footsteps; he did not even bestir himself to journey to Rome during his reign. Instead, he left it to his son, the emperor Lothar, to maintain law and order in the city of the apostles and in the kingdom of Italy.

Just one or two years after Einhard wrote his reminiscences of Charlemagne, the famous letter of 494 from Pope Gelasius I to Emperor Anastasius I—which would henceforth become renowned and be cited over and over again—was rediscovered and read out at the Synod of Paris in 829. It juxtaposed and contrasted the "sacred authority of the popes" (*sancta auctoritas pontificum*) with "kingly power" (*regalis potestas*), and expressly set the former above the latter. This was also to be construed as a warning to the emperor, who was intent on treating the pope like any other bishop. Immediately, Louis's opponents both harked back to the time of Charlemagne and looked forward to a future where they anticipated the pope being deemed of equal rank with, or even above, the emperor. In other words, they referenced what was presumed to be Charlemagne's final capitulary, which had formulated the principle of the subordination of the secular regional powers of counts and "judges" to the bishops,[20] before moving forward in time to the *Pseudo-Isidorian Decretals,* the monumental counterfeit work of canon law created by the circle of scholars around Wala of Corbie and his assistant, Paschasius Radbertus. This work likewise saw the king and emperor as subject to the spiritual leadership of the pope.

The *Pseudo-Isidorian Decretals* consciously picked up on the substance of the Gelasius decretal and in so doing retained the legal argument, which had been repeatedly cited ever since, for the strict separation of the "two powers," that of the king or emperor from the spiritual "power" of the bishop of Rome, before which every crowned head was expected to bow. Although Einhard's *Life of Charlemagne* was not a response to the Paris Synod, it nevertheless stood in the context of the very same "political" discourse that led to that meeting. It showed that its author had a close affinity to those enemies of Louis who forced Charlemagne's successor to do penance and who even sought—albeit in vain—to depose him.

Most of the contemporary figures who had direct experience of Charlemagne's reign—Adalhard, Theodulf, Wala, and the rest—would have had a different recollection of the great Carolingian ruler than Einhard, notwithstanding how close the latter may have been to his master in the final years of his rule. The contradictions in the historical record reveal a ruling elite under Louis the Pious that was deeply divided. The monastically minded but unnamed biographer of Alcuin of Tours, who was writing at the same time as Einhard, noted that Charlemagne had been "terrible and pious" (*terribilis et pius*) when he wanted to curry favor with Charlemagne's emperor-son Louis.[21] The former emperor had, he claimed, refused to let his Anglo-Saxon scholar-adviser, who by then was afflicted by advancing age and ill-health, to retire to a monastery, an act that bordered on blasphemy.

Nithard, the historian and illegitimate grandson of Charlemagne, who was almost certainly brought up at his court and who fell in battle against the Northmen in 845, idealized this institution in noting its "humanistic nature" but also, in regard to Einhard's biography, the actions of his grandfather: "He is said to have been fearsome, yet in the same measure endearing and admirable" (*History* 1.1). In a description reminiscent of Virgil (*Aeneid* 1.302), Nithard claimed that Charlemagne, imbued with "every kind of wisdom and virtue," had managed by means of "mild terror" to tame the wild and iron hearts (*ferocia ac ferrea corda*)[22] of the Franks and the barbarians alike—something not even the might of Rome had been able to do—so effectively that the only actions they undertook within his realm (*imperium*) were those that accorded with the "general good" (*publica utilitas*), that is, were to the benefit of the royal-imperial authority and its helpers, not the "common good."[23]

Yet Nithard was writing at a time when Charlemagne's legitimate grandsons were at war with one another over their inheritance and the Carolingian Empire was disintegrating. This ruptured state was to be permanent. Henceforth, rulers with an equal claim to the throne were to reign concurrently in the West and the East of the broken realm, with one or another of them repeatedly attaining the title of emperor, although this bespoke only a degree of temporary precedence rather than any absolute supremacy over the other. In attempting to legitimize their position, all these subsequent rulers could invoke the name of Charlemagne.[24] In the East, the reign of Otto the Great (912–973) saw the start of the tradition of the "Aix monarchy," that is, the coronation of the "German" kings in Charlemagne's cathedral at Aix-la-Chapelle (Aachen) and their enthronement on the throne that he had set up there. Yet even as early as the twelfth century, "Kaerlingen," the "Land of the Carolingians/Charlemagne," became synonymous with the realm of the "Franks," that is, France, while the East, the *imperium,* constituted a "Roman empire." Increasingly, the founder figure Charlemagne merged with France; and by the time the "Chanson de Roland" was composed there, in the first half of the twelfth century, it described Charlemagne ruling over only "sweet France," *la France dulce.*

The royal dynasty of the Capetians, which began when Hugh Capet drove the last Carolingians from power and ascended the throne in the final years of the tenth century, was constantly having to allay doubts about its legitimacy. This situation changed only with the marriage of Philip II to Isabella of Hennegau in 1180, for the new queen was, it was said, a latter-day granddaughter of "Charlemaine," and with her son Louis VIII the monarchy reverted to the lineage of Charlemagne. Before long, this had been developed into a new doctrine of legitimacy, the so-called return of the monarchy to the lineage of Charlemagne (*reditus regni ad stirpem Karoli*). Around 1274, the *Grandes chroniques de France*—a history of France through a chronography of its kings, which drew on numerous strands of tradition, including Einhard's *Life of Charlemagne*—adopted this doctrine and made it an integral part of how the French monarchy perceived itself.[25] The *stirps Karoli* ("la lignée de Challemaine le Grant") came to be fully identified with the Capetian monarchy. From the fifteenth century onward, France therefore trod auspiciously in the footsteps of Charlemagne and began to base and to justify territorial demands on these grounds. Soon it was being claimed that Charlemagne had appointed the twelve "pairs de France" (peers of France, the highest-ranking members of the country's aristocracy), founded the tribunal of the Parlement, and endowed the University of Paris—all of them symbolic identifiers of late medieval France.

The "imperial" eastern region of the former Carolingian Empire identified no less strongly with "Charles the Great," beginning with Otto I and continuing with the Salian dynasty, Frederick Barbarossa and the Guelfs, Charles IV (from the House of Luxembourg), and all subsequent incumbents of the post of Holy Roman emperor down the centuries. Every coronation of a Frankish-German king that took place in Aix-la-Chapelle (Aachen) from 936 or 961 until the end of the Middle Ages was in some way reminiscent of Charlemagne.[26] For example, the *Kaiserchronik* (Imperial chronicle), a verse epic in Middle High German composed sometime before the mid-twelfth century, is an eloquent testimony to the veneration of Charlemagne that had set in by that stage; it hailed the Carolingian ruler as a hero and lawgiver. Yet although Charlemagne never ceased to be associated with France and its ruling dynasty, no such tradition of identification with the monarchy developed in the East. Indeed, to cite just one instance, the late fifteenth-century Nuremberg chronicler Hartmann Schedel characterized Charlemagne simply as a *franckreichish könig* (French king). All subsequent centuries up to the present have continued to evoke memories of the Frankish ruler, and his name has been co-opted by all the various "trends" that (Western) European intellectual history has gone through over this period. Machiavelli, Hugo Grotius, Montesquieu, and Voltaire, to name but four key thinkers, all wrote about Charlemagne.[27]

In attempts to pin down Charlemagne's role in history and his personality, a multitude of extremely diverse recollections have merged in the collective cultural consciousness. Despite having initially concentrated all remembrance of Charlemagne into an idealized image of the ruler, Einhard's compact and much-admired *Vita* in no way dominated these uniformly selective, uncertain, and highly mutable recollections. With growing temporal distance from his lifetime, the folk memory of him as a hero broadened and changed into anecdote and myth, a development that first became evident in Notker of St. Gall's *Gesta Karoli* and was subsequently repeated endlessly in popular and scholarly accounts.

The honorific title of "the Great" (*Carolus magnus*), which became firmly established only around 1000, stuck to him forever thereafter; in German he is known as "Karl der Große," while in French the honorific became an integral part of a new name. "Charlemagne." As Charlemagne, he remained for centuries the hero of French history. Louis XIV appealed to his memory when he sent his troops across the Rhine, and Montesquieu praised him as a constitutional monarch—"The prince was great, the man was even greater"; "His genius spread over all the parts of the empire"; "One sees in the laws of this prince a spirit of foresight that includes everything, and a certain force that carries everything along."[28] Only Voltaire saw fit to criticize the great ruler ("the son of a servant") for being a usurper and a despot and for having put to death thousands of Saxons.[29] Like Schedel before him, the most important German constitutional lawyer of the eighteenth century, Johann Jacob Moser, saw Charlemagne primarily as a French king, from whose realm Germany later split and developed as an independent state.[30] Finally, Napoleon had ambitions to resurrect Charlemagne's empire and to this end invaded Italy and crossed the Rhine.[31] In 1804, on the occasion of Bonaparte's coronation as emperor of France, the *Journal de Paris* noted: "In Europe, there is only one hand worthy of wielding the sword of Charlemagne, and it belongs to Bonaparte the Great."[32]

The study of history as an academic subject, which blossomed during the nineteenth century and the first half of the twentieth, mostly interpreted the material on Charlemagne in a nationalistic light. Only tentatively, in the writings of August Wilhelm Schlegel, did a different viewpoint begin to emerge, one that dared to regard Charlemagne from a European perspective. Leopold von Ranke returned to a nationalistic interpretation, seeing in

Charlemagne the ideal German and the "executor of world history."[33] Thereafter, horizons narrowed even further, at least in Germany. One further German voice should be cited at this juncture, the novelist Gustav Freytag, who—elegantly but erroneously—said of Charlemagne, "He was a German from head to toe, hard as steel yet soft as a child, in need of education yet thoughtful, capable of lenience and clarity in his judgments and of contented abandon to the mood of the moment, surely the greatest prince of German stock known to history. . . . The sense of order that Charlemagne imposed marks the beginning of Germany's history as an autonomous nation."[34] No sooner had the idea of Europe—however cautiously—been associated with the Carolingian monarch than it vanished once more. As a consequence, no Dane, Pole, Hungarian, Greek, or Russian celebrated his reign, although among the Slavs, his name came to be used as a ruler's title: *korol, król,* or *král.*

Finally, scholars have also considered the influence that Charlemagne had on cultural history, a phenomenon often apostrophized as the "Carolingian Renaissance."[35] This had to overtrump any nationalism. Perhaps for that reason, it took a "neutral" Swiss with no allegiance to either France of Germany, namely, the historian Jacob Burckhardt from Basel, to draw attention to this perspective. However briefly Burckhardt may have treated this subject, his Charlemagne was nevertheless one of the few historical figures, if not the only one, who managed to move this archskeptic to indulge in unashamed speculation:[36]

> Indeed, if we imagine the heyday of Charlemagne's empire
> lasting for a century, then over this period culture would surely
> have gained precedence, moving from the third most important
> aspect [that is, after the state and the Church] to the first. Then
> city life, art, and literature would have formed the general
> tenor of the age, and there would have been no Middle Ages.
> The world would simply have leapfrogged this phase and
> flowed seamlessly into the High Renaissance (rather than just
> offered tentative beginnings of such a development); and the
> Church, however greatly Charlemagne favored this institution,
> would never have gained remotely the power it later did.

Yet, Burckhardt lamented, too many "only seemingly tamed forces of barbarianism" contrived to thwart any such trajectory. "The culture of which Charlemagne was a representative was, in view of the barbarism of the seventh and eighth centuries, essentially a Renaissance in itself and could appear under no other guise" was the same author's laconic summation in his work *The Civilization of the Renaissance in Italy,* a work that played a key role in shaping the entire conception of the Renaissance in academic research.[37] So, under Charlemagne, a Renaissance "essentially" occurred, or perhaps more accurately a pre- or proto-Renaissance.

This assessment, however, was neither entirely false nor completely true. The fruitful and enduring cultural effect of Charlemagne's long reign is undeniable, but it was not sought for its own sake; rather, it was intended to consolidate the Church and royal authority. To put it simply, the true end-product of the civilization that Charlemagne revived was the grandiose forgery that was the *Pseudo-Isidorian Decretals*—characterized by a combination of knowledge and aptitude, rationality and faith, and innovation and inertia—rather than, as Burckhardt suggested, a mode of thinking that in any way resembled the genuinely secular mind-set of the late medieval Renaissance.[38]

Some remarkable works of art were dedicated to the hero Charlemagne in Italy, France, and Germany. The most famous and frequently reproduced images of the ruler are the portrait busts of Charlemagne in Aachen, most likely commissioned by Charles IV, and the idealized portrait created by Albrecht Dürer for the Nuremberg treasure chamber (Figure 60). The early Baroque fresco of Charlemagne by Taddeo Zuccaro in the Sala Regia, the magnificent state room at the Vatican, is an imaginative rendition of the ruler's donation of territories to the Roman Church, which is still regarded today as the historical origin of the Papal States. Since 1846, frescoes of Charlemagne by Alfred Rethel have adorned the banqueting hall of Aachen town hall,[39] which was built on the site of Charlemagne's former *Aula Regia*.

The brothers Charles and Louis Rochet cast an impressive bronze statue of Charlemagne on horseback and his paladins (*Charlemagne et ses leudes*); completed in 1882, this work was installed at a highly symbolic location, in front of Notre-Dame Cathedral on the Île de la Cité in Paris, in the very heart of France, so to speak—a defiant gesture of self-assertion by a nation that had suffered a humiliating defeat at the hands of Prussia in 1870/1871. During this conflict, a scurrilous caricature by an unknown artist, titled "Entrée du Charlemagne moderne à Paris—accompagné par son ministre" (Entry of the new Charlemagne into Paris, accompanied by his minister), showed Wilhelm I, sitting astride a pig, and his chancellor, Otto von Bismarck, heading down the Champs-Elysées; the Prussian king sports the crown and the extravagant mustache of the defeated French emperor, Napoleon III.[40]

CAROLVS·MAGNVS IN PATRIMONII·POSSESSIONEM
ROMANAM·ECCLESIAM·RESTITVIT

FIGURE 56 Charlemagne signing his renewal of the Donation of Pepin; detail from a fresco in the Sala Regia of the Vatican by Taddeo Zuccaro (sometime after 1573).

On the opposing side, Bismarck had originally proposed a statue of Charlemagne as a monument to commemorate the founding of the German Empire, rather than the symbolic figure of Germania that was ultimately sculpted and inaugurated at Rüdesheim am Rhein in the state of Hesse in 1883.[41]

Was this dual Carolus Magnus to be interpreted as symbol of confrontation or as a sign of peace stressing the common origin of the opposing nations? It was easy to recast the legend of Charlemagne as political prop-

FIGURE 57 *Charlemagne and His Paladins* (*Charlemagne et ses leudes*), bronze sculpture by Charles and Louis Rochet, 1882, Île de la Cité, Paris.

aganda. Protestants hailed Charlemagne as a forerunner of the Reformation.[42] Others have even claimed him as an enlightened monarch,[43] while romanticism retrospectively idealized the figure of Charlemagne beyond all recognition. The philosopher of the Sturm und Drang movement, Johann Gottfried Herder, composed a poignant obituary for him: "Rest in peace, then, o great king, you who in the long run were too great for your successors. . . .

Perhaps you will reappear in the year 1800 and reset the machine that began running in 800. . . . Great Charlemagne, the empire that fell apart immediately after your death is your monument. France, Germany, and Lombardy are its ruins."[44] Admittedly, the post-Napoleonic restoration that began soon after Herder wrote these words would preserve these ruins.

Charlemagne as the Hero of Myth

The trope of Charlemagne as the hero of legend[45] appears to reiterate the fundamental trait of real historical events, namely, the subjugation of foreign peoples. Accordingly, the brothers Grimm found Saxony and Lombardy particularly fertile hunting grounds when they were tracking down the (German) myth of Charlemagne. "Only after the eradication of the Merovingians does a luxuriant thicket of rich legend begin to grow up around Charlemagne. Hereafter, the cultural traditions of the tribes who populate the north of Germany, namely, the Saxons, the Westphalians, and the Frisians, are lost almost entirely and obliterated virtually at a stroke. . . . Such wanton destruction would be barely comprehensible were it not explained by the cruel subjugation of these peoples by Charlemagne; hand in hand with the destruction of all ancient customs and observances came the introduction of Christianity."[46] A millennium before the Grimms, Notker of St. Gall had provided some initial material for the legend of Charlemagne, which then continued to grow and proliferate. Over the ages, around one hundred instances of mythologizing tales appear; Charlemagne duly became the "supreme figure of legend, bar none."[47] He was even mentioned in books of spells and magic incantations: the so-called "Charlemagne's Prayer," used to invoke Jesus's help in resisting the devil, could supposedly also protect a person against enemies, fire, water, evil spirits, or illness.[48]

The cycle of motifs around what would later (from the late eleventh century) coalesce into the "Chanson de Roland" seems to have begun to expand from the second half of the ninth century on and spread throughout France, Spain, Germany, and Italy. The genesis of the "Chanson" can be followed over two centuries. Other poetic compositions soon added to the canon of works on this subject.[49] They provide examples of the transformation of the figure of Charlemagne from secular emperor to crusader and ultimately saint.[50] As early as the tenth century, writers such as the monk Benedict of Sant'Andrea del Soratte depicted Charlemagne as a pilgrim in the Holy Land, a motif that later, during the era of the Crusades, became ever more commonplace. Around that time, and certainly sometime before

1130, the *Historia Caroli Magni et Rotholandi* (*History of the Life of Charlemagne and Roland*) was published, written by the so-called Pseudo-Turpin. This forged chronicle of legends surrounding Charlemagne's supposed capture of Spain from the Moors became particularly influential; it was instrumental in Charlemagne's complete transfiguration to sainthood[51] and to a kind of precursor of the emperor at the End of Days.[52] France and Spain in particular were central to this development, but the legend of Charlemagne (*Karlamagnús saga*) spread as far afield as Norway and Iceland. A wide variety of social and political needs was reflected in the different manifestations of the Charlemagne saga and legend down the ages.

A process not only of hero worship and sanctification but also of devaluation of the king and emperor is evident in these legends. Especially during the High Middle Ages, disparagement of Charlemagne took hold in the south of France, which was far removed from the center of monarchy in Paris. A series of so-called rebel epics mirrored this development—to cite just one example, the chanson de geste of *The Four Sons of Haimon* (also known as *Rainaut de Montauban*). This tale relates the adventures of the children of the legendary Count Haimon and his wife Aja, supposedly a sister of Charlemagne. These sons, foremost among whom is Rainaut/Renart, find themselves opposed to Charlemagne and are condemned to death but manage to survive. They then exact revenge on Charlemagne by killing his son Louis but are ultimately forced to bend the knee to the ruling authorities.

This tale was translated into several languages and had various new elements constantly added to it (for instance, Rainaut's involvement in the building of Cologne Cathedral) according to the social context in which the story was related. It was one of the earliest books of folktales to be published. Its basic theme was the tension between the loyalty of vassals and aristocratic resistance to an overbearing king. At the time this verse epic was composed, it broached the issue of opposition to the trend toward centralization on the part of the French Crown in the late twelfth and early thirteenth centuries. The folktale version of *The Four Sons of Haimon* fired Goethe's imagination when he read it in childhood: "We children had the good fortune to find these precious remains of the Middle Ages every day on a little table outside the door of a secondhand bookseller, and to buy them at the cost of just a few kreuzer: *Till Eulenspiegel, The Four Sons of Haimon, The Fair Melusine . . . The Wandering Jew* were all to hand whenever we relished works of this kind rather than sweet things."[53]

In the High Middle Ages, even the Jewish community invoked the memory of the great Frankish ruler.[54] Recollections of him illuminate Jewish stories from this period like bright beams of light. Some writers credited Charlemagne with the Jewish settlement of southern Gallia. For example, the chronicle written by Abraham ben David (*Sefer Ha-kabbalah* [*The book of tradition*]) recounted that Charlemagne asked Harun al-Rashid to send him a rabbi from the House of David, and that this scholar, a man by the name of Rabbi Makhir, duly came to the West and, after Charlemagne had captured Narbonne from the Saracens, was granted a third of this city and founded an important Talmudic school there. The chronicler claimed that a special privilege issued by the king confirmed this grant of land and placed the Jewish community in Narbonne under royal protection. In actual fact, Narbonne had already been incorporated into the Frankish Empire in 759 under Pepin the Short.

This story was repeated in a slightly different form, but still in the twelfth or early thirteenth century, by the *Gesta Karoli Magni ad Carcassonam et Narbonam*, which was disseminated in both Latin and the Provençal language. According to this account, when Charlemagne was besieging Narbonne, the Jews living in the city sent him 70,000 marks in silver, offering to let him storm the city through that section of the walls that they were charged with defending. In return, all they asked of him was that their "king from the House of David" (*rex de gente nostra . . . de genere Davidis*) should always retain authority over the city. Charlemagne gave them his promise and, after taking the city, ascended the royal throne surrounded by a great crowd, scepter in hand. He summoned the local nobleman Aimeric of Narbonne and told him, "Aimeric, I am granting one-third of the city to the archbishop and one-third to the Jews; the remainder is yours." In this version, too, he confirmed everything by granting a royal privilege.[55] This story, slightly altered, was also recounted of other places. It was also said that Charlemagne was the first person to relocate Jews from Italy to the Rhineland.[56] The actual situation was quite different.[57]

These sagas all served to idealize the Christian ruler. They could sometimes take on mythical elements. This is the case, for instance, in the decoration of a valuable limewood panel painting by the artist Albrecht Altdorfer, which is thought to have come originally from Regensburg and is dated 1518; it is now kept at the German National Museum in Nuremberg.[58] This painting, titled *The Victory of Charlemagne over the Avars near Regensburg,* depicts Charlemagne doing battle in front of an idealized townscape and, supported by an avenging angel, striking down heathens. In the myth that is attached to this picture, the angel revealed to Charlemagne the countries and the peoples that he was destined to convert to Christianity. Pope Celestine, the legend continued, had blessed this struggle and sent his legate Appollonius to support the king. With heavenly assistance, Charlemagne proceeded to bring Sicily, Apulia, the Terra di Lavoro (Liburia), Tuscia, and all the surrounding lands into the Christian fold. Only the Lombard king Desiderius clung resolutely to paganism, before the emperor was finally able to forcibly baptize the people of this region too. The Bavarians promptly accepted baptism voluntarily, except for the "square city" of Regensburg (the former Roman settlement of Castra Regina). Besieged by Charlemagne from the "Siegbühel" hill outside the city, Regensburg put up stern resistance and fell only after fierce fighting, in which the angel intervened. To give thanks for his victory, Charlemagne founded the Church of Weih St. Peter on the burial ground beside his tent. At the time when this legend was published and the painting was completed, the Bavarian city requested that relics of the sacred emperor be sent from Aachen.

Charlemagne as Saint

The figure of Charlemagne as the hero of legend already had a distinct aura of saintliness about it.[59] Corresponding intimations appear as early as 900 in the writings of the anonymous "Poeta Saxo." This poet, who to a large extent drew his material from the *Royal Frankish Annals,* made Charlemagne into a herald of the Christian faith to the Saxons. Evangelization of the region was a way of overcoming the inglorious past of the Saxons, the disgrace of a defeat by the Franks.[60] But the first attempt to raise Charlemagne to the status of sainthood in 1000, by the young Holy Roman emperor Otto III and his ecclesiastical aides Heribert of Cologne and Bernward of Hildesheim, came to nothing.[61] The fact that the young ruler died less than two years after the opening of Charlemagne's grave caused this pious act to be retrospectively interpreted as one of desecration.

The Salians, German kings and emperors from a Frankish dynasty, claimed to be able to trace their line back to Charlemagne via Gisela, the wife of Conrad II. But it was Frederick Barbarossa who finally succeeded in getting Charlemagne canonized on 29 December 1165. The emperor found himself in a tricky political situation at the time and hoped that he might gain some kudos by elevating this heroic figure from the past to sainthood. The Hohenstaufen monarch was supported by two leading clerics, Rainald von Dassel, the archbishop of Cologne, and the bishop of Liège, and the antipope Paschal III agreed to the canonization. Sacred relics were distributed, and the first reliquaries were donated, foremost among them the golden casket of Charlemagne's remains in Aachen Cathedral, which Barbarossa's grandson and namesake Frederick II ceremonially closed in 1215. However, the political circumstances of the canonization disbarred the new saint from gaining general liturgical recognition by the Catholic Church: "Charlemagne was never a 'popular saint'; his canonization was the result of political considerations, and his cult never anything more than a minor local one."[62] The cult of St. Charlemagne gained a foothold only in a few places, notably Aachen, Reims, Frankfurt am Main, Zurich, and Regensburg. The twelfth century witnessed the composition of the beautiful prayer known as the "Karlssequenz" (Charles's sequence), which is still sung today as part of the Karlsamt, a Holy Mass for Charlemagne celebrated in these cities:

> *Urbs Aquensis, urbs regalis,*
> *Regni sedes principalis,*
> *Prima regum curia,*
> *Regi regum pange laudes,*
> *Quae de magni regis gaudes*
> *Karoli praesentia.*[63]

(City of Aachen, royal city,
Principal seat of the kingdom,
First court of kings,
Sing to the king of kings
The praises with which you
Celebrate the presence of King Charles.)

In France, the liturgical veneration of Charlemagne—accompanied by aspirations of renewal—began in earnest in the fourteenth century under the French king Charles V; this too has survived to the present day.[64] Charles commissioned a golden royal scepter with a statuette of Charlemagne seated on his throne at its tip. Underneath, three medallions show three scenes from the legend of Charlemagne as related by Pseudo-Turpin. Napoleon later took possession of this treasure[65]—the very emperor who saw himself as the true successor to the great and sainted Carolingian ruler. Bonaparte revived the cult of St. Charlemagne; just as it had done under Louis XIV, this appropriation of Charlemagne served to legitimize France's expansion under the Corsican dictator to the east and beyond the Rhine. In Germany, though, the Reformation, the Enlightenment, and the gradual process of secularization in the nineteenth century saw the Charlemagne cult recede to just Aachen and Frankfurt.[66]

Yet Charlemagne the "saint" also proved highly effective in secularized form, as a national hero. A nationalistic narrowing of cultural horizons and the formulation of anachronistic opinions among scholars did the rest, turning Charlemagne into a hero of the French and then, in turn, of the Germans. In both of these countries, intellectuals competed to prove Charlemagne's nationality. "Charlemagne" was regarded as a Frenchman, and his empire as a forerunner of France. Louis XIV and Napoleon both made full use of this intellectual construct. Meanwhile, "Karl der Große" arose as a distinctly German hero figure.

To be sure, the Scottish historian and king's chaplain William Robertson, writing in 1769, provided some gentle hints of a "European" Charlemagne. Yet these had to wait for the era of Napoleonic hegemony to end before they bore riper, though not always more assertive, fruit. Even Napoleon, after conquering Lombardy, had entertained the ambition of becoming a new Charlemagne: "*Pour le Pape, je suis Charlemagne*" (In the pope's eyes, I am Charlemagne), he is supposed to have claimed.[67] In the course of lectures on modern history that he delivered in 1810 in Vienna, the German romantic Friedrich Schlegel was the first person, it would appear, to sketch an image of Charlemagne as the "lawgiver for the whole of Western Europe." The great Corsican dictator may well have been the inspiration behind this notion. Schlegel certainly knew of Napoleon's assertion that "a great European federative system alone can be favorable to the development of civilization." But it was Charlemagne, the German historian claimed, who first lent Europe tangible form as a "Christian union of all Western nations," and who laid the foundations of a "European republic." However we may choose to evaluate Charlemagne's achievements, this is most decidedly not one of them.

The French and the Germans especially cherished an abiding memory of "Charlemagne" and "Karl der Große," respectively, as a framer of legislation and a judge, as a celebrated precursor and ancestor of their own ruling dynasties, as the founder of the Electoral College of German princes and the University of Paris, as a warrior against paganism, as a crusader, and as a saint—in short, as the embodiment of everything they had held dear since time immemorial.

Around the same time as Schlegel's Vienna lectures, Goethe recalled, "We heard many a legend told about Charlemagne, but our interest in real, historical events began with Rudolf of Habsburg, who by his courage put an end to such violent disorder."[68] This testifies to a remarkable lack of interest on Goethe's part in a ruler during whose reign, after all, the writer's own birthplace, Frankfurt, entered history. Certainly, Charlemagne the saint may well have held little fascination for the Protestant Goethe. Or was he, as a humanist, not particularly interested in this warlike emperor? Then there was the folktale of "Iron Charles," which the brothers Grimm had recorded in their *German Legends* of 1816–1818. This Charles was "bold, handsome, merciful, blessed, humble, constant, praiseworthy, and fearless." And legend had it that he would return at the End of Days. So perhaps Charlemagne was an emperor for the Apocalypse after all.

Malicious Misrepresentation

The differences among nations deformed the figure of the great Frankish king, traces of whose rule can still be found in France, Germany, Italy, and Catalonia. Over time, he atrophied into little more than a figurehead for various mundane political objectives. In the later years of the nineteenth century, the British historian Houston Stewart Chamberlain was responsible for sowing many weeds in this particular field with his work *The Foundations of the Nineteenth Century*—an unspeakable piece of historical misrepresentation that nevertheless was widely and eagerly read by the German bourgeoisie of the time. The weeds Chamberlain sowed fell on particularly fertile soil in Germany and grew rampant. According to this Germanophile writer, Charlemagne had it in his power to separate the Germans definitively from Rome but in fact did just the opposite. "This so fatally enthusiastic admirer of Rome was nevertheless a good German, and nothing lay nearer his heart than reforming from top to bottom, and freeing from the clutches of heathenism this Church which he so passionately prized as an ideal." But nothing Charlemagne achieved in his struggle against Rome was permanent, claimed Chamberlain. Instead, his actions had been determined by "inconsistencies"; "by his activity in the interests of culture and his Teutonic attitude of mind," Chamberlain maintained, "[he had] contributed more than any other to the unfettering of nationalities and to the gagging of the Roman idea."[69]

Before long, even worse liberties were being taken with the name of Charlemagne. "A region fell under the suzerainty of the Teutons—a region as great as the people themselves. An extensive homeland was made ready on Earth for this race. That was the end result of Charlemagne's policies." Thus wrote the influential cultural commentator Arthur Moeller van den Bruck, the man who claimed to have coined the term "the Third Reich." In his eight-volume work *The Germans: Our People's History,* which appeared from 1905 onward, Moeller van den Bruck expanded on his idea of Charlemagne as a key figure in the genesis of the German race: "It was by the grace of the emperor, not of the pope, that Christianity, Germanic culture, and the force that bound together and promoted these two realms—namely, the Nordic emperorship—survived." Yet Charlemagne's empire collapsed, the upshot of which was that "German culture could not make its way through history as a single, distinct race but only in the form of individual nations."[70] Tendentious statements such as this, which were doubtless far more influential than scholarly university history, were to shape the political opinions of the following generation with disastrous consequences.

The image of Charlemagne thus sparkled like some multifaceted diamond. In the ideologically discordant National Socialist period, the picture of the Frankish ruler, Holy Roman emperor, and saint underwent a number of confusing transformations.[71] In the spirit of Alfred Rosenberg, the anti-Italian and antipapal editor of the Nazi newspaper *Völkischer Beobachter* (who admittedly never used the phrase directly himself), some commentators at the time repeatedly defamed Charlemagne as a "butcher of the Saxons."[72] This term can almost certainly be traced back to the journalist and regional writer Hermann Löns, whose virulently anti-Charlemagne short story "Die rote beeke" (The Red Brook) of 1912 gave a dramatic account of the "bloody assizes" of Verden in 782: "I'm telling you, boy, run as fast as your legs will carry you. Charlemagne is already at the river crossing and is holding an assizes to judge thousands of men." Charlemagne is painted in the blackest hues: "The wine and women of the South had made him heavy and sluggish." "And Renke [the fictional bard of the story] starts shouting, louder than anyone around him: 'All hail! All hail!' and waving his cap in the air and staring at the king." And finally: "In a hollow whisper . . . Renke, the avenger, . . . brings news of the terrible slaughter . . . and of the dreadful day when the waters of the brook ran red with blood, on the orders of King Charlemagne." Löns's story ends with a rendition of the (again fictional) "Ballad of the Shameful Butcher and the Red Brook."[73]

Hermann Löns's story found favor with both Hitler and the Baltic German Rosenberg, who added and emphasized racist and anticlerical elements. According to Rosenberg, Charlemagne had suppressed the freedom and the religion of the Nordic race and in return for this "crime against the German people" had been canonized.[74] Voltaire had already leveled this latter false accusation at Charlemagne.[75] By contrast, the Saxon leader Widukind advanced to the status of an alternative hero, a warrior and king on a par with Charlemagne. Indeed, as early as 1653, the illustrated title page of the engraver Matthäus Merian's *Topographia Saxoniae Inferioris* (*Topography of Lower Saxony*) depicted him opposite Charlemagne, labeling them respectively as *Witekind M(agnus)* and *Carolus M(agnus)*.[76]

But the worst example of Charlemagne's reputation being traduced occurred in Münster. There, shortly after the Nazis' "seizure of power," a drama with the title *Wittekind* was given its premiere; although the play's eponymous hero had to submit to the victor Charlemagne and be baptized, as had happened in reality, he agreed to do so only because the Frankish ruler and "admirer of Rome" had threatened to let 60,000 Saxon women be raped by "foreign races, Jews, and Huns" if he refused.[77]

Eight highly respected German historians were moved to write a monograph condemning such defamation "for the sake of the truth . . . and for the sake of Germany, which would only harm itself if it were to abandon this outstanding personality." As the foreword, which may well have been the work of Karl Hampe, at that time the doyen of German medieval scholarship, stated, Charlemagne was the person who united the "tribes of the Franks, Saxons, Frisians, Thuringians, Swabians, and Bavarians in a single realm." This sentiment was not all that far removed from that of Moeller van den Bruck ("It was his [i.e., Charlemagne's] work that enabled a unified Germany to develop in the first place"). Moreover, the academics identified Voltaire (i.e., a Frenchman) as the instigator of all the "accusations leveled at Charlemagne." They were intent on ensuring that the French Enlightenment philosopher "gained no more disciples . . . in his denigration of the first emperor of Germanic stock." But, they stated, they were not going to demonstrate Charlemagne's "achievements on the stage of world history" in their ensuing essays but instead would endeavor to paint "a rounded picture of him, as a person of Teutonic-German character and descent." The figure of "Charlemagne" was a reinterpretation that had always been conjured up to justify "French expansionist policies toward the Rhine and toward regions on the right bank of the river."[78] The eminent medievalist chose to completely blank out the long tradition of divergence in the naming of the ruler from the Middle Ages onward. Instead, all of a sudden, his name was seen to reflect a supposedly traditional enmity between Germany and France. In the following contributions to this monograph, the careful reader needed to be alive to nuances rather than focus on the "official" line of argument, which tended to actually obscure the high regard in which these authors held Charlemagne.

Without mentioning him by name, the adversary these historians were tilting at was the powerful Rosenberg. All the same, they did not represent a single political standpoint. Nor was their aim to correct the National Socialist image of Charlemagne either within or outside Germany. Quite the contrary: even Carl Erdmann, who took a critical and hostile stance toward the Nazi regime, who drew a clear distinction between "Teutons" and "Germans" and explicitly refused to recognize the latter as Teutons, and who saw the Roman, Christian, and Catholic elements that Nazi ideology so reviled as an integral part of the Teutonic-German character—even he concluded his essay with an observation that chimed in with the general tenor of the times: "Charlemagne . . . was ultimately responsible for deciding that Germany should evolve in accordance with the ideals of antiquity and Christendom, and set an example in his own person that the Teutonic-German character would not thereby be lost, only deepened. The service he rendered to the development of the German character was incomparable."[79] Opposing Rosenberg, then, did not mean opposing a nationalistic interpretation of Charlemagne.

Such interpretations, though, scarcely did justice to the Carolingian ruler either. At least some of the theories advanced by the eight historians chimed in with Hitler's views on the subject. Shortly after, in his concluding address to the Nuremberg Party Congress of 1935, without mentioning Charlemagne or the Saxons by name, he offered the following overview of German history, which ran counter to Rosenberg's assessment: "The first joining together of the German people into a state could come about only through the violation of the independent existence of individual German tribes. . . . We should not condemn history because the path that led from dozens of German tribes to a single German nation proceeded—and had to proceed— through the more or less unforgiving violation of tens of thousands of people."[80] This was a brutal vindication of the use of force and—tacitly—of Hitler's future wars of conquest: Charlemagne the violator and Hitler his follower. The Frankish king would, admittedly, have acknowledged the other peoples in their differentness; achieving conformity through oppression was Hitler's objective.

Rosenberg therefore found himself obliged to perform an ideological about-face.[81] The very next year, 1936, his Reich Office for the Promotion of Literature for the Total Spiritual and Ideological Education of the German

National Socialist Workers' Party published a textbook that peddled this new party line, titled *Geschichtsunterricht als nationalsozialistische Erziehung* (*History Teaching as National Socialist Education*). Its author, Dietrich Klagges, the distinctly menacing premier of the state of Braunschweig, celebrated the figure who had so recently been reviled: "The Frankish king Charlemagne acknowledged the security of Germanic Europe as the greatest political objective of his life," a "unified Teutonic empire under the hegemony of the Franks" (p. 315). "Charlemagne was the first Teuton to be the master and guardian of the whole of Europe. His capital city of Aachen supplanted Rome as the center of world politics" (p. 320). However, "the Teutonic global empire, Emperor Charlemagne's greatest creation, was smashed to pieces" (p. 322); Klagges concluded that it would rise again, all the more gloriously, only under Hitler: "In protecting themselves, the German people at the same time guard and preserve Nordic culture throughout the whole of Europe and worldwide" (p. 328).[82]

Dictatorships have always sought to appropriate history for their own ends, and Hitler certainly exploited the figure of Charlemagne. Had he taken on board the ideas put forward in the monograph by the eight historians? Hitler's "table talk" during the war years (recorded at his headquarters by the Nazi lawyer Henry Picker) would certainly suggest that this was so:[83] "He said . . . he had drawn Rosenberg's attention to the fact . . . that it was improper to call a hero like Charlemagne 'the butcher of the Saxons.' " "The German nation was, he claimed, . . . a product of compulsion, ancient philosophy, and Christianity. In Imperial times, it was through compulsion that the German nation had welded itself together into a coherent whole under the aegis of a Christianity represented by a universal church and in the image of ancient Rome. It was certain that a man like Charlemagne was not motivated merely by a desire for political power but sought instead—in adherence to the ancient idea—for an expression of civilization." "Guided by these maxims, which were quite simple and natural, Charlemagne had organized the Germans into a tight-knit community, he said, and created an empire that was still worthy of the name long after his death. This empire comprised the best elements of the old Roman Imperium, with the result that for centuries the peoples of Europe have regarded it as a continuation of the global empire of the Caesars." This conception of Charlemagne and the Holy Roman Empire provided rich propaganda pickings for the Nazis in justifying their policies.

The misappropriation of Charlemagne at this time knew no bounds. On 2 April 1942, the twelve hundredth anniversary of the emperor's conjectured

FIGURE 58 Special postmark of the German Imperial Postal Service introduced in 1942 to mark the supposed twelve hundredth anniversary of Charlemagne's birth.

birth, the German Postal Service (Reichspost) issued a special postmark that read "Greater Germany commemorates Charlemagne" and showed a right-facing profile of the famous equestrian statuette.[84] Hitler had a clear motive in commemorating the French emperor Charlemagne, namely, to win support for his plans in France. This son of a customs official enjoyed comparison with the great medieval ruler; it served to gloss over his own crimes. A further, more grandiose gesture of the same kind came in 1943, when Hitler commissioned a commemorative plate manufactured from fine Sèvres porcelain (Figure 59). Once again, its face was decorated with a relief image of the equestrian statuette from the Louvre (Figure 23), while the reverse bore the following Latin inscription, directed at the people of Europe: *IMPERIUM / CAROLI MAGNI / DIVISUM PER NEPOTES / ANNO DCCCXLIII / DEFENDIT / ADOLPHUS HITLER / UNA CUM / OMNIBUS EUROPAE POPULIS / ANNO MCMXLIII* (The empire of Charlemagne, divided by his grandsons in the year 843, Adolf Hitler is now defending, together with all the peoples of Europe. In the year 1943).

The message was crystal clear: Hitler was the new Charlemagne. Whoever the aggressor may have been, Hitler was presented here as the person to unite the shattered Carolingian Empire, served by the peoples of Europe and acting as a ruler by force who, in the words of the 1935 Nuremberg

FIGURE 59 This plate in Sèvres porcelain was produced for Adolf Hitler to distribute as a commemorative gift, in most instances to members of the French SS Division "Charle-magne." Paris, Musée de l'Armée.

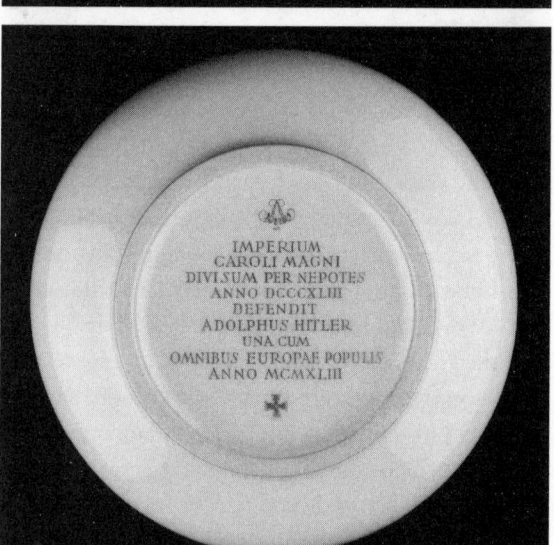

speech, intended to bring these nations to heel through "violation of their independent existence." Most of the recipients of the commemorative china plate were members of the SS division "Charlemagne," a unit made up of French volunteers who had made themselves willing accomplices of that vi-olation. The chauvinistic policy of the National Socialist regime toward Eu-rope used the great Frankish leader as a symbolic figure to rally around.

Professional German historians like Hermann Aubin, a professor at Breslau and later Hamburg who had been a contributor to the 1935 monograph, voiced much the same kind of sentiment as Hitler in offering a speciously positive analysis of Germany's actions in the so-called Lightning War invasion of Poland and France in 1939–1940. "The masterful hand of Charlemagne," wrote Aubin in the (then as now) most prestigious German historical journal, *Historische Zeitschrift*,[85] "put in place the essential elements for a satisfactory settlement between the interests of the German masters and the foreign subject races." Aubin was not forced to kowtow in this way to the evil spirit of the age, but his utter contempt for foreign peoples was shameful all the same.

In 1997, in a lecture delivered in Aachen in honor of Charlemagne, the director of the German Historical Institute in Paris, Karl Ferdinand Werner, delivered the following highly pertinent verdict: "It is not our history as such that led to disaster, but rather the evolution of certain ideas for which the conceited academic disciplines of the nineteenth century were largely to blame. This process succeeded in crowning us Germans, we who were once so proud of our education, with the dunce cap of the politically stupidest people in Europe."[86] The distortion of the historical Charlemagne was a prime example of such arrant folly.

Charlemagne and the Modern Age

"Who was Charlemagne? When did he live? I have been posing these questions for quite some time . . . and have had cause to notice, albeit with a certain degree of incredulity and notwithstanding the existence of the annual 'Charlemagne Prize' and the magnificent Cathedral at Aachen, how far he has receded in people's historical consciousness." These were the opening sentences of a radio lecture given by Horst Fuhrmann, the long-serving president of the Monumenta Germaniae historica, the leading medieval research archive in Germany, in 1983.[87] Nor has the situation got any better in the thirty-plus years that have elapsed since then—despite the epoch-making exhibition organized by the Council of Europe in Aachen in 1965 to mark the eight hundredth anniversary of Charlemagne's canonization,[88] or the one put on in Paderborn in 1999 to commemorate Pope Leo III's visit to Charlemagne there twelve hundred years earlier, and despite the existence of many fine historical studies on the first emperor of the Carolingian dynasty, and even several substantial novels about him.[89] "Schoolchildren no longer have any conception of key events," lamented a 2012 article in a leading German newspaper,[90] while a political science study identified all manner of shortcomings in the teaching of history.[91] Similarly, a nation-wide survey conducted in Germany in 2012 on students' aptitude for higher education revealed a shocking deterioration in their command of language and their levels of reading literacy—both essential requirements for political, social, and cultural orientation with regard to both history and the present.[92] Yet a lack of orientation still continues to bedevil studies of Charlemagne.

Charlemagne was neither German nor French but Frankish—that is the prevailing verdict of current academic historians. Alongside this view, a few isolated images of him from the past—also the fruit of scholarship, though factually inaccurate—still enjoy a certain currency.[93] In these circumstances, after 1945 it was all too easy, especially in Germany, to co-opt Charlemagne for a new role and install him as a figurehead for the newly favored idea of a united Europe. The British historian Christopher Dawson had already set the tone for this conception of the ruler in 1932, in his work *The Making of Europe*. Dawson's view was at variance with the then still-current denigration of Charlemagne as a "Saxon-slayer": "The historical importance of the Carolingian age far transcends its material achievement. The unwieldy Empire of Charles the Great did not long survive the death of its founder, and it never really attained the economic and social organisation of a civilised state. But, for all that, it marks the first emergence of the European culture from the twilight of pre-natal existence into the consciousness of active life. Hitherto the barbarians had lived passively on the capital they had plundered; now they began to co-operate with it in a creative social activity."[94] It is easy to see how such a view could gain purchase after the war, particularly in Germany: "It is striking how there is a studied avoidance of the 'national question' in recent German historiography, especially in comparison to history writing in neighboring countries, which have retained their traditional conception of history."[95] Yet propagating the new ideal of Europe merely as an antidote to the kind of abuse of Charlemagne perpetrated earlier by, say, Klagges or Hitler was not a universal critical response. The Polish historian Oskar Halecki, for instance, writing in 1957, instead stressed that Charlemagne's achievement was to have "integrated Germanic peoples who had remained outside the boundaries of the old Roman Empire into the community of historical Europe"; one key indicator of this, in Halecki's view, was the way in which Christendom had extended its boundaries far to the northeast.[96]

Yet even this "European" role of Charlemagne is no longer accepted by all academic historians. "Unless I am very much mistaken, Charlemagne will remain just as bland as a symbol of European unity as he has been in all the previous roles assigned to him," the Czech historian František Graus,[97] who had been forced into exile by the Prague Spring of 1968, presciently noted. The French historian Jacques Le Goff was also somewhat skeptical on this point. In his 2005 work *The Birth of Europe,* he posed the question "Was Charlemagne—the First European?" before answering, "In my view . . . to present Charlemagne as the father of Europe is . . . a distortion of history." And although he fully recognized that Charlemagne and his counselors left Europe with the blueprint of a common culture and were responsible for the first European "renaissance," Le Goff was careful to qualify this assertion: "The Carolingian renaissance that developed around Charlemagne was somewhat more limited than is suggested by the triumphal and brilliant image that is sometimes purveyed of it."[98] Certainly, although it encompassed the whole of Western Europe, at no time did it include the British Isles or Spain west of the river Ebro, let alone Byzantium, "Greece," the Slavic lands, or Hungary.

Younger historians in France, Germany, Italy, England, and the United States are generally even more reserved in their judgment; Michael Borgolte's wide-ranging overview of the history of Europe offers a clear-sighted analysis.[99] One exception is Alessandro Barbero, whose monograph on Charlemagne, while stopping short of calling him "the father of Europe," nevertheless still refers to him as "a father of Europe."[100] Jean Favier's major 1999 biography of Charlemagne, meanwhile, avoids the catchword "Europe" altogether.[101]

Historians are unanimous, however, in acknowledging Charlemagne's importance for the cultural development of Western Europe and for the more or less uniform way in which the intellectual character of this region was determined by the spread of the cultural and scholarly Latin language and the Roman Church, including the anticlerical opposition that was to erupt openly just a few centuries after Charlemagne's death. The systematic recourse to the work of grammarians from the golden age of classicism and late antiquity and to both Christian and pagan literature represent key factors in this cultural renewal, as does the writing reform instituted under Charlemagne that led to Carolingian minuscule and hence to the basic form of the script that is still in use today, and to the revival of monastic culture, which in turn became the bedrock of a new educational system. Modes of categorical and dialectical thinking were imparted to the Carolingian Empire from the reign of Charlemagne on through Boethius's translations of and commentaries on the methodology of Aristotle, while the ancient art of rhetoric—itself a form of epistemology—was gleaned from the works of Cicero. The fruits ultimately borne by these intellectual disciplines gave Western civilization a "unique selling proposition" that had worldwide repercussions. Last but not least, Europe had Charlemagne to thank for the calendar that, in the increasingly globalized world of the twentieth century, established itself internationally as the most widely used system for determining time.

Indeed, over the course of centuries, this "Western" culture radiated out to the entire world and in so doing was instrumental in changing the world and giving rise to a new "global present." We must, of course, be careful to distinguish any such long-term effects from original intentions and so resist declaring Charlemagne, on the basis of his own aims, either a "European" or a pioneer of globalization. One might profitably cite here the philosopher Karl Löwith's analysis of the approach Jacob Burckhardt adopted in his *Reflections on History* (published posthumously in 1905). Burckhardt's self-confessed modus operandi, in deliberate contrast to, say, Hegel's attempts to explain history by subordinating it to a principle, was merely "to link up a number of observations and enquiries to a series of half-random thoughts."

The permanent center of history, in Burckhardt's view, is "man, as he is and was and ever shall be, striving, acting, and suffering." There is no ultimate meaning in history, but rather an ongoing antagonism between, on the one hand, continuity and the "continuation of history as a tradition" and, on the other, "a revolutionary will to permanent revisions."[102] If one follows this reasoning, Charlemagne may be regarded as one of the "men of action" who wanted to preserve and renew things at the same time and yet achieved something genuinely new. If we are to do justice to such a figure, we need to judge him by the standards of his own time, and not to misappropriate him symbolically or propagandistically to serve the purposes of any particular subsequent age.

Modern historians who find themselves confronted by globalization never choose to focus merely on individual personalities but rather on social groups and societies worldwide; in the process, they also inevitably relativize Charlemagne's role. Recent mass migrations around the world and the need to formulate new "master narratives" of world history do not sit at all easily alongside notions of the "father of Europe," the founding-hero myth of France and Germany, the guardian of the Roman Church, or the image of a new Constantine, although all these conceptions may well have been perfectly justified at the time they were created. Such a viewpoint would be completely antiquated, for all that a resurgence of old nationalisms is discernible in the modern world. What is required is a global perspective.

A new departure in this respect was marked by the publication of the brilliant work *Mahomet et Charlemagne* by the Belgian historian Henri Pirenne, which appeared posthumously in 1937.[103] In actual fact, it is less the results of his research that draw our attention than his aims. At a time when nationalistic approaches to history were at their height, Pirenne's book was an audacious attempt at an objective standpoint that eschewed all nationalism. He planned the first draft of his work during his internment in a German prisoner-of-war camp in 1916. As an economic and cultural historian, Pirenne did not take as his starting point the narrow perspective and the restricted, self-reinforcing tendencies of his own European cultural milieu, the Frankish Empire, Roman traditions, or the Latin Church, but instead his profound knowledge of the Mediterranean economic area in the early medieval period, an area whose ancient unity he saw as shattered by the spread of Islam. This rupture made possible the relocation of the centers of power in the West from the south to the north, from Italy or southern Gallia to the region around the rivers Rhine and Meuse (Maas), and hand in hand with this development the rise of the Carolingians and Charlemagne. Viewed in this light, the Prophet Muhammad provided the springboard for Charlemagne's ascent to power.

Pirenne's theory was well received at the time; even today, it still has its defenders. Yet in the interim, archaeological evidence and painstaking research into the history of travel and trade in particular have shown that even as far back as the reign of the Byzantine emperor Justinian, the great lawgiver, who attempted to restore the unity of the empire through costly wars against the Vandals and the Goths, this unity was nevertheless immediately lost once more, and also that momentous events like the plague epidemic of the sixth century had lasting deleterious effects on communication in the Mediterranean. Before long, the extensive empire of Justinian and other early Byzantine rulers, which had spanned the entire Mediterranean, had become little more than the hinterland of Constantinople, the imperial city around which the whole empire coalesced but that also absorbed and used up all its potential.[104] The former "unity" of the Mediterranean had, so to speak, dwindled to nothing but Constantinople long before the warriors of Allah launched their assaults against the Roman provinces. Yet the methodological approach applied by Pirenne was new and fruitful, revealing as it did a very real intercultural interplay that was in no way intentional on the part of the former protagonists; alongside this extensive culture-endowing interaction, other novel elements contained in his study were the insights it afforded into communication processes that were equally capable of engendering friendship or enmity, and into a systemic dynamism that was detached from any human will. Pirenne's influential work gave rise to further studies of this kind and still continues to do so.[105]

Retaining as he did a keen awareness of a world in a state of flux, Charlemagne indisputably continually widened his horizons. "Through its confrontation with the emperorship in Constantinople and the papacy in Rome, the Frankish empire found its new form and ultimately its own version of a restricted universalism," the historian Peter Classen wrote in the 1960s.[106] Although this is undoubtedly true, it does not convey the whole truth of the matter. The Muslim world, through its economic relations and its exchange of technology and knowledge, exerted a far-longer-lasting influence on the Frankish Empire than even recent historians have assumed.[107] Even the office of emperor profited from the active contacts Charlemagne maintained with Muslim rulers in both the East and the West, as demonstrated not least by the obverse and reverse of the programmatic portrait coinage he had minted.[108]

All the same, the principal aim for scholars has been to comprehend in the context of his contemporary milieu the king and emperor under whom renewal took place, and to offer an appraisal of his impact on history. Yet from his youth, Charlemagne had been accustomed to looking beyond his narrow homeland around Paris and Soissons toward Saxony, Italy, and Spain, toward Córdoba, Constantinople, and Pannonia, toward Jerusalem, Kairouan, and Baghdad, from the Western to the Oriental world, with which he exchanged ambassadors and initiated trade contacts, and through which intercultural learning processes were stimulated within his own realm. Our evaluation of Charlemagne thus calls for a similarly broad view, taking in Europe, Asia, and Africa, and indeed the whole world that was known to him at that time.

Therefore, the image of Charlemagne continues to change. Admittedly, academic knowledge cannot be equated with the kind of historical knowledge current among the "general public" of central and Western Europe or the United States. If Charlemagne continues to live on at all in popular consciousness, it is as some vague, shadowy figure often consigned to a timeless realm of legend. Does this process have its roots in the material, spiritual, and cultural needs of a changed world that is steadily coalescing within a global framework? Or in the meeting or clash of a plethora of cultures with their own traditions and a high degree of self-awareness, to whom a distant hero figure means very little? Or in people's incapacity to fathom the depths of the globalization process?

FIGURE 60 Albrecht Dürer, idealized portrait of Charlemagne, 1512.
Germanisches Nationalmuseum, Nuremberg.

To be sure, within this general blurring of borders, the lasting impact that Charlemagne and his counselors had in strengthening the Roman Church and the universal papacy remains undimmed, even if it is rarely called to mind by the general public, as does the decisive impulse he and his court gave to the revival of a reason-based intellectual culture of the Latin Western world. In the millennium after Charlemagne's death, this culture would duly gain in strength and hold the world under its spell. Finally, one tangible reminder of Charlemagne still remaining is the veneration of Charlemagne the saint at a few locations in Western Europe, notably St. Mary's Cathedral in Aachen and St. Bartholomew's Cathedral in Frankfurt. In the Karlsamt, the Holy Mass sung there for Charlemagne, the Frankish ruler becomes timeless, completely divested of his earthly existence:

> *Regali natus*
> *de stirpe deoque probatus*
> *Karolus illicitae*
> *sprevit contagia vitae*
> *Angelica cultus*
> *dulcedine miles adultus*
> *dum sublimatur*
> *celesti pane cibatur.*

> (Born of royal lineage,
> And tested by God,
> Charles spurned
> Any contact with an illicit life.
> The strong hero,
> Adorned with the sweetness of angels,
> Will be lifted up and be
> Fed with the Bread of Heaven.)[109]

This Latin "rhymed office" (a service in which all the musical items were turned into verse), which is thought to have been composed as early as the twelfth century, eulogizes a Charlemagne from whom all the burden of sin has been cast off and who has been washed clean of all his former transgressions. This paean of praise continues to ring out every year without fail on the anniversary of his death.

ABBREVIATIONS

NOTES

SELECTED BIBLIOGRAPHY

ILLUSTRATION CREDITS

INDEX

ABBREVIATIONS

AM	anno mundi (=year date after the creation of the world)
AMP	*Annales Mettenses priores* (Earlier annals of Metz)
ArF	*Annales regni Francorum* (Royal Frankish annals)
ArFqdE	*Annales regni Francorum qui dicuntur Einhardi* (Royal Frankish annals reputed to be by Einhard)
BM²	J. F. Böhmer, *Regesta Imperii*, vol. 1, *Die Regesten des Kaiserreichs under den Karolingern, 751–918*, revised by Eberhard Mühlbacher and completed by Johann Lechner, with a foreword, concordance tables, and supplements by Carlrichard Brühl and Hans H. Kaminsky, Hildesheim 1966.
CC	Codex Carolinus
CdV	*Capitulare de villis*
CE	common era
D	Diplom (=record; the abbreviations that follow it, signifying the name of the relevant king and the number, identify the record in the edition of the MGH)

DA   Deutsches Archiv für Erforschung des Mittelalters (German Archive for Medieval Research)

DKDG   MGH Diplomata Karolinorum, records of Charlemagne with record number

FmaSt   *Frühmittelalterliche Studien* (Early medieval studies)

HJb   *Historisches Jahrbuch der Görres Gesellschaft* (Historical yearbook of the Görres Society)

HZ   *Historische Zeitschrift* (Historical journal)

LP   *Liber pontificalis* (Book of the popes; book of biographies of popes from St. Peter to the fifteenth century)

MGH   Monumenta Germaniae historica (collection of medieval historical sources covering the period ca. 500–1500)

Migne   see under *PL*

MIÖG   *Mitteilungen des Instituts für Österreichische Geschichtsforschung* (Communications of the Institute for Austrian Historical Research)

Ms.   manuscript

NA   *Neues Archiv der Gesellschaft für Ältere Deutsche Geschichtskunde* (New archive of the Society for Older German History)

PL   Migne, *Patrologia latina* (with volume number; collection of the writings of the Church Fathers and other ecclesiastical authors, published by Jacques-Paul Migne between 1840 and 1855)

Rhein. Vjbll.   *Rheinische Vierteljahrsblätter* (quarterly journal for regional studies of the Rhineland)

SB   Sitzungsbericht (minutes of proceedings of a given German historical research institute, indicated by the name of its location)

Settimane Spoleto   *Settimane di Studi del Centro Italiano di Studi sull'Alto Medioevo* (Papers of the Italian Center for Study of the Middle Ages, Spoleto)

SS	Scriptores
UB	Urkundenbuch (document/record book)
VuF	Vorträge und Forschungen hg. vom Konstanzer Arbeit-skreis für mittelalterliche Geschichte (Lectures and researches published by the Konstanz Working Group in Medieval History)
ZRG Kan	*Zeitschrift der Savigny-Stiftung für Rechtsgeschichte Kanonistische Abteilung* (Journal of the Savigny Institute of Legal History, Canon Law Division)

NOTES

1   Heito von Reichenau, *Visio Wettini,* chap. 11 (MGH Poetae 2 p. 271), in verse: Walahfrid Strabo vv. 446–65, both texts with translation: *Visio Wettini,* ed. Knittel, pp. 48–50 and pp. 92–4. On "dream literature" in general, see: Paul Edward Dutton, *The Politics of Dreaming in the Carolingian Empire,* Lincoln/London 1994, on Charlemagne pp. 50–80.

2   Mettke, *Älteste deutsche Dichtung,* pp. 156–65; Schlosser, *Althochdeutsche Literatur,* pp. 200–4.

3   Einhard states his intention of memorializing Charlemagne no fewer than five times in the preface, Einhard, *Vita Karoli,* ed. Holder-Egger, p. 1, 13–4, lines 17, 24, p. 2, 13 and line 27; see also his personal remembrance, pp. 2, 6. Cicero's *Tusculan Disputations* was itself a book of remembrance that recalled literary figures and heroes of Rome's past. – On the *Vita,* cf. Tischler, *Einharts "Vita Karoli";* and Steffen Patzold, Einhards erste Leser: Zu Kontext und Darstellungsabsicht der "Vita Karoli," in: *Viator Multilingual* 42 (2011) pp. 33–55.

4   Einhard, *Vita Karoli,* chap. 4. Education with Adalhard: Paschasius Radbertus, *Vita Adalhardi,* chap. 7, Migne *PL* 120 col. 1511. The only clue for assigning a date to the *Vita* comes from the text itself. I have adhered to 826 as a *terminus post quem.* In addition, some allusions in the text have led me to regard the years immediately before 830 as the period when the *Vita Karoli* was written, cf. finally: Johannes Fried, Ein Gastmahl Karls des Großen, in: Fried, *Zu Gast im Mittelalter,* Munich 2007, pp. 13–46, and the first section of Chapter 5 in this book.

5   H. F. Haefele, Notker der Stammler, Taten Kaiser Karls des Großen (Notkeri Balbuli Gesta Karoli Magni imperatoris), MGH Script. rer. Germ. N.S., 12, 1959 (2nd edition 1980); on interpretation: Heinz Löwe, Das Karlsbuch Notkers von St. Gallen und sein zeitgeschichtlicher Hintergrund, in: Löwe, *Von Cassiodor zu Dante. Ausgewählte Aufsätze*

zur Geschichtsschreibung und politischen Ideenwelt des Mittelalters, Berlin/New York 1973, pp. 123–48.

6   Werner, Karl der Große oder Charlemagne?, pp. 33–7.

7   Johannes Fried, Karl der Große. Geschichte und Mythos, in: *Mythen Europas. Schlüsselfiguren der Imagination. Mittelalter,* ed. Inge Milfull and Michael Neumann, Regensburg 2004, pp. 15–46.

8   See the section "The *Opus Caroli* regis" in Chapter 7.

9   The *Annales regni Francorum (ArF;* Royal Frankish annals) also exists in a revised edition (*ArFqdE; Annales regni Francorum qui dicunter Einhardi* [Royal Frankish annals reputed to be by Einhard]), which was produced sometime between 801 and 829; the exact date of the revision is contested. The *ArF* was not written in one go and is the work of a number of different authors. Where it was compiled is unknown, but its compilers are thought to have been court insiders. See also: McKitterick, *Karl der Große,* pp. 38–58.

10   Becher, *Eid und Herrschaft;* cautiously in agreement with this is: Rudolf Schieffer, Ein politischer Prozeß des 8. Jahrhunderts im Vexierspiegel der Quellen, in: *Frankfurter Konzil von 794,* vol. 1, pp. 167–82; more in opposition is: Philippe Depreux, Tassilon III et le roi des Francs. Examen d'une vassalité controversée, in: *Révue Historique* 293 (1995) pp. 23–73; for a summary, see: Matthias Becher, Zwischen Macht und Recht. Der Sturz Tassilos III. von Bayern 788, in: *Tassilo III. von Bayern,* pp. 39–55.

11   This kind of reading for approval is known from the so-called *Libri Carolini;* on this subject, see the section "The *Opus Karoli* regis" in Chapter 7; further relevant references can be found there.

12   For more on this subject, see Chapters 1 and 3.

13   *Gesta episcoporum Mettensium,* MGH SS 2 pp. 260–70, with reference to Charlemagne and praise of the ruler: pp. 264–5.

14   On the cult of St. Arnulf: Oexle, Karolinger und die Stadt des heiligen Arnulf, here especially pp. 361–2; on Charlemagne's relation to the saint: Oexle, pp. 273–9.

15   Cf. Heinz Löwe in: Wattenbach and Löwe, *Deutschlands Geschichtsquellen im Mittelalter. Vorzeit und Karolinger,* pp. 245–66, Roger Collins, The "Reviser" Revisited: Another Look at the Alternative Version of the *Annales Regni Francorum,* in: *After Rome's Fall. Narrators and Sources of Early Medieval History. Essays Presented to Walter Goffart,* ed. Alexander Callander Murray, Toronto 1998, pp. 191–213; cf. above note 11. On the archchaplain, see the section "Organization Requires a Hierarchy" in Chapter 5.

16   See additional discussion in Chapters 1 and 3.

17   *AMP;* see Hoffmann, *Untersuchungen.*–On Charlemagne's visit to Chelles in 804: *AMP* ed. Simson p. 92.

18   *AMP* ed. Simson p. 4, 9–13 and lines 20–4.

19   Johannes Fried, *Der Schleier der Erinnerung. Grundzüge einer historischen Memorik,* Munich 2004; new edition, including an afterword, Munich 2012.

20   O. Holder-Egger in his edition of the *Vita Karoli Magni* (MGH SS rer. Germ. [25]) pp. 48–50.

21   On Alcuin's eschatology: Josef Adamek, *Vom römischen Endreich der mittelalterlichen Bibelerklärung,* Würzburg 1938, pp. 65–8; Arno Borst, Alkuin und die Enzyklopädie von 809, in: *Science in Western and Eastern Civilization in Carolingian Times,* ed. Paul Leo

Butzer and Dietrich Lohrmann, Basel 1993, pp. 53–78, here p. 67; Wolfram Brandes, *Tempora periculosa sunt.* Eschatologisches im Vorfeld der Kaiserkrönung Karls des Großen, in: *Frankfurter Konzil von 794,* vol. 1, pp. 49–79.–Donald Bullough, Alcuin before Frankfort, in: *Frankfurter Konzil von 794,* vol. 2, pp. 571–85.

22 Amy G. Remensnyder, *Remembering Kings Past: Monastic Foundation Legends in Medieval Southern France,* Ithaca/London 1996.

23 *Opus Caroli,* ed. Freeman; the importance of the marginal notes in Tironian notes was first identified by Steinen, Randbemerkungen; after some interim skepticism, his findings were confirmed through new studies of the text by Freeman pp. 48–50.

24 These examples and the translation follow Steinen, Randbemerkungen p. 35 (first published 1931); cf. Steinen, Karl der Große und die *Libri Carolini,* pp. 252–3. The texts themselves are in: *Opus Caroli* 1.7 and 3.3, ed. Freeman, p. 139, 8–10, p. 140, 13–5, and p. 349, 9–10; this last passage may refer to the (immediately following) *filioque* creed (*ex Patre et Filio*), as followed by "the entire Catholic Church."

25 Knut Görich, *Friedrich Barbarossa. Eine Biographie,* Munich 2011, pp. 633–7.

CHAPTER 1. BOYHOOD

1 Carlrichard Brühl, *Palatium und Civitas. Studien zur Profantopographie spätantiker Civitates vom 3. bis zum 13. Jahrhundert,* 2 vols., Cologne/Vienna 1975–1990 (1991).

2 On Charlemagne's birthdate (2 April 748), cf. Matthias Becher, Neue Überlegungen zum Geburtsdatum Karls des Großen, in: *Francia* 19 (1992) pp. 37–60, here pp. 50–4; Becher, *Karl der Große,* [2]Munich 2000, pp. 41–2; Jean Favier, *Charlemagne,* Paris 1999, pp. 142–6, unconvincingly reverts to Einhard's dubious assessment of Charlemagne's date of birth. Cf. Johannes Fried, Wann verlor Karl der Große seinen ersten Zahn?, in: *DA 56* (2000) pp. 573–83; the defense of the historicity of the episode offered by Janet L. Nelson, Charlemagne the Man, in: *Charlemagne. Empire and Society,* ed. Joanna Story, Manchester/New York 2005, pp. 22–37, here pp. 24–8, ignores the problems of dating and the historical record that are posed by the sole surviving interpolated translation report. For an evaluation of all the evidence, see: Wilfried Hartmann, *Karl der Große,* pp. 39–45.

3 Werner, Karl der Große oder Charlemagne?, pp. 20–1.

4 Eduard Hlawitschka, Die Vorfahren Karls des Großen, in: *Karl der Große,* vol. 1, *Persönlichkeit und Geschichte,* ed. Helmut Beumann, Düsseldorf 1965 (=[3]1967), pp. 51–82, on Rothaid and Adelheid p. 82.

5 Cf. Martina Hartmann, *Königin,* pp. 95–8.

6 On the princes' instruction in the liberal arts, cf. Alfred Wendehorst, Wer konnte im Mittelalter lesen und schreiben? in: *Schulen und Studium im sozialen Wandel des hohen und späten Mittelalters,* ed. Johannes Fried (VuF 30), Sigmaringen 1986, pp. 9–33. Reading was taught independently from writing (which was regarded as a handicraft). On Charlemagne's knowledge of Latin: Johannes Fried, Karl der Große, die *Artes liberales* und die karolingische Renaissance, in: *Karl der Große und sein Nachwirken. 1200 Jahre Kultur und Wissenschaft in Europa,* vol. 1, *Wissen und Weltbild,* ed. P. Butzer, M. Kerner, and W. Oberschelp, Turnhout 1997, pp. 25–43.

7 Kasten, *Königssöhne und Königsherrschaft,* pp. 238–49, highlights these difficulties associated with biographies of medieval childhood; on royal childhood in a later age, see

Carola Föller, Königskinder. Erziehung am Hof Ludwigs IX. des Heiligen von Frankreich, typewritten dissertation, Frankfurt a. M. 2011.

8   On the epitaph for Charlemagne's sister Rothaid: MGH SS 2 p. 265.

9   Cf. the Prologue of this book.

10   This "continuation" by two authors related to the royal household is the most important contemporary account up to the year 750. Comparison with the *ArF* reveals their bias. Investigated in exemplary fashion by: Matthias Becher, Eine verschleierte Krise. Die Nachfolge Karl Martells 741 und die Anfänge der karolingischen Hofgeschichtsschreibung, in: *Von Fakten und Fiktionen. Mittelalterliche Geschichtsdarstellungen und ihre kritische Aufarbeitung*, ed. Johannes Laudage, Cologne/Weimar/Vienna 2003, pp. 95–133.

11   Cf. Hoffmann, *Untersuchungen*.

12   Rosamond McKitterick, Constructing the Past in the Early Middle Ages: The Case of the *Royal Frankish Annals*, in: *Transactions of the Royal Historical Society*, 6th ser., vol. 7, Cambridge 1997, pp. 101–29, here p. 126, speculates that the *ArF* may have been disseminated by the scriptorium of Lorsch Abbey. In McKitterick, *Karl der Große*, pp. 49–58, the question of the royal commission of the *ArF* and its possible origin in the Abbey of St-Denis is considered.

13   The *Annales Laureshamenses* for the year 759 (also the *Ann. Petav.* for 759) mentions this Pepin clearly on account of the transfer of the name: "Mutavit rex Pippinus nomen suum in filio suo," MGH SS 1 p. 28 (resp. p. 11). However, there is no indication where the boy was buried; this means that we cannot postulate that any allusion in the text to a particular abbey proves that it was the place where the annals were compiled.

14   BM² 92i (761) and 93c (762).

15   The year when this Pepin was born is unknown. K. F. Werner's assumption (see the table of descendants in Die Nachkommen Karls des Großen) that he was born in or around 770 presumably supposes that—since Pepin's mother, Himiltrud, is not known to have had any other offspring—Charlemagne's first son must have been born shortly before his marriage to the Lombard princess. Yet all the pointers to this Pepin occur far too late to have necessitated mentioning any siblings who might have died at a young age.

16   These form an integral part of Paulus's *Liber de episcopis Mettensibus:* MGH SS 2 pp. 265–6. Cf. note 8.

17   Cf. the discussion later in this chapter of Charlemagne's first meeting with a pope.

18   Cf. discussion later in this chapter.

19   Notker, *Gesta Karoli* 2.15, ed. Haefele, p. 80.

20   Andreas Schaub and Tanja Kohlberger-Schaub, Archäologische Untersuchungen im Aachener Dom. Ein Arbeitsbericht, in: *Geschichte im Bistum Aachen* 9 (2007/2008) pp. 15–36, here pp. 21–7. On the palace at Aix/Aachen in Charlemagne's reign, cf. Chapter 6.

21   *De Karolo rege et Leone papa,* vv. 294–7, ed. Hentze, p. 30, translated by Franz Brunhölzl in *Karolus magnus et Leo papa* p. 31.

22   Cf. the section "King Charles the Wise" in Chapter 5.

23   MGH Capit. 1 No. 30 p. 80, 22–8.–On *reparare* as a royal obligation, cf. also Chapter 8, section "Organizing the Succession."

24 Paschasius Radbertus, *Vita b. Adalhardi* chap. 7, Migne *PL* 120 col. 1511. Adalhard's own writings attest to his knowledge of the quadrivium; see Kasten, *Adalhard von Corbie,* pp. 110–37.

25 Cf. Epilogue, section "Charlemagne as Saint."

26 Fischer, Bibeltext und Bibelreform unter Karl dem Großen, in *Karl der Große, Lebenswerk und Nachleben,* vol. II, *Das geistige Leben,* ed. Bernhard Bischoff and Wolfgang Braunfels, Düsseldorf 1965, pp. 156–216; here p. 186.

27 Ibid., p. 216. Guy Lobrichon, Le texte des bibles alcuiniennes, in: Alcuin, de York à Tours, pp. 209–19.

28 Fischer, Bibeltext und Bibelreform, p. 173.–On Theodulf's Bible, see the discussion later in this chapter.

29 Anton, *Fürstenspiegel.*

30 *Epistolae variorum Carolo magno regnante scriptae* 7 [Cathuulfus to Charlemagne], ed. Ernst Dümmler, MGH Epp. 4, Berlin 1895, pp. 501–5. Cf. Hans Hubert Anton, Pseudo-Cyprian. *De duodecim abusivis saeculi* und sein Einfluß auf den Kontinent, insbesondere auf die karolingischen Fürstenspiegel, in: *Die Iren und Europa im frühen Mittelalter,* vol. 2, ed. Heinz Löwe (Veröffentlichungen des Europa-Zentrums Tübingen. Kulturwissenschaftliche Reihe), Stuttgart 1982, pp. 568–617, especially pp. 597–600.

31 On the cult of relics, see Arnold Angenendt, *Heilige und Reliquien. Die Geschichte ihres Kultes vom frühen Christentum bis zur Gegenwart,* Munich 1994; Anton Legner, *Reliquien in Kunst und Kult. Zwischen Antike und Aufklärung,* Darmstadt 1995.

32 Henry Mayr-Harting, Charlemagne's Religion, in: *Am Vorabend der Kaiserkrönung,* pp. 113–24.–In his letter to Ghaerbald of Liège in the famine year of 807, Charlemagne did not exempt himself from the act of collective self-abasement to appease divine wrath: MGH Capit. 1 pp. 245–6 (No. 124).

33 From the early ninth-century Bavarian *Exhortatio ad plebem Christianam,* transl. Mettke, *Älteste deutsche Dichtung,* pp. 136–9; Schlosser, *Althochdeutsche Literatur,* pp. 208–11.

34 See Schlosser, *Althochdeutsche Literatur,* p. 253.

35 See ibid., p. 255.

36 Cf., for instance, the *Admonitio generalis* of 789, chap. 65.

37 Cf. the section "Signs in the Heavens" in Chapter 8.

38 See the Georgetown University website on Augustine's *De doctrina christiana,* http://faculty.georgetown.edu/jod/augustine/ddc.html., with a full translation of Augustine's text into English, reproduced from Philip Schaff (ed.) *A Select Library of the Nicene and Post-Nicene Fathers of the Christian Church,* Buffalo, NY, 1886.

39 Trier, Stadtbibliothek, Cod. 31, facsimile edition by Richard Laufner and Peter K. Klein, Graz 1975.

40 Cf., for example, MGH Capit. 1 No. 124 (to Ghaerbald of Liège) p. 245, 33–46, 14.

41 Pseudo-Cyprian, *De XII Abusivis,* ed. with introduction and indexes by A. Breen (Celtic Studies), Dublin 1996 (I was unable to consult the earlier edition); the earlier edition was edited by Siegmund Hellmann (Texte und Untersuchungen, 3. Reihe, 4. Band, Heft 1), Leipzig 1908, pp. 51–3.

42 These examples occur in the so-called *Continuations of the Chronicle of Fredegar* (by Count Childebrand and his son Count Nibelung), chaps. 8–11, and come from the period that is decisive in the rise of the Carolingians, around 715. On the subject of the continuity from late antiquity and the Merovingian period, see principally Werner, *Naissance*.

43 Paulus Diaconus, *Gesta episcoporum Mettensium*, MGH SS 2 p. 264.

44 Both texts edited by Bruno Krusch: MGH SS rer. Merov. 2.

45 The most recent monograph on this topic is Andreas Fischer, *Karl Martell. Der Beginn karolingischer Herrschaft*, Stuttgart 2012.

46 On the deliberate policy of conquest and expansion pursued by the Carolingians from the reign of Charles Martel on, see: Bachrach, *Early Carolingian Warfare*.

47 Jean François Verbruggen, L'armée et la strategie de Charlemagne, in: *Karl der Große. Lebenswerk und Nachleben*, vol. 1, ed. Helmut Beumann, ³Düsseldorf 1967, pp. 420–36, here p. 420; on criticism of Verbruggen's work, see Bernard S. Bachrach, Charlemagne's Cavalry. Myth and Reality, in: Bachrach, *Armies and Politics in the Early Medieval West*, London 1993, pp. 1–20.

48 Ulrich Nonn, Das Bild Karl Martells in den lateinischen Quellen vornehmlich des 8. und 9. Jahrhunderts, in: *FmaSt* 4 (1970) pp. 70–137, here p. 115 (Adrevald von Fleury, *Tudites*, MGH SS 15, 1, p. 483) and p. 116 (*Vita Rigoberti*: "vir bellicosus et robore fortissimus, postmodum Martellus cognominatus," MGH SS rer. Merov. 7 p. 66).

49 From Childebrand's *Continuation of Fredegar*, chap. 30.

50 *Vita Bonifatii*, ed. Wilhelm Levison (MGH SS rer. Germ. 57), p. 44: "Pippinus domino donante . . . regnum suscepit, et iam aliquantulum sedante populorum perturbatione in regem sublevatus est." See also: Matthias Becher, Drogo und die Königserhebung Pippins, in: *FmaSt* 23 (1989) pp. 131–53.

51 See the *AMP* for the year 750, ed. Simson p. 42. Also the *ArF* for 749 and 750.

52 Cf. Childebrand's *Continuation of Fredegar*, chap. 33; *ArF* for 749 and 750 (*consecratio*). The "Clausula de Pippini consecratione" (MGH SS 15, 1, p. 1) talks of *unctio*. On the question of authenticity, see below note 68; correspondingly: *ArF* for 750 (with the use of older evidence: *unctus*) and the *ArFqdE* for 750 (*unctio*). Cf. BM² 64a.

53 Conflicting historical records preclude a definitive overall picture: Philippe Buc, Warum weniger die Handelnden selbst als eher die Chronisten das politische Ritual erzeugten und warum es niemandem auf die wahre Geschichte ankam, in: *Macht des Königs*, pp. 27–37. Yet every official reception required a formal ceremonial.

54 For the earliest surviving wording, see the section "The Fascination of Rome" in Chapter 5.

55 *LP* 1 Vita Stephani II, pp. 440–55. On the basis of later comparative material, Hack, *Empfangszeremoniell*, pp. 409–78, especially pp. 425–6, has made it clear that Pope Stephen's reception by Pepin most likely did take place in roughly the manner described in the *Liber pontificalis (LP)*.–Nibelung's *Continuation of Fredegar* (chap. 36) mentions no rituals, no proskynesis, and no acts of servitude. It merely gives a brief description of the young Charlemagne meeting the pope and escorting him to Ponthion and an equally short account of the meetings between the pope and the king there and at St-Denis.–Hack doubts whether Pepin performed the so-called strator service for the pope. His argument that the sentence supposedly indicating this—which occurs in all the manuscripts—was added to the *Vita Karoli* retrospectively and around the same time as the *Constitutum Constantini* is unconvincing, since the *Constitutum* is not a Roman invention but an early

Frankish one, cf. Fried, *Donation of Constantine*. The pope rode to the services held at the Stations of the Cross, while strators (grooms) on foot led his horse by the reins (cf., for instance, Ordo Rom. I). Church dignitaries rode behind the pope, while the mass of common people proceeded on foot, accompanied by religious singing. The entry into Ponthion would not have been very different from this. The king and the pope would scarcely have traveled three miles on foot. The *LP* does not mention every detail; for instance, there is no reference to the change of clothes that must have taken place, with the pope exchanging his riding habit for his pontifical robes.

56 *AMP* for the year 753, ed. Simson, pp. 44–5.

57 On this question, see Classen, Karl der Grosse, das Papsttum, and Byzanz, p. 18 and p. 59.

58 *Opus Caroli* 1.6, ed. Freeman, p. 136; Charlemagne's exclamation can be surmised only from a very unclear and poor carbon copy on the facing page.

59 *Opus Caroli* 1.1, ed. Freeman, p. 132.

60 Wolfgang H. Fritze, *Papst und Frankenkönig. Studien zu den päpstlich-fränkischen Rechtsbeziehungen von 754 bis 824* (VuF Sonderband 10), Sigmaringen 1973, pp. 63–94.

61 Arnold Angenendt, Das geistliche Bündnis der Päpste mit den Karolingern (754–796), in: *HJb* 100 (1980) pp. 1–94.

62 MGH Epp. 3 No. 21 (761). See also Arnold Angenendt, Mensa Pippini Regis. Zur liturgischen Präsenz der Karolinger in Sankt Peter, in: *Hundert Jahre Deutsches Priesterkolleg beim Campo Santo Teutonico, 1876–1976. Beiträge zu seiner Geschichte*, ed. Erwin Gatz (Römische Quartalschrift für christliche Altertumskunde und Kirchengeschichte, Suppl. 35), Rome/Freiburg/Vienna 1977, pp. 52–68; Bauer, *Bild der Stadt Rom im Frühmittelalter*, pp. 94–6.

63 Bauer, *Bild der Stadt Rom im Frühmittelalter*, pp. 91–4 and plate 36 (p. 83).

64 Cf. MGH Epp. 3 No. 14 (757) pp. 524–8.

65 On the royal unction of 754 (and of 751), cf. Arnold Angenendt, Pippins Königserhebung und Salbung, in: *Dynastiewechsel von 751*, pp. 179–209.

66 *LP* 1 Vita Stephani II pp. 447–9. On the formula quoted, cf. Erich Caspar, *Pippin und die römische Kirche. Kritische Untersuchungen zum fränkisch-päpstlichen Bunde im VIII. Jahrhundert*, Berlin 1914, p. 156n3.–For more on the "Roman Republic of St. Peter," see later in this section.

67 BM[2] 74.

68 "Clausula de unctione Pippini," MGH SS 15, 1, p. 1. On the question of authenticity, see: Olaf Schneider, Die Königserhebung Pippins 751 in der Erinnerung der karolingischen Quellen: Die Glaubwürdigkeit der Reichsannalen und die Verformung der Vergangenheit, in: *Dynastiewechsel von 751*, pp. 243–75, here pp. 268–75.

69 The passage on the exclusivity of the Carolingians has given cause for considering the "Clausula," which enters the historical record only at the end of the tenth century, as a forgery designed to stave off a Capetian monarchy and to strengthen the legitimacy of the deposed Carolingians. Yet the sentence may have been directed instead against Drogo, the son of the older Carloman. Pope Stephen III's recollection of Stephen's II's admonishing of Pepin that he should never abandon his wife may have been connected with the "blessing" of Bertrada: Cod. Carol. No. 45 MGH Epp. 3 pp. 561–2. After all, this note is embedded in a passage recalling the royal unction of the Carolingians by Stephen II and the sworn *amicitia* with that very pope.

70 CC 10 (756).

71 On this and the following, cf. LP 1 Vita Stephani II., pp. 452–3; cf. also CC 11 MGH Epp. 3 pp. 505–6.

72 Cf. Wolfram Brandes, *Finanzverwaltung in Krisenzeiten. Untersuchungen zur byzantinischen Administration im 6.–9. Jahrhundert* (Forschungen zur byzantinischen Rechtsgeschichte 25), Frankfurt am Main 2002, pp. 368–78; see also Sebastian Scholz, Das Papsttum, Roms wirtschaftliche Lage und die Enteignung der päpstlichen Patrimonien in der Mitte des 8. Jahrhunderts, in: *Päpstliche Herrschaft im Mittelalter. Funktionsweisen, Strategien, Darstellungsformen,* ed. Stefan Weinfurter, Ostfildern 2012, pp. 11–31.

73 Kasten, *Königssöhne und Königsherrschaft,* p. 129.

74 This may even have occurred one or two years earlier, cf. the opening section of this chapter.

CHAPTER 2. THE FRANKISH EMPIRE AND THE WIDER WORLD

1 Cf. the beginning of Chapter 8.

2 François Louis Ganshof, On the Genesis and Significance of the Treaty of Verdun (843), in: Ganshof, *The Carolingians and the Frankish Monarchy. Studies in Carolingian History,* London 1971, pp. 289–302.

3 On this, see the section "Center and Periphery" in Chapter 4.

4 For the figure 4,500, cf. the section "Thirty Years of War in Saxony" in Chapter 3; 1,600: Heinz Löwe, Eine Kölner Notiz zum Kaisertum Karls des Großen, in: *Rhein. Vjbll.* 14 (1949) pp. 7–34, here pp. 10–12.

5 Kuchenbuch, *Bäuerliche Gesellschaft,* pp. 174–9.

6 Werner, Nachkommen, pp. 403–82 and tables.

7 Fried, Fulda in der Bildungs- und Geistesgeschichte.

8 Cf. the section "Knowledge Concentrates at the Court" in Chapter 6.

9 Cf. Chapter 7 and its note 85.

10 *Vita Willibaldi episcopi Eichstetensis*, chap. 4, MGH SS 15, 1, pp. 92–102, here pp. 101–2 (*insula Vulcani*).

11 *Vita Willibaldi episcopi Eichstetensis,* chap. 4, MGH SS 15, 1, p. 95, 7 (title), p. 97, 10–25 (Holy Sepulchre).

12 Cf. the prologue of his *Vita sancti Galli,* most recent edition with a German translation by Franziska Schnoor, and with notes and an epilogue by Ernst Tremp, Stuttgart 2012, pp. 10–15.

13 *Die Kosmographie des Aethicus,* ed. Otto Prinz (MGH Quellen zur Geistesgeschichte des Mittelalters 14), Munich 1993; quotation: p. 27; same location also for the following quotation. *The Cosmography of Aethicus Ister,* ed. Michael Herren (Publications of the Journal of Medieval Latin 8), Turnhout 2011. – At the time of writing, the latest study on Aethicus and his (possible) sources, in addition to the introduction by Herren, is: Richard Matthew Pollard, Denuo on Lucan, the "Orpheus" and "Aethicus Ister," in: *Journal of Medieval Latin* 20 (2010), pp. 58–69.

14 Adamnan, *De locis sanctis,* ed. Denis Meehan (Scriptores Latini Hiberniae 3), Dublin 1958.

15 The manuscript Paris, Bibl. nat. Lat. 13048, comes from Corbie; as in the Reichenau manuscript (Zurich, Rheinau 73, ninth century, cf. Meehan, Introduction [as note 14] p. 32), the *Carmina* of Venantius Fortunatus, which are still written in transcript, follow the text by Adamnan, cf. Davis Ganz, *Corbie in the Carolingian Renaissance* (Beihefte der Francia 20), Sigmaringen 1990, p. 142.

16 *Bedae Venerabilis De locis sanctis,* ed. J. Fraipont, in: *Itineraria et alia geographica,* vol. 1 (Corpus Christianorum, Series Latina 175), Turnhout 1965, pp. 245–80.

17 *De situ et nominibus locorum Hebraicorum,* Migne *PL* 23 cols. 903–76.

18 Hugeburc, *Vita Willibaldi,* chap. 4, MGH SS 15, 1, pp. 97–8.

19 Dicuil, *Liber de mensura orbis terrae,* ed. J. J. Tierney with contributions by Ludwig Bieler (Scriptores Latini Hiberniae 6), Dublin 1967. On the appraisal of this work, cf. Werner Bergmann, Dicuils "De mensura orbis terrae," in: *Science in Western and Eastern Civilization,* pp. 525–36. Godescalc's dedicatory poem in his evangeliary for Charlemagne (on this, see the section "The Lack of Information on Spain and Benevento" in Chapter 3) appears to quote an expression from the "Mensuratio," cf. Peter Orth, Das Widmungsgedicht, in: Crivello, Denoël, and Orth, *Godescalc-Evangelistar,* pp. 40–1.

20 On the tradition of Ultima Thule, see Klaus von See, "Ultima Thule" als Versatzstück der literarischen Bildung, in: See, *Ideologie und Philologie. Aufsätze zur Kultur- und Wissenschaftsgeschichte,* Heidelberg 2006, pp. 70–89, here p. 64 on Dicuil (first published 2004).

21 Johannes Fried, Der karolingische Herrschaftsverband im 9. Jahrhundert zwischen "Kirche" und "Königshaus," in: *HZ* 235 (1982) pp. 1–43; Fried, "Gens" und "regnum." Wahrnehmungs- und Deutungskategorien politischen Wandels im früheren Mittelalter. Bemerkungen zur doppelten Theoriebindung des Historikers, in: *Sozialer Wandel im Mittelalter. Wahrnehmungsformen, Erklärungsmuster, Regelungsmechanismen,* ed. Jürgen Miethke and Klaus Schreiner, Sigmaringen 1994, pp. 74–104; also in an abbreviated and slightly altered form in: *Macht des Königs,* pp. 72–89.

22 CC 59 p. 585; cf. Classen, *Karl der Große,* p. 27.

23 But cf. Cathuulf's monitory letter to Charlemagne, discussed in the section "Education as a Scholar and Instruction in the Christian Faith" in Chapter 1.

24 For a summary of these various etymologies, see the Wikipedia article on Radhanite.

25 On the concept of *amicitia* in the Carolingian period, see: Wolfgang H. Fritze, *Papst und Frankenkönig. Studien zu den päpstlich-fränkischen Rechtsbeziehungen von 754–824* (VuF Sonderband 10), Sigmaringen 1973; cf. also: Reinhard Schneider, *Brüdergemeine und Schwurfreundschaft* (Historische Studien 388), Lübeck/Hamburg 1964; and Heinhard Steiger, *Die Ordnung der Welt. Eine Völkerrechtsgeschichte des karolingischen Zeitalters* (741 bis 840), Cologne/Weimar/Vienna 2010.

26 Daniel Ziemann, *Vom Wandervolk zur Großmacht. Die Entstehung Bulgariens im frühen Mittelalter (7.–9. Jh.)* (Kölner Historische Abhandlungen 43), Cologne/Weimar/ Vienna 2007.

27 Theophanes on the year AM 6251.

28 Cf. the section "The *Opus Caroli regis*" in Chapter 7.

29 On the following, see Gerhard P. Wolf, *Salus Populi Romani. Studien zur Geschichte römischer Kultbilder im Mittelalter,* Heidelberg 1990; Belting, *Bild und Kult,* pp. 131–148 and pp. 348–68; and Noble, *Images,* pp. 127–34.

30 *LP* 1 p. 443.

31 Cf. Belting, *Bild und Kult,* p. 78 with plate 192 p. 362; illustration in: Bauer, *Bild der Stadt Rom im Frühmittelalter,* p. 79.

32 *LP* 1 Vita Stephanin II, pp. 452–3; *Cont. Fredegarii* chap. 40. Cf. Classen, *Karl der Große,* p. 25.

33 Cf. the section "The Young Charlemagne's First Encounter with a Pope" in Chapter 1.

34 The sole source for this is a brief note by Stephen III, CC 45 p. 562; cf. Classen, *Karl der Große,* pp. 25–6.

35 Cf. McCormick, Textes, images et iconoclasme; Willjung, Das Konzil von Aachen 809, pp. 12–15; and Noble, *Images,* pp. 142–7.

36 *ArF* for 767; especially CC 36 pp. 544–5 and CC 37 p. 549; on Paul I's delighted reaction to Pepin's rejection of Constantine V's request ("quae ab eo [i.e., the emperor] vobis intimata sunt") and its impact, ibid. 37: "quae ad exaltationem . . . Romanae ecclesiae . . . pertinere noscuntur."

37 Cf. the section "A Late Peace Agreement with Byzantium" in Chapter 8.

38 Borgolte, *Gesandtenaustausch;* in general, see: *Geschichte der arabischen Welt,* ed. Ulrich Haarmann, Munich 1987; and Krämer, *Geschichte des Islam.*

39 McCormick, *Origins of the European Economy,* especially pp. 431–43.

40 On this topic, see: Jim al-Khalili, *The House of Wisdom. How Arabic Science Saved Ancient Knowledge and Gave Us the Renaissance,* London 2011; al-Khalili reproduces the quotation by al-Mansur from Michael Cooperson, *Al-Ma'mun. Makers of the Muslim World,* Oxford 2005, p. 21.

41 Drews, *Karolinger und die Abbasiden von Bagdad,* pp. 262–3.

42 Quoted from *Islamische Geschichte Spaniens,* presented by Wilhelm Hoenerbach on the basis of the Kitab A'mal al-a'lam (*Book of the Deeds of the Illustrious*) by Ibn al-Hatib and associated writings (Bibliothek des Morgenlandes), Zurich/Stuttgart 1970, p. 65.

43 Drews, *Karolinger und die Abbasiden von Bagdad.*

44 I glean the idea that the initiative came from al-Mansur from a remark in the *Continuation of Fredegar,* chap. 51, the only evidence for 764/765, which states that Pepin "once more" sent the next embassy from the caliph back three years later (768) with gifts: "Iterum ipsos Sarracinos, qui ad eum missi fuerant, munera dedit." When this second legation of the caliph came to Aix in 768, it was accompanied by Frankish envoys from the court in Baghdad. Conversely, these envoys may already have gone to Baghdad in the first place in the company of legates of the caliph.

45 See Michael McCormick, Pippin III, the Embassy of Caliph al Mansur, and the Mediterranean World, in: *Dynastiewechsel von 751,* pp. 221–41.

46 On the gold imitation dinar of Offa of Mercia, see the British Museum website: http://www.bmimages.com/preview.aspimage=00031108001&imagex=1&searchnum =0002.

47 MGH Epp. 4 p. 147 No. 101.

48 Ibid., pp. 144–8 Nos. 100–1.

49 Cf., for example, ibid., pp. 127–8 No. 85 and BM² 333 (793/796).

50 Erwin Herrmann (ed.), *Slawisch-germanische Beziehungen im südostdeutschen Raum von der Spätantike bis zum Ungarnsturm. Ein Quellenbuch mit Erläuterungen* (Veröffentlichungen des Collegium Carolinum 17), Munich 1965, pp. 212–21 with illustration.

51 Walter Pohl, *Die Awaren. Ein Steppenvolk in Mitteleuropa, 567–822 n. Chr.*, ²Munich 2002.

52 MGH Capit. 1 No. 44, chap. 7, p. 123; cf. also the section "Organizing the Succession" in Chapter 8.

53 Alheydis Plassmann, *Die Normannen. Erobern, Herrsche, Integrieren*, Stuttgart 2008; Föller, *Wikinger.*

54 Klaus von See, *Skaldendichtung. Eine Einführung*, Munich/Zurich 1980.

55 On the military campaigns of the Vikings, cf. Daniel Föller, Verflochtenes Denken. Kognitive Strategien im wikingerzeitlichen Skandinavien, typewritten doctoral dissertation, Frankfurt a. M. 2012; cf. the section "A New Enemy Appears: The 'Northmen' " in Chapter 8.

56 Rudolf Simek, *Die "Edda,"* Munich 2007.

Chapter 3. The Warrior King

1 On this and the following, see: Classen, *Karl der Große*, pp. 9–14.

2 CC 16 (758), MGH Epp. 3 pp. 513–4.

3 CC 44, MGH Epp. 3 p. 560.

4 Noble, *Images*, pp. 146–9.

5 LP 1 p. 476 (chap. XXi).

6 CC 45 (769/770), MGH Epp. 3 p. 561.

7 CC 47, MGH Epp. 3 pp. 565–6.

8 Unless otherwise stated, where dating is concerned, in all relevant genealogical questions I have followed: K. F. Werner, Nachkommen, p. 443. The date of this marriage follows from his ensuing marriage to Hildegard, which—according to her epitaph—must have taken place in the first half of 771. Cf. below note 15.

9 *Annales Admontenses* for 772, MGH SS 9 p. 572. Cf. Peter Classen, Bayern und die politischen Mächte im Zeitalter Karls des Großen und Tassilos III., in: Classen, *Ausgewählte Aufsätze*, pp. 231–48, here p. 237.

10 CC 48 (Spring 771), MGH Epp. 3 pp. 566–7.

11 Vita Stephani III *LP* 1 p. 480.

12 CC 46 (770/71), MGH 3 pp. 564–5.

13 Einhard, *Vita Karoli*, chap. 18, maintains that this marriage lasted for more than a year (*post annum*). I do not share the supposition of Janet L. Nelson, Making a Difference in Eighth-Century Politics: The Daughters of Desiderius, in: *After Rome's Fall. Narrators and Sources of Early Medieval History. Essays Presented to Walter Goffart*, ed. Alexander

Callender Murray, Toronto 1998, pp. 171–90, here p. 183, that the unknown daughter of Desiderius was called Gerberga. The evidence she adduces does not prove this. The ninth-century historian Andreas of Bergamo (MGH SS rer. Langob. pp. 223–4) did not know the name of the princess. The manuscripts give the name Berterad, sometimes as the result of a correction. The *Annales Lobienses* for the year 771 (MGH SS 2 p. 195) must be read in conjunction with its entry for 747: *Carlomannus imperator,* a name—bearing in mind the comparatively late manuscript—that surely signifies Charlemagne rather than Carloman. In other words, the wives have not been confused with one another here, but the two brothers. The name of his Lombard wife does not appear here.

14 We may deduce this from the date of his marriage to Hildegard, cf. the following note.

15 The date of the marriage can be calculated only approximately from Hildegard's epitaph (written by Paulus Diaconus: MGH SS 2 p. 266) and from the dates of birth of her children; cf. Werner, Nachkommen, p. 443 No. 1c.

16 Not all of Charlemagne and Hildegard's nine children survived; the youngest, their daughter Adelheid, was born in 782 and died when she was still less than a year old, forty days after her mother: for her epitaph (by Paulus Diaconus), see: MGH SS 2 p. 267.

17 At least this is how it is presented by Paschasius Radbertus in his *Life of Adalhard,* chap. 7, Migne PL 120 col. 1511. On this subject, cf. Kasten, *Adalhard von Corbie,* pp. 18–24.

18 On the relationship with the Agilolfing dynasty and on the *amicitia* between Charlemagne and Tassilo, see Jarnut, Genealogie.

19 Einhard, *Vita Karoli,* chap. 3.

20 Cf. BM² 128a.

21 The *ArF* for 771 and the *AMP* for the same year both mention the royal unction; cf. BM² 142a.

22 *LP* 1 Vita Hadriani I p. 488, 29–37.

23 Ibid., p. 494, 11–15.

24 Ibid., p. 494, 21–2; *ArF* for 773.

25 The location of the Irminsul (Old Saxon for "great pillar," probably of oak) is unclear. The *ArF* for 772 reports that after destroying Eresburg, Charlemagne "reached the Irminsul" (*ad Ermensul usque pervenit*), which would appear to suggest that it was some distance from Eresburg; on the other hand, the revision of the annals leaves out the word *usque,* making it seem as though the pillar-shrine was close to the settlement. All we know for sure is that it was not located at the Externsteine prehistoric monument; cf. Uta Halle, *"Die Externsteine sind bis auf weiteres germanisch!" Prähistorische Archäologie im Dritten Reich* (Sonderveröffentlichungen des Naturwissenschaftlichen und Historischen Vereins für das Land Lippe 68), Bielefeld 2002. Halle (pp. 295–305, especially pp. 301–2) points out that the pottery finds at this site, dating at the earliest from the tenth and eleventh centuries, rule out any possibility of this.

26 Distribution of the war booty is recorded in the *AMP* for 772, ed. Simson, p. 58.

27 *LP* 1 Vita Hadriani I p. 495.

28 *Chronicon Novaliciense* 3.8 (MGH SS 7 p. 99); also in wikisource.org/wiki/Chronicon _Novaliciense.

29 *Chronicon Anianense (Moissiacense)* for 773, MGH SS 1 p. 295, 23; ed. Kettemann, pt. 2, p. 40.

30 *LP* 1 Vita Hadriani I p. 496, 18–20.

31 *A Deo protectus magnus rex:* Ibid., p. 495, 1; *christianissimus rex:* used repeatedly, e.g., p. 494, 27.

32 The *LP* 1 Vita Hadriani I p. 496, 15–6, recounts that Charlemagne's wife and son followed him on campaign only as far as Pavia; Charlemagne would have left them there under the protection of the army when he hurried to Rome at Easter. On his reception in Rome, cf. Classen, *Karl der Große,* pp. 17–21; and Scholz, *Politik, Selbstverständnis, Selbstdarstellung,* pp. 78–85.

33 *LP* 1 Vita Hadriani I pp. 496–7. On the reception of the "Laudes" in Rome: Kantorowicz, *Laudes regiae,* pp. 53–4; on how Charlemagne was received: Kantorowicz, pp. 75–6.–In the following exposition I fall back, sometimes verbatim, on my earlier work: Fried, Karl der Große, Rom und Aachen; the necessary supporting documentary evidence is cited there.

34 Cf. on Charlemagne's route in Rome: according to the Anonymus Einsidlensis, Bauer, Bild der Stadt Rom in karolingischer Zeit, map p. 195; Bauer, in: *799. Kunst und Kultur,* vol. 2, p. 707, with a map on p. 608.

35 Cf. the section "The Young Charlemagne's First Encounter with a Pope" in Chapter 1.

36 On the attitude toward Constantine in the early Middle Ages, see: Eugen Ewig, Das Bild Constantins des Großen in den ersten Jahrhunderten des abendländischen Mittelalters, reprinted most recently in: *Das byzantinische Herrscherbild,* ed. Herbert Hunger (Wege der Forschung 341), Darmstadt 1975, pp. 133–92.–St. Augustine: *De civitate Dei* 5.25.–The *LP* lists the emperor's "gifts" in minute detail.

37 Paschasius Radbertus, *Vita s. Adalhardi,* chap. 22, Migne *PL* 120 col. 1519D.

38 Wilhelm Levison, Kirchenrechtliches in den *Actus Silvestri,* in: *ZRG Kan* 15 (1926) pp. 501–11, in: Levison, *Aus rheinischer und fränkischer Frühzeit,* pp. 390–465, pp. 466–73, quotation: p. 466.

39 Cf. CC 60.

40 See also Oexle, Karolinger und die Stadt des heiligen Arnulf, pp. 301–11.

41 On this and the following, see Fried, *Donation of Constantine,* pp. 71–86; cf. also the following note. It should be emphasized here that the *Constitutum Constantini,* the *Donation of Constantine,* did not yet exist in Charlemagne's time. It is therefore not permissible to adduce its topography to aid our understanding of conditions in the Carolingian period.

42 According to Bauer (*Bild der Stadt Rom im Frühmittelalter,* pp. 49–61), to see the decoration of churches with images as—in the words of the *LP*—"manifestations of papal independence" from the emperor is valid only for the eighth century; earlier measures (pp. 61–3) should be regarded as endowments, not in the context of power politics. Talk of the "papal palace" is anachronistic. On the *patriarchium,* cf. Manfred Luchterhandt, Päpstlicher Palastbau und höfisches Zeremoniell unter Leo III., in: *799. Kunst und Kultur,* 3, pp. 109–22.

43 Michel Andrieu, *Les ordines Romani du haut moyen âge,* vol. 3, *Les textes (ordines XIV–XXXIV)* (Spicilegium sacrum Lovaniense. Études et documents 24), Louvain 1961, Ordo 24, 3, p. 288; on the time of writing, Andrieu, p. 282.

44 For a summary of this process, see, for example: Peter Classen, Italien zwischen Byzanz und dem Frankenreich, in: Classen, *Ausgewählte Aufsätze,* pp. 85–115.

45 Cf. the section "The Young Charlemagne's First Encounter with a Pope" in Chapter 1.

46 LP 1 Vita Hadriani I p. 498.

47 The absolute consonance of the *AMP,* the *ArF,* and the *Chronicon Moissiacense (Anianense)* on this point is noteworthy.

48 Angela Böck, *Die Sala Regia im Vatikan als Beispiel der Selbstdarstellung des Papsttums in der zweiten Hälfte des 16. Jahrhunderts* (Studien zur Kunstgeschichte 112), Hildesheim 1997, pp. 35–6 plus plate 12 (Charlemagne) and plate 11 (Pepin).–On discussion of the object of Charlemagne's donation, cf. Florian Hartmann, *Hadrian I.,* pp. 119–29. But his hypothesis (pp. 115–8) that the king's visit to Rome culminated in "the stay in Rome taking a distinct turn for the worse and a correspondingly strained farewell ceremony" (p. 118), supposedly because Charlemagne left Rome prematurely on the Wednesday after Easter, is incorrect. Hartmann fails to take into account that—in a significant departure from the customary order of the Services of the Stations of the Cross, which would have required that Mass be celebrated on this particular Wednesday in the Church of San Lorenzo—the final and elaborately arranged meeting between the pope and the king, which is mentioned only in the *LP* (1 p. 498), actually took place in St. Peter's Basilica. In other words, Charlemagne, who was no doubt well aware of how lavishly the event would be staged, had been extremely eager to have this meeting, and Hadrian was prepared to deviate from the liturgical order of the Roman Catholic Church to facilitate it.–In any event, factoring in the time it took for Charlemagne to travel to and from Rome, plus his stay there, Charlemagne had already been away from his siege army outside Pavia for several weeks.

49 On this, see Scholz, *Politik, Selbstverständnis, Selbstdarstellung,* pp. 89–93.

50 On coins, see ibid., p. 95; on military campaigns: ibid., p. 96.

51 Cf. Martina Hartmann, *Königin,* p. 99.

52 Verbruggen, Armée; Bachrach, *Early Carolingian Warfare,* passim. The number of troops is disputed; cf. Busch, *Herrschaften der Karolinger,* p. 76.

53 On the decades-long discussion over the obligation for military service, cf. Hechberger, *Adel,* pp. 202–12.

54 MGH Capit. 1 p. 123 No. 44 chap. 6 (806).

55 Heiko Steuer, Bewaffnung und Kriegsführung der Sachsen und Franken, in: 799. *Kunst und Kultur* pp. 310–22; Herbert Westphal, Zur Bewaffnung und Ausrüstung bei Sachsen und Franken. Gemeinsamkeiten und Unterschiede am Beispiel der Sachkultur, in: 799. *Kunst und Kultur* pp. 323–7.

56 Steuer, Bewaffnung (as above note 55), p. 320.

57 Simson, *Jahrbücher des Fränkischen Reiches,* vol. 1, pp. 116–7.

58 MGH Capit. 2 p. 5 No. 185A; cf. Simson, *Jahrbücher des Fränkischen Reiches,* vol. 1, p. 311.

59 For an example from the reign of Louis the Pious. see: Form. Imp. 7 MGH Form. p. 292.

60 MGH Capit. 1 p. 168 No. 75.

61 *Althochdeutsche Literatur,* v. 6 and vv. 63–7, transl. into German by Schlosser, pp. 265–7.

62 *Waltharius,* vv. 180–97, ed. Karl Strecker, transl. into German by Peter Vossen, Berlin 1947, pp. 33–5.

63 Cf. Padberg, *Christianisierung,* p. 76.

64 Ibid., p. 78.

65 Springer, *Sachsen,* passim.

66 Cf. Becher, *Non enim habent regem,* p. 2.

67 Peter Johanek, Der Ausbau der sächsischen Kirchenorganisation, in: *799. Kunst und Kultur,* vol. 2, pp. 496–506.

68 *ArF* for 775.

69 This is corroborated by the *Capitulatio de partibus Saxoniae,* chaps. 19–21, MGH Capit. 1 p. 69.

70 *Vita Lebuini antiqua,* chap. 6, MGH SS 30, 2, p. 793.–On territorial law codes, cf. Becher, *Non enim habent regem.*

71 See Becher, *Non enim habent regem,* pp. 4–18.

72 *Vita Lebuini antiqua,* chap. 6, MGH SS 30, 2, p. 794.

73 *Capitulatio de partibus Saxoniae,* chap. 34, MGH Capit. 1 p. 70 No. 26.

74 Jörg Jenal, Gregor der Große und die Anfänge der Altsachsenmission (596–604), in: Angli e Sassoni al di qua e al di là del mare, *Settimane Spoleto* 32 (Spoleto 1982), pp. 793–857.

75 Padberg, Mission und Christianisierung, pp. 44–8.

76 *Die Vita Sturmi des Eigil von Fulda. Literarkritisch-historische Untersuchung und Edition,* ed. Pius Engelbert (Veröffentlichungen der Historischen Kommission für Hessen und Waldeck 29), Marburg 1968, chap. 23, p. 158. In contrast to this editor, I place the origin of this *Vita* only at "around 819"; cf. Fried, Fulda, note 63.

77 *ArFqdE* for 774, p. 41.

78 Die Übertragung des hl. Alexander von Rom nach Wildeshausen durch den Enkel Widukinds 851. Das älteste niedersächsische Geschichtsdenkmal, in: *Nachrichten Göttingen,* 1933, pp. 406–36, here chap. 3, p. 426.

79 MGH Capit. 1 p. 222 No. 107.

80 *Indiculus superstitionum,* MGH Capit. 1 pp. 22–3.

81 *Capitulatio de partibus Saxoniae,* chaps. 7, 9, and 21, MGH Capit. 1 p. 69.

82 *Translatio s. Liborii,* chap. 5, MGH SS 4 p. 15.

83 Cf. Padberg, Mission und Christianisierung, pp. 71–89.

84 *Vitae Sancti Liudgeri,* pp. 3–53.

85 Cf. Padberg, Mission und Christianisierung, pp. 79–82.

86 *Vita Gregorii abbatis Traiectensis,* chap. 8, MGH SS 15, 1, p. 73, 39.

87 Altfrid, *Vita s. Liudgeri* I, chap. 21, in: *Vitae Sancti Liudgeri,* p. 25.

88 Cf. Altfrid, *Vita s. Liudgeri* I, chap. 16, in: *Vitae Sancti Liudgeri,* p. 20.

89 For a summary, cf. Schieffer, *Zeit des karolingischen Großreiches,* pp. 58–61.

90 The first mention of Widukind in the *ArFqdE* occurs in 777, while in the *ArF* it is 782. Since we cannot rely unconditionally on both versions of the *Royal Frankish Annals,* there is no certainty in this matter.

91 *ArF* for the year 782, pp. 62 and 63.

92 Eckhard Freise, Widukind in Attigny. Taufpatronat und Treueidleistung als Ziele der sächsischen Unterwerfungs- und Missionskriege Karls des Großen, in: *1200 Jahre Widukinds Taufe,* ed. Gerhard Kaldewei, Paderborn 1985, pp. 12–45.

93 MGH Capit. 1 No. 26 pp. 68–71. This capitulary has been preserved in a single, undated manuscript; it may have been promulgated in either 782 or 785, cf. Mordek, *Bibliotheca,* p. 770.

94 Cf., for example, the *Capitulare Saxonicum* of 797: MGH Capit. 1 pp. 71–2.

95 *ArFqdE* for 795, p. 97. It is not possible to treat in detail here the differences between this and the older version of the *ArF*; cf. Johannes Fried, Bardowick, Sachsen und Karl der Große, in: *Lüneburger Blätter* 30 (1998) pp. 61–84.

96 On the palace, see: Gerhard Roeder, Die Pfalz und die frühen Kirchen in Paderborn nach den schriftlichen Quellen, in: *Westfälische Forschungen* 19 (1966) pp. 137–60; and Uwe Lobbedey, *Die Ausgrabungen im Dom zu Paderborn 1978–80 and 1983,* 4 vols. (Denkmalpflege und Forschung in Westfalen 11), Bonn 1986.

97 Citations from: *Karolus magnus et Leo Papa,* vv. 520–4, ed. Brunhölzl, p. 56 (96).

98 The tradition of illustrated manuscripts of the commentary begins in the tenth century. The set of illustrations is, with very few exceptions, uniform, suggesting that they may have originated with Beatus himself. Cf. John Williams, *The Illustrated Beatus. A Corpus of Illustrations of the Commentary on the Apocalypse,* 5 vols., London 1994–2003.

99 *Cronica Mozarabe de 754,* ed. and transl. José Roduardo López Pereira (Textos medievales 58), Zaragoza 1980.

100 *ArF* for 777. BM² 211a.

101 *AMP* for 778.

102 *ArFqdE* for 777.

103 On attempts at legitimation, see: Achim Thomas Hack, Karl der Große, Hadrian I. und die Muslime in Spanien. Weshalb man einen Krieg führt und wie man ihn legitimiert, in: *Faszination der Papstgeschichte. Neue Zugänge zum frühen und hohen Mittelalter,* ed. Wilfried Hartmann and Klaus Herbers, Cologne/Weimar/Vienna 2008, pp. 229–54 (comparative evaluation of the descriptions in the *ArF,* the *ArFqdE,* CC 61, and the *AMP*).

104 On the following, see Rotter, *Abendland und Sarazenen,* p. 281 (index of the Venerable Bede), esp. pp. 231–64; for the following quotation, see p. 232; cf. also pp. 248–9 (servants of the devil).

105 The *AMP* for 778 adds the word *victor* to the account copied from the *ArF.*

106 Walther Björkman, Karl und der Islam, in: *Karl der Große,* vol. 1 (1965) pp. 672–82, here p. 675.

107 Cf. BM² 840a and 841b.

108 Oexle, Karolinger und die Stadt des heiligen Arnulf, pp. 270–2.

109 Cf. Fried, *Der Schleier der Erinnerung. Grundzüge einer historischen Memorik,* Munich 2004; new edition, including an afterword, Munich 2012, p. 343.

110 Erwin Rosenthal, Der Plan eines Bündnisses zwischen Karl dem Großen und 'Abdurrahman in der arabischen Überlieferung, in: *NA* 48 (1928) pp. 441–5.

111 On the ballad tradition, cf. "Nachwort" by Dieter Kartschoke, in: *Das Rolandslied des Pfaffen Konrad,* Middle High German/New High German parallel text, edited, translated, and annotated by Dieter Kartschoke, Stuttgart 1993.

112 Cf. the section "Reforms Are Long Overdue, but Where to Begin?" in Chapter 5.

113 CC 57 (Late 775).

114 CC 59. Cf. the opening section of Chapter 2.

115 Classen, *Karl der Große,* p. 27.

116 CC 60 (May 778).

117 Fried, Zu Herkunft und Entstehungszeit, pp. 609–10.

118 *ArF* and *AMP* for the 780.

119 Paris, Bibl. nat. nouv. acq. lat. 1203. On the manuscript: Bruno Reudenbach, *Das Godescalc-Evangelistar. Ein Buch für die Reformpolitik Karls des Grossen,* Frankfurt a. M. 1998; the following quotation on p. 7; see also Crivello, Denoël, and Orth, *Godescalc-Evangelistar.*

120 *ArF* for 781.

121 Classen, *Karl der Große,* p. 29; Angilbert: Fleckenstein, *Hofkapelle,* vol. 1, p. 67.

122 Walahfrid Strabo, *Visio Wettini,* vv. 391–9, ed. Knittel.

123 Cf. the section "Increasing Rivalry with Byzantium" in this chapter.

124 Classen, *Karl der Große,* pp. 29–30, with reference to the "Ludovicianum" of 817.

125 See the section "Reforms Are Long Overdue, but Where to Begin?" in Chapter 5.

126 BM² 279a.

127 On the following, see Belting, Studien zum beneventanischen Hof, pp. 142–93 with 6 plates; the following quotation comes from the prince's foundation charter, Belting, p. 182.

128 C. V. B. West, Charlemagne's Involvement in Central and Southern Italy: Power and the Limits of Authority, in: *Early Medieval Europe* 8 (1999, published 2000) pp. 341–67.

129 Elias Avery Lowe, *The Beneventan Script. A History of the South Italian Minuscule,* Oxford 1914.

130 Belting, Probleme der Kunstgeschichte Italiens.

131 BM² 282b. On the visit, see Glatthaar, Zur Datierung der *Epistola generalis.*

132 Letter of Abbot Theodemar of Montecassino to Charlemagne: MGH Epp. 4, 510; Paulus Diaconus, *Historia Langobardorum* 6.40 (MGH SS rer. Lang. 179, 2–5).

133 BM² 285.

134 MGH Capit. 1 pp. 80–1 No. 30; see also Glatthaar, Zur Datierung der *Epistola generalis,* with his conclusion p. 469.–See the section "Reforms Are Long Overdue, but Where to Begin?" in Chapter 5.

135 On the following, see Classen, *Karl der Große,* pp. 33–4.

136 MGH Poetae 1 pp. 66–8 No. 33.

137 Quotation: Classen, *Karl der Große,* p. 33.

138 CC 58, p. 583; cf. Classen, *Karl der Große,* p. 27.

139 Theophanes for AM 6274.

140 *Annales Laureshamenses* for the year 781, MGH SS 1 p. 32; *Chronicon Moissiacense* for 781, MGH SS 1 p. 297.

141 *ArFqdE* for 787 p. 75: "[legati], qui propter petendam filiam suam ad se [sc. Karolum] missi fuerant."

142 The *Lorsch Annals* and the *AMP* do not contain any reference to the end of the engagement either.

143 *ArFqdE* for 788: "Constantinus . . . propter negatam sibi regis filiam"; cf. Classen, *Karl der Große,* pp. 32–3.

144 Gesta sanctorum patrum Fontanellensis coenobii (Gesta abbatum Fontanellensium), chap. 12, ed. Fernand Lohier and Jean Laporte (Société d'histoire de Normandie), Rouen/Paris 1936, p. 84 = *Chronique des Abbés de Fontenelle (Saint-Wandrille)* (Les Classiques de l'Histoire de France au Moyen Age 40), Paris 1999.

145 Cf. the section "The Nearest Neighbors" in Chapter 2.

146 *Fragmentum Annalium Chesnii* for 786, MGH SS 1 p. 33.

147 Agnellus, *Liber pontificalis ecclesiae Ravennatis,* chap. 165, ed. Deborah Mauskopf Deliyannis, Turnhout 2006, pp. 342–3.

148 On the inscription, cf. Peter Classen, *Ausgewählte Aufsätze,* p. 204; on Frankish master builders in 821 in Grado, cf. Belting, Probleme der Kunstgeschichte Italiens, p. 96.

149 Fastrada's second daughter, Hiltrud, may have been born around the time in question, cf. K. F. Werner, Nachkommen, table.

150 See further discussion of the campaign against Tassilo later in this section.

151 Cf. the discussion in the opening section of Chapter 6.

152 Seminal studies on Tassilo include: Becher, *Eid und Herrschaft;* Becher, Zwischen Macht und Recht: Der Sturz Tassilos III. von Bayern 788, in: *Tassilo III. von Bayern,* pp. 39–55; and Freund, *Von den Agilolfingern zu den Karolingern,* pp. 120–60.

153 Jahn, *Ducatus,* pp. 335–550.

154 Arbeo, *Vita et passio Sancti Haimhrammi martyris,* chap. 6, ed. Bruno Krusch, MGH SS rer. Germ. [13] p. 32.

155 Freund, *Von den Agilolfingern zu den Karolingern,* pp. 84–143.

156 Ibid., pp. 107–20; Hammer, *From* Ducatus *to* Regnum, pp. 137–200.

157 MGH LL 3 pp. 459–61; Karl-Ludwig Ay, *Altbayern vom Frühmittelalter bis 1800,* vol. 1, *Altbayern bis 1180* (Dokumente zu Staat und Gesellschaft in Bayern I, 1), Munich 1974, p. 102 No. 63; cf. Wilfried Hartmann, *Synoden,* pp. 90–6; Jahn, *Ducatus,* pp. 512–4; Freund, *Von den Agilolfingern zu den Karolingern,* pp. 93–107.

158 Jahn, *Ducatus,* pp. 475–7.

159 Ay, *Altbayern,* p. 104 No. 66 (Synod of Aschheim; see also Jahn, *Ducatus,* pp. 344–8).

160 *Kasseler Glossen,* in: *Die althochdeutschen Glossen* (4 vols.), compiled and edited by Elias Steinmeyer and Eduard Sievers, Berlin 1895; here vol. 3, p. 13.

161 Ay, *Altbayern,* p. 98 No. 57. Cf. Franz-Reiner Erkens, Summus princeps und dux quem rex ordinavit. Tassilo III. im Spannungsfeld von Fürstlichem Selbstverständnis und königlichem Auftrag, in: *Tassilo III. von Bayern,* pp. 21–38, here pp. 25–6.

162 *Fragmentum Annalium Chesnii* for 787, MGH SS 1 p. 33.

163 Cf. the discussion at the beginning of this section.

164 *Ann. Nazariani Cont.* for 787, MGH SS 1 p. 43.

165 Paulus Diaconus, *Gedicht* 35, ed. Neff, vv. 43–50, p. 149.

166 *Fragmentum Annalium Chesnii* for 788, MGH SS 1 p. 33.

167 See Peter Classen, Bayern und die politischen Mächte im Zeitalter Karls des Großen und Tassilos III. (first published 1978), in: Classen, *Ausgewählte Aufsätze,* pp. 231–48.

168 On this and the following, see Becher, *Eid und Herrschaft;* and, briefly, Becher, Zwischen Macht und Recht (as above note 152). Also see Bernhard Bischoff, *Salzburger Formelbücher und Briefe aus Tassilonischer und Karolingischer Zeit* (SB Munich 1973/1974), Munich 1973, pp. 22–6 with the letters 3.19–23 pp. 54–7.

169 *Ann. Nazariani Cont.* for 788, MGH SS 1 p. 44. Cf. the discussion above (after the *Annals* fragment).

170 Cf. the opening section of Chapter 6. On Gerold: Michael Mitterauer, *Karolingische Markgrafen im Südosten. Fränkische Reichsaristokratie und bayerischer Stammesadel im österreichischen Raum* (Archiv für österreichische Geschichte 123), Vienna 1963, pp. 8–16; Borgolte, *Grafen Alemanniens,* pp. 122–6.

171 On the genealogical connection, see: Jarnut, Genealogie. On the "political" significance for Charlemagne of the group of relatives to which his wife Hildegard belonged, cf. the opening section of this chapter.

172 Michel Germain first made this observation as early as 1675, cf. Astrid Krüger, *Litanei-Handschriften der Karolingerzeit* (MGH Hilfsmittel 24), Hanover 2007, pp. 78–90, on the litany of the psalter, here p. 79 (on the appearance of only the saints of Soissons in this litany). However, Krüger does not commit herself to a definitive identification of the place of origin of the psalter.

173 The identity of the Rotrude of the psalter is the subject of debate; it has been speculated whether the *soror* might not be Tassilo's daughter of the same name, cf. Krüger (as above note 172) pp. 81–2; Bernhard Bischoff pronounces in favor of Rotrude being the daughter of Charlemagne; the same view is taken by Maximilian Diesenberger, Spuren des Wandels. Bayerische Schriftkultur zwischen Agilolfinger- und Karolingerzeit, in: *Tassilo III. von Bayern,* pp. 175–89, here p. 177 and note 7.

174 On the history of the psalter to the present day, see: Hammer, *From* Ducatus *to* Regnum, pp. 182–91.

175 Walahfrid Strabo, *Visio Wettini,* vv. 802–26, ed. Knittel, p. 116.

176 Becher, *Eid und Herrschaft,* pp. 30–5.

177 On the following, see Pohl, *Awaren,* pp. 170–4; this is also the source of the quotations here.

178 Cf. on these conflicts: Pohl, *Awaren,* pp. 312–21.

179 MGH Epp. 4 pp. 528–9 No. 20 (791).

180 Theodulf, carmina. 25, vv. 33–40, MGH Poetae 1 p. 484; on Theodulf's poem: D. Schaller, Vortrags- und Zirkulardichtung, pp. 14–36, here pp. 17–9.

181 On the *filioque* controversy, cf. Willjung, *Konzil von Aachen 809*, introduction; Bernd Oderdorfer, *Filioque. Geschichte und Theologie* (Forschungen zur systematischen und ökumenischen Theologie 96), Göttingen 2001; Gemeinhardt, *Filioque-Kontroverse*, pp. 108–64; and Michael Böhnke, Assaad Elias Kattan, and Bernd Oberdorfer, *Die Filioque-Kontroverse. Historische, ökumenische und dogmatische Perspektiven 1200 Jahre nach der Aachener Synode*, Freiburg i. Br. 2011; cf. the section "The *Opus Karoli regis*" in Chapter 7.

182 *Annales Laureshamenses*, chap. 34 (801), MGH SS 1 p. 38.

183 On the capitularies, cf. Chapter 4; on the pope's admonition, cf. Hadrian's dedicatory poem (MGH Poetae 1 pp. 90–1, lines 10–5) accompanying his dispatch to Charlemagne of the collection of canon-law decrees known as the *Dionysio-Hadriana*.

184 CC 50, p. 570.

185 Werner, Karl der Große oder Charlemagne?, pp. 22–3.

CHAPTER 4. POWER STRUCTURES

1 On monetary policy in the early Middle Ages, cf. Michael McCormick, Was der frühmittelalterliche König mit der Wirtschaft zu tun hatte, in: *Macht des Königs*, pp. 55–71.

2 *CdV*, MGH Capit. 1 pp. 82–91, here chap. 1.

3 For a useful overview, see: Metz, *Zur Erforschung.* – On the economy and trade in the early Middle Ages: McCormick, *Origins of the European Economy.*

4 See the section "Signs in the Heavens" in Chapter 8.

5 For a useful summary, see: Metz, *Zur Erforschung;* relating to a limited region only: Dietmar Flach, *Reichsgut, 751–1024* (Geschichtlicher Atlas der Rheinlande. Beiheft 5), Bonn 2008.

6 On Adalhard's economic planning, cf. the section "How Were the Estates Managed?" in this chapter.

7 MGH Form. pp. 201–2 No. 36. Cf. Walter Schlesinger, Der Markt als Frühform der deutschen Stadt, in: *Vor- und Frühformen der europäischen Stadt im Mittelalter,* vol. 1, ed. Herbert Jankuhn et al. (Abhandlungen der Akademie der Wissenschaften in Göttingen 1973), pp. 262–93, here p. 265.

8 As an example of such continuity, cf. the formula for the monastery at Jumièges: MGH Form. Imp. p. 303 No. 24.

9 DKDG 88 (774–5).

10 MGH Capit. 1 p. 139 and Form. Imp. pp. 314–5 No. 37.

11 On this and the following, cf. Patzold, Normen im Buch, pp. 331–50.

12 On the literature and the historical record, cf. Mordek, *Bibliotheca,* passim.

13 MGH Capit. 1 pp. 82–91 No. 32; now: *Capitulare de villis. Cod. Guelf. 254 Helmst. der Herzog August Bibliothek Wolfenbüttel,* ed. Carlrichard Brühl, Stuttgart 1971. This sole copy, bound together in a slim volume with the *Brevium exempla* (see the section

"How Were the Estates Managed?" in this chapter) may have been the working copy of one of Charlemagne's *missi,* cf. Mordek, *Bibliotheca,* pp. 946–9 (with bibliography); on Louis: Hägermann, *Karl der Große,* p. 670 (but St. Andrew's Day, 30 November, may have been set as a deadline for the delivery of wax for the upcoming Advent period, in much the same way as the delivery date in the Lenten period was determined by the impending Easter festival rather than by specific veneration of the saint on the part of Louis the Pious); on Charlemagne: Tobias Weller in: *Otto der Große und das Römische Reich,* pp. 418–9; the idea that Pope Leo III's letters were originally an addendum at the end of the manuscript is incorrect: Hägermann, *Karl der Große,* pp. 669–70.

14 Metz, *Karolingische Reichsgut,* pp. 53–9.

15 Federico Patetta, Frammento di un Capitolare Franco nel codice A 220 Inf. della Biblioteca Ambrosiana, in: *Atti della Reale Accademia delle Scienze di Torino* 33, disp. 3a (1897/1898) pp. 187–92; Mordek, *Bibliotheca,* pp. 978–9 (for 811?).

16 Metz, *Karolingische Reichsgut,* pp. 60–5.

17 For instance, the *Brevium exempla:* MGH Capit. 1 pp. 250–6 No. 128.

18 On the plan of St. Gall, cf. Peter Ochsenbein and Karl Schmucki (eds.), *Studien zum St. Galler Klosterplan,* vol. 2 (Mitteilungen zur vaterländischen Geschichte 52), St. Gall 2002. Deviations from the monastery reforms of Louis the Pious and the *Rule of St. Benedict* are highlighted by Hanns-Christoph Picker, Der St. Galler Klosterplan als Konzept eines weltoffenen Mönchtums—Ist Walahfrid Strabo der Verfasser?, in: *Zeitschrift für Kirchengeschichte* 119 (2008) pp. 1–29.

19 DKDG 81 (774) for St. Martin in Tours.

20 MGH Capit. 1 pp. 83–91, chap. 16, plus chaps. 27, 47, and 58.

21 *CdV,* chap. 44, MGH Capit. 1 p. 87.

22 On the *Brevium exempla,* cf. the section "How Were the Estates Managed?" in this chapter; on St-Wandrille, cf. the section "Instituting Practical Measures" in Chapter 5.

23 Werner, *Missus;* a partially different interpretation: Hannig, Pauperiores vassi.

24 Schlesinger, Hufe, pp. 41–70.

25 See the section "How Were the Estates Managed?" in this chapter.

26 Schlesinger, Hufe, pp. 56–7.

27 *CdV,* chap. 62 p. 89.

28 Recent excavations have brought some remains of these oak pilings to light, cf. Chapter 7, note 110.

29 As, for example in the Frankfurt capitulary of 794.

30 Mordek, *Bibliotheca,* p. 979, chap. 22.

31 See the section "A Hidden Failure: The Synod of Frankfurt" in Chapter 7.

32 Chap. 79, ed. Mordek, Zechiel-Eckes, and Glatthaar, pp. 230–3.

33 On this, see Ludolf Kuchenbuch, *Opus feminile.* Das Geschlechterverhältnis im Spiegel von Frauenarbeiten im früheren Mittelalter, in: Kuchenbuch, *Reflexive Mediävistik,* pp. 278–315, here pp. 280–1.

34 Cf., for example, *CdV,* chap. 64, MGH Capit. 1 p. 89.

35 Fred Schwind, Zu karolingerzeitlichen Klöstern als Wirtschaftsorganismen und Stätten handwerklicher Tätigkeit, in: *Institutionen, Kultur und Gesellschaft im Mittelalter. Festschrift für Josef Fleckenstein,* ed. Lutz Fenske, Werner Rösener, and Thomas Zotz, Sigmaringen 1984, pp. 101–24.

36 MGH Capit. 1 p. 123 No. 44, 7 (805).

37 Ibid., pp. 250–6 No. 128 (ca. 811). On the census of manorial estates through figures, cf. Kuchenbuch, Zahlendenken und Zahlengebrauch, in: Kuchenbuch, *Reflexive Mediävistik.*

38 On the analysis of this estate: Konrad Elmshäuser, Untersuchungen zum Staffelseer Urbar, in: *Strukturen der Grundherrschaft,* pp. 335–69; on women's work there: Kuchenbuch, *Opus feminile,* in: Kuchenbuch, *Reflexive Mediävistik,* pp. 294–5.–The example of a monastery (St-Wandrille) is presented in the section "Instituting Practical Measures" in Chapter 5.

39 On the Annappes estate: Helmar Härtel, in: *799. Kunst und Kultur,* vol. 1, p. 93; cf. the section "Instituting Practical Measures" in Chapter 5 on St-Wandrille.

40 Cf. Kuchenbuch, *Opus feminile,* in: Kuchenbuch, *Reflexive Mediävistik,* p. 297.

41 BM^2 351b–353a.

42 *Statuta seu brevia Adalhardi,* in: *Corpus Consuetudinum Monasticarum,* vol. 1, ed. Kassius Hallinger, Siegburg 1963, pp. 357–408. For a summary, see: Kasten, *Adalhard von Corbie,* pp. 110–37.

43 Brevis chap. 3 (as note 42), p. 376.

44 Ibid., chap. 7 (as note 42), pp. 403–8.

45 Ibid., chap. 1 (as note 42), pp. 365–72.

46 Ibid., chap. 6.2 (as note 42), p. 390.

47 Ibid., chap. 3 (as note 42), p. 376.

48 DKDG 73 = *Codex Laureshamensis, Chronik,* ed. Karl Glöckner (Arbeiten der Historischen Kommission für den Volksstaat Hessen), Darmstadt 1929, chaps. 6 and 6a, pp. 277–82 = BM^2 152. On Lorsch: Josef Semmler, Die Geschichte der Abtei Lorsch von der Gründung bis zum Ende der Salierzeit (764–1125), in: *Die Reichsabtei Lorsch. Festschrift zum Gedenken an ihre Stiftung 764,* pt. 1, ed. Friedrich Knöpp, Darmstadt 1975, pp. 75–173.

49 On this (including an edition and reports of epigraphic and philological experts), see: Wilhelm Metzendorf, Die Steinurkunde von St. Peter in Heppenheim, in: *Geschichtsblätter Kreis Bergstraße* 16 (1983) pp. 27–64 (805). Granted, the phrase "great Charles" (instead of "the great emperor") suggests a period after Charlemagne, at least for the creation of the dating on the stone plaque.

50 *CdV,* chap. 36, MGH Capit. 1 p. 86.

51 MGH Capit. 1 pp. 81–2 No. 31 (800).

52 Harald Witthöft, Thesen zu einer karolingischen Metrologie, in: *Science in Western and Eastern Civilization,* pp. 503–24; Witthöft, "Denarius novus," "modius publicus" und "libra panis" im Frankfurter Kapitulare. Elemente und Struktur einer materiellen Ordnung in fränkischer Zeit, in: *Frankfurter Konzil von 794,* vol. 1, pp. 219–52.–Cf. the section "A Hidden Failure: The Synod of Frankfurt" in Chapter 7.

53 MGH Conc. 2, 1 p. 166 No. 19G, 4.–Cf. the section "A Hidden Failure: The Synod of Frankfurt" in Chapter 7.

54 MGH Conc. 2, 1 p. 166 No. 19G, 4; the following quotation: p. 167.

55 Alcuin, *De virtutibus et vitiis liber ad Widonem comitem,* Migne *PL* 101, cols. 613–38, here cols. 613 613C–614C (with omissions not indicated in the translation). On this, see: Alain Dubreucq, Autour du *De virtutibus et vitiis* d'Alcuin, in: Alcuin, de York à Tours, pp. 269–88 (with a bibliography of older titles).

56 Walahfrid Strabo, *Visio Wettini,* vv. 481–508, for the quotation: v. 492, ed. Knittel, pp. 94–6. Cf. the discussion at the beginning of the Prologue.

57 As in Heito's description of the monk Wetti's vision: ed. Knittel, p. 50.

58 Form. Imp. 5, MGH Form. p. 291.

59 For a general account of Charlemagne's adversaries: Karl Brunner, *Oppositionelle Gruppen* (Veröffentlichungen des Instituts für Österreichische Geschichtsforschung 25), Vienna 1979; on Hardrat's rebellion, pp. 48–52; see also Janet L. Nelson, *Opposition to Charlemagne* (German Historical Institute in London, Annual Lecture 2008), London 2009.

60 Capitulare missorum (uncertain dating; 789 or 792), MGH Capit. 1 p. 66 No. 25 chaps. 1–2, p. 67 chap. 4, cf. Mordek, *Bibliotheca,* p. 472. On the dating to 789, cf. Becher, *Eid und Herrschaft,* pp. 79–85.

61 MGH Capit. 1 p. 63 No. 23 chap. 18 from 789 (?). On its implementation, see the discussion later in this section and the section "Internal Order within the Empire" in Chapter 8.

62 MGH Capit. 1 p. 67 No. 23 chap. 6.

63 For example, the Herstal capitulary of 779 (MGH Capit. 1 p. 48 chap. 9) drew a distinction between *vassi casati* and *vassi non casati* (vassals with and without a fief).

64 On the abbot Adalhard of Corbie as a *vassus domini Caroli imperatoris:* Kasten, *Adalhard von Corbie,* pp. 69–70 (812); on a count as a royal *vassus:* Michael Borgolte, *Geschichte der Grafschaften Alemanniens in fränkischer Zeit* (VuF Sonderband 31), Sigmaringen 1984, p. 226 (816); the sons of Louis the Pious as *vassalli* of the emperor: Susan Reynolds, *Fiefs and Vassals. The Medieval Evidence Reinterpreted,* Oxford 1994, p. 86 (=Paschasius Radbertus, *Epitaphium Arsenii,* ed. Ernst Dümmler, Preussische Akademie der Wissenschaften Berlin, Abhandlungen der historisch-philologischen Klasse, 1900, pp. 18–98, here p. 85; certainly, this was not a customary designation for princes with manorial rights deriving from the father, but it occurred in an extraordinary context and at the same time represented the only contemporary piece of evidence in which a king/emperor addressed his rebellious sons; in this regard, Reynolds's interpretation misses the point of the *Epitaphium Arsenii* as an exception).

65 Cf. Bullough, *Karl der Große,* p. 113 (with the notes on p. 291).

66 Regarding research into the nobility of the eighth and ninth centuries, cf. here only a selection of groundbreaking studies: Tellenbach, *Königtum und Stämme; Studien und Vorarbeiten zur Geschichte des großfränkischen und frühdeutschen Adels,* ed. Gerd Tellenbach (Forschungen zur Oberrheinischen Landesgeschichte 4), Freiburg i. Br. 1957; further studies on the subject by Tellenbach in his *Ausgewählte Abhandlungen,* vol. 3; Schmid, *Gebetsgedenken;* Werner, Bedeutende Adelsfamilien im Reich Karls des Großen, in W. Braunfels (ed.), *Karl der Große,* vol. I, Düsseldorf 1965; Werner, *Naissance de la Noblesse;* Störmer, *Früher Adel;* and Hechberger, *Adel.*

67 Stieldorf, *Marken und Markgrafen,* pp. 36–40 and elsewhere.

68 Tellenbach, Großfränkische Adel, p. 54.

69 On the usage and the limitations of the term: Hechberger, *Adel,* pp. 186–94.

70 Although the king's approving comment on this remark was cut out of the original manuscript of the *Opus Caroli* by the bookbinder (3.13, ed. Freeman, p. 388 note d), it was definitely there beforehand.

71 MGH Capit. 1 p. 67 No. 23 chap. 5.

72 Cf. ibid., p. 125 No. 44 chap. 16.

73 Examples: W. Hartmann, *Karl der Große,* p. 280n29.

74 See the discussion later in this section.

75 *AMP* for 790 (ed. Simson p. 78); *Ann. S. Amandi* for 789 (MGH SS 1 p. 12).

76 Charles the Younger's subkingship does not stand out as clearly as the two outposts of Italy and Aquitaine. Even so, traces of his reign are evident: cf. Peter Classen, Karl der Große und die Thronfolge im Frankenreich, in: Classen, *Ausgewählte Aufsätze,* pp. 205–29, here pp. 206–7.–On Pepin "the Hunchback" (not discussed by Classen), cf. the opening section of Chapter 6.

77 MGH SS 1 p. 12.

78 Cf. the opening section of Chapter 6.

79 See the following text.

80 See the section "Italy—A Special Case" in this chapter.

81 Cf. the section "Instituting Practical Measures" in Chapter 5.

82 Astronomus, *Vita Hludowici imperatoris,* ed. Ernst Tremp MGH SS rer. germ. i.u.s. 64, Hanover 1995, here chap. 7, p. 304. See the section "'Opposing the Enemies of Truth'" in Chapter 7.

83 The beginning of capitulary No. 51, MGH Capit. 1 p. 138 (808), was cited as an example.

84 On the *Admonitio generalis,* cf. the section "Even a King Has Worries" in Chapter 5. On its dissemination: *Admonitio generalis,* ed. Mordek, Zechiel-Eckes, and Glatthaar, introduction, pp. 86–110 (Zechiel-Eckes).

85 Mordek, *Bibliotheca,* pp. 210–7, here pp. 215–6; *Admonitio generalis,* ed. Mordek, Zechiel-Eckes, and Glatthaar, introduction. pp. 86–110 (Zechiel-Eckes), pp. 93–5.

86 On the process of taking the oath, see the discussion earlier in this section. On the Herstal capitulary, cf. the section "Reforms Are Long Overdue, but Where to Begin?" in Chapter 5; on the *Admonitio,* see the section "Even a King Has Worries" in Chapter 5.

87 Werner, *Missus,* pp. 203–4.

88 MGH Capit. 1 No. 58 pp. 145–6.

89 MGH Epp. 4 pp. 528–9 No. 20 (791); cf. the section "Conflict Grows with Bavaria and Pannonia" in Chapter 3 and the section "Diversity of Forms of Worship" in Chapter 5.

90 But cf. MGH Capit. 1 p. 137 No. 50, 1.

91 First attested in ibid. (808).

92 Cf. the section "How Were the Estates Managed?" in this chapter.

93   *Tabula Peutingeriana. Codex Vindobonnensis 324*, Vollständige Faksimile-Ausgabe im Originalformat, Graz 1976; with a commentary by E. Weber, Graz, 2004.

94   Arnold Esch, *Wege nach Rom. Annäherungen aus zehn Jahrhunderten*, Munich 2003, pp. 9–29.

95   Arnold Esch, *Zwischen Antike und Mittelalter. Der Verfall des römischen Straßensystems in Mittelitalien und die Via Amerina*, Munich 2011. On Charlemagne's processions through his realm: McKitterick, *Karl der Große*, pp. 165–71.

96   *ArFqdE* for 793, ed. Kurze, p. 93.

97   Hanns Hubert Hofmann, *Kaiser Karls Kanalbau*, ²Sigmaringen 1976. The so-called *Annals* of Einhard (as in the preceding note) clearly shows the failure of this undertaking.

98   Einhard, *Vita Karoli*, chap. 17.

99   *ArF* for 793, ed. Kurze, pp. 92–4.

100 For a brief treatment of this subject, cf. Carlrichard Brühl, Die wirtschaftliche Bedeutung der Pfalzen für die Versorgung des Hofes von der fränkischen bis zur Stauferzeit, in: Brühl, *Aus Mittelalter und Diplomatik*, vol. 1, Hildesheim 1989, pp. 222–32; for a more extensive account, Brühl, *Fodrum, Gistum, Servitium regis. Studien zu den wirtschaftlichen Grundlagen des Königtums im Frankenreich und in den fränkischen Nachfolgestaaten Deutschland, Frankreich und Italien vom 6. bis zur Mitte des 14. Jahrhunderts*, Cologne/Vienna 1968.

101 Cf. the section "The Call of Italy" in Chapter 3.

102 Einhard ep. 5, MGH Epp. 5 p. 111.

103 Einhard ep. 9, MGH Epp. 5 p. 113.

104 Einhard ep. 56, MGH Epp. 5 p. 137.

105 For example, DKDG 81 (774) for St. Martin in Tours; particular mention is made here of a *senodochium*, in other words, a hospice; or DKDG 112 (776) for the grammarian Paulinus of Aquileia.

106 *Instituta regalia et ministeria camere regum Lombardorum et honorantie civitatis Papie*, chap. 1, MGH SS 30, 2 p. 1451.

107 Bernhard Bischoff assigned this inventory to the court library of Charlemagne; in contrast, cf. its reassignment to Verona or northern Italy by Villa, *Horazüberlieferung*, pp. 29–52.

108 MGH Capit. 1 pp. 187–8 No. 88 (20 February [most likely 774]).

109 On the manuscript: Mordek, *Bibliotheca*, pp. 676–80.

110 See the section "Reforms Are Long Overdue, but Where to Begin?" in Chapter 5.

111 See the section "Even a King Has Worries" in Chapter 5.

112 MGH Capit. 1 pp. 203–4 No. 97.

Chapter 5. The Ruler

1   Alcuin ep. 93, MGH Epp. 31, 136–8, for the quotation pp. 137–8 (796); Scholz, *Politik, Selbstverständnis, Selbstdarstellung*, pp. 109–10.

2   Cf. the Prologue.

3   Theodulf Carmina vv. 32, 32–4, MGH Poetae 1 pp. 523–4.

4   MGH Epp. 4 p. 503, 3–6.

5   MGH Conc. 2 p. 242, 13–4.

6   Cf. the section "Conflict Grows with Bavaria and Pannonia" in Chapter 3.

7   Arnold Esch, Überlieferungs-Chance und Überlieferungs-Zufall als methodologisches Problem des Historikers, in: *HZ* 240 (1985) pp. 529–70 (again in: Esch, *Zeitalter und Menschenalter. Der Historiker und die Erfahrung vergangener Gegenwart,* Munich 1994, pp. 39–69).

8   Johannes Fried, Der karolingische Herrschaftsverband im 9. Jahrhundert zwischen "Kirche" und "Königshaus," in: *HZ* 235 (1982) pp. 1–43.

9   As ultimately attested by the *Admonitio generalis* of 789, ed. Mordek, Zechiel-Eckes, and Glatthaar, p. 238; or the proceedings of the Synod of Frankfurt in 794: MGH Conc. 2, 1 p. 119 (Spanish bishops to their Frankish colleagues), less clearly p. 120 (the Spanish bishops to Charlemagne), p. 162 (Charlemagne to the Spanish bishops).

10   Pseudo-Cyprian, *De XII abusivis,* ed. with introduction and indexes by A. Breen, Dublin 1996.

11   Cf. the section "Education as a Scholar and Instruction in the Christian Faith" in Chapter 1.

12   Orosius, *Historiarum adversum paganos libri VII,* ed. Carl Zangemeister (Corpus Scriporum Ecclesiasticorum Latinorum 5), Vienna 1882, 7.43.5–6, p. 300: "de restituendo in integrum."

13   For a brief but useful overview: Rosamond McKitterick, Die karolingische Renovatio, in: *799. Kunst und Kultur,* vol. 2, pp. 668–85.

14   I am following here the observations of Bernhard Jussen (in a conversation with me).

15   Cf. Katharina Bierbrauer, Le miniature, in: *I Goti (Milano, Palazzo Reale 28 gen.-8 marzo 1994),* ed. Ermanno A. Arslan, Volker Bierbrauer, and Otto Von Hessen, Milan 1994, pp. 268–9, No. III.39.

16   Cf. the section "Education as a Scholar and Instruction in the Christian Faith" in Chapter 1.

17   *Heliand und Genesis,* ed. Otto Behagel, 9th ed. revised by Burkhard Taeger (Althochdeutsche Textbibliothek 4), Tübingen 1984; Otfrid von Weißenburg, *Evangelienbuch,* ed. Wolfgang Kleiber and Rita Heuser, 2 vols., Tübingen 2004.

18   Cf. the section "Education as a Scholar and Instruction in the Christian Faith" in Chapter 1.

19   MGH Conc. 2, 1 pp. 3–4 No. 1 cc. 5 and 6 (742 or 743).

20   Ibid., p. 53 No. 7 c. 13 (740/50).

21   Tellenbach, *Königtum und Stämme,* chaps. 3 and 4. Cf. also Tellenbach, Vom karolingischen Reichsadel zum deutschen Reichsfürstenstand, most recently in Tellenbach, *Ausgewählte Abhandlungen und Aufsätze,* vol. 3, Stuttgart 1988, pp. 889–940 (first published 1943). Cf. Hechberger, *Adel,* pp. 186–94.

22   Cf. also, for example, *Opus Caroli,* ed. Freeman, p. 50, and the author index, p. 607; Borst, *Schriften zur Komputistik,* vol. 1, p. 87.

23 MGH DKarol 55.

24 Cf. the section "The Call of Italy" in Chapter 3. For a brief account of the church constitution of Saxony: Peter Johannek, Der Ausbau der sächsischen Kirchenorganisation, in: 799. Kunst und Kultur, vol. 2, pp. 494–506.

25 On the following, cf. Classen, Karl der Große, pp. 17–25; and Scholz, Politik, Selbstverständnis, Selbstdarstellung, pp. 78–96.

26 A wall was built around the Vatican only in the mid-ninth century under Pope Leo IV.

27 Cf. the section "The Call of Italy" in Chapter 3.

28 CC 45, MGH Epp. 3 p. 562, 4–5.

29 On this, see the section "Diversity within Church Law" in this chapter. Cf. Horst Fuhrmann, Das Papsttum und das kirchliche Leben im Frankenreich, in: Settimane Spoleto 27 (1979; published 1981) pp. 419–56, here esp. p. 438, the following quotation p. 450.

30 These quotations are from Hadrian I's poem accompanying his dispatch to Charlemagne of the Dionysio-Hadriana: MGH Epp. 1 pp. 90–1. Cf. (with translation into German) Scholz, Politik, Selbstverständnis, Selbstdarstellung, pp. 82–5.

31 On the genesis of the laudes sung to the Frankish monarch and their incorporation into the Easter festivities of 774: Kantorowicz, Laudes regiae, pp. 53–4.

32 From the Montpellier Codex H409 in: Die Kaiserkrönung Karls des Großen, compiled and with an introduction by Kurt Reindel (Historische Texte Mittelalter 4), Göttingen 1970, pp. 38–9. The words in brackets cannot have been a constituent part of the laudes at Easter 774.

33 AMP for 774, pp. 61–2; repeated in Chronicon Anianense (Moissiacense) for 774, MGH SS 1 p. 295; ed. Kettemann, Subsidia Anianensia, pt. 2, p. 41.

34 Because of the destruction of the Irminsul in that year, Charlemagne called the annals for 772 gloriosus.

35 CC No. 55 (774), MGH Epp. 3 pp. 568–9.

36 Chronicon Anianense (Moissiacense) for 772, MGH SS 1 p. 295; ed. Kettemann, Subsidia Anianensia, pt. 2, p. 39.

37 Cf. Scholz, Politik, Selbstverständnis, Selbstdarstellung, pp. 86–9.

38 Wolfgang H. Fritze, Papst und Frankenkönig. Studien zu päpstlich-fränkischen Rechtsbeziehungen von 754 bis 824 (VuF Sonderband 10), Sigmaringen 1973, pp. 49–62.

39 Cf. the section "The Young Charlemagne's First Encounter with a Pope" in Chapter 1.

40 Alcuin ep. 93 (796), MGH Epp. 4 pp. 136–8; on the letter: Bullough, Alcuin, pp. 455–8.

41 For Alcuin's verses, see: MGH Poetae 1 pp. 113–4 No. 9; for Theodulf's, MGH Poetae 1 pp. 489–90 No. 26. On the epitaph in Rome: Scholz, Karl der Große und das "Epitaphium Hadriani," in: Frankfurter Konzil von 794, vol. 1, pp. 373–94, here p. 381.

42 See the section "Even Priests Clash" in this chapter.

43 On Alcuin, cf. Bullough, Alcuin and the Kingdom of Heaven, in: Carolingian Essays pp. 1–69; Bullough, Alcuin; also the relevant essays in: Science in Western and Eastern Civilization, pp. 3–114; on Theodulf: Ann Freeman, introduction to Opus Caroli.

44 *Annales Laureshamenses* for 796, MGH SS 1 p. 36.

45 Angilbert's verses, MGH Poetae 1 p. 360 vv. 19–21: "David habere cupit sapientes mente magistros / Ad decus, ad laudem cuiuscumque artis in aula, / Ut veterum renovet studiosa mente sophiam."

46 These quotations from Wilhelm Levison in: Wilhelm Wattenbach and Wilhelm Levison, *Deutschlands Geschichtsquellen im Mittelalter. Vorzeit und Karolinger*, vol. 2, *Die Karolinger vom Anfang des 8. Jahrhunderts bis zum Tode Karls des Großen*, edited by Wilhelm Levison and Heinz Löwe, Weimar 1953, p. 194.

47 For Charlemagne's monitory letter to the monks of Fulda, tentatively dated to the 780s, see: UB Fulda 1 pp. 251–6 (the following quotations also come from this).

48 *Disputatio de vera philosophia* (=introduction to Alcuin's *On Grammar*), in: *Alcuini Opera*, ed. Frobenius Forster, vol. 2, 4, Regensburg 1777, pp. 265–8, here p. 268.

49 Quotation: Alcuin ep. 145 (798), MGH Epp. 4 p. 233, 5–6. On this subject, cf. Springsfeld, *Alkuins Einfluß*.

50 Cf. the section "Signs in the Heavens" in Chapter 8.

51 MGH Epp. 4.

52 Notker, *Gesta Karoli* I, 2, ed. Reinhold Rau, Quellen zur karolingischen Reichsgeschichte 3, Darmstadt 1960, pp. 321–427; Notker, *Gesta Karoli Magni* 1.I, 2, ed. Rau; here p. 324.

53 On the following, see Florian Hartmann, Vitam litteris ni emam, nihil est, quod tribuam. Paulus Diaconus zwischen Langobarden und Franken, in: *FmaSt* 43 (2009) pp. 71–93.

54 This evaluation of Theodulf's achievement can be found in: Horst Fuhrmann, *Cicero und das Seelenheil; oder, Wie kam die heidnische Antike durch das christliche Mittelalter?* (Lectio Teubneriana 12), Munich/Leipzig 2003, p. 16.

55 Paris, Bibl. nat. Lat. 9380 f. 347r. The two distichs read, in English prose: "Live long in God, dear reader, and I pray that you will think of your Theodulf. This work is now ended. To those who have completed it, including yourself, dear reader, I wish peace, a good life, and salvation. Farewell!"

56 Rosamond McKitterick, *The Carolingians and the Written Word*, Cambridge 1989; on the problem of the monastery school for "externs" who did not belong to the convent, see: M. M. Hildebrandt, *The External School in Carolingian Society* (Education and Society in the Middle Ages and the Renaissance 1), Leiden 1992.

57 As noted in the introduction of the "Epistola de litteris colendis," UB Fulda, vol. 1, pp. 251–6.

58 Cf. Bischoff, Bibliothek im Dienst der Schule, p. 215.

59 See Walter Berschin, *Biographie und Epochenstil im lateinischen Mittelalter*, vol. 3, Stuttgart 1991, p. 146.

60 Cf. the section "Reforms Are Long Overdue, but Where to Begin?" in this chapter.

61 For an overview of early Irish history, see: Dáibhí Ó Cróinín (ed.), *Prehistoric and Early Ireland*, vol. 1 of *A New History of Ireland*, Oxford 2008.

62 Michael Richter, *Bobbio in the Early Middle Ages. The Abiding Legacy of Columbanus*, Dublin/Portland, OR, 2008.

63 These verses were discovered by Bischoff, *Theodulf und der Ire Cadac-Andreas,* pp. 19–25, here pp. 21–2; cf. the section "Knowledge Concentrates at the Court" in Chapter 6.

64 Cf. Einhard, *Vita Karoli,* chap. 21 (p. 26).

65 MGH Capit. 1 pp. 349–52 No. 171 (819).

66 Hoffmann, *Untersuchungen;* Bernhard Bischoff, Die Kölner Nonnenhandschriften und das Skriptorium von Chelles, in: Bischoff, *Mittelalterliche Studien,* vol. 1, Stuttgart 1966, pp. 16–34.

67 MGH Poetae 1 pp. 93–4 No. 6.

68 On Corbie: David Ganz, *Corbie in the Carolingian Renaissance* (Beihefte der Francia 20), Sigmaringen 1990; on fraternization: MGH Conc. 2 pp. 72–3; see also Karl Schmid and Otto Gerhard Oexle, Voraussetzungen und Wirkungen des Gebetsbundes von Attigny, in: *Francia* 2 (1972) pp. 71–122.

69 Tino Licht, Die älteste karolingische Minuskel, in: *Mittellateinisches Jahrbuch* 47 (2012) pp. 337–46.

70 Bruno Reudenbach, *Das Godescalc-Evangelistar. Ein Buch für die Reformpolitik Karls des Großen,* Frankfurt a. M. 1998. Crivello, Denoël, and Orth, *Godescalc-Evangelistar,* pp. 38–48, on the dedicatory poem, with a corrected edition and translation (P. Orth). In the dedicatory poem the name is spelled with a double *s: Godesscalc.* On the image of the fountain of life in the evangelistary: Crivello, Denoël, and Orth, p. 54 plate 6.

71 Cf. the section "Conflict Grows with Bavaria and Pannonia" in Chapter 3.

72 *Mittelalterliche Bücherverzeichnisse des Klosters Fulda und andere Beiträge zur Geschichte der Bibliothek des Klosters Fulda im Mittelalter,* ed. Gangolf Schrimpf (Fuldaer Studien 4), Frankfurt am Main 1992, pp. 12–3 and 94–7.

73 On tracking down manuscripts, cf. Philippe Depreux, Büchersuche und Büchertausch im Zeitalter der karolingischen Renaissance am Beispiel des Briefwechsels des Lupus von Ferrières, in: *Archiv für Kulturgeschichte* 76 (1994) pp. 267–84.

74 Cf. the sections "King Charles the Wise" in this chapter and "Charlemagne and the Modern Age" in the Epilogue.

75 MGH Capit. Episcop. 1 pp. 73–142.

76 Hubert Mordek, Fränkische Kapitularien und Kapitulariensammlungen, in: Mordek, *Studien zur fränkischen Herrschergesetzgebung. Aufsätze über Kapitularien und Kapitular-iensammlungen, ausgewählt zum 60. Geburtstag,* Frankfurt am Main 2000, pp. 1–53.

77 Josef Fleckenstein, Karl der Große und sein Hof, in: *Karl der Große,* vol. 1, pp. 24–50, here pp. 32–3.

78 Cf. the section "The Call of Italy" in Chapter 3.

79 This is evident from the poem in the letter.

80 Alcuini *Carmen* 4, MGH Poetae 1 pp. 220–23; see Schaller, Vortrags- und Zirkulard-ichtung, p. 19.–According to Bernhard Bischoff, the sole manuscript of the poem was written in in St-Denis, cf. Schaller, note 18.

81 Cf. the section "The Rules of the Court" in Chapter 6 on the royal court and the court chapel.

82 MGH Capit. 1 No. 20. It is not clear whether No. 21, as had been previously supposed (cf. Wilfried Hartmann, *Synoden,* pp. 101–2), comes from approximately the same time or was written only in 792/793, as Mordek, *Bibliotheca,* p. 1082, assumes. The following references to individual chapters refer to this capitulary.

83 On this and the following, see Daniel Carlo Pangerl, *Die Metropolitanverfassung des karolingischen Frankenreiches* (Schriften der MGH 63), Hanover 2011, pp. 35–9; p. 41, 3; pp. 106–9.

84 Boniface ep. 50, MGH Epp. sel. 1 p. 82 (742).

85 MGH Auct. Ant. 9 pp. 552–612, the text: pp. 584–612.

86 On the context, cf. Fuhrmann, Papsttum und das kirchliche Leben, pp. 428–9.

87 MGH Capit. 1 No. 22; see the section "Even a King Has Worries" in this chapter.

88 MGH Epp. 4 p. 532 No. 22; see also Glatthaar, Zur Datierung der *Epistola generalis,* pp. 462–3.

89 MGH Capit. 1 pp. 80–1 No. 30; on the dating to 787, cf. Glatthaar, Zur Datierung der *Epistola generalis.*

90 *Ann. Nazariani cont.,* MGH SS 1 pp. 41–3.

91 MGH Capit. 1 p. 66 No. 25. On tensions among the aristocracy: Regine Lejan, Der Adel um 800: Verwandtschaft, Herrschaft, Treue, in: *Am Vorabend der Kaiserkrönung,* pp. 257–68.

92 *Admonitio generalis,* ed. Mordek, Zechiel-Eckes, and Glatthaar, introduction, p. 29.

93 Arno Borst, *Die karolingische Kalenderreform* (MGH Schriften 46), Hanover 1998, p. 236, referred to Justianian (*Nov.* 7) in this context; in general on the *Admonitio generalis,* pp. 234–8. The idea that the *Admonitio generalis* was modeled on the *Edictus* of the Lombard king Rothari (see, for example, *Admonitio generalis,* ed. Mordek, Zechiel-Eckes, and Glatthaar, introduction, p. 47) seems to me less probable, since Charlemagne's list of titles in the *Admonitio* notably leaves out the title of king of the Lombards, which Charlemagne customarily used.

94 *Admonitio generalis,* ed. Mordek, Zechiel-Eckes, and Glatthaar, introduction, p. 182, 26–30.

95 On the following, cf. the introduction to *Admonitio generalis,* ed. Mordek, Zechiel-Eckes, and Glatthaar. On Alcuin's authorship: ibid., pp. 47–63 (after Bullough, *Alcuin*).

96 *Admonitio generalis,* ed. Mordek, Zechiel-Eckes, and Glatthaar, p. 86.

97 Now: Wolfenbüttel, Cod. Guelf. 496a, cf. Mordek, *Bibliotheca,* pp. 949–52; and Hubert Mordek, Frühmittelalterliche Gesetzgeber und Iustitia in Miniaturen weltlicher Rechtshandschrifte, in: La Giustizia nell'Alto Medioevo (Secoli V–VIII), *Settimane Spoleto* 42 (1995), pp. 997–1052 with plates I–XL, here pp. 1018–22 with plates XIV–XV.–Illustration of the first page: Marco-Aeilko Aris and Regina Pütz, *Bibliotheca Fuldensis. Ausgewählte Handschriften und Handschriftenfragmente aus der mittelalterlichen Bibliothek des Klosters Fulda,* Fulda 2010, pp. 74–5; illustration of fol. 4r: *Admonitio generalis,* ed. Mordek, Zechiel-Eckes, and Glatthaar, plate 1.

98 Cf. Hubert Mordek and Michael Glatthaar, Von Wahrsagerinnen und Zauberern. Ein Beitrag zur Religionspolitik Karls des Großen, in: *Archiv für Kulturgeschichte 75* (1993) pp. 33–64.

99 Cf. the section "Internal Order within the Empire" in Chapter 8.

100 This sentiment is expressed in the preamble to the *Epistola de litteris colendis:* UB Fulda, vol. 1, pp. 251–6.

101 *Aristoteles Latinus* I,1–5, ed. L[orenzo] Minio-Paluello, Bruges/Paris 1961, pp. 129–75, along with the introduction, pp. lxxvii–xxxiv. See also: "Categoriae decem" in Wikipedia, which contains a link to a scan of the text.

102 Cf. the author list in *Opus Caroli*, ed. Freeman, MGH Concilia 2 Suppl. 1, pp. 60–1.

103 These characteristics of "oral culture" were highlighted—with reference to Alexander Luria's researches among the Kirgiz people—by Walter J. Ong, *Oralität und Literalität. Die Technologisierung des Wortes*, Opladen 1987.

104 *Admonitio generalis*, chap. 70, ed. Mordek, Zechiel-Eckes, and Glatthaar, pp. 222–4.

105 MGH Conc. 2 No. 38, 17 p. 288.

106 *De Karolo rege et Leone papa*, vv. 73–5, p. 14 [64].

107 Menso Folkerts, *Die älteste mathematische Aufgabensammlung in lateinischer Sprache. Die Alkuin zugeschriebenen "Propositiones ad acuendos iuvenes." Überlieferung, Inhalt, Kritische Edition* (Österreichische Akademie der Wissenschaften, Mathematische-Naturwissenschaftliche Klasse Denkschriften 116, 6), Vienna 1978, pp. 15–80, here p. 63 No. 32; Folkerts, Die Alkuin zugeschriebenen *Propositiones ad acuendos iuvenes*, in: *Science in Western and Eastern Civilization*, pp. 273–81, see also Folkerts and Helmut Gericke, in: Folkerts, Die Alkuin zugeschriebenen *Propositione*, pp. 283–362, edition and translation (No. 32 p. 336).

108 Jochen Splett, Der Abrogans und das Einsetzen althochdeutscher Schriftlichkeit im 8. Jahrhundert, in: *Typen der Ethnogenese unter besonderer Berücksichtigung der Bayern*, vol. 1, ed. Herwig Wolfram and Walter Pohl (Österreich. Akad. d. Wiss. Phil.-Hist. Kl. Denkschriften 201), Vienna 1990, pp. 235–41.

109 *Die althochdeutschen Glossen*, compiled and edited by Elias Steinmeyer and Eduard Sievers, vol. 1, Berlin 1879, pp. 1–270; Bernhard Bischoff (ed.), *Die "Abrogans"-Handschrift der Stiftsbibliothek St. Gallen. Das älteste deutsche Buch*, 2 vols. (facsimile and commentary), St. Gall 1977.

110 *Vita Alcuini*, chap. 16, MGH SS 15, 1 p. 193.

111 For an overview, see: Birger Munk Olsen, *Catalogue des manuscrits classiques latins copiés du IXe au XIIe siècles*, vol. 1, *Apicius–Juvénal* (Documents, études et répertoire publ. par l'Institut de recherche des texts), Paris 1982; vol. 2, *Livius–Vitruvius. Florileges— Essais de plume*, Paris 1985.–On the literature of the Carolingian period, cf. Gröber, *Übersicht*; Brunhölzl, *Geschichte*, vol. 1; Berschin, *Biographie und Epochenstil*, vol. 3; and Peter Godman, *Poets and Emperors. Frankish Politics and Carolingian Poetry*, Oxford 1987, pp. 1–92.

112 *Glossaria latina iussu Academiae Britannicae edita*, vol. 1, *Glossarium Ansileubi sive Librum Glossarum*, ed. W. M. Lindsay, J. F. Mountford, and J. Whatmough, Paris 1926. A new edition is currently in preparation; cf. on the Internet under the search term "LibGloss."—Bischoff, Bibliothek im Dienst der Schule, assumes involvement on the part of the Carolingian court.–Cf. also David Ganz, The "Liber Glossarum": A Carolingian Encyclopedia, in: *Science in Western and Eastern Civilization*, pp. 127–35.

113 Ms. Florence, Bibl. Laurenziana Plut. xxix.32, cf. Florentine Mütherich, Der Agrimensoren-Codex in Rom, in: *Aachener Kunstblätter* 45 (1974) pp. 59–74, here p. 71.

114 Summaries of these reforms in Josef Fleckenstein, *Die Bildungsreform Karls des Großen als Verwirklichung der Norma rectitudinis*, Bigge (Ruhr) 1953; Fleckenstein, Karl der Große und sein Hof, in: Fleckenstein, *Ordnungen und formende Kräfte des Mittelalters. Ausgewählte Aufsätze*, Göttingen 1989, pp. 28–66; *Science in Western and Eastern Civilization; The Gentle Voices of Teachers. Aspects of Learning in the Carolingian Age*, ed. Richard E. Sullivan, Columbus, OH, 1995; Rosamond McKitterick, *Karl der Große* (in addition to her previous studies); also Johannes Fried, In den Netzen der Wissensgesellschaft. Das Beispiel des mittelalterlichen Königshofes, in: *Wissenskulturen. Beiträge zu einem forschungsstrategischen Konzept*, ed. Johannes Fried and Thomas Kailer, Berlin 2003, pp. 141–93 (some passages from this have been used here, with minor changes).

115 Einhard, *Vita Karoli*, chap. 25.

116 On the schools, cf. the sections "Teachers from Foreign Climes" and "Schools, Scriptoria, and Prayers" in this chapter; on Fulda, cf. *Epistola de litteris colendis*, ed. Edmund E. Stengel, *Urkundenbuch des Klosters Fulda*, vol. 1 (Veröffentlichungen der Historischen Kommission für Hessen und Waldeck 10/1), Marburg 1958, No. 166 pp. 246–54, here p. 252, see also Fried, Fulda, pp. 3–38.

117 Cf. the section "King Charles the Wise" in this chapter.

118 Theodulf *Carm.* 46, MGH Epp. Poetae 1 pp. 544–7 with App. pp. 629–30.

119 Springsfeld, *Alkuins Einfluß*, pp. 38–59, an overview of the relevant letters.

120 Theodulf *Carm.* 45, MGH Poetae 1 pp. 543–4; the parenthesis in the text follows vv. 21–2.

121 Einhard's later prologue to his *Vita Karoli*. On its interpretation cf. the Prologue of this book.

122 MGH Poetae 1 p. 92 No. IV, 12–3, v. 18 and v. 8.

123 Alcuin, *Rhetorica*, chaps. 1–2, ed. Howell, p. 68.

124 Ibid., chap. 36, ed. Howell, pp. 128–30.

125 Ibid., chap. 30, ed. Howell, pp. 116–8.

126 Petrus: *Grammatici Latini*, vol. 8, ed. Hermann Hagen, Leipzig 1870, p. 159.–"Philosophers": Alcuin ep. 148 (798), MGH Epp. 1 p. 239, 18–23.

127 Boethius, *Liber de divisione*, Migne *PL* 64 col. 877C/D.

128 Cf. Alcuin ep. 155 (798) MGH Epp. 4 pp. 249–53; the following quotations can be found on p. 252.

129 Cf. Louis Holtz, Le dialogue de Franco et de Saxo, in: Alcuin, de York à Tours, pp. 133–45.

130 Alcuin's *On Grammar*, including its foreword: Froben Forster von St. Emmeram (ed.), *Beati Flacci Albini seu Alcuini . . . Opera* 2, 2, Regensburg 1777, pp. 265–300, Migne *PL* 101, cols. 849–902; Pierre Swiggers, Alcuin et les doctrines grammaticales, in: Alcuin, de York à Tours, pp. 147–61.

131 Froben Forster (ed.), *Alcuini . . . Opera* 2, 2, pp. 265–8, Migne *PL* 101, cols. 849–54.

132 Alcuin, *Rhetorica*, chap. 47 (at the end), ed. Howell, p. 154.

133 Quotations, see the section "The Fascination of Rome" in this chapter; Hadrian: see that same section. – On the following, see most recently Wilfrid Hartmann, *Kirche und Kirchenrecht um 900,* pp. 62–4 and 66.

134 Cf. the section "Reforms Are Long Overdue, but Where to Begin?" in this chapter.

135 For a brief overview of the collections, see: Wilfried Hartmann, *Kirche und Kirchenrecht um 900,* pp. 62–8.

136 *Opus Caroli* 1.26, ed. Freeman, p. 218 with note 3.

137 On the following, cf. Ubl, *Inzestverbot und Gesetzgebung;* also Johannes Fried, Kanonistik und Mediävistik. Neue Literatur zu Kirchenrecht, Inzest und zur Ehe Pippins von Italien, in: *HZ* 294 (2012) pp. 115–41, here esp. pp. 124–41.

138 JE 2277 = CC 3, chap. 22; on the norm of incest, see MGH Epp 3 p. 485.

139 Ubl, *Inzestverbot und Gesetzgebung,* pp. 261–6.

140 MGH Capit. 1 No. 13.

141 Ubl, *Inzestverbot und Gesetzgebung,* p. 270n257, points to two problematic capitularies: Capit. I No. 83 chap. 6 (an episcopal capitulary of 813? Grenze 3:3; cf. Mordek, *Bibliotheca,* pp. 828–9) and Capit. I No. 114 chap. 2 (doubtless from Italy, Grenze 3:2; cf. Mordek, *Bibliotheca,* p. 929), which are unreliably dated to the reign of Charlemagne, although the author does add the note: "Presumably both chapters do not date right back to Charlemagne himself."

142 Fried, Papst Leo III. besucht Karl den Großen.

143 Cf. the fragment from Laon: Mordek, *Bibliotheca,* pp. 980–1 (before 814?).

144 For a summary, see: Heinrich Tiefenbach, Wessobrunner Schöpfungsgeschichte, in: *Reallexikon der Germanischen Altertumskunde,* ²vol. 33, Berlin/New York 2006, pp. 513–6.

145 For an overview: Herbert Schneider, Karolingische Kirchen- und Liturgiereform, ein konservativer Neuaufbruch, in: *799. Kunst und Kultur,* vol. 2, pp. 772–81.

146 Glatthaar, Zur Datierung der *Epistola generalis,* pp. 467–9. Cf. Philippe Bernard, Benoît d'Aniane est-il auteur de l'avertissement "Hucusque" et du Supplement au sacramentaire "Hadrianum"?, in: *Studi medievali,* 3rd ser., 39 (1998) pp. 1–120.

147 For Charlemagne's letter to Queen Fastrada: MGH Epp. 4 pp. 528–9 No. 20 (791).

148 Cf. the sections "The Palace in Aix Recalls the Palace of Constantine the Great," "A Prayer in Stone," and "Charlemagne's Other Palace Buildings" in Chapter 6.

149 Barbara H. Rosenwein, Perennial Prayer at Agaune, in: *Monks and Nuns, Saints and Outcasts. Religion in Medieval Society. Essays in Honor of Lester K. Little,* ed. Sharon Farmer and Barbara H. Rosenwein, Ithaca, NY, 2010, pp. 37–56.

150 *Angilberti abbatis De ecclesia Centulensi libellus,* MGH SS 15, 1 pp. 173–9. On Centula, cf. most recently Michael S. Driscoll, Church Architecture and Liturgy in the Carolingian Era, http://theology.nd.edu/graduate-program/master-of-sacred-music/faculty /documents/NAAL2009Driscoll.pdf. The description of the church in the eleventh century comes from Hariulf, who was a monk at Centula at that time, and who later became abbot of Oudenburg: *Chronique de l'abbaye de Saint Riquier* 2.8, ed. Ferdinand Lot (Collections de textes), Paris 1894, pp. 57–61; 2.9 on relics, pp. 61–7; 2.10 on altars, pp. 67–70; on the liturgy, pp. 296–303, here pp. 305–6.

151 MGH SS rer. Merov. 4 pp. 381–401.

152 The dedication of the *Vita Richarii:* MGH SS rer. Merov. 4 p. 389. See also the information on the history of the monastery at St-Riquier in the introduction by Bruno Krusch (pp. 381–9). Cf. Berschin, *Biographie,* vol. 3, pp. 139–46.

153 Steinen, Karl der Große und die *Libri Carolini.*–Cf. Prologue.

154 Cf., for example, Alcuin ep. 145 MGH Epp. 4 p. 233, 27–30, and ep. 172 (799) p. 284, 13–5 (the quotation is from here); see Steinen, Karl der Große und die *Libri Carolini,* p. 217.

155 Alcuin ep. 202 MGH Epp. 4 p. 335, 27–30.

156 Einhard, *Translatio ss Petri et Marcellini* 2.1, MGH SS 15, 1 pp. 245–6. Although this report related to the reign of Louis the Pious, the circumstances mentioned may not have been very different in Charlemagne's time.

157 Cf. the opening section of this chapter.

158 Cf. the section "The Rules of the Court" in Chapter 6.

159 Cf. the section "Reforms Are Long Overdue, but Where to Begin?" in this chapter (on 779).

160 MGH Conc. 2, 1 No. 19G p. 169 cc. 26 and 27.

161 Ibid., c. 5 and 4 p. 165. Cf. also the opening section of Chapter 4 and the section "A Hidden Failure: The Synod of Frankfurt" in Chapter 7. See also Harald Witthöft, Münze, Maß und Gewicht im Frankfurter Kapitular, in: Johannes Fried et al. (eds.), 794—*Karl der Große in Frankfurt am Main,* pp. 124–8.

162 See the section "Schools, Scriptoria, and Prayers" in this chapter.

163 See: Willy Szalvert, Die Entstehung und Entwicklung der Klosterexemtion bis zum Ausgang des 11. Jahrhunderts, in: *MIÖG* 59 (1951) pp. 265–98, here p. 271.

164 MGH Capit. 1 No. 20, 3 p. 47, and No. 22, 73 p. 60.

165 Cf. the section "The Lack of Information on Spain and Benevento" in Chapter 3.

166 Johannes Fried, Ungeschehenes Geschehen. Implantate ins kollektive Gedächtnis— Eine Herausforderung für die Geschichtswissenschaft, in: *Millennium 5* (2008) pp. 1–36, here pp. 29–34.

167 Cf. the sections "Center and Periphery" in Chapter 4 and "Even a King Has Worries" in this chapter.

168 Schlesinger, Hufe im Frankenreich.–Cf. the opening section of Chapter 4.

169 *Gesta sanctorum patrum Fontanellensis coenobii (Gesta abbatum Fontanellensium),* chap. 11, ed. Fernand Lohier and Jean Laporte (Société d'histoire de Normandie), Rouen/ Paris 1936, pp. 82–3. On the problem of surveying manorial estates in figures, cf. Kuchenbuch, Zahlendenken und Zahlengebrauch.

170 Fleckenstein, *Hofkapelle,* vol. 1, pp. 48 and 51. On Hildebald, cf. the section "A Hidden Failure: The Synod of Frankfurt" in Chapter 7 (and elsewhere).

171 *Vita Alcuini,* chap. 9, MGH SS 15 p. 190.

172 Charlemagne appointed Einhard abbot of the Cathedral of Saint Bavo/Sint Baaf in Ghent, as is made clear in Louis the Pious's declaration of immunity; cf. [Einhard], *Charlemagne's Courtier,* ed. Dutton, pp. 49–53 (English translation).

173 See the section "Thirty Years of War in Saxony" in Chapter 3.

174 Alcuin ep. 281 (793/804), MGH Epp. 4 p. 440, 6–7.

175 On the dispute between these two scholars: Hélène Noizet, Alcuin contre Théodulphe: Un conflit producteur de normes, in: Alcuin, de York à Tours, pp. 113–29.

176 Cf. the section "The Fascination of Rome" in this chapter.

177 Theodulfi Carmina 25, vv. 191–8, MGH Poetae 1, p. 488; these verses evoke Alcuin's Carmen 26, v. 49 (MGH Poetae 1, p. 245); cf. Dieter Schaller, Vortrags- und Zirkulardichtung, 14–36.

178 Cf. the sections "Education as a Scholar and Instruction in the Christian Faith" in Chapter 1 and "Teachers from Foreign Climes" in this chapter.

179 MGH Epp. 4 pp. 393–404 epp. 245–6, 248–9; on the emperor's decision: MGH Epp. 4 pp. 399–401 No. 247.

180 Ardo, Vita Benedicti Aninanensis, chaps. 29–30, MGH SS 15, 1 pp. 211–2; ed. Kettemann, Subsidia Anianensia, pt. 1, pp. 188–92. On this subject, see most recently Melville, Welt der mittelalterlichen Klöster, pp. 42–4.

181 On this and the following, see: Kasten, Adalhard von Corbie, pp. 93–100.

182 Cf. the section "The Lack of Information on Spain and Benevento" in Chapter 3.

183 Chronicon Moissiacense for 802, MGH SS 1 p. 306. Cf. BM² 390a; see also Wilfried Hartmann, Synoden, pp. 124–6; on the implementation of the Benedictine Rule: Oexle, Forschungen, pp. 134–57.

184 Augustine of Hippo, De civitate Dei 4.4; Dei cultus: ibid., 5.24.

185 Given his active support for the emperor, Einhard is likely to have already owned property in Aix under Charlemagne. Even before 804, he was Charlemagne's familiaris adiutor ("household assistant"; Alcuin ep. 172), while in 806 he delivered the so-called Divisio regnorum to Rome, in 811 he was almost certainly responsible for drafting the so-called testament of Charlemagne (without, however, signing it), and in 813, undoubtedly with Charlemagne's approval, he proposed Louis the Pious as successor to his father as emperor; he was in all likelihood also active at the imperial court as a "goldsmith," cf. Einhard, ed. Schefers, pp. 36–7.

CHAPTER 6. THE ROYAL COURT

1 Alcuin ep. 262 (798/803), MGH Epp. 4 p. 420, 10–2. The pupil in question was Nathanael-Fredegisus. Charlemagne's words at the beginning of the chapter are loosely modeled on Alcuin's introduction to his work On Rhetoric. The fact that horse breeding was a particular passion of Charlemagne comes across from the CdV; see the opening section of Chapter 4.

2 Angilbert carm. 2, vv. 1–2 and v. 50, MGH Poetae 1 p. 360; translated into German by Paul Klopsch, Lateinische Lyrik des Mittelalters. Lateinisch/Deutsch, Stuttgart 1985, p. 105 and p. 109.

3 On the poem, see: D. Schaller, Vortrags- und Zirkulardichtung. Liutgard also appears in the procession of courtly society depicted in the epic De Karolo rege et Leone papa (undoubtedly ca. 800), where she is now called regina and coniux: vv. 181–94 (Karolus magnus et Leo papa, ed. Brunhölzl, p. 22 [73]), although the poet mainly extols her magnificent clothing.

4   Werner, *Nachkommen*, pp. 442–3 No. 1a–k places Charlemagne's liaison with the mother of Hruodhaid, whom he identifies with the concubine whom Einhard (c. 18) does not mention by name, between his marriages to Fastrada and Liutgard. Yet it is by no means impossible that Charlemagne entered into this relationship while he was still married to Fastrada.

5   So DKDG 149 (Deed of Donation for the commemoration of Hildegard).

6   MGH Epp. 4 p. 528 No. 20: "Dilecte nobis et valde amabili coniuge . . . regine. Salutem amabilem tibi . . . mittere studuimus et per te dulcissimis filiabus nostris et ceteris fidelibus nostris tecum commarantibus."

7   MGH Capit. 1 pp. 83–91, here chap. 16, cf. chaps. 27, 47, and 58.

8   MGH SS 2 p. 266.

9   Cf. Charlemagne's aforementioned latter to her, see above note 6. Fastrada's role or function in the execution of a certain Hortlaicus in Frankfurt, possibly in the winter of 793/794, remains unclear: MGH Form. p. 323 No. 49. Was she perhaps acting as the king's representative in this matter?

10   *Annales Laureshamenses*, MGH SS 1 p. 31.

11   Nelson, *Opposition to Charlemagne*, p. 11.

12   This theory is advanced by Carl I. Hammer, "Pippinus rex": Pippin's Plot of 792 and Bavaria, in: *Traditio* 63 (2008) pp. 235–72, on the basis of a dedicatory entry in the liturgical manuscript Praha, Knihovna Metropolitní Kapituli, O. LXXXIII of 792, which was originally written for Tassilo of Bavaria; cf. Hammer, The Social Landscape of the Prague Sacramentary: The Prosopography of an Eighth-Century Mass-Book, in: *Traditio* 54 (1999) pp. 42–80, here p. 49, and Hammer, *From* Ducatus *to* Regnum, pp. 248–51. This thesis was first put forward by Nelson, *Opposition to Charlemagne*, p. 10.–Cf. also the section "Conflict Grows with Bavaria and Pannonia" in Chapter 3.

13   Cf. the section "Reforms Are Long Overdue, but Where to Begin?" in Chapter 5.

14   The poem appears in a shorter version in MGH Poetae 1 pp. 526–7 carm. 35 but also exists in a hitherto-unpublished longer version discovered in Würzburg by Franz Fuchs, which, it is hoped, will be published in due course. In the following, I have relied heavily on Franz Fuchs's essay on these verses (Theodulf von Orléans, Alkuins Gegenspieler?), which exists only in manuscript form. I am very grateful to my colleague Fuchs for kindly sending me a copy of the manuscript.

15   Alcuin ep. 294 (795 or earlier), MGH Epp. 4 pp. 451–2 (with no mention of names).

16   Alcuin ep. 188, MGH Epp. 4 p. 315.

17   Alcuin ep. 10 (797/798), MGH Epp. 4 p. 36; cf. John Boswell, *Christianity, Social Tolerance, and Homosexuality. Gay People in Western Europe from the Beginning of the Christian Era to the Fourteenth Century*, Chicago/London 1980, pp. 188–91. Bullough, *Alcuin*, pp. 110–7, rejects Boswell's interpretation.

18   On Louis's court in Aquitania, see: Egon Boshof, *Ludwig der Fromme*, Darmstadt 1996, pp. 54–70.

19   Nithard 1.2; Thegan, *Vita Hludowici.* chap. 24; Astronomus, *Vita Hludowici,* chap. 35 ed. Tremp pp. 214, 406.

20   Alcuin ep. 244 (801/802), MGH Epp. 4 pp. 392–3, to Nathanael-Fredegisus.

21   Alcuin ep. 241 (ca. 800), MGH Epp. 4 pp. 386–7.

22 Fleckenstein, *Hofkapelle*, vol. 1, pp. 66–7.

23 Cf. Werner, Nachkommen, p. 444 No. II, 8 and p. 448 No. III, 19.

24 Janet L. Nelson, Women at the Court of Charlemagne: A Case of Monstrous Regiment?, in: *Medieval Queenship*, ed. John Carmi Parsons, Phoenix Mill 1994, pp. 43–61 and 203–6, goes too far, in my opinion, when she suggests that Charlemagne may have had incestuous relationships with his daughters; the term *contubernium*, which she cites in this regard, does not support this contention in the context in which it is used.

25 *De Karolo rege et Leone papa*, vv. 29–30, *Karolus magnus et Leo papa*, ed. and trans. Brunhölzl, pp. 10–1.

26 Theodulf, *Carm.* 25 MGH Poetae 1 pp. 483–96; cf. D. Schaller, Vortrags- und Zirkulardichtung.

27 Peter Classen, Bemerkungen zur Pfalzenforschung am Mittelrhein, in: Classen, *Ausgewählte Aufsätze*, pp. 475–501.

28 Zotz, Palatium publicum, nostrum, regium, pp. 71–101.

29 Classen, Geschichte der Königspfalz Ingelheim, pp. 87–105.

30 See the sections "The Palace in Aix Recalls the Palace of Constantine the Great," "A Prayer in Stone," and "Charlemagne's Other Palace Buildings" in this chapter.

31 On this finding, see: Thomas Zotz, Palatium et curtis. Aspects de la terminologie palatiale au Moyen Age, in: *Palais royaux et princiers au moyen âge. Actes du colloque international tenu au Mans les 6–7 et 8 octobre 1994,* under the direction of Annie Renoux, Le Mans 1996, pp. 7–17.

32 Alcuin ep. 50 (794? 795?), MGH Epp. 4 p. 94. On Charlemagne's "travels": McKitterick, *Karl der Große*, pp. 165–79.

33 Hincmarus, *De ordine palatii*, chap. 5, p. 74.

34 Cf. the opening section of Chapter 4.

35 Cf. also Notker, *Gesta Karoli* 1.34.

36 Hincmarus, *De ordine palatii*, introduction, pp. 10–1.

37 Hincmarus, *De ordine palatii*, chap. 3 at the end of p. 54 and chap. 4 (introduction), where reference is made to Adalhard's work (*dicens*). Unless indicated otherwise, the folowing references to the court personnel follow the information given in chap. 4 (pp. 60–6).

38 The best work on this subject remains Treitinger, *Die oströmische Kaiser- und Reichsidee.*

39 See Steinen, Randbemerkungen, p. 34.

40 Notker, *Gesta Karoli* 2.6 and 2.8.

41 *De Karolo rege et Leone papa*, vv. 176–325; vv. 433–50; the "chair" is also mentioned in v. 463; *Karolus magnus et Leo papa*, ed. Brunhölzl, pp. 22–32, 40, 42.

42 For instance, in DKDG 162.

43 Notker, *Gesta Karoli* 1.4.

44 Fundamental information on the court chapel: Fleckenstein, *Hofkapelle*, vol. 1, esp. pp. 44–112.

45 As in Fleckenstein, *Hofkapelle*, vol. 1, p. 75; on Charlemagne's "production of documents": McKitterick, *Karl der Große*, pp. 181–90.

46 Fleckenstein, *Hofkapelle*, vol. 1, p. 76.

47 Hagen Keller, Zu den Siegeln der Karolinger und Ottonen. Urkunden als Hoheitszeichen in der Kommunikation des Herrschers mit seinen Getreuen, in: *FmaSt* 32 (1998) pp. 400–41, here pp. 404–10.

48 Fleckenstein, *Hofkapelle*, vol. 1, p. 47.

49 Cf. the section "Center and Periphery" in Chapter 4. On notaries at Charlemagne's court: McKitterick, *Karl der Große*, pp. 185–90.

50 Hincmarus, *De ordine palatii*, chap. 6, p. 84.

51 Ibid., chap. 7, p. 92.

52 Ibid., chap. 6, p. 86.

53 MGH Epp. 4 pp. 529–31 No. 21 (ca. 794).

54 *De Karolo rege et Leone papa*, vv. 18–23, *Karolus magnus et Leo papa*, ed. Brunhölzl, pp. 10–11, followed by a translation into German.

55 Cf. Fried, *Gastmahl*, pp. 44–45.

56 Bischoff, Theodulf und der Ire Cadac-Andreas, pp. 21–2; cf. the section "Schools, Scriptoria, and Prayers" in Chapter 5.

57 Cf. Franz Brunhölzl, Der Bildungsauftrag der Hofschule, in: *Karl der Große II. Das geistige Leben*, ed. Bernhard Bischoff, Düsseldorf 1965, pp. 28–41.

58 Alcuin ep. 121 (796/797), MGH Epp. 4 p. 177, 29–32.

59 Cf. the section "King Charles the Wise" in Chapter 5.

60 Alcuin ep. 121 (796/797), MGH Epp. 4 p. 177.

61 I hold to the view that this list of books is connected with the court at Aachen: Fried, Karl der Große, die *Artes liberales,* und die karolingische Renaissance, in: *Karl der Große und sein Nachwirken. 1200 Jahre Kultur und Wissenschaft in Europa*, vol. 1, *Wissen und Weltbild,* ed. P. Butzer, M. Kerner, and W. Oberschelp, Turnhout 1997, p. 33 note 36; Villa, Horazüberlieferung, analyzes only the list, not the structure of the whole manuscript; cf. *Sammelhandschrift Diez. B Sant. 66. Grammatici Latini et catalogus librorum,* with introduction by Bernhard Bischoff, Graz 1973. See also McKitterick, *Karl der Große*, pp. 314–7, who regards this not as a library catalog but as a list of important instructional books (but there was a school at the court; why should no important "schoolbooks" have been made available to it?); on Charlemagne's library: McKitterick, pp. 312–9. This discussion was surveyed by Jürgen Geiss in: *Otto der Große und das Römische Reich*, pp. 451–3.

62 For the best overview, see: Bernhard Bischoff, Die Hofbibliothek Karls des Großen, in: Bischoff, *Mittelalterliche Studien*, vol. 3, pp. 149–69. Cf. Chapter 4, note 107.

63 On Plato's *Timaios*: Raymond Klibansky, *The Continuity of the Platonic Tradition with a New Preface and Four Supplementary Chapters Together with Plato's "Parmenides" in the Middle Ages and the Renaissance*, Millwood, NY, 1982, p. 6. "Codex argenteus": see the section "'Restitution' and 'Renovation'" in Chapter 5.

64 Bernhard Bischoff, Kölner Nonnenhandschriften; Ulla Ziegler, Das Sacramentarium Gelasianum der Bibl. Vat. Reg. Lat. 316 und die Schule von Chelles, in: *Archiv für Geschichte des Buchwesens* 16 (1976) pp. 1–142.

65 Einhard, *Vita Karoli,* chap. 1, 33 (at the end).

66 Fried, Fulda, pp. 3–38.

67 See also: Tilman Seebass, Die Bedeutung des Utrechter Psalters für die Musik-geschichte, in: J. H. A. Engelbregt and Tilman Seebass, *Kunst- en muziekhistorische bijdragen tot de bestudering van het Utrechts Psalterium,* Utrecht 1973, pp. 33–48 with eight plates.

68 Cf. Figure 29.

69 *Das Einhardkreuz. Vorträge und Studien der Münsteraner Diskusion zum arcus Einhardi,* ed. Karl Hauck, Göttingen 1974; [Einhard], *Charlemagne's Courtier,* pp. 63–7.

70 Genevra Kornbluth, *Engraved Gems of the Carolingian Empire,* University Park, PA, 1995, pp. 125–6 No. 24.

71 On the statuette, see Figure 23 and Epilogue: Commemorating Charlemagne.

72 Hack, Karl der Große hoch zu Roß, p. 351, cf. the Epilogue, note 2.

73 Moduin, *Ecloga* 1.24–7 and v. 40, ed. Ernst Dümmler, in: *NA* 11 (1886) pp. 82–3.

74 *De Karolo rege et Leone papa,* v. 94; on Einhard as the possible author: Schaller, Aachener Epos, pp. 163–8.

75 Horst Fuhrmann, Einladung ins Mittelalter, Munich 1987, p. 75. In the following, I have taken over some passages verbatim (while omitting the corroborating references) from: Fried, Karl der Große, Rom und Aachen.

76 On Charlemagne's sojourns in Aachen: McKitterick, *Karl der Große,* pp. 150–2.

77 BM² 101a/b.

78 Cf. the opening section of Chapter 1.

79 *Capitulare de disciplina palatii Aquisgranensis,* MGH Capit. 1 No. 14j chap. 2 p. 298 (from the reign of Louis the Pious); Flach, *Untersuchungen,* especially pp. 280–2 (*actor*).

80 See the opening section of Chapter 4.

81 BM² 130e.

82 First reference: DKDG 179; cf. Falkenstein, Pfalz und *vicus* Aachen; Dietmar Flach, Pfalz, Fiscus und Stadt Aachen im Lichte der neuesten Pfalzenforschung, in: *Zeitschrift des Aachener Geschichtsvereins* 98/99 (1992/1993) pp. 31–56.–The term *palacio nostro* is also used of the palace at Ingelheim: DKDG 206 (807). From 811 on, *palacio regio* (first mentioned in DKDG 212) is regularly used to refer to Aachen.

83 BM² 301b–27c (789–94).

84 *De Karolo rege et Leone papa,* vv. 99–100 (transl. Brunhölzl).

85 Ibid., vv. 101–16.

86 The wooden connecting walkway between the Church (*basilica*) and the Council Hall (*regia*) had already collapsed once in 813 (Einhard, chap. 32) and did so again on Maundy Thursday in 817 (Astronomus, *Vita Hludowici,* chap. 28, ed. Tremp, pp. 372–4), an accident in which Emperor Louis was injured. On bathing in hot springs: *De Karolo rege et Leone papa,* vv. 106–11.

87 Cf. Wolfram Giertz, Zur Archäologie von Pfalz, *vicus* und Töpferbezirk Franzstraße in Aachen, in: *Zeitschrift des Aachener Geschichtsvereins* 107/108 (2005/2006) pp. 7–89, here pp. 45–8.

88   Notker, *Gesta Karoli* 1.30, ed. Haefele, pp. 40–1.

89   The documentary evidence for this is given in Falkenstein, Pfalz und *vicus* Aachen, pp. 139–42.

90   *De Karolo rege et Leone papa*, v. 121 (transl. Brunhölzl).

91   Ibid., vv. 94–105.

92   I am indebted to the archaeologists Sebastian Ristow and Andreas Schaub, as well as Judith Ley, for information on the palace complex at Aachen/Aix.–On the settlement there: *Capitulare de disciplina palatii Aquis.*, MGH Capit. 1 No. 146 chap. 2 p. 298; Flach, *Untersuchungen*, pp. 56–77.

93   This is clearly evident in the reign of Louis the Pious: *Capitulare de disciplina palatii Aquis.*, MGH Capit. 1 No. 146 chap. 3 p. 298; Flach, *Untersuchungen*, pp. 56–77.

94   MGH Epp. 3 p. 614 No. 81 (for the year 787?).

95   Cf. Figure 10.

96   On the equestrian figure: Walahfrid Strabo, *De imagine Tetrici*; Agnellus von Ravenna, *Liber pontificalis ecclesiae Ravennati*, chap. 94, ed. Deborah Mauskopf Deliyannis (CCCM 199), Turnhout 2006, pp. 258–60. Denigration of Theoderic begins with Walahfrid Strabo's poem *De imagine Tetrici* of 829/830, e.g., vv. 30–45.

97   Werner, Nachkommen, p. 445 No. II, 18; water: v. 67.

98   *Chronicon Moissiacense* for the year 796, MGH SS 1 p. 303; ed. Kettemann, Subsidia Anianensia, pt. 2, p. 85. Soldiers returned from three campaigns "to the palace at Aachen" (*ad Aquis palacium*). "For there [*ibi*, namely, in Aachen] Charlemagne had established his royal seat [*firmaverat*], and there too [*ibi*] he had erected a church of magnificent size. . . . There [*ibi*] he also built the palace that he named 'at the Lateran' [*palatium, quod nominavit Lateranis*]." The term *palatium*, used twice here, must refer to the entire palace complex; the second mention could hardly mean the Great Hall, let alone the *secretarium*, which was later referred to as *ad Lateranis* (see also the following note). On the date of this report—presumably 802—cf. Fried, Karl der Große, Rom und Aachen, esp. note 99.

99   MGH Capit. 1 p. 344 No. 170 = *Corpus Consuetudinum monasticarum*, vol. 1, ed. Josef Semmler, p. 457. The texts on this name have been conveniently collected by Falkenstein, *"Lateran,"* pp. 3–4. For an interpretation that diverges from that of Falkenstein, cf. Fried, Karl der Große, Rom und Aachen, note 99. How the name "Lateran" came to be used in a more restricted sense is no longer known.

100   *Actus b. Silvestri*, ed. Boninus Mombritius, Sanctuarium seu Vitae Sanctorum 2, Paris 1910, pp. 508–31. Here p. 514, 22.

101   My interpretation here is at variance with that of Falkenstein, *"Lateran,"* passim.

102   Ulrike Heckner and Christoph Schaab, Baumaterial und Bauausführung der Aachener Pfalzkapelle, in: *Karolingische Pfalzkapelle*, pp. 117–228, here p. 149. Odo's background is unknown; on Odo as master builder, see: Einhard, *Vita Karoli*, ed. Holder-Egger, p. vii note 1; he was buried in Metz.–Theodulf carm. 27, vv. 93–4 (*construit*).

103   The masonry of both of these polygons was secured by iron ring anchors, which have survived to this day.

104   *Einhard*, ed. Schefers, p. 8 with notes 33–4.

105 These have been preserved: Aachen, Domschatz Inv. No. G8. See Rainer Kahsnitz, "Die Elfenbeinskulpturen der Adagruppe." Hundert Jahre nach Adolph Goldschmidt, in: *Zeitschrift des Deutschen Vereins für Kunstwissenschaft* 64 (2010) pp. 9–172, here No. 13 pp. 100–4.

106 Cf. Fried, Karl der Große, Rom und Aachen, note 103.

107 Hugo Brandenburg, *Roms frühchristliche Basiliken des 4. Jahrhunderts* (Heyne Stilkunde 14), Regensburg 1979, p. 23.

108 On the consecration days of 17 July and 8 September (*dedicatio parva*), see: Falkenstein, *Karl der Große und die Entstehung des Aachener Marienstifts*, pp. 141n457 and 94n268; also Fried, Karl der Große, Rom und Aachen, note 96.–I am grateful to Sible de Blauuw for the information (told to me in a discussion) that in the Carolingian period, services of consecration for churches did not necessarily have to take place on Sundays.–On the year 796 as the date of the dedication given in the *Chronicon Moissiacense*, cf. Fried, Karl der Große, Rom und Aachen, note 99, and above note 98.–Theodulf's poems: carm. 25, 59–62, MGH Poetae 1 p. 485.

109 Cf. Alcuin ep. 145 (end of March 798), MGH Epp. 4 p. 235, 5–8 (Palm Sunday celebration?), ep. 149 (July 798), MGH Epp. 4 p. 244, 24–5 (capital decorations and vespers). The Paderborn Epic vv. 111–3 and 177–8 describes building work still ongoing in 799 but claims that the church itself was completed to the extent that Charlemagne was described as leaving the building after morning mass before going hunting.–On the debate on this issue, cf. Fried, Karl der Große, Rom und Aachen, note 93.

110 A discussion by the author with the archaeologists Sebastian Ristow und Andreas Schaub on 18 January 2013 in Aachen ascertained that dendrochronological analysis of an oak pillar from the foundations of Aachen Cathedral had established the year 798 (plus or minus five years) as the date when building work on the church began (calculated on the basis of seventeen sapwood rings; cf. Burghart Schmidt et al., Die Hölzer aus dem karolingischen Oktogon der Aachener Pfalzkapelle—Möglichkeiten einer dendrochronologischen Datierung, in: *Jahrbuch der Rheinischen Denkmalpflege* 40/41 [2009], pp. 220–35, here esp. pp. 228–34). On the earthquake damage that supposedly occurred in 803, cf. K. Reichert et al., Historische Erdbebenschäden im Dom zu Aachen: Aquisgrani terrae motus factus est, in: *Dombaumeistertagung*, pp. 109–26. Yet oaks of the age in question from the Eifel region or the Ardennes Forest—the most likely sources of timber used in the construction of the cathedral in Aachen—have on average only 16.2 sapwood rings with a standard deviation of 4.89 or 4.85 years (cf. Burghart Schmidt et al., *Auf den Spuren alter Häuser. Jahrringdatierung und Bauweise* [Schriftenreihe zur Dendrochronologie und Bauforschung 2], Marburg 2001, p. 35). In all probability, then, this dates the age of the oak pillar in question to 797 (plus or minus five years). From this, we can reasonably deduce that building work in Aachen would have started in 792, or even somewhat earlier if the standard deviation is higher.–Furthermore, the date of the destructive earthquake is uncertain. Einhard (chap. 32) speaks of "frequent earth tremors" (*creber Aquensis palatii tremor*) as omens of Charlemagne's death; the biographer goes on to state, "The palace at Aix-la-Chapelle frequently shook, and the roofs of whatever buildings he [i.e., Charlemagne] stayed in kept up a continual crackling noise." Certainly earthquakes were reported in 801 along the Rhine, as well as in Gallia, which would also have included the region around Aachen (on the use of language: *ArF*; cf. BM² 327d/e or h/i). A severe earthquake was said to have hit Aachen itself in 829; it was accompanied by a violent storm that ripped lead tiling off the cathedral roof (*ArF*). It is entirely conceivable that earlier tremors also affected this earthquake-prone region. If these caused only negligible damage, they were not recorded. But it may have been for this reason that a number of

ring anchors to shore up the two polygons at the heart of the cathedral were included in the construction plans. We do not know when the particular earthquake occurred that caused fissures in the foundations of the church and in the floor pavement of the hexadecagon, although this may have happened soon after 790. The split in the roof of the ambulatory may have occurred in 803 or 829.

111 *Faksimileedition der Handschrift Vienna Weltliche Schatzkammer, Inv. XIII 18,* Munich 2012; plus the volume of commentary edited by Franz Kirchweger, Munich 2012.

112 Fried, Karl der Große, Rom und Aachen, with notes 104 and 106.

113 D Lothars I. 136. Falkenstein, Kirche der hl. Maria zu Aachen und Saint-Corneille zu Compiègne; Falkenstein, *Karl der Große und die Entstehung des Aachener Marienstifts.* – Its decoration by Louis the Pious is attested by a register of deaths (ibid. p. 55n73). The estates and incomes cited in pp. 59–78 cannot be attributed to a particular ruler. – The sequence of the selection of patron saints for the church—first the Virgin Mary, then Christ the Redeemer (see Falkenstein, *"Lateran,"* p. 71)—may perhaps be explained by the fact that in legal terms two originally quite separate institutions were concerned, namely, the cathedral chapter of the Virgin Mary in the lower church and the parish church in the upper church (*Hochmünster*).

114 Cf. the section "A Prayer in Stone" in this chapter.

115 Cf. the verses dedicated to Odo in Theodulf carmina 27, vv. 93–4: "Hiram bene construit aedem / Altithrono: Christus auxilietur opus"; MGH Poetae 1 p. 493. On the poem and its dating (probably 798/800): Dieter Schaller, Der junge "Rabe" am Hof Karls des Großen (Theodulf. carm. 27), in: *Festschrift Bernhard Bischoff zu seinem 65. Geburtstag,* ed. Johanne Autenrieth and Franz Brunhölzl, Stuttgart 1971, pp. 123–41.

116 Even so, the verbs that Theodulf uses—*construit* and *auxilietur*—suggest that the building was not completely finished. This, however, would not preclude a consecration ceremony in 796, cf. the discussion earlier in this section and note 108 above. The cupola image would almost certainly not have been a mosaic at this stage: Wehling, *Mosaiken,* p. 33.

117 Wehling, *Mosaiken,* pp. 31–4 and 38. St. Peter: Ursula Nilgen in: *799. Kunst und Kultur,* vol. 2, pp. 611–3.

118 Zurich, Zentralbibliothek Ms. C 80, fol. 83r; cf. Euw, Karl der Große als Schüler Alkuins with plate 1 p. 199.

119 Wehling, *Mosaiken,* pp. 24–5 and 33.

120 On the church in Aachen: Falkenstein, *Karl der Große und die Entstehung des Aachener Marienstifts;* Falkenstein, Kirche der hl. Maria zu Aachen und Saint-Corneille zu Compiègne; for a summary, see also: Johannes Schlütter, Wi(e)der die Pfalzkapelle. Das Bild der Aachener Marienkirche in der historischen Forschung, in: *Aachener Dom,* pp. 13–25. On Constantine's church: *Actus b. Silvestri.*

121 Falkenstein, Kirche der hl. Maria zu Aachen und Saint-Corneille zu Compiègne, p. 17 (based on the *ArF* for 812).

122 On this and the following, see Ulrike Heckner, Der Tempel Salomos in Aachen: Datierung und geometrischer Entwurf der karolingischen Pfalzkapelle, in: *Karolingische Pfalzkapelle,* pp. 25–62.

123 On the number six (regarded as a perfect number, being divisible by one, two, and three, which in turn make six when multiplied together): Meyer and Suntrup, *Lexikon,* cols. 442–79. – On the number eight: ibid., col. 80.

124 Cf. MGH Epp. 4 pp. 477–8: A letter by Alcuin (No. 309 of 801/804) to the emperor's cousin Gundrada, who was resident at the court, expressly refers the addressee to the emperor's knowledge of such matters; cf. *Opus Caroli*, 4.13, ed. Freeman, p. 521, 19–32.

125 Cf. figure 41 and the last paragraph of this section; 144 stars: Wehling, *Mosaiken*, pp. 27 and 37; on their meaning: Meyer and Suntrup, *Lexikon*, cols. 896 and 809.

126 Meyer and Suntrup, *Lexikon*, cols. 214–331.

127 MGH Poetae 1 p. 432 No. 3; cf. Günther Binding, Zur Ikonologie der Aachener Pfalzkapelle nach den Schriftquellen, in: *Mönchtum, Kirche, Herrschaft, 750–1000*, ed. Dieter R. Bauer et al., Sigmaringen 1998, pp. 187–211, here pp. 200–8; Binding, Kirchenbau als Bedeutungsträger, in: *Wallraf-Richartz-Jahrbuch* 73 (2012) pp. 97–106; for a partially divergent view, see Bayer, Karolingische Bauinschrift. On the image of the "living stone": J. C. Plumpe, Vivum saxum, vivi lapides. The Concept of "Living Stone" in Classical and Christian Antiquity, in: *Traditio* 1 (1943) pp. 1–14. Flach, *Untersuchungen*, pp. 38–45 misinterpreted the *aula* (King's Hall) in Aachen.

128 Cf. the section "Education as a Scholar and Instruction in the Christian Faith" in Chapter 1.

129 Cf. the section "The Lack of Information on Spain and Benevento" in Chapter 3.

130 Dieter P. J. Wynands, Zur Symbolik der Zahl Acht—ausgehend von Aachener Marienkirche, in: *Aachener Dom*, pp. 165–83. On interpretation of the number sixteen: Meyer and Suntrup, *Lexikon*, cols. 659–61.

131 Cf. Henry Ashworth, "Urbs beata Ierusalem": Scriptural and Patristic Sources, in: *Ephemerides Liturgicae* 70 (1956) pp. 238–41. The hymn has survived in versions with eight and sixteen strophes.

132 See Bayer, Karolingische Bauinschrift, p. 187, with reference to Alcuin's *De clade Lindisfarnensis monasterii* (On the destruction of the monastery at Lindisfarne), MGH Poetae 1 p. 234 No. 9, 201.

133 *Analecta Hymnica Medii Aevi* (Medieval Latin hymns of the Catholic Church, 500–1400, in 55 volumes), 51, 110–2. See Josef Szövérffy, *Die Annalen der lateinischen Hymnendichtung*, vol. 1, Berlin 1964, pp. 151–2. In English translation, these verses read: "O blessed city of Jerusalem, a vision of peace / Which has been raised to the heavens in living stones. . . . Christ was sent as a foundation and cornerstone / To hold the walls together in a twofold way. . . . That city consecrated in God's name and loved by Him . . . Proclaims the Trinity to everyone."

134 On the dedication of churches, including those in the early Middle Ages, cf. *Reallexikon für Antike und Christentum* 20 (2004) cols. 1139–69.–On the altar to the Trinity: see the discussion later in this section.

135 For a summary, see: Euw, Karl der Große als Schüler Alkuins.

136 On Charlemagne's knowledge of number theory: above note 124.–On the *Admonitio:* see the section "Even a King Has Worries" in Chapter 5.

137 Alcuin: ep. 145 (798), MGH Epp. 4 pp. 231–5.–The Holy Cross: Philippe Lauer, *Le Palais de Latran. Étude historique et archéologique*, Paris 1911, pp. 57–64 and 90–1; for a brief summary, see Bauer, *Bild der Stadt Rom im Frühmittelalter*, p. 62.

138 Cf. the section "Diversity of Forms of Worship" plus note 150 in Chapter 5.

139 On the throne, see Schütte, Forschungen; Werner Georgi, *Sedes Karoli*—Herrschersitz oder Reliquienthron? Ein historischer Versuch zum Karlsthron der Aachener Marienkirche, in: *Aachener Dom*, pp. 107–30; in the fall of 2012 the archaeologists Uwe Lobbedey, Sebastian Ristow, and Andreas Schaub conducted a new investigation of the throne plinth and the surface below the throne; although their findings have not been published to date, the most important insights resulting from this study have been shared with me by Max Kerner and Harald Müller, who were present at the inspection. I have incorporated these here.

140 It is hardly surprising that signs of wear and tear are evident on the throne.

141 Widukind von Corvey, *Rerum gestarum Saxonicarum* 2.1, ed. H.-E. Lohmann and Paul Hirsch (MGH SS rer. Germ. 60), p. 66, 20–3.

142 Schütte, Forschungen, pp. 138–40 with plates 14–15.

143 Widukind, *Rerum gestarum Saxonicarum* 2.1.

144 Georgi, *Sedes Karoli* (see note 139 above), pp. 107–30; his findings have been taken up by Max Kerner, Aachen und der Kult Karls des Großen, in: *Welt des Mittelalters*, pp. 45–57, here pp. 47–8.

145 Anna Angiolini, *La capsella eburnea di Pola* (Studi di antichità christiane 7), Bologna 1970.

146 There are many indications of figurative wall paintings or mosaics from the Carolingian period; cf. Wehling, *Mosaiken*, pp. 39–41; see also the catalog of the exhibition in Aachen: *Krönungen. Könige in Aachen—Geschichte und Mythos. Katalog der Ausstellung*, ed. Mario Kramp, Mainz 2000, p. 227 (illustration) and pp. 235–6 Nos. 2–9 and 2–10.

147 Cf. Clemens M. M. Bayer, Die Aachener Marienkirche in der Diözese Lüttich, in: *Dombaumeistertagung*, pp. 55–74, here p. 62. On adoptionism, see the section "'Opposing the Enemies of Truth'" in Chapter 7.

148 See the *Actus b. Silvestri*, ed. Mombritius, p. 513, 41–4.

149 See, for example, Hans-Karl Siebigs, Neue Untersuchungen der Pfalzkapelle zu Aachen, in: *Einhard. Studien zu Leben und Werk*, pp. 95–137, esp. pp. 108–9; in an eschatalogical context: McCormick, *Charlemagne's Survey of the Holy Land*, pp. 184–96.

150 Cf. the section "Thirty Years of War in Saxony" in Chapter 3.

151 Ermoldus Nigellus, *In honorem Hludowici* 4.245–82, MGH Poetae 2, pp. 65–6; ed. Edmond Faral, *Ermold le Noir, Poème sur Louis le Pieux et épitres au roi Pépin*, vv. 2126–63, Paris 1932, pp. 163–4. On the cycle, cf. the section "The Prelude to Imperial Rule" in Chapter 7.

152 Ermoldus Nigellus, *In honorem Hludowici* 4.189–243 = Faral's edition, vv. 2068–124, cf. Chapter 7, note 98.

153 Some outline sketches are preserved in the church: Paul Clemen, *Die romanische Monumentalmalerei in den Rheinlanden*, Düsseldorf 1916, plates II and III.

CHAPTER 7. REVIVING THE TITLE OF EMPEROR

1 *Opus Caroli* 1.25, ed. Freeman, p. 217.

2 *Opus Caroli* 2.6, ed. Freeman, p. 250 note c; the Tironian note that was once present at this point has been cut off and can no longer be deciphered.

3   Quotation from Alcuin ep. 193 (fall [?] of 798), MGH Epp. 4 p. 320, 8–12.–The following excerpts from the "Wessobrunn Prayer" and the "Muspilli" follow Schlosser Althochdeutsche Literatur.

4   Arno Borst, *Die karolingische Kalenderreform* (MGH Schriften 46), Hannover 1998, p. 298; cf. ibid., note 37.

5   Paulus Diaconus, *Die Gedichte des Paulus Diaconus,* ed. Neff, pp. 7–10 No. 2. "Iudex veniet supernus velut fulgor caelitus / dies set aut hora quando non patet mortalibus / felix erit, quem paratum invenerit dominus. // Ante tuum, iuste iudex, dum steterit solium / Arechis, benignus ductor cum praeclara coniuge, / dona eis cum electis laetari perenniter."

6   Johannes Fried, Die Endzeit fest im Griff des Positivismus? Zur Auseinandersetzung mit Sylvain Gouguenheim, in: *HZ* 275 (2002) pp. 281–321, here esp. pp. 301–11.

7   Cf. the section "The Lack of Information on Spain and Benevento" in Chapter 3.

8   *Beati in Apocalipsin libri duodecim,* ed. Henry A. Sanders (Papers and Monographs of the American Academy in Rome 7), Rome 1930, pp. 368–9.

9   *Cronica Mozarabe de 754,* ed. and transl. José Riduardo López Pereira (Textos medievales 58), Zaragoza 1980, passim.

10 Bullough, *Alcuin,* p. 10.

11 Schlosser, *Althochdeutsche Literatur,* p. 220; see also pp. 358–9 (the creed in the so-called *Weissenburg Catechism*).

12 For the latest study of this doctrine, see: John C. Cavadini, *The Last Christology of the West. Adoptianism in Spain and Gaul, 785–820,* Philadelphia 1993.

13 CC ep. 95, MGH Epp. 3 pp. 636–43 (the quotation can be found there on p. 637, 6). See also Kurt Schäferdiek, Der adoptianische Streit im Rahmen der spanischen Kirchengeschichte, in: Schäferdiek, *Schwellenzeit. Beiträge zur Geschichte des Christentums in Spätantike und Frühmittelalter,* Berlin/New York 1996, pp. 381–416, and also the brief account in: Scholz, *Politik, Selbstverständnis, Selbstdarstellung,* pp. 104–5.

14 Letter from Charlemagne to the Frankfurt Synod of 794: MGH Conc. 2, 1 p. 113, 19–22; the following quotation is from lines 29–30. Cf. also p. 117, 6–9. For a comprehensive historical-theological appraisal: Gemeinhardt, *Filioque-Kontroverse,* pp. 90–107.

15 MGH Conc. 2, 1 p. 113, 10–7.

16 On the following, cf. also Wilhelm Hell, *Alkuinstudien,* vol. 1, *Zur Chronologie und Bedeutung des Adoptianismusstreites,* Düsseldorf 1970; several synods were convened to discuss this issue: Wilfried Hartmann, *Synoden,* pp. 104–8, 117–22.

17 Response of the Frankish bishops in 794 to their Spanish counterparts: MGH Conc. 2, 1 p. 145, 35–40.

18 CC ep. 95, MGH Epp. 3 pp. 636–43 (quotation on p. 637, 6) and epp. 96 and 97, pp. 643–8. On Charlemagne's knowledge: ep. 97, p. 648, 5–8.–On the doctrine of Migetius: Albert Hauck, *Kirchengeschichte Deutschlands,* [8]Berlin/Leipzig 1954, vol. 2, pp. 298–301; Schäferdiek, Adoptianische Streit (see note 13 above), pp. 381–416.

19 The counterarguments of the pope can be found in epistles 95 and 96, mentioned in note 18.

20 Touched on only fleetingly by the *ArFqdE* for 793; more extensively in: *Chronicon Moissiacense (Anianense),* ed. Kettemann, Subsidia Anianensia, pt. 2, pp. 65–6.

21 MGH Capit. 1 p. 169 No. 76 (2 April 812). At that time, forty-two "Spaniards," mentioned by name, had complained to Charlemagne about oppression by the counts who governed their regions; cf. the section "The End Is Nigh" in Chapter 8. Charlemagne stressed that these people had been settled there thirty or more years previously, since his Spanish campaign of 778 and especially in the 780s.

22 Cf. Eckhardt Müller-Mertens, *Karl der Große, Ludwig der Fromme und die Freien. Wer waren die liberi homines der karolingischen Kapitularien (742/743–832)? Ein Beitrag zur Sozialgeschichte und Sozialpolitik des Frankenreiches* (Forschungen zur mittelalterlichen Geschichte 66), Berlin 1963.

23 Astronomus, *Vita Hludowici,* chaps. 6–7, ed. Tremp, pp. 302–4; cf. BM² 515a (also on the following) (814).

24 Astronomus, *Vita Hludowici,* chaps. 7–8, ed. Tremp, pp. 304–8.

25 Alcuin ep. 148 (798), MGH Epp. 4 p. 231, 25–31.

26 For the synod's "records": MGH Conc. 2, 1 pp. 110–71 No. 19.

27 MGH Conc. 2, 1 pp. 120–1 No. 19B.

28 MGH Conc. 2, 1 p. 161, 23–5.

29 MGH Conc. 2, 1 pp. 162 and 163.

30 Cf. the section "Far-off Byzantium and the Even More Remote Dar al-Islam" in Chapter 2; summarizing from a Western viewpoint: Ann Freeman, introduction to *Opus Caroli,* pp. 1–12; from a Byzantine perspective: Peter Schreiner, Der byzantinische Bilderstreit: Kritische Analyse der zeitgenössischen Meinungen und das Urteil der Nachwelt bis heute, in: Bisanzio, Roma e l'Italia nell'Alto Medioevo, *Settimane Spoleto* 34 (Spoleto 1988), pp. 319–427. For a fundamental account: Noble, *Images.*

31 Theophanes on the year AM 6234.

32 MGH Conc. 2, 2 No. 44A pp. 478–9 (824).

33 Concilium Parisiense 825, MGH Conc. 2, 2 p. 482, 28–9: "Pars illa [a respectful periphrasis for the Roman episcopal teaching authority] non solum resistere, verum etiam incauta defensione contra auctoritatem divinam et sanctorum partum dicta nitebatur suffragari."

34 Illustration in: Bauer, *Bild der Stadt Rom im Frühmittelalter,* p. 79 with the accompanying text, pp. 75–80. Cf. also the section "Far-off Byzantium and the Even More Remote Dar al-Islam" in Chapter 2.

35 Pohl, *Awaren,* pp. 318–21.

36 Einhard, *Vita Karoli,* chap. 16, ed. Holder-Egger, p. 20.

37 *Opus Caroli,* ed. Freeman, p. 97, 13–5, and p. 98, 19–34.

38 Known only from Hadrian I's answer: MGH Epp. 5 pp. 5–57 No. 2, here chap. 1 pp. 7–11 on the *per filium* doctrine. On the context of the tradition, cf. Gemeinhardt, *Filioque-Kontroverse,* pp. 107–64.

39 Thus the king's official designation of the work: *Opus Caroli,* ed. Freeman, p. 97. The introduction summarizes earlier studies by this scholar and lays the foundation for her assessment of this manuscript.

40 *Opus Caroli* 2.1, ed. Freeman, p. 105, 11–2 and lines 20–3, in addition to the preface, p. 99, 11–8.

41 Ibid., p. 275 note b (the precise wording has admittedly been lost).

42 *Ornamenta: Opus Caroli* praef. 1, ed. Freeman, p. 99, 10, and p. 100, 32; Gregory: ibid., 2.23, pp. 278–80 with note k on p. 279. The quotation is from St. Gregory the Great ep. 11, 10; on the *Opus Caroli* as an aide-mémoire: *Opus Caroli* 2.30, p. 303, 26–30; Charlemagne may also have approved this last aspect, cf. p. 303 note i.–On word and image in the *Opus Caroli*, Lieselotte E. Saurma-Jeltsch, Das Bild in der Worttheologie Karls des Großen. Zur Christologie in karolingischen Miniaturen, in: *Frankfurter Konzil von 794*, vol. 2, pp. 635–75.

43 MGH Epp. 5 pp. 5–57 No. 2.

44 Noble, *Images*, p. 123, drew attention to this with an analysis of the *Liber pontificalis*.

45 The German translation from the Greek church council acts follows Gemeinhardt, *Filioque-Kontroverse*, p. 82.

46 Cf. the penultimate paragraph of the Prologue.

47 Noble, *Images*, p. 149.

48 MGH Epp. 5 p. 6.

49 Ibid., p. 7.

50 Noble, *Images*, p. 168, follows the observations of Ann Freeman.

51 Cf. the section "The Results of Charlemagne's Wars" in Chapter 3, the section "The Prelude to Imperial Rule" in this chapter, and the opening section of Chapter 8.

52 On the Frankfurt capitulary: MGH Conc. 2, 1 pp. 165–71 No. 19G; also, Johannes Fried et al. (ed.), *794—Karl der Große in Frankfurt am Main*, and *Frankfurter Konzil von 794*, and especially in that work, Hubert Mordek, Aachen, Frankfurt, Reims. Beobachtungen zu Genese und Tradition des Capitulare Francofurtense, vol. 1, pp. 125–48. Cf. also the section "How Were the Estates Managed?" in Chapter 4.

53 For the context of the East-West and the Western controversies: Noble, *Images*, pp. 169–80.

54 *Fragmentum annalium Chesnii* for 788, MGH SS 1 p. 33.

55 Quotation: Frankfurt capitulary, chap. 4 (grain prices); chap. 5 (coinage reform). On the following, see: Harald Witthöft, Münze, Maß und Gewicht im Frankfurter Kapitular, in: Fried et al. (eds.), *704—Karl der Große in Frankfurt am Main*, pp. 124–8.

56 On portrait coinage, cf. the sections "Knowledge Concentrates at the Court" in Chapter 6 and "Attention Turns to the Near East" in Chapter 8.

57 Cf. MGH Capit. 1 p. 150 No. 62, 8 and p. 152 No. 63, 8 (both 809) (both presumably from the same decree).

58 As, for example, in MGH Capit. 1 p. 152 No. 63, 7 (809).

59 Cf. MGH Capit. 1 p. 116 No. 40, 28 (803), then p. 125 No. 44, 18 (805); p. 140 No. 52, 7 (808); cf. also No. 53, 5.

60 Cf. the section "The Young Charlemagne's First Encounter with a Pope" in Chapter 1; Fried, *Donation of Constantine*, pp. 59, 70–1, and 106–7.

61 Oexle, Karolinger und die Stadt des heiligen Arnulf.

62 Manuscripts: Plotzek, Zur Geschichte der Kölner Dombibliothek, pp. 16–27 and 65–156. Significance for Charlemagne: see the section "Signs in the Heavens" in Chapter 8; for

Aachen: see the section "Knowledge Concentrates at the Court" in Chapter 6. On Charlemagne as benefactor, see Clemens M. M. Bayer, in: Ulrich Back et al., *Der alte Dom zu Cologne* (Studien zum Kölner Dom 12), Cologne 2012, pp. 213–29.

63   MGH Conc. 2, 1 pp. 119–20.

64   Ibid., p. 162.

65   Ibid., p. 143.

66   On the following, cf. Walther Björkman, Karl der Große und der Islam, in: *Karl der Große,* vol. 1 (1965), pp. 672–82.

67   MGH Conc. 2, 1 pp. 162–3.

68   Alcuin ep. 174, MGH Epp. 4 p. 288, 21 and lines 32–3. The context is "tota Spania errat in adoptione."

69   Alcuin ep. 146 (798), MGH Epp. 4 p. 236, 11–13; the Cologne manuscript: as below note 70.

70   The doctrine of the seventh and eighth eons was probably explained to the emperor in 802; the text occurs in the same manuscript from the Cologne Diocesan and Cathedral Library, 83 II, that also contained the aforementioned news concerning the end of the world: Arno Borst (ed.), *Schriften zur Komputistik,* p. 835: see also note 72.

71   Cf. the section "Signs in the Heavens" in Chapter 8.

72   Cologne Diocesan and Cathedral Library 83[II]; on the manuscript, see: Joachim M. Plotzek and Ulrike Surmann, Glaube und Wissen im Mittelalter. On the Cologne Cathedral Library, p. 136–56 (Anton von Euw). On the text (the so-called "Cologne Memo," fol. 14v), see: Borst (ed.), *Schriften zur Komputistik,* pp. 773, 780–4. The finding reached in the text above runs counter to notes 36 and 37 in Borst.–On the end of the world: Borst, pp. 781–2.

73   Alcuin's response: ep. 163 (before 799), MGH Epp. 4 pp. 263–5.

74   Cf. the opening section of Chapter 2 and the section "King Charles the Wise" in Chapter 5.

75   Alcuin epp. 148, 149, and 155 (all 798), MGH Epp. 4 pp. 237–41, 243, and 249–53.

76   Johannes Fried, *Aufstieg aus dem Untergang. Apokalyptisches Denken und die Entstehung der modernen Naturwissenschaft im Mittelalter,* Munich 2001.

77   Cf. Dietrich Lohrmann, Alcuins Korrespondenz mit Karl dem Großen über Kalender und Astronomie, in: *Science in Western and Eastern Civilization,* pp. 79–114; Stephen C. McCluskey, Astronomies in the Latin West from the Fifth to the Ninth Centuries, ibid., pp. 139–60.

78   Borgolte, Papst Leo III., Karl der Große und der Filioquestreit in Jerusalem; McCormick, *Charlemagne's Survey of the Holy Land.* Cf. the section "Attention Turns to the Near East in Chapter 8.

79   Alcuin ep. 193, MGH Epp. 4 p. 320, 11–2.

80   Evident in the familiar enquiry to Pope Zacharias, as recorded in the *ArF* for 749, regarding who should be named king (*vocari*): the person who wields power (*potestas*) or the one who does not.

81   Krämer, *Geschichte des Islam,* p. 84.

82 On the designation "Persians," cf. the discussion later in this section.

83 Cf. Collins, *Charlemagne*, p. 148; McCormick, *Charlemagne's Survey of the Holy Land*, passim.

84 Cf. Borgolte, *Gesandtenaustausch*, pp. 45–107.

85 On the following, cf. Lutz Ilisch, Arabische Kupfermünzen an der Ostsee und die Gesandtschaft Karls des Großen an den Kalifen, in: *Numismatisches Nachrichtenblatt* 61 (August 2012) pp. 296–302. I am grateful to my Frankfurt colleague Maria R.-Alföldi for alerting me to this article. The finds and their interpretation are confirmed in McCormick, *Origins*.

86 On cash remittances: see the section "Attention Turns to the Near East" in Chapter 8. This long-distance trade was also verified by finds of Arabic gold and silver coins in the former Carolingian Empire: Michael McCormick, Charlemagne and the Mediterranean World: Communications, Arab Coins and Commerce at the Time of the Paderborn Meeting, in: *Am Vorabend der Kaiserkrönung*, pp. 193–218.

87 Pilgrims: *Ex miraculis s. Genesii*, MGH SS 15, 1 pp. 169–72. – *Angilberti abbatis De ecclesia Centulensi libellus*, chap. 2, MGH SS 15, 1 p. 175, 39 and p. 176.

88 Cf. the compilation of the texts in Borgolte, *Gesandtenaustausch*, pp. 47–8 note 237.

89 See McCormick, *Charlemagne's Survey of the Holy Land*.

90 Cf. the section "Attention Turns to the Near East" in Chapter 8.

91 *Fredegar Cont.*, chap. 51 (765/768). This chronicler used the name "Saracen" exclusively, on a total of three occasions. Charlemagne himself may have encountered these "Saracens" around this same time. The change from *Sarracenus* to *Persa* cannot therefore simply be explained by the change of authors. On the terms *Maurus and Sarracenus* for the Muslim inhabitants of Spain: *ArF* for 806, used here in contradistinction to *rex Persarum* (p. 122).

92 I have used the bilingual edition by Herwig Wolfram (ed.), *Quellen zur Geschichte des 7. und 8. Jahrhunderts* (Ausgewählte Quellen zur deutschen Geschichte des Mittelalters. Freiherr vom Stein–Gedächtnisausgabe 4a), Darmstadt 1982.

93 On his father's side, Harun (786–809) belonged to the Quraysh tribe, whereas his mother was a Yemeni slave; Krämer, *Geschichte des Islam*, p. 82; he lived mostly in Syria (ibid., p. 84) but died while on campaign in Iran. None of this information permits us to identify him as a "Persian." Only in 810, in other words, after Harun's death, did the "Persian" designation disappear, and the caliph was referred to once more as a *Sarracenus*.

94 The so-called *Chronicle of Fredegar* contained a series of corresponding indications; cf. Johannes Fried, Religionsbegegnungen im Wandel. Beobachtungen zu Reiseberichten vom frühen zum späten Mittelalter, in: *Religiostità e civiltà. Conoscenze, confronti, influssi reciproci tra le religioni (secc. X–XIV)*, ed. Giancarlo Andenna, Milan 2013, pp. 3–34.

95 *AMP, ARF*, and Einhard's *Vita Karoli* all concur on this point. The fragment of the *Lorsch Annals* (777–801) makes no mention of the exchange of envoys; *Chron. Lauriss. breve* 4.34 but see *Amormulus Saracenorum rex*, ed. Schnorr von Carolsfeld, *NA* 36 (1911) p. 35.

96 Fried, Papst Leo III. besucht Karl den Großen, pp. 281–326.

97 *ArF* for 799 and 800, ed. Kurze, pp. 108 and 112.

98 Ermoldus Nigellus, *In honorem Hludowici* 4.245–82, ed. Ernst Dümmler (MGH Poetae 2), pp. 65–6; ed. Edmond Faral, *Ermold le Noir, Poème sur Louis le Pieux et épitres*

au roi Pépin, vv. 2126–63, Paris 1932, pp. 163–4. On the picture cycle: Lammers, Karolingisches Bildprogramm, esp. pp. 247–72; corrections: Nees, *Tainted Mantle,* pp. 270–7; Noble, *Images,* pp. 354–5.–The authenticity of the descriptions has been called into doubt by Christine Ratkowitsch, Die Fresken im Palast Ludwigs des Frommen in Ingelheim (Ermold., Hlud4,181ff.): Realität oder poetische Fiktion?, in: *Wiener Studien* 107/108 (1994/1995) pp. 553–81. However, the type of text does not necessarily require that we should question the existence of the fresco cycle as such. Literary form is no argument against historicity. Moreover, the absence of any other testimonies, a fact that Ratkowitsch and others make much of (p. 555), means nothing. For example, all authors, including Einhard, say nothing about pictorial decoration in Aachen. The example of Boudri de Bourgeuil, from three hundred years later, which Ratkowitsch cites by way of comparison (pp. 556–7), derives from a much-changed context and in any event clearly proclaims itself to be a piece of poetic whimsy. The Ingelheim cycle culminated in a double portrait of Charlemagne, not of Louis the Pious, in whose physical presence Ratkowitsch might wish the cycle to culminate (p. 558). In fact, this ruling emperor is not represented by any image but instead was present in person in this hall, where he dispensed justice amid the frescoes. The fact that no image of the current ruler is cited by Ermoldus Nigellus not only serves to indicate that the fresco cycle was completed before Louis ascended the throne but also points to the very real existence of these imaginative works. Furthermore, there is nothing to refute the supposition that Ermoldus visited the hall at an earlier juncture in the service of "his" king Pepin, for instance, on the occasion of the court assembly held there in 819. Later, then—around 830—he would have described the palace and the frescoes relying either on his own memories from ten years or so previously or on a mixture of others' descriptions and the evidence of his own eyes. This process left plenty of scope for errors to creep in. Cf. note 102 below.–On the cycle, cf. also the section "The Palace in Aix Recalls the Palace of Constantine the Great" in Chapter 6.

99   "Carpets" (no doubt meaning "tapestries") are mentioned in regard to Charlemagne's palace in Paderborn, cf. Lammers, Karolingisches Bildprogramm, p. 223 (after the epic *Karolus magnus et Leo papa,* v. 525).

100   The archaeological record appears to corroborate doubts over the existence of the picture cycle; according to findings by the archaeologist Holger Grewe, only an extremely small proportion of fragments of plaster among the many found at the site of the King's Hall indicates possible figures. Yet the fact that they are not totally lacking may be a decisive factor. The palace at Ingelheim continued to be used by kings until the reign of Charles IV, when the ruler handed it over to the Charles Monastery that had just been founded in (Nieder-)Ingelheim in 1354 as an offshoot of its parent institution in Prague to house four Bohemian canons. This religious institution then established its church in the former King's Hall; cf. Classen, Geschichte der Königspfalz Ingelheim, pp. 138–40. Admittedly, it may be the case that the Carolingian frescoes—if we can presume that they took this form rather than that of tapestries—even survived the Ottonian period, when the church was given a new floor pavement. We simply do not know the extent to which the Ottonians rebuilt the palace complex.

101   I customarily, though at variance with Lammers, date this picture cycle to the period just before 800; cf. Johannes Fried, Imperium Romanum. Das römische Reich und der mittelalterliche Reichsgedanke, in: *Millennium* 3 (2006) pp. 1–42, here pp. 8–9 with note 11. Cf. the section "Charlemagne's Other Palace Buildings" in Chapter 6.

102   It is unclear to which church Ermoldus's imaginative description of a sacred space for baptism refers. There does not appear to have been any such large palace chapel or church in Ingelheim at that time (or perhaps it is still to be unearthed). The poet may not have witnessed firsthand the christening of the "Dane" Harald Klak Halfdansson. There is no

way of ascertaining what information he processed, or in what way. Other historical records name the Church of St. Alban in Mainz as the place where the Danish king was baptized. It is possible, then, that Ermoldus drew together various events into one place and embellished the images of the church in Mainz rather than the chapel at Ingelheim; cf. above note 100.

103 Ermoldus Nigellus, *In honorem Hludowici* 4.266. Cf. Nees, *Tainted Mantle,* p. 295n61.

104 "Caesareis actis Romanae sedis opimae / Iunguntur Franci gestaque mira simul," 4:269–70.

105 "Romam dimittit amore," 4.271. On interpretation of this statement, cf. Fried, Imperium Romanum.

106 MGH SS 1 p. 38: (Carolus) "qui ipsam Romam tenebat, ubi semper Caesares sedere soliti erant . . . quia Deus omnipotens has omnes sedes in potestate eius concessit."

107 Fried, Papst Leo III. besucht Karl den Großen, pp. 281–326; *Rudolf Schieffer, Neues von der Kaiserkrönung Karls des Großen* (SB Munich 2004/2), Munich 2004, pp. 9–25, here pp. 9–14. Janet L. Nelson, Warum es so viele Versionen von der Kaiserkrönung Karls des Großen gibt, in: *Macht des Königs,* pp. 38–54, p. 51.

108 Cologne Diocesan and Cathedral Library 83 II. For the text (the so-called "Cologne Memo," fol. 14v), see: Borst (ed.), *Schriften zur Komputistik im Frankenreich von 721 bis 818,* p. 793; on the manuscript, see esp. p. 773.

109 *Annales Northumbrenses* for the year 800, MGH SS 13 p. 156, 19–20. The phrase *regnum et imperium* makes it clear that this was really about the emperorship and not—as has sometimes been assumed—simply about the cession of territory. There can be no question of confusion with the negotiations of 802, since on that occasion only a Frankish legation hurried to Constantinople (after the deposition of Empress Irene, a Byzantine counterlegation failed to appear in Aachen); the *Royal Frankish Annals,* however, definitely refers to a legation from Constantinople. In addition, the *Annals* accurately mentions a legation from Jerusalem that came to Aachen at precisely this time, namely, 800. This mission may indeed have witnessed Charlemagne's coronation as emperor; cf. the discussion earlier in this section. Reports concerning the Byzantine Greeks can therefore only have referred to the legations of 798 or 799.–*ArF* for 798 and 799.

110 Cf. Classen, *Karl der Große,* p. 49 with supplementary literature and pp. 77–9.

111 Cf. ibid., pp. 57–87.

112 Cf. Wattenbach and Levison, *Deutschlands Geschichtsquellen,* vol. 2, p. 249n284. The Anglo-Saxon communication cannot go back the "Cologne Memo," since the manuscript in question (Cologne Diocesan and Cathedral Library 83 II) has never left either the royal court or Cologne; rather, it entails them having their own informant in the city.–The ArF for the year 798 (ed. Kurze, p. 104) expressly records a legation dispatched by Empress Irene from Constantinople to Aachen to conduct negotiations "solely on the subject of peace," or—according to the *AMP* p. 83, 1–2—"on ecclesiastical peace and unity"; for the following year, the *Annals* reports an envoy from the Byzantine prefect of Sicily paying a visit to the Frankish king, again without mentioning the subject of their negotiations (p. 108, 1–3). Unlike the contemporaneous "Cologne Memo," the entries in the ArF were made only retrospectively and so hint at a noticeably new interpretation of events at the Carolingian court directly after the coronation.

113 *ArF* for 798; see Noble, *Images,* pp. 161–2.

114 Cf. the section "Increasing Rivaly with Byzantium" in Chapter 3 (betrothal of Constantine VI to Charlemagne's daughter Rotrude).

115 *ArF* for 797, ed. Kurze, p. 100.

116 This phrase comes from Borst, *Buch der Naturgeschichte,* p. 151.

117 Cf. the section "Signs in the Heavens" in Chapter 8.

118 On the following, see: Scholz, *Politik, Selbstverständnis, Selbstdarstellung,* pp. 113–26.

119 The mosaic in Santa Susanna depicts (from the center to the outside) Christ in the middle, and on his right hand the Mother of God and Saint Susanna, on his left presumably St. Paul together with St. Gaius (Susanna's father) and Gabinius (her uncle) and Charlemagne; cf. Bauer, *Bild der Stadt Rom im Frühmittelalter,* pp. 107–8. On this and the following mosaic in the Triclinium, cf. also Manfred Luchterhandt, *Famulus Petri.* Karl der Große in den römischen Mosaikbildern Leos III., in: *799. Kunst und Kultur,* vol. 3, pp. 55–70.

120 Scholz, *Politik, Selbstverständnis, Selbstdarstellung,* pp. 125–6, cites Charlemagne's gifts to Rome from the treasures he seized from the Avars as the reason for Leo's gratitude. This may or may not be the case. The much more lavish gifts of Pepin and his son Charlemagne were never celebrated by Hadrian I in a comparable way. Charlemagne is not recognizable as the benefactor in the drawings of the mosaic preserved in Santa Susanna.

121 Earlier studies repeatedly maintained that the left end wall was the location of a mosaic depicting Christ giving keys to St. Peter and a flag to Constantine the Great, but this has since been shown to be a seventeenth-century invention; cf. Bauer, *Bild der Stadt Rom im Frühmittelalter,* pp. 111–4.

122 The mosaic in the apse may well have been created at roughly the same time the Triconchos was built; for a summary, cf. Scholz, *Politik, Selbstverständnis, Selbstdarstellung,* pp. 114–6. Yet the mosaic on the wall facing the apse is not dated alongside all the available information on the time of construction. It may even have been created in 798, after Pope's Leo's return from Paderborn. This is strongly suggested by the content of the accompanying title, which wishes "life" to the pope and "victory" to the king. This is more in keeping with the situation after the assassination attempt on Leo rather than before. Cf. the discussion later in this section.

123 On the following, cf. Fried, Papst Leo III. besucht Karl den Großen, pp. 281–326; Rudolf Schieffer, Das Attentat auf Papst Leo III., in: *Am Vorabend der Kaiserkrönung,* pp. 75–85 (especially on the "miracle").

124 On such images, cf., for example, the Synod of Rome of 761, MGH Conc. 2, 1, here pp. 67–9.

125 *LP* 2 Vita Leonis III p. 5, 17–20.

126 Alcuin ep. 174, MGH Epp. 4 p. 288, 17–22.

127 Ibid., 32–3. Cf. also ep. 173, pp. 286–7, and ep. 234 (801), pp. 379–80 to Leo III: the entire letter reflects the demands of the end time.

128 Alcuin ep. 193, MGH Epp. 4 p. 320, 10–2.

129 Alcuin ep. 177, MGH Epp. 4 p. 293, 5, and ep. 178, pp. 295–6.

130 Alcuin ep. 174, MGH Epp. 4 p. 289, 1.

131 Cf. ibid., 8–9: "si tamen illa patria [i.e., Saxonia] Dei electione digna habetur."

132 *De civitate Dei* 5.24 (the italicized words show how strictly Charlemagne followed St. Augustine): "*Neque* enim nos christianos quosdam *imperatores ideo felices* dicimus, *quia* vel diutius imperarunt, vel imperantes filios morte placida reliquerunt, vel *hostes rei publicae domuerunt vel inimicos cives adversus se insurgentes* et cavere et opprimere potuerunt. . . . *Sed* felices eos dicimus, si iuste imperant, si . . . se homines esse meminerunt, *si suam potestatem ad Dei cultum maxime dilatandum maiestati eius famulam faciunt,* si Deum timent, diligunt, colunt. . . . *Tales christianos imperatores* dicimus esse *felices* interim spe, postea re ipsa futuros, *cum id, quod expectamus, advenerit,*" ed. Bernhard Dombart and Alphons Kalb (Corpus Christianorum, Series Latina 47), Turnhout 1955, p. 160.

133 According to Einhard, *Vita Karoli,* chap. 24, Augustine's *City of God* was one of Charlemagne's favorite books.

134 Alcuin ep. 173, MGH SS 4 p. 286, 16–31. See Fried, Papst Leo III. besucht Karl den Großen, p. 299.

135 Alcuin ep. 184, MGH Epp. 4 p. 309, 6–12. See also Alcuin ep. 179, MGH SS 4 p. 297, 14–15.

136 On the assassination attempt: Matthias Becher, Die Reise Papst Leos III. zu Karl dem Großen. Überlegungen zu Chronologie, Verlauf und Inhalt der Paderborner Verhandlungen des Jahres 799, in: *Am Vorabend der Kaiserkrönung,* pp. 87–112.

137 In this portrayal of events, I adhere closely to the account given in Becher, Karl der Große und Papst Leo III., pp. 23–6. In my view, Becher convincingly demonstrates that Wirund and Arn were sent to Rome long before the assassination attempt and that in all likelihood they were resident in Rome, awaiting instructions from the king, for the two months or so during which Pope Leo was effectively deposed from the papal throne.

138 Theodulf carm. 32, MGH Poetae 1, pp. 523–4 lines 15–24; Helmut Beumann, Paderborner Epos, in *Karolus magnus et Leo papa,* p. 9, overlooks the ironic tone of Theodulf's commentary, as does Padberg, Paderborner Treffen, p. 49. On the dating, see: Classen, *Karl der Große,* p. 57n203. On the palace at Paderborn: see the section "Thirty Years of War in Saxony" in Chapter 3.

139 Alcuin to Arn of Salzburg: MGH Epp. 4 p. 297, 21–4 (ep. 179, 799 Aig.).

140 *LP* 2 pp. 5–6.

141 On the pope's retinue consisting of 203 Roman *consiliatores* (counselors), cf. BM[2] 350 and the relevant passage from the *Annales Guelferbytani* for the year 799. The so-called Paderborn epic spoke of *iustum iudicium,* vv. 388–9, ed. Franz Brunhölzl, in: *De Karolo rege et Leone papa. Supplement.* – See also Dieter Schaller, Das Aachener Epos für Karl den Kaiser, in: *Frühmittelalterliche Studien* 10 (1976) pp. 134–68; Schaller, De Karolo rege et Leone papa, in: *Die deutsche Literatur des Mittelalters. Verfasserlexikon* 4 (1983) cols. 1041–5.

142 *Karolus magnus et Leo Papa,* vv. 504–5, ed. Brunhölzl in *De Karolo rege et Leone papa,* pp. 44–5, with a translation.

143 *LP,* ed. Duchesne, vol. 2, p. 6.

144 See the opening section of Chapter 8.

145 BM[2] 353 (St-Bertin), 353a (Centula), 353b (Rouen), ArF (Tours).

146 *ArFqdE* for 800; *Annales Lauresbamenses* for 800.

147 Repeatedly, modern historical research has suggested a visit to Alcuin as the reason for the king's detour; Charlemagne allegedly wanted to seek his adviser's counsel on how to proceed against the heavily indebted Pope Leo III; but Alcuin accompanied the king on the return journey to Aachen, where the circumstances for the march on Rome were discussed. In any event, Charlemagne could have summoned Alcuin to Aachen without more ado and spared himself the trouble of making a long journey to Tours.

148 *AMP* for 800.

149 *Chronicon Moissiacense* for 800, ed. Kettemann, Subsidia Anianensia, pt. 2, p. 96.

150 See Peter Classen, Karl der Große und die Thronfolge im Frankenreich, in: Classen, *Ausgewählte Aufsätze*, pp. 205–29, here pp. 211–3.

151 BM² 358b.

152 Theodulf carm. 32 vv. 25–6, MGH Poetae 1 p. 524. Cf. Scholz, *Politik, Selbstverständnis, Selbstdarstellung*, p. 129.

153 Cf. BM² 369a–c.

154 Both the *ArF* for 800 and the *Annales Maximiani*, MGH SS 13 p. 23, mention the meeting at Nomento; the latter source also gives the exact date.

155 *ArF* for 800 (in both versions); cf. Classen, *Karl der Große*, pp. 58–60. The following description also diverges in many of its details and evaluations from Becher, Kaiserkrönung. Even so, I constantly referred to these two studies in formulating my interpretation.

156 Cf. the discussion earlier in this section.

157 Cf. note 122 above.

158 This is the picture that emerges from the *Annales Laureshamenses* for 800: "comitibus seu reliquo christiano populo." MGH SS 1 p. 58.

159 Cf. the section "The Rules of the Court" in Chapter 6.

160 MGH Epp. 5 pp. 63–4 No. 6; the form of oath cited in the *LP* is shorter and less stringent. See also Max Kerner, Der Reinigungseid Leos III. vom Dezember 800. Die Frage seiner Echtheit und frühen kanonistischen Überlieferung. Eine Studie zum Problem der päpstlichen Immunität im frühen Mittelalter, in: *Zeitschrift des Aachener Geschichtsvereins* 84/85 (1977/1978) pp. 131–60.

161 *Annales Laureshamenses* for 800, MGH SS 1 p. 38.

162 For an overview of critical analyses of Charlemagne's coronation, see Schieffer, *Neues von der Kaiserkrönung*.

163 On the Laudes, see the section "The Fascination of Rome" in Chapter 5 and the discussion later in this section.

164 Likewise the *Annales Maximiani*, MGH SS 13 p. 23.

165 For a discussion of the *nomen imperatoris*, cf. Thomas Ertl, Byzantinischer Bilderstreit und fränkische Nomentheorie. Imperiales Handeln und dialektisches Denken im Umfeld der Kaiserkrönung Karls des Großen, in: *FmaSt* 40 (2006, published 2007) pp. 13–42.

166 Cf., for example, Alcuin ep. 174, MGH Epp. 4 p. 288; ep. 177 (*imperium christianum*), p. 292; and ep. 217, p. 361.–Cf. Classen, *Karl der Große*, pp. 48–9; Arno

Borst, Kaisertum und Namentheorie im Jahr 800, in: *Zum Kaisertum Karls des Großen. Beiträge und Aufsätze,* ed. Gunther Wolf (Wege der Forschung 38), Darmstadt 1972, pp. 216–39.

167 Similarly, the later emperorship of Louis the Pious did not have a specifically Roman tenor.

168 Alcuin, *De grammatica,* ed. Froben Forster, *Beati Flacci Albini Opera,* vol. 2, 2, Regensburg 1777, p. 271.

169 Cf. Johann Peter Kirsch, *Die Stationskirchen des Missale Romanum. Mit einer Untersuchung über Ursprung und Entwicklung der liturgischen Stationsfeier* (Ecclesia Orans), Freiburg i. Br. 1926, pp. 236–9.

170 *LP* 2 p. 7.

171 *LP* 2 p. 110 (XVII).

172 Johannes Fried, Endzeiterwartung um die Jahrtausendwende, in: *DA* 45 (1989) pp. 381–473, here pp. 449–50.

173 Wendling, Erhebung, has demonstrated that this was the case in 813.

174 On the liturgical procedure: Karl Josef Benz, "Cum ab oratione surgeret." Überlegungen zur Kaiserkrönung Karls des Großen, in: *DA* 31 (1975) pp. 337–69; the legal ramifications that Benz deduces from the procedural "analogy," however, are in no way compelling. Benz ignores the fact that Charlemagne's elevation to emperor was a succession of ritual acts, a practice borrowed from Byzantine ceremonial.

175 Cf. the examples cited in Treitinger, *Oströmische Kaiser- und Reichsidee,* according to their designation: in 457, Leo I being crowned with a torque before the acclamation (p. 9); in 491, Anastasius's coronation by the patriarch before the acclamation (pp. 10–1); and in 518, Justin I being crowned with a torque and crown by the patriarch before the acclamation by the people (pp. 11–2). In cases where the (principal) emperor elevated a co-emperor, the emperor assumed the function of the Senate, and the coronation and acclamation followed. No acclamations appear to have been attested from Byzantium in the course of the eighth century (which is not to say that they did not occur). Classen, *Karl der Große,* pp. 62–6, takes no account of this. On the coronation: R.-J. Lilie, Krönung, in: *Reallexikon zur byzantinischen Kunst* 5 (1995) cols. 439–54, esp. cols. 448–9 (my thanks to Wolfram Brandes for directing me to this study).

176 Charlemagne's coronation was not that of a co-emperor, and the pope was no "principal emperor appointing a co-emperor," as Becher, Kaiserkrönung, pp. 18–9 (quotation p. 19) has suggested. Rather, Charlemagne's coronation corresponded to a procedure practiced in Byzantium, cf. above note 175. The frequently encountered reference to the essay by W. Sickel, Das byzantinische Krönungsrecht bis zum 10. Jahrhundert, in: *Byzantinische Zeitschrift* 7 (1898) pp. 511–57, is misleading insofar as Sickel does not address the question of the acclamation. Sickel clarified that the coronation was and remained an act within the framework of "constitutional law" and did not mutate into an independent ecclesiastical responsibility.

177 *Annales Laureshamenses,* MGH SS 1 p. 38 chap. 34 (for the year 801).

178 Although the title βασιλεὺς τῶν Ῥομαίων was perfectly possible before 812, it was not customary; in 812 the title was put forward programmatically, but it became common practice only in the later course of the ninth century; cf. Rösch, *ONOMA BAΣIΛEIAΣ,* pp. 38 and 111–6.

179 On the "Laudes," cf. Kantorowicz, *Laudes regiae*, pp. 13–111. Admittedly, only the Frankish royal acclamations have survived from the time of Charlemagne, but no imperial acclamations from Rome, cf. ibid., pp. 103–4.

180 On the date of writing of the "Vita Leonis" in the *LP*, cf. Classen, *Karl der Große*, p. 43; on its possible dispatch to Aachen: Schaller, Aachener Epos, p. 148.

181 The imperial title in the form *Romanum gubernans imperium* (see the opening section of Chapter 8) employed the only official imperial title found in the Latin West that referred explicitly to Rome, as Peter Classen has demonstrated: *Romanum gubernans imperium*. Zur Vorgeschichte der Kaisertitulatur Karls des Großen, in Classen, *Ausgewählte Aufsätze*, pp. 187–204.

Chapter 8. Imperator Augustus

1 *De Karolo rege et Leone papa*, vv. 14–6, p. 10 [60]; for the following quotations, vv. 12–3 and v. 21. Cf. also Chapter 7 note 141. The poem is now dated to the period after Charlemagne's coronation as emperor.

2 Modoin, *Ecloga* 2.93, MGH Poetae 1 p. 390; translated into German in Steinen, Karl und die Dichter, p. 68. For an edition that corrects the one in MGH Poetae 1: Ernst Dümmler, Nasos (Modoins) Gedichte an Karl den Großen, in: *NA* 11 (1886) pp. 75–91; the Ecloga is on pp. 86–91.

3 Modoin, *Ecloga* 2; cf. Steinen, Karl und die Dichter, p. 68.

4 Modoin, *Ecloga* 2.115–7, MGH Poetae 1 p. 391.

5 Cf. mentions of this later in this section and in the sections "Attention Turns to the Near East" and "A New Enemy Appears: The 'Northmen'" in this chapter.

6 Alcuin ep. 178, MGH Epp. 4 p. 294.

7 See Klaus Schreiner, "Gerechtigkeit und Frieden haben sich geküßt" (Ps. 84, 11). Friedensstiftung durch symbolisches Handeln, in: *Träger und Instrumentarien des Friedens im hohen und späten Mittelalter*, ed. Johannes Fried (VuF 43), Sigmaringen 1996, pp. 37–86.

8 Leo's response has survived: MGH Epp. 5 pp. 93–4 No. 4 (809).

9 Willjung, *Konzil von Aachen 809*, p. 290.

10 François Louis Ganshof, La fin du règne de Charlemagne, une décomposition, in: *Zeitschrift für schweizerische Geschichte* 28 (1948) pp. 533–52.

11 Alcuin ep. 254, MGH Epp. 4 p. 411, 23–5.–Pope Zachary spoke of a *norma rectitudinis* in a letter to Boniface: MGH Epp. Sel. 1 p. 108 No. 58, and of the *via rectitudinis* in his letter to the mayors of the palace Pepin and Carloman, ibid., pp. 125–7 No. 61 (both letters in 745), cf. Fleckenstein, Die Bildungsreform Karls des Großen als Verwirklichung der norma rectitudinis, Bigge 1953; here p. 10 with note 16. *Norma rectitudinis* is a key concept of monastic life according to the *Dialogues* of Gregory the Great (2.3.3). There is little wonder, then, that Zachary, as a great admirer of Gregory, adopted the phrase.

12 *Annales Laureshamenses*, chap. 34 for 801, MGH SS 1 p. 38; *Chronicon Moissiacense* for 800 and 801, MGH SS 1 pp. 305–6; ed. Kettemann, Subsidia anianensia, pt. 2, p. 100.

13 Cf. Hageneder, *Crimen maiestatis*, pp. 55–79 (Hageneder also corrects some earlier opinions on this).–Theodulf: BM² 369f.

14 *Libellus de imperatoria potestate*, ed. Valentini and Zucchetti, p. 199. On the Roman judicial system of this period, see Theodor Hirschfeld, Das Gerichtswesen der Stadt Rom vom 8. bis 12. Jahrhundert wesentlich nach stadtrömischen Urkunden, in: *Archiv für Urkundenforschung* 4 (1912) pp. 419–562, here esp. pp. 420–40.

15 On the distinction between the old imperial palace (the *palatium Lateranense* of Constantine the Great) and the papal *patriarchium* (which can be verified as a *palatium* only from the reign of Pope Leo II and the year 813), cf. Fried, *Donation of Constantine*, pp. 74–88.

16 *LP* 2 p. 8.

17 *LP*, "Vita Leonis," chaps. 84–5, p. 26. Cf. the sections "The *Opus Caroli regis*" in Chapter 7 and "Signs in the Heavens" in this chapter.

18 *ArF* and *AMP* for the year 801.

19 *Libellus de imperatoria potestate*, ed. Valentini and Zucchetti, p. 199.

20 Ibid. On the legal position of Rome after Charlemagne, see: Hageneder, *Crimen maiestatis*, pp. 74–7.

21 This is clearly evident from both the text of the document and the reference to Leo's verdict (DKDG 196 from 4 March 801, esp. also lines 26–8).

22 Heinrich Fichtenau, Genesius, Notar Karls des Großen (797–803), in: *Folia Diplomatica* 1 (Brno 1971) pp. 75–87 (quotations from here); again in Fichtenau, *Beiträge zur Mediävistik. Ausgewählte Aufsätze*, vol. 2, *Urkundenforschung*, Stuttgart 1977, pp. 100–14.

23 *Annales Laureshamenses* Chap. 33, MGH SS 1 p. 38.

24 Becher, Kaiserkrönung, pp. 24–5, appears to adopt this latter position, but the *crimen laesae majestatis* argues against this.

25 The *Lorsch Annals* (MGH SS 1 p. 38) states that "et ibi [i.e., in Rome] celebravit pascha." Charlemagne would have celebrated this festival as he did otherwise in Rome, namely, by attending Mass in the most important patriarchal churches; cf. the section "The Call of Italy" in Chapter 3. Becher, however (Kaiserkrönung, pp. 17–8) raises doubts on this score.

26 Whether this departure date—three years to the day after Leo II was attacked—was indicative of serious differences between the emperor and the pope is a moot point; this is the surmise of Becher, Kaiserkrönung, pp. 17–8. Even so, Charlemagne may have been symbolically present during the procession, for the jewelled cross that he had donated to the Church of St. Savior on the day of his coronation was always carried in front of the pope during the *Letania maior* procession: *LP* 2 p. 110 (XVII).

27 This earthquake was also registered in Rome on 30 April: *LP* 2 p. 9.

28 *Annales Laureshamenses*, chap. 34 for 801, MGH SS 1 p. 38.

29 DKDG 197.

30 This did not exclude other formulations; notable here is the deliberately archaizing title used in the "Divisio regnorum" of 806: "Imperator Caesar Karolus rex Francorum invictissimus et Romani rector imperii pius felix victor ac triumphator semper augustus"; see the section "Organizing the Succession" in this chapter.

31 Cf. the section "The Prelude to Imperial Rule" in Chapter 7. On the context, see: Ernst Tremp, Zwischen Paderborn und Barcelona: König Ludwig von Aquitanien und die

Auseinandersetzung des Karlsreichs mit dem Islam, in: *Am Vorabend der Kaiserkrönung*, pp. 283–99.

32 Cf. the following section.

33 Theophanes on AM 6294–95.

34 Krämer, *Geschichte des Islam*, p. 84.

35 This unrest and destruction are mentioned by Theophanes on AM 6301. On this subject, cf. McCormick, *Charlemagne's Survey of the Holy Land*.

36 On this liturgical controversy, cf. the preceding section. On the diverse correspondence to and from Jerusalem, Rome, and the imperial court, cf. Borgolte, Papst Leo III., Karl der Große und der Filioque-Streit von Jerusalem, pp. 403–27, esp. the diagram on p. 414.

37 The suggestion by Philip Grierson, Money and Coinage, pp. 524–7, that the rarity of portrait coins had to do with the edict that coins could be regularly minted only in a single palace is unconvincing, given the fact that around thirty examples have now been found, minted in at least seven different years. Moreover, such a decree—as Bernd Kluge, Nomen imperatoris und christiana religio. Das Kaisertum Karls des Großen und Ludwigs des Frommen im Licht der numismatischen Quellen, in: *799. Kunst und Kultur*, p. 87, points out—would have jeopardized the coinage reform of 794 (Frankfurt). Kluge therefore prefers to interpret the portrait coins as special mintings to mark the coronation; however, this would have been a unique occurrence in Carolingian times and clearly takes later circumstances as its model.

38 One example of the second group lacking the inscription "xpictiana religio" may represent a posthumous minting under Louis the Pious.

39 Kluge, Nomen imperatoris und christiana religio (see note 37 above), pp. 82–90; on Einhard, cf. Heinz Löwe, "Religio christiana." Rom und das Kaisertum in Einhards *Vita Karoli magni*, in: *Storiografia e storia. Studi in onore di Eugenio Duprè Theseider*, ed. Massimo Petrocchi, Rome 1974, pp. 1–20. Löwe speculated whether St. Peter's Basilica in Rome might have acted as a model for the coin image (cf. esp. p. 11); but Einhard clearly places this building in second place, behind the cathedral in Aachen, not to mention the Church of the Holy Sepulchre. The xpictiana religio type of coin has also been found with the legend d(ominus) n(oster) karolus imp aug rex f(rancorum) et l(angobar-dorum); such coins are attributed to an Italian mint, almost certainly Milan.

40 Cf. Maria R.-Alföldi, Münze, in: *Reallexikon für Antike und Christentum* 25 (2012) cols. 115–62, here col. 131 and plates 33–4 (Maxentius).

41 Grierson, Money and Coinage, pp. 519–20.

42 MGH Capit. 1 No. 64, 18 p. 154: "propter aecclesias Dei restaurandas"; the later Byzantine emperor Constantine VII Porphyrogennetos certainly knew of Charlemagne's aid payments and alludes to them in *De adminstrando imperio*, chap. 26, 5–10, ed. Gy. Moravcsik, transl. R. J. H. Jenkins, Budapest 1949, p. 108 (I was unable to consult the revised edition: Dumbarton Oaks Center for Byzantine Studies, Washington, DC, 1967). On conditions in Palestine in the period in question, cf. Moshe Gil, *A History of Palestine, 634–1099*, Cambridge/New York 1992 (my thanks are due to Mordechai Levy for this reference).

43 Cf. the illustration in McCormick, *Charlemagne's Survey of the Holy Land*, pp. 190–1.

44 It should also be borne in mind that the usual pennies minted by Charlemagne, while far more frequently represented in archaeological finds, have never been found in the Holy

Land or Africa, despite the fact that Charlemagne's coinage, at least according to Einhard, was in circulation there.

45 See the section "A Late Peace Agreement with Byzantium" in this chapter.

46 This earthquake occurred in 774, https://en.wikipedia.org/wiki/Al-Aqsa_Mosque.

47 McCormick, *Charlemagne's Survey of the Holy Land,* pp. 199–217, for the edition and pp. 218–37 for the specific commentary on it.

48 Notker, *Gesta Karoli* 2.8.

49 Anton Baumstark, *Abendländische Palästinapilger des ersten Jahrtausends und ihre Berichte,* Cologne 1906; Colin Morris, *The Sepulchre of Christ and the Medieval West from the Beginnings to 1600,* Oxford 2005.

50 But cf. the trade relations between Africa and Charlemagne, discussed in the section "The Prelude to Imperial Rule" in Chapter 7.

51 Cf. Michael Borgolte, Der Elefant des Kalifen reiste nach Aachen, review of Heinhard Steiger, *Die Ordnung der Welt. Eine Völkerrechtsgeschichte des karolingischen Zeitalters (741 bis 840),* Cologne/Weimar/Vienna 2010, in: *Frankfurter Allgemeine Zeitung,* 7 July 2011, p. 34.

52 Cf. the section "Organizing the Succession" in Chapter 8.

53 This fact was pointed out by Arnold Bühler, Capitularia relecta. Studien zur Entstehung und Überlieferung der Kapitularien Karls des Großen und Ludwigs des Frommen, in: *Archiv für Diplomatik* 32 (1986) pp. 305–501; cf. Hartmann, *Karl der Große,* p. 134.–These figures follow the hitherto-definitive edition of the capitularies in MGH Capit. 1. The planned new edition of the MGH will have to undertake extensive modifications, but the overall impression of the welter of capitularies immediately after Charlemagne's coronation as emperor will likely remain unchanged.

54 MGH Capit. 1 pp. 204–6 No. 98 (801); cf. Hageneder, *Crimen maiestatis,* pp. 65–6.

55 Wilfried Hartmann, *Kirche und Kirchenrecht um 900,* pp. 93–9; for a summary, see Wilfried Hartmann, *Karl der Große,* pp. 139–41.

56 MGH Capit. 1 pp. 157–9 Nos. 68–9.

57 Hannig, Pauperiores vassi; Hannig, Zentrale Kontrolle.

58 MGH Capit. 1 p. 112 No. 39 (803); the addressee of the memo was Count Stéphane of Paris.

59 MGH Capit. 1 p. 113 No. 39, 5 (803).

60 Chap. 35, MGH SS 1 p. 38.

61 In assessing this measure, I follow, albeit with certain reservations, Hannig, Pauperiores vassi; older studies of the *missi* are also cited there; cf. Hannig, Zentrale Kontrolle. As early as 787, an abbot and a count met as *missi* in St-Wandrille, see the sections "Center and Periphery" in Chapter 4 and "Instituting Practical Measures" in Chapter 5; for 793/794, see "Center and Periphery" and the section "'Opposing the Enemies of Truth'" in Chapter 7. I interpret these dates in accordance with Werner, *Missus,* who contends that although royal messengers were certainly appointed at an earlier date, it was only from 802 on that clearly defined *missatica,* that is, areas of inspection under the control of the *missi,* were established.

62 For the quotations, see: *Annales Laureshamenses,* chap. 35 for 802, MGH SS 1 pp. 38–9; cf. also *Chronicon Moissiacense (Anianense)* for 802, ed. Kettemann, Subsidia anianensia, pt. 2, p. 101.

63 Hannig, Zentrale Kontrolle.

64 Ibid., pp. 28–36.

65 Although mutilated at the beginning, Wulfar's letter to Fardulf was preserved for posterity in the specimen collection of St-Denis (No. 24): MGH Form. p. 509; cf. Patzold, Normen im Buch, p. 345.

66 MGH Capit. 1 pp. 91–9 No. 33. For a fundamental treatment, see: Patzold, Normen im Buch, passim.

67 Mordek, *Bibliotheca,* p. 474.

68 Mordek and Schmitz, Neue Kapitularien, p. 414 No. II chap. 3.

69 On the form of the oath: MGH Capit. 1 p. 101 No. 34. On the capitulary and the various surviving versions intended for different *missatica,* cf. Wilhelm Alfred Eckhardt, Die Capitularia missorum specialia von 802, in: *DA* 12 (1956) pp. 498–516; and Patzold, Normen im Buch, pp. 341–5.

70 On this and the following: MGH Capit. 1 No. 33 (cf. BM² 380c). The introductory passage on the reason for the oath reflects the relevant article of the *Lex Romana Visigothorum,* cf. the opening section of this chapter.

71 Leidrad to Karl, MGH Epp. 4 pp. 540–1 No. 29, here p. 541, 10–3.

72 BM² 390a and MGH Capit. 1 pp. 99–102 No. 34 (?).

73 The most significant testimony on synods and court assemblies *is Chronicon Moissia-cense (Anianense)* for 802, ed. Kettemann, Subsidia anianensia, pt. 2, pp. 102–3.

74 Chap. 36 for 803, MGH SS 1 p. 39. This is the last entry of these annals to have survived.

75 MGH Capit. 1 pp. 170–2 No. 77.

76 Detlev Zimpel, Unliebsame Herrscher-Erlasse im Frankenreich. Über die Sabotage von Kapitularien, in: *Scientia veritatis. Festschrift für Hubert Mordek zum 65. Geburtstag,* ed. Oliver Münsch und Thomas Zotz, Ostfildern 2004, pp. 127–36. The examples cited here relate to a later period.

77 Cf., for example, Mordek and Schmitz, Neue Kapitularien, p. 423 No. II chap. 40 (probably 813).

78 The letters of Pope Leo III to Charlemagne, possibly gathered into one volume by the emperor himself, Nos. 1–10: MGH Epp. 5 pp. 85–104 (808).

79 MGH Epp. 5 p. 102 No. 10 (808–14?).

80 Cf. the opening section of this chapter.

81 MGH Epp. 5 pp. 87–8 No. 1.

82 MGH Epp. 5 p. 89, 35–7 No. 2.

83 BM² 431b.

84 On the *palatium:* Fried, *Donation of Constantine,* pp. 74–88. On the Polyconchos: Bauer, *Bild der Stadt Rom im Frühmittelalter,* pp. 68–9.

85 Bauer, *Bild der Stadt Rom im Frühmittelalter,* pp. 115–7. The suggestion by Bauer that Charlemagne was represented here seems improbable to me. The Frankish ruler would

have to have been depicted as an emperor, but Leo did his utmost to play down imperial sovereignty over Rome.

86   Hageneder, *Crimen maiestatis,* pp. 72–4.

87   For a good overview, see: Horst Zettel, Karl der Große, Siegfried von Dänemark und Gottfried von Dänemark, in: *Zeitschrift für Schleswig-Holsteinische Geschicte* 110 (1985) pp. 11–25; on the Vikings: Föller, *Wikinger.*

88   Cf. Harald Neifeind, Verträge zwischen Normannen und Franken im neunten und zehnten Jahrhundert, dissertation, Heidelberg 1971; Daniel Föller, Verflochtenes Denken. Kognitive Strategien im wikingerzeitlichen Skandinavien, typewritten dissertation, Frankfurt am Main 2012, pp. 234–7.

89   MGH Capit. 1 p. 139 No. 51, 10. On the Franks' use of ships for military purposes before the reign of Charlemagne: Bernard S. Bachrach, *Early Carolingian Warfare,* pp. 247–57.

90   MGH Capit. 1 No. 74 pp. 166–7.

91   Ibid., 11 p. 167.

92   On this, cf. the section "The End Is Nigh" in this chapter.

93   MGH Epp. 5 p. 90 No. 2 (808).

94   Revised *ArF* for the year 797. Ursula Vones-Liebenstein, Katalonien zwischen Maurenherrschaft und Frankenreich. Probleme um die Ablösung westgotisch-mozarabischer Kirchenstrukturen, in: *Frankfurter Konzil von 794,* vol. 1, pp. 453–505. Cf. the section "A Hidden Failure: The Synod of Frankfurt" in Chapter 7.

95   This emerges from a comparison of the *ArF* for 778 with the *ArFqdE* for the same year.

96   MGH Capit. 1 p. 97 No. 33, 32 (802).

97   Cf. the opening words of the so-called Divisio regnorum of 806: MGH Capit. 1 No. 45 p. 127: "ad occasum tendentia secula"; on this, see also Wolfram Brandes, *Tempora periculosa sunt.* Eschatologisches im Vorfeld der Kaiserkrönung Karls des Großen, in: *Frankfurter Konzil von 794,* vol. 1, pp. 49–79.

98   Cf. the section "Thirty Years of War in Saxony" in Chapter 3.

99   Cf., for example, MGH Capit. 1 pp. 134–5 No. 48, 2 (807).

100 MGH Capit. 1 p. 130 No. 49, 4 (806).

101 Ibid., pp. 121–2 No. 43.

102 Mordek and Schmitz, Neue Kapitularien, p. 399 No. 1 chap. 23 (805/813).

103 MGH Capit. 1 pp. 122–6 No. 44.

104 I have corroborated my view of this division elsewhere: Fried, Erfahrung und Ordnung, pp. 145–92.

105 *ArF* for 806, ed. Kurze, p. 121. Einhard is regarded as the author of the "private" will of Charlemagne, which was handed down solely by him (*Vita Karoli,* chap. 33). Certainly, it is striking that Einhard says absolutely nothing about the whole succession system instituted in 806; cf. the section "The End Is Nigh" in this chapter.

106 Cf. the section "Organizing the Succession Revisited" in this chapter.

107 On the motif of *reparare,* cf. the section "Education as a Scholar and Instruction in the Christian Faith" in Chapter 1.

108 Cf., for example, Lactantius, *Divinae institutiones* 7.25.6–9, ed. Stefan Freund, *Laktanz, Divinae institutiones Buch 7: De vita beata. Einleitung, Text, Übersetzung und Kommentar,* Berlin 2009, pp. 186–7.

109 Cf. the opening section of Chapter 6.

110 MGH Capit. 1 p. 136 No. 49 chap. 2 (806).

111 Ibid., p. 123 No. 44, 7 (805). On the border, cf. the section "The Call of Italy" in Chapter 3.

112 Ibid., pp. 130–2 No. 46.

113 Ibid., p. 131 No. 46, 4 (806).

114 Ibid., p. 152 No. 63, 13 (809).–MGH Capit. 1 pp. 258–9 No. 131 is now—if it is not categorized as a forgery—generally dated to the reign of Louis the Pious or even later.

115 Johannes Heil, *Kompilation oder Konstruktion? Die Juden in den Pauluskommentaren des 9. Jahrhunderts* (Forschungen zur Geschichte der Juden, Abteilung A: Abhandlungen, vol. 6), Hanover 1998.

116 The true author was Quodvultdeus Carthaginiensis (the so-called Pseudo-Augustinus); the manuscript is Munich, Bavarian State Library, clm 14098 (part 2); the incomplete "Muspilli" poem appears in Carolingian minuscule on the page margins of this manuscript. Cf. Elisabeth Wunderle, *Katalog der lateinischen Handschriften der Bayerischen Staatsbibliothek Munich: Die Handschriften aus St. Emmeram in Regensburg,* vol. 1, Wiesbaden 1995, pp. 238–41. The treatise was edited (without reference to clm 14098) by René Braun (Corpus Christianorum, Series Latina 60), Turnhout 1976.

117 Similar measures were called for in MGH Capit. 1 p. 136 No. 49 chap. 4 (806).

118 Mordek and Schmitz, Neue Kapitularien, p. 414 No. 2 chap. 9.

119 MGH Capit. 1 p. 135 No. 49 chap. 1 (806).

120 Ibid., p. 146 No. 59.

121 Ibid., pp. 134–5 No. 48 (807).

122 Cf., for example, ibid., pp. 136–8 No. 50 (808).

123 MGH Capit. 1 pp. 164–5 No. 73 (811).

124 *Chronicon Moissiacense* for 808, MGH SS 1 p. 307; ed. Kettemann, Subsidia Anianensia, pt. 2, p. 111.

125 Borst (ed.), *Schriften zur Komputistik,* with an extensive introduction (pp. 1–326) summarizing the entire subject; Supplements: Warntjes, Irische Komputistik, esp. pp. 23–9.

126 Borst (ed.), *Schriften zur Komputistik.* vol. 2, pp. 820–84; important corrections and a reinterpretation: Hartmut Hoffmann, *Abisag calefaciente* oder Der karolingische Traktat *De sole et luna,* in: *DA* 68 (2012), pp. 445–77.

127 But cf. the section "The Prelude to Imperial Rule" in Chapter 7.

128 On the manuscript: Anton von Euw, Kompendium der Zeitrechnung, Naturlehre und Himmelskunde, in: *Glaube und Wissen im Mittelalter. Die Kölner Dombibliothek. Katalogbuch zur Ausstellung,* ed. Erzbischöfliches Diözesanmuseum Cologne: Joachim M.

Plotzek et al., Munich 1998, pp. 136–56; Borst, *Schriften zur Komputistik,* vol. 2, pp. 773–94 and 885–950. – On the Irish: Warntjes, Irische Komputistik; a *Computus Rhenanus* is known from Cologne as early as 775, while in 789—perhaps in conjunction with the *Admonitio generalis*—a *computus* was also published in Fulda.

129 The *ArF* for 810 reported two solar eclipses (on 7 June and 30 November) and two lunar eclipses (21 June and 15 December) (p. 133) and for 812 one solar eclipse (on 15 May); cf. also *Annales S. Amandi breves,* MGH SS 2 p. 184.

130 MGH Epp. 4 pp. 552–5. The dating is uncertain; formerly the assumption was 804–814, more recently 800; cf. Symke Haverkamp, Making Something from Nothing. Content and Context of Fredegisus of Tours' *De substantia nihili et tenebrarum,* dissertation, Utrecht 2006, p. 39 (for April 800); see also Borst, *Schriften zur Komputistik,* vol. 2, pp. 820–84. Yet the indications of Charlemagne's imperial title, which appear both in the letter to Dungal that originally preceded (Haverkamp p. 10) the small treatise by the deacon Fredegisus (*Romanum gubernans imperium*) and in Fredegisus's little work itself (*princeps* and *sacrum palatium*) do not accord with the early date of 800 that Borst proposes. I therefore continue to prefer the later dating. In 811, the "reviewer" Dungal, a monk at St-Denis, explained the solar eclipses of the previous year in terms on the basis of Macrobius's *Commentary on the Dream of Scipio:* MGH Epp. 4 pp. 570–8 ep. 1. Around this time Fredegisus was also resident at the court in Aix, where as principal abbot (of Tours) he countersigned Charlemagne's testament. His predecessor Alcuin was also "only" a deacon (cf., for example, Einhard, *Vita Karoli,* chap. 25).

131 MGH Epp. 4 p. 553, 29–33 (*nihil*), and p. 555, 13–5 (*tenebrae*).

132 Borst, *Schriften zur Komputistik,* vol. 2, pp. 820–84, attempts to attribute the treatise *De sole et luna,* which is replete with allegorical interpretations of physical phenomena, to Arn of Salzburg and to interpret it as a response to Fredegisus; for an opposite view, see Hoffmann (as note 126). Furthermore, the supposed allusions to Fredegisus that Borst claims are present in this text are far too weak and general to be convincing. The manuscript of Fredegisus's small treatise offers as a preamble (cf. above note 131) Charlemagne's request to Dungal that he should explain "nothingness" and "darkness" without recourse to allegory. In the light of this, Fredegisus's work, as a piece of "plain science," might conversely have been a response to *De sole et luna.*

133 On the following, see cf. Borst, *Schriften zur Komputistik,* vol. 2, pp. 951–1020 Nos. 13 and 14.

134 Borst, *Schriften zur Komputistik,* vol. 3, p. 142 No. 16 chap. 4.

135 Ibid., pp. 1145–6 No. 17 2.1; *Ebraice veritatis:* ibid., p. 1042 No. 16 chap. 4.

136 *Der Karolingische Reichskalender und seine Überlieferung bis ins 12. Jahrhundert,* ed. Arno Borst (MGH Libri Memoriales 2, 1–3), Hanover 2001, here vol. 2, 1, p. 751 (cf. the illustrations in vol. 2, 1 after p. 74 plate 2).

137 Cf. the section "The *Opus Caroli regis*" in Chapter 7.

138 Borgolte, Papst Leo III., Karl der Große und der filioque-Streit, pp. 401–27; Scholz, *Politik, Selbstverständnis, Selbstdarstellung,* pp. 139–42; Willjung, *Konzil von Aachen 809,* pp. 20–9. – The doubts raised by Daniel F. Callahan, The Problem of the "Filioque" and the Letter from the Pilgrim Monks of the Mount of Olives to Pope Leo III and Charlemagne, *Revue Bénédictine* 108 (1992) pp. 75–134, over the authenticity of the letter from the Frankish monks at the Convent of the Mount of Olives have not been borne out.

139 For this assessment, cf. Max Kerner, Karl der Große—Gestalter des Glaubens?, in: Böhnke, Kattan, and Oberdorfer, *Filioque-Kontroverse* (see note 181 of Chapter 3),

pp. 14–29, here pp. 25–7. On the theological context: Gemeinhardt, *Filioque-Kontroverse*, pp. 141–64.

140 *LP*, "Vita Leonis," chaps. 84–5, p. 26. Cf. the section "The Results of Charlemagne's Wars" in Chapter 3 and the opening section of this chapter. Andrea Sterk, "The Silver Shields of Pope Leo III: A Reassessment of the Evidence," in: *Comitatus* 19(1) (1988) pp. 62–79.

141 Willjung, *Konzil von Aachen 809*, p. 290, 6–7: the quotation from 2 Timothy 3:1 represents one of the central eschatological promises.

142 MGH Epp. 4 pp. 533–4 No. 24, here p. 534.

143 Ibid., p. 556 No. 37 (Spring 813).

144 Theophanes on the year AM 6304, also *ArF* for 812.

145 Notker, *Gesta Karoli* 2.6.

146 Ibid., 2.7.

147 Cf. the brief account by Herbert Hunger *in Geschichte der Textüberlieferung der antiken und mittelalterlichen Literatur,* vol. 1, Zurich 1961, p. 94.

148 Cf. the sections "The Nearest Neighbors" in Chapter 2 and "A New Enemy Appears: 'The Northmen' " in this chapter.

149 BM² 450a.

150 BM² 458 (early 811).

151 My thanks are due to Ernst Mutschler, my colleague at the Mainz Academy, for his advice on these medical questions.

152 Cf. the section "Even Priests Clash" in Chapter 5.

153 MGH Capit. 1 pp. 161–2 No. 71 (811).

154 See, for example, Hägermann, *Karl der Große*, pp. 577–8.

155 MGH Capit. 1 pp. 245–6 No. 124 (November 807).

156 Reference to empire-wide fasting: Ibid., p. 162 No. 72 chap. 1 (811, looking back at 810).

157 On the following, see: Ibid., pp. 162–4 No. 72 (811). This capitulary may have come from the same collection as the previously cited capitulary No. 71.

158 Ibid., chap. 11.

159 MGH Capit. 1 p. 162 No. 71 chap. 13 (811).

160 Ibid., p. 169 No. 76 (2 April 812)=DKDG 217.

161 Ibid., 1 pp. 176–7 No. 80 (811).

162 Cf. Glatthaar, in: *Admonitio Generalis,* ed. Mordek, Zechiel-Eckes, and Glatthaar, pp. 115–47.

163 Mordek and Schmitz, Neue Kapitularien, pp. 413–4 chap. 1 on the appeal for peace; see also the following capitulary (805–13, possibly September 813).

164 Leidrad to Charlemagne: MGH Epp. 4 pp. 542–4 No. 30.

165 On the following, see: Fried, Elite und Ideologie, esp. pp. 95–6; on the contemporary issue of incest, see: Fried, Erfahrung und Ordnung, pp. 177–9. I have attempted to rebut

the objections to my interpretation raised by Ubl, *Inzestverbot und Gesetzgebung,* p. 379n428, and by Martina Hartmann, *Königin,* p. 105, in Fried, Kanonistik und Mediävistik.

166 Alcuin ep. 119 (796).

167 Werner, Nachkommen, p. 417, and Wikipedia, "List of Counts of Vermandois" (Carolingian counts).

168 After Thegan, *Gesta Hludowici imperatoris,* chap. 22.

169 Fried, Elite und Ideologie.

170 Stiftsbibl. 4/1; cf. Mordek, Frühmittelalterliche Gesetzgeber, pp. 1005–18 with plates VI–VIII.

171 Wendling, Erhebung.

172 Paschasius Radbertus, *Vita s. Adalhardi,* chap. 50, Migne *PL* 120 col. 1534C.

173 The first false decretals seem to have appeared in 834, i.e., during Wala's time as abbot of Corbie. It is inconceivable that his close confidant Paschasius Radbertus could have posed as Isidor without his knowledge or agreement. Thus, Adalhard's brother, who had not been raised in a monastery but instead had been educated for worldly affairs, may have been the "political" brains behind the forgery, while the scholarly Paschasius Radbertus was the canon-law expert who compiled the work; cf. Fried, *Donation of Constantine,* pp. 88–109.

174 Cf. Paschasius Radbertus, *Vita s. Adalhardi,* chaps. 20 and 22, with a reflection on the reading of the *Acta s. Silvestri.*

175 Fried, *Donation of Constantine;* Fried, Die Konstantinische Schenkung, in: *Welt des Mittelalters,* pp. 295–311.

176 MGH Conc. 2, 2 pp. 610–1.

177 Ernst Dümmler, Radbert's Epitaphium Arsenii, in: *Abhandlungen der königlichen Akademie der Wissenschaften zu Berlin,* 1899/1900.

178 Astronomus, *Vita Hludowici,* chap. 20, ed. Tremp, p. 342.

179 Mordek and Schmitz, Neue Kapitularien, p. 399 No. 1 chap. 2 (805/813); cf. the section "The End Is Near" in this chapter.

180 Ibid., pp. 408–9 No. 1 chap. 25 (805/813).

181 As, for example, in a letter to Archbishop Odilbert of Milan, MGH Capit. 1 pp. 246–7 No. 125 (probably 812).

182 Mordek and Schmitz, Neue Kapitularien, p. 414 No. 2 chap. 1.

183 Namely, in the form of the one hundred fabricated papal decretals of the so-called Pseudo-Isidor, closely associated with Abbot Wala of Corbie.

184 Mordek and Schmitz, Neue Kapitularien, pp. 413–4 No. 1 chap. 43 (805/813).

185 MGH Conc. 2, 1 pp. 245–306 Nos. 34–8. For a summary, see: Wilfried Hartmann, *Synoden,* pp. 128–40.

186 MGH Conc. 2, 1 p. 248. On adoption of the decretals: Horst Fuhrmann, Das Papsttum und das kirchliche Leben im Frankenreich, in: *Settimane Spoleto* 27 (1979) pp. 419–56, here p. 443n41.

187 The contention that MGH Conc. 2, 1 pp. 197–201 App. B represents this conclusion, as has been suggested (cf. Wilfried Hartmann, *Synoden,* p. 140), cannot be proved. The tersely formulated chapters here read more like a preview or a draft resolution for a synod rather than the canons issued by a synod. The *ArF* for 813 explicitly indicates that no new synod was held, but instead that just the resolutions from the five individual foregoing synods were available.

188 MGH Conc. 2, 1 pp. 301–6 App. C.

189 As noted in the *ArF.* This "collation" might be represented by MGH Conc. 2, 1 pp. 197–201 App. B; however, this text already incorporated the emperor's capitulary (App. A).

190 MGH Conc. 2, 1 pp. 294–7 App. A.

191 *Einhard,* ed. Schefers, p. 12 with note 56.

192 BM[2] 479a. For the following quotation, see: *Chronicon Moissiacense* for 813, MGH SS 1 p. 310. On this topic, see: Wendling, Erhebung.

193 Cf. Einhard, *Vita Karoli,* chap. 32: "Adpropinquantis finis conplura fuere prodigia, ut non solum alii, sed et ipse hoc minitari sentiret."

194 Cf. the section "The End Is Nigh" in this chapter.–The soul-searching by Charlemagne portrayed here is conceivable but, of course, wholly fictitious.

195 This account of the emperor's final hours is from Thegan of Trier's *Gesta Hludowici imperatoris,* chap. 7, ed. Tremp, pp. 186–8.

Epilogue

1 Percy Ernst Schramm, Karl der Große im Lichte seiner Siegel und Bullen sowie der Bild- und Wortzeugnisse über sein Aussehen, in: *Karl der Große,* vol. 1 ([3]1967), pp. 15–23.

2 Like other commentators before him, Hack, Karl der Große hoch zu Roß, ascribes the equestrian statuette to Charles (II) the Bald. The supposed evidence for this, namely, the orb the rider is holding in his right hand, does not furnish conclusive proof because of the paucity of pictorial material on Charlemagne; the famous stylized images on coins of the Carolingian ruler as a Roman emperor are irrelevant here, so not a single portrait specific to the king or emperor or commissioned by him has come down to us from the kingdom of the Franks. Furthermore, images of Charles the Bald usually show him without a royal orb. Cf. also Wilfried Hartmann, *Karl der Große,* pp. 71–3.

3 Cf. the next-to-last paragraph of the Prologue.

4 Preserved among the letters of St. Boniface: MGH Epp. Sel. 1 pp. 125–7 No. 61 (end of October 745), here p. 126, 2. The *principes* Pepin and Carloman are named here. On the *norma rectitudinis,* cf. the opening section of Chapter 8 with note 11.

5 On the history of the research: Kerner, *Karl der Große,* pp. 51–63.

6 *Opus Caroli* 1.25, ed. Freeman, p. 218 with note 3.

7 Cf. the sections "A New Enemy Appears: 'The Northmen,'" and "Contacts with Foreigners" and "The End Is Nigh" in Chapter 8.

8 Cf. the section "The *Opus Caroli regis*" in Chapter 7.

9 Johann Wolfgang von Goethe, Die Externsteine, in: Sophien-Ausgabe Sect. I vol. 49b, pp. 46–52. On the Externsteine prehistoric monument, see above, note 25 of Chapter 3.

10 Migne *PL* 106, 121–278.

11 The text from Bobbio: *Einhardi Vita Karoli Magni*, ed. Holder-Egger, pp. 50–2. On the following, see: Julian Ellmann, Der Proserpina-Sarkophag: Vom römisch-antiken Zeugnis zur Grablege Karls des Großen, in: *Aachener Dom*, pp. 61–83, and Gunnar Heuschkel, Überlegungen zum Grab Karls des Großen, ibid., pp. 85–105.

12 This suggestion is made by Danielle Gaborit-Chopin, *La statuette équestre de Charlemagne* (Collection solo 13), Paris 1999. Despite the opposing view of Hack, Karl der Große hoch zu Roß, pp. 356–60, I still consider the dating and the interpretation offered by Gaborit-Chopin extremely plausible. She demonstrated that the horse is a piece of work from late antiquity that was reused for the Charlemagne statuette. It is therefore not inconceivable that this horse may originally have been regarded as a sacred relic. The question of the material used to sculpt the rider (not costly enough for a memorial statue) would thereby be obviated. The orb proves nothing, cf. the section "Knowledge Concentrates at the Court" in Chapter 6 and the Epilogue, note 2.–On the silver statue: Hack, Karl der Große hoch zu Roß, p. 351.–The image on Charlemagne's grave may have been carved from stone from the outset, showing him with a cross and the imperial orb in his hands; cf. the testimony of Antonio de Beatis from 1517, quoted in Ellmann (as per the preceding note) pp. 75–6.

13 Cf. the Prologue.

14 Fried, Ludwig der Fromme, das Papsttum und die fränkische Kirche, in: *Charlemagne's Heir. New Perspectives on the Reign of Louis the Pious (814–840)*, ed. Peter Godman and Roger Collins, Oxford 1990, pp. 231–73.

15 Fried, Kanonistik und Mediävistik, pp. 127–41. On the dating of the *Vita Karoli*, cf. the Prologue.

16 Fried, Zu Herkunft und Entstehungszeit, pp. 605–6.

17 Cf. the section "Charlemagne's Final Decrees and Death" in Chapter 8.

18 Tischler, *Einharts "Vita Karoli,"* pp. 153–62, refers to Louis as the first reader of Einhard's biography.

19 Alexander Weihs, *Pietas und Herrschaft. Das Bild Ludwigs des Frommen in den "Vitae Hludowici"* (Theologie 65), Münster 2004.

20 Mordek and Schmitz, Neue Kapitularien, pp. 414ff. No. 2 chap. 2.

21 MGH SS 15, 1 pp. 184–87, here chap. 11 p. 191, 12.

22 Nithard, Historiae 1.1.

23 MGH SS rer. Germ [44] pp. 2–3.

24 Cf. Werner, Karl der Große oder Charlemagne?, pp. 23–31. Cf. also Joachim Ehlers, Charlemagne—Karl der Große, in: *Deutsche Erinnerungsorte*, vol. 1, ed. Etienne François und Hagen Schulze, ²Munich 2001, pp. 41–55.

25 Karl Ferdinand Werner, Die Legitimität der Karolinger und die Entstehung des "Reditus Regni ad stirpem Karoli," in: *Die Welt als Geschichte* 12 (1952) pp. 203–25; Gabrielle M. Spiegel, "The Reditus Regni ad Stirpem Karoli Magni: A New Look," in: *French Historical Studies* 7 (1971) pp. 145–71.

26 Cf. Kerner, *Karl der Große*, pp. 256–63.

27 Borst, Karlsbild, p. 377. Cf. also Joachim Ehlers, *Charlemagne. L'Européen entre la France et l'Allemagne* (Conférences annuelles de l'Institut Historique Allemand 7), Stuttgart 2001.

28 Montesquieu, *De l'esprit des lois* 31.18 (first published in Geneva in 1748). For an online translation of Montesquieu's work (*The Spirit of Laws*) into English, see the website of the Constitution Society: http://www.constitution.org/cm/sol_31.htm.

29 On both, see: Borst, Karlsbild, p. 378.

30 Cf., for example, Johann Jacob Moser, *Compendium iuris publici Regni Germanici oder Grund-Riss der heutigen Staats-Verfassung des Teutschen Reichs,* Frankfurt/Leipzig 1738, pp. 88–9.

31 Pape, Karlskult, pp. 138–81. On Napoleon and Charlemagne, cf. the depiction (albeit without documentary evidence) by Berthold Vallentin, *Napoleon,* Berlin 1923, pp. 121–32.

32 Quoted in Pape, Karlskult, p. 146.

33 Borst, Karlsbild, pp. 387–8.

34 Gustav Freytag, *Bilder aus der deutschen Vergangenheit,* vol. 1, *Das Mittelalter,* ed. G. A. E. Bogeng, Leipzig n.d., p. 291.

35 For a more recent example, the reader is referred to Favier, *Charlemagne,* pp. 435–515.

36 *Weltgeschichtliche Betrachtungen,* ed. Jakob Oeri, quotations from the 4th ed., 1921, Berlin, p. 130 (long the standard edition).

37 Jacob Burckhardt, *Die Cultur der Renaissance in Italien. Ein Versuch,* first published Leipzig 1860, ²1869; multiple editions thereafter; forthcoming in vol. 4 of the complete critical edition. I quote here from the following edition: Jacob Burkhardt, *Gesammelte Werke,* vol. 3, Darmstadt 1962, p. 117.

38 Burckhardt, *Cultur der Renaissance in Italien.*

39 Illustration and interpretation: Kerner: *Karl der Große,* pp. 191–211.

40 Maria Effinger, Aufbruch zwischen Zeitkritik und Zensur, in: *Forschung. Das Magazin der Deutschen Forschungsgemeinschaft* 4/2012, pp. 16–21, here p. 21 (digital version at: http://artjournals.uni-hd.de).

41 Lothar Gall, *Germania. Eine deutsche Marianne?,* Bonn 1993, pp. 29–30; see also p. 78n35.

42 Borst, Karlsbild, p. 373.

43 Cf. ibid., p. 377.

44 Quoted from Pape, Karlskult, pp. 143–4; cf. Borst, Karlsbild, pp. 381–2.

45 For a general account of legend as the source of history: František Graus, Die Herrschersagen des Mittelalters als Geschichtsquelle, in: Graus, *Ausgewählte Aufsätze,* pp. 3–27; on Charlemagne in particular: Robert Folz, *Le souvenir et la légende de Charlemagne dans l'empire germanique médiéval,* Paris 1950; Kerner, *Karl der Große,* pp. 157–80.

46 *Deutsche Sagen,* ed. by the brothers Grimm with illustrations by Otto Ubbelohde, 2 vols., Frankfurt am Main 1981, here vol. 2, introduction, pp. 11–2. The legends: pp. 89–117. Here is not the place to go into the brothers' conception of legends.

47   Friedrich Wolfzettel, Karl der Große, in: *Enzyklopädie des Märchens* 7 (1993) cols. 982–1002, here col. 984.

48   *Handwörterbuch des deutschen Aberglaubens* 4 (1931/1932) cols. 1006–7.

49   *Karl der Große in den europäischen Literaturen des Mittelalters. Konstruktion eines Mythos,* ed. Bernd Bastert, Tübingen 2004.

50   Fried, Karl der Große. Geschichte und Mythos; Matthew Gabriele and Jace Stuckey (eds.), *The Legend of Charlemagne in the Middle Ages: Power, Faith, and Crusade,* New York 2008.

51   Gerhard Rauschen, *Die Legende Karls des Großen im 11. und 12. Jahrhundert* (Publikationen der Gesellschaft für Rheinische Geschichtskunde 7), Leipzig 1890; Maximilian Kerner, ed., Der verschleierte Karl. Karl der Große zwischen Mythos und Wirklichkeit und Mythos, Aachen 1999.

52   The most recent studies are: Matthias M. Tischler, Modes of Literary Behaviour in Christian-Islamic Encounters in the Iberian Peninsula: *Pseudo-Turpin* versus Peter the Venerable, in: *Languages of Love and Hate: Conflict, Communication, and Identity in the Medieval Mediterranean,* ed. Sarah lambert and Helen Nicholson (International Medieval Research 15), Turnhout 2012, pp. 201–21; and Hannes Möhring, Karl der Große und die Endkaiser-Weissagung. Der Sieger über den Islam kommt aus dem Westen, in: *Montjoie. Studies in Crusade History in Honour of Hans Eberhard Mayer,* ed. Benjamin Z. Kedar, Jonathan Riley-Smith, and Rudolf Hiestand, Aldershot 1997, pp. 1–19.

53   Goethe, *Dichtung und Wahrheit,* pt. 1, bk. 1, Sophien-Ausgabe Sect. 1, vol. 26, p. 9.

54   On the following, see A. Graboïs, Souvenir et légendes de Charlemagne dans les textes hébraïques médiévaux, in: *Le Moyen Âge* 72 (1966) pp. 5–41.

55   On interpretation, cf. Michael Toch, Mehr Licht: Eine Entgegnung zu Friedrich Lotter, in: *Aschkenas* 11 (2001), pp. 465–87. According to Toch, such stories may have been devised to absolve communities from earlier traditional story motifs showing them committing this kind of "treachery" in favor of the Moors.

56   Mark R. Cohen, *Under Crescent and Cross. The Jews in the Middle Ages,* Princeton, NJ, 1994, p. 80.

57   Cf. the section "Signs in the Heavens" in Chapter 8.

58   Ekkehard Schenk zu Schweinsberg, *Die letzte Schlacht Karls d. Gr. Die bemalte Tischplatte von 1518 und die Regensburger Karlslegende am Anfang des 16. Jahrhunderts* (Hefte des Kunstgeschichtlichen Instituts der Universität Mainz 1), Mainz 1972; including a facsimile of Hain 4525 "Daz ist die loblich legend / von des grossen Kayser Karls streyt vor der stat Regenspurg geschehen" (The praiseworthy legend of the great emperor Charles's battle outside the town of Regensburg; undated).

59   On the cult of Charlemagne: Robert Folz, *Étude sur le culte liturgique de Charlemagne dans les églises de l'Empire,* Paris 1951; Kerner, *Karl der Große,* pp. 97–156; cf. also Pierre Monnet, Charlemagne à Franc-fort. Mémoire et espace urbain, in: *Geschichtliche Landeskunde* 60 (2007) pp. 117–30.

60   Helmut Beumann, Hagiographie "bewältigt." Unterwerfung und Christianisierung der Sachsen durch Karl den Großen, most recently in: Beumann, *Ausgewählte Aufsätze aus den Jahren 1966–1986,* Sigmaringen 1987, pp. 289–323.

61   Knut Görich, Otto III. öffnet das Karlsgrab in Aachen. Überlegungen zu Heiligen-verehrung, Heiligsprechung und Traditionsbildung, in: *Herrschaftsrepräsentation im*

ottonischen Sachsen, ed. Gerd Althoff and Ernst Schubert (VuF 46), Sigmaringen 1998, pp. 381–430; Görich, Erinnerung und ihre Aktualisierung: Otto III., Aachen und die Karlstradition, in: *Robert Folz (1910–1996). Mittler zwischen Frankreich und Deutschland,* ed. Franz Felten et al. (Geschichtliche Landeskunde 60), Stuttgart 2007, pp. 97–116.

62 František Graus, *Volk, Herrscher und Heiliger im Reich der Merowinger. Studien zur Hagiographie in der Merowingerzeit,* Prague 1965, p. 426.

63 *Analecta Hymnica Medii Aevi* (Medieval Latin hymns of the Catholic Church, 500–1400, in 55 volumes) 251. These verses were later reworked to relate to Frankfurt and Zurich.

64 Favier, *Charlemagne,* pp. 651–715.

65 Now in the Louvre; cf. the gallery catalog *Le trésor de Saint-Denis,* Paris 1991, pp. 264–71 No. 57.

66 Pape, Karlskult, pp. 138–81.

67 Recorded in [Pierre] Lanfrey, *Vie [Histoire] de Napoleon I,* vol. 3, pp. 417 and 420, quoted from James Bryce, *The Holy Roman Empire,* ³London 1871, pp. 358–9 notes c and d.

68 Goethe, *Dichtung und Wahrheit,* pt. 1, bk. 1, Sophien-Ausgabe, vol. 26, p. 27.

69 Houston Stewart Chamberlain, *Die Grundlagen des neunzehnten Jahrhunderts 2. Hälfte,* ⁵Munich 1904, pp. 617–9 and 666. This English translation from the website http://www.hschamberlain.net/grundlagen/division3_chapter7.html.

70 Quoted from: Arthur Moeller van den Bruck, *Das Ewige Reich,* ed. Hans Schwarz, Breslau 1933, pp. 92, 95, and 98. The original version (*Die Deutschen*) appeared in several volumes before 1914.

71 Cf. Henry Picker, *Hitlers Tischgespräche im Führerhauptquartier, 1941–1942,* new ed., ed. Percy Ernst Schramm in collaboration with Andreas Hillgruber and Martin Vogt, Stuttgart 1963, p. 230. Picker's record became available in English as *Hitler's Table Talk, 1941–1944: His Private Conversations,* trans. Norman Cameron and R. H. Stevens, ed. Hugh Trevor-Roper, London 1953 (reprinted New York 2000). Hitler himself warned Rosenberg not to portray Charlemagne as a slayer of the Saxons. One example of the negative portrayal of Charlemagne in this period is Ferdinand Thürmer, Karl der Große—Charlemagne—Karl der Sachsenschlächter, in: *Der Hammer* 33 (1934) pp. 231–2 (cited by Reinhard Bollmus, *Das Amt Rosenberg und seine Gegner. Studien zum Machtkampf im nationalsozialistischen Herrschaftssystem,* Munich 2006 [first published 1969], p. 349); Pape, Karlskult; Kerner, *Karl der Große,* pp. 181–91.

72 Rolf Köhn, Kirchenfeindliche und antichristliche Mittelalter-Rezeption im völkisch nationalsozialistischen Geschichtsbild. Die Beispiele Widukind und Stedinger, in: *Mittelalter-Rezeption. Ein Symposion,* ed. Peter Wapnewski, Stuttgart 1986, pp. 581–616, here pp. 594–602.

73 Hermann Löns, "Die rote Beeke," in: Löns, *Sämtliche Werke in acht Bänden,* ed. Friedrich Castelle, vol. 7, Leipzig 1928, pp. 29–41, with striking woodcuts by Erich Feyerabend (first published in Hanover 1912).

74 Alfred Rosenberg, *Der Mythus des 20. Jahrhunderts. Eine Wertung der seelisch-geistigen Gestaltenkämpfe unserer Zeit,* Munich, numerous editions. On this subject, see Borst, Karlsbild, pp. 397–8.

75 Cf. the section "Commemorating Charlemagne" above.

76 Edition: Frankfurt 1653. Cf. *Widukind. Forschungen zu einem Mythos*, ed. Stefan Brakensiek, Bielefeld 1997.

77 Quoted from Ludwig Quidde, "Karl der Grosse—Der Sachsenschlächter?," in: *Pariser Tageblatt* 3, Nos. 491–2 (17 and 18 April 1935), in each case p. 4, here No. 491. The *Pariser Tageblatt* was a German-language newspaper for émigrés.

78 *Karl der Große oder Charlemagne? Acht Antworten deutscher Geschichtsforscher,* Karl Hampe, Hans Naumann, Hermann Aubin, Martin Lintzel, Friedrich Baethgen, Albert Brackmann, Carl Erdman, and Wolfgang Windelband (Probleme der Gegenwart), Berlin 1935; all quotations here from the foreword, pp. 5–6.–On the foreword, cf. Werner, *Karl der Große in der Ideologie des Nationalsozialismus*, pp. 50–5. The Nobel Peace Prize laureate Ludwig Quidde (cf. the previous note) also added his voice to this protest.

79 *Karl der Große oder Charlemagne?*, p. 105.

80 *Die Reden Hitlers am Parteitag der Freiheit 1935,* Munich 1935, p. 73. Cf. Reinhard Bollmus, *Amt Rosenberg und seine Gegner. Studien zum Machtkampf im nationalsozialistischen Herrschaftssystem,* ²Munich 2006, pp. 195–6; this is the source of the following quotation by Rosenberg: "I have never referred to Charlemagne as a 'slayer of the Saxons,' let along condoned anything that might lead to Charlemagne being banished from German history."

81 Rosenberg, *Der Mythus des 20. Jahrhunderts,* 1942 edition (edition number not given), does not actually contain the term *Sachsenschlächter* (slayer of the Saxons); on p. 186 it is simply stated that Charlemagne "used religion as a way of sanctifying his own status" and that "although Widukind fought for himself, at the same time, he was also fighting for the freedom of all Nordic peoples. Even so, Charlemagne remained the basic founder of the German Empire."

82 A second edition was published in 1937.

83 Trevor-Roper, *Hitler's Table Talk,* pp. 287–88.

84 Kerner, *Karl der Grosse,* plate 24.

85 Hermann Aubin, Vom Aufbau des mittelalterlichen Deutschen Reiches, in: *HZ* 162 (1940) pp. 479–508, here pp. 480–1, 485, and 507.

86 Werner, *Karl der Große in der Ideologie des Nationalsozialismus,* pp. 23–4.

87 Horst Fuhrmann, Kaiser Karl der Große. Geschichte und Geschichten, most recently in: Fuhrmann, *Einladung ins Mittelalter* (Beck'sche Reihe), Munich 2000, pp. 65–76.

88 This anniversary exhibition resulted in the publication of four monumental volumes of academic studies of Charlemagne and his age (*Karl der Große. Lebenswerk und Nachleben,* 1965–1967).

89 For example: Hans-Jürgen Ferdinand, *Karl der Große: Visionär und Reformer.* Historischer Roman, Aachen 2008.

90 Josef Kraus, Der historische Analphabetismus greift um sich. Schüler wissen mit zentralen Ereignissen nichts mehr anzufangen. Geschichtsunterricht ohne Geschichte, in: *Frankfurter Allgemeine Zeitung,* 21 June 2012, No. 142 p. 6.

91 Klaus Schroeder, Monika Deutz-Schroeder, Rita Quasten, and Dagmar Schulze Heuling, *Später Sieg der Diktaturen? Zeitgeschichtliche Kenntnisse und Urteile von Jugendlichen,* Frankfurt 2012.

92   On this subject, cf. the interview with Gerhard Wolf, who conducted and evaluated the findings of the survey, in: *Frankfurter Allgemeine Sonntagszeitung,* 8 July 2012, No. 27.

93   Examples in Werner, Karl der Große oder Charlemagne?, pp. 3–4.

94   Christopher Dawson, *The Making of Europe: An Introduction to the History of European Unity,* London 1932, p. 192.

95   František Graus, Die Einheit der Geschichte, in: Graus, *Ausgewählte Aufsätze,* pp. 197–211, here p. 204.

96   Oskar Halecki, *The Limits and Divisions of European History,* London/New York 1950.

97   František Graus, *Lebendige Vergangenheit. Überlieferung im Mittelalter und in den Vorstellungen vom Mittelalter,* Cologne/Vienna 1975.

98   Jacques Le Goff, *The Birth of Europe,* Oxford 2005, pp. 32 and 37.

99   Borgolte, *Christen, Juden, Muselmanen,* p. 305.

100 Alessandro Barbero, *Carlo Magno. Un padre dell'Europa,* Rome/Bari 2000. Cf. also Rosamond McKitterick, *Charlemagne: The Formation of a European Identity,* Cambridge 2008.

101 Favier, *Charlemagne.*

102 Karl Löwith, *Meaning in History: The Theological Implications of the Philosophy of History,* Chicago 1957, pp. 20–21.

103 Henri Pirenne, *Mahomet et Charlemagne,* Paris/Brussels 1937; translated into German with the title *Mohammed und Karl der Große. Untergang der Antike am Mittelmeer und Aufstieg des germanischen Mittelalters,* most recently Frankfurt am Main 1985.

104 Cf., for example, Richard Hodges and David Whitehouse, *Mohammed, Charlemagne and the Origins of Europe,* London 1983; Dietrich Claude, *Der Handel im westlichen Mittelmeer während des Frühmittelalters. Bericht über ein Kolloquium der Kommission für Altertumskunde Mittel- und Nordeuropas im Jahr 1980,* Göttingen 1985; and especially McCormick, *Origins.*

105 As an example, see: Borgolte, *Christen, Juden, Muselmanen,* cf. the index of persons.

106 Classen, *Karl der Große,* p. 1.

107 Cf. the section "The Prelude to Imperial Rule" in Chapter 7.

108 Cf. the section "Attention Turns to the Near East" in Chapter 8.

109 Text in Ewald Jammers, *Das Karlsoffizium "Regali natus." Einführung, Text und Übertragung in moderne Notenschrift,* Strasbourg 1934 (reprinted 1984).

SELECTED BIBLIOGRAPHY

Der Aachener Dom als Ort geschichtlicher Erinnerung. Werkbuch der Studierenden des Historischen Instituts der RWTH Aachen, ed. and with an introduction by Max Kerner, Cologne 2004.

Die Admonitio generalis Karls des Großen, ed. Hubert Mordek, Klaus Zechiel-Eckes, and Michael Glatthaar (MGH Fontes iuris Germ. ant. 16), Hanover 2012.

[Alcuin]. *The Rhetoric of Alcuin and Charlemagne. A Translation, with an Introduction. The Latin Text, and Notes,* by Wilbur Samuel Howell, New York 1965.

Alcuin, de York à Tours. Écriture, pouvoire et réseaux dans l'Europe du haut Moyen Âge, ed. Philippe Depreux and Bruno Judic, in: *Annales de Bretagne et des Pays de l'Ouest* 111/3 (2004), Rennes 2004.

Am Vorabend der Kaiserkrönung. Das Epos "Karolus Magnus et Leo papa" und der Papstbesuch in Paderborn 799, ed. Peter Godman, Jörg Jarnut, and Peter Johanek, Berlin 2002.

Annales Mettenses priores primum recensuit B(ernhardus) de Simson (MGH SS rer. Germ. [10]).

Annales regni Francorum . . . qui dicuntur Annales Laurissenses maiores et Einhardi, ed. Friedrich Kurze (MGH SS rer. Germ. [6]). German edition: see *Quellen zur karolingischen Reichsgeschichte,* vol. 1.

Anton, Hans Hubert, *Fürstenspiegel und Herrscherethos in der Karolingerzeit* (Bonner Hist. Forschungen 32), Bonn 1968.

Bachrach, Bernard S., *Early Carolingian Warfare. Prelude to Empire,* Philadelphia 2001.

Bauer, Franz Alto, Das Bild der Stadt Rom in karolingischer Zeit: Der Anonymus Einsidlensis, in: *Römische Quartalschrift* 92 (1997) pp. 190–228.

———, *Das Bild der Stadt Rom im Frühmittelalter. Papststiftungen im Spiegel des Liber Pontificalis von Gregor dem Dritten bis zu Leo dem Dritten* (Palilia 14), Wiesbaden 2004.

Bayer, Clemens M. M., Die karolingische Bauinschrift des Aachener Domes, in: *Der Aachener Dom*, pp. 185–95.

Becher, Matthias, *Eid und Herrschaft. Untersuchungen zum Herrscherethos Karls des Großen* (VuF Sonderband 39), Sigmaringen 1993.

———, Karl der Große und Papst Leo III. Die Ereignisse der Jahre 799 und 800 aus der Sicht der Zeitgenossen, in: *799. Kunst und Kultur der Karolingerzeit*, pp. 22–36.

———, *Non enim habent regem—Antiqui Saxones . . .* Verfassung und Ethnogenese in Sachsen während des 8. Jahrhunderts, in: *Studien zur Sachsenforschung* 12 (1999) pp. 1–31.

———, Die Kaiserkrönung im Jahr 800. Eine Streitfrage zwischen Karl dem Großen und Papst Leo III., in: *Rhein. Vjbll.* 66 (2002) pp. 1–38.

Belting, Hans, Studien zum beneventanischen Hof im 8. Jahrhundert, in: *Dumbarton Oaks Papers* 16 (1962) pp. 142–93 with 6 plates.

———, Probleme der Kunstgeschichte Italiens im Frühmittelalter, in: *FmaSt* 1 (1967) pp. 94–143.

———, *Bild und Kult. Eine Geschichte des Bildes vor dem Zeitalter der Kunst,* ²Munich 1991.

Berschin, Walter, *Biographie und Epochenstil im lateinischen Mittelalter,* vol. 3, *Karolingische Biographie, 750–920,* Stuttgart 1991.

Bischoff, Bernhard, Die Bibliothek im Dienst der Schule, in: Bischoff, *Mittelalterliche Studien,* vol. 3, pp. 213–33.

———, Die Kölner Nonnenhandschriften und das Skriptorium von Chelles, in: Bischoff, *Mittelalterliche Studien,* vol. 1, pp. 16–34.

———, *Mittelalterliche Studien. Ausgewählte Aufsätze zur Schriftkunde und Literaturgeschichte,* 3 vols., Stuttgart 1966–1981.

———, Theodulf und der Ire Cadac-Andreas, in: Bischoff, *Mittelalterliche Studien,* vol. 2, pp. 19–25.

Borgolte, Michael, *Der Gesandtenaustausch der Karolinger mit den Abbasiden und den Patriarchen von Jerusalem* (Münchener Beiträge zur Mediävistik und Renaissance-Forschung 25), Munich 1976.

———, Papst Leo III., Karl der Große und der Filioquestreit in Jerusalem, in: *Byzantina* 10 (1980) pp. 403–27.

———, *Die Grafen Alemanniens in merowingischer und karolingischer Zeit. Eine Prosopographie* (Archäologie und Geschichte 2), Sigmaringen 1986.

———, *Christen, Juden, Muselmanen. Die Erben der Antike und der Aufstieg des Abendlandes, 300 bis 1400* (Siedler Geschichte Europas), Munich 2006.

Borst, Arno, Das Karlsbild in der Geschichtswissenschaft vom Humanismus bis heute, in: *Karl der Große,* vol. 4 pp. 364–402.

———, *Das Buch der Naturgeschichte. Plinius und seine Leser im Zeitalter des Pergaments* (Abhandlungen Heidelberg 1994, 1), Heidelberg 1994.

——— (ed.), *Schriften zur Komputistik im Frankenreich von 721 bis 818* (MGH Quellen zur Geistesgeschichte des Mittelalters 21/I–III), Hanover 2006.

Brunhölzl, Franz, *Geschichte der lateinischen Literatur*, vol. 1, *Von Cassiodor bis zum Ausklang der karolingischen Erneuerung*, Munich 1975.

Bullough, Donald A., *The Age of Charlemagne*, London 1965 (2nd ed. 1973, reissued 1980). German translation: *Karl der Große und seine Zeit*, Wiesbaden 1966.

———, *Alcuin. Achievement and Reputation* (Education and Society in the Middle Ages and the Renaissance 16), Leiden 2002.

Busch, Jörg W., *Die Herrschaften der Karolinger, 714–911* (Enzyklopädie deutscher Geschichte 88), Munich 2011.

Capitulare de villis. Cod. Guelf. 254 Helmst. der Herzog August Bibliothek Wolfenbüttel, ed. Carlrichard Brühl, Stuttgart 1971; also: MGH Capit. 1 pp. 82–91.

Carolingian Essays. Andrewa W. Mellon Lectures in Early Christian Studies, ed. Uta-Renate Blumenthal, Washington, DC 1983.

Chronicon Anianense, cf. Kettemann.

Chronicon Moissiacense, cf. Kettemann.

Classen, Peter, Die Geschichte der Königspfalz Ingelheim bis zur Verpfändung an Kurpfalz 1375, in: *Ingelheim am Rhein. Forschungen und Studien zur Geschichte Ingelheims*, ed. Johanne Autenrieth, Ingelheim am Rhein 1964, pp. 87–146.

———, *Ausgewählte Aufsätze*, with Carl Joachim Classen and Johannes Fried, ed. Josef Fleckenstein (VuF 28), Sigmaringen 1983.

———, *Karl der Große, das Papsttum und Byzanz. Die Begründung des karolingischen Kaisertums*, ed. Horst Fuhrmann and Claudia Märtl (Beiträge zur Geschichte und Quellenkunde des Mittelalters 9), Sigmaringen 1985.

Codex Carolinus, ed. Wilhelm Gundlach, MGH Epp. 3, pp. 467–657.

Collins, Roger, *Early Medieval Europe, 300–1000,* Basingstoke/London 1991.

———, *Charlemagne*, Basingstoke/London 1998.

Continuator Fredegarii (so-called), see Fredegar und Continuationes.

Crivello, Fabrizio, Charlotte Denoël, and Peter Orth, *Das Godescalc-Evangelistar. Eine Prachthandschrift für Karl den Großen*, with a preface by Florentine Mütherich, Gütersloh/Munich/Darmstadt 2011.

Depreux, Philippe, *Prosopographie de l'entourage de Louis le Pieux (781–840)* (Instrumenta 1), Sigmaringen 1997.

Dombaumeistertagung in Aachen 2009. Vorträge zum Aachener Dom, ed. Helmuth Maintz (Karlsverein-Dombauverein Schriftenreihe 13), Aachen 2011.

Drews, Wolfram, *Die Karolinger und die Abbasiden von Bagdad. Legitimationsstrategien frühmittelalterlicher Herrscherdynastien im transkulturellen Vergleich* (Europa im Mittelalter 12), Berlin 2009.

Dutton, Paul Edward, cf. Einhard.

Der Dynastiewechsel von 751. Vorgeschichte, Legitimationsstrategien und Erinnerung, ed. Matthias Becher and Jörg Jarnut, Münster 2004.

[Einhard], *Charlemagne's Courtier. The Complete Einhard*, ed. and transl. Paul Edward Dutton (Readings in Medieval Civilizations and Cultures 3), Peterborough, Ontario 1998.

Einhard. Studien zu Leben und Werk, ed. Hermann Schefers (Arbeiten der Hessischen Historischen Kommission, Neue Folge 12), Darmstadt 1997.

Einhardi Vita Karoli Magni, ed. O. Holder-Egger (MGH SS rer. Germ. [25]); for an English translation of Einhard's *Life of Charlemagne*, see the online medieval sourcebook resource created by Fordham University, http://legacy.fordham.edu/halsall/basis/einhard.asp.

Euw, Anton von, Karl der Große als Schüler Alkuins, das Kuppelmosaik des Aachener Domes und das Maiestasbild in Codex C 80 der Zentralbibliothek Zürich, in: *Der Aachener Dom*, pp. 197–217.

Falkenstein, Ludwig, *Der "Lateran" der karolingischen Pfalz zu Aachen* (Kölner Historische Abhandlungen 13), Cologne/Graz 1966.

———, *Karl der Große und die Entstehung des Aachener Marienstifts* (Quellen und Forschungen aus dem Gebiet der Geschichte, Neue Folge 3), Paderborn 1981.

———, Die Kirche der hl. Maria zu Aachen und Saint-Corneille zu Compiègne, in: *Celica Jherusalem. Festschrift für Erich Stephany*, ed. Clemens Bayer, Theo Jülich, and Manfred Kuhl, Siegburg/Cologne 1986, pp. 13–70.

———, Pfalz und *vicus* Aachen, in: *Orte der Herrschaft. Mittelalterliche Königspfalzen*, ed. Caspar Ehlers, Göttingen 2002, pp. 131–81.

Favier, Jean, *Charlemagne*, Paris 1999.

Flach, Dietmar, *Untersuchungen zur Verfassung und Verwaltung des Aachener Reichsgutes von der Karolingerzeit bis zur Mitte des 14. Jahrhunderts* (Veröffentlichungen des Max-Planck-Instituts für Geschichte 46), Göttingen 1976.

Fleckenstein, Josef, *Die Hofkapelle der deutschen Könige*, vol. 1, *Die karolingische Hofkapelle* (Schriften der MGH 16/1), Stuttgart 1959.

Föller, Daniel, *Wikinger. Wissen, was stimmt*, Freiburg/Basel/Vienna 2011.

Das Frankfurter Konzil von 794. Kristallisationspunkt karolingischer Kultur, ed. Rainer Berndt (Quellen und Abhandlungen zur mittelrheinischen Kirchengeschichte 80), 2 vols., Mainz 1997.

[Fredegar und Continuationes]: *Quellen zur Geschichte des 7. und 8. Jahrhunderts. Die vier Bücher der Chroniken des sogenannten Fredegar. Die Fortsetzungen der Chroniken des sogenannten Fredegar. Das Buch von der Geschichte der Franken. Das alte Leben Lebuins. Jonas erstes Buch vom Leben Columbans*, ed. and trans. Herwig Wolframs, Andreas Kusternig, and Herbert Haupt (Ausgewählte Quellen zur Geschichte des Mittelalters. Freiherr vom Stein–Gedächtnisausgabe IVa), Darmstadt 1982.

Freund, Stephan, *Von den Agilolfingern zu den Karolingern. Bayerns Bischöfe zwischen Kirchenorganisation, Reichsintegration und Karolingischer Reform (700–847)* (Schriftenreihe zur bayerischen Landesgeschichte 144), Munich 2004.

Fried, Johannes, *Der Weg in die Geschichte. Die Ursprünge Deutschlands bis 1024* (Propyläen Geschichte Deutschlands 1), Berlin 1994.

———, Fulda in der Bildungs- und Geistesgeschichte des früheren Mittelalters, in: *Kloster Fulda in der Welt der Karolinger und Ottonen*, ed. Gangolf Schrimpf, Frankfurt am Main 1996, pp. 3–38.

——, Elite und Ideologie; oder, Die Nachfolgeordnung Karls des Großen vom Jahre 813, in: *La royauté et les élites dans l'Europe Carolingienne (du début du IXe aux environs de 920)*, ed. Régine Lejan (Centre d'Histoire de l'Europe du Nord-Ouest), Lille 1998, pp. 71–109.

——, Papst Leo III. besucht Karl den Großen in Paderborn; oder, Einhards Schweigen, in: *HZ* 272 (2001) pp. 281–326.

——, Karl der Große. Geschichte und Mythos, in: *Mythen Europas. Schlüsselfiguren der Imagination. Mittelalter,* ed. Inge Milfull and Michael Neumann, Regensburg 2004, pp. 15–46.

——, Imperium Romanum. Das römische Reich und der mittelalterliche Reichsgedanke, in: *Millennium* 3 (2006) pp. 1–42.

——, *Donation of Constantine and Constitutum Constantini. The Misinterpretation of a Fiction and Its Original Meaning. With a Contribution of Wolfram Brandes: "The Satraps of Constantine"* (Millennium-Studien 3), Berlin/New York 2007.

——, Ein Gastmahl Karls des Großen, in Fried, *Zu Gast im Mittelalter,* pp. 13–46.

——, *Zu Gast im Mittelalter,* Munich 2007.

——, Zu Herkunft und Entstehungszeit des "Constitutum Constantini." Zugleich eine Selbstanzeige, in: *DA* 63 (2007) pp. 603–11.

——, Erfahrung und Ordnung. Die Friedenskonstitution Karls des Großen vom Jahr 806, in: *Herrscher- und Fürstentestamente im westeuropäischen Mittelalter,* ed. Brigitte Kasten, Cologne/Weimar/Vienna 2008, pp. 145–92.

——, Kanonistik und Mediävistik. Neue Literatur zu Kirchenrecht, Inzest und zur Ehe Pippins von Italien, in: *HZ* 294 (2012) pp. 115–41.

——, Karl der Große, Rom und Aachen. *Actus b. Silvestri* und *Constitutum Constantini* als Wegweiser zur Pfalz Karls des Großen, in: *Von Kreuzburg nach Munich. Lebensstationen von Horst Fuhrmann,* ed. Martina Hartmann and Claudia Märtl, Hanover 2013.

Fried, Johannes, et al. (eds.), *794—Karl der Große in Frankfurt am Main. Ein König bei der Arbeit. Ausstellung zum 1200-Jahre-Jubiläum der Stadt Frankfurt am Main* (catalog), Sigmaringen 1994.

Fuhrmann, Horst, Das Papsttum und das kirchliche Leben im Frankenreich, in: *Settimane Spoleto 1979* (published 1981), pp. 419–56.

Gemeinhardt, Peter, *Die Filioque-Kontroverse zwischen Ost- und Westkirche im Frühmittelalter* (Arbeiten zur Kirchengeschichte 82), Berlin/New York 2002.

Glatthaar, Michael, Zur Datierung der *Epistola generalis* Karls des Großen, in: *DA* 66 (2010) pp. 455–77.

Graus, František, *Ausgewählte Aufsätze,* ed. Jürgen Gilomen, Peter Moraw, and Rainer C. Schwinges (VuF 55), Stuttgart 2002.

Grierson, Philip, Money and Coinage under Charlemagne, in: *Karl der Große,* vol. 1 (1965), pp. 501–36.

Gröber, Gustav, *Übersicht über die lateinische Literatur von der Mitte des VI. Jahrhunderts bis zur Mitte des XIV. Jahrhunderts* (Grundriß der romanischen Philologie 2, 1), Straßburg 1902; ed. Walter Bulst, Munich (undated).

Hack, Achim Thomas, *Das Empfangszeremoniell bei mittelalterlichen Papst-Kaiser-Treffen* (Forschungen zur Kaiser- und Papstgeschichte des Mittelalters. Beihefte zu J. F. Böhmer, Regesta Imperii 18), Cologne/Weimar/Vienna 1999.

———, *Codex Carolinus. Päpstliche Epistolographie im 8. Jahrhundert* (Päpste und Papsttum 35), 2 vols., Stuttgart 2006/2007.

———, Karl der Große hoch zu Roß. Zur Geschichte einer (historisch falschen) Bildtradition, in: *Francia* 35 (2008) pp. 349–79.

Hageneder, Othmar, Das *crimen maiestatis,* der Prozeß gegen die Attentäter Papst Leos III. und die Kaiserkrönung Karls des Großen, in: *Aus Kirche und Reich. Studien zu Theologie, Politik und Recht im Mittelalter. Festschrift für Friedrich Kempf,* ed. Hubert Mordek, Sigmaringen 1983, pp. 55–79.

Hägermann, Dieter, *Karl der Große. Herrscher des Abendlandes,* Berlin 2000.

Hammer, Carl I., *From* Ducatus *to* Regnum. *Ruling Bavaria under the Merovingians and Early Carolingians* (Collection Haut Moyen Âge 2), Turnhout 2007.

Hannig, Jürgen, Pauperiores vassi de infra palatio? Zur Entstehung der karolingischen Königsbotenorganisation, in: *MIÖG* 91 (1983) pp. 309–74.

———, Zentrale Kontrolle und regionale Machtbalance. Beobachtungen zum System der karolingischen Königsboten am Beispiel des Mittelrheingebietes, in: *Archiv für Kulturgeschichte* 66 (1984) pp. 1–46.

Hartmann, Florian, *Hadrian I. (772–795). Frühmittelalterliches Adelspapsttum und die Lösung Roms vom byzantinischen Kaiser* (Päpste und Papsttum 34), Stuttgart 2006.

Hartmann, Martina, *Die Königin im frühen Mittelalter,* Stuttgart 2009.

Hartmann, Wilfried, *Die Synoden der Karolingerzeit im Frankenreich und in Italien* (Konziliengeschichte, Reihe A), Paderborn 1989.

———, *Kirche und Kirchenrecht um 900. Die Bedeutung der spätkarolingischen Zeit für Tradition und Innovation im kirchlichen Recht* (Schriften der MGH 58), Hanover 2008.

———, *Karl der Große,* Stuttgart 2010.

Hechberger, Werner, *Adel im fränkisch-deutschen Mittelalter. Zur Anatomie eines Forschungsproblems,* Ostfildern 2005.

Hentze, Wilhelm (ed.), cf. *De Karolo rege et Leone papa.*

Hincmarus, *De ordine palatii,* ed. Thomas Gross and Rudolf Schieffer (MGH Fontes iuris Germanici antiqui 3), Hanover 1980.

Hoffmann, Hartmut, *Untersuchungen zur karolingischen Annalistik* (Bonner Historische Forschungen 10), Bonn 1958.

Ilisch, Lutz, Arabische Kupfermünzen an der Ostsee und die Gesandtschaft Karls des Großen an den Kalifen, in: *Numismatisches Nachrichtenblatt* 61 (August 2012) pp. 296–302.

Jahn, Joachim, *Ducatus Baiuvariorum. Das bairische Herzogtum der Agilolfinger* (Monographien zur Geschichte des Mittelalters 35), Stuttgart 1991.

Jarnut, Jörg, Genealogie und politische Bedeutung der agilolfingischen Herzöge, *MIÖG* 99 (1991) pp. 1–22, also in: Jarnut, *Herrschaft und Ethnogenese im Frühen Mittelalter.*

Gesammelte Aufsätze, ed. Matthias Becher, Stefanie Dick, and Nicola Karthaus, Münster 2002, pp. 139–60.

Kantorowicz, Ernst H., *Laudes regiae. A Study in Liturgical Acclamations and Mediaeval Ruler Worship,* [2]Berkeley/Los Angeles 1958.

Karl der Große. Lebenswerk und Nachleben, ed. Wolfgang Braunfels, 4 vols., Düsseldorf 1965–1967.

Karl der Große oder Charlemagne? Acht Antworten deutscher Geschichtsforscher. Karl Hampe, Hans Naumann, Hermann Aubin, Martin Lintzel, Friedrich Baethgen, Albert Brackmann, Carl Erdmann, and Wolfgang Windelband (Probleme der Gegenwart), Berlin 1935.

Karl der Große und das Erbe der Kulturen, ed. Franz-Reiner Erkens (Akten des 8. Symposiums des Mediävistenverbandes), Berlin 2001.

Die karolingische Pfalzkapelle in Aachen. Material, Bautechnik, Restaurierung, ed. Andrea Pufke (Arbeitsheft der rheinischen Denkmalpflege 78), Worms 2012.

De Karolo rege et Leone papa. Der Bericht über die Zusammenkunft Karls des Großen mit Leo III. in Paderborn 799 in einem Epos für Karl den Kaiser. Mit vollständiger Farbeproduktion nach der Handschrift der Zentralbibliothek Zürich, Ms. C 78, und Beiträgen von Lutz E. v. Padberg, Johannes Schwind and Hans-Walther Stork, ed. Wilhelm Hentze, Paderborn 1999, Beiheft.

Karolus magnus et Leo papa. Ein Paderborner Epos vom Jahre 799. Mit Beiträgen von Helmut Beumann, Franz Brunhölzl, Wilhelm Winkelmann (Studien und Quellen zur westfälischen Geschichte 8), Paderborn 1966.

Kasten, Brigitte, *Adalhard von Corbie. Die Biographie eines karolingischen Politikers und Klostervorstehers* (Studia humaniora 3), Düsseldorf 1986.

———, *Königssöhne und Königsherrschaft. Untersuchungen zur Teilhabe am Reich in der Merowinger- und Karolingerzeit* (Schriften der MGH 44), Hanover 1997.

Kerner, Max, *Karl der Große. Entschleierung eines Mythos,* Cologne/Weimar/Vienna [2]2001.

Kershaw, Paul J. E., *Peaceful Kings: Peace, Power, and Early Medieval Political Imagination,* Oxford 2011.

Kettemann, Walter, Subsidia Anianensia. Überlieferungs- und textgeschichtliche Untersuchungen zur Geschichte Witiza-Benedikts, seines Klosters Aniane und zur sogenannten "anianischen Reform" mit kommentierten Editionen der *"Vita Benedicti Anianensis,"* "Notitia de servitio monasteriorum," des ‹Chronicon Moissiacense/Anianense› sowie zweier Lokaltraditionen aus Aniane, 2 parts, doctoral thesis, Duisburg 2000: duepublico.uni-duisburg-essen.de/servlets/DerivateServlet/Derivate-19910/ Kettemann_Diss.pdf.

Knittel, Hermann, see *Visio Wettini.*

Krämer, Gudrun, *Geschichte des Islam,* Munich 2005.

Krönungen. Könige in Aachen—Geschichte und Mythos. Katalog der Ausstellung, ed. Mario Kramp, Mainz 2000.

Kuchenbuch, Ludolf, *Bäuerliche Gesellschaft und Klosterherrschaft im 9. Jahrhundert. Studien zur Sozialstruktur der Familia der Abtei Prüm* (Vierteljahrschrift für Sozial- und Wirtschaftsgeschichte, Beiheft 66), Wiesbaden 1978.

——, *Grundherrschaft im früheren Mittelalter* (Historisches Seminar, Neue Folge 1), Idstein 1991.

——, *Reflexive Mediävistik. Textus, Opus, Feudalismus,* Frankfurt/New York 2012.

——, Zahlendenken und Zahlengebrauch in Registern der seigneurialen Güter- und Einkünftekontrolle im 9. Jahrhundert, in: *Was zählt. Ordnungsangebote, Gebrauchsformen und Erfahrungsmodalitäten des "numerus" im Mittelalter,* ed. Moritz Wedell, Cologne/Weimar/Vienna 2012, pp. 235–72.

Lammers, Walther, Ein karolingisches Bildprogramm in der Aula regia von Ingelheim, in: Lammers, *Vestigia Mediaevalia. Ausgewählte Aufsätze zur mittelalterlichen Historiographie, Landes- und Kirchengeschichte* (Frankfurter Historische Abhandlungen 19), Wiesbaden 1979, pp. 219–83.

Levison, Wilhelm, *Aus rheinischer und fränkischer Frühzeit. Ausgewählte Aufsätze,* Düsseldorf 1948.

Libellus de imperatoria potestate in urbe Roma, ed. Roberto Valentini and Giuseppe Zucchetti, *Codice topografico della Città di Roma,* vol. 2 (Fonti per la Storia d'Italia 88), Rome 1942. regis.

Liber pontificalis: L(éopold) Duchesne, *Le Liber pontificalis. Texte, introduction et commentaire,* vol. 1 (Textes Bibliothèque des Écoles Françaises d'Athènes et de Rome, ser. 2, vol. 1), Paris 1886.

Löwe, Heinz, Das Karlsbuch Notkers von St. Gallen und sein zeitgeschichtlicher Hintergrund, in: Löwe, *Von Cassiodor zu Dante. Ausgewählte Aufsätze zur Geschichtsschreibung und politischen Ideenwelt des Mittelalters,* Berlin/New York 1973, pp. 123–48.

Die Macht des Königs. Herrschaft in Europa vom Frühmittelalter bis in die Neuzeit, ed. Bernhard Jussen, Munich 2005.

McCormick, Michael, Textes, images et iconoclasme dans le cadre des relations entre Byzance et l'occident carolingien, in: *Settimane Spoleto* 41 (1994) pp. 95–158.

——, *Origins of the European Economy. Communications and Commerce, A.D. 300–900,* Cambridge 2001.

——, *Charlemagne's Survey of the Holy Land: Wealth, Personnel, and Buildings of a Mediterranean Church between Antiquity and the Middle Ages* (Dumbarton Oaks Medieval Humanities), Washington, DC, 2011.

McKitterick, Rosamond (ed.), *Carolingian Culture, Emulation, and Innovation,* Cambridge 1984.

——, *Charlemagne. The Formation of a European Identity,* Cambridge 2008. German translation: *Karl der Große,* Darmstadt 2008.

Melville, Gerd, *Die Welt der mittelalterlichen Klöster. Geschichte und Lebensformen,* Munich 2012.

Mettke, Heinz, *Älteste deutsche Dichtung und Prosa. Ausgewählte Texte,* Leipzig 1976.

Metz, Wolfgang, *Das karolingische Reichsgut. Eine verfassungs- und verwaltungsgeschichtliche Untersuchung,* Berlin 1960.

——, *Zur Erforschung des karolingischen Reichsgutes* (Erträge der Forschung 4), Darmstadt 1971.

Meyer, Heinz, and Rudolf Suntrup, *Lexikon der mittelalterlichen Zahlenbedeutungen* (Münstersche Mittelalterschriften 56), Munich 1987.

Migne, see *PL.*

Mordek, Hubert, *Bibliotheca capitularium regum Francorum manuscripta. Überlieferung und Traditionszusammenhang der fränkischen Herrschererlasse* (MGH Hilfsmittel 15), Munich 1995.

———, Frühmittelalterliche Gesetzgeber und iustitia in Miniaturen weltlicher Rechtshandschriften, in: La giustizia nell'alto medioevo (sec. V–VIII), in: *Settimane Spoleto* 42 (1994, published 1995) pp. 997–1052.

Mordek, Hubert, and Gerhard Schmitz, Neue Kapitularien und Kapitulariensammlungen, in: *DA* 43 (1987) pp. 361–439.

Murbach Annals = various annals derived from this putative original source (now lost) and recorded in: MGH SS 1 pp. 22–44.

Nees, Laurence, *A Tainted Mantle. Hercules and the Classical Tradition at the Carolingian Court* (University of Pennsylvania Press, Middle Ages Series), Philadelphia 1991.

Nelson, Janet L., *Opposition to Charlemagne* (German Historical Institute in London, 2008 Annual Lecture), London 2009.

Noble, Thomas F. X., *Images, Iconoclasm, and the Carolingians,* Philadelphia 2009.

Notker, *Gesta Karoli,* ed. Hans F. Haefele (MGH SS rer. Germ., Neue Folge 12); bilingual: Notker, *Taten Karls,* in: *Quellen zur karolingischen Reichsgeschichte,* vol. 3.

Oexle, Otto Gerhard, Die Karolinger und die Stadt des heiligen Arnulf, in: *FmaSt* 1 (1967) pp. 250–364.

———, *Forschungen zu monastischen und geistlichen Gemeinschaften im Westfränkischen Bereich,* Munich 1978.

Opus Caroli regis contra synodum (Libri Carolini), ed. Ann Freeman with the assistance of Paul Meyvaert (MGH Concilia 2 Suppl. 1), Hanover 1998.

Otto der Große und das Römische Reich. Kaisertum von der Antike bis zum Mittelalter, Ausstellungskatalog, ed. Matthias Puhle and Gabriele Köster, Regensburg 2012.

Padberg, Lutz E. von, *Mission und Christianisierung. Formen und Folgen bei Angelsachsen und Franken im 7. und 8. Jahrhundert,* Stuttgart 1995.

———, Das Paderborner Treffen von 799 im Kontext der Geschichte Karls des Großen, in: *De Karolo rege et Leone papa,* pp. 9–104.

———, *Christianisierung im Mittelalter,* Darmstadt/Mainz 2006.

Pape, Matthias, Der Karlskult an Wendepunkten der neueren deutschen Geschichte, in: *HJb* 120 (2000) pp. 138–81.

Patzold, Steffen, Normen im Buch. Überlegungen zu Geltungsansprüchen sogenannter "Kapitularien," in: *FmaSt* 41 (2007, published 2008) pp. 331–50.

Paulus Diaconus = Karl Neff, *Die Gedichte des Paulus Diaconus und erklärende Ausgabe* (Quellen und Untersuchungen zur lateinischen Philologie des Mittelalters III/4), Munich 1908.

PL (Patrologia Latina) = Jacques-Paul Migne, *Patrologiae cursus completus sive bibliotheca universalis integra, uniformis, commoda, oeconomica omnium ss. patrum, doctorum scriptorumque ecclesiasticorum qui ab aevo apostolico ad usque Innocentii III tempora floruerunt*, Paris 1844–, with volume number.

Plotzek, Joachim M., Zur Geschichte der Kölner Dombibliothek, in: *Glaube und Wissen im Mittelalter. Die Kölner Dombibliothek*, ed. Joachim M. Plotzek et al., Munich 1998.

Pohl, Walter, *Die Awaren. Ein Steppenvolk in Mitteleuropa, 567–822 n. Chr.*, ²Munich 2002.

Quellen zur karolingischen Reichsgeschichte, 3 vols. (Freiherr vom Stein–Gedächtnisausgabe 5–7), Darmstadt 1955–1960 (with translations into German of, among other works and authors, the *ArF*, the *Vita Karoli*, Notker, Thegan, and the so-called Astronomus).

Regino von Prüm, *Das Sendhandbuch des Regino von Prüm*, ed. Wilfried Hartmann (Ausgewählte Quellen zur deutschen Geschichte des Mittelalters. Freiherr vom Stein–Gedächtnisausgabe 42), Darmstadt 2004.

Rösch, Gerhard, ONOMA ΒΑΣΙΛΕΙΑΣ. *Studien zum offiziellen Gebrauch der Kaisertitel in spätantiker und frühbyzantinischer Zeit* (Byzantina Vindobonensia 10), Vienna 1978.

Rotter, Ekkehart, *Abendland und Sarazenen. Das okzidentale Araberbild und seine Entstehung im Frühmittelalter* (Studien zur Sprache, Geschichte und Kultur des islamischen Orients 11), Berlin/New York 1986.

Schaller, Dieter, Vortrags- und Zirkulardichtung am Hof Karls des Großen, in: *Mittellateinisches Jahrbuch* 6 (1970) pp. 14–36.

——, Das Aachener Epos für Karl den Kaiser, in: *FmaSt* 10 (1976) pp. 134–68.

Schefers, Hermann, see *Einhard*.

Schieffer, Rudolf, *Neues von der Kaiserkrönung Karls des Großen* (SB Munich 2004, 2), Munich 2004.

——, *Die Zeit des karolingischen Großreiches, 714–887* (Gebhardt, Handbuch der Deutschen Geschichte 2), Stuttgart 2005.

——, *Die Karolinger*, ⁴Stuttgart 2006.

Schlesinger, Walter, Die Hufe im Frankenreich, in: *Untersuchungen zur eisenzeitlichen und frühmittelalterlichen Flur in Mitteleuropa und ihrer Nutzung*, vol.1, ed. Heinrich Beck, Dietrich Denecke, and Herbert Jan-Kuhn (Abhandlungen Göttingen Phil.-Hist. Kl., III. Folge Nr. 115), Göttingen 1979, pp. 41–70.

Schlosser, Horst Dieter, *Althochdeutsche Literatur. Ausgewählte Texte mit Übertragungen*, Frankfurt a. M. 1989.

Schmid, Karl, *Gebetsgedenken und adliges Selbstverständnis im Mittelalter. Ausgewählte Beiträge*, Sigmaringen 1983.

Schmitz, Gerhard, cf. under Hubert Mordek.

Scholz, Sebastian, *Politik, Selbstverständnis, Selbstdarstellung. Die Päpste in karolingischer und ottonischer Zeit* (Historische Forschungen im Auftrag der Historischen Kommission der Akademie der Wissenschaften und der Literatur 36), Stuttgart 2006.

Schütte, Sven, Forschungen zum Aachener Thron, in: *Dombaumeistertagung in Aachen 2009*, pp. 127–42.

Science in Western and Eastern Civilization in Carolingian Times, ed. Paul Leo Butzer and Dietrich Lohrmann, Basel/Boston 1993.

799. Kunst und Kultur der Karolingerzeit. Karl der Große und Papst Leo III. in Paderborn. Beiträge zum Katalog der Ausstellung. Katalog der Ausstellung Paderborn 1999, 2 vols., ed. Christoph Stiegemann and Matthias Wemhoff, Mainz 1999.

Simson, Bernhard von, *Jahrbücher des Fränkischen Reiches unter Ludwig dem Frommen,* 2 vols., Leipzig 1874–1876.

Springer, Matthias, *Die Sachsen,* Stuttgart 2004.

Springsfeld, Kerstin, *Alkuins Einfluß auf die Komputistik zur Zeit Karls des Großen* (Sudhoffs Archiv Beihefte 48), Stuttgart 2002.

Steiger, Heinhard, *Die Ordnung der Welt. Eine Völkerrechtsgeschichte des karolingischen Zeitalters (741 bis 840),* Cologne/Weimar/Vienna 2010.

Steinen, Wolfram von den, Karl der Große und die *Libri Carolini.* Die tironischen Randglossen zum Codex authenticus, in: *NA* 49 (1931) pp. 207–80.

——, Karl und die Dichter, in Steinen, *Menschen im Mittelalter,* pp. 37–77 (first published 1965).

——, *Menschen im Mittelalter. Gesammelte Forschungen. Betrachtungen. Bilder,* ed. Peter von Moos, Bern/Munich 1967.

——, Randbemerkungen Karls des Großen. Eine Selbstanzeige, in: Steinen, *Menschen im Mittelalter,* pp. 32–6.

Stieldorf, Andrea, *Marken und Markgrafen. Studien zur Grenzsicherung durch die fränkisch-deutschen Herrscher* (Schriften der MGH 64), Hanover 2012.

Störmer, Wilhelm, *Früher Adel. Studien zur politischen Führungsschicht im fränkisch-deutschen Reich vom 8. bis 11. Jahrhundert,* 2 vols., Stuttgart 1973.

Strukturen der Grundherrschaft im frühen Mittelalter, ed. Werner Rösener (Veröffentlichungen des Max-Planck-Instituts für Geschichte 92), Göttingen 1992.

Suntrup, Rudolf, cf. Heinz Meyer.

Tassilo III. von Bayern. Großmacht und Ohnmacht im 8. Jahrhundert, ed. Lothar Kolmer and Christian Rohr, Regensburg 2005.

Tellenbach, Gerd, *Königtum und Stämme in der Werdezeit des Deutschen Reiches,* Weimar 1939.

——, Der großfränkische Adel und die Regierung Italiens in der Blütezeit des Karolingerreiches, in: *Studien und Vorarbeiten zur Geschichte des großfränkischen und frühdeutschen Adels,* ed. Gerd Tellenbach (Forschungen zur Oberrheinischen Landesgeschichte 4), Freiburg i. Br. 1957, pp. 40–70; also in Tellenbach, *Ausgewählte Abhandlungen,* vol. 3, pp. 795–825 (with original pagination).

——, *Ausgewählte Abhandlungen und Aufsätze,* 5 vols., Stuttgart 1988–1996.

Tischler, Matthias M., *Einharts "Vita Karoli." Studien zur Entstehung, Überlieferung und Rezeption* (Schriften der MGH 48/I/II), 2 vols., Hanover 2001.

Treitinger, Otto, *Die oströmische Kaiser- und Reichsidee nach ihrer Gestaltung im höfischen Zeremoniell. Vom oströmischen Staats- und Reichsgedanken,* [2]Darmstadt 1956.

Ubl, Karl, *Inzestverbot und Gesetzgebung. Die Konstruktion eines Verbrechens (300–1100)* (Millennium-Studien 20), Berlin/New York 2008.

Verbruggen, Jean François, L'armée et la strategie de Charlemagne, in: *Karl der Große. Lebenswerk und Nachleben,* vol. 1, ed. Helmut Beumann, [3]Düsseldorf 1967, pp. 420–36.

Villa, Claudia, Die Horazüberlieferung und die "Bibliothek Karls des Großen." Zum Werkverzeichnis der Handschrift Berlin, Diez B. 66, in: *DA* 51 (1995) pp. 29–52.

Visio Wettini, introduction, Latin-German edition, and commentary by Hermann Knittel, 3rd enl. ed., with an introduction by Walter Berschin (Reichenauer Texte und Bilder 12), Heidelberg 2009.

Die Vitae Sancti Liudgeri, ed. Wilhelm Diekamp (Die Geschichtsquellen des Bistums Münster 4), Münster 1881.

Walahfrid Strabo, *De imagine Tetrici,* ed. Ernst Dümmler, MGH Poetae 2 pp. 370–78; with a German translation: Alois Däntl, Walahfrid Strabos Widmungsgedicht an die Kaiserin Judith und die Theoderichstatue vor der Kaiserpfalz zu Aachen, in: *Zeitschrift des Aachener Geschichtsvereins* 52 (1930, published 1931) pp. 3–23.

Warntjes, Immo, Irische Komputistik zwischen Isidor von Sevilla und Beda Venerabilis: Ursprung, karolingische Rezeption und generelle Forschungsperspektiven, in: *Viator Multilingual* 42 (2012) pp. 1–31.

Wattenbach, Wilhelm, and Wilhelm Levison, *Deutschlands Geschichtsquellen im Mittelalter. Vorzeit und Karolinger,* vol.Heft 2, *Die Karolinger vom Anfang des 8. Jahrhunderts bis zum Tode Karls des Großen,* ed. Wilhelm Levison and Heinz Löwe, Weimar 1953.

Wehling, Ulrike, *Die Mosaiken im Aachener Münster und ihre Vorstufen* (Arbeitsheft der rheinischen Denkmalpflege 46), Cologne/Bonn 1995.

Weinrich, Lorenz, *Wala. Graf, Mönch und Rebell. Die Biographie eines Karolingers* (Historische Studien 386), Lübeck/Hamburg 1963.

Die Welt des Mittelalters. Erinnerungsorte eines Jahrtausends, ed. Johannes Fried and Olaf B. Rader, Munich 2011.

Wendling, Wolfgang, Die Erhebung Ludwigs d. Fr. zum Mitkaiser im Jahr 813 und ihre Bedeutung für die Verfassungsgeschichte des Frankenreiches, in: *FmaSt* 19 (1985) pp. 201–38.

Werner, Karl Ferdinand, Die Nachkommen Karls des Großen bis um das Jahr 1000, in: *Karl der Große. Lebenswerk und Nachkommen,* vol. 4, ed. Wolfgang Braunfels and Percy Ernst Schramm, Düsseldorf 1967, pp. 403–82 with 2 tables.

———, *Missus, marchio, comes.* Entre l'administration centrale et l'administration locale de l'Empire carolingien, in: *Histoire comparée de l'administration (IVe–XVIIIe siècles),* ed. Werner Paravicini and Karl Ferdinand Werner (Beiheft der Francia 9), Munich 1980, pp. 191–239; again in: Werner, *Vom Frankenreich,* pp. 108–156 (also with original pagination).

———, *Vom Frankenreich zur Entfaltung Deutschlands und Frankreichs. Ursprünge, Strukturen, Beziehungen. Ausgewählte Beiträge. Festgabe zu seinem sechzigsten Geburtstag,* Sigmaringen 1984.

———, Karl der Große oder Charlemagne? Von der Aktualität einer überholten Fragestellung (SB Munich 1995/4).

————, Karl der Große in der Ideologie des Nationalsozialismus. Zur Verantwortung deutscher Historiker für Hitlers Erfolge, in: *Zeitschrift des Aachener Geschichtsvereins* 101 (1997/1998) pp. 9–64.

————, *Naissance de la noblesse. L'essor des élites politiques en Europe,* ²Paris 1998.

Willjung, Harald, *Das Konzil von Aachen 809* (MGH Conc. 2 Suppl. 2), Hanover 1998.

Zotz, Thomas, Palatium publicum, nostrum, regium. Bemerkungen zur Königspfalz in der Karolingerzeit, in: *Die Pfalz. Probleme einer Begriffsgeschichte vom Kaiserpalast auf dem Palatin bis zum heutigen Regierungsbezirk,* ed. Franz Staab, Speyer 1990, pp. 71–101.

ILLUSTRATION CREDITS

acquerelli romani di Ettore Roesler Franz dal 1876 al 1895/Landscapes of Memory: The Roman Watercolours of Ettore Roesler Franz, 1876–95. Exhibition Catalog: Rome, Museo di Roma in Trastevere, 19 December 2007–24 March 2008. Florence: Mandragora Srl, 2008.

Figure 12 (p. 110) From Christoph Stiegemann and Matthias Wemhoff, eds., *799. Kunst und Kultur der Karolingerzeit. Karl der Große und Papst Leo III. in Paderborn. Katalog der Ausstellung Paderborn.* Mainz: Verlag Phillip von Zabern in Wissenschaftliche Buchgesellschaft, 1999.

Figure 13 (p. 111) akg-images / Andrea Jemolo

Figure 14 (p. 113) Zentralinstitut für Kunstgeschichte, Photothek, München

Figure 15 (p. 115) © The Fitzwilliam Museum, Cambridge, UK

Figure 16 (p. 137) akg-images / Bayerische Staatsbibliothek, München (clm 22053)

Figure 17 (p. 148) akg-images

Figure 18 (p. 160) From Michael Imhof and Christoph Winterer, *Karl der Grosse. Leben und Wirkung, Kunst und Architektur.* Petersberg: Michael Imhof Verlag, 2005.

Figure 19 (p. 166) Wuerttembergische Landesbibliothek, Stuttgart (Cod. bibl. fol. 23, f. 124v)

Figure 20 (p. 173) Wuerttembergische Landesbibliothek, Stuttgart (Cod. bibl. fol. 23, f. 96v)

Figure 21 (p. 176) University Library, Utrecht, Ms. 32, fol. 84r

Figure 22 (p. 209) Erich Lessing / Art Resource, NY

Figure 23 (p. 216) Author's collection

Figure 24 (p. 228) Scala / Art Resource, NY

Figure 25 (p. 233) Zentralinstitut für Kunstgeschichte, Photothek, München

Figure 26 (p. 244) From *Zeitschrift des Deutschen Vereins für Kunstwissenschaft,* vol. 64. Berlin: Gebr. Mann Verlag, 2010.

Figure 27 (p. 245) From *Zeitschrift des Deutschen Vereins für Kunstwissenschaft,* vol. 64. Berlin: Gebr. Mann Verlag, 2010.

Figure 28 (p. 249) Österreichische Nationalbibliothek, Vienna (Cod. 1861, fol. 24v–25r)

Figure 29 (p. 262) Herzog August Bibliothek, Wolfenbüttel (Cod. Guelf. 496a Helmst., Einbandzeichnung)

Figure 30 (p. 280)   Bayerische Staatsbibliothek München (clm 14377)

Figure 31 (p. 282)   Parker Library, Master and Fellows of Corpus Christi College, University of Cambridge, Ms. 206, f. 101r

Figure 32 (p. 299)   Zentralinstitut für Kunstgeschichte, Photothek, München

Figure 33 (p. 329)   Wikimedia Commons (CC BY-SA 3.0)

Figure 34 (p. 343)   From Christoph Stiegemann and Matthias Wemhoff, eds., 799. *Kunst und Kultur der Karolingerzeit. Karl der Große und Papst Leo III. in Paderborn. Katalog der Ausstellung Paderborn.* Mainz: Verlag Phillip von Zabern in Wissenschaftliche Buchgesellschaft, 1999.

Figure 35 (p. 345)   Zentralinstitut für Kunstgeschichte, Photothek, München

Figure 36 (p. 347)   © The Trustees of the British Museum / Art Resource, NY

Figure 37 (p. 352)   Foto Marburg / Art Resource, NY

Figure 38 (p. 353)   Museen der Stadt Aachen, Museum Burg Frankenberg. From *Aachen im Bild, IX: Ausstellungs- und Dokumentationsreihe zur Geschichte der Stadt Aachen, 1979–1982*

Figure 39 (p. 355)   From *Die karolingische Pfalzkapelle in Aachen. Material, Bautechnik, Restaurierung*, ed. Andrea Pufke (Arbeitsheft der rheinischen Denkmalpflege 78).Worms: Wernersche Verlagsgesellschaft, 2012.

Figure 40 (p. 359)   From *Die karolingische Pfalzkapelle in Aachen. Material, Bautechnik, Restaurierung*, ed. Andrea Pufke (Arbeitsheft der rheinischen Denkmalpflege 78).Worms: Wernersche Verlagsgesellschaft, 2012.

Figure 41 (p. 362)   Foto Marburg / Art Resource, NY

Figure 42 (p. 365)   Foto Marburg / Art Resource, NY

Figure 43 (p. 366)   Zentralinstitut für Kunstgeschichte, Photothek, München

Figure 44 (p. 367)   Zentralinstitut für Kunstgeschichte, Photothek, München

Figure 45 (p. 368)   Photograph by Georges Jansoone. Wikimedia Commons. (CC BY-SA 3.0)

Figure 46 (p. 371)   © Kaiserpfalz Museum, Ingelheim

Figure 47 (p. 384)   Hans Belting, *Bild und Kult. Eine Geschichte des Bildes vor dem Zeitalter der Kunst.* München: C. H. Beck, 2000.

Figure 48 (p. 387)   Werner Forman Archive / Bridgeman Images

Figure 49 (p. 411)   From Christoph Stiegemann and Matthias Wemhoff, eds., 799. *Kunst und Kultur der Karolingerzeit. Karl der Große und Papst Leo III. in Paderborn. Katalog der Ausstellung Paderborn.* Mainz: Verlag Phillip von Zabern in Wissenschaftliche Buchgesellschaft, 1999.

Figure 50 (p. 421)   Francesco Paolo Rizzo, *Rom. Die Stadt der Päpste.* Photographs by Takashi Okamura. Freiburg im Breisgau: Herder Verlag, 1983.

Figure 51 (p. 435)   Author's collection

Figure 52 (p. 444)   bpk, Berlin / Muenzkabinett, Staatliche Museen, Berlin / Photo: Lutz Jürgen Lübke / Art Resource, NY

Figure 53 (p. 445)   From Michael McCormick, *Charlemagne's Survey of the Holy Land: Wealth, Personnel, and Buildings of a Mediterranean Church between Antiquity and the Middle Ages.* Washington, DC: Dumbarton Oaks Research Library and Collection, 2011.

Figure 54 (p. 484)   Erich Lessing / Art Resource, NY

Figure 55 (p. 522)   From Michael Imhof and Christoph Winterer, *Karl der Grosse. Leben und Wirkung, Kunst und Architektur.* Petersberg: Michael Imhof Verlag, 2005.

Figure 56 (p. 532)   Scala / Art Resource, NY

Figure 57 (p. 533)   akg-images

Figure 58 (p. 545)   Author's collection

Figure 59 (p. 546)   © Musée de l'Armée / Dist. RMN-Grand Palais / Art Resource, NY

Figure 60 (p. 553)   bpk, Berlin / Germanisches Nationalmuseum, Nuremberg / Photo: Lutz Braun / Art Resource, NY

Color plates follow page 338

Plate I   Gianni Dagli Orti / The Art Archive at Art Resource, NY

Plate II   Bibliothèque nationale de France, Département des Manuscrits, NAL 1203

Plate III   Bibliothèque nationale de France, Département des Manuscrits, NAL 1203

Plate IV   KHM-Museumsverband

Plate V	KHM-Museumsverband
Plate VI	Stiftsbibliothek St. Gallen
Plate VI	Stiftsbibliothek St. Gallen
Plate VIII	bpk, Berlin/ Kupferstichkabinett, Staatliche Museen, Berlin /Photo: Joerg P. Anders / Art Resource, NY

INDEX